T0212504

Lecture Notes in Computer Science 10070

More information about this series at http://www.springer.com/series/7409

Carmelo R. García · Pino Caballero-Gil
Mike Burmester · Alexis Quesada-Arencibia (Eds.)

Ubiquitous Computing and Ambient Intelligence

10th International Conference, UCAmI 2016
San Bartolomé de Tirajana, Gran Canaria, Spain,
November 29 – December 2, 2016
Proceedings, Part II

Springer

Editors
Carmelo R. García
University of Las Palmas de Gran Canaria
Las Palmas
Spain

Mike Burmester
Florida State University
Tallahassee, FL
USA

Pino Caballero-Gil
Departamento de Estadistica
Universidad La Laguna
La Laguna
Spain

Alexis Quesada-Arencibia
University of Las Palmas de Gran Canaria
Las Palmas
Spain

ISSN 0302-9743 ISSN 1611-3349 (electronic)
Lecture Notes in Computer Science
ISBN 978-3-319-48798-4 ISBN 978-3-319-48799-1 (eBook)
DOI 10.1007/978-3-319-48799-1

Library of Congress Control Number: 2016955505

LNCS Sublibrary: SL3 – Information Systems and Applications, incl. Internet/Web, and HCI

Printed on acid-free paper

This Springer imprint is published by Springer Nature
The registered company is Springer International Publishing AG
The registered company address is: Gewerbestrasse 11, 6330 Cham, Switzerland

Preface

The UCAmI Conference brings together the fields of ubiquitous computing (UC), which is defined as the integration of human factors, computer science, engineering and social sciences, with a paradigm built upon UC, called ambient intelligence (AmI), which refers to sensitive electronic environments responsive to the presence of people. Thus, altogether, the core of the conference is a complete notion that mutually inspires UC and AmI. In particular, UCAmI 2016 focused on research topics related to ambient assisted living, Internet of Things, smart cities, ambient intelligence for health, human–computer interaction, ad hoc and sensor networks, and security.

This year we celebrated in Gran Canaria, Canary Islands, Spain, the 10th International Conference on Ubiquitous Computing and Ambient Intelligence (UCAmI 2016), which included the International Work Conference on Ambient Assisted Living (IWAAL), and the International Conference on Ambient Intelligence for Health (AmIHEALTH). The program of this joint event included a rich variety of technical sessions to cover the most relevant research topics of each conference. Since its first meeting back in 2005 the event has grown significantly, as shown by its increasing number of participants. For UCAmI 2016, a total of 145 submissions were received, and the acceptance rate for long papers and doctoral consortium papers was 51 %. All submissions were peer reviewed by at least three members of the Program Committee. The reviewers' comments and recommendations were taken into consideration while selecting submissions for inclusion in the proceedings, and were communicated to the authors. Authors whose manuscripts were accepted were asked to address the reviewers' comments. We would like to thank all the authors who submitted their work for consideration and also the reviewers for providing their detailed and constructive reviews in a timely manner.

Furthermore, in an effort to increase the visibility of the contributions of UCAmI, selected papers were invited for submission as extended versions in the journals: *Sensors*, *Mobile Information Systems*, *Journal of Ambient Intelligence and Humanized Computing*, and *International Journal of Computational Intelligence Systems*. We would like to thank the distinguished editors of these journals for providing us with these opportunities.

Finally, we would like to thank all organizers (i.e., University of Las Palmas de Gran Canaria and MAmI Research group), and the reviewers (members of the Program Committee) for helping us by contributing to a high-quality event and proceedings book on the topics of ubiquitous computing and ambient intelligence. Special thanks are due to the staff of Springer in Heidelberg for their valuable support.

November 2016

Carmelo R. García
Pino Caballero-Gil
Mike Burmester
Alexis Quesada

Organization

General Chair

Jose Bravo	University of Castilla La Mancha, Spain

Local Organizing Chair

Alexis Quesada	University of Las Palmas de Gran Canaria, Spain

UCAmI PC Co-chairs

Carmelo R. García	University of Las Palmas de Gran Canaria, Spain
Pino Caballero-Gil	University of La Laguna, Spain
Mike Burmester	University of State of Florida, USA

Publicity Chairs

Jesús Fontecha Diezma	University of Castilla-La Mancha, Spain
Vladimir Villarreal	Technological University of Panama, Panama

Web Master

Iván González Díaz	University of Castilla-La Mancha, Spain

Steering Committee

Xavier Alaman, Spain
Jose Bravo, Spain
Jesus Favela, Mexico
Juan Manuel García Chamizo, Spain
Luis Guerrero, Costa Rica
Ramón Hervás, Spain
Rui Jose, Portugal
Diego López-De-Ipiña, Spain
Chris Nugent, UK
Sergio F. Ochoa, Chile
Gabriel Urzáiz, Mexico
Vladimir Villareal, Panama

Organizing Committee

Jezabel Molina-Gil, Spain
Cádido Caballero-Gil, Spain
Candelaria Hernández-Goya, Spain
Alexandra Rivero-García, Spain
Iván Santos-González, Spain
Tania Mondéjar, Spain
Justyna Kidacka, Spain
Merce Naranjo, Spain
Elitania Jiménez, Spain
Carlos Gutiérrez, Spain
Esperanza Johnson, Spain
María Martínez, Spain
Carlos Dafonte, Spain

Tracks Chairs

AAL (IWAAL)

Riitta Hellman, Norway
Jesus Fontecha, Spain
Juan M. García-Chamizo, Spain

Health (AmIHEALTH)

Ramón Hervás, Spain
Oresti Baños, Spain

Ad-Hoc Sensor Networks

Jezabel Molina-Gil, Spain
Mike Burmester, USA

Security

Pino Caballero-Gil, Spain
Slobodan Petrovic, Norway

Human-Computer Interaction

Jesús Favela, Mexico
Nadia Bethouze, UK

Smart Cities

Diego López-De-Ipiña, Spain
Erik Mannens, Belgium

IoT

Candido Caballero-Gil, Spain
Haibo Chen, UK

Program Committee

Hindusthan A.V. Senthil	Hindusthan College of Arts and Science, India
Ricardo Aguasca-Colomo	Universidad de Las Palmas de Gran Canaria, Spain
Ramón Aguero Calvo	Universidad de Cantabria, Spain
Mónica Aguilar Igartua	Universidad Politécnica de Cataluña, Spain
Xavier Alamán	UAM, Spain
Francisco Alayón	Universidad de Las Palmas de Gran Canaria, Spain
Rosa Arriaga	Georgia Institute of Technology, USA
Mohamed Bakhouya	University of Technology of Belfort Montbeliard, France
Nelson Baloian	University of Chile, Chile
Jean-Paul Barthès	UTC, France
Oresti Baños	University of Twente, The Netherlands
Paolo Bellavista	University of Bologna, Italy
Jessica Beltrán	CICESE, Mexico
Nadia Berthouze	University College London, UK
Stephane Bouchard	Uqo, Canada
Ljiljana Brankovic	The University of Newcastle, UK
Jose Bravo	Universidad de Castilla La Mancha, MAmI Research Lab, Spain
Willem-Paul Brinkman	Delft University of Technology, The Netherlands
Mike Burmester	Florida State University, USA
Cándido Caballero-Gil	Universidad de La Laguna, Spain
Pino Caballero-Gil	Universidad de La Laguna, Spain
Eduardo Calvillo	City of San Luis Potosí, Mexico
Karina Caro	CICESE, Mexico
Giorgio Carpino	CIR, University Campus Bio-Medico of Rome, Italy
Luis Castro	Instituto Tecnologico de Sonora, Mexico
Filippo Cavallo	The BioRobotics Institute, Italy
Sophie Chabridon	Institut Telekom and Management SudParis/CNRS UMR SAMOVAR, France
Haibo Chen	University of Leeds, UK
Walter Colitti	ModoSmart S.L., Spain
Diane Cook	Washington State University, USA
Ray Cornejo	Northwestern, USA
Domenico Cotroneo	University of Naples Federico II, Italy
Michael P. Craven	University of Nottingham, UK
Dagoberto Cruz	CICESE, Mexico
Gabriel de Blasio	Universidad de Las Palmas de Gran Canaria, Spain
Fabio De Felice	Università degli Studi di Cassino, Italy

Boris De Ruyter	Philips Research, The Netherlands
Stefan Decker	RWTH Aachen, Germany
Anna Doreen Robin	University of India, India
Rachael Dutton	Accord Group, UK
Kholoud Elbast	Gaza University, Palestine
Lizbeth Escobedo	UABC, Mexico
Jesus Favela	CICESE, Mexico
Anna Fensel	Semantic Technology Institute (STI) Innsbruck, University of Innsbruck, Austria
Antonio Fernández-Caballero	Universidad de Castilla-La Mancha, Spain
Carlo Ferrari	University of Padova, Italy
Giuseppe Fico	Universidad Politécnica de Madrid, Spain
Laura Fiorini	The BioRobotics Institute, Italy
Jesus Fontecha	Universidad de Castilla La Mancha, MAmI Research Lab, Spain
Antonio Fratini	Aston University, UK
Andrea Gaggioli	Catholic University of Milan, Italy
Juan Manuel Garcia-Chamizo	University of Alicante, Spain
Carmelo R. García	University of Las Palmas de Gran Canaria, Spain
Jorge García Vidal	Universidad Politécnica de Cataluña, Spain
Lilia Georgieva	Heriot-Watt University, UK
Roberto Gil Pita	University of Alcala, Spain
Victor Gonzalez	Instituto Tecnológico Autónomo de México, Mexico
Dan Grigoras	UCC, Ireland
Terje Grimstad	Karde AS, Norway
Luis Guerrero	Universidad de Chile, Chile
Juan Carlos Guerri Cebollada	Universidad Politécnica de Valencia, Spain
Antonio Guerrieri	University of Calabria, Italy
Bin Guo	Institut Telecom SudParis, France
Sofiane Hamrioui	University of Haute Alsace, France
Maria Haritou	Institute of Communication and Computer Systems - National Technical University of Athens, Greece
Jan Havlik	Czech Technical University in Prague, Czech Republic
Riitta Hellman	Karde AS, Norway
Daniel Hernandez	CICESE, Mexico
Netzahualcoyotl Hernández	CICESE, Mexico
Candelaria Hernández-Goya	Universidad de La Laguna, Spain
Valeria Herskovic	Pontificia Universidad Católica de Chile, Chile
Ramon Hervas	Universidad de Castilla La Mancha, MAmI Research Group, Spain
Jesse Hoey	University of Waterloo, Canada
Alina Huldtgren	Eindhoven University of Technology, The Netherlands
Marjan Hummel	University of Twente, The Netherlands

Eduardo Jacob	Universidad del País Vasco, Spain
Martin Jaekel	ZHAW Zurich University of Applied Sciences, Switzerland
Alan Jovic	University of Zagreb, Croatia
Martin Kampel	Vienna University of Technology, Computer Vision Lab, Austria
Wolfgang Kastner	TU Vienna, Austria
Mariano Lamarca Lorente	Ayuntamiento de Barcelona, Spain
Sungyoung Lee	KyungHee University, South Korea
Ernst Leiss	University of Houston, USA
Lenka Lhotska	Czech Technical University in Prague, Czech Republic
Jaime Lloret Mauri	Universidad Politécnica de Valencia, Spain
Vincenzo Loia	Università degli Studi di Salerno, Italy
Tun Lu	Fudan University, China
Jens Lundström	Högskolan i Halmstad, Sweden
Wolfram Luther	University of Duisburg-Essen, Germany
Diego López-De-Ipiña	Deusto Institute of Technology, University of Deusto, Spain
Elsa María Macías López	Universidad de Las Palmas de Gran Canaria, Spain
Ratko Magjarevic	University of Zagreb, Croatia
Domingo Marrero Marrero	University of Las Palmas de Gran Canaria, Spain
Alicia Martinez	CENIDET, Mexico
Ana Martinez	CICESE, Mexico
Francisco José Martínez Saldivar	Universidad Politécnica de Cataluña, Spain
Oscar Mayora	CREATE-NET, Italy
Paolo Melillo	Second University of Naples, Italy
Vicente E. Mena Santana	ULPGG, Spain
Singidunum Milos Stojmenovic	Singidunum University, Serbia
Jezabel Molina-Gil	Universidad de La Laguna, Spain
Alberto Moran	UABC, Mexico
Tatsuo Nakajima	Waseda University, Japan
Julián Navajas Fernández	Universidad de Zaragoza, Spain
Rene Navarro	Universidad de Sonora, Mexico
Panagiota Nikopoulou-Smyrni	Brunel Univesrity, UK
Chris Nugent	University of Ulster, UK
Sergio Ochoa	Universidad de Chile, Chile
Mof Otoom	Yarmouk University, Jordan
Mwaffaq Otoom	Yarmouk University, Jordan
Gabino Padrón	Instituto de Ciencias y Tecnologías Cibernéticas, Universidad de Las Palmas de Gran Canaria, Spain
Philippe Palanque	ICS-IRIT, University Toulouse 3, France
Nicolas Pallikarakis	University of Patras, Greece
Pablo Pancardo	Universidad Juárez Autónoma de Tabasco, Mexico

George Papadopoulos	University of Cyprus, Cyprus
Lorenz Pascal	University of Haute Alsace, France
Leandro Pecchia	University of Warwick, UK
Antonella Petrillo	University of Cassino and Southern Lazio, Italy
Slobodan Petrović	NTNU, Norway
Rainer Planinc	Vienna University of Technology, Austria
Till Plumbaum	DAI-Labor, Technische Universität Berlin, Germany
Octavian Postolache	Instituto de Telecomunicacoes, Portugal
José Antonio Pow-Sang	Pontificia Universidad Católica del Perú, Peru
Alexis Quesada-Arencibia	Universidad de Las Palmas de Gran Canaria, Spain
Boris Ramos Sánchez	Escuale Politécnica del Litoral, Ecuador
Giuseppe Riva	Università Cattolica del Sacro Cuore, Italy
Joel Rodrigues	Instituto de Telecomunicacoes, University of Beira Interior, Portugal
Marcela Rodriguez	UABC, Mexico
Manuel Rosa Zurera	Universidad de Alcalá de Henares, Spain
Cristian Rotariu	UMF Iasi, Romania
Kohat S. Khan	University of Science and Technology, Pakistan
Albert Ali Salah	Bogazici University, Turkey
Javier Sanchez Galan	Universidad Tecnologica de Panama, Panama
José A. Santana Almeida	Universidad de Las Palmas de Gran Canaria, Spain
Uli Sattler	University of Manchester, UK
Markus Schneider	University of Florida, USA
Sandra Sendra Compte	Universidad de Málaga, Spain
Weiming Shen	National Research Council, Canada
Francois Siewe	De Montfort University, USA
Antonio Skarmeta Gomez	Universidad de Murcia, Spain
Valeria Soto	CICESE, Mexico
Alvaro Suarez Sarmiento	Universidad de Las Palmas de Gran Canaria, Spain
Jonathan Synnott	University of Ulster, UK
Chantal Taconet	Télécom SudParis, France
Monica Tentori	CICESE, Mexico
Gabriel Urzaiz	Universidad Anahuac Mayab, Mexico
Tito Vargas	Universidad Santo Tomás, Colombia
Natalia Villanueva-Rosales	University of Texas at El Paso, USA
Vladimir Villarreal	Technological University of Panama, Panama
Benjamin Weyers	University of Duisburg-Essen, Germany
Rainer Wieching	University of Siegen, Germany
Erik Wilde	Siemens, USA
Juan Ye	University of St Andrews, UK
Zhejiang Gongshang Yuxin Mao	University of China, China
Rui Zhang	IBM Research - Almaden, USA
Kayhan Zrar Ghafoor	Koya University, Iraq

Additional Reviewers

Acerbi, Giorgia
Aguilera, Unai
Almeida, Aitor
Alvarez-Díaz, Néstor
Azkune, Gorka
Brewer, Robin
Buján-Carballal, David
Emaldi, Mikel
Fankhauser, David
Fernbach, Andreas
Fiorini, Laura
Fuentes, Carolina
González Díaz, Iván
Guidi, Gabriele
Iadanza, Ernesto
Ibarra-Esquer, Jorge Eduardo
Landaluce, Hugo
Limosani, Raffaele
Lodeiro-Santiago, Moisés
Lopez, Unai
López-De-Armentia, Juan
Marrero Marrero, Domingo
Pijoan, Ander
Pretel, Ivan
Raich, Philipp
Razzaq, Asif
Rivero-Cáceres, Alexandra
Rivero-García, Alexandra
Rodriguez, Iyubanit
Santana, Jose
Santos-González, Iván
Suárez-Armas, Jonay

Contents – Part II

AAL (IWAAL)

Ad-hoc and Sensors Networks

IoT

Smart Cities

Security

Contents – Part I

Health (AmIHEALTH)

AAL (IWAAL)

Probability and Common-Sense: Tandem Towards Robust Robotic Object Recognition in Ambient Assisted Living

J.R. Ruiz-Sarmiento(✉), C. Galindo, and J. Gonzalez-Jimenez

Machine Perception and Intelligent Robotics Group,
System Engineering and Automation Department, University of Málaga,
Campus de Teatinos, 29071 Málaga, Spain
{jotaraul,cgalindo,jgonzalez}@uma.es

Abstract. The suitable operation of mobile robots when providing Ambient Assisted Living (AAL) services calls for robust object recognition capabilities. Probabilistic Graphical Models (PGMs) have become the de-facto choice in recognition systems aiming to efficiently exploit contextual relations among objects, also dealing with the uncertainty inherent to the robot workspace. However, these models can perform in an incoherent way when operating in a long-term fashion out of the laboratory, e.g. while recognizing objects in peculiar configurations or belonging to new types. In this work we propose a recognition system that resorts to PGMs and common-sense knowledge, represented in the form of an ontology, to detect those inconsistencies and learn from them. The utilization of the ontology carries additional advantages, e.g. the possibility to verbalize the robot's knowledge. A primary demonstration of the system capabilities has been carried out with very promising results.

Keywords: AAL · Robotics · Object recognition · Probabilistic graphical models · Ontologies · Environmental information

1 Introduction

Ambient Assisted Living (AAL) aims to facilitate and extend the independence of elderly people by means of cutting-edge solutions from Information and Communication Technologies (ICT). Mobile robots have stood out as valuable ICT systems to improve the quality of life of the elderly, being applied with success to a variety of services: health care, companion, entertainment, household maintenance, etc [1]. A required robotic ability to provide those services with guarantees is such of object recognition. Moreover, the robot should exhibit the capability to reason about what it is perceiving and, if needed, to react in consequence. For example, if the robot recognizes a pill box on a counter, and it knows

Work supported by the research projects TEP2012-530 and DPI2014-55826-R, funded by the Andalusia Regional Government and the Spanish Government, respectively, both financed by European Regional Development's funds (FEDER).

C.R. García et al. (Eds.): UCAmI 2016, Part II, LNCS 10070, pp. 3–8, 2016.
DOI: 10.1007/978-3-319-48799-1_1

that its content is perishable and needs refrigeration, it should infer the need to put it into the fridge or alert the elder – this option also requires Human-Robot Interaction (HRI) capacities.

A renowned tool to tackle the robotic object recognition problem is such of Probabilistic Graphical Models (PGMs), and concretely Conditional Random Fields (CRFs) [2]. These graph-based models provide a mathematically-grounded framework for the recognition of objects exploiting their contextual relations, also dealing with uncertainty. Home environments are rich in contextual information, which is useful to disambiguate recognition results, e.g. a white box near a fridge is more probable to be a microwave than a night-stand [3]. Typically, mobile robots employ CRFs that are pre-tuned with a certain dataset in order to recognize a fixed range of object categories. However, this configuration lacks of the flexibility demanded by robots performing in home environments, e.g. it is (of course) unable to recognize new types of objects not appearing in the training dataset, or instances of learned ones showing peculiar features, which can lead to an incoherent performance.

In this paper we propose a CRF-based object recognition system that relies on common-sense knowledge about home environments to detect and learn from incoherent recognition results. Concretely, common-sense knowledge is codified as an ontology [4], which allows for a natural definition of the properties of concepts in the domain (object types in this case) and their relations. For example, we can define the concept `Fridge` codifying that they are usually tall, box-shaped objects, and the `Pill_box` one stating that they are small boxes related to fridges by `Pill_box placedInto Fridge`. In the proposed system, the recognition results yielded by probabilistic inference over the CRF are checked for coherence against the common-sense representation. If any of them is detected as incoherent (for example, a middle-size object is classified as a fridge), then it is annotated for its posterior evaluation by the user through a simple dialogue. This human-robot interaction is greatly supported by the ontology, since its content can be verbalized in a straightforward way. Finally, the feedback from the user is back-propagated in order to tune the CRF accordingly (see Fig. 1 for a complete overview of the system). It is worth to mention that ontologies also suppose a basic way to *understand* the robot workspace, enabling the detection of object configurations that can be hazardous, e.g. the pill box found out of the fridge.

Summarizing, the presented object recognition system is able to: (i) exploit contextual relations, (ii) handle uncertainty, (iii) detect incoherent results, (iv) learn from experience, and (v) verbalize its outcome. In this paper we introduce the ongoing research towards capabilities (iii) and (iv). To illustrate the system capabilities we have conducted a proof-of-concept demonstration showing promising results.

2 Proposed Robotic Object Recognition System

This section, first, gives some brief background on the theoretical concepts that support our recognition system, and ends up with a description of its operation.

2.1 Conditional Random Fields for Object Recognition

In order to recognize the objects appearing in a given scene, Conditional Random Fields (CRFs) [2] build a graph representation of it according to the objects' layout. In this graph, usually denoted by $\mathcal{G} = (\mathcal{V}, \mathcal{E})$, the nodes $\mathcal{V}$ represent random variables, and the edges $\mathcal{E} \subseteq \mathcal{V} \times \mathcal{V}$ link nodes that are related in some way. The random variables, commonly represented as $\boldsymbol{y} = [y_1, ..., y_n]$, take values from a set $\mathcal{L}$ of considered object types, e.g. chair, table, tv, fridge, etc., and are associated with the vector of n object observations $\boldsymbol{x} = [x_1, ..., x_n]$. In this way, only the nodes representing objects that are close to each other in the scene are linked with an edge (see Fig. 1a and b). CRFs efficiently encode the probability distribution $p(\boldsymbol{y}|\boldsymbol{x})$ over this graph representation by:

$$p(\boldsymbol{y}|\boldsymbol{x}; \boldsymbol{\theta}) = \frac{1}{Z(\boldsymbol{x}, \boldsymbol{\theta})} \prod_{c \in C} \exp(\langle \phi(x_c, y_c), \boldsymbol{\theta} \rangle) \tag{1}$$

where $\mathcal{C}$ is the set of maximal cliques of the graph $\mathcal{G}$ (in this work we consider cliques of size one, nodes, and two, neighboring nodes), $Z(\cdot)$ is the also called partition function, which plays a normalization role so $\sum_{\xi(\boldsymbol{y})} p(\boldsymbol{y}|\boldsymbol{x}; \boldsymbol{\theta}) = 1$, being $\xi(\boldsymbol{y})$ a possible assignment to the variables in $\boldsymbol{y}$. $\langle \cdot, \cdot \rangle$ stands for the inner product, and $\phi(x_c, y_c)$ are the sufficient statistics of the variables in the clique c. These sufficient statistics comprise the salient features of the data, e.g. features characterizing nodes in $\mathcal{V}$ are the height of the object, orientation, color, etc., while features about the relations in $\mathcal{E}$ are difference in height, difference of orientation, etc. The vector $\boldsymbol{\theta}$ stands for the model parameters (or weights) to be tuned during the CRF training.

Once the scene and the objects observed therein have been represented as a graph, a probabilistic inference algorithm can be executed over it in order to retrieve the recognition results. This is usually carried out by algorithms computing the Maximum a Posteriori (MAP) assignment [2], i.e. the assignment $\hat{\boldsymbol{y}}$ to the variables in $\boldsymbol{y}$ that maximizes Eq. 1 (see Fig. 1c).

2.2 Common-Sense Knowledge Representation

Ontologies are widely-resorted representations for codifying common-sense knowledge about a certain domain. They are often created by an expert in that domain, and consist of: a number of descriptions of concepts arranged hierarchically, relations among them, and instances of those concepts [4]. For example, concepts codifying the types of objects often appearing in home environments are `Fridge`, `Cereal_box`, or `Cabinet`, with properties like `Fridge has_orientation Vertical` or `Cereal_box has_shape Box`. Relations set associations between concepts, e.g. `Cereal_box isNear Cabinet`, which expresses that cereal boxes can be found near cabinets. Knowledge about the objects from a particular scenario and their properties can be stated in the ontology through instances, e.g. `cereal_box-1`, `cabinet-1`, and instantiations of relations, `cereal_box-1 is_near cabinet-1`. Figure 1(d) shows the simplified ontology used in this work

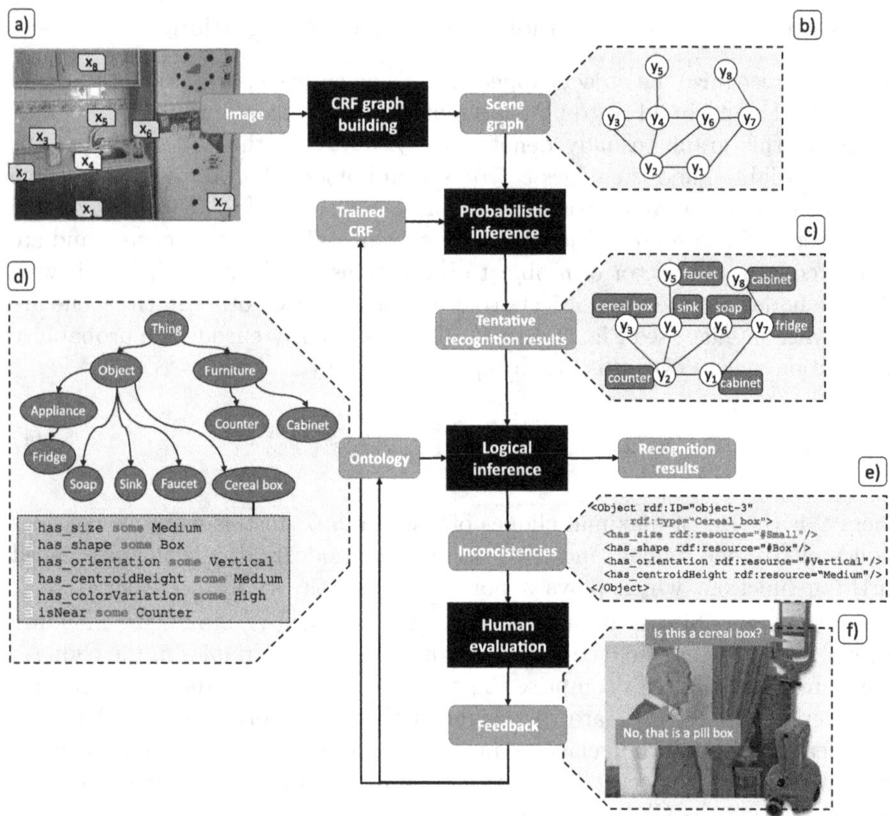

Fig. 1. Overview of the proposed object recognition system. Information about the sub-figures from (a) to (f) is detailed in the text

describing objects typically appearing in kitchens, and the detail of the description of the concept `Cereal_box`.

2.3 System Overview

An overview of the complete system is depicted in Fig. 1. The recognition pipeline starts by capturing an image of the scene to be processed, and the posterior building of its CRF graph representation. This graph, along with the pre-trained CRF parameters, is exploited by a probabilistic inference algorithm to provide a set of tentative object recognition results. These results are then inserted as instances in the Ontology, which checks their consistency with respect to the codified common-sense knowledge by employing a logical reasoner. This permits the robot to detect incoherent results that are subsequently evaluated by the user. The evaluation of a conflicting object starts by showing him/her a cropped image of it. Three different scenarios are then possible:

Case 1: the user determines that the recognition result is right. This means that the CRF performed correctly, but the codified common-sense knowledge was somehow *too strict*. The ontology learns from this outcome by relaxing the codified object property that produced the inconsistency.

Case 2: the recognition result is wrong, and:

- **Case 2.1:** the object type is already present in the CRF/ontology. In this case the CRF misclassified the object. To learn from the mistake, the gathered object information is used to re-tune the CRF parameters.
- **Case 2.2:** the object type is new. The relevant information from the object is used to automatically generate a new concept in the ontology, and the CRF is also re-trained taking into account this new object type.

The re-training of a CRF model entails the utilization of a dataset with a considerable number of samples covering all the relevant object types. Since this dataset consist of the sufficient statistics extracted from objects and relations, and raw data are not required (e.g. images), its size in memory is usually small. However, if the robot storage is quite limited, we have shown in a previous work [5] how an ontology can be also exploited to successfully train CRFs.

3 System Demonstration

To carry out a primary demonstration of the system capabilities we trained a CRF to recognize the same object types that were codified into the ontology. This training was carried out through the UPGMpp library [6], relying on the pseudo-likelihood objective function and the L-BFGS optimization method. Regarding the ontology design, we resorted to Protégè[1]. The CRF and the ontology were then plugged into the recognition system as shown in Fig. 1, which was integrated into the mobile robot Giraff [7] (see Fig. 1f). This robot is built upon a motorized wheeled platform endowed with a 2D laser scanner, a RGB-D camera, and a videoconferencing set: microphone, speaker, and screen.

The robot was deployed into an apartment and performed a primary task: to check the configuration of the objects in the kitchen. Concretely, during the robot operation, the RGB-D camera was used to capture both intensity and depth images when reaching certain locations in the kitchen. For brevity we analyze one system trace reported while detecting an inconsistency due to a new object category. This is the most complete case of the three aforementioned ones.

The described trace is fully depicted in Fig. 1. It starts with the robot capturing the image shown in Fig. 1a, and the recognition system building its corresponding CRF-graph (Fig. 1b). After a probabilistic inference process [2], the MAP assignment yields the tentative object recognition results (Fig. 1c). These results are inserted as instances of objects in the ontology, which checks their consistency with respect to the encoded knowledge. The logical inference process [8] detects an inconsistency: the object x_3 was recognized as a cereal box, but it does not exhibit the common size of cereal boxes (Fig. 1e, expressed as OWL).

[1] http://protege.stanford.edu/.

The remaining results are considered as valid, while the inconsistent one has to be evaluated by the user. Through a simple dialogue (Fig. 1f), the user determines that the object (x_3) is in fact a pill box, and that it must be stored in the fridge. This information is then back-propagated to both: (i) the ontology, where the system creates a new concept `Pill_box`, inheriting from the `Object` one, and describes it with the information gathered from the human and from the collected sensory data, and (ii) to the CRF model, which re-tunes its parameters according to the new information. The learning success was evaluated in later observations of pill boxes, where the robot was able to successfully recognize this new type of object.

4 Discussion and Future Work

In this work we have proposed a robust robotic object recognition system for providing AAL services consisting of two parts: a Conditional Random Field (CRF), and an ontology. The system is able to detect incoherent recognition results and learn from them including a human in the loop, aiming to improve its performance and robustness in the long-term operation within home environments. A demonstration of its suitability has been carried out, showing promising results.

There is significant room to explore possible system improvements or applications, including a thorough evaluation of the system with more complex CRFs and ontologies. On the other hand, both CRFs and ontologies could be extended to also consider information relative to rooms, opening new possibilities to exploit object-room relations, e.g. that fridges are usually in kitchens. The system could also benefit from a study of when would be more appropriate to ask the user about inconsistent results in order to not bother him/her.

References

1. Payr, S., Werner, F., Werner, K.: Potential of robotics for ambient assisted living. Technical report, Austrian Research Institute for Artificial Intelligence (2015)
2. Koller, D., Friedman, N.: Probabilistic Graphical Models: Principles and Techniques. MIT Press, Cambridge (2009)
3. Ruiz-Sarmiento, J.R., Galindo, C., González-Jiménez, J.: Joint categorization of objects and rooms for mobile robots. In: IEEE/RSJ International Conference on Intelligent Robots and Systems (IROS) (2015)
4. Uschold, M., Gruninger, M.: Ontologies: principles, methods and applications. Knowl. Eng. Rev. **11**, 93–136 (1996)
5. Ruiz-Sarmiento, J.R., Galindo, C., González-Jiménez, J.: Exploiting semantic knowledge for robot object recognition. Know. Based Syst. **86**, 131–142 (2015)
6. Ruiz-Sarmiento, J.R., Galindo, C., González-Jiménez, J.: UPGMpp: a software library for contextual object recognition. In: 3rd. REACTS Workshop (2015)
7. Gonzalez-Jimenez, J., Galindo, C., Ruiz-Sarmiento, J.: Technical improvements of the giraff telepresence robot based on users' evaluation. In: RO-MAN, September (2012)
8. Sirin, E., Parsia, B., Grau, B.C., Kalyanpur, A., Katz, Y.: Pellet: a practical owl-dl reasoner. Web Seman. Sci. Serv. Agents WWW **5**(2), 51–53 (2007)

Ensemble Learning-Based Algorithms for Aggressive and Agitated Behavior Recognition

Belkacem Chikhaoui(✉), Bing Ye, and Alex Mihailidis

IATSL Laboratory, Toronto Rehab Institute, University of Toronto, Toronto, Canada
{belkacem.chikhaoui,alex.mihailidis}@utoronto.ca, bing.ye@uhn.ca

Abstract. This paper addresses a practical and challenging problem concerning the recognition of behavioral symptoms dementia (BSD) such as aggressive and agitated behaviors. We propose two new algorithms for the recognition of these behaviors using two different sensors such as a Microsoft Kinect and an Accelerometer sensor. The first algorithm extracts skeleton based features from 3D joint positions data collected by a Kinect sensor, while the second algorithm extracts features from acceleration data collected by a Shimmer accelerometer sensor. Classification is then performed in both algorithms using ensemble learning classifier. We compared the performance of both algorithms in terms of recognition accuracy and processing time. The results obtained, through extensive experiments on a real dataset, showed better performance of the Accelerometer-based algorithm over the Kinect-based algorithm in terms of processing time, and less performance in terms of recognition accuracy. The results also showed how our algorithms outperformed several state of the art methods.

1 Introduction

Globally we are facing a healthcare crisis related to caring for a rapidly aging population who are suffering from a variety of chronic medical conditions, such as dementia. Caring for people with dementia is more complicated given the severity of dementia they suffer from and the degree of autonomy they need for the completion of their activities of daily living [1]. Disruptive behaviors, such as agitation and aggression, are very common in people with dementia and regarded as part of behavioral symptoms of dementia (BSD) [2].

These disruptive behaviors can cause great suffering for persons with dementia and a great deal of distress and burden for caregivers. Early recognition of these behaviors can help effectively provide better treatment for persons with dementia. This, in turn will help reduce caregiver's burden [2]. Direct observation from family caregivers and the care staff is usually used to identify disruptive behaviors. However, this method is subjective, time consuming and could increase the workload of care staff and caregivers [2]. Therefore, researchers

C.R. García et al. (Eds.): UCAmI 2016, Part II, LNCS 10070, pp. 9–20, 2016.
DOI: 10.1007/978-3-319-48799-1_2

have focused on developing smart systems to automatically monitor and recognize aggression and agitation [3], as these systems will significantly reduce the manpower and time needed to observe and detect these behaviors [4].

Various types of sensors have been used for behavior recognition such as accelerometers, cameras, and Kinects. However, particular attention has been devoted recently to the use of Kinect and the accelerometer sensors given the rich information they provide of a person's behaviors comparing to other sensors [5]. Kinect, which is a vision sensor, allows collecting different types of data such as individual movements, physical and verbal behaviors in skeleton, depth or color data format. Kinect sensors have been gaining momentum in different domains to monitor people behaviors and considered more accurate than many other 3D sensors [6]. Accelerometer sensor, as opposed to Kinect sensor, is a wearable sensor that can provide acceleration data of person's behaviors. The acceleration data could be used to develop applications such as recognition of a person's activity [7] and individual postural tracking [8].

Although Kinect and accelerometer sensors have been used in behavioral recognition, both sensors have not yet been compared for their accuracy in recognition of aggressive and agitated behaviors. In this paper, we use the two sensors to explore their capabilities for the recognition of aggressive and agitated behaviors. We propose two novel algorithms for the recognition of aggressive and agitated behaviors using data collected form a Kinect and an accelerometer sensor. The algorithms extract useful features, which will be combined with an ensemble learning classifier for behavior classification. The primary contributions of this paper can be summarized as follows:

- This work is, to the best of our knowledge, the first formal study that compares Kinect and accelerometer sensors for agitated and aggressive behavior recognition purposes.
- Proposing two novel algorithms for aggressive and agitated behavior recognition using Kinect sensor and accelerometer sensor.
- Collecting real data and conducting extensive experiments to validate the proposed algorithms.

The rest of the paper is organized as follows. First, we give an overview of related work in Sect. 2. Section 3 describes the proposed algorithms in terms of feature extraction, learning and recognition using ensemble method. The results of our experiments on real dataset are presented in Sect. 4. Finally, Sect. 5 presents our conclusions and highlights future work directions.

2 Related Work

Various research studies have been done on normal human action and activity recognition using Kinect and cameras [9,10] and accelerometers [7]. However, very little work has been done on the recognition of aggressive and agitated behaviors using these two sensors. Here we report only research studies interested in aggressive and agitated behavior recognition using Kinect and accelerometer sensors.

2.1 Vision-Based Research Studies

Little work has been done on the recognition of aggressive and agitated behaviors using a Kinect sensor. Nirjon et al. [11] proposed a system to detect aggressive actions such as hitting, kicking, pushing, and throwing from streaming 3D skeleton joint coordinates obtained from a Kinect sensor. The authors combined supervised and unsupervised learning for behavior classification. However, the unsupervised learning used in [11] needs more interventions from the system's users in order to label the behaviors, which is not practical in real settings. Even though their work is similar to our work in terms of aggressive behaviors recognition using skeleton data, the main difference relies on the methodological side in terms of the features used and the classification algorithms employed. In addition, we use two more actions namely the wandering and tearing, which makes our data richer.

Other studies used cameras to monitor [12] and quantify agitation in intensive care unit patients [13]. For example, Chase et al. [13] used patient motion that is sensed using digital video image processing. Then a fuzzy inference system is developed to classify levels of motion that correlate with observed patient agitation. Biswas et al. [14] used multimodal sensors to monitor agitation in people with dementia. The agitation was detected and monitored by the sensors based on the intensity of the movements such as sitting and standing. However, the authors consider only limited movements such as sitting and standing. Siang et al. [4] used a video camera-based method to recognize agitated behaviors. The recorded video data were then annotated based on the gold standard agitation assessment tool to classify agitated behaviors and non-agitated behaviors. Skin color segmentation techniques were used in order to analyse video data and extract relevant features describing agitated behaviors. However, this technique present some limitations in terms of the difficulty in detecting the skin regions during the night and when the person is not facing the camera, which could affect the feature extraction.

2.2 Accelerometer-Based Research Studies

Various studies have been performed on the acceleration of the body joints to understand their association with agitation [15]. However, these studies looked at acceleration data combined with physiological features, such as the galvanic skin response [15], heart rate [16], and skin temperature [16] to train models of agitated behaviors. For instance, Wenhui et al. [15] combined evidences of different modalities to infer stress level. These evidences include physical appearance (facial expression, eye movements, and head movements) extracted from video via visual sensors, physiological conditions (heart rate, skin temperature, Galvanic skin response (GSR) and finger pressure) collected from an emotional mouse, behavioral data from user interaction activities with the computer, and performance measures. Inferring the stress level was modeled using a dynamic Bayesian network. Sakr et al. [16] used wearable sensors to detect agitation. They used bio-physiological measures to detect agitation by monitoring the changes of the heart rate, galvanic skin response and skin temperature of the participants. Classification is then performed using a support vector machine classifier.

Several other studies [17–19] looked at the correlation between acceleration data and agitated behaviors measured using conventional scales such as Cohen-Mansfield Agitation Inventory (CMAI) and Neuropsychiatric Inventory (NPI) scales. However, no formal methods were proposed in these studies and only correlation measures were investigated. In addition, the weakness of these methods is that, they require an active engagement of the person while collecting data and require physiological data to assess the agitation level, which is obtrusive. In our work, we consider only acceleration data, which can be collected unobtrusively using accelerometers worn on the wrists for example like watches. No physiological data is used in our work.

3 Our Approach

In this section we discuss our proposed algorithms such as the feature extraction and classification using ensemble learning.

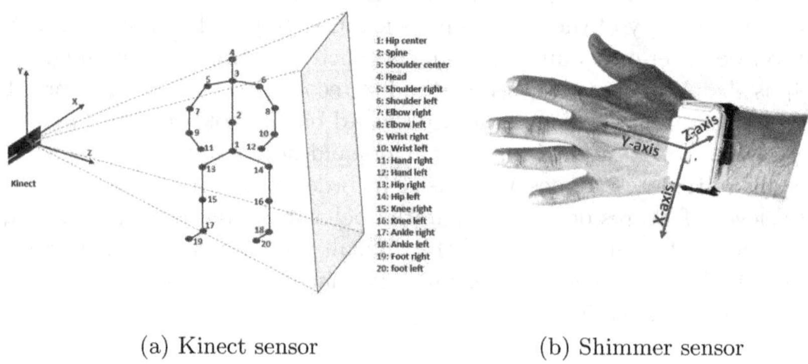

(a) Kinect sensor (b) Shimmer sensor

Fig. 1. Kinect and Shimmer sensors used in our experiments

3.1 Kinect-Based Algorithm

This algorithm describes how the recognition of aggressive and agitated behaviors can be achieved using skeleton data collected with a Kinect sensor[1]. Figure 1(a) shows the different skeleton joints captured by a Kinect sensor.

A human skeleton can be represented by a hierarchy of joints that are connected with bones. The spatiotemporal features are local descriptions of human motions [20]. Therefore, an action can be described as a collection of time series of 3D positions. The time series of 3D positions represent 3D trajectories of the

[1] http://www.microsoft.com/en-us/kinectforwindows/purchase/.

joints in the skeleton hierarchy. In order to accurately represent and differentiate between human actions, taking only 3D positions of the joints and how they evolve over time are not sufficient given the similarity between human actions. In order to obtain a better description and representation of human actions, we extracted the following features:

1. **Relative and absolute joint angles**: they are computed between each two connected limbs, and we represent the skeleton motion data as the changes over time of joint angles computed at each time frame. The aim of computing relative and absolute joint angles is to understand the contribution of each body part in performing actions.
2. **Distance to the hip center**: it represents the distance between the different joints and a fixed point of the skeleton, which is the hip center. The aim of computing this distance is to give more information of the body parts involved in each movement over time.
3. **Distance between current and initial position of joints**: it represents the distance between the position of a joint at time t and its initial position at time t_0 (initial frame). The aim of computing this distance is to characterize the spatial information of each joint, and will further indicate how far the joint will be with respect to its initial position.

These features will be used by the ensemble learning algorithm to perform behavior classification.

3.2 Accelerometer-Based Algorithm

This algorithm describes how the recognition of aggressive and agitated behaviors can be achieved using acceleration data captured using an accelerometer sensor. Figure 1(b) shows the different axis of the accelerometer sensor (Shimmer[2]) used in our work.

Features were extracted from the filtered accelerometer data using a sliding window ($\mathbf{w}$). We empirically choose a window size of $\mathbf{w} = 14$ with 50 % samples overlapping between consecutive windows. Feature extraction on windows with 50 % overlap has demonstrated success in previous work [21]. At a sampling frequency of 50Hz, each window represents data for 0.28 s, which is reasonable given that aggressive actions are usually performed quickly [22]. The window size of 14 yielded better results as well as many training examples. The extracted features are described as follows: Mean, Standard deviation, 25th percentile, 75th percentile, Average Absolute Difference (AAD) [23], Average Resultant Acceleration, Entropy and Covariance. The extracted features take into account the description of the three axis when they are taken separately, two axis conjointly and all the axis together. This will allow to extract rich information about each behavior.

[2] www.shimmersensing.com.

3.3 Classification

Once the features are computed for skeleton and acceleration data, we can now build a classification model for the aggressive and agitated behaviors. Several classification methods could be used such as SVM, decision trees, and naive Bayes to perform classification. However, these methods have shown to be less accurate when compared to ensemble methods [24]. This motivates us to incorporate ensemble methods to build our classification model. The reason to use ensemble methods is to improve the predictive performance of a given model through combining several learning algorithms. We used rotation forest ensemble method to perform classification.

Rotation forest [25] is an ensemble method proposed to build a classifier based on independently trained decision trees. It is found to be more accurate than bagging, AdaBoost and Random Forest ensembles across a collection of benchmark datasets. The advantage of rotation forests lies in the use of principal component analysis (PCA) to rotate the original feature axes so that different training sets for learning base classifiers can be formed.

Formally, let $\mathbf{x} = [x_1, ..., x_n]^T$ be a data point described by n features, and let X be an $m \times n$ matrix containing the training example. Let $Y = [y_1, ..., y_m]^T$ be a vector of class labels for the training data, where y_j takes a value from the class labels $\{w_1, ..., w_c\}$. Let $D = \{D_1, ..., D_L\}$ be the ensemble of L classifiers and $\boldsymbol{F}$ be a feature set. The idea is that all classifiers can be trained in parallel. Therefore, each classifier D_i is trained on a separate training set T_{D_i} to be constructed as follows [25]:

1. split the feature vector $\boldsymbol{F}$ into K subsets. The subsets may be disjoint or intersecting. Note that rotation forest aims at building accurate and diverse classifiers. Therefore, to maximize the chance of getting high diversity, it is suggested to take disjoint subsets of features. For the sake of simplicity, if K is a factor of n, so that each subset contains $M = n/K$ features.
2. for each of the subsets, select randomly a nonempty subset of classes and then draw a bootstrap sample of objects.
3. run PCA using only the M features in $\boldsymbol{F}_{i,j}$ and the selected subset of X, where j is the jth subset of features for the training set of classifier D_i. Then, store the obtained coefficients of the principal components $\mathbf{a}_{i,j}^1, ..., \mathbf{a}_{i,j}^{M_j}$ in a matrix $C_{i,j}$.
4. rearrange the columns of the matrix $C_{i,j}$ in a new matrix B_i^a so that they correspond to the original features in matrix X.
5. the training set for classifier D_i is XB_i^a.
6. to classify a new sample $\mathbf{x}$, we compute the confidence ψ for each class as follows:

$$\psi_j(\mathbf{x}) = \frac{1}{L}\sum_{i=1}^{L} d_{i,j}(\mathbf{x}B_i^a), j = 1, ..., c \tag{1}$$

   where $d_{i,j}(\mathbf{x}B_i^a)$ is the probability assigned by the classifier D_i indicating that $\mathbf{x}$ comes from class w_j. Therefore, $\mathbf{x}$ will be assigned to the class having the highest confidence value.

Due to space limitations, the reader is referred to [25] for more details about the rotation forest ensemble method. The next section presents the validation of the two algorithms.

4 Validation

We evaluate the performance of our algorithms on a real human behavior dataset, that contains aggressive and agitated human behaviors obtained by conducting an experiment in Toronto Rehabilitation Institute-UHN (TRI-UHN). Ten (10) participants (6 males and 4 females, 3 among them were left-handed) were involved in this experiment to conduct six (6) aggressive and agitated behaviors (hitting, pushing, throwing, tearing, kicking and wandering) in front of a Kinect sensor v2 by wearing a Shimmer accelerometer sensor. These behaviors have been identified as the most common challenging aggressive and agitated behaviors[3] observed from persons with dementia. These behaviors were selected from Cohen-Mansfield Agitation Inventory (CMAI) Scale and are described as follows: **hitting**, **pushing**, **throwing**, **tearing**, **kicking**, and **wandering**.

Participants were asked to perform the full set of actions using the right side of the body. For instance, hitting and kicking with the right hand and the right foot respectively. Note that two of these actions, pushing and wandering, are not specific to one side of the body. In order to ensure the study is generic and takes into account both left-handed and right-handed people, participants were then requested to repeat the four laterally specific actions, hitting, kicking, throwing and tearing, using the left side of the body. Participants performed all the actions in front of a Kinect sensor five times while facing each of three directions (front, left and right). For example, during the hitting action, participants did first the action facing the Kinect sensor five times, then repeated the action another five times with their left side facing the Kinect and then another five times with their right side facing the Kinect. This is to ensure that we take into account different situations that might occur when a person is being monitored. A total of 1500 behavior instances have been collected in our experiment from both Kinect and accelerometer sensor. A Research Ethics Board (REB) approval was obtained prior to collecting the data.

Each action was performed using three different directions with respect to the Kinect sensor: front side facing the Kinect, right side facing the Kinect and left side facing the Kinect. Each skeleton data consists of 3D coordinates of 25 joints with time stamp indicating the time when the joint coordinates were recorded at each frame. All the skeleton data were recorded at 30 frame per second rate. The acceleration data ware recorded using the Shimmer connect application[4]. All the acceleration data were recorded at 50 Hz frequency. A total of 75 features were extracted from Kinect data and 48 features from the Accelerometer data.

[3] Here we use the terms Behavior and Action interchangeably.

[4] http://www.shimmersensing.com/shop/shimmer3.

4.1 Experimental Results

We evaluate the performance of the two proposed algorithms using the TRI dataset. In our experiments, we used the F-Measure to present the results. We used the Leave-One-Out cross validation method to validate our algorithms. In this experiment, we used all behavior instances from 9 participants for training and the behavior instances of the remaining participant for testing. We performed the experiment 10 times, excluding one participant at each time. The benefit of such setup is twofold. First, it allows detecting problematic participants and analyzing the sources of some of the classification errors caused by these participants. A problematic participant means his/her behaviors were performed differently compared to other participants. Second, it allows testing the inter-participant generalization of the algorithms, which constitutes a good indicator about the practicability of our algorithms. For classification performance comparison purposes, we also reported the results using different other single and ensemble classifiers such as random forest, decision tree, Bayesian net, AdaBoost, and Bagging. Table 1 shows the classification results obtained for each algorithm.

Table 1. Recognition results (F-Measure) obtained using the kinect-based and accelerometer-based algorithms

	Kinect-based algorithm		Accelerometer-based algorithm	
	Left handed	Right handed	Left handed	Right handed
Our approach	**0.88**	**0.93**	**0.85**	**0.94**
Random forest	0.77	0.92	0.81	0.87
Decision tree	0.7	0.83	0.72	0.77
Bayesian net	0.8	0.79	0.45	0.5
AdaBoost	0.44	0.38	0.45	0.51
Bagging	0.72	0.89	0.75	0.83

The results obtained using the Right-handed dataset are promising compared to those obtained using the Left-handed dataset. The good results obtained using the Right-handed dataset can be explained by the fact that the majority of the participants (n = 7) were right handed so that behaviors were performed as they normally perform their behaviors. Investigation of the participant errors, in each of the 10 leave one out experiments on the Left-handed dataset, revealed that the most problematic behavior instances belonged to participants number 6 and 7. Indeed, by inspecting the behavior classes with high error rate for participant 7, we found that the participant performed the Hitting behavior by rising the hand behind the head and pretend to hit in exactly the same way as the Throwing behavior, while the other participants punch when performing this behavior without rising their hands behind their head.

Similarly, participant number 6 performed the Throwing behavior with additional movements such as moving left and back while the behavior should be performed only by hands. Moving left and back when performing the Throwing behavior created confusions with the Wandering behavior where participants were asked to move forward and backward and left and right. Moreover, the participant performed the Tearing behavior by moving the hands forward in the same way as the Pushing behavior, and then performed the Tearing behavior. This creates a confusion with the Pushing behavior. The variability observed in the ways participants performed the different behaviors constitutes a good validation setting for our algorithms. This is demonstrated by the promising results obtained using the Right-handed and the Left-handed datasets.

4.2 Execution Time

The execution time is an essential part in the development of real time applications. We compared the execution time of both algorithms in order to identify which algorithm is more efficient. Although both algorithms use the same ensemble learning classifier, the difference in the execution time will give a good indication about the influence of the number of features used in each algorithm. To measure the execution time, a machine with 6 GB of memory and 2.5 GHz processor is used to perform these experiments. Figure 2 shows the execution time taken by each algorithm to train and classify the data in the Left-handed and Right-handed datasets.

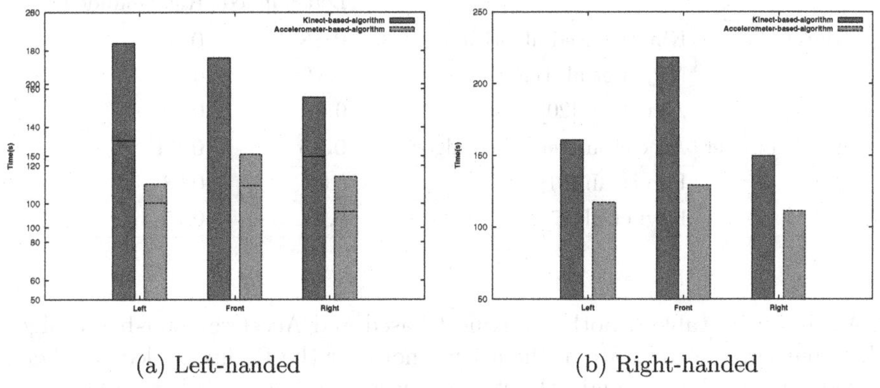

(a) Left-handed (b) Right-handed

Fig. 2. Execution time taken by each algorithm in the left-handed and right-handed datasets

As shown in Fig. 2, the Accelerometer-based algorithm takes lower time compared to the Kinect-based algorithm in the Left-handed and Right-handed datasets. For instance, the Kinect-based algorithm takes 217.99 s to train and classify the Front side data in the Right-handed dataset, while the Accelerometer-based algorithm takes only 129.34 s as shown in Fig. 2(a). The same observations were found in the Left-handed dataset. This can be explained by the number of frames the Kinect sensor captured for each behavior. In fact, data were collected at 30 fps for each behavior, which generates more training samples compared to the acceleration data.

5 Comparison

In order to compare our algorithms with the state of the art methods, we compared the Kinect-based algorithm with the approach of Nirjon et al. [11] for aggressive and agitated behavior recognition using skeleton data collected using a Kinect sensor, and the approach of Zhu et al. [20] for behavior recognition using random forest based classification. Similarly, we compared the Accelerometer-based algorithm with the approach of Bao et al. [21] for human activity recognition using accelerometer data, and the approach of Ravi et al. [7] for activity recognition using acceleration data. The comparison of the Accelerometer-based algorithm with the approaches of [7,21] is justified by the lack of work reported in the literature about the recognition of aggressive and agitated behaviors using only acceleration data. These two approaches are the most cited works on activity recognition using acceleration data. Table 2 shows the results obtained for each approach.

Table 2. Comparison results for each approach

		Left-handed	Right-handed
Kinect	Kinect-based algorithm	**0.88**	**0.93**
	Nirjon et al. [11]	0.31	0.46
	Zhu et al. [20]	0.61	0.65
Accelerometer	Accelerometer-based algorithm	**0.85**	**0.94**
	Bao et al. [21]	0.82	0.68
	Ravi et al. [7]	0.78	0.75

As shown in Table 2, both the Kinect-based and Accelerometer-based algorithms outperform the state of the art methods for the Right-handed and Left-handed datasets. Interestingly, the state of the art methods based on acceleration data perform also well compared to our algorithm. Indeed, the method of [21] achieves an accuracy of 0.82 for the Left-handed dataset, while the method of [7] achieves an accuracy of 0.78 for the same dataset. However, the state of the art methods based on the Kinect data achieves low accuracy in both datasets. Therefore, this confirms the effectivness and suitability of our algorithms.

6 Conclusion

In this paper we have studied the problem of agitated and aggressive behavior recognition. We have proposed and compared two effective algorithms. The first algorithm used skeleton data collected using a Kinect sensor, while the second algorithm used acceleration data collected using an accelerometer sensor. We have illustrated the effectiveness and suitability of the proposed algorithms through experiments on a real agitated and aggressive behavior dataset. The preliminary results show the suitability of the two algorithms in representing behaviors and distinguishing between them. In addition, we have also illustrated how our algorithms outperformed several of the state-of-the-art methods.

We are currently exploring the fusion of Kinect data and Accelerometer data to improve the recognition accuracy of agitated and aggressive behaviors.

References

1. Mihailidis, A., Boger, J., Craig, T., Hoey, J.: The coach prompting system to assist older adults with dementia through handwashing: an efficacy study. BMC Geriatr. **8**(1), 28 (2008)
2. Desai, A., Grossberg, G.: Recognition and management of behavioral disturbances in dementia. Prim. Care Companion J. Clin. Psychiatry **3**(3), 93 (2001)
3. Qiu, Q., Foo, S., Wai, A., Pham, V., Maniyeri, J., Biswas, J., Yap, P.: Multimodal information fusion for automated recognition of complex agitation behaviors of dementia patients. In: 2007 10th International Conference on Information Fusion, pp. 1–8. IEEE (2007)
4. Foo, S., Pham, V., Htwe, T., Qiu, Q., Wai, A., Maniyeri, J., Biswas, J., Yap, P.: Automated recognition of complex agitation behavior of demented patient using video camera. In: Conference One-Health Networking, Application and Services, pp. 68–73 (2007)
5. Wouter, V., Egon, V., Reinier, K., Schavemaker, J.: Towards sensing behavior using the kinect. In: 8th International Conference on Methods and Techniques in Behavioural Research, pp. 372–375. Noldus Information Technology (2012)
6. Banos, O., Calatroni, A., Damas, M., Pomares, H., Rojas, I., Sagha, H., Milln, J., Troster, G., Chavarriaga, R., Roggen, D.: Kinect=imu? learning mimo signal mappings to automatically translate activity recognition systems across sensor modalities. In: ISWC, pp. 92–99 (2012)
7. Nishkam, R., Nikhil, D., Preetham, M., Littman, M.: Activity recognition from accelerometer data. AAAI **5**, 1541–1546 (2005)
8. Yun, X., Bachmann, E., Moore, H., Calusdian, J.: Self-contained position tracking of human movement using small inertial/magnetic sensor modules. In: IEEE International Conference on Robotics and Automation, pp. 2526–2533. IEEE (2007)
9. Xia, L., Chen, C., Aggarwal, J.: View invariant human action recognition using histograms of 3d joints. In: CVPR Workshops, pp. 20–27 (2012)
10. Chen, C., Jafari, R., Kehtarnavaz, N.: A survey of depth and inertial sensor fusion for human action recognition. Multimed. Tools Appl., 1–21 (2015)
11. Nirjon, S., Greenwood, C., Torres, C., Zhou, S., Stankovic, J., Yoon, H., Ra, H., Basaran, C., Park, T., Son, S. Kintense: a robust, accurate, real-time and evolving system for detecting aggressive actions from streaming 3d skeleton data. In: ACM Conference on Embedded Networked Sensor Systems, pp. 1–9 (2013)
12. Martinez, M., Stiefelhagen, R.: Automated multi-camera system for long term behavioral monitoring in intensive care units. In: Proceedings of the 13 IAPR International Conference on Machine Vision Applications, MVA, pp. 97–100 (2013)

13. Chase, J.G., Agogue, F., Starfinger, C., Lam, Z.H., Shaw, G.M., Rudge, A.D.: Quantifying agitation in sedated ICU patients using digital imaging. Comput. Method Prog. Biomed. **76**, 131–141 (2004)
14. Biswas, J., Jayachandran, M., Thang, P., Fook, V., Choo, T., Qiang, Q., Takahashi, S., Jianzhong, E., Feng, C., Yap, P.: Agitation monitoring of persons with dementia based on acoustic sensors, pressure sensors, ultrasound sensors,: a feasibility study. In: International Conference on Aging, Disability and Independence, pp. 3–15 (2006)
15. Wenhui, L., Weihong, Z., Zhiwei, Z., Qiang, J.: A real-time human stress monitoring system using dynamic bayesian network. In: CVPR 2005, pp. 70–77 (2005)
16. Sakr, G., Elhajj, I., Huijer, H.: Support vector machines to define and detect agitation transition. IEEE Trans. Affect. Comput. **1**(2), 98–108 (2010)
17. Pan, W., Yoshida, S., Liu, Q., Wu, C., Wang, J., Zhu, J., Cai, D.: Quantitative evaluation of severity of behavioral and psychological symptoms of dementia in patients with vascular dementia. Transl. Neurodegener. **2**(9), 2–7 (2013)
18. Tractenberg, R., Singer, C., Cummings, J., Thal, L.: The sleep disorders inventory: an instrument for studies of sleep disturbance in persons with alzheimer's disease. J. Sleep Res. **12**(4), 331–337 (2003)
19. Knuff, A.: Application of actigraphy to the measurement of neuropsychiatric symptoms of agitation in dementia. Master's thesis, Queen's University, Canada (2014)
20. Zhu, Y., Wenbin, C., Guodong, G.: Fusing spatiotemporal features and joints for 3d action recognition. In: CVPRW, pp. 486–491 (2013)
21. Bao, L., Intille, S.S.: Activity recognition from user-annotated acceleration data. In: Ferscha, A., Mattern, F. (eds.) PERVASIVE 2004. LNCS, vol. 3001, pp. 1–17. Springer, Heidelberg (2004)
22. Stern, T.: Massachusetts General Hospital Handbook of General Hospital Psychiatry, 6th edn. Saunders, Elsevier, New York (2010)
23. Kwapisz, J., Weiss, G., Moore, S.: Activity recognition using cell phone accelerometers. SIGKDD Explor. Newsl. **12**(2), 74–82 (2011)
24. Opitz, D., Maclin, R.: Popular ensemble methods: an empirical study. J. Artif. Intell. Res. **11**, 169–198 (1999)
25. Rodriguez, J., Kuncheva, L., Alonso, C.: Rotation forest: a new classifier ensemble method. IEEE Trans. Pattern Analy. Mach. Intell. **28**(10), 1619–1630 (2006)

Motorized Multi-camera Slider for Precise Monitoring of Physical Rehabilitation

Ramón Panduro, Miguel Oliver, Rafael Morales, Pascual González, and Antonio Fernández-Caballero(✉)

Universidad de Castilla-La Mancha, 02071 Albacete, Spain
antonio.fdez@uclm.es

Abstract. This paper introduces the description of the design and operation of a motorized multi-camera slider. The slider has been developed as part of an assistive technology aimed at monitoring physical rehabilitation exercises from different views. The monitoring of the exercises is performed from a couple of RGB-D Kinect cameras that are placed on the most convenient positions of the slider in an intelligent manner to capture the best views of the patient's important body parts. This paper focuses mainly on the description of the dynamic model of the platform and the control of the motorized slider.

Keywords: Motorized slider · RGB-D camera · Rehabilitation · Control system

1 Introduction

Assistive technologies aim to bring technology to the disabled and use specialized hardware, specifically designed to solve a human-machine interaction problem. Disabled people can actually interact with a computer system by using new hardware addressing their disability. One class of assistive technology is associated with the area of computer-assisted rehabilitation, which designs specialized hardware and software to help patients in their rehabilitation exercises and therapists in monitoring the patients' activities [1].

A rehabilitation system of two young adults using the Kinect sensor has been developed by [2]. Another example of a system that uses the Kinect device to capture the patient's movements during rehabilitation exercises has been described [3]. Applications developed in our proper research team are some other examples aimed at assisting aging adults [4]. There are also commercial rehabilitation systems based on this affordable sensor, such as KineLabs, Reflexion, Toyra, TeKi and VirtualRehab.

Although mono-camera rehabilitation systems work well enough in most situations, if we need to monitor more than one part of the patient's body, such systems have several limitations. This article describes the operation of a motorized slider capable of moving a couple of RGB-D cameras in an intelligent way for monitoring the patient's body.

C.R. García et al. (Eds.): UCAmI 2016, Part II, LNCS 10070, pp. 21–27, 2016.
DOI: 10.1007/978-3-319-48799-1_3

2 System Description

The number of cameras that a physical rehabilitation system should support is an important key in the design of the motorized slider. In our case, two Kinect cameras are sufficient to monitor the exercises. The first camera should follow the patient's forehead, and the second has to track one of his/her sides. This may leave dead angles in certain cases. However, it is a sufficiently good solution for most real cases. Another key to be treated in depth is the rail type to use. In most cases, a rectilinear slider along each wall is sufficient. This option even facilitates mounting the system in a normal room. However, the design could be an understatement. Indeed, a curved channel gives more tracking freedom to the cameras, specially when the patient makes difficult maneuvers such as turning on him/herself. This is why, we have finally envisioned an arrangement consisting in a circle that surrounds the monitored patient.

The next question to be addressed is the kind of movement that the lane can perform. In our case, the slider needs only to move horizontally, as Kinect cameras rotate with an independent motor rail. The camera movements to cover all angles are the pitch and the lead, which is fair enough to observe all angles. Also, it is interesting to discuss the issue on the number of lanes to be used. A cheaper solution is to mount both cameras on a same lane, but there are more difficulties in programming the system so that the cameras do not collide.

Finally, the problem of distances and weight measurements in the platform have been faced. The optimum viewing distance of the Kinect 2.0 is between 1.8 and 2.5 m. Based on the layout chosen for the cameras, they will be placed in a circular rail whose radius is 2.2 m. Thus, the patient is perfectly monitored during the physical rehabilitation exercises. The next measurement is the height at which the cameras should be placed. The optimum height of the Kinect 2.0 cameras is between 0.6 and 1.8 m. This is why the cart is sized to place the cameras at a height of 1 m. Lastly, the weight of the Kinect 2.0 camera along with its cables has been measured, obtaining a weight of 931 g. All the information has been transferred to the control system.

3 Dynamic Model of the Platform

The dynamical model of the platform has been set up from the description of the system. To calculate the balance of forces, the cart has been separated into three subsystems: the Kinect camera, the cart body and the sprocket. The calculations have been performed starting from the camera and following the transmission of forces to the engine that would move the sprocket. To obtain the dynamic model, at first we must get the function that provides the moment generated by the engines. Figure 1 illustrates a sketch with the forces balance to obtain the equations that determinate our torques.

Lat us emphasize that the torque caused by the movement of the camera in the Y-axis has not been taken into account in the other bodies, because it

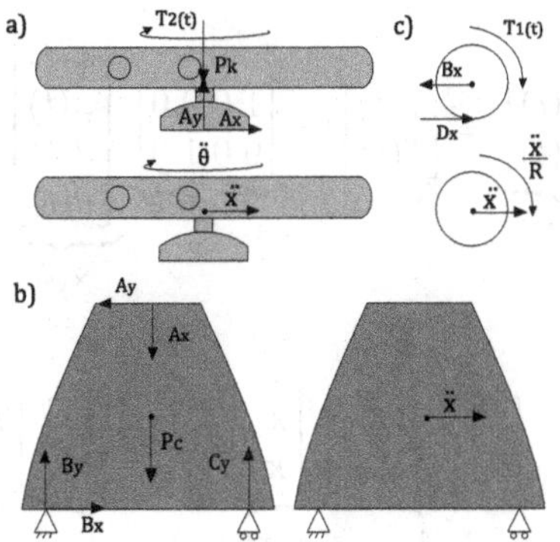

Fig. 1. Force and acceleration balances: (a) in the Kinect camera, (b) in the cart body, (c) in the sprocket.

is absorbed by the axes and the rail. The equations obtained for the engines' moments are the following ones:

$$T_1(t) = I_g \frac{\ddot{x}(t)}{R} + mR_r\ddot{x}(t); \quad T_2(t) = I_{gk}\ddot{\theta}(t) \tag{1}$$

where I_{gk} represents the inertial moment of the gyratory body of the camera, I_g expresses the inertial moment of the sprocket, $T_1(t)$ is the torque caused by the engines of the cart; $T_2(t)$ is the torque caused by the engines of the camera engine, m denotes the mass of the whole system, R_r and R_c represent the radius of the sprocket and the rail, respectively, $x(t)$ is the linear position of the track, and $\theta(t)$ represents the angular position of the camera. When solving the values of the acceleration, $\ddot{x}(t)$, and the angular acceleration, $\ddot{\theta}(t)$, one obtains:

$$\ddot{x}(t) = \frac{R_r}{I_g + mR_r^2}T_1(t); \quad \ddot{\theta}(t) = \frac{1}{I_{gk}}T_2(t) \tag{2}$$

Bearing in mind that the multi-camera slider moves on a rail with circular shape of radius R_c, it is necessary to convert the linear acceleration component for the cart's engine, $\ddot{x}(t)$, into an angular acceleration, defined as $\ddot{\varphi}(t)$, around the circle that forms the rail. Therefore, the dynamic model is as follows:

$$\ddot{\varphi}(t) = \frac{R_r R_c}{I_g + mR_r^2}T_1(t); \quad \ddot{\theta}(t) = \frac{1}{I_{gk}}T_2(t) \tag{3}$$

Finally, the dynamic system (3) is expressed in space-state form as:

$$\underbrace{\frac{d}{dt}\begin{bmatrix}\varphi(t)\\ \dot{\varphi}(t)\\ \theta(t)\\ \dot{\theta}(t)\end{bmatrix}}_{\dot{\mathbf{x}}(t)} = \underbrace{\begin{bmatrix}0&1&0&0\\0&0&0&0\\0&0&0&0\\0&0&0&0\end{bmatrix}}_{\mathbf{A}}\underbrace{\begin{bmatrix}\varphi(t)\\ \dot{\varphi}(t)\\ \theta(t)\\ \dot{\theta}(t)\end{bmatrix}}_{\mathbf{x}(t)} + \underbrace{\begin{bmatrix}0&0\\ \beta_\varphi&0\\0&0\\0&\beta_\theta\end{bmatrix}}_{\mathbf{B}}\underbrace{\begin{bmatrix}T_1(t)\\T_2(t)\end{bmatrix}}_{\mathbf{u}(t)} \tag{4}$$

$$\underbrace{\begin{bmatrix} y_1(t) \\ y_2(t) \end{bmatrix}}_{\mathbf{y}(t)} = \begin{bmatrix} \varphi(t) \\ \theta(t) \end{bmatrix} = \underbrace{\begin{bmatrix} 1\,0\,0\,0 \\ 0\,0\,1\,0 \end{bmatrix}}_{\mathbf{C}} \underbrace{\begin{bmatrix} \varphi(t) \\ \dot{\varphi}(t) \\ \theta(t) \\ \dot{\theta}(t) \end{bmatrix}}_{\dot{\mathbf{x}}(t)} \tag{5}$$

or

$$\underbrace{\begin{bmatrix} \dot{\mathbf{x}}_\varphi(t) \\ \dot{\mathbf{x}}_\theta(t) \end{bmatrix}}_{\dot{\mathbf{x}}(t)} = \underbrace{\begin{bmatrix} \mathbf{A}_\varphi & \mathbf{0}_{2\times 2} \\ \mathbf{0}_{2\times 2} & \mathbf{A}_\theta \end{bmatrix}}_{\mathbf{A}} \underbrace{\begin{bmatrix} \mathbf{x}_\varphi(t) \\ \mathbf{x}_\theta(t) \end{bmatrix}}_{\mathbf{x}(t)} + \underbrace{\begin{bmatrix} \mathbf{B}_\varphi \\ \mathbf{B}_\theta \end{bmatrix}}_{\mathbf{B}} \underbrace{\begin{bmatrix} T_1(t) \\ T_2(t) \end{bmatrix}}_{\mathbf{u}(t)} \tag{6}$$

$$\mathbf{y}(t) = \begin{bmatrix} \varphi(t) \\ \theta(t) \end{bmatrix} = \underbrace{\begin{bmatrix} \mathbf{C}_\varphi & \mathbf{0}_{1\times 2} \\ \mathbf{0}_{1\times 2} & \mathbf{C}_\theta \end{bmatrix}}_{\mathbf{C}} \underbrace{\begin{bmatrix} \mathbf{x}_\varphi(t) \\ \mathbf{x}_\theta(t) \end{bmatrix}}_{\mathbf{x}(t)} \tag{7}$$

where $\beta_\varphi = \frac{R_r R_c}{I_g + m R_r^2}$ and $\beta_\theta = \frac{1}{I_{gk}}$ have been defined in order to simplify the calculations and ease the management of the dynamic model.

4 Control Design

After inspection of expressions (6) and (7), one observes that these two systems can be controlled in an uncoupled form. Indeed, they can work independently each other. This allows to design independent controller actions for the wheel platform and the camera subsystems. The fundamental idea in regulating the motorized multi-camera slider is to use the dynamic model represented by expressions (6) and (7). To accomplish this, we primarily estimate the time derivatives of the measured variables, $\hat{\mathbf{w}}(t) = [\hat{\dot{\varphi}}(t), \hat{\dot{\theta}}(t)]^T$, by means of a reduced order observer, and then asymptotically impose a linear stable closed loop dynamics by using a linear space state feedback with an additional output feedback [5–8]. Figure 2 illustrates the proposed scheme. Then, the observer-based feedback controller is conceived as follows:

$$\mathbf{u}(t) = \begin{bmatrix} T_1(t) \\ T_2(t) \end{bmatrix} = \mathbf{K}_0 \left[\mathbf{r}(t) - \mathbf{y}(t)\right] + \mathbf{K}\mathbf{x}(t) = \mathbf{K}_0 \mathbf{r}(t) - \left[\mathbf{B}\mathbf{K}_0\mathbf{C} + \mathbf{B}\mathbf{K}\right]\mathbf{x}(t) \tag{8}$$

with

$$\mathbf{K} = \begin{bmatrix} 0 & k_{\varphi 1} & 0 & 0 \\ 0 & 0 & 0 & k_{\theta 1} \end{bmatrix} = \begin{bmatrix} \mathbf{K}_{1\varphi} & \mathbf{0}_{1\times 2} \\ \mathbf{0}_{1\times 2} & \mathbf{K}_{1\theta} \end{bmatrix}; \quad \mathbf{K}_0 = \begin{bmatrix} k_{\varphi 0} & 0 \\ 0 & k_{\theta 0} \end{bmatrix} \tag{9}$$

where variables, $\hat{\mathbf{w}}(t) = [\hat{\dot{\varphi}}(t), \hat{\dot{\theta}}(t)]^T$, used in (8), are generated by the following reduced order observer:

$$\dot{\hat{\mathbf{w}}}(t) = \mathbf{F}\hat{\mathbf{w}}(t) + \mathbf{G}\mathbf{u}(t) + \mathbf{H}_1\mathbf{y}(t) + \mathbf{H}_2\mathbf{A}_{11}\mathbf{y}(t) + \mathbf{H}_2\mathbf{A}_{12}\mathbf{w}(t) + \mathbf{H}_2\mathbf{B}_1\mathbf{u}(t) \tag{10}$$

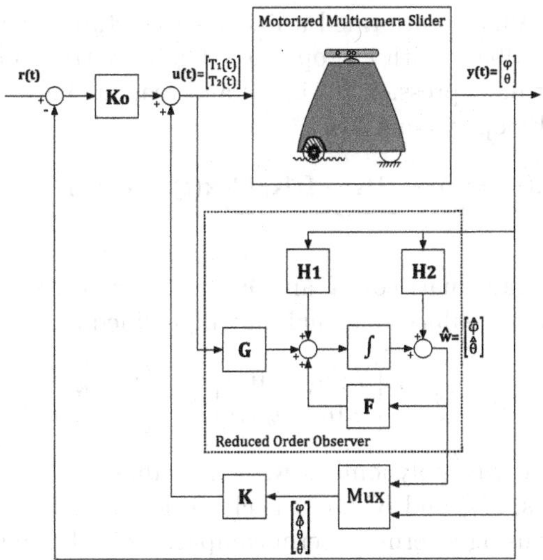

Fig. 2. Proposed control scheme.

where $\mathbf{F}$ represents the desired closed-loop dynamics of the observer and $\mathbf{A}_{11}$, $\mathbf{A}_{12}$, $\mathbf{A}_{21}$, $\mathbf{A}_{22}$, $\mathbf{B}_1$ and $\mathbf{B}_2$ matrices are given by the following values:

$$\mathbf{A}_{11} = \mathbf{A}_{21} = \mathbf{A}_{22} = \mathbf{B}_1 = \begin{bmatrix} 0 & 0 \\ 0 & 0 \end{bmatrix}; \quad \mathbf{A}_{12} = \begin{bmatrix} 1 & 0 \\ 0 & 1 \end{bmatrix}; \quad \mathbf{B}_2 = \begin{bmatrix} \beta_\varphi & 0 \\ 0 & \beta_\theta \end{bmatrix} \tag{11}$$

The estimation error vector, $\mathbf{e_w}(t) = \dot{\hat{\mathbf{w}}}(t) - \dot{\mathbf{w}}(t)$, evolves according with the following linear dynamics:

$$\dot{\hat{\mathbf{w}}}(t) - \dot{\mathbf{w}}(t) = \mathbf{F}\hat{\mathbf{w}}(t) - [\mathbf{A}_{22} - \mathbf{H}_2\mathbf{A}_{12}]\,\mathbf{w}(t) + [\mathbf{H}_1 + \mathbf{H}_2\mathbf{A}_{11} - \mathbf{A}_{21}]\,\mathbf{y}(t) + [\mathbf{G} + \mathbf{H}_2\mathbf{B}_1 - \mathbf{B}_2]\,\mathbf{u}(t) \tag{12}$$

Starting from the knowledge of the matrices $\mathbf{A}_{11}$, $\mathbf{A}_{12}$, $\mathbf{A}_{21}$, $\mathbf{A}_{22}$, $\mathbf{B}_1$ and $\mathbf{B}_2$, in order to achieve a convergence to the origin of the phase space of the observer estimation error, $\mathbf{e_w}(t)$, the coefficients of the constant gain matrix $\mathbf{F}$ were designed to locate the desired observer closed-loop poles at a common root of the real line, given by $\mathbf{I}^{2\times2}s = -\mathbf{f_o}$, where $\mathbf{f_o} = diag[f_{o\varphi}, f_{o\theta}]$ is a diagonal matrix which terms are clearly strictly positive. On the other hand, the definition of the constant gain matrices $\mathbf{H}_1$, $\mathbf{H}_2$ and $\mathbf{G}$ were designed to fulfill the following three conditions:

$$\mathbf{F} = \mathbf{A}_{22} - \mathbf{H}_2\mathbf{A}_{12} \tag{13}$$

$$\mathbf{H}_1 + \mathbf{H}_2\mathbf{A}_{11} - \mathbf{A}_{21} = \mathbf{0} \tag{14}$$

$$\mathbf{G} + \mathbf{H}_2\mathbf{B}_1 - \mathbf{B}_2 = \mathbf{0} \tag{15}$$

Then, the trajectory of the estimation error, $\mathbf{e_w}(t)$, converges to the origin of the phase space of the observer estimation error. On the other hand, and according to expression (8), we have performed a linear space state feedback through an additional output feedback with a proportional gain matrix to regulate the system. After substituting expression (8) in (6) and rearranging terms, one obtains the following closed loop system:

$$\dot{\mathbf{x}}(t) = \underbrace{[\mathbf{A} - \mathbf{BK} - \mathbf{BK}_0\mathbf{C}]}_{\mathbf{A}_r}\mathbf{x}(t) + \mathbf{BK}_0\mathbf{r}(t) \tag{16}$$

where the constant gain matrices $\mathbf{K}$ and $\mathbf{K}_0$ are designed so as to render the following 2×2 complex valued diagonal matrix, defined as:

$$\mathbf{p_c}(s) = \mathbf{I}^{2\times2}s^2 + \begin{bmatrix} \beta_\varphi k_{1\varphi} & 0 \\ 0 & \beta_\theta k_{1\theta} \end{bmatrix} s + \begin{bmatrix} \beta_\varphi k_{0\varphi} & 0 \\ 0 & \beta_\theta k_{0\theta} \end{bmatrix} \tag{17}$$

as second degree Hurwitz polynomials with desirable root locations. The constant controller gains, $\mathbf{K_D^m}$ and $\mathbf{K_P^m}$, of the closed loop characteristic polynomial were determined by using a term-by-term comparison with the following desired Hurwitz 2×2 complex valued diagonal matrix:

$$\mathbf{p_{c_d}}(s) = \mathbf{I}^{2\times2}s^2 + 2\mathbf{a}s + \mathbf{a}^2 \tag{18}$$

where $\mathbf{a} \in \mathbb{R}^{2\times2}$ is a diagonal positive definite matrix representing the natural frequency.

Acknowledgements. This work was partially supported by Spanish Ministerio de Economía y Competitividad/FEDER under TIN2015-72931-EXP, TIN2013-47074-C2-1-R and TIN2012-34003 grants. Miguel Oliver holds an FPU scholarship (FPU13/03141) from the Spanish Government.

References

1. Oliver, M., Montero, F., Molina, J.P., González, P., Fernández-Caballero, A.: Multi-camera systems for rehabilitation therapies: a study of the precision of Microsoft Kinect sensors. Front. Inf. Technol. Electron. Eng. **17**(4), 348–364 (2016)
2. Chang, Y., Chen, S., Huang, J.: A Kinect-based system for physical rehabilitation: a pilot study for young adults with motor disabilities. Res. Dev. Disabil. **32**(6), 2566–2570 (2011)
3. Freitas, D., Da Gama, A., Figueiredo, L., Chaves, T., Marques-Oliveira, D., Teichrieb, V., Araújo, C.: Development and evaluation of a Kinect based motor rehabilitation game. In: Simposio Brasileiro de Jogos e Entretenimento Digital, pp. 144–153 (2012)
4. Oliver, M., Montero, F., Fernández-Caballero, A., González, P., Molina, J.P.: RGB-D assistive technologies for acquired brain injury: description and assessment of user experience. Expert Syst. **32**(3), 370–380 (2015)
5. Morales, R., Somolinos, J.A., Morón, C., García, A.: Space-state robust control of a Buck converter with amorphous core coil and variable load. Measurement **46**, 3863–3870 (2013)
6. Morales, R., Sira-Ramírez, H., Somolinos, J.A.: Linear active disturbance rejection control of the hovercraft vessel model. Ocean Eng. **96**, 100–108 (2015)

7. Morales, R., Feliu, V., Jaramillo, V.: Position control of very lightweight single-link flexible arms with large payload variations by using disturbance observers. Robot. Auton. Syst. **60**, 532–547 (2012)
8. Morales, R., Somolinos, J.A., Sira-Ramírez, H.: Control of a DC motor using algebraic derivative estimation with real time experiments. Measurement **47**, 401–417 (2014)

Machine Learning Method to Establish the Connection Between Age Related Macular Degeneration and Some Genetic Variations

Antonieta Martínez-Velasco[1(✉)], Juan Carlos Zenteno[2], Lourdes Martínez-Villaseñor[1], Luis Miralles-Pechúan[1], Andric Pérez-Ortiz[1], and Francisco Javier Estrada-Mena[1]

[1] Universidad Panamericana Campus México, Augusto Rodin 498, Col. Insurgentes-Mixcoac, Ciudad de México, Mexico
{amartinezv, lmartine, lmiralles, festrada}@up.edu.mx, andricc@me.com

[2] Instituto de Oftalmología Conde de Valenciana, Chimalpopoca 14, Col.Obrera, Ciudad de México, Mexico
jczenteno@institutodeoftalmologia.org

Abstract. Medicine research based in machine learning methods allows the improvement of diagnosis in complex diseases. Age related Macular Degeneration (AMD) is one of them. AMD is the leading cause of blindness in the world. It causes the 8.7 % of blind people. A set of case and controls study could be developed by machine-learning methods to find the relation between Single Nucleotide Polymorphisms (SNPs) SNP_A, SNP_B, SNP_C and AMD. In this paper we present a machine-learning based analysis to determine the relation of three single nucleotide SNPs and the AMD disease. The SNPs SNP_B, SNP_C remained in the top four relevant features with ophthalmologic surgeries and bilateral cataract. We aim also to determine the best set of features for the classification process.

Keywords: Single nucleotide polymorphisms · Macular degeneration · Machine learning · Polymorphism relation

1 Introduction

Age related macular degeneration (AMD) is the leading cause of visual dysfunction and blindness in developed countries, and a rising cause in underdeveloped countries. In the United States, its prevalence in the population over age 65 years is 9 % and increases to 28 % in those over 75 years [1, 2]. AMD is characterized by progressive degeneration of the macula, causing central field vision loss. A characteristic feature of AMD is the formation of deposits in the macula, called drusen, which may progress to either geographic atrophy (dry form) or subretinal neovascularization (wet form), manifestations of late AMD. Several genetic and environmental risk factors influence disease susceptibility. AMD is a multifactorial disease, typically caused by many genetic variants, each with modest effect on the risk and also influenced by non-genetic/environmental factors, such as diet and smoking [3].

C.R. García et al. (Eds.): UCAmI 2016, Part II, LNCS 10070, pp. 28–39, 2016.
DOI: 10.1007/978-3-319-48799-1_4

Multiple studies have assessed the role of genetic variants on AMD risk and progression. Some of them are consistently associated with the disease in Caucasians [4, 5], and in ethnic groups with a complex admixture of ancestral populations such as Mexican mestizos [6]. Sivakumaran et al. [7] have identified a set of SNPs for relation with AMD. This is evidence that the aforementioned genes may confer increased risk for AMD.

The prevalence of AMD varies widely across different ethnic groups in the world. However, it has been observed that in the United States is estimated there are more than 7 million individuals with early changes in the retina that places them at high risk to develop the disease. Thirty per cent of them could develop macular degeneration consistent with the early form of AMD [3].

In other populations such as Oriental, it has also become a health problem due to demographic changes, senescence and lifestyle [8–10]. It is estimated that by 2020, at least 80 million people globally, may be affected with AMD [11].

This substantial increase in public health burden could lead to a collapse in health systems worldwide. Not only envisages the poor response of these systems to care for these patients, and the AMD has a tremendous impact not only on physical health, also in mental health and in the economy of the geriatric population and their families [12, 13].

One of the factors that make this disease a problem of major health is that its incidence continues to rise due to the increasing number of elderly people in the world. AMD is also the leading cause of lower disability, affecting progressively central vision.

There are few studies on Mexican population. It is important to study the relation between the genetic variation in populations not traditionally studied to find the relation between ethnic differences in each genetic variants to modify disease risk [6, 14].

Usually the relation is determined by statistics techniques. Obtaining the odds ratio and p value which indicates the risk or protection against the disease [3].

Machine learning methods have been used to study the relation between SNPs and complex diseases such as cancer [15], schizophrenia [16], even AMD [17] some SNPs for Caucasian population mainly.

Currently medical research is made to relate mutations in some particular genes associated with this disease. In order to establish the relationship between risk factors and AMD, statistical information management is usually used. These studies asses the presence of Single Nucleotide Polymorphisms (SNPs) to establish the relation between them and the disease, but the results of this analysis only give the possibilities of having the disease. An improved model can be generated using machine learning techniques. This will allow more reliable and accurate predictions for the risk of developing the disease.

We constructed a dataset with 119 patients and 137 healthily subjects. Criteria for patient inclusion were as follows: (1) age 60 years or older, (2) diagnosis by a retina specialist of AMD grades 4 or 5 in both eyes or AMD grades 4 or 5 in one eye and any type of drusen in the fellow eye, (3) no relation with other retinal disease, and (4) a negative history of vitreous-retinal surgery. Subjects were classified according to Clinical Age Related Maculopathy Staging System (CARMS) where grade 4 corresponds to geographic atrophy, while grade 5 corresponds to choroidal neovascularization [3, 18]. The AMD stage assigned was based on the most affected eye at the time of recruitment. Control subjects were enrolled from the outpatient department throughout routine ophthalmic examination. They were aged 60 years or older, had no drusen or retinal pigment epithelium (RPE) changes under dilated fundus examination, and informed a negative family history of AMD. Informed consent was signed by all subjects before they participated in the study.

In this paper we present a machine-learning based analysis to determine the relation of three single nucleotide SNPs and the AMD disease. One hundred and nineteen patients and 137 controls — persons without visual injury— were recruited following a standard ophthalmologic examination protocol. This investigation was a hospital-based, case-control relation study done in a Mexican population. We included 30 clinical features for each one of the cases and controls.

We found an accuracy of 85.5 % in the supervised analysis for the three Single Nucleotide Polymorphism (SNPs) to predict the disease. It is a promising result which motivates us to continue studying and testing with larger databases to improve the predictability of the disease.

The rest of the paper is as follows. A brief state of the art of the analysis of associations in complex diseases is presented in Sect. 2. In Sect. 3, we propose our machine-based analysis to determine the relation of three single nucleotide SNPs and the AMD disease. In Sect. 4, experiments and results are shown and discussed. Section 5 concludes the paper and highlights future work in this context.

2 Determining Relation Between SNPs and Complex Diseases

A complex disease is the medical condition that arises from an intricate interaction of inherited nature and environmental factors. Examples of them are cancer, AMD, bipolar disorder, obesity, and schizophrenia [19].

Traditionally statistical analysis is applied to determining the association between SNPs in genes and complex diseases. Various features should be considered to analyze a complex disease for sick and healthy subjects. In the main, continuous variables are compared with the Student t test, and corrected chi- square statistics are applied for categorical variables. Univariate and multivariate non conditional logistic regressions are developed to determine risk magnitude comparing each allele and genotype with the main effect employed as the binary variable [20].

Machine learning is also used to detect patterns and relations between SNPs and AMD [21]. Machine learning models generate inference rules that serve to generate new knowledge from initial data collections. The accuracy of the model will be proportional to the amount of data. Those models will predict with high accuracy the cases where the disease is present in a patient [22].

Machine learning models consider relationships among input data that cannot always be recognized by conventional analyses. In the future, complex medical diagnostic and treatment decisions will be increasingly based in machine learning models [23].

The growing interest in individualized medicine reinforces the role of predictive models, particularly of diagnostic processes. These are intended to establish a relationship between a set of variables and dependence of them have AMD, to make reliable and accurate predictions of the risks of developing the disease.

It is important to determine the risk of having the disease as soon as possible given that, as it appears in elderly subjects, it leaves us a long time to prevent the disease.

Until today machine learning methods have been used to study the relation between SNPs and complex diseases such as cancer [15], schizophrenia [16] and AMD [21].

3 Machine Learning Based Method for Relation of SNPs and AMD

In order to find the relation of single nucleotide polymorphisms SNP_A, SNP_B, and SNP_C we followed the procedure shown in Fig. 1.

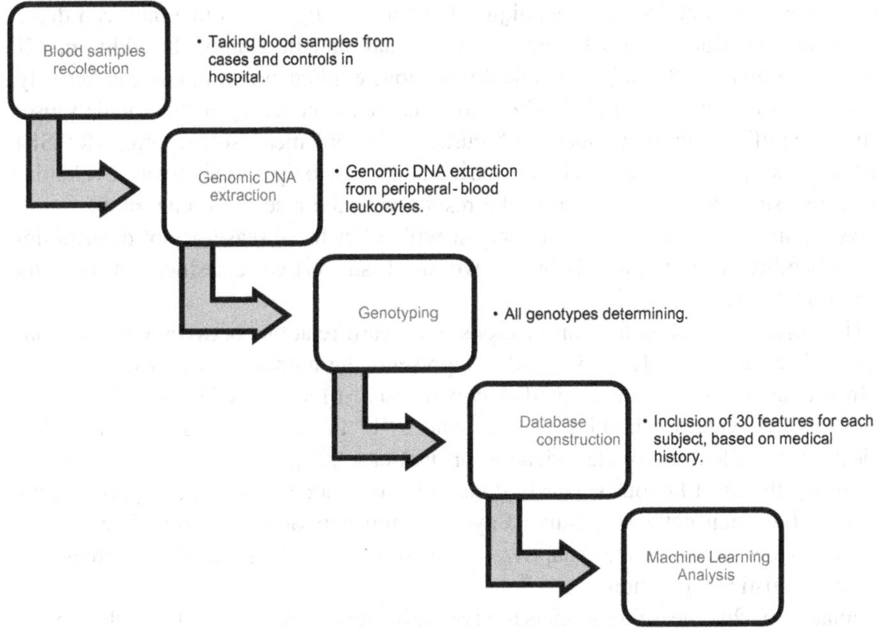

Fig. 1. Procedure to determine the relation

3.1 Data Collection Procedure

The first step was to obtain the blood samples from patients and healthy subjects in the ophthalmologic hospital.

Then genomic DNA was extracted from peripheral- blood leukocytes using the QIAamp DNA Blood Maxi Kit (Qiagen, Hilden, Germany).

The next step was to genotyping DNA samples with Taqman probes (Applied Biosystems). All genotypes were determined in a Real Time PCR instrument PikoReal (Thermo Scientific). The probes were acquired directly from tests on demand service Applied Biosystems as quality control verification process for genotyping. The assay was done for all samples twice.

The last step was to build the data base with the data obtained from the clinical history of each one of subjects. The data base includes 30 features as ophthalmic surgery, cataract both eyes, alcoholism, visual acuity left eye, visual acuity right eye, glaucoma, cataract left eye, pterygium, diabetic retinopathy, altered glucose, diabetes, vitreous hemorrhage, age, obesity, sex, hypercholesterolemia, xerosis both eyes, cataract right eye, presbyopia, astigmatism, smoking, hole in macula, blepharitis, posterior vitreous detachment, choroidal fracture, dyslipidemia, ectropion. The last feature is group which values "1" for cases and "0" for controls.

3.2 Analysis and Information Processing

We proposed to improve the analysis with machine learning modeling. The main reason to use machine learning techniques for our investigation is that they can detect patterns and relations than a human, or traditional statistic cannot. In addition, ML methods are able to "learn" automatically without explicit programming, effectively, and with less cost and effort [15]. These models are evaluated by metrics widely used by the scientific community such as accuracy, the root mean square error (RMSE), sensitivity or specificity [24]. These metrics allow not only to effectively evaluating model precision, but also comparing the results with the research community.

As we must predict whether the patient will suffer the disease or not determining the probability with great reliability, we used supervised classification machine learning methods.

The objective of classification methods is to learn relations between entries X and outputs Y, where $Y \in \{1, \ldots, C\}$ and C represents the number of classes.

In our experiment, models predict two outputs. Models predict the class group which has two values. The class has the value "1" for patients and "0" for healthy subjects. It is called binary classification or dual-case [25].

Among the most famous supervised classification models there are Support Vector Machine, Bayesian networks, Naive Bayes, Neural networks, Random Forest, C5.0, C4.5-like Trees, Multivariate Adaptive Regression Spline, Logistic Model Trees, and Boosted Logistic Regression.

Finally, machine learning models are typically created from a set of samples known as training set and evaluated with a different set of samples called test set. The data sets are composed of the training set that usually has the major part of the data set samples and the test set that usually has a small part of the data set samples, depending on the experimentation settings.

4 Experiments and Results

In this work, we designed two sets of experiments. The goal of the first set was to find the importance of each feature in order to determine the relevance for the classification process of SNP_A, SNP_B, and SNP_C. We aim also to determine the best set of features for the classification process. The second set of experiments compared the performance of ten well-known supervised machine learning techniques in the classification process. The goal of these experiments is to prove the predictive power of all combinations of features, preferably testing SNP's sets of features.

4.1 Data Set

The data set used in the experiment is composed by 256 samples. Each one has 30 features, where "Group" variable represents the output of the model and the remaining 29 represent the model entries. The "Group" column has the value "1" for patients or "0" for healthy subjects. Therefore, we have a binary classification problem. Data were standardized as nominal variables, except age that remained in numeric format.

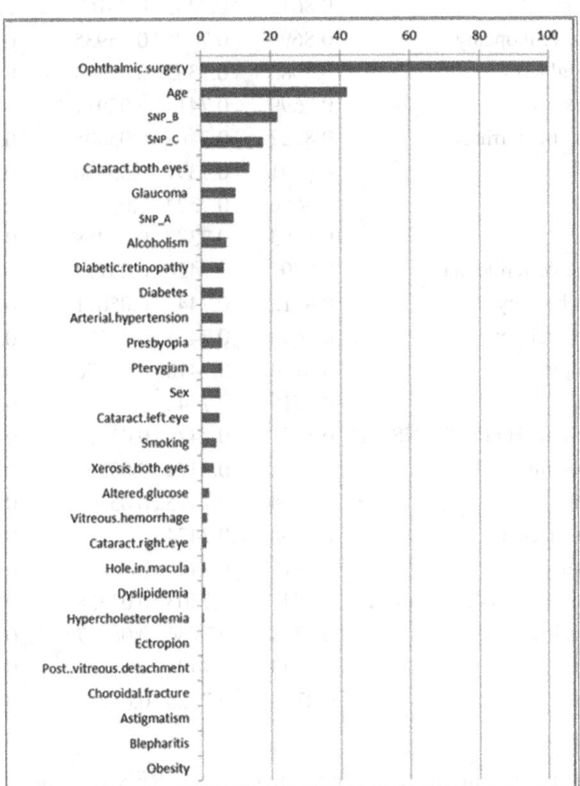

Fig. 2. Ranking of 30 features in relation with AMD.

4.2 Feature Ranking and Best Feature Set Selection

Recursive Feature Elimination (RFE) was used in order to perform feature ranking. RFE method provides high quality results. This method is a wrapper type. This technique uses Random Forest to measure the quality of each combination of features. Accuracy of generated models is the evaluation measure to determine the predictive

Table 1. Feature importance and combination set accuracy

N°	Feature	Accuracy	Kappa	AccuracySD	KappaSD
1	Ophthalmic surgery	0.7969	0.6024	0.05913	0.1130
2	SNP_B	0.8242	0.6537	0.05837	0.1129
3	Cataract both eyes	0.8332	0.6708	0.06078	0.1183
4	SNP_C	0.8245	0.653	0.06297	0.1233
5	Alcoholism	0.8258	0.6549	0.06180	0.1211
6	Visual acuity left eye	0.8184	0.6397	0.06295	0.1236
7	Visual acuity right eye	0.8188	0.6398	0.06689	0.1318
8	Glaucoma	0.8368	0.6755	0.07229	0.1432
9	Cataract left eye	0.8501	0.7012	0.06397	0.1271
10	Pterygium	0.861	0.7233	0.06167	0.1218
11	Diabetic retinopathy	0.8695	0.7405	0.05935	0.1171
12	Altered glucose	0.8683	0.7383	0.05875	0.1158
13	Diabetes	0.8699	0.7411	0.05917	0.1172
14	Vitreous hemorrhage	0.8722	0.746	0.05805	0.1146
15	Age	0.8691	0.7397	0.05900	0.1163
16	Obesity	0.8656	0.7324	0.05705	0.1127
17	Sex	0.8683	0.7377	0.05258	0.1044
18	Hypercholesterolemia	0.8707	0.7426	0.05774	0.1144
19	Xerosis both eyes	0.8715	0.744	0.05671	0.1125
20	Cataract right eye	0.8696	0.7401	0.05762	0.1144
21	Presbyopia	0.8704	0.7418	0.05670	0.1127
22	SNP_A	0.8715	0.7442	0.05557	0.1101
23	ARTERIAL HYPERTENSION	0.8735	0.7479	0.05511	0.1092
24	Astigmatism	0.868	0.7374	0.05862	0.1161
25	Smoking	0.8708	0.7425	0.05397	0.1072
26	Hole in macula	0.8708	0.7424	0.05478	0.1088
27	Blepharitis	0.8715	0.744	0.05447	0.1082
28	Posterior vitreous detachment	0.8747	0.7503	0.05358	0.1063
29	Choroidal fracture	0.8738	0.7486	0.05617	0.1114
30	Dyslipidemia	0.8743	0.7493	0.05606	0.1113
31	Ectropion	0.8758	0.7526	0.05625	0.1115

power of the feature set in the classification process. RFE provides high levels of accuracy and optimal amount of time.

As is shown in Fig. 2, the ranking of the variables was found by RFE method. We can observe that the SNP_B and SNP_C remained in the top four relevant features with ophthalmologic surgeries and bilateral cataract.

In the first place, RFE algorithm fits the model to all variables. Each variable is classified according to the importance to the model as it can be seen in Fig. 3. Then, the RFE algorithm begins to create models using the S_i variables from i = 1 … S. RFE algorithm tries all possible combinations and keeps in a list the variables combination and its performance.

For each iteration, all variables are again classified. At the end of the algorithm execution, a ranking list is done using the results of all iterations as it is shown in Table 1. That explains why the variable order in Fig. 2 is different from the variable order in Table 1. Finally, it is selected the combination with the highest accuracy.

As we can see in Fig. 3, from the combination of ten features, models do not improve significantly with the inclusion of more features. It could be useful to include only the set of the first ten features. Because the small number of samples we used all features in the classification process in Sect. 4.3.

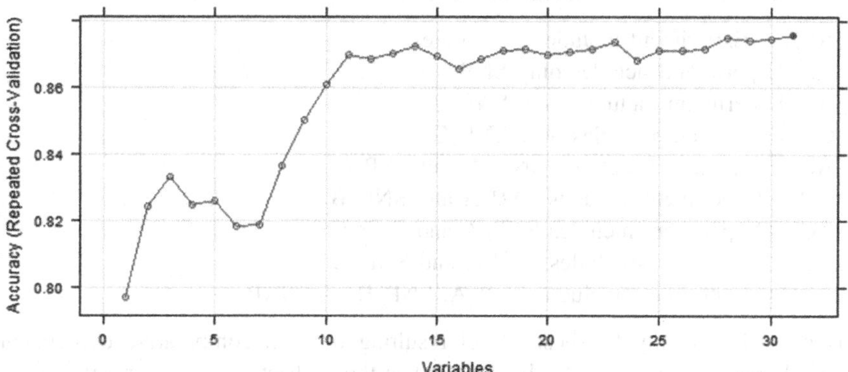

Fig. 3. RFE feature sets accuracy analysis using CV

4.3 Classification Process

The second set of experiments compared the performance of ten well-known supervised machine learning techniques in the classification process: Random Forest, Neural Networks, Naïve Bayes, Multivariate Adaptive Regression Splines, C3.4-like Trees, Stochastic Gradient Boosting and C5.0. The complete analysis were done using R software [27]. We performed the analysis with case and controls samples.

We applied the cross-validation (CV) technique given the small size of our dataset, to obtain more reliable results. CV makes different partitions and combines these to generate many models. The global accuracy is calculated as the average accuracy of all models. Models' performance was analyzed with the means of accuracy, sensitivity and specificity.

To perform the experiments, we used the Caret package of R Studio. We use as measure the accuracy, because it is measuring is the most widely used classification models [28]. Our problem is the classification as we must predict whether a patient has the disease according to the features extracted. We decided to apply CV technique with 10 partitions and 10 repetitions. The algorithm generated 100 models and the model accuracy was calculated as the average of the 100 created models. We used the same methodology and configuration for the generation of models with all selected techniques. We have 4 methods, Random Forest, C5.0, Single C5.0 Ruleset, Single C5.0

Tree, with a number of hits higher than 88 %. The results of the rest of the compared techniques were not very good.

Balance accuracy, is very useful when the samples are not balanced, i.e., when we have a higher number of samples of one class to another. This happens in our case, as we have 119 and 137 by what find us interesting show this value. Giving the same weight to each class. On the other hand, in general gives equal importance to each element. Have also shown the number of configurations that have been tested by the time expressed in thousandths of a second to build each model and each model.

The following comparison experiments were designed to determine the relevance of the three SNPs in the classification process:

(1) ALL. – Experiment includes all features.
(2) A. - Experiment includes only SNP_A
(3) B. - Experiment includes only SNP_B
(4) C. - Experiment includes only SNP_C
(5) AC. - Experiment includes SNP_A and SNP_C
(6) AB. – Experiment includes SNP_A and SNP_B
(7) AC. – Experiment includes SNP_A and SNP_C
(8) BC. – Experiment includes SNP_B and SNP_C
(9) ABC. - Experiment includes SNP_A, SNP_B, and SNP_C

Table 2 shows only the best model resulting of each comparative experiment. Random Forest method is better because it has the highest accuracy, specificity and sensitivity. A good binary classification test always results with high values for all the three factors whereas a poor binary classification test results with low values for all.

"If Sensitivity is high and Specificity is low then, there is no need to worry about the excellent candidates but the poor candidates must be reexamined to eliminate false positives. If Sensitivity is low and Specificity is high, there is no need to bother about the poor candidates but the excellent candidates must be reexamined to eliminate false negatives. An average binary classification test always results with average values which are almost similar for all the three factors." [26]

Table 2. Comparative experiment results (A = SNP_A, B = SNP_B, C = SNP_C)

	Method	Acc	Sens	Spec	Prec	F1	B.Acc	Conf	Time (ms)
ALL	Random forest	0.8585	0.9045	0.8188	0.8528	0.8779	0.8616	3	231.0
A	Neural network	0.5666	0.4397	0.6769	0.6103	0.5112	0.5583	9	15.3
B	Naive bayes	0.5548	0.9579	0.2046	0.5809	0.7232	0.5812	2	20.3
C	Multivariate adaptive regression splines	0.6761	0.5549	0.7814	0.7450	0.6361	0.6682	1	21.2
AC	C4.5-like trees	0.6757	0.5543	0.7812	0.7446	0.6355	0.6678	1	100.4
AB	Stochastic gradient boosting	0.5912	0.4438	0.7192	0.6453	0.5259	0.5815	9	8.4
AC	C4.5-like trees	0.6757	0.5543	0.7812	0.7446	0.6355	0.6678	1	100.4
BC	Random forest	0.7317	0.5488	0.8907	0.8525	0.6677	0.7197	1	80.1
ABC	C5.0	0.7305	0.5465	0.8904	0.8516	0.6658	0.7185	12	7.8

It is remarkable the BC experiment (which includes only SNP_B and SNP_C) because it has high predictive power with 73.17 % Accuracy, 54.88 % Sensitivity, and 89.07 % Specificity.

The combination of the SNP_A and SNP_B shows the same behavior of them separately. Which means that they are correlated and show the same information: 59.12 % accuracy. It was found that the combination of SNP_B and SNP_C results 67.57 % accuracy, which means that 67.57 % of the tests in the diagnosis hit AMD. As it was expected.

5 Conclusions

In this work, we used a machine learning method to develop a classification model to determine if an individual is likely to suffer AMD disease. We also proved the relevance of SNP_A, SNP_B, and SNP_C to the classification process and hence to predict if an individual will have the disease or not. For this purpose, we designed two sets of experiments. The first experiment we performed a feature ranking with RFE. The SNPs SNP_B, and SNP_C remained in the top four relevant features with ophthalmologic surgeries and bilateral cataract. The best combination is the one that includes all the variables, based on measurements of accuracy, sensitivity and specificity. It was obtained by the Random Forest technique using all features. The second set of experiments compared the performance of ten well-known supervised machine learning techniques in the classification process. Random Forest method is best because it has the highest accuracy, specificity and sensitivity.

Based on our results, we conclude that models generated with machine learning techniques support the diagnosis of AMD disease. This shows a promising scenario for the handling of large amounts of data and inference of more precise results.

For future work, we will intend to improve our model including a larger data set. It may help to refine the model and allow to improve the prediction disease. Future studies should evaluate the possibility of extending this model to other diseases.

References

1. Hageman, G.S., Gehrs, K., Johnson, L.V., Anderson, D.: Age-Related Macular Degeneration (AMD) (2008)
2. Congdon, N., et al.: Causes and prevalence of visual impairment among adults in the United States. Arch. Ophthalmol. **122**, 451–452 (2004)
3. Friedman, D.S., et al.: Prevalence of age-related macular degeneration in the United States. Arch. Ophthalmol. (Chicago, Ill. 1960) **122**, 564–572 (2004)
4. Jager, R.D., Mieler, W.F., Miller, J.W.: Age-related macular degeneration. N. Engl. J. Med. **358**, 2606–2617 (2008)
5. Patel, N., Adewoyin, T., Chong, N.V.: Age-related macular degeneration: a perspective on genetic studies. Eye (Lond). **22**, 768–776 (2008)

6. Buentello-Volante, B., et al.: Susceptibility to advanced age-related macular degeneration and alleles of complement factor H, complement factor B, complement component 2, complement component 3, and age-related maculopathy susceptibility 2 genes in a Mexican population. Mol. Vis. **18**, 2518–2525 (2012)
7. Sivakumaran, T.A., et al.: A 32 kb critical region excluding Y402H in CFH mediates risk for age-related macular degeneration. PLoS ONE **6**, e25598 (2011)
8. Gupta, S.K., et al.: Prevalence of early and late age-related macular degeneration in a rural population in Northern India: the INDEYE feasibility study. Invest. Ophthalmol. Vis. Sci. **48**, 1007–1011 (2007)
9. Nirmalan, P.K., et al.: Prevalence of vitreoretinal disorders in a rural population of Southern India. Arch. Ophthalmol. **122**, 581 (2004)
10. Krishnaiah, S., et al.: Risk factors for age-related macular degeneration: findings from the Andhra Pradesh eye disease study in South India. Investig. Opthalmology Vis. Sci. **46**, 4442 (2005)
11. Clemons, T.E., et al.: Risk factors for the incidence of advanced age-related macular degeneration in the age-related eye disease study (AREDS) AREDS report no. 19. Ophthalmology **112**, 533–539 (2005)
12. Berman, K., Brodaty, H.: Psychosocial effects of age-related macular degeneration. Int. Psychogeriatr. **18**, 415–428 (2006)
13. Rovner, B.W., et al.: Effect of depression on vision function in age-related macular degeneration. Arch. Ophthalmol. **120**, 1041 (2002)
14. Klein, R., et al.: Inflammation, complement factor h, and age-related macular degeneration: the multi-ethnic study of atherosclerosis. Ophthalmology **115**, 1742–1749 (2008)
15. Kourou, K., Exarchos, T.P., Exarchos, K.P., Karamouzis, M.V., Fotiadis, D.I.: Machine learning applications in cancer prognosis and prediction. Comput. Struct. Biotechnol. J. **13**, 8–17 (2015)
16. Cardoso, L., et al.: Abstract computation in schizophrenia detection through artificial neural network based systems. Sci. World J. **2015**, 1–10 (2015)
17. Fraccaro, P., et al.: Combining macula clinical signs and patient characteristics for age-related macular degeneration diagnosis: a machine learning approach. BMC Ophthalmol. **15**, 10 (2015)
18. Seddon, J.M., Sharma, S., Adelman, R.A.: Evaluation of the clinical age-related maculopathy staging system. Ophthalmology **113**, 260–266 (2006)
19. Marchini, J., Donnelly, P., Cardon, L.R.: Genome-wide strategies for detecting multiple loci that influence complex diseases. Nat. Genet. **37**, 413–417 (2005)
20. Hadley, D., et al.: Analysis of six genetic risk factors highly associated with AMD in the region surrounding ARMS2 and HTRA1 on chromosome 10, region q26. Investig. Ophthalmol. Vis. Sci. **51**, 2191–2196 (2010)
21. Simonett, J.M., et al.: A validated phenotyping algorithm for genetic association studies in age-related macular degeneration. Sci. Rep. **5**, 12875 (2015)
22. Dasgupta, A., Sun, Y.: Brief review of regression based and machine learning methods in genetic epidemiology: the genetic analysis workshop 17 experience. Genet. Epidemiol. **35**, 1–13 (2011)
23. Hu, X., et al.: Artificial neural networks and prostate cancer–tools for diagnosis and management. Nat. Rev. Urol. **10**, 174–182 (2013)
24. Sokolova, M., Lapalme, G.: A systematic analysis of performance measures for classification tasks. Inf. Process. Manag. **45**, 427–437 (2009)
25. Kotsiantis, S.B.: Supervised machine learning: a review of classification techniques. Informatica **31**, 249–268 (2007)

26. The R Foundation: The R Project for Statistical Computing. (2016). www.r-project.org. Accessed 13 June 2016
27. Kuhn, M., et al: Caret: classification and regression training. R package version 6.0–24. (2014)
28. Aswathi, B.L.: Sensitivity, Specificity, Accuracy and the relationship between them. Lifescience (2009). http://www.lifenscience.com/bioinformatics/sensitivity-specificity-accuracy-and. Accessed 13 June 2016

Ambient Displays to Assist Caregivers Monitoring the Sleep of People with Dementia

Carlos A. Alemán(✉) and Jesús Favela

Computer Science Department, CICESE, Ensenada, Mexico
caleman@cicese.edu.mx, favela@cicese.mx

Abstract. Ambient displays provide peripheral awareness of an event or situation of importance, but not critical. One such situation is monitoring the sleep of people with dementia (PwD). They frequently exhibit problematic behaviors at night, such as waking up often or wandering, which cause significant burden to caregivers. In this paper we propose the use of ambient displays for caregivers in a geriatric residence to be aware of the sleep of PwD. We report the results of a user study conducted in a geriatric residence to determine potential applications of ambient displays. From an ethnographic analysis of the data gathered in the study we derive design insights and application scenarios. We validated these results with caregivers who work in two geriatric residences.

1 Introduction

Human behavior and context sensing via UbiComp can help understand different aspects of human lives as well as to intervene to improve their wellbeing. Within the domain of healthcare, the monitoring of people with dementia (PwD) provides an opportunity to assist both the person being monitored, as well as the caregiver.

PwD often exhibit behavioral problems that are exacerbated in the afternoon and night, as part of a syndrome known as Sundowning [1]. These behaviors include mood changes, agitation, sleep wake disturbances and wandering. Professional caregivers are normally trained to deal with these disturbances, however when the PwD are alone in their rooms, the caregiver might not notice these behaviors, which could potentially put the PwD at harm. Wandering is especially dangerous due to the fact that poor lighting conditions augment the risk of falling. The above underlines the importance of monitoring sleep disturbances experienced by PwD at night.

Sleep monitoring and awareness of problematic behaviors at night is particularly challenging for caregivers in a residence, who care for multiple PwD. In this work we focus on the design of UbiHealth technology to assist them, particularly with the use of an ambient display to serve as a sleep-wake awareness monitors. We describe an observational study conducted in a residence of people with dementia, the results obtained from the qualitative analysis of the data gathered, and the validation of these results with caregivers from two residences.

C.R. García et al. (Eds.): UCAmI 2016, Part II, LNCS 10070, pp. 40–45, 2016.
DOI: 10.1007/978-3-319-48799-1_5

2 Sleep Monitoring

Sleep monitoring, in its simplest form, consists of visually observing patients to verify their status. In a medical context, sleep studies involve a series of tests wrapped in a polysomnography study which is used to diagnose a sleep disorder [2], in which various sensors are attached to the patient to analyze the physiological changes the body experiences across sleep phases [3]. These studies are typically made in a sleep clinic supervised by a specialist.

Most research on HCI related to sleep involves smart alarms and accelerometer-based systems that monitor sleep-wake cycles [4], but with social awareness associated to sleep health. This research is mostly focused on technologies that improve sleep hygiene from individual [5] to collective perspectives [4]. Another current focus is on proactive and knowledge-enhanced sleep environments that react to the user's current sleep state and necessities [6]. This kind of sleep monitoring environments could be useful in an elderly home where caregivers must be aware of the current state of multiple residents at night. We aim to explore the use of ambient displays as a multiple PwD sleep monitoring tool to assist caregivers during nightshifts.

3 Ambient Displays

Ambient displays are aesthetical means to deliver information to the periphery of the user's perception via subtle pulses that somehow reach the user without increasing his a cognitive load [7]. Ambient displays provide an opportunity to abstract different kinds of concepts and big bulks of data into simple and understandable stimulus that reside within the user's environment and specific context.

The broad range of stimulus and interaction forms that an ambient display provide, presents a challenge to ambient displays designers. The abstraction of different types of information, whether simple or complex in an elementary and uncomplicated form, yields some advantages such as data privacy in public schemes, undisruptive notification of non critical events and global awareness of data to multiple selected users [7]. These characteristics make them a feasible technology to support caregivers in an elderly home accommodating multiple PwD residents with diverse sleep problems.

4 Case Study and Methodology

In order to design a usable and useful ambient display, we conducted a contextual study in an elderly home with PwD in northern Mexico. We made 7 semistructured interviews [8] (4H:35 M:13S) with sleep doctors, the manager of geriatric residence, and caregivers to better understand the issues of caring for PwD during the night shift. The interviews were complemented with non participatory shadowing observation [8] of the night shift of the night caregivers at the elderly home (24H51 M). The transcripts of the interviews and observation sessions were analyzed in two interpretation sessions using grounded theory and affinity diagramming [8].

5 Qualitative Study Results: Scenarios and Low-Fidelity Prototypes

From the analysis of the data we derived four scenarios and five personas (four residents and one generic caregiver) [8] in which the night shift caregivers would benefit from non-critical contextual information for PwD monitoring, as well as 4 PwD personas that modeled prototypical residents to be monitored. For these scenarios, we proposed different ambient displays that could be used to address these problems, and designed five low fidelity prototypes. These scenarios are described in Table 1, along with the Persona associated to that scenario.

Table 1. Scenario descriptions with assigned persona

Scenario	Description	PwD Persona
S1 PwD in deep sleep or REM interrupted by the caregiver's activities.	At night, caregivers patrol each of the resident's rooms. During these lookouts they might disrupt the PwD sleep. This alters the rest sleep cycle of the PwD.	Alice is the newest resident at the elderly home and she doesn't trust the caregivers. She tends to wake up angry at night when a caregiver enters her room to check up on her.
S2 The PwD awakes and wanders unsupervised	At night, the PwD tends to wake up and start wandering. Poor illumination, stuff misarranged on the floor and night disorientation, are factors that increase the risk of falling at night.	Jackson suffers from severe dementia. He discontinuously sleeps during the day provoking high activity especially after dinner. Caregivers frequently find him wandering in his dark room or halls; sometimes even crawling.
S3 The PwD awakes and urinates or defecates in their rooms	Some PwD wake up at night and take off their diapers and urinate in the floor. When a caregiver notices, they have to clean the PwD, the bed and the room. This extra activity disturbs the PwD sleep cycle and deprives the caregiver's attention to the other residents.	Patty has always been an erratic resident. Caregivers are always checking on her, especially at night because she tends to be aggressive. She is often disoriented. When she wakes up at night, she tends to urinate or defecate in her room or walk to the other residents' rooms.
S4 The Pwd suffers night pains	Because of the temperature, humidity, ailments, etc. some PwD can't sleep at night due to intense pain and frequently demand the caregiver's attention to ask for pain killers or make them company.	Jackie is a 72 woman with fibromyalgia. At nights she constantly buzzes the caregivers to ask them for extra pain killers. Other nights when she suffers from insomnia she keeps calling them just to talk.

5.1 Prototypes

Considering ambient as "*of or relating to the immediate surroundings of something*" [9], we based the prototypes on different ways of perceiving subtle stimulus (Table 2). Most ambient displays relay on a traditional visual stimulus to lock the targets' attention and deliver data, our prototypes also take advantage of other kind of perception channels such ambient sounds and haptic stimulation.

Table 2. Ambient display prototypes description.

Ambient display	Description	Data output	Perception channel
Door lights	Color lights on the door frame	The color of the light represents the type of event	Visual
White noises	Nature ambient sounds	Each sound represents the location of the event	Auditory
Vibration morse code	Haptic interface	Each haptic morse code indicate the type of event or location	Kinesthetic
Light path	Light patterns and colors	Indicates the path to a current event of interest	Visual
Tempescope	Sound and light awareness	The color of the light and water display indicate the type of event	Visual/Auditory
Live portrait	Light and sound awareness	The image and audio displayed represent the type of event.	Visual/Auditory

6 Validation Design Insights and Discussion

To corroborate their feasibility of implementation and use in the elderly home, we presented the scenarios, personas and ambient displays proposed to four nigh shift caregivers in two elderly homes and their night shift supervisor.

During the first presentation we exposed the results of our analysis of the contextual study and showed them the collected scenarios and personas. We then asked their feedback on the validity of the scenarios and personas. A second presentation was made in which we presented animations and a video prototype of the proposed ambient displays. The animations included the functioning of the prototypes in the presented scenarios. This helped to demonstrate the versatility of ambient displays.

After both presentations, we conducted semi-structured interviews to record additional feedback on the specific topics we were interested. This allowed us to further validate the scenarios breakdowns, realism of the personas, perception on ambient displays in their work environment and define ambient display design insights for the semi-hospitalized supervising context of an elderly home (Table 3).

Table 3. Ambient display prototypes description.

Scenario description	Perception channel
Scenario realism. According to all the informants, the proposed scenarios were relevant and true to the source. This validates the results based on the concept analysis made during the interviews and observation.	*"…the scenarios you outlined are the common ones.. The scenario in which the PwD wakes up in the middle of the night; often they are confused, their dementia exacerbates at night. In the day they are more calmed, at night they don't stop!"*
Importance of sleep monitoring. The informants stated that night monitoring on PwD is crucial because i.e. a doctor can change the medication of a patient depending on the sleep quality and their night behavior. Another fact is that without a proper night rest the PwD might promt additional workload to the dayshift caregivers.	*"For us, sleep data is essential because for example, there are some meds that provoke secondary effects like insomnia, and when they go to the doctor, they can change the treatment so that there are no effects like that."*
Perception on the prototypes implementation in-site. All the prototypes were viewed as applicable in the residency. On behalf of the caregivers there were concerns on the cost of the hardware necessary to implement the ambient displays in a realistic scenario	*"Maybe those are difficult to install in the infrastructure, but once installed they should be easy to use"* *"[The implementation] depends on the cost of installation"*
User personalization. Because of the many illnesses and different treatments that each PwD has, the caregivers stressed that each PwD requires a customization that is adequate to each ailment.	*"These are more suitable for PwD that wander at night. We wouldn't check up on them on every chance and we could dedicate more time to the others…"*
Sound as a perceptive data channel. Caregivers expressed that different types of sounds are a reliable way to get their attention. They liked the use of white noises to raise awareness while not disturbing other PwD	*"It's suitable for night use because there's less noise"* *"[with an] ambient sound like that helps to build a more relaxing work environment"*
Lights as perceptive data channel. Caretakers found the use of light patterns or in different colors as a reliable and comfortable way to become aware night events with the advantage of not disturbing them during the night shift.	*"I don't think that lights would affect our work. On the contrary, we could do our check ups on them with more confidence if we know what's happening"*
Perception of ambient displays. All models were perceived as a valid and comfortable way to obtain non-critical input on the PwD. They also noted that compared to other types of notifications, these are a non stressful ways to recognize events that otherwise might go unnoticed.	*"With the current alarm system the residents call us when they need something, but with this we get awareness of what's happening"*

From the feedback and the validation received by the caregivers and further examination on the data, we identified wandering as the more crucial event they deal with at night. The risk of falling increases at night due to poor visibility and sundowning. One caregiver reported that while she was cleaning a resident's urine on the floor next to her bed, she noticed that there was another resident wandering unsupervised in the hall. Another resident due to his sundowning tends to empty his closet and leave everything on the floor leaving him vulnerable to a dangerous fall.

7 Conclusions and Future Work

Given the positive response of the stakeholders to the prototypes, we have implemented and are currently evaluating some of these ambient displays. This evaluation in-site will serve to gauge the influence and repercussion in the caregiver's routine behaviors and (in long term) the PwD residents sleep health.

The results of this study can be used as design insights for ambient displays and other kind of ambient intelligence technologies in similar semi-hospitalized contexts.

References

1. Bachman, D., Rabins, P.: "Sundowning" and other temporally associated agitation states in dementia patients. Annu. Rev. Med. **57**, 499–511 (2006)
2. Bliwise, D.L.: Sleep disorders in Alzheimer's disease and other dementias. Clin. Cornerstone. **6** (Suppl 1A), S16–S28 (2004)
3. Harding, S.M., Hawkins, J.W.: What is a necessary knowledge base for sleep professionals? Sleep Breath. **5**, 101–107 (2001)
4. Aliakseyeu, D., Du, J., Zwartkruis-Pelgrim, E., Subramanian, S.: Exploring interaction strategies in the context of sleep. In: Campos, P., Graham, N., Jorge, J., Nunes, N., Palanque, P., Winckler, M. (eds.) INTERACT 2011, Part III. LNCS(LNAI, LNB), vol. 6948, pp. 19–36. Springer, Heidelberg (2011)
5. Bauer, J.S., Consolvo, S., Greenstein, B., Schooler, J., Wu, E., Watson, N.F., Kientz, J.A: ShutEye: encouraging awareness of healthy sleep recommendations with a mobile, peripheral display. In: Conference on Human Factors Computer System, CHI pp. 1401–1410 (2012)
6. Haba-Rubio, J., Krieger, J.: Introduction to Modern Sleep Technology. Springer, Dordrecht (2012)
7. Mankoff, J., Dey, A.K., Hsieh, G., Kientz, J., Lederer, S., Ames, M.: Heuristic evaluation of ambient displays. In: Proceedings of the SIGCHI Conference on Human Factors Computer System, pp. 169–176 (2003)
8. Sharp, H., Rogers, Y., Preece, J.: Interaction Design: Beyond Human - Computer Interaction. Wiley, Chichester (2007)
9. Oxford Dictionaries: British & World definition on Ambient, http://www.oxforddictionaries.com/us/definition/english/ambient

Physiological Data Acquisition System Based on Mobile Computing

Ezekiel Sarasua, Maider Simón, Borja Gamecho, Edurne Larraza-Mendiluze, and Nestor Garay-Vitoria(✉)

Egokituz Laboratory, Informatika Fakultatea (UPV/EHU), Manuel Lardizabal pasealekua 1, 20018 Donostia, Gipuzkoa, Spain
nestor.garay@ehu.eus

Abstract. The way to achieve enough data for data mining is by accessing existing databases or directly acquiring data with the aim of creating new databases. In this paper we present the DAFIESKU system built to acquire different types of physiological data via experiments and the factors taken into account when developing it, in order to facilitate the creation of new datasets by means of mobile and wearable devices. DAFIESKU has been evaluated on a case study associated to non-classroom learning.

Keywords: Physiological data acquisition · Data storage · Mobile and wearable computing · Design of experiments

1 Introduction

Before analyzing or applying machine learning techniques to physiological signals, datasets have to be obtained. There are a huge number of public repositories storing datasets which are available online. Nevertheless, in some cases researchers need to create new datasets with which to work, making the task of acquiring the datasets an essential step in the research process.

The way data are obtained is an important issue which bears upon the validity of the data under consideration. The main approaches to recording data are in controlled environments or in uncontrolled environments.

In this paper authors review the issues to be taken into account and present a system aimed at acquiring physiological data in a mobile uncontrolled environment named DAFIESKU, which allows researchers to conduct experiments remotely with the collaboration of participants, taking both ethical and privacy issues into account.

2 Related Work

It is not surprising that many frameworks, toolkits and platforms are to be found devoted to the remote evaluation in scientific literature [1, 2]. During the last decade, the high popularity of smart phones and its applications, commonly called apps, presented an opportunity to carry out remote evaluations in mobile environments (for instance, Funf [3]

C.R. García et al. (Eds.): UCAmI 2016, Part II, LNCS 10070, pp. 46–51, 2016.
DOI: 10.1007/978-3-319-48799-1_6

and Aware [4]). In recent years, the use of physiological signals has emerged in the computer science area due to the vast amount of wireless wearable devices that provide such signals. Thus, we can find similar systems in the literature for the recording and storing of physiological signals such as the Biosignal Ignitor toolkit [5] and the Physiodroid system [6].

The main objective of DAFIESKU is to provide resources and tools to researchers, are not usually covered in the references found in literature, which facilitate the deployment of an experiment from its design to the analysis of its results.

3 Design Issues

Design issues on the development of DAFIESKU system are explained below.

3.1 Mobile Sensors, Data Acquisition and Transmission

Nowadays, sensors are becoming ever more comfortable due to miniaturization. Normally, these sensors are integrated in all-in-one hardware platforms, such as Biosignalsplux [7] or Shimmer [8]. Nevertheless, these platforms still have limited storage capabilities and personal area network connectivity.

In order to overcome these limitations, a common solution is to combine sensor platforms with mobile phones carried by users. Thanks to mobile devices, data obtained from sensors are transmitted first to the storage of the mobile device and finally to a system server available on the Internet. The main idea of the DAFIESKU system is to enable the acquisition of data in real life, without limiting it to controlled environments. These data will better reflect natural user characteristics and behavior.

3.2 Ethical Data and Privacy for Storage

Ethical and privacy issues have also to be taken into account. Physiological data are personal in most of cases and have to be securely stored in order to ensure the people behind these data are not identified.

3.3 Further Data Analysis

Once all the ethical and privacy issues have been considered, data should be processed and filtered, and in order to make further analysis easier, standards, such as HDF5 [9] should be followed.

4 DAFIESKU System

The DAFIESKU system has been designed to take advantage of wireless devices in order to obtain the least intrusive environment for the participants during the data acquisition. DAFIESKU consists of a set of wearable devices with physiological sensors coordinated by a server. Wearable devices with wireless connections usually offer Bluetooth based connectivity which can be used to send physiological data to any computer. For this reason, a mobile device (e.g. smart phone or tablet) is used as intermediary between the server and the wearable devices (see Fig. 1). The main advantage of this approach is the possibility it gives to configure the data acquisition in each experiment and to guide and support the participants during the experiments.

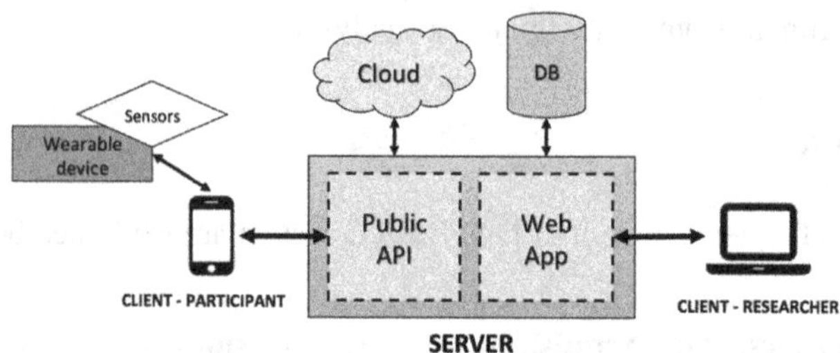

Fig. 1. Architecture of the DAFIESKU system.

4.1 Configuring Data Acquisition

With DAFIESKU, researchers may establish what data will be acquired for creating databases with physiological information as well as how they will be acquired and during what time period. The data to be gathered depends on the scope of the studies that the researchers plan for future development, the sensors that are available for acquisition, the population, etc.

The DAFIESKU system gives the researchers a web client, which offers the possibility to define how the sensors (among those available) will be used, whether they will be used together or separately, and what kind of information will be recorded.

4.2 Providing Guidance to the Participants

In the DAFIESKU system, participants play a key role in the data acquisition. Among other things, they decide when to start the experiments and when to provide feedback to label the physiological data. In order to facilitate these activities, the researcher must also: (1) specify the experiment description and define the tasks for the participants, (2) describe the instructions for attaching the sensors, and (3) set a list of predefined marks or activities related to the experiment in order to label the data set. All these texts must be fully understandable for the participants in order to avoid problems during the experimentation.

4.3 Experiment Development

The participants will be able to download the experiment to their Android mobile device (smart phone or tablet). Having done this, they will have to set the sensors and connect them to the mobile device via Bluetooth. Finally they will have to start recording data and labeling moments, following the instructions of each experiment. These last two actions will be simple "push button" or "select from list" tasks.

Tasks are classified as being pending or finished, depending on their status. In order to perform a task, it has to be selected from the pending tasks list. Clicking on a finished task name gives you the task feedback.

Once the user has selected a task from the pending list, a screen shows all the information regarding to the selected task (description, sensors to be worn by the participant, maximum time estimation, and activities to be performed). In order to make accurate recordings, the user can check whether the sensors are correctly adjusted before performing the activities related to the tasks.

5 Case Study to Evaluate DAFIESKU System on Non-classroom Learning Experimentation

A case study was carried out to test the adequacy of the described system. For this purpose a representative experiment in non-classroom learning was designed for DAFIESKU in order to test both roles in the system. As a researcher, the experimental subject introduced the information to set up the experiment. Then, as a participant in the experiments, the same experimental subject performed fixed tasks while his/her physiological data were gathered. The usability of both web and mobile applications was measured through SUS questionnaires [10].

5.1 Method

Participants and Apparatus. Five volunteers (two females) were recruited from the surrounding research laboratories of the Faculty of Informatics of the University of the Basque Country. The experimental subjects ranged from 30 to 57 years old (41.2 ± 10). Informed consent was obtained from all individual experimental subjects included in the study.

The Web service for designing experiments run on a virtual machine with Ubuntu 14.04 LTS operating system. This Web service was used when playing the researcher role in this experiment using a laptop. Designed Apps for acquiring data run on a Samsung Galaxy Tab 2.7.0 with Android 4.2.2 operating system (RAM: 1 GB; 1.0 GHz dual core processor; 7″ screen with 1024*600 pixels). A BITalino [11] sensor platform was used to collect physiological data from the Electrocardiography (ECG) and Electro Dermal Activity (EDA) sensors. The virtual machine running on the laptop and the tablet were connected wirelessly using a WiFi router. The tablet and the BITalino were connected via Bluetooth interface.

Procedure. After consent had been obtained from experimental subjects, their demographic data were gathered and a paper with the tasks to be completed was delivered to them.

Task 1 was defining an experiment with certain characteristics by using the Web client of DAFIESKU. This was carried out in the researcher role. Task 2 was carried out as a participant. The subjects prepared the equipment needed in the experiment, verified it was working correctly and then they performed the required activities for the experiment defined in Task 1: reading a text printed on paper, and then reading and answering, on paper with a pen, several questions relating to that text, just as if they were doing exercises in a classroom. Participants had to indicate, using the system, when they were reading the text, when they were reading questions and when answering questions. After finishing the experiment, they had to disconnect the sensors. Once more as a researcher, in Task 3 they verified, by using the Web client again, that the data of the experiment had been stored on the server.

After finishing these three tasks, the experimental subjects provided quantitative feedback by completing two SUS questionnaires, one as researcher and the other as participant in a physiological experiment. Finally, they were interviewed by up to two DAFIESKU design team members in order to get qualitative feedback.

Design. Experimental subjects had to follow a routine composed of Tasks 1, 2 and 3. The times required to complete each task were measured. The experimental subjects provided feedback by means of two SUS questionnaires, along with the final interviews.

5.2 Results and Discussion

All the experimental subjects successfully completed the required tasks. Task 2 was the one which required the most time while Task 3 was the one needing the least time. The number of minutes needed for completing the three tasks went from 25' (User07) to 44' (User03). With regard to the usability of the system, the SUS scores were 78,5 $\pm$ 11,25 for the researchers Web client application and 71 $\pm$ 15,62 for the Android application. These scores are over 70 and therefore both applications may be considered acceptable from the usability point of view [10].

Experimental subjects also suggested several enhancements, almost all with the aim of making a better participant experience for data acquisition. As DAFIESKU aims to create experiments and register data, including in the app help or instructions for correctly adjusting the sensors is a good idea for future versions.

6 Conclusions and Future Work

In this paper we have presented the DAFIESKU system, developed to configure data acquisition, collect and finally store the data. Its initial aim is to prepare experiments aimed to be carried out by students to analyze their physiological characteristics while participating in non-classroom learning, but it could be generalized to other experimental topics and settings such as accessing public sector Web sites.

A case study has been carried out to test the validity and usability of the described system. Participants completed fixed tasks such as reading texts and questions, and answering questions. The results achieved are promising and also led to several enhancements that are being currently made to the DAFIESKU system.

Next, a new version of DAFIESKU will be deployed to define experiments and acquire physiological data. Once the acquisition has been finished, data will be filtered and processed, taking into account all the relevant ethical, legislation security and validity issues, in order to make data available for further research.

Acknowledgements. This work has been supported by the Ministry of Economy and Competitiveness of the Spanish Government and by the European Regional Development Fund (projects TIN2013-41123-P and TIN2014-52665-C2-1-R), and by the Department of Education, Universities and Research of the Basque Government under grant IT395-10. The last three authors belong to the Basque Advanced Informatics Laboratory (BAILab), grant UFI11/45, supported by the University of the Basque Country (UPV/EHU). B. Gamecho is backed by the "Convocatoria de contratación de doctores recientes hasta su integración en programas de formación postdoctoral en la UPV/EHU 2015".

References

1. Paternò, F.: Tools for remote web usability evaluation. In: HCI International, pp. 828–832. Lawrence Erlbaum Associates, Inc. (2003)
2. Christos, F., Christos, K., Eleftherios, P., Nikolaos, T., Nikolaos, A.: Remote usability evaluation methods and tools: a survey. In: Proceedings of the 11th Panhellenic Conference in Informatics (PCI 2007), pp. 151–162. New Technologies Publications (2007)
3. Aharony, N., Pan, W., Ip, C., Khayal, I., Pentland, A.: Social fMRI: investigating and shaping social mechanisms in the real world. Pervasive Mob. Comput. **7**(6), 643–659 (2011)
4. Ferreira, D.: Aware: a mobile context instrumentation middleware to collaboratively understand human behavior. In: Ph.D. dissertation, University of Oulu, Faculty of Technology (2013)
5. Silva, H.P., Lourenço, A., Fred, A., Martins, R.: BIT: biosignal igniter toolkit. Comput. Methods Programs Biomed. **115**(1), 20–32 (2014)
6. Banos, O., Villalonga, C., Damas, M., Gloesekoetter, P., Pomares, H., Rojas, I.: Physiodroid: combining wearable health sensors and mobile devices for a ubiquitous, continuous, and personal monitoring. Sci. World J. **2014**, 11 (2014). Article ID 490824
7. Biosignalsplux. http://biosignalsplux.com/index.php/en/
8. Shimmer. http://www.shimmersensing.com/
9. Folk, M., Heber, G., Koziol, Q., Pourmal, E., Robinson, D.: An overview of the HDF5 technology suite and its applications. In: Proceedings of the EDBT/ICDT 2011 Workshop on Array Databases, pp. 36–47. ACM (2011)
10. Brooke, J.: SUS: a retrospective. J. Usability Stud. **8**(2), 29–40 (2013)
11. Silva, H., Fred, A., Martins, R.: Biosignals for everyone. IEEE Pervasive Comput. **13**(4), 64–71 (2014)

Do We Need an Integrated Framework for Ambient Assisted Living?

Ashalatha Kunnappilly(✉), Cristina Seceleanu, and Maria Lindén

Mälardalen University, Västerås, Sweden
{ashalatha.kunnappilly,cristina.seceleanu,maria.linden}@mdh.se

Abstract. The significant increase of ageing population calls for solutions that help the elderly to live an independent, healthy and low risk life, but also ensure their social interaction. The improvements in Information and Communication Technologies (ICT) and Ambient Assisted Living (AAL) have resulted in the development of equipment that supports ubiquitous computing, ubiquitous communication and intelligent user interfaces. The smart home technologies, assisted robotics, sensors for health monitoring and e-health solutions are some examples in this category. Despite such growth in these individualized technologies, there are only few solutions that provide integrated AAL frameworks that interconnect all of these technologies. In this paper, we discuss the necessity to opt for an integrated solution in AAL. To support the study we describe real life scenarios that help us justify the need for integrated solutions over individualized ones. Our analysis points to the clear conclusion that an integrated solution for AAL outperforms the individualized ones.

Keywords: Ambient Assisted Living · Assisted robotics · e-Health

1 Introduction

The society is now witnessing a demographic change towards an ageing population. Demographic statistics reports [1] show that the elderly population, that is, people who are older than 60 years of age constitutes about one-fourth of the total population in Europe and is expected to increase in the coming years. A similar ageing trend is also witnessed around the world. The technological boom and the need to support an increasing elderly population have prompted the research community to focus on the field of Ambient Assisted Living (AAL). There are numerous Ambient Intelligent (AI) systems that have been developed to support the elderly in their independent living. In addition, there are significant advances in the field of smart homes, wireless sensor technology, assisted robotics, e-health etc., which have created a breakthrough development in the AAL domain [2,3]. However, a survey of the existing AAL solutions reveals a potential research gap regarding solutions that integrate all relevant technologies into a common framework.

C.R. García et al. (Eds.): UCAmI 2016, Part II, LNCS 10070, pp. 52–63, 2016.
DOI: 10.1007/978-3-319-48799-1_7

In practice, almost all of the AAL solutions are found to be fragmented, with limited support of only few integrated functionalities. Nevertheless, it is also possible that one uses various independent systems to build up multiple functionalities. For instance, if an elderly person's home is equipped with an AAL solution that does not have an automatic fall detection system, the user can purchase it separately, as there exist readily available, wearable separate solutions that detect a fall and raise an alarm. This functionality of a fall detection system remains the same whether it is an independent system or part of an integrated framework.

If this is the case, we need to answer an important question - if the individualized solutions can perform their functionality without integration, then do we really need to integrate all of them into a single framework bearing additional cost overheads? This paper focuses on answering such a question. The most obvious reason for a positive answer would be the difficulty encountered in using separate solutions as compared to a single integrated one; however, there might exist a more important reason - the fact that the performance of individualized solutions differ dramatically if they are integrated into a coherent framework, versus the case when they are employed in isolation. We discuss this issue in detail in Sect. 3.

The paper is organized as follows. In Sect. 2, we review some of the prominent AAL solutions with respect to their functionalities. Section 3 reasons about the necessity of developing integrated solutions rather than individualized ones. We show this by selecting representative scenarios that we simulate via sequence diagrams, and check their offline schedules against real-time deadlines. In Sect. 4, we show the functional components of an integrated AAL system by constructing a feature diagram representation. Section 5 concludes the paper and gives some directions for future work.

2 Literature Survey

In this section, we survey some of the most relevant AAL frameworks developed during the last two decades. The search is restricted to the platforms with multi-functionality support, their availability in the market (or at least at a prototype level) and documented user acceptance. Below, we first list the main functionalities required by AAL systems, and then identify AAL solutions supporting such functionalities. We summarize the results in Table 1, that is, the chosen solutions and their supported functionalities, which justify the rest of the paper.

The functionalities that we have chosen are: health monitoring, fall detection, communication and socialization, support for supervised physical exercises, personalized intelligent and dynamic program management, robotics platform support, intelligent personal assistant that takes orders, gives advice and reminders etc., support for vocal interface, mobility assistance, and home and environment management.

1. *Health monitoring and care:* Health monitoring is an important functionality of AAL systems. The parameters to monitor depend on the health status

of older adults. The major health monitoring frameworks are inCASA [4], Reaction [5], UniversAAL [6], Diabetic Support Systems, Automated Memory Support for Social Interaction (AMSSI) [2] etc.
2. *Fall detection:* The risk of falling is one of the critical hazardous situations that needs to be addressed in an AAL system [7]. Examples of existing solutions include the Tunstall fall alarm, the Bay Alarm sensor etc. The inCASA architecture [4] comprises fall detection for elderly people. The GiraffPlus project [8] uses both the smart phone fall detection application and the Tunstall fall detection sensor.
3. *Communication and social inclusion:* Communication to health care professionals and social inclusion is another vital functionality of AAL systems. Among the existing frameworks, inCASA [4], Reaction [5], GiraffPlus [8], MobiServ [9] support this functionality.
4. *Supervised physical exercises:* Mobility problems are very common for elderly people. Exergames are video games that combine traditional game play with physical activity. The most common sensors available for physical activity detection are Webcamera and Kinect sensors. The Mobiserv [9] framework supports supervised physical exercises.
5. *Personalized, intelligent and dynamic program management:* An AAL system should allow the storage of the user's personal data like medication plan, daily, weekly, monthly program planning, exercise planner, record of medical data obtained from sensors, etc. The major frameworks that support this functionality are listed in Table 1.
6. *Robotic platforms support:* The service robots like the Pearl, Care-o-Bot, Cero, PR2, Robocare etc. play a significant role in the AAL domain. Another major category is the companion robots, like the robotic baby seal Paro [2]. The major platforms with robotic support include Domeo AAL project [10], GiraffPlus [8], Mobiserv [9] etc.
7. *Intelligent personal assistant:* The cognitive abilities of elderly people decrease with age, hence the functionality provided by an intelligent informed friendly collaborator is crucial to AAL systems. Two of the frameworks that support this functionality are inCASA [4], and Reaction [5].
8. *Vocal interface:* Most of the elderly regard traditional computer interfaces as overly technical and difficult to use. Hence, support for vocal commands is necessary. There are many existing software systems for speech recognition and synthesis, out of which CMU Sphinx, Julius, Google Speech API are among the most popular. Some of the platforms that support vocal interfaces are listed in Table 1.
9. *Mobility assistance:* Many of the elderly lack the ability to move independently and require mobility support. There are many smart wheel chairs devised for this purpose, like NavChair, Wheelesley, VAHM, PerMMa etc. Apart from wheel chairs, mobility scooters and smart vehicles are prominent in this category [2].
10 *Home and environment management:* The most recognized smart home systems that take care of one's home, and perform environment management are iDorm, PERSONA (PERceptive Spaces prOmoting iNdependent Aging),

CASAS Smart Home Project, MavHome, and Aware Home Research Initiative (AHRI) [2].

Table 1. Functionalities supported by various AAL frameworks

AAL platforms	1	2	3	4	5	6	7	8	9	10
inCASA	✓	✓	✓	✗	✗	✗	✓	✗	✗	✓
iCarer	✗	✗	✓	✗	✓	✗	✓	✗	✗	✓
Persona	✗	✗	✓	✗	✓	✗	✓	✓	✗	✓
Reaction	✓	✗	✓	✗	✓	✗	✓	✗	✗	✗
UniversAAL	✓	✓	✓	✗	✓	✗	✓	✗	✗	✗
iDorm	✗	✗	✗	✗	✓	✗	✗	✗	✗	✓
Robocare	✗	✓	✗	✗	✓	✓	✓	✓	✗	✓
Aware Home	✗	✗	✓	✗	✓	✗	✗	✗	✗	✓
Mav Home	✗	✗	✗	✗	✓	✗	✓	✗	✗	✓
CASAS	✗	✗	✗	✗	✓	✗	✗	✗	✗	✓
GiraffPlus	✓	✓	✓	✗	✓	✓	✓	✗	✗	✓
MobiServ	✗	✓	✓	✓	✓	✓	✗	✓	✗	✓

Table 1 gives a synthetic account of various AAL frameworks in terms of supported functionalities. By inspecting the table one can notice that none of the platforms that we have reviewed supports all the functionalities that we have selected. This finding gives rise to a straightforward research question: "Are there any critical performance differences in using an integrated framework versus using individual systems side by side, for achieving the desired functionality?". The answer to this question is elaborated in the next section.

3 Analysis of Independent vs. Integrated AAL Solutions

In the previous section we have established the fact that none of the reviewed frameworks acts as a fully integrated solution for AAL. In order to answer our original question, we proceed to analyzing a real life scenario involving a fire event and a fall event, possibly occurring simultaneously.

The motivation for choosing this scenario is based on actual data on fall and fire incidents. According to statistics, the fall incidents among elderly people over the age of 75 is at least 30 % every year, and 40 % of them fall more than once, turning this incident into one of the major risk factors for elderly people, which can sometimes lead to death [11]. Besides falls, the number of fire incidents occurring at home has also been increasing at an alarming rate. According to the report given by Nation Fire Protection, the number of fire incidents reported in 2013 is 369.500, causing 2755 civilian deaths [12]. The fire and fall incidents statistics implies that there is a high likeliness of both events happening at the same time.

We perform our behavioral analysis of solutions by modeling the sequence of message exchanges in the automatic fire and fall detection systems, and by simulating the execution traces of the resulting sequence diagrams in Visual Paradigm [13]. Fire and fall events have hard deadlines associated with their resolution, that is, if a proper timely action is not guaranteed, they will have catastrophic consequences. Therefore, we add response times to individual messages in the sequence diagrams, and thereby calculate the response times of fire detection and fall detection systems, respectively. Next, we analyze the actions schedule of each independent system by using offline scheduling, which is the most suited type of scheduling for hard real time applications [14].

3.1 Sequence Diagrams and Schedule Analysis

In this paper, we aim our analysis to understanding the behavior of automatic fire detection and fall detection systems when:

1. Both systems are independent, and:
   (a) Fire and fall events occur at different times.
   (b) Fire and fall events occur simultaneously.
2. Both systems are integrated into a common framework, and:
   (a) Fire and fall events occur at different times.
   (b) Fire and fall events occur simultaneously.

We also annotate duration constraints to the message interactions in both scenarios, in their respective sequence diagrams. A fall event is usually detected by various feature extraction techniques and fall detection algorithms running in the fall sensor [7]. Most of the fall sensors take approximately 255 ms to get activated on the occurrence of a fall event [15], and take 5 to 6 s to detect a fall [16]. Some of the fall sensors available in the market can raise a fall alarm at 30 s after the detection of a fall [17].

Let us assume that the fall alarm is communicated to a caregiver via an automatic call that takes about 1 min. The average time for the caregiver to respond to the fall alarm call is 2.96 min [18]. The caregiver can validate the fall through a telepresence system (if available), in order to reduce the risk of false alarms. This timing constraint is a variable based on the design aspects of the system. Let us assume that validation takes another 1 min. In case of a real fall, the caregiver should provide assistance immediately. The time taken for providing the required assistance varies, and depends on many factors like the distance from the hospital to the patient's house, type of action taken, etc. For our analysis, we assume a fair time of about 15 min during which proper medical care should reach the person who has fallen.

The fire sensors do not fall under the category "wearable", and hence the system's performance depends on a variety of physical factors like the place of installation, height of installation, type of fire etc. There are now various categories of fire sensors such as ionization sensors, photoelectric sensors, and dual sensors. In this paper, we analyze the performance of a photoelectric sensor

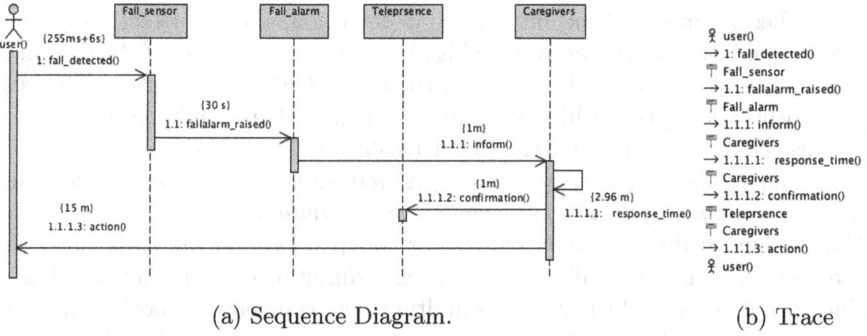

(a) Sequence Diagram. (b) Trace

Fig. 1. Message sequence for fall event.

installed in a bedroom of a two storey house, which can detect a fire due to flaming, and raise an alarm within 54 s [19]. Let us split this into 2 actions: fire detection within 45 s, and alarm raising within 9 s from detection, in order to carry out a similar analysis like for the fall event. The fire alarm is sent to the firefighter in 30 s [20]. Due to a high number of false alarms, there is a need for confirming the alarm before taking an action. This is usually achieved via telephone call confirmations. All these actions take about 1 min [20]. For detailed analysis, we split this action into 3 subactions: 10 s response time of firefighters, 25 s for call confirmation, and another 25 s for confirmation reply. The volunteer firefighters should arrive at the spot within 9 min from fire alarm confirmation. The fire's put out time is 60 s [20], so the total time for the whole response action is 10 min.

Once we have assigned duration constraints to individual messages in each system, we can analyze both independent and integrated solutions, based on sequence diagram simulations, and then construct their offline schedules.

1. *Behavior of independent, automatic fire detection system, and fall detection system, assuming fire and fall events occur at different times.*
   The sequence diagrams for the individual systems, and their execution traces are described in Figs. 1 and 2, with their respective duration constraints. The duration constraints are assigned as previously discussed in this section. In case of automatic fall detection systems, the total response time is calculated by adding the individual response times of all messages in the sequence diagram of Fig. 1.

$$R_{fall} = \sum_{i=1}^{6} R_i = 20.56 \text{ min} \tag{1}$$

   In case of automatic fire detection systems, the response time is calculated in a similar way:

$$R_{fire} = \sum_{i=1}^{7} R_i = 12.36 \text{ min} \tag{2}$$

The schedule graphs of the automatic fall detection, and fire detection systems are shown in Fig. 3, respectively. This gives a clear indication of the deadlines associated with each of the events in the context of our analysis: a fall event has to be addressed within 20.56 min to ensure safety, and the fire, once it occurs, has to be extinguished within 12.36 min.

2. *Behavior of independent, automatic fire detection system, and fall detection system, assuming fire and fall events occur simultaneously.*
   The sequence diagram interactions for independent fire and fall detection systems, with fire and fall events occurring simultaneously is shown in Fig. 4. In order to better illustrate the simultaneous occurrence of both events, we restrict to a single sequence diagram that shows the interaction of both systems. However, note that these systems are still independent, without any mutual interactions.
   When the fall and fire events occur simultaneously, the fall event follows the usual sequence of events, but in case of a fire event, the confirmation call of fire event is not answered as the user has fallen (shown as a lost message in the sequence diagram of Fig. 4). Consequently, it is highly possible that firefighters ignore the fire alarm. Let us imagine the worst case scenario where the fire gets notified to firefighters only when the caregiver arrives to help the fallen individual, that is, the fire event is notified after 20.56 min from start, which is far beyond the deadline of 12.36 min, associated with the fire event. A real catastrophe could occur in this scenario, as the fire is not extinguished in due time.
   The deadline miss of the fire event is clearly depicted in the schedule diagram described in Fig. 6a.
3. *Behavior of an integrated fire detection system and fall detection system, assuming fire and fall events occur at different times.*
   When the fire and fall events occur at disjoint points, the integrated system follows the same sequence of events described by the sequence diagrams in Figs. 1 and 2; the response times for both the events remain the same as in the case of independent systems, and both events are addressed within their deadlines, respectively, as shown in the diagram of Fig. 3.
4. *Behavior of an integrated fire detection system and fall detection system, assuming fire and fall events occur simultaneously.*
   We have seen earlier that if both fire and fall events occur simultaneously in independent systems, the fire event misses its deadline, which might have catastrophic consequences. Let us now check if the integrated system can address this issue. The sequence diagram in this case is shown in Fig. 5. As described by the scenario, both individual systems are integrated into a common framework, so both fall and fire events are first communicated to the integrated framework now.

There exists a design constraint associated with the integrated system requiring that the system has to wait for an arbitrary time to check whether some other events are activated at the same time. In our case, when the fall event is sent first to the integrated system, it waits arbitrarily for 0.5 s, such that the fire event

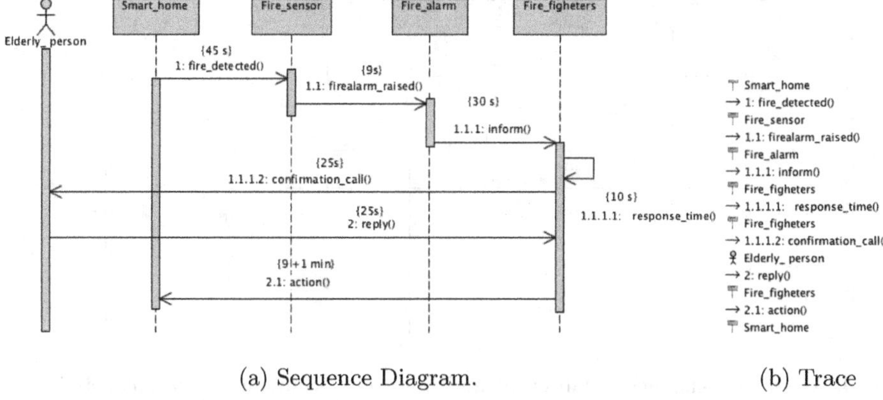

(a) Sequence Diagram. (b) Trace

Fig. 2. Message sequence for fire event.

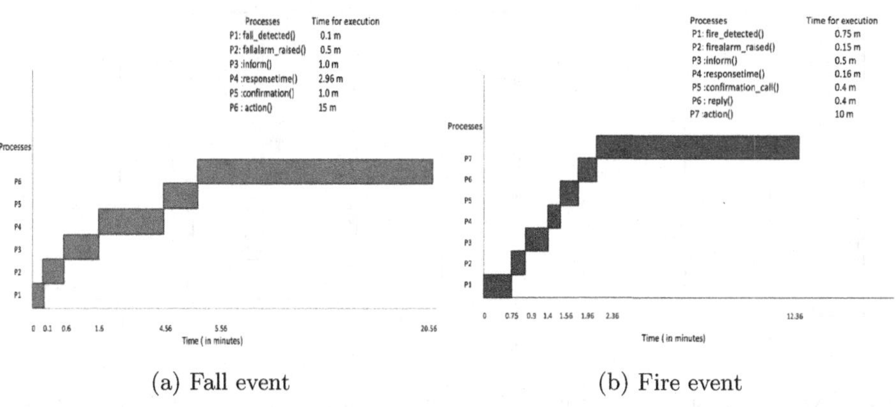

(a) Fall event (b) Fire event

Fig. 3. Offline scheduling of fire and fall event messages.

that occurred at the same point of time also gets accounted for. We can chose this waiting time, depending on the design constraints, such that the system registers multiple events and does not miss individual deadlines associated with the events. In this case, the integrated framework communicates to the firefighters and caregiver that there is fire, and a fall event has occurred also. As such, the firefighters prioritize their rescuing action without requiring a confirmation call, thus completing their action well before the associated deadline. Similarly, the caregiver does not spend time with confirmation, as there are two critical events reported at the same time, so he/she takes his/her action within the associated deadline of 20.53 s. The schedule of this scenario is shown in Fig. 6b.

The scenario that we have analyzed is one among many scenarios that highlight the necessity of an integrated AAL solution. With the help of this scenario, we could clearly identify that there is a significant performance difference between independent and integrated systems, when multiple critical events

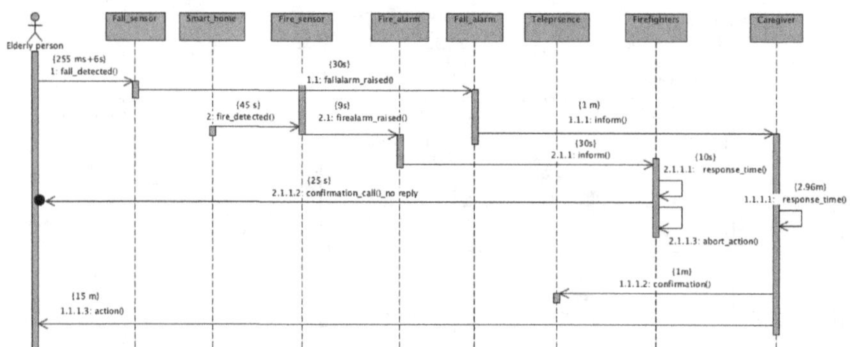

Fig. 4. Message exchanges of fall event and fire event occurring simultaneously in an independent system.

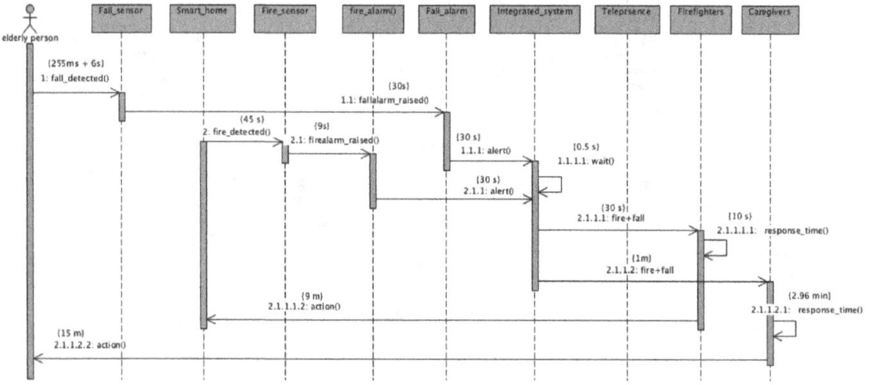

Fig. 5. Message exchanges of fall event and fire event occurring simultaneously in an integrated system.

occur simultaneously. Due to such evaluations, we can generalize and infer that a potential AAL framework that integrates all the functionalities ranging from health monitoring systems to assisted robotic systems is highly essential to be able to tackle multiple simultaneous events. We need a solution that is capable of making a decision by interconnecting and prioritizing the events in case more than one critical situation occurs. In short, such intelligence can be developed only if one analyzes the scenarios collaboratively, which is only possible if one uses an integrated framework of AAL functions.

4 A Feature Diagram of Integrated AAL Functions

Until now we have analyzed whether one should develop or not an integrated architectural solution for AAL. As a first step towards the design of such an integrated architecture for AAL, we capture the functionality features of such a system using a feature diagram reprsentation [21].

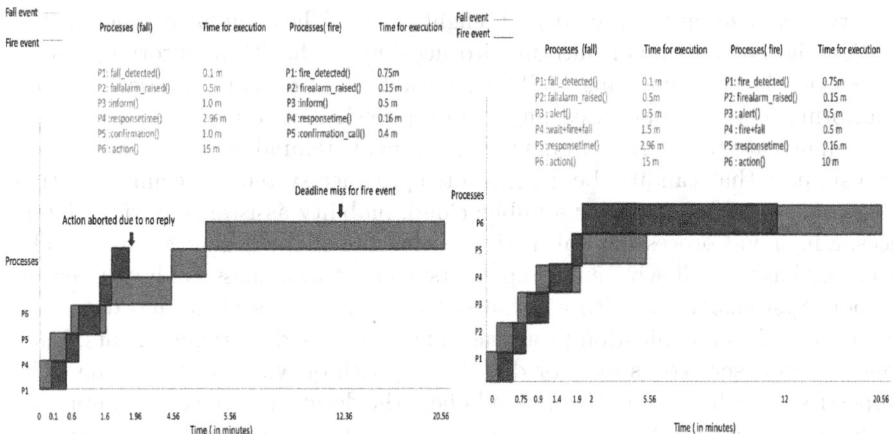

(a) Fall and fire events occuring simultaneously in independent systems.

(b) Fall and fire events occuring simultaneously in an integrated system

Fig. 6. Offline schedules of fire event and fall event messages.

The feature diagram depicting the functional components and attributes of an integrated AAL system is shown in Fig. 7. In a feature diagram, a node with a solid circle represents a mandatory feature of any AAL system. A node with an empty circle represents an optional feature that can be selected by a particular system. Several nodes associated with a spanning curve represent a group of alternative features, from which a feature must be selected for a particular system.

As one can notice, the AAL system is composed of users, components, and communication protocols. The primary users of the system are elderly adults, but there are also secondary users like the caregivers, family, friends, etc., and also

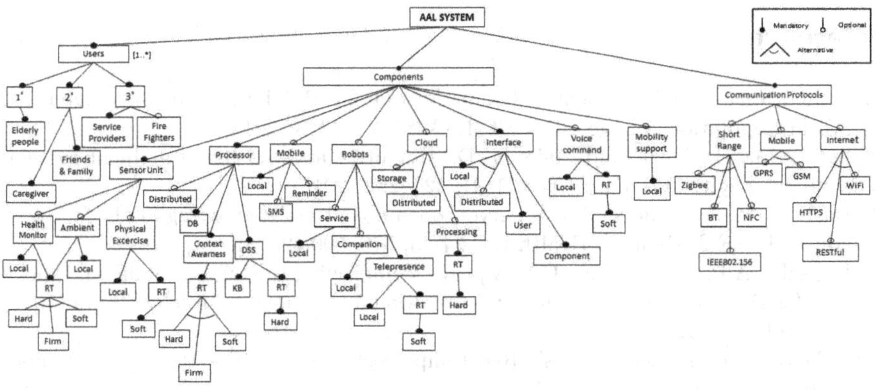

Fig. 7. Feature Diagram capturing the Functions of an Integrated AAL system.

tertiary users like service providers, firefighters, etc. The components include the sensor unit that contains health monitoring sensors (health monitoring), ambient sensors (home monitoring), fall sensors (fall detection), and physical exercise monitoring sensors (supervised physical exercises), mobile phone of the elderly to communicate to external users via SMS, provide reminders, etc., robotic platform support that can also be used as a telepresence system for communication to external users, a private or a public cloud, mobility assistance devices, interfaces, a high end processing unit acting as the core of the AAL system, etc. The processor has the following subcomponents: context awareness module, Decision Support Systems (DSS) with associated Knowledge Bases (KB) and database. The choice of communication protocols is flexible, based on requirements. Each node is also described as local or distributed, with or without Real Time (RT) properties. The diagram in Fig. 7 should help the designer to select the appropriate features of a new AAL system, as well as figure out infeasible combinations of features.

5 Conclusions and Future Works

In this paper, we have highlighted the significance of developing an integrated framework for Ambient Assisted Living by analyzing real-life scenarios that justify such a solution. The emergent behavior that arises by integrating the various functionalities like health monitoring, smart homes, physical exercise monitoring systems, robotic platform systems, fall alarms, intelligent friendly collaborator systems, multi modal user interface systems, etc., are essential for ensuring the success of any AAL system. We have also provided a feature diagram representation of the functionalities of an integrated AAL framework, which can serve as design reference of existing or future solutions.

As part of the future work, we plan to propose a fully integrated AAL architecture, which we plan to further model and verify formally against functional and real-time requirements.

References

1. United Nations, Department of Economic and Social Affairs, Population Division. World Population Ageing 2013. ST/ESA/SER.A/348 (2013)
2. Li, R., Lu, B., McDonald-Maier, K.D.: Cognitive assisted living ambient system: a survey. Digit. Commun. Netw. **1**(4), 229–252 (2015)
3. Rashidi, P., Mihailidis, A.: A survey on ambient-assisted living tools for older adults. IEEE J. Biomed. Health Inf. **17**(3), 579–590 (2013)
4. Kapsalis, A.P., et al.: The inCASA project: improving the quality of life and social care for the ageing population. In: International Congress on Telehealth and Telecare, vol. 6 (2012)
5. "The Reaction Project - News". Reactionproject.eu. N.p. 2014. Web. 18 September 2016
6. "Home: Universaal". Universaal.sintef9013.com. N.p. 2010. Web. 18 September 2016

7. Delahoz, Y.S., Labrador, M.A.: Survey on fall detection and fall prevention using wearable and external sensors. Sensors **14**(10), 19806–19842 (2014)
8. Kristoffersson, A., Coradeschi, S., Loutfi, A.: A review of mobile robotic telepresence. Adv. Hum. Comput. Inter. **2013**, 3 (2013)
9. Heuvel, H., et al.: Mobiserv: a service robot and intelligent home environment for the provision of health, nutrition and safety services to older adults. Gerontechnology **11**(2), 373 (2012)
10. Rumeau, P., et al.: Home deployment of a doubt removal telecare service for cognitively impaired elderly people: a field deployment. In: IEEE 3rd International Conference on Cognitive Infocommunications (CogInfoCom). IEEE (2012)
11. Dai, J., Bai, X., Yang, Z., Shen, Z., Xuan, D.: Mobile phone-based pervasive fall detection. Pers. Ubiquit. Comput. **14**(7), 633–643 (2010)
12. "NFPA Statistics - Home Fires". www.Nfpa.org. N.p. 2013. Web. 18 September 2016
13. "Software Design Tools for Agile Teams, with UML, BPMN and More". http://www.visual-paradigm.com. N.p. 2016. Web. 18 September 2016
14. Burns, A.: Scheduling hard real-time systems: a review. Softw. Eng. J. **6**(3), 116–128 (1991)
15. Yang, B., Lee, Y., Lin, C.: On developing a real-time fall detecting and protecting system using mobile device. In: Proceedings of the International Conference on Fall Prevention and Protection, Tokyo (2013)
16. Kostopoulos, P., et al.: F2D: a fall detection system tested with real data from daily life of elderly people. In: 17th International Conference on E-health Networking, Application & Services (HealthCom). IEEE (2015)
17. "The Best Fall Detection Sensors of 2016—Top Ten Reviews". TopTenREVIEWS. N.p. 2016. Web. 18 September 2016
18. Tzeng, H.M., Yin, C.Y.: Nurses' response time to call lights and fall occurrences. MEDSURG Nurs. **19**(5), 266–272 (2010)
19. Kasperczyk, C.: Smoke Alarms:: Comparing the Differences in Response Times and Nuisance Alarms (2010). Print
20. Flynn, J.D.: Fire Service Performance Measures. National Fire Protection Association, Fire Analysis and Research Division (2009)
21. Batory, D.: Feature models, grammars, and propositional formulas. In: Obbink, H., Pohl, K. (eds.) SPLC 2005. LNCS, vol. 3714, pp. 7–20. Springer, Heidelberg (2005)

Recognition of Activities in Resource Constrained Environments; Reducing the Computational Complexity

M. Espinilla[1(✉)], A. Rivera[1], M.D. Pérez-Godoy[1], J. Medina[1], L. Martínez[1], and C. Nugent[2]

[1] Computer Sciences Department, University of Jaén, Campus Las Lagunillas S/n, 23071 Jaén, Spain
{mestevez,arivera,lperez,jmquero,martin}@ujaen.es

[2] School of Computing and Mathematics, University of Ulster, Jordanstown BT37 0QB, UK
cd.nugent@ulster.ac.uk

Abstract. In our current work we propose a strategy to reduce the vast amounts of data produced within smart environments for sensor-based activity recognition through usage of the nearest neighbor (NN) approach. This approach has a number of disadvantages when deployed in resource constrained environments due to its high storage requirements and computational complexity. These requirements are closely related to the size of the data used as input to NN. A wide range of prototype generation (PG) algorithms, which are designed for use with the NN approach, have been proposed in the literature to reduce the size of the data set. In this work, we investigate the use of PG algorithms and their effect on binary sensor-based activity recognition when using a NN approach. To identify the most suitable PG algorithm four datasets were used consisting of binary sensor data and their associated class activities. The results obtained demonstrated the potential of three PG algorithms for sensor-based activity recognition that reduced the computational complexity by up to 95 % with an overall accuracy higher than 90 %.

Keywords: Activity recognition · Resource constrained environments · Nearest Neighbor (NN) · Prototype generation (PG) · Computational complexity

1 Introduction

Sensor-based activity recognition [1] is at the core of smart environments. This recognition aims to recognize the actions of one or more persons within the environment based on a series of observations of sub-actions and environmental conditions over a period of finite time. It can be deemed as a complex process that involves the following steps: (i) select and deploy the appropriate sensors to be attached to objects within the smart environment; (ii) collect, store and

C.R. García et al. (Eds.): UCAmI 2016, Part II, LNCS 10070, pp. 64–74, 2016.
DOI: 10.1007/978-3-319-48799-1_8

pre-process the sensor related data and, finally, (iii) to classify activities from the sensor data through the use of activity models.

Advances in technology developments have mainly focused around the provision of a wide range of low cost devices, with low-power requirements and decreased form factor that implies constrained resource environments. An example are the inexpensive micro boards, such as Raspberry Pi [2] or Arduino [3]. These devices allow information to be read from sensors, in addition to the processing of sensor data to extract relevant information from the smart environments. These small computer boards, however, offer limited processing capacity and low storage capacity hence a key factor with their usage is to reduce the computational complexity of any tasks they must undertake [4,5].

Approaches used for sensor-based activity recognition have been divided into two main categories: Data-Driven (DDA) and Knowledge-Driven (KDA) Approaches. The former, DDA, are based on machine learning techniques in which a preexistent dataset of user behaviors is required (and available). A training process is carried out, usually, to build an activity model which is followed by a testing processes to evaluate the generalization of the model in classifying unseen activities [6–8]. With KDA, an activity model is built through the incorporation of rich prior domain knowledge gleaned from the application domain, using knowledge engineering and knowledge management techniques [9,10].

This contribution is focused on the most popular algorithm among all of the DDA solutions namely, the nearest neighbour (NN) [11] that provides simplicity and overall good levels of accuracy [12]. The approach is based on the concept of similarity patterns that can be allocated to the same class label (activity) [13–15].

The NN approach does, however, suffer from several shortcomings. These mainly relate to high storage requirements and high levels of computational complexity [16]. These requirements are closely related to the size of the dataset. The computational complexity of the linear search method of NN is $O(n\ d)$ where n is the size of the dataset and d is the dimensionality, i.e., the number of sensors. This fact is even more relevant in the application domain of activity recognition where the size of the data is related to a vast amount of generated-sensor data within smart environments.

For this reason, the PG algorithms [17] are a suitable choice given their focus on recognizing an optimal subset of representative samples from the original training data. This is achieved by removing noisy and redundant examples in order to generate and replace the original data with new artificial data [18].

In order to maximise the advantages provided by the NN approach and avoiding the drawbacks associated with the size of the datasets in resource constrained environments, the contribution of the current work proposes to use PG algorithms to reduce the size of the data in order to (i) decrease the storage requirements and computational complexity with the NN approach, (ii) maintain classification accuracy.

An evaluation is undertaken with four datasets to consider the effects of the reduction of the computational complexity in terms of overall accuracy for activity recognition based on sensor data gleaned from smart environments.

The remainder of the paper is structured as follows: Sect. 2 reviews the NN approach in addition to PG algorithms. Section 3 presents an empirical study that analyzes PG algorithms in terms of their accuracy and reduction for the purpose of activity recognition based on four datasets using binary sensors within smart environments. Finally, in Sect. 4, Conclusions and Future Work are presented.

2 Prototype Generation Algorithms Designed for the NN Approach

In this Section, we present an overview of the NN approach in addition to consider the notion of PG algorithms.

2.1 Nearest Neighbor Approach

The NN approach [11] is one of the most successfully used techniques for classification and pattern recognition tasks. It is based on the concept of similarity [19] and the fact that patterns that are similar, usually, have the same class label. The method is categorized as lazy learning [20] given it classifies the class label from raw training samples.

In order to recognize an unseen sample, representative training samples are stored within the activity model. Each training sample, which is annotated with a class label, is essentially a vector in a multidimensional feature space. In the case of activity recognition, each feature corresponds to each sensor of the network. During the testing process, a non-annotated vector i.e., a new sample, is classified. To do so, a parameter k is fixed that means the k training samples nearest to the new sample will be used to classify. The non-annotated vector, i.e., the new sample, is classified with the activity label corresponding to the most frequent label among the k training samples nearest to it. When $k = 1$ in the NN approach, i.e., the activity label of the non-annotated vector is the activity label of its single most closest neighbour.

The NN approach is based on the similarity of its k closest neighbours and has the ability to attain good levels of performance [12], however it suffers from the following three weaknesses [16]:

1. High storage requirements in order to retain the set of training samples.
2. High computational complexity in order to search through the training samples and classify a new sample.
3. Low tolerance to noise given that it considers all data relevant, even when the training set may contain incorrect data.

A successful technique, which has been shown to address these challenges, is based on PG algorithms. The following Section provides further details on PG algorithms and their use with NN approach.

2.2 Prototype Generation Algorithms

PG algorithms are a form of data reduction technique [21] that aim to identify an optimal subset from the original training set, by discarding noisy and redundant examples and by modifying the value of some features of the samples to build new artificial samples that are known as prototypes [18].

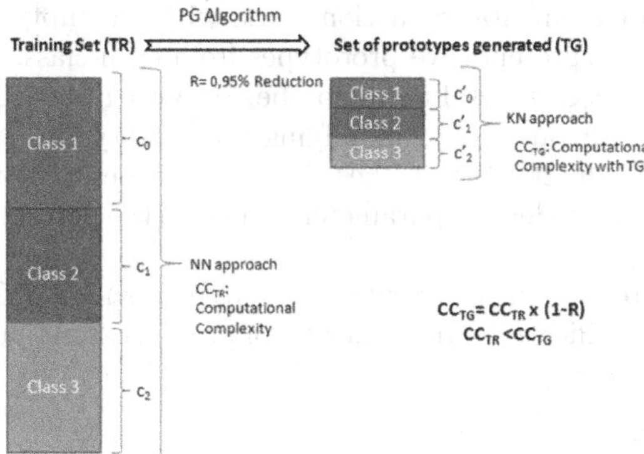

Fig. 1. Reduction through usage of PG algorithms in the number of stored instances with the ability to reduce the computational complexity of the NN

PG algorithms are therefore designed to obtain a set of prototypes generated TG, which has a smaller size of the data than the original training set TR. The cardinality of the TG is sufficiently small and has the subsequent effect to reduce both the storage requirements and computational complexity spent by the NN approach.

A wide range of PG algorithms have been designed for the NN approach to reduce the size of the dataset. Figure 1 illustrates the objective of these algorithms which have been categorized into a taxonomy based on the following four mechanisms of prototyping [17]:

- *Positioning adjustment* [22–24]: This technique corrects the position of a subset of prototypes from the initial set by using an optimization procedure. New positions of the prototype can be obtained by using the movement idea in the multidimensional feature space by adding or subtracting some quantities to the feature values of the prototypes.
- *Class relabeling* [25,26]: This generation mechanism consists of changing the class labels of samples from TR, which are considered as having errors and/or belonging to other different classes than to those which they have been labeled.
- *Centroid based* [27,28]: These techniques are based on generating artificial prototypes by merging a set of similar examples. The merging process is usually made from the computation of averaged attribute values over a selected set, yielding the so-called centroids.

- *Space splitting* [29,30]: These techniques are based on different heuristics to partition the feature space, along with several mechanisms to define new prototypes. The idea consists of dividing TR into regions, which will be replaced with representative examples establishing the decision boundaries associated with the original TR.

The PG algorithms can be associated with four types of reduction [17].

- *Incremental*: An incremental reduction starts with an empty reduced set TG or with only some representative prototypes from each class.
- *Decremental*: The decremental reduction begins with $TG = TR$, and then the algorithm starts reducing TG or modifying the prototypes in TG.
- *Fixed.* The fixed reduction establishes the final number of prototypes for TG using a user previously defined parameter related to the percentage of retention of TR.
- *Mixed.* A mixed reduction starts with a pre-selected subset TG, and following this, additions, modifications and removals of prototypes are performed in TG.

3 Case Study

This Section details the evaluations under taken to investigate the effects of the performance of the PG algorithms to decrease the size of the dataset for use with NN as a means of classification in the process of activity recognition.

3.1 Activity Recognition Datasets

The case study presented in this contribution uses four datasets collected from multiple smart environments all of which used binary sensors.

Each instance of the dataset is a vector with $d + 1$ components; the first d components correspond to the value of the d sensors involved in the smart environment and the last component, $d+1$ corresponds to the activity performed (class label). The value of a sensor is represented as a binary variable that takes the value 1 if the sensor had a change of state and 0 otherwise.

Following, the four datasets are described:

- *Casas* [31]. This dataset was collected from the smart apartment test-bed of the Washington State University that contains 121 instances that was generated using 39 binary sensors with five types of activities.
- *ODI1 and ODI2* [32].[1] *ODI* datasets were generated within the IE Sim intelligent environment simulation tool. The first ODI contains 308 observations generated using 21 binary sensors with 11 types of activities. The second *ODI* dataset contains 616 observations that was generated using also 21 binary sensors with the same 11 types of activities that *ODI1*

[1] *ODI*1 and *ODI*2 datasets were generated by Ulster University thanks to the Open Data Initiative (ODI) [33] for Activity Recognition consortium that aims to create a structured approach to provide annotated datasets in an accessible format.

– *VanKasteren* [34]. This dataset was compiled in a house environment and contains 245 observations that were generated using 14 binary sensors with seven types of activities.

Depending on each person within the smart environment, it is usual that the same activity may be performed in a number of different ways over a range of durations. Thus, depending on the activity performance the sensors' interactions can be different.

3.2 Evaluated PG Algorithms

Twelve PG algorithms, which are presented in see Table 1, have been considered in order to identify the most suitable PG algorithms for binary sensor-based activity recognition that reduce the computational complexity.

Table 1. Taxonomy of PG algorithms evaluated

PG algorithm	Mechanisms of prototyping	Reduction type
LVQ3	Positioning Adjustment	Fixed
VQ	Positioning Adjustment	Fixed
LVQTC	Positioning Adjustment	Fixed
MSE	Positioning Adjustment	Mixed
HYB	Positioning Adjustment	Mixed
LVQPRU	Positioning Adjustment	Mixed
PSCSA	Positioning Adjustment	Mixed
ENPC	Positioning Adjustment	Mixed
GENN	Class Re-labeling	–
MixtGauss	Centroids	Fixed
MCA	Centroids	Decremental
POC	Space Splitting	Incremental

Each PG algorithm requires a set of parameters. In this contribution, the fixed configuration has been the configuration proposed in [17] due to the successful results previously achieved.

Given that activities of the four datasets are annotated, we are able to evaluate the accuracy of the resulting subset of prototypes from each PG algorithm. In this way, the classification percentage is related to the accuracy percentage using the complete dataset to evaluate the NN classifier for a given prototype in the activity recognition process. Specifically, the accuracy percentage is defined as the proportion of true results among the total number of classes examined.

The set of evaluated PG algorithms are presented in Table 1, which were run using Keel software [35], an open source Java software tool with evolutionary learning and soft computing based techniques for different kinds of data mining problems. To assess the performance of the PG algorithms, a 10-fold Cross-Validation was used to evaluate the accuracy percentage of each PG algorithm. The main advantage of this validation is that all the samples in the dataset are eventually used for both training and testing [36]. With this approach less of an emphasis is placed on how much the data becomes divided.

3.3 Results

Table 2 presents the average results obtained by the set of PG algorithms evaluated over the four datasets with the NN approach with $k = 1$ ($1NN$). The value of the parameter $k = 1$ is selected because this value presents low tolerance to noise in the NN approach.

Table 2 indicates the accuracy percentage in addition to the percentage reduction in terms of computational complexity for each PG algorithm and dataset. So, the reduction represents the percentage of instances that are included in the activity model of the original training set. For example, in the $ODI2$ dataset contains 616 observations, if the training size is reduced by 95 %, the set of prototypes generated contains 31 samples, which will be included in the activity model of the NN approac. Furthermore, the accuracy average percentage and the reduction average percentage are indicated in Table 2.

The PG algorithms reduced the size of the training data and also reduced the computational complexity when classifying a new activity based on binary sensor-based activity recognition with a $1NN$ approach. The PG algorithms with a reduction around 95 %, significantly decreased the size of the initial training data. Therefore, the computational complexity is clearly reduced in the same proportion, i.e., 95 %, to classify a new activity.

Nevertheless, in some PG algorithms, the reduction of the size of the training data implies a reduction in the percentage accuracy. This fact is dramatic due to the fact that the accuracy average does not exceed 85 % in the following PG algorithms: $LVQ3$, VQ, $LVQTC$, $ENPC$, $GENN$ and MCA. In these cases, the PG algorithms generalize the inconsistency, incoherence or noise in the dataset, implying negative results in the use of these PG algorithms to classify a new activity based on binary sensor-based activity recognition with a $1NN$ approach.

There are PG algorithms with an excellent performance in terms of accuracy percentage and reduction percentage of computational complexity in the four datasets. It is noteworthy that *MixtGauss* is the best PG algorithm that obtains an average percentage accuracy of 95 % with a reduction average percentage of 95 %.

Analyzing the results, we can point out that the PG algorithms: $MixtGauss$, $PSCSA$ and $LVQPRU$ obtain successful results in terms of accuracy percentage with the average accuracy above 90 %. This PG algorithms prefer numerical datasets, especially binary as the dataset used in this case study, which offers excellent reduction percentage without losing performance accuracy. Therefore, these PG algorithms used for activity recognition can be deemed as being very

Table 2. Results obtained of the PG algorithms with the four datasets

PG algorithms	Dataset	Accuracy (%)	Reduction (%)	Accuracy Av. (%)	Reduction Av. (%)
LVQ3	Odi1	49.92	95.00	72.00	95.00
LVQ3	ODI2	59.56	95.00		
LVQ3	VanKasteren	82.70	95.00		
VQ	Casas	88.33	95.00	68.63	95.00
VQ	ODI1	56.14	95.00		
VQ	ODI2	57.78	95.00		
VQ	VanKasteren	72.27	95.00		
LVQTC	Casas	94.17	95.00	76.89	95.00
LVQTC	ODI1	69.39	95.00		
LVQTC	ODI2	55.51	95.00		
LVQTC	VanKasteren	88.50	95.00		
MSE	Casas	93.33	63.00	86.50	86.75
MSE	ODI1	82.48	94.00		
MSE	ODI2	80.86	97.00		
MSE	VanKasteren	89.33	93.00		
HYB	Casas	93.33	95.00	81.95	95.00
HYB	ODI1	68.52	95.00		
HYB	ODI2	72.09	95.00		
HYB	VanKasteren	93.85	95.00		
LVQPRU	Casas	96.67	95.00	89.87	95.00
LVQPRU	ODI1	84.40	95.00		
LVQPRU	ODI2	84.58	95.00		
LVQPRU	VanKasteren	93.82	95.00		
PSCSA	Casas	86.67	95.00	91.98	96.25
PSCSA	ODI1	94.12	96.00		
PSCSA	ODI2	91.23	98.00		
PSCSA	VanKasteren	95.92	96.00		
ENPC	Casas	93.33	89.00	78.14	93.25
ENPC	ODI1	65.91	93.00		
ENPC	ODI2	68.02	96.00		
ENPC	VanKasteren	85.28	95.00		
GENN	Casas	95.00	95.00	73.89	95.00
GENN	ODI1	56.82	95.00		
GENN	ODI2	60.55	95.00		
GENN	VanKasteren	83.20	95.00		
MixtGauss	Casas	94.17	95.00	94.57	95.00
MixtGauss	ODI1	96.42	95.00		
MixtGauss	ODI2	93.84	95.00		
MixtGauss	VanKasteren	93.85	95.00		
MCA	Casas	6.67	95.00	67.36	96.00
MCA	ODI1	84.42	96.00		
MCA	ODI2	84.10	97.00		
MCA	VanKasteren	94.25	96.00		
POC	Casas	90.00	63.00	84.65	53.75
POC	ODI1	81.48	23.00		
POC	ODI2	72.87	70.00		
POC	VanKasteren	94.23	59.00		

useful given that a reduction in the number of stored instances corresponds to a reduction in the computational complexity, reducing the number of instances that are contained in the activity model.

4 Conclusions

This work has been focused on the identification of the prototype generation algorithms for the purpose of binary sensor-based activity recognition with NN approach in order to reduce the computational complexity of the classification process to be deployed in low cost devices. Twelve PG algorithms have been evaluated with four activity datasets. Results from the evaluation demonstrated the ability of the *MixtGauss*, *PSCSA* and *LVQPRU* PG algorithms to provide good performance and percentage reduction of approximately 95 % with an average accuracy percentage higher than 90 %.

Acknowledgments. This contribution has been supported by research projects: TIN2015-66524-P and UJAEN/2014/06/14. Invest Northern Ireland is acknowledged for partially supporting this project under the Competence Centre Program Grant RD0513853 - Connected Health Innovation Centre.

References

1. Chen, L., Hoey, J., Nugent, C., Cook, D.J., Yu, Z.: Sensor-based activity recognition. IEEE Trans. Syst. Man Cybern. Part C: Appl. Rev. **42**(6), 790–808 (2012)
2. Maksimovic, M., Vujovic, V., Davidovic, N., Milosevic, V., Raspberry, P.B.: Pi as internet of things hardware: performances and constraints. Des. Issues **3**(8), 8 (2014)
3. Doukas, C.: Building Internet of Things with the ARDUINO. CreateSpace Independent Publishing Platform, USA (2012)
4. Botta, A., Donato, W., Persico, V., Pescape, A.: Integration of cloud computing and internet of things: a survey. Future Gener. Comput. Syst. **56**, 684–700 (2016)
5. Chui, M., Loffler, M., Roberts, R.: The Internet of Things (Process Optimization). McKinsey Quarterly, Germany (2010)
6. Gu, T., Wang, L., Wu, Z., Tao, X., Lu, J.: A pattern mining approach to sensor-based human activity recognition. IEEE Trans. Knowl. Data Eng. **23**(9), 1359–1372 (2011)
7. Li, C., Lin, M., Yang, L.T., Ding, C.: Integrating the enriched feature with machine learning algorithms for human movement and fall detection. J. Supercomput. **67**(3), 854–865 (2014)
8. San Martin, L.A., Pelaez, V.M., Gonzalez, R., Campos, A., Lobato, V.: Environmental user-preference learning for smart homes: an autonomous approach. J. Ambient Intell. Smart Environ. **2**(3), 327–342 (2010)
9. Chen, L., Nugent, C.: Ontology-based activity recognition in intelligent pervasive environments. Int. J. Web Inf. Syst. **5**(4), 410–430 (2009)
10. Chen, L., Nugent, C.D., Wang, H.: A knowledge-driven approach to activity recognition in smart homes. IEEE Trans. Knowl. Data Eng. **24**(6), 961–974 (2012)
11. Cover, T., Hart, P.: Nearest neighbor pattern classification. IEEE Trans. Inf. Theor. **13**(1), 21–27 (1967)

12. Wu, X., Kumar, V.: The Top Ten Algorithms in Data Mining, 1st edn. Chapman & Hall/CRC, Boca Raton (2009)
13. Al-Faiz, M.Z., Ali, A.A., Miry, A.H.: A k-nearest neighbor based algorithm for human arm movements recognition using EMG signals. In: EPC-IQ 2010, pp. 159–167 (2010)
14. Jafari, R., Li, W., Bajcsy, R., Glaser, S., Sastry, S.: Physical activity monitoring for assisted living at home. In: Leonhardt, S., Falck, T., Mähönen, P. (eds.) BSN 2007. IFMBE, vol. 13, pp. 213–219. Springer, Heidelberg (2007)
15. Moayeri Pour, G., Troped, P.J., Evans, J.J.: Environment feature extraction and classification for context aware physical activity monitoring. In: SAS 2013, pp. 123–128 (2013)
16. Kononenko, I., Machine, K.M., Learning, D.M.: Introduction to Principles and Algorithms. Horwood Publishing Limited, Chichester (2007)
17. Garcia, S., Derrac, J., Cano, J.R., Herrera, F.: Prototype selection for nearest neighbor classification: taxonomy and empirical study. IEEE Trans. Pattern Anal. Mach. Intell. **34**(3), 417–435 (2012)
18. Lozano, M., Sotoca, J.M., Sanchez, J.S., Pla, F., Pekalska, E., Duin, R.P.W.: Experimental study on prototype optimisation algorithms for prototype-based classification in vector spaces. Pattern Recognit. **39**(10), 1827–1838 (2006)
19. Chen, Y., Garcia, E.K., Gupta, M.R., Rahimi, A., Cazzanti, L.: Similarity-based classification: concepts and algorithms. J. Mach. Learn. Res. **10**, 747–776 (2009)
20. Garcia, E.K., Feldman, S., Gupta, M.R., Srivastava, S.: Completely lazylearning. IEEE Trans. Knowl. Data Eng. **22**(9), 1274–1285 (2010)
21. Wilson, D.R., Martinez, T.R.: Reduction techniques for instance-based learning algorithms. Mach. Learn. **38**(3), 257–286 (2000)
22. Geva, S., Site, J.: Adaptive nearest neighbor pattern classifier. IEEE Trans. Neural Netw. **2**(2), 318–322 (1991)
23. Kim, S.W., Oomenn, A.: A brief taxonomy and ranking of creative prototype reduction schemes. Pattern Anal. Appl. **6**, 232–244 (2003)
24. The, K.T.: The self-organizative map. Proc. IEEE **78**(9), 1464–1480 (1990)
25. Koplowitz, J., Brown, T.A.: On the relation of performance to editing in nearest neighbor rules. Pattern Recognit. **13**, 251–255 (1981)
26. Sanchez, J.S., Barandela, R., Marques, A.I., Alejo, R., Badenas, J.: Analysis of new techniques to obtain quaylity training sets. Pattern Recognit. Lett. **24**, 1015–1022 (2003)
27. Chang, C.L.: Finding prototypes for nearest neighbor classifiers. IEEE Trans. Comput. **23**(11), 1179–1184 (1974)
28. Fayed, H.A., Hashem, S.R., Atiya, A.F.: Self-generating prototypes for pattern classification. Pattern Recognit. **40**(5), 1498–1509 (2007)
29. Raicharoen, T., Lursinsap, C.: A divide-and-conquer approach to the pairwise opposite class-nearest neighbor (POC-NN) algorithm. Pattern Recognit. Lett. **26**(10), 1554–1567 (2005)
30. Sanchez, J.S.: High training set size reduction by space partitioning and prototype abstraction. Pattern Recognit. **37**, 1561–1564 (2004)
31. Cook, D.J., Schmitter-Edgecombe, M.: Assessing the quality of activities in a smart environment. Method Inf. Med. **48**(5), 480–485 (2009)
32. Synnott, J., Chen, L., Nugent, C.D., Moore, G.: The creation of simulated activity datasets using a graphical intelligent environment simulation tool, pp. 4143–4146 (2014)

33. Nugent, C., Synnott, J., Santanna, A., Espinilla, M., Cleland, I., Banos, L.J.O., et al.: An initiative for the creation of open datasets within the pervasive healthcare, pp. 180–183 (2016)
34. Van Kasteren, T., Noulas, A., Englebienne, G., Krse, B.: Accurate activity recognition in a home setting, pp. 1–9 (2008)
35. Alcalá, J., Fernández, A., Luengo, J., Derrac, J., García, S., Sánchez, L.: KEEL data-mining software tool: data set repository, integration of algorithms and experimental analysis framework. J. Multiple-Valued Logic Soft Comput. **17**(2–3), 255–287 (2011)
36. Devijver, P.A., Kittler, J.: Pattern Recognition: A Statistical Approach. Prentice Hall, London (1982)

Activity Recognition Using Dynamic Instance Activation

Alberto Calzada[1], Chris Nugent[1(✉)], Macarena Espinilla[2], Jonathan Synnott[1], and Luis Martinez[2]

[1] School of Computing and Mathematics, University of Ulster, Jordanstown, Northern Ireland, UK
{a.calzada,cd.nugent,j.synnott}@ulster.ac.uk

[2] Department of Computer Sciences, University of Jaen, Jaen, Spain
{mestevez,martin}@ujaen.es

Abstract. Dynamic Instance Activation (DIA) is a newly developed data-driven classification algorithm. It was designed to minimise the negative impact in situations of data incompleteness and inconsistency. To achieve this, the proposed methodology attempts to maximise the accuracy of the classification process in a way that does not compromise the overall computational effort.

In this research, DIA was evaluated in the context of Human Activity Recognition (HAR) for Smart Environments, using datasets consisting of binary sensor data and their associated class labels (activities). This scenario was selected as an ideal case study to illustrate the usefulness of DIA considering the wide range of domains in which HAR is applied. It was also considered adequate given the simplicity of the data involved in the process, which allows using relatively simple similarity functions, therefore placing the main focus on DIA's performance.

In this context, DIA was compared with other state-of-the-art classifiers, delivering promising results in terms of percentage of activities correctly identified over the total. It is important to note that these results could be further improved if other similarity functions or data representation schemes were selected.

Keywords: Activity recognition · Classification · Smart environments · Similarity measures

1 Introduction

Over the last decade, Human Activity Recognition (HAR) has emerged as a prominent field of study from which several research areas have directly benefited. These areas include pervasive, mobile and context-aware computing, surveillance and ambient-assisted living, to name but a few. This increased attention in the study of HAR has been driven by two main aspects: technological advances in sensor devices and application-domain demands [1]. On the one hand, innovations in miniaturization, wired and wireless communications, reduced costs, decrease in energy consumption and increased capacity have increased the use of sensing devices.

C.R. García et al. (Eds.): UCAmI 2016, Part II, LNCS 10070, pp. 75–83, 2016.
DOI: 10.1007/978-3-319-48799-1_9

One particular application domain that has greatly benefited from the advances in sensor devices is that of Smart Environments, which often require extensive sensor-based monitoring across a particular scenario [1]. Among all the types of Smart Environments, the scenarios consisting solely of binary sensors can be considered as one of the simplest. In this regard, Binary Smart Environments (BSEs) provide an ideal framework in which to test new concepts and procedures that can be applied in the entire HAR field. The research presented in this paper can be considered as an example of research within this BSE domain.

The activities performed in BSE scenarios in a certain period of time are described as sequences of one or more sensors. The status of a sensor is represented as a binary variable that takes the value 1 if the sensor was activated and 0 otherwise. When these sequences of sensor statuses (state sequences) and their associated class label (the activity performed when the sequence of sensor activations occurred) are collected within a dataset, a data-driven machine learning (ML) algorithm can be used to classify new sequences of events and identify the activity being performed [1, 2].

In this regard, HAR can be described as a classification problem. As such, it can be negatively impacted by situations of incompleteness and inconsistency of instances (in this case, sequences of binary sensor state sequences). On the one hand, a situation of incompleteness occurs when the data does not contain an exact match for a new instance that needs to be classified, and therefore a new activity cannot be identified. On the other hand, a situation of incompleteness arises when a group of similar instances included in the dataset are labelled with different activities. In this case, when a new instance that needs to be classified is assessed, the classification algorithm is prone to misclassify the new activity.

Situations of incompleteness and inconsistency can be considered as opposite: while the former occurs due to a lack of data, the latter can originate due to an excess of data. The proposed Dynamic Instance Activation (DIA) approach in the current work balances these two situations by finding a non-empty set of instances similar to the one being classified and with minimum inconsistency between them [2]. Hence, only the most relevant and consistent observations are then aggregated, therefore producing a more clear output. DIA can be considered as a generalization of the recently-proposed Dynamic Rule Activation (DRA) algorithm [3], which was designed to work solely on Extended Belief Rule-Based systems (E-BRB) [4]. DIA removes the need for rule-based datasets that DRA had, and is able to operate over any type of dataset, provided that a similarity and an aggregation function are provided.

The following Section illustrates the concepts of incompleteness and inconsistency of information in a BSE and Sect. 3 details the DIA process. Section 4 briefly introduces several BSE case studies where DIA and other popular ML classifiers were applied and in Sect. 5 their results are highlighted. Finally, the conclusions are outlined in Sect. 6.

2 Data Incompleteness and Inconsistency

In a BSE, incomplete and inconsistent situations are likely to occur due to the nature of the data and the elements related to its generation. For example, a human might perform the different tasks of an activity in a different order, timescale or miss an optional task. Also, a sensor device might be faulty, out of battery, misplaced or not connected to the network. Any of these situations introduce some noise in the dataset being compiled which affects the quality of the data. Therefore, an HAR algorithm should be designed to acknowledge these situations and have the capability to minimise their impact in the activity recognition process. Two of the undesirable data issues commonly encountered are incompleteness and inconsistency, which are briefly detailed in an BSE context in the following Sections.

2.1 Incompleteness

In a BSE, a situation of incompleteness occurs when the sensor state sequence analyzed to determine the activity performed does not exactly match any instance of the BSE training dataset. This can be due to some noise which was induced in the data as previously mentioned, or due to the activity which was being performed having not been recorded previously.

For example, in a basic BSE consisting of two sensors placed in a bathroom: one of them activates when the door is open (Bathroom Door Sensor) and another one when the toilet is flushed (Toilet Sensor). Consider the dataset presented in Table 1, consisting of three instances.

Table 1. Example of a basic BSE dataset

Instance number	Bathroom door sensor status	Toilet sensor status	Activity
1	1	1	Use toilet
2	1	0	Use toilet
3	1	1	Clean toilet

Considering the BSE dataset illustrated in Table 1, and the sensor state sequence: *{(Bathroom Door Sensor,* 0*), (Toilet Sensor,* 1*)}*. Since such a sequence is not represented in the BSE dataset, which is being used for training a HAR algorithm, will not be able to exactly match any instance in order to confidently identify an activity based on the examples. Hence, the BSE dataset can be considered as incomplete.

2.2 Inconsistency

A situation of inconsistency occurs when the sensor state sequence of an activity needs to be recognized matches two or more different activities recorded in the dataset. In such a situation, a HAR algorithm would typically be unable to select between the range of matched activities.

In the example represented in Table 1, the sensor state sequence *{(Bathroom Door Sensor,* 1*), (Toilet Sensor,* 1*)}* matches two instances labelled with different activities (*Use Toilet* and *Clean Toilet*). These two instances are said to be inconsistent between them, and it will be difficult for a HAR algorithm to discern which one of the two activities was the one performed.

The following Section describes the DIA algorithm, which aims to address these two situations simultaneously, subsequently minimizing their impact.

3 Dynamic Instance Activation

In many classification algorithms, two differentiated steps can be identified: similarity evaluation and aggregation. In the first step, the similarities between the instances in the training dataset and the unlabelled instance (the one being classified) are measured in order to select the most relevant instances from the dataset. In the second step, these relevant instances and their similarities are aggregated in a certain way in order to assign a label to the unlabelled instance. In terms of HAR, this process is used to assign an activity to the unlabelled instance (i.e. sensor state sequence).

The DIA process sits between these two steps. Its main aim is to minimize the incompleteness and inconsistency in the set of instances obtained after the similarity evaluation step. Therefore, a more suitable set of instances is aggregated in the subsequent step, eventually increasing the accuracy of the classifier.

As illustrated in Fig. 1, DIA focuses on the set of relevant instances obtained from the similarity step. It increases the size of this set if incompleteness is found, and reduces it when a situation of inconsistency occurs. This is how DIA attempts to minimize incompleteness and inconsistency simultaneously. Once a suitable size of relevant instances is identified, it can be processed in the final aggregation step.

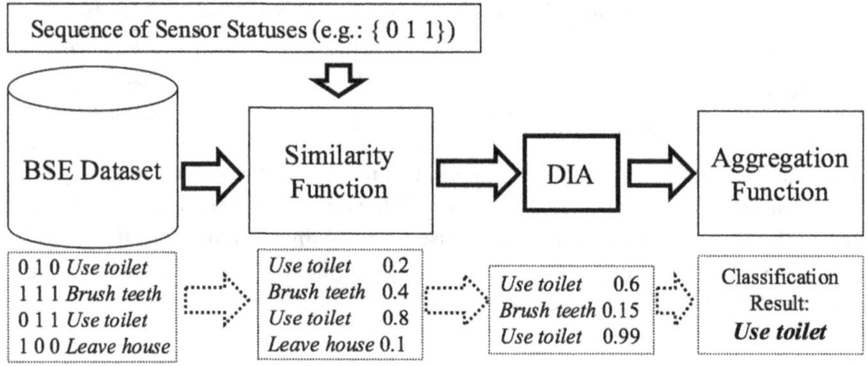

Fig. 1. The function of DIA embedded in a classification process. Example elements added for clarification are contained within dotted rectangles.

The increase and reduction process in which DIA is based is achieved by optimizing one single parameter, named λ. This parameter modifies the original similarities provided by a similarity function as follows:

$$S_{\lambda}(X, I_i) = (S(X, I_i))^{\lambda} \quad (1)$$

where X is the unlabelled sensor state sequence being classified, and I_i is the sensor state sequence of the ith instance of the BSE dataset. S is a similarity function that retrieves values within the [0, 1] range when comparing two sensor state sequences, where 0 and 1 denote total dissimilarity and exact match, respectively.

By augmenting the value of λ, the set of relevant instances is reduced as an attempt to minimize inconsistency. Likewise, as the value of λ is decreased, the set of instances is enlarged, reducing the effects of incompleteness. For each λ value, an agreement function is necessary to compare the sets produced against other λ values. In this research, the agreement function is defined as the highest percentage of instances whose label is the same over the total set of instances contained in the set. Once a series of λ values is evaluated, the set of instances with the highest agreement is passed onto the aggregation step.

DIA allows the modification of the similarity and aggregation functions of the classifier where it is being used. Nevertheless, for Eq. 1 to function correctly, the selected similarity function S needs to return values within the interval [0, 1], as previously described.

4 Case Studies

The Hamming distance [5, 6], was selected as the similarity function since it is designed to compare different sequences of binary values. Therefore, it is ideal in order to compare sensor state sequences for different activities stored in a BSE.

In addition, in order to place the main focus on DIA, the aggregation function selected was the average of the similarity values (after being tuned by DIA) per each activity included in the set of instances retrieved by DIA. The activity with the highest average is chosen as the classification result. Average was selected as it is probably one of the simplest aggregation functions to work on.

This simple DIA-focused classifier was called Dynamic Instance Activation with Hamming and Average (DIAHA). Hence, its equivalent without using DIA can be named HA.

A total of 4 datasets collected from distinct BSEs were inputted into DIA in order to measure its accuracy, in terms of percentage of instances correctly predicted.

The first activity recognition dataset tested has been widely used in research publications and it was presented in [7]. It was compiled in a house environment consisting of three rooms in which a male participant performed 7 types of ADLs during 25 days. The information about each one of the 245 observations recorded was generated using 14 binary sensors placed across the home setting.

The second dataset (WSU) utilized in this study was collected from the smart apartment test-bed of the Washington State University (WSU) by 24 participants who completed five activities [8]. These activities consisted of the following: Make a phone call, Wash hands, Cook, Eat and Clean. Activities were annotated by the participants while performing each activity. In this paper, the original dataset was transformed into a set of activity binary vectors where each vector was an activity and each component of the vector represented the sensor state sequence during the performance of the activity.

As for the rest of the datasets generated from BSEs, a sensor status with a value of one indicates that the sensor was activated at least once, while a value of zero indicates that the sensor was not activated. The number of sensors was 39, and can be categorized as: M01… M26: motion sensor, I01: item sensors for oatmeal, I02: raisins, I03: brown sugar, I04: bowl, I05: measuring spoon, I06: medicine container sensor, I07: pot sensor, I08: phone book sensor, D01: cabinet sensor, AD1-A: water sensor, AD1-B: water sensor, AD1-C: burner sensor, asterisk: phone usage.

The remaining two datasets were generated thanks to the Open Data Initiative (ODI) for Activity Recognition consortium, which currently consists of researchers from Ulster University (UK), Luleå Technical University (Sweden), Halmstad University (Sweden), University of Jaén (Spain), and the University of Twente (The Netherlands) [9]. The consortium was recently created recognising that the development of novel activity recognition approaches requires access to high quality, annotated datasets capturing activity performance through sensor data. Large amounts of efforts have been put in place internationally for the designing of experiments, collecting and analyzing data. Nevertheless, the size, diversity and availability of datasets is limited due to significant financial and time costs associated with running experiments within intelligent environments. There is a general appreciation that further efforts should be made to streamline existing approaches to define common data formats, data collection protocols, data aggregation platforms and approaches for comparison of analysis techniques. The ODI has been established to address this, by aiming to create a structured approach to provide annotated datasets in an accessible format.

The first ODI dataset (ODI_1), consisted of sensor data generated by 4 participants within the IE Sim intelligent environment simulation tool [10]. Each participant completed 11 activities 7 times (having a total of 308 observations). These activities consisted of the following typical household activities: Go to Bed, Use toilet, Watch Television, Prepare Breakfast, Take Shower, Leave House, Get Cold Drink, Get Hot Drink, Prepare Dinner, Get Dressed and Use Telephone. These activities were annotated by the participants, while performing them. The dataset was provided in 2 formats: MySQL database entry and activity vector. The latter version is the one being utilized in this study, given that it matches the format of the datasets previously presented. The second dataset generated by the ODI (ODI_2) consists of the previous dataset with an additional 4 participants performing the same 11 activities 7 times each (having a total of 616 observations). Using these four datasets, DIAHA, HA and four popular state-of-the-art classifiers were tested running a series of 50 10-fold cross-validation (CV) tests. In each test of the series of 50, the observations in each dataset were randomly permuted. In this way, the CV tests in each series are based on different training/testing instances.

A selection of some of the most popular classifiers used in literature was used to compare the performance of HA with and without the DIA boost. The selected classifiers were: Naive Bayes classifier (NB) [11], Nearest Neighbor (NN) [12], Decision Table (DT) [13] and Support Vector Machines (SVM) [14].

5 Results

After running the series of tests specified in Sect. 4, the accuracy of each method, measured as the percentage of activities correctly classified over the total, was used to measure the performance of each classification method used for HAR. Table 2 summarizes the results obtained from the tests, with the results of the two best classifiers in each dataset highlighted in bold.

Table 2. Average accuracy results obtained from the 50 10-fold cross-validation tests for all the classifiers and datasets evaluated.

Method	Dataset				Mean
	Van Kasteren	WSU	ODI_1	ODI_2	
HA	46.53 %	55.03 %	70.04 %	79.72 %	62.83 %
DIAHA	**96.26 %**	**94.51 %**	**95.38 %**	93.28 %	**94.85 %**
DT	95.19 %	88.22 %	95.24 %	93.26 %	92.08 %
NN	95.94 %	93.40 %	95.01 %	91.65 %	94.00 %
NB	**96.78 %**	**94.18 %**	**96.37 %**	**94.04 %**	**95.34 %**
SVM	96.05 %	93.08 %	95.36 %	**94.55 %**	94.76 %

As illustrated in Table 2, when the HA method is complemented with the DIA enhancement, its results considerably increase. Note that, even if HA initially produces considerably worse results than the rest of classifiers, its performance is brought into competitive levels when it is boosted with DIA. This difference in performance helps quantifying the amount of incompleteness and inconsistency that the DIA boost is able to eliminate from a classifier (in this case: HA). In fact, this is the same reason why DIAHA is slightly better than NN on every occasion: DIAHA is able to detect when a nearest neighbor is an inconsistent sample, so it always looks to other surrounding neighbors for a greater agreement level. Such an agreement level is measured by an agreement function, as explained in Sect. 4.

One of the reasons why DIAHA outperforms DT and SVM in most cases is because DIA does not produce boundaries within the data set. Therefore, it does not classify based on the region in which a new observation falls, like DT and SVM do [13, 14] (although in different ways). On the contrary, DIA can be considered as an NN-based booster algorithm that dynamically selects the optimal number of neighbors to be considered when classifying each new observation.

A possible reason why DIAHA was slightly outperformed by NB in many cases is because NB considers the class probabilities in addition to the distribution of the values for each feature when producing a classification probability [12]. This suggests that one of the ways to improve DIA is to assume either or both of these factors in the selection of the λ parameter. A possible way of doing so is by use of either of those probabilities/distributions to weight the relevant samples obtained for each λ value and produce a distribution of class probabilities as a result; as opposed to the single class value being produced at the moment. Another possibility to improve the results provided by this research is to use a base classifier slightly more complex than HA. In this situation, DIA would have better *initial predictions* to optimise/boost, instead of those rather low accuracies provided by HA.

Taking these results into consideration, the DIA booster will outperform other conventional classification methods in situations where the classes of the dataset (in this case activities to be recognised) cannot be separated in regions, taking their features as coordinates. This is the reason why DIAHA was able to improve the results of both DT and SVM. However, it was just slightly better than NN. In this regard, DIA is ideal in situations where NN already performs well, however, it still misclassifies observations due to high inconsistency levels.

In summary, it can be considered that the optimal situation for use of DIA is when similar instances have associated different classes and the dataset classes are not easily divided into regions by one or more features (in our case, binary sensor values).

It is important to note, however, that despite the simplicity of both the distance and aggregation functions utilized in HA, the DIAHA algorithm performs better than any other classifier in the WSU dataset. In addition, it obtains the second best result in the van Kasteren and ODI_1 dataset and it ranks second when the results from all the datasets are averaged, only behind the NB method.

6 Conclusion

This research demonstrated the value of the DIA method as an algorithm able to outperform the performance of other classifiers based on similarity and aggregation functions. Such an enhancement is based on identifying and minimising situations of incompleteness and/or inconsistency in the data being considered.

In order to illustrate these capabilities, the field of HAR based on binary sensors was selected as an ideal scenario where the data collected from different sensor devices is both as simple as possible and prone to be noisy. In such scenarios DIA could be easily exemplified, as found in the case studies when the performances of HA and DIA-HA were compared. Although a very simple classifier based on the Hamming distance similarity and a Weighted Average aggregation was proposed (HA), DIA has a great potential to be further improved if other more advanced similarity and aggregation functions were utilized.

Further research will therefore be focused on developing similarity and aggregation functions specialised on specific features of HAR, such as imbalanced classification or missing values. The development of algorithms able to include data from different types of sensors, rather than just from binary sensors, is also an aim to be addressed in the foreseeable future.

Acknowledgements. Invest Northern Ireland partially supported this project under the Competence Centre Program Grant RD0513853 – Connected Health Innovation Centre.

References

1. Chen, L., Hoey, J., Nugent, C.D., Cook, D.J., Yu, Z.W.: Sensor-based activity recognition. IEEE Trans. Syst. Man Cybern. Part C **42**(6), 790–808 (2012)
2. Calzada, A., Nugent, C., Espinilla, M., Martinez, L.: Generalized dynamic instance activation for activity recognition. In: 38th Annual International Conference of the IEEE Engineering in Medicine and Biology Society (EMBS), Orlando, Florida, US, 17–20 August 2016
3. Calzada, A., Liu, J., Wang, H., Kashyap, A.: A new dynamic rule activation method for extended belief rule-bases. IEEE Trans. Knowl. Data Eng. **27**(4), 880–894 (2014)
4. Liu, J., Martinez, L., Calzada, A., Wang, H.: A novel belief rule base representation, generation and its inference methodology. Knowl. Based Syst. **53**, 129–141 (2013)
5. Hamming, R.W.: Error detecting and error correcting codes. Bell Syst. Tech. J. **29**(2), 147–160 (1950)
6. Norouzi, M., Fleet, D.J., Salakhutdinov R.R.: Hamming distance metric learning. In: Advances in Neural Information Processing Systems, pp. 1061–1069 (2012)
7. van Kasteren, T.L.M., Englebienne, G., Kröse, B.J.A.: Transferring knowledge of activity recognition across sensor networks. In: Floréen, P., Krüger, A., Spasojevic, M. (eds.) Pervasive 2010. LNCS, vol. 6030, pp. 283–300. Springer, Heidelberg (2010)
8. Cook, D., Schmitter-Edgecombe, M.: Assessing the quality of activities in a smart environment. Methods Inf. Med. **48**(5), 480–485 (2009)
9. Nugent, C., Synnott, J., Santanna, A., Espinilla, M., Cleland, I., Banos, O., Lundström, J., Hallberg, J., Calzada, A.: An initiative for the creation of open datasets within the pervasive healthcare. In: 10th EAI International Conference on Pervasive Computing Technologies for Healthcare, Cancun, Mexico, 16–19 May 2016
10. Synnott, J., Chen, L., Nugent, C.D., Moore, G.: The creation of simulated activity datasets using a graphical intelligent environment simulation tool. In: 36th Annual International Conference of the IEEE Engineering in Medicine and Biology Society (EMBS), Chicago, IL, USA, 26–30 August 2014
11. Domingos, P., Pazzani, M.: On the optimality of the simple bayesian classifier under zero-one loss. Mach. Learn. **29**, 103–137 (1997)
12. Cover, T., Hart, P.: Nearest neighbor pattern classification. IEEE Trans. Inf. Theory **13**(1), 21–27 (1967)
13. Kohavi, R.: The power of decision tables. In: Lavrač, N., Wrobel, S. (eds.) ECML 1995. LNCS, vol. 912, pp. 174–189. Springer, Heidelberg (1995)
14. Cortes, C., Vapnik, V.: Support vector networks. Mach. Learn. **20**, 273–297 (1995)

Fall Detection Through Thermal Vision Sensing

Joseph Rafferty[1(✉)], Jonathan Synnott[1], Chris Nugent[1], Gareth Morrison[2], and Elena Tamburini[3]

[1] School of Computing and Mathematics, University of Ulster, Coleraine, Northern Ireland, UK
{j.rafferty,j.synnott,cd.nugent}@ulster.ac.uk
[2] Lava Group, 17 Falcon Road, Belfast, UK
g.morrison@thelavagroup.co.uk
[3] I+ S.R.L, Piazza Puccini 26, Florence, Italy
e.tamburini@i-piu.it

Abstract. Accidental falls can cause serious injury to at risk individuals. This is especially true in the elderly community where falls are the leading cause of hospitalization, injury-related deaths and loss of independence. Detecting and rapidly responding to falls has shown to reduce the long-term impact of and risks associated with falls. A number of real time fall detection solutions exist, however, these have some deficiencies relating to privacy, maintenance, and correct usage. This study introduces a novel fall detection approach that aims to address some of these deficiencies through use of computer vision processes and ceiling mounted thermal vision sensors. A preliminary evaluation has been performed on this process showing promising results, with an accuracy of 68 %, however, highlighting a number of issues related to false positives. Future work will improve this approach and provide extended evaluation.

Keywords: Fall detection · Assistive technologies · Computer vision · Sensors · Thermal vision

1 Introduction

Accidental falls can cause serious injury to at risk individuals, such as the elderly and those with bone disease. Falls can cause a variety of injuries including broken bones and significant bruising. In particular, broken bones can represent a significant risk to the immediate health of an individual and can negatively affect their long term Quality of Life (QOL) [1, 2]. This is especially true in elderly communities where falls are the leading cause of hospitalization, injury-related deaths and loss of independence [1–4]. Fall prevention may not be realistically feasible in all cases [5, 6], however, detection of falls and rapidly responding to them has shown to be highly beneficial. Rapid response addresses injury earlier and can help prevent fall-related death and can increase the long-term QOL of elderly individuals who suffered a fall [4, 7, 8].

A number of solutions currently exist to provide real-time fall detection and alerting. These solutions have shown promising results. They have, however, some deficiencies related to correct usage, privacy and maintenance. In order to address some of these

C.R. García et al. (Eds.): UCAmI 2016, Part II, LNCS 10070, pp. 84–90, 2016.
DOI: 10.1007/978-3-319-48799-1_10

deficiencies, this study investigates the feasibility of a novel approach to fall detection that is based upon thermal sensing and computer vision.

The remaining Sections of this paper are arranged as follows; Sect. 2 provides a summary of related work; Sect. 3 introduces the novel approach used within this study; Sect. 4 provides an evaluation of the approach and, finally, Sect. 5 concludes the paper with a reflection on the utility of the approach and future work.

2 Related Work

A number of related works exist within the domain of fall detection [9–12]. These are roughly separated into two classes of approach as dictated by their operational model. These classes are Wearable-sensor based and environmental based.

Wearable-sensor based approaches typically use signals from sensors to detect falls through classifying signals [13]. These sensors include accelerometers, gyroscopes and barometers [14]. These approaches may use dedicated fall detection devices, such as those in [15] or use smartphone based apps [16, 17].

Wearable-sensors have shown extremely promising results with accuracy reaching over 90 % [8], however, have a disadvantage where they need to be worn to function. This represents a problem for use within the elderly population where cognitive impairment may lead to these wearable devices not being used correctly [9–12]. In addition, wearable sensors need to have their power source maintained by a recharging process or battery replacement, representing an additional barrier to adoption.

Environmental approaches rely upon sensors deployed in a location of interest. A range of sensors have been used to in this approach, including acoustic sensors [18], visual/infrared vision cameras [10, 19, 20], vibration detection [21], positional/pressure tracking [22–24] and thermal vision [25].

Acoustic sensors detect noises which may represent falls. This approach has issues related to noisy environments where its accuracy and utility may be diminished. Visual/ infrared cameras show promise, however, represent a potential violation of privacy as they transmit/record highly detailed imagery of an environment. Depth cameras address the privacy issues of visual/thermal camera solutions, however, have a limited field of view and require an unobscured side-profile view of their subjects, introducing problems with deployment. Vibration detection based solutions detect vibrations in a locale that may represent a fall but are subject to false positives. Positional tracking, incorporating technology such as pressure-sensitive floors or radar, are effective, however, expensive and require an extensive retrofitting of an environment. Thermal vision has been previously investigated using neural networks and the vertical-velocity of a person. This solution had issues related to low detection rate, limited field of view, requirement for an unobscured side-profile view and was easily confused by a person sitting down.

In order to address these shortcomings, a novel approach to detecting falls, related to the work in [25] has been proposed. This approach uses ceiling mounted thermal vision sensors in conjunction with an advanced computer vision based mechanism which identifies potential falls. Potential falls are logged with alerts being passed to caregiving staff who can then intervene appropriately. In this approach, an individual's environment is monitored in a way that is non-invasive and respects privacy.

3 Detecting Falls Through Thermal Vision

The devised fall detection approach observes an inhabitant through a thermal vision sensor and identifies likely fall events. Thermal sensors are placed on a ceiling and generate a 32*31 frame of temperature readings for the area directly below at a rate of 6 Hz. This sensor has an extremely wide field of view of 86° by 83°, allowing perception of a large area; at a deployment of height of 2.5 meters the viewable areas is approximately 6 meters by 5.6 meters. This sensor is shown in Fig. 1(a) and its perception of the world is shown in Fig. 1(b).

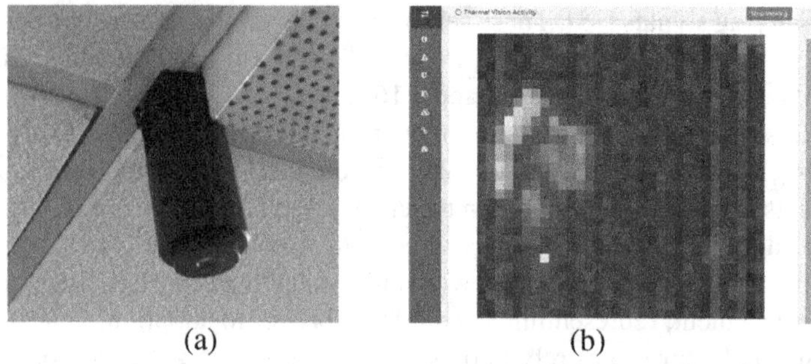

Fig. 1. The thermal vision sensor used in this study (a). The environment as perceived by the sensor and presented in a web interface, the hot readings are represented by white pixels (b).

Frames are read from the sensor through a listener program placed on the local network. This listener reads raw frame data from this sensor and interleaves it to generate frames with usable values in Celsius, to 2 decimal places. The listener then forwards these usable frames to a web service endpoint. This web service endpoint then stores the frame in a Time Series Database (TSDB) and an in-memory cache.

A computer vision process retrieves the frame data from the endpoint and performs blob and entity detection. Initially, the process filters thermal pixels which are outside of the likely range of human emissive temperatures or occurred through gradually raised temperature. These filtered readings are subsequently used to identify thermal pixels that are significantly above unfiltered background temperatures through comparison with previous frame data. These identified thermal pixels are then grouped as blobs, representing occupants, and a number of metrics are generated. These metrics include thermal pixel count, blob location, blob emissive temperature, blob width, blob height and blob aspect ratio. Finally, blobs that have a thermal pixel count less than 6 are discarded, as these would be too small to represent a human at the intended sensor deployment height, as determined though a small number of evaluations. Further information on this process can be obtained in [26, 27].

This blob detection process then stores these blob in the TSDB and memory cache. A Fall Detection Process (FDP) subsequently consumes these recorded blob[1]. If the FDP detects a fall, it is recorded in a Relational Database which is presented in a web interface. The overall architecture of this approach is presented in Fig. 2 and is followed by a description of the FDP.

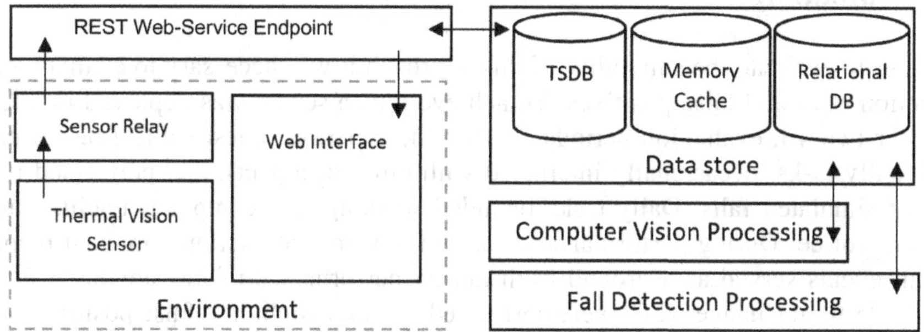

Fig. 2. The architecture of the developed fall detection platform.

The FDP reasons upon the blob records generated by the computer vision process. Central to this process is the hypothesis that rapid and significant expansion of a blob in a localized area could indicate a fall.

Blobs under consideration are those within body temperate range, 26C - 41C. Only blobs that have fully entered the frame are considered, as the rapid blob expansion from an inhabitant entering a scene could mislead the FDP. Blobs are considered to be in scene when they are not touching the outer pixels of the frame. Although this reduces the usable area of sensor frames, uncertainty related to partial observability is reduced. Events in which multiple blobs converge into one, potentially representing close conversation, are ignored by the FDP to reduce false positives.

When a single, unconverged and in scene blob is present the FDP is eligible and so performed. The FDP operates on a window of 4 frames; where f_n is the current frame and f_{n-3} is the 4th most current frame. A reference blob size value, $blob_{rs}$, is produced by averaging the size of a blob from f_{n-3} and f_{n-2}. Averaging over 2 frames introduces a smoothing factor, reducing the impact of anomalous readings and accommodating movement. $blob_{rs}$ is assumed to initially indicate the size of a blob in a non-fall state, such as standing. If at any point, the blob size in f_n expands more than 1.8 times larger than $blob_{rs}$ it will be assumed that a fall has occured. Frame f_{n-1} is not considered to facilitate transitioning from a normal posture to a fall. The value of 1.8 was arose through sequential analysis of values between 1.2 and 3.4 incremented in steps of 0.2.

This analysis incorporated 4 test cases, involving one subject; 2 test falls and 2 postural changes incorporating sitting to seating and vice versa. 1.8 was the lowest value to reliably detect test falls and not be triggered on posture transitions. Higher values may

[1] It should be noted that this detection process is designed to operate within a single occupant environment, when a fall is most dangerous and there is no immediate assistance available.

reduce false positives, however, not detect falls. If other blobs enter the scene, this process is reset and halted until its eligibility is restored. Following this initial development, this FDP was then evaluated; the scenario and results of which are presented in the following Section.

4 Evaluation

In order to evaluate the suitability of this approach it was necessary to evaluate fall detection rates and false positives. To achieve this, a sensor was deployed in a test area for two 4-h evaluation periods. During these periods a test subject performed their daily tasks, occasionally interacted with other occupants, and performed two sets of simulated falls. Daily tasks included working at a computer, reading, and making coffee. During performance of daily tasks and interaction a manual record of fall events served as a ground truth during performance of the simulated falls. Thirty Postural Changes (PC) were performed to gain insight into false positives and false negatives. PCs are significant changes in blob size through normal activity, such as reaching across a desk or moving from seated to standing. The results of this evaluation are presented in Table 1.

Table 1. Accuracy of fall detection through the thermal vision-based FDP devised in this study.

Set	Simulated falls	Detected falls	Detection rate	PC Count	PC Errors	True Positive/ False Positive/ True Negative/ False Negative	Sensitivity/ Specificity
I	15	10	66.7 %	20	4	10/4/16/5	66.7 %/ 80.0 %
II	10	7	70 %	10	3	7/3/7/3	70.0 %/ 70.0 %

The preliminary results show that this approach has promise, though a number of issues were highlighted. In some cases, PCs were incorrectly identified as falls. Incorrectly classified PCs included reaching across a desk with a leg extended for balance, which is not likely to be performed by an elderly person in the home, and quickly transitioning from standing to seated while arms were simultaneously being fully extended. Some falls were not correctly identified when the subject limbs where partially obscured by desks and other fixtures. In another case a slow fall was not detected where the subject partially stopped their fall by pushing against a support. Potential mechanisms to address these errors are presented in the conclusion of this paper.

5 Conclusion

In this paper we present a novel approach to fall detection that utilizes thermal vision sensors and a computer vision based FDP. This approach addresses some issues with previous fall detection works by respecting privacy, not requiring an extensive retrofitting process and eliminating the need for wearable devices. Although this study is in its early stage, preliminary evaluation shows accuracy of 68 %, comparing favorably with previous thermal vision fall detection that was 35 % accurate [25].

A number of deficiencies have been identified and efforts are underway to address these. Specifically, edge and shape detection will be added to the computer vision process to reduce misclassification of unusual PCs. Additional work, will investigate use of shape detection to help address issues with falls where the subject becomes partially obscured. Finally, adaptive generation of $blob_{rs}$ across a dynamic frame window will be investigated to accommodate variance in fall rates.

Following development of these improvements, a more thorough evaluation will be undertaken involving a number of subjects and a larger sample size. Following evaluation, trialing this approach in a suitable population will be investigated.

Acknowledgments. Invest Northern Ireland is acknowledged for supporting this project under the Competence Centre Programs Grant RD0513853 – Connected Health Innovation Centre.

References

1. Evans, D., Pester, J., Vera, L., Jeanmonod, D., Jeanmonod, R.: Elderly fall patients triaged to the trauma bay: age, injury patterns, and mortality risk. Am. J. Emerg. Med. **33**, 1635–1638 (2015)
2. González, N., Aguirre, U., Orive, M., Zabala, J., García-Gutiérrez, S., Las Hayas, C., Navarro, G., Quintana, J.M.: Health-related quality of life and functionality in elderly men and women before and after a fall-related wrist fracture. Int. J. Clin. Pract. **68**, 919–928 (2014)
3. Stevens, J.A., Corso, P.S., Finkelstein, E.A., Miller, T.R.: The costs of fatal and non-fatal falls among older adults. Inj. Prev. **12**, 290–295 (2006)
4. Masud, T., Morris, R.O.: Epidemiology of falls. Age Ageing **30**, 3–7 (2001)
5. El-Khoury, F., Cassou, B., Charles, M.-A., Dargent-Molina, P.: The effect of fall prevention exercise programmes on fall induced injuries in community dwelling older adults: systematic review and meta-analysis of randomised controlled trials. BMJ **347**, f6234 (2013)
6. Coppedge, N.: Using a standardized fall prevention tool decreases fall rates. Nurs. (Lond.) **46**, 64–67, 4p (2016)
7. Lord, S.R., Sherrington, C., Menz, H.B., Close, J.C.T.: Falls in Older People: Risk Factors and Strategies for Prevention. Cambridge University Press, Cambridge (2007)
8. Bagal, F., Becker, C., Cappello, A., Chiari, L., Aminian, K., Hausdorff, J.M., Zijlstra, W., Klenk, J.: Evaluation of accelerometer-based fall detection algorithms on real-world falls. PLoS One **7**, 1–9 (2012)
9. Khan, S.S., Hoey, J.: Review of fall detection techniques: a data availability perspective (2016)
10. Zhang, Z., Conly, C., Athitsos, V.: A survey on vision-based fall detection. In: Proceedings of 8th ACM International Conference on PErvasive Technologies Related *to* Assistive Environments, pp. 46:1–46:7 (2015)
11. Schwickert, L., Becker, C., Lindemann, U., Maréchal, C., Bourke, A., Chiari, L., Helbostad, J.L., Zijlstra, W., Aminian, K., Todd, C., Consensus Group.: Fall detection with body-worn sensors. Z. Gerontol. Geriatr. **46**, 706–719 (2013)
12. Pannurat, N., Thiemjarus, S., Nantajeewarawat, E.: Automatic fall monitoring: a review. Sens. (Basel) **14**, 12900–12936 (2014)

13. Ciuti, G., Ricotti, L., Menciassi, A., Dario, P.: MEMS sensor technologies for human centred applications in healthcare, physical activities, safety and environmental sensing: a review on research activities in Italy. Sensors **15**, 6441–6468 (2015)
14. Tsai, P., Yang, Y., Shih, Y., Kung, H.: Gesture-aware fall detection system: design and implementation, pp. 88–92 (2015)
15. Lee, J.K., Robinovitch, S.N., Park, E.J.: Inertial sensing-based pre-impact detection of falls involving near-fall scenarios. IEEE Trans. Neural Syst. Rehabil. Eng. **23**, 258–266 (2015)
16. Rakhman, A.Z., Nugroho, L.E., Widyawan, K.: Fall detection system using accelerometer and gyroscope based on smartphone. In: Proceedings of 2014 1st International Conference on Information Technology, Computer, Engineering Engineering Green Technology. Its Application a Better Future, ICITACEE 2014, pp. 99–104 (2015)
17. Aguiar, B., Rocha, T., Silva, J., Sousa, I.: Accelerometer-based fall detection for smartphones. In: Proceedings of IEEE MeMeA 2014 - IEEE International Symposium on Medical Measurements and Applications (2014)
18. Khan, S., Yu, M., Feng, P., Wang, L., Chambers, J.: An unsupervised acoustic fall detection system using source separation for sound interference suppression. Signal Process. **110**, 199–210 (2015)
19. Sokolova, M.V., Serrano-Cuerda, J., Castillo, J.C., Fernndez-Caballero, A.: A fuzzy model for human fall detection in infrared video. J. Intell. Fuzzy Syst. **24**, 215–228 (2013)
20. Debard, G., Baldewijns, G., Goedem, T., Tuytelaars, T., Vanrumste, B.: Camera-based fall detection using a particle filter, pp. 6947–6950 (2015)
21. Zigel, Y., Litvak, D., Gannot, I.: A method for automatic fall detection of elderly people using floor vibrations and sound-proof of concept on human mimicking doll falls. IEEE Trans. Biomed. Eng. **56**, 2858–2867 (2009)
22. Chaccour, K., Darazi, R.: Smart carpet using differential piezoresistive pressure sensors for elderly fall detection. Presented at the (2015)
23. Amin, M.G., Zhang, Y.D., Ahmad, F., Ho, K.C.D.: Radar signal processing for elderly fall detection: the future for in-home monitoring. IEEE Signal Process. Mag. **33**, 71–80 (2016)
24. Loncomilla, P., Tapia, C., Daud, O., Ruiz-del-Solar, J.: A novel methodology for assessing the fall risk using low-cost and off-the-shelf devices. IEEE Trans. Hum. Mach. Syst. **44**, 406–415 (2014)
25. Sixsmith, A., Johnson, N.: A smart sensor to detect the falls of the elderly. IEEE Pervasive Comput. **3**, 42–47 (2004)
26. Rafferty, J., Synnott, J., Nugent, C.: A hybrid rule and machine learning based generic alerting platform for smart environments. Engineering in medicine and biology society. In: 2016 38th Annual International Conference of the IEEE Engineering in Medicine and Biology Society (EMBC) (2016)
27. Synnott, J., Nugent, C., Jeffers, P.: A thermal data simulation tool for the testing of novel approaches to activity recognition. In: Pecchia, L., Chen, L.L., Nugent, C., Bravo, J. (eds.) IWAAL 2014. LNCS, vol. 8868, pp. 10–13. Springer, Heidelberg (2014)

The Intelligent Environment Experiment Assistance Tool to Facilitate Partial Environment Simulation and Real-Time Activity Annotation

Jonathan Synnott[1(✉)], Celeste Gabrielli[2], and Chris Nugent[1]

[1] School of Computing and Mathematics, University of Ulster, Jordanstown, Northern Ireland
{j.synnott,cd.nugent}@ulster.ac.uk
[2] Dipartimento dell'ingegneria dell'informazione, Universita Politecnica Delle Marche, Ancona, Italy
s1052886@univpm.it

Abstract. The development of novel activity recognition approaches requires access to high quality, annotated datasets. When designing an experiment, researchers may not have access to the complete set of equivalent sensors required. A viable solution to this barrier has been the use of completely simulated environments. Nevertheless, an optimal solution may be to allow researchers to use the equipment they do have, and simulate missing sensors. This paper aims to address this scenario through the proposal of the Intelligent Environment Experiment Assistance Tool. The approach facilitates real-time partial simulation of an environment in addition to a real-time annotation component which aims to maximize the accuracy and consistency of dataset annotations. The concept has received feedback from 19 international researchers who are involved in Intelligent Environments research. This feedback provides an insight into the prevalence, type and impact of limitations in physical IE usage. Additionally, 84.3 % of the researchers stated that the real-time annotation would be very useful or quite useful, and 52.6 % stated that the partial simulation component would be very useful or quite useful.

Keywords: Dataset annotation · Intelligent environments · Simulation

1 Introduction

Intelligent Environments (IEs) are used within a wide range of domains including healthcare, security and energy efficiency. A common theme within these domains is the development of novel approaches to activity recognition for the purpose of metric generation, trend analysis and anomaly detection. The development of such approaches requires access to high quality annotated datasets describing a diverse range of activities performed within IEs. Access to such datasets, and the ability to generate such datasets, may be limited due to several factors. These factors include expense and availability of sensor technology, the expense, physical space required, and the time consuming nature of IE construction, and the ethical and practical limitations associated with data

C.R. García et al. (Eds.): UCAmI 2016, Part II, LNCS 10070, pp. 91–97, 2016.
DOI: 10.1007/978-3-319-48799-1_11

collection on human participants. Ultimately, such limitations are detrimental to the progress of research, slowing down advances in the development of new approaches [1].

The use of simulation software is one approach that has been investigated by researchers in the field as a solution to mitigate these limitations, particularly in the earlier stages of solution development. These approaches facilitate low-cost, flexible and rapid experimentation, allowing researchers to quickly change environment configuration and assess the impact upon algorithm performance without the need for infrastructure investment [2]. While the use of simulation software provides a wide range of advantages, particularly during the earlier stages of solution development, researchers must ultimately test their solutions in real environments with real participants. This step is crucial as it exposes these solutions to variables which may not have been considered during the modelling process. There is therefore the need for an approach that can facilitate the transition between reliance on entirely simulated environments, and entirely physical environments. Such an approach should provide the advantages of both simulated and physical environments, whilst addressing the limitations of both.

In addition to high quality sensor data collection, high quality annotation of activities recorded within the datasets is critical to ensure the usability of the data. Many researchers rely on the use of pen and paper or spreadsheets with stop watches in order to record the start and end of events within a scenario. Such annotations must then be manually inserted into the dataset in the correct location once the experiment is complete. This is a time consuming and error-prone process, and often requires that a member of a research team is dedicated to this task while the principle investigator monitors other elements of the experiment.

The paper introduces a novel approach to data collection which aims to capitalize upon the advantages of both physical and simulated IEs while mitigating some of the limitations of each. The approach consists of "partial simulation" in which experiments are completed within physical IEs, and the physical sensor set is complemented with simulated sensors where necessary. The approach also incorporates a solution to real-time activity annotation, facilitating accurate timestamping and removing the need for manually appending annotations to the dataset after the experiment has concluded. Both approaches will be incorporated into the Intelligent Environment Experiment Assistance Tool (IEEAT), and made freely available to the research community. Section 2 details related work and current limitations. Section 3 provides further details of the IEEAT and its core functionality. Section 4 presents community feedback. Finally, Sect. 5 provides a conclusion and proposes future work.

2 Related Work

There is currently a wide range of approaches to environment simulation, each with associated advantages and limitations. Persim [3] is an example of an event-driven simulation approach, facilitating rapid creation of vast datasets for use within activity recognition research. The approach facilitates the modelling of activities by specifying parameters including typical duration, and maximum and minimum sensor values, amongst others. Persim 3D [4] is an evolution of the Persim software, offering context-based simulation of human activities within 3D virtual IEs. IE Sim is an interactive approach to IE Simulation, facilitating the rapid creation of virtual IEs populated with simulated sensors. Such IEs can be interacted with through the use of an avatar which can passively or actively interact with sensors including floor pressure, chair pressure, PIR and contact sensors [5].

Several approaches have investigated alternative methods of dataset annotation. These approaches focus on increasing the quality and accuracy of annotation through intuitive user interfaces. For example, the Dynamic Annotation System for Smart Environments (DANTE) [6] is a system which incorporates the use of stereoscopic cameras for offline annotation of activity performance. The system is capable of tracking object position and orientation in 3D space using fiducial markers, and allowing users to annotate recorded datasets by navigating through captured videos on a frame-by-frame basis. IE Sim facilitates the annotation of simulated datasets by providing an interface to allow users to indicate the start and end of each activity within a pre-defined activity list. While this facilitates real-time annotation during simulated activity performance, it was found that annotations were occasionally omitted or delayed as a result of users becoming fixated on activity performance.

There is a need for an approach that can facilitate the transition from reliance on fully simulated environments to fully physical environments, and offer a more intuitive and effective method of dataset annotation. As a result, this work proposes the development of the IEEAT, which has been designed to combine the advantages of simulated and physical environments whilst mitigating their limitations, in addition to assisting with real-time annotation.

3 The Intelligent Environment Experiment Assistance Tool

The IEEAT is designed to enable researchers to generate datasets more easily that are high quality, sensor-rich, and accurately annotated. The concept was first realized through hands-on experience within Ulster University's Smart Environments Research Group (SERG) [7] during the performance of experiments within SERG's smart lab. The concept was later designed and refined through feedback collected from researchers within the field of IE data processing from institutes including Ulster University, University of Jaén, Spain, University of Genoa, Italy and Halmstad University, Sweden, as detailed in Sect. 4. The IEEAT contains two areas of key functionality: Partial simulation of experiments and real-time annotation. These features are described in more detail in the following sub-sections. The tool will generate data in both the HomeML and activity vector format, with options for generation in CSV and JSON.

3.1 Partial Simulation of Experiments

The concept of partial simulation of experiments is centered around the principle of combining the benefits of IE simulation with the benefits of physical IE use, while mitigating many of the limitations associated with both. This concept facilitates the use of IEs which may contain a limited selection of sensors, allowing researchers to simulate sensors which are required but not present.

One use case involves a researcher who wishes to re-create an experiment which focused on the use of contact or pressure sensors throughout an environment for activity classification. Nevertheless, the environment at the researcher's institution may not have the complete set of sensors required to fully replicate the experiment. Another use case includes the scenario in which a researcher would like to assess the impact of adding additional contact sensors to an environment when evaluating a novel activity recognition approach. Rather than investing in additional sensors, a partially simulated approach would allow such experiments to be performed by simulating the presence of additional sensors within the environment while experiments are performed.

Within the IEEAT, partial simulation will be performed in two stages: Pre-experiment and during the experiment. Pre-experiment, the researcher would complete an assessment of all sensors required within the environment, taking note of any sensors required that are not present. These sensors would then be recorded within the IEEAT, in which the researcher specifies a sensor type, name and description. This would form the simulated sensor list. During the experiment, the researcher could access the list of simulated sensors and select a simulated sensor at the same time as it would have been activated in the real environment. For example, when an experiment participant opens a door, the researcher can select the corresponding simulated sensor, changing its state to "open", and sending simulated data to the sensor database. If the door is then closed at some point, the researcher selects the sensor again to change the state to "closed", sending the simulated data once again to the sensor database. A similar method would be used for pressure sensors, in which the researcher could select the sensor once to indicate activation, and select again to indicate de-activation.

This simple user interface facilitates the insertion of simulated data into the dataset in real-time in the same format as data from the physical sensors used in the experiment. An additional flag would be sent along with the simulated data to indicate that it is simulated, providing researchers with the option to exclude this data should they wish to complete a simulation impact assessment.

3.2 Real-Time Annotation

The real-time annotation component of the IEEAT has been designed to minimize effort, time and risk of user error when annotating the data collected during an experiment. Additionally, it aims to increase the accuracy of timestamps associated with annotations. Similar to the partial simulation component, the real-time annotation component requires user input pre-experiment and during the experiment. Pre-experiment, the researcher must identify a list of all annotations that may be recorded during the experiment. For each annotation, the researcher will specify whether the annotation is single state (i.e. "Fall"), or double state (i.e. "Started Making Coffee" and "Finished Making Coffee"). During the experiment, the researcher simply selects the appropriate annotation at the time of relevance. This will upload and insert the time-stamped annotation into the dataset in real-time. For double state annotations, the annotation will switch between the first and second state each time the annotation is selected, uploading the current state each time. This approach facilitates more advanced annotations including interleaved activities.

4 Community Feedback

The concept of the IEEAT was introduced to 19 members of the research community. These researchers were from institutions including Ulster University in Northern Ireland, University of Jaén in Spain, University of Genoa, Italy and Halmstad University, Sweden. These researchers had backgrounds in a wide range of areas including assisted living, activity recognition, wearables, machine learning, affective computing, computer vision, and visualization. These researchers were presented with a questionnaire accompanied by an overview of the key concepts of partial simulation and real-time annotation. The purpose of the questionnaire was to collect further information on the prevalence of issues during data collection in physical IEs, and to receive feedback on the initial design of the IEEAT in order to ensure key issues were addressed.

The questions throughout the questionnaire prompted for responses on likert scales and checkboxes. The questionnaire consisted of two sections. The first section asked 13 questions about the researcher, their research background, and issues they may have while completing experiments. In particular, the questions investigated how often the researcher uses environment sensors, wearable sensors, or simulation software to generate datasets. Information was also collected on the researcher‘s experience with limitations in physical IEs, including the frequency, significance, impact and type of limitations. Finally, the researchers were asked about their preferred annotation approach, including when they perform the annotation, how time consuming it is, and how often errors are made. The second section asked 10 questions about the researcher's opinion on the partial simulation and real-time annotation features of the IEEAT and the potential usefulness in their research. Additionally, the questionnaire collected responses on the usefulness of filtering out simulated data, awareness of similar approaches, and the preferred platform for the IEEAT to be developed upon. Space was also provided at the end of the questionnaire for any further comments.

4.1 Results

Of the 19 participants who completed the questionnaire, 31.6 % very regularly used IEs, 42.1 % sometimes or regularly used IEs, and 26.3 % did not currently use IEs, however, were involved in the analysis of IE data. One user very regularly used simulation for the generation of IE data, 42.1 % sometimes or regularly, and 52.6 % had never used simulation. 10.5 % were very regularly limited by not having the optimal amount of sensors for an experiment, 21.0 % were regularly limited, 42.1 % occasionally limited and 15.8 % never limited. Of those who did experience limitations, 52.6 % found these limitations to be significant or very significant, and 15.8 % found them to be not significant. The most common impact such limitations had on experiments included: reduction in environment types used, reduction in amount of data collected, reduction in the number of metrics generated, reduction of activities performed, reduction in statistical significance of metrics collected, and time delays. Contact, Pressure, and PIR sensors were the most common sensors that were in limited supply. Other sensors included electrodes, cameras, audio, and thermal vision.

In terms of dataset annotation, 63.1 % annotated the dataset after the experiment was complete, 26.3 % annotated during the experiment, and 10.5 % annotated during the experiment and refined the annotations after the experiment was complete. 68.4 % found dataset annotation to be quite to very time consuming, 26.3 % found it somewhat time consuming, and one user did not find it to be time consuming. Common annotation approaches included review of camera footage, NFC tags, pen and paper, and stopwatch. 15.8 % made mistakes in annotations often to very often, 68.4 % sometimes made mistakes in annotations, and 15.8 % never made mistakes in annotation.

63.1 % stated that they would find the IEEAT useful to very useful within their research. 36.8 % wound find it somewhat useful. In particular, the simulation of additional sensors was useful or very useful for 52.6 %, and 2 users stated it would not be useful. 84.2 % would find the real-time annotation to be useful or very useful. 73.7 % stated that the IEEAT would assist with international collaboration, and 84.2 % stated that it would assist with replication of experiments. 78.9 % would find the ability to filter out simulated data as useful or very useful. 15.8 % were aware of other investigations into realtime dataset annotation. When asked about the preferred platform on which the IEEAT should be developed, HTML5 (47.4 %) was the most popular, followed by Android (36.8 %).

When asked for further comments with regards to the app, users expressed concern about latency in real time annotation and requested the ability to perform collaborative simultaneous annotation, and the ability to include contextual information during annotation, such as audio notes and photographs.

5 Conclusion and Future Work

Limitations associated with the collection of sensor data within IEs can result in the slowing down of progress within the activity recognition domain. Additionally, dataset annotation is a time consuming and often error prone process, yet is vital to ensuring the quality of the associated dataset. This paper has introduced the IEAAT, an approach which has been designed to combine the advantages of simulated and physical environments while mitigating their limitations, in addition to assisting with real-time annotation. The approach facilitates two key features: partial simulation of IE experiments, and real-time annotation. 19 researchers within the field provided feedback on the proposed approach, and results were consistently positive. Future work will involve incorporating additional researcher feedback into the approach design, before beginning implementation and testing. Additionally, difficulties in the implementation of the tool will need to be further considered and addressed. These include support for bespoke data formats and data repositories, in addition to support for an extensible range of sensor types. Once complete, the resulting tool will be made available to the research community.

Acknowledgments. Invest Northern Ireland is acknowledged for supporting this project under the Competence Centre Programme Grant RD0513853 - Connected Health Innovation Centre.

References

1. Helal, S., Kim, E., Hossain, S.: Scalable approaches to activity recognition research. Paper presented at Pervasive 2010, Helsinki, Finland, 17–20 May 2010 (2010)
2. Synnott, J., Nugent, C., Jeffers, P.: Simulation of smart home activity datasets. Sensors **15**, 14162–14179 (2015)
3. Helal, S., Lee, J.W., Hossain, S., Kim, E., Hagras, H., Cook, D.: Persim - simulator for human activities in pervasive spaces. In: Paper Presented at the 7th International Conference on Intelligent Environments, Nottingham, UK, 25–28 July 2011 (2011)
4. Lee, J.W., Cho, S., Liu, S., Cho, K., Helal, S.: Persim 3D: context-driven simulation and modeling of human activities in smart spaces. IEEE Trans. Autom. Sci. Eng. **12**, 1243–1256 (2015)
5. Synnott, J., Chen, L., Nugent, C.D., Moore, G.: The creation of simulated activity datasets using a graphical intelligent environment simulation tool. In: Paper Presented at the 36th Annual International Conference of the IEEE Engineering in Medicine and Biology Society, Chicago, IL, USA, 26–30 August 2014 (2014)
6. Cruciani, F., Donnelly, M.P., Nugent, C.D., Parente, G., Paggetti, C., Burns, W.: DANTE: a video based annotation tool for smart environments. In: Par, G., Morrow, P. (eds.) S-CUBE 2010. LNICST, vol. 57, pp. 179–188. Springer, Heidelberg (2011)
7. Nugent, C., Mulvenna, M., Hong, X., Devlin, S.: Experiences in the development of a Smart lab. Int. J. Biomed. Eng. Technol. **2**(4), 319–331 (2009)

Impact of Medical History on Technology Adoption in Utah Population Database

Priyanka Chaurasia[1(✉)], Sally I. McClean[2], Chris D. Nugent[1], Ian Cleland[1], Shuai Zhang[1], Mark P. Donnelly[1], Bryan W. Scotney[2], Chelsea Sanders[3], Ken Smith[4], Maria C. Norton[3], and JoAnn Tschanz[3]

[1] School of Computing and Mathematics, University of Ulster, Newtownabbey, Co. Antrim BT37 0QB, Northern Ireland
{p.chaurasia,cd.nugent,i.cleland,s.zhang, mp.donnelly}@ulster.ac.uk

[2] School of Computing and Information Engineering, University of Ulster, Coleraine BT52 1SA, Northern Ireland
{si.mcclean,bw.scotney}@ulster.ac.uk

[3] Department of Psychology, Utah State University, Logan, UT 84322-4440, USA
{chelsea.saunders,maria.norton,joann.tschanz}@usu.edu

[4] Population Sciences, Huntsman Cancer Institute, University of Utah, Salt Lake City, UT 84112, USA
ken.smith@fcs.utah.edu

Abstract. In this paper we study the use of medical history information extracted from the Utah Population Database (UPDB) to predict adoption of a reminder solution for people with dementia. The adoption model was built using 24 categorised features. The *k*NN classification algorithm gave the best performance with 85.8 % accuracy. Whilst data from the UPDB is more readily available than that in our previous work, the results highlight the benefit of including psychosocial and background information within an adoption model.

Keywords: Technology adoption · Prediction modelling · Assistive technology · Dementia

1 Introduction

The rising numbers of older patients aged 65 and above are putting a massive strain on current social and health care systems [1]. The rise in the number of older patients leads to an increase in workload for caregivers and an increase in the demand for the number of hospital beds. The challenges of caring will consequently become larger in the near future with limited facilities. Nevertheless, decentralization of healthcare coupled with the willingness of older patients to stay at home have led to developments in the area of assistive technologies [2]. The aim of these tools is to provide assistance through technology-based solutions that can assist in performing activities, remote healthcare assessments and monitoring and managing social interactions. The success of these tools are highly dependent on the acceptance by the target end users. It is therefore vitally

C.R. García et al. (Eds.): UCAmI 2016, Part II, LNCS 10070, pp. 98–103, 2016.
DOI: 10.1007/978-3-319-48799-1_12

important to understand the factors that affect technology adoption to make it successful in the long-term. Incorporating such information into prediction models that predict adoption has proved to be valuable and is a relatively new area of research.

Considering these challenges, our research aims to investigate the factors that affect technology adoption with a specific focus on reminding technologies for persons with dementia (PwD) [3]. In the related work on this area, we identified multiple features that impacted on PwD's decision in adopting video based reminding technology [4, 5], and a mobile-based reminder app [6]. The current work studies medical history features from the UPDB and considered how these affect the rate of adoption. The remainder of the paper is organised as follows: related work is discussed in Sect. 2; Sect. 3 describes the methodology used in the current study. Section 4 details the results attained from the adoption modelling and finally, Sect. 5 provides details of the conclusion to the work and possible future work.

2 Related Work

With the aim of modelling factors that affect acceptance of technology, it has been found that a limited amount of research has been carried out in this area. The psychosocial impact of assistive device scale (PIADS) [7] and technology acceptance model (TAM) [8] have been developed for modelling adoption of technologies. TAM is based on reasoning action and work under the assumption that user behavior is subjective to the perceived usefulness and ease of use. Nevertheless, the perceived usefulness of a particular technology may differ due to context of use, an individual's background and type of technology. PIADS is an extension of TAM and includes personal factors as well as external factors, for example people and society that may have an impact on usage. As a further extension to these findings, the unified theory of acceptance and use of technology (UTAUT) [9] has been developed that incorporates more reliable factors into the model. Following the evaluation of UTAUT, it was found that gender, age, experience and willingness to use directly affected adoption whereas attitude, self-efficacy and anxiety did not affect adoption. A Mobile Phone Technology Adoption Model (MOPTAM) has been built by integrating TAM and the influential factors from UTAUT. The MOPTAM has been used to model personal phone usage in university students. Preliminary evidence has been found in recent studies that different age groups follow a different approach to the use of technology and its subsequent adoption [10]. Older people realise the benefits of technology, however, consider themselves less capable of using technology based solutions [11]. As a result they report negative impact on themselves such as technology anxiety and lower self-efficacy [12]. It has also been found that older people have less interest towards high end technology products, however, have an appreciation for simple technology products that are easy to use, convenient to learn with additional features of safety and security [10]. It has been reported that technologies that assist in completing activities and convenient to use leave a positive impact on older people [11]. Factors influencing acceptance of technologies was studied in [13] and it was found that the factors affecting the acceptance were mostly studied in the pre-implementation stage.

Taking into consideration these findings the rationale to determine factors that affect adoption and how these could be improved so as to avoid negative outcomes and misuse of resources becomes increasingly important. Limited research has been undertaken to explore the factors that affect technology adoption among PwDs and their caregivers. In our previous research we identified that features such as gender, age, profession, experience, Mini-mental State Exam (MMSE) score, mobile reception, living arrangement and access to broadband were influential in an individual decision to adoption [4, 5]. Building on this work the Technology Adoption and Usage Tool (TAUT) project analysed data from the Cache County Study on Memory and Aging (CCSMA) [14] for participants who agreed to engage with a mobile based reminding solution [3]. The CCSMA dataset has a rich set of features consisting of patient medical data and self-proclaimed information, which was collected through consultation with the participant. Through undertaking analysis on this dataset it was found that the prediction of technology adoption could be achieved with a prediction accuracy of 92.48 % [15]. The aim of the current study is to model technology adoption using objective medical history information relating to the participants which was gleaned from the UPDB and subsequently study the impact of medical history on adoption of technology.

3 Methodology

The TAUT project actively engaged participants from the CCSMA to undertake the evaluation of TAUT reminder app for 12 months. For each participant additional information relating to their medical history was available from the UPDB dataset. This data was analysed in the current work. The current evaluation is based on a cohort of 169 subjects who were screened and contacted by the research team. Following this exercise 30 subjects met the inclusion criteria and agreed to participate in the study. For the purposes of the study a class name 'adopter' was used to represent those engaging with the app (consisting 30 recruits) and a 'non-adopter' class (containing the remaining 139 subjects contacted) was used to represent the remainder.

3.1 UPDB Dataset

The UPDB at the University of Utah is a rich dataset comprising information relating to the genetics, genealogy, demography, epidemiology and public health of the citizens within Utah. At present it contains information on approximately nine million people within the state of Utah. Participants from the CCMSA were linked to the UPDB, a procedure approved by the IRB of the University of Utah. From this dataset we considered information about the number of times a TAUT participant was hospitalized in the category of inpatient discharge/hospitalizations (HOSP) and Ambulatory Surgery (AS) from 1996 to 2013 for the 10 most prevalent diseases (Heart disease, Cancer, Chronic lower respiratory diseases, Accidents, Stroke (cerebrovascular diseases), Alzheimer disease (AD), Diabetes, Influenza/Pneumonia, Nephritis/nephrotic syndrome/nephrosis and Septicemia). Considering the huge number of features in the dataset, reduction of features was managed by merging features as follows: (1) Total year of Hospitalization

(Total HOSP), (2) Total year of Ambulatory Surgery (Total AS), (3) Total year of all 10 disease (HOSP + AS), (4) Recent three years of HOSP (5) Recent three years of AS and (6) Recent three years for all disease (HOSP + AS). The feature reduction resulted in a total of 24 features, providing information relating to the number of times a participant was hospitalized in each category.

3.2 Modelling Adoption

Each of the features in the UPDB dataset has continuous values resulting in a number of categories, hence posing challenges for the development of the prediction models. As a solution to this problem, the variables were discretized [15]. We categorized each feature into fewer categories. For example, Total AS feature that represents the total number of times a participant was hospitalized in ambulatory surgery was categorized into fewer categories of NoneAS, FewAS and LotAS based on 0 times, 1 to 5 times and more than 5 times respectively. To find the best model that can predict adoption we considered a range of classification algorithms following our previous work reported in [4]. The algorithms considered were: C4.5 Decision Tree (DT), Neural Network (NN), Support Vector Machine (SVM), *k*-nearest-neighbour (*k*NN), Adaptive Boosting (AB), Naïve Bayes (NB) and Classification and Regression Trees (CART).

4 Results

Following the resampling of the UPDB dataset, the new data were used to build the prediction models by applying classification algorithms described in the previous section. The UPDB dataset consisted of 139 non-adopters and 30 adopters. Such an imbalance in the dataset may lead to bias towards the majority class [4, 5]. To handle the imbalance in the dataset the Synthetic Minority Over-Sampling Technique (SMOTE) was applied. Following application of SMOTE the adopter minority class was given a 363 % (100*(139−30)/30) boost to make it equivalent to the non-adopter class. Each model was built with 24 labelled features. SMOTE was only applied to the training dataset. Original data was used for testing. This gave us the chance to predict the model's performance in real world scenarios where the given dataset may have had imbalance. Table 1 presents average prediction accuracies of the models built with the SMOTE data and tested on the real data for a range of algorithms. In comparison to the results obtained for the CCSMA dataset, the results obtained for the UPDB dataset have lower accuracy. In the CCSMA dataset with a reduced set of labeled features, it was possible to differentiate between the non-adopters and adopters with an average prediction accuracy of 92.48 % for the *kNN* model [15]. Although the results using only the UPDB do not perform as well as the data collected from the cohort using the reminder app, the results indicate that from the technology side there is merit to consider the integration with other data for the purpose of modelling adoption.

Table 1. Average prediction accuracies (%) of the models learnt.

Dataset	NN	C4.5 DT	SVM	NB	AB	*k*NN	CART
All 24 features SMOTE model + test original data	84.02	74.56	72.78	59.17	66.86	85.80	77.25

5 Conclusion and Future Work

The acceptance of technology based assistive solutions is critical for their long term success. In this paper we studied the UPDB dataset in an effort to understand the impact of medical history of a patient's likelihood to adopt a technology based service. The prediction model was built using 24 features on a SMOTE dataset and was tested on the original data. Taking into consideration only the medical history, the *k*NN classification algorithm gave the best performance of 85.8 % accuracy. The UPDB dataset is unique in itself, however, it requires more information about the individuals. It would be useful to merge the CCSMA and the UPDB dataset together so that the prediction models have both information related to (1) user background such as age, gender, profession and (2) medical history. The inputs from these datasets could lead to the development of a better technology adoption model. Future work will be undertaken to merge these datasets and to subsequently find a sub-set of features that could model adoption more effectively.

Acknowledgements. The Alzheimer's Association is acknowledged for supporting the TAUT project under the research grant ETAC-12-242841. Partial support for all data sets within the UPDB was provided by the University of Utah Huntsman Cancer Institute and the Huntsman Cancer Institute Cancer Center Support grant, P30 CA42014 from the National Cancer Institute.

References

1. Chaurasia, P., McClean, S.I., Nugent, C.D., Scotney, B.W.: A duration-based online reminder system. Int. J. Pervasive Comput. Commun. **10**(3), 337–366 (2014)
2. Cook, D.J., Augusto, J.C., Jakkula, V.R.: Ambient intelligence: technologies, applications, and opportunities. Pervasive Mob. Comput. **5**(4), 277–298 (2009)
3. Hartin, P.J., Nugent, C.D., McClean, S.I., Cleland, I., Norton, M.C., Sanders, C., Tschanz, J.T.: A smartphone application to evaluate technology adoption and usage in persons with dementia. In: Proceeding of Annual International Conference on IEEE Engineering in Medicine and Biology Society, vol. 2014, pp. 5389–5392 (2014)
4. Zhang, S., McClean, S.I., Nugent, C.D., Donnelly, M.P., Galway, L., Scotney, B.W., Cleland, I.: A predictive model for assistive technology adoption for people with dementia. IEEE J. Biomed. Heal. Inf. **18**(1), 375–383 (2014)
5. O'Neill, S.A., Parente, G., Donnelly, M.P., Nugent, C.D., Beattie, M.P., McClean, S.I., Scotney, B.W., Mason, S.C., Craig, D.: Assessing task compliance following mobile phone-based video reminders. In: Proceedings of Annual International Conference on IEEE Engineering and Medical Biology Society, EMBS, pp. 5295–5298 (2011)

6. Chaurasia, P., McClean, S.I., Nugent, C.D., Cleland, I., Zhang, S., Donnelly, M.P., Scotney, B.W., Sanders, C., Smith, K., Norton, M.C., Tschanz, J.: Technology adoption and prediction tools for everyday technologies aimed at people with dementia. In: 38th Annual International Conference of the IEEE Engineering in Medicine and Biology Society, EMBC 2016, Florida, USA, 16–20 August 2016 (2016)
7. Day, H., Jutai, J.: Measuring the psychosocial impact of assistive devices: the PIADS. Can. J. Rehabil. **9**(2), 159–168 (1996)
8. Scherer, M., Jutai, J., Fuhrer, M., Demers, L., Deruyter, F.: A framework for modelling the selection of assistive technology devices (ATDs). Disabil. Rehabil. Assist. Technol. **2**(1), 1–8 (2007)
9. Venkatesh, V., Morris, M.G., Gordon, B.D., Davis, F.D.: User acceptance of information technology: toward a unified view. MIS Q. **27**, 425–478 (2003)
10. Chen, K., Chan, A.H.S.: A review of technology acceptance by older adults. Gerontechnology **10**(1), 1–12 (2011)
11. Mitzner, T.L., Boron, J.B., Fausset, C.B., Adams, A.E., Charness, N., Czaja, S.J., Dijkstra, K., Fisk, A.D., Rogers, W.A., Sharit, J.: Older adults talk technology: technology usage and attitudes. Comput. Hum. Behav. **26**(6), 1710–1721 (2010)
12. Czaja, S.J., Charness, N., Fisk, A.D., Hertzog, C., Nair, S.N., Rogers, W.A., Sharit, J.: Factors predicting the use of technology: findings from the center for research and education on aging and technology enhancement (CREATE). Psychol. Aging **21**(2), 333–352 (2006)
13. Peek, S.T.M., Wouters, E.J.M., van Hoof, J., Luijkx, K.G., Boeije, H.R., Vrijhoef, H.J.M.: Factors influencing acceptance of technology for aging in place: a systematic review. Int. J. Med. Inf. **83**(4), 235–248 (2014)
14. Tschanz, J.T., Norton, M.C., Zandi, P.P., Lyketsos, C.G.: The cache county study on memory in aging: factors affecting risk of Alzheimer's disease and its progression after onset. Int. Rev. Psychiatry **25**(6), 673–685 (2013)
15. Chaurasia, P., McClean, S.I., Nugent, C.D., Cleland, I., Zhang, S., Donnelly, M.P., Scotney, B.W., Sanders, C., Smith, K., Norton, M.C., Tschanz, J.: Modelling assistive technology adoption for people with dementia. J. Biomed. Inform. **63**, 235–248 (2016)

Improving the Quality of User Generated Data Sets for Activity Recognition

Chris Nugent[1,4(✉)], Jonathan Synnott[1], Celeste Gabrielli[2], Shuai Zhang[1], Macarena Espinilla[3], Alberto Calzada[1], Jens Lundstrom[4], Ian Cleland[1], Kare Synnes[5], Josef Hallberg[5], Susanna Spinsante[2], and Miguel Angel Ortiz Barrios[6]

[1] School of Computing and Mathematics, Ulster University, Jordanstown, Northern Ireland, UK
{cd.nugent, j.synnott, s.zhang, a.calzada, i.cleland}@ulster.ac.uk

[2] Dipartimento dell'ingegneria dell'informazione, Universita Politecnica Delle Marche, Ancona, Italy
s1052886@univpm.it, s.spinsante@staff.univpm.it

[3] Department of Computer Sciences, University of Jaen, Jaen, Spain
mestevez@ujaen.es

[4] School of Information Technology, Halmstad University, Halmstad, Sweden
Jens.lundstrom@hh.se

[5] Department of Computer Science, Electrical and Space Engineering, Lulea Technical University, Luleå, Sweden
{unicorn, Josef.hallberg}@ltu.se

[6] Industrial Engineering Department, Universidad de La Costa CUC, Barranquilla, Colombia
mortizl@cuc.edu.co

Abstract. It is fully appreciated that progress in the development of data driven approaches to activity recognition are being hampered due to the lack of large scale, high quality, annotated data sets. In an effort to address this the Open Data Initiative (ODI) was conceived as a potential solution for the creation of shared resources for the collection and sharing of open data sets. As part of this process, an analysis was undertaken of datasets collected using a smart environment simulation tool. A noticeable difference was found in the first 1–2 cycles of users generating data. Further analysis demonstrated the effects that this had on the development of activity recognition models with a decrease of performance for both support vector machine and decision tree based classifiers. The outcome of the study has led to the production of a strategy to ensure an initial training phase is considered prior to full scale collection of the data.

Keywords: Activity recognition · Open data sets · Data validation · Data driven classification

C.R. García et al. (Eds.): UCAmI 2016, Part II, LNCS 10070, pp. 104–110, 2016.
DOI: 10.1007/978-3-319-48799-1_13

1 Introduction

It is fully appreciated that data driven approaches developed for the purposes of activity recognition are being constrained due to the lack of the availability of large annotated data sets which provide a high level of quality in terms of both ground truth and the underlying data. A number of efforts have been made towards the creation of such datasets, however, this has led to a number of individual studies being undertaken and the generation of datasets, which although have aimed to address the same problem, have resulted in non-common protocols being used with differing technologies providing data of different formats. In an effort to address these problems a number of organisations have worked together to define both common protocols and technology platforms to support the collection and storage of data. Through this collaboration the Open Data Initiative was conceived [1]. By adopting such an approach it becomes possible to collect data at different sites and aggregate into one common dataset.

In our previous work the aspirations of the ODI were followed in being able to generate data and make it available to independent researchers. This provides the ability for researchers to compare and contrast innovative approaches on exactly the same data and therefore being able to make true comparisons between approaches [2]. To facilitate this approach required the generation of a simulated dataset. Four researchers were asked to complete a series of activities within a smart environment by following a predefined protocol. Analysis of this data demonstrated that there was a large variance in the initial iterations of data collection [3]. The work presented within this paper proposes strategies to both assess and improve the quality of user generated data sets and highlights the importance for appropriate user training.

The remainder of the paper is structured as follows. Section 2 presents background to generation of activity related data sets and introduces the ODI. Section 3 explains the process by which the data was collected using IESim and Sect. 4 presents the results from various activity recognition models. Section 5 summarises the paper with an overview of the findings and recommendations.

2 Related Work

There is evidence that the research community have not only recognised the importance of having large, high quality datasets, however, there are now efforts being made to create data sets which can be shared. This will have the desired knock-on effect of improving the efficiency with which data is stored and aggregated in addition to the improved development of data driven algorithms themselves.

A number of crowd sourced approaches have emerged as potential solutions to this problem. Crowdsignals.io and the UbiHealth Sensing Campaign [4] have both launched strategies to support the definition of protocols for the collection of data in addition to the collection and annotation of data sets which can then be made publically available.

The European Union funded Project OPPORTUNITY in their work created a common platform whereby researchers working in different organisations could have access to a common data set and therefore were able to compare their results with others [5]. A limited number of online repositories have supported the notion of shared datasets. Two notable examples are the UC Irvine Machine Learning repository [6] and Physionet [7]. The former has recently extended its datasets to include a small number of activity recognition related resources.

The ODI, an initiative established by the authors of this paper aimed to address both the definition of a protocol for the collection of data at different sites in addition to a framework for evaluation [1]. To date efforts from the ODI have led to the development of a common dataset which has-been collected in different organisations using a mix of both real and simulated sensing environments. The work has been subsequently extended to provide a platform whereby a comparison of a range data driven approaches, independently developed by researchers from different organisations, has been undertaken [2].

Although all of these studies have embraced the notion of creating easily accessible resources for the sharing of protocols and data, little effort has been reported whereby the quality of the data and guidance provided to those who are collecting the data has been considered.

3 Generation of Data Sets in Simulated Environments

Initial efforts of those involved with the ODI have led to the development of a number of simulated datasets using the IESim platform [8]. IESim is a simulation tool which supports the replication of real environments through the creation of a simulated environment. Sensors can be added within the simulated environment to replicate their placement within the real environment. Users can then engage with the simulated environment through use of an avatar and generate data relating to interaction with sensorised objects [8]. Figure 1 presents an overview of a real test bed environment (from Ulster University) and its subsequent realisation within IESim. The format of the data produced by IESim can be tailored to meet the requirements of any future processing modules. At present IESim can support up to 4 differing types of data formats.

In the current study IESim was used to create an environment with 5 rooms. Throughout the environment 21 sensors were included to record the activities being

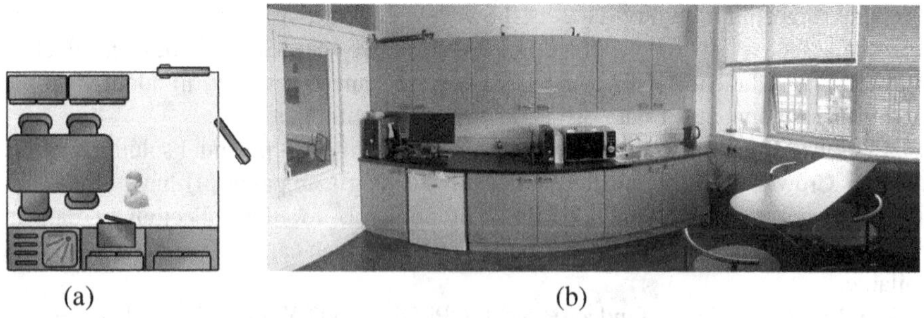

Fig. 1. (a) Overview of IESim replicating smart kitchen environment from the (b) Smart Environments Research Group at Ulster University's smart labs.

undertaken. Figure 2 provides the layout for the environment and an overview of the activities each participant was asked to undertake. Data was collected from 8 participants who used the simulation tool to complete the predefined set of activities. Each participant repeated each of the 11 activities 7 times, producing a data set with a total of 616 instances. The time taken for each participant to complete the set of activities (n = 77) was less than 30 min.

Upon analysis of the data collected it was found that the initial recordings made by participants using IESim varied (Fig. 3). Based on visual inspection it can be viewed that the 1st and 2nd replication tend to be different than the others for both activities presented in Fig. 3 (*WatchTV* and *LeaveHouse*). An outlier may be used an indication of bad-quality data. If detected, the outlying value must be deleted to avoid significant statistical changes in the distribution of the data. In the current work a Grubb' s test was performed with a 95 % level of confidence as an outlier identification test [10, 11].

Activity 1 – Go to Bed
Activity 2 – Use Toilet
Activity 3 – Watch TV
Activity 4 – Prepare Breakfast
Activity 5 – Take Shower
Activity 6 – Leave House
Activity 7 – Get Cold Drink
Activity 8 – Get Hot Drink
Activity 9 – Prepare Dinner
Activity 10 – Get Dressed
Activity 11 – Use Telephone

(a)

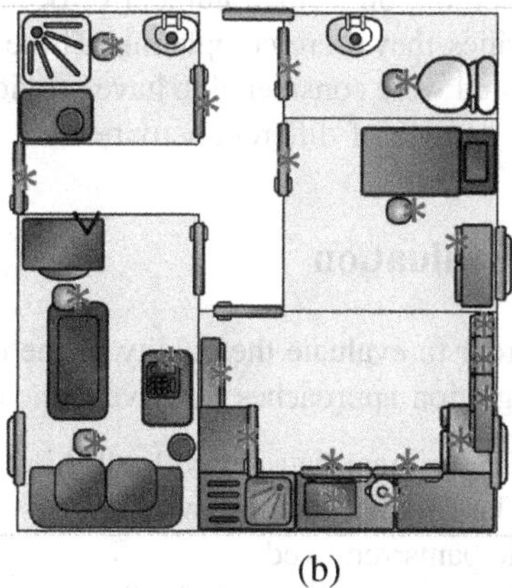

(b)

Fig. 2. (a) List of activities undertaken by participants. (b) Environment used for data collection. Each sequence of 11 activities was repeated 7 times by each participant. Stars indicate where the sensors (n = 21) were placed.

It was found that the 1st replication of User 2 was identified as an outlier with a p-value = 0.00307 (α = 0.05) and 1.92069 standard deviations from the sample mean. This is an indication that this point does not follow the statistical behaviour of the sample and must be removed since it generates a significant variance change. To further elaborate on this occurrence the same analysis was carried out for the *Leave-House* activity. By applying the outlier identification technique it was found that the 1st replication of User 3 was identified as an outlier with a p-value = 0.0114 (α = 0.05) and 2.13201 standard deviations from the sample mean. This is an indication that this point does not follow the statistical behaviour of the sample and must be removed as it causes a significant variance change.

Although participants found IESim intuitive to use a number of usability errors were recorded. The main error was one of incorrect self-annotation. The effects of this process were sensor events being assigned to either the previous or following activity.

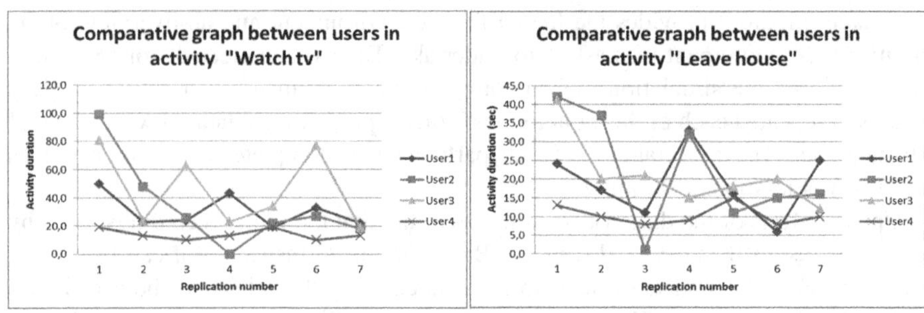

Fig. 3. Examples of assessment of time of 4 participants completing activities *WatchTV* and *LeaveHouse* completed using IESim. Each replication represents the completion of the set of 11 activities.

In addition, on a small number of occasions, participants skipped sub-tasks within the activities they were completing. These errors had a minor effect on the quality of the data and were considered to have provided a more realistic distribution of sensor events over a range of different activities.

4 Evaluation

In order to evaluate the quality of the data on the development of data driven activity recognition approaches three versions of the dataset were considered:

1. The original data set with all 7 iterations from all participants.
2. The original data set with the first iteration of experiments performed by all participants removed.
3. The original data with the first and second iteration of experiments performed by all participants removed.

Removal of replications 1 and 2 was intended to avoid the effects of non-representative completion of activities during a period of time of first usage with IESim when participants made themselves familiar with the simulator.

Two classification models have been considered; support vector machines (SVM) and decision trees. SVM algorithms use a non-linear kernel to discriminate the feature space into various classes. This approach offers the advantage in our current problem where the activity classes may have a non-linear relationship with the captured data. Additionally, SVMs handle a high dimensionality of the feature space, in our case represented by the large number of sensors deployed to monitor the designed activities. The decision tree approach, in particular, offers the advantage of intuition, where both the methodology, the derived model and the results are coherent. This has the potential to provide additional valuable information on the discriminative ability of the sensors in the environment. The decision tree approach may, however, suffer from differentiating classes which are not linearly separable. Decision tree approaches have demonstrated their superior performance over other popular machine learning approaches, i.e., decision table, instance-based learning or nearest neighbour, and Naive Bayes classifiers in activity recognition tasks [9]. Table 1 presents the results attained with both classifiers using 10 fold cross validation on the 3 datasets.

Table 1. Summary of results from usage of 2 classifiers with 3 different datasets.

	Accuracy with 7 repetitions (n = 616)	Accuracy with 6 repetitions (n = 528)	Accuracy with 5 repetitions (n = 440)
Support vector machine (10 fold cross validation)	93,83 %	94,69 %	94,32 %
Decision tree (10 fold cross validation)	93,83 %	94,51 %	94,77 %

5 Summary

In this paper we have demonstrated the effects that poor quality data can have when developing data driven approaches to activity recognition. Upon closer examination of a dataset which was previously collected by the ODI it was found that the initial 1–2 replications through the data, when those generating the data where learning the approach to adopt for data collection, where largely different to data collected in later cycles. As such it was found that this data was not representative of the target activities and should be removed. This was further evidenced through the application of outlier detection testing. To mitigate the impact of such data in the development of the classification process it is recommended that participants are provided with an opportunity to be trained with the simulation tool and that the initial replications are not recorded in the final dataset until the point in time when the participant can use the system confidently. This approach can be extended into the more general domain of pervasive healthcare where data is both generated and collected in the wild. There is the potential to improve the quality of such data through periodic training sessions. It may also be the case that algorithms developed will never reach 100 % accuracy due to the complexity of the problem, however, efforts should be made to provide the training process with as high a quality data set as possible. Future work will involve testing of this concept further through the collection of new datasets and generation and analysis of a range of classification models. In addition, further efforts will be made to analyze the effects on an activity per activity basis.

Acknowledgments. Invest Northern Ireland partially supported this project under the Competence Centre Program Grant RD0513853 – Connected Health Innovation Centre.

References

1. Nugent, C., Cleland, I., Epsinilla, M., Santanna, A., Synnott, J., Banos, O., Lundstrom, J., Hallberg, J., Calzada, A.: An initiative for the creation of open datasets within pervasive healthcare. In: Future of Pervasive Health Workshop. ACM (2016). doi:10.4108/eai.16-5-2016.2263830
2. Synnott, J., Nugent, C., Zhang, S., et al.: Environment simulation for the promotion of the open data initiative. In: SmartSys Workshop (2016)
3. Ortiz Barrios, M., Nugent, C., Synnott, J.: A methodology for assessing the quality of datasets in support of data driven activity recognition. In: EMBC 2106 (2016, in press)
4. Ubihealth project. http://www.ubihealth-project.eu/index.php. Accessed 8 March 2016
5. Sagha, H., et al.: Benchmarking classification techniques using the opportunity human activity dataset, In: 2011 IEEE International Conference on Systems, Man, and Cybernetics (SMC), Anchorage, AK, pp. 36–40 (2011)
6. UCI machine learning repository. http://archive.ics.uci.edu/ml/. Accessed 08 March 2016
7. PhysioNet: the research resource for complex physiologic signals. https://www.physionet.org/. Accessed 08 March 16
8. Synnott, J., Chen, L., Nugent, C.D., Moore, G.: The creation of simulated activity datasets using a graphical intelligent environment simulation tool. In: Engineering in Medicine and Biology Society (EMBC), pp. 4143–4146 (2014)
9. Bao, L., Intille, S.S.: Activity recognition from user-annotated acceleration data. In: Ferscha, A., Mattern, F. (eds.) PERVASIVE 2004. LNCS, vol. 3001, pp. 1–17. Springer, Heidelberg (2004)
10. Barrios, M.O., Jiménez, H.F.: Reduction of average lead time in outpatient service of obstetrics through six sigma methodology. In: Bravo, J., Hervás, R., Villarreal, V. (eds.) AmIHEALTH 2015. LNCS, vol. 9456, pp. 293–302. Springer, Heidelberg (2015)
11. Herazo-Padilla, N., Montoya-Torres, J.R., Muñoz-Villamizar, A., Isaza, S.N., Polo, L.R.: Coupling ant colony optimization and discrete-event simulation to solve a stochastic location-routing problem. In 2013 Winter Simulations Conference (WSC), pp. 3352–3362, December 2013. IEEE (2013)

Personalizing Physical Effort Estimation in Workplaces Using a Wearable Heart Rate Sensor

Pablo Pancardo(✉), J.A. Hernández-Nolasco, Francisco D. Acosta, and Miguel A. Wister

DAIS, Juarez Autonomous University of Tabasco, Cunduacan, Tabasco, Mexico
{pablo.pancardo,adan.hernandez,francisco.acosta,miguel.wister}@ujat.mx

Abstract. Sensor technology for personalized physiologic monitoring contributes to health and safety in workplaces. Wearable devices represent an efficient way to capture physiological values to obtain individual efforts for each worker due to physical activities. Heart rate based ergonomic methods provide results that show drudgery of a work activity for each person. In this paper, we show some experiments that highlight the importance when using custom methods to estimate the effort of people doing physical work. Previous works have already validated some benefits in using sensor technology to estimate physical efforts and energy consumption in the workplace. The results in our experiments applied to cleaning staff demonstrate how important is to use personalized measurements for more objective effort estimation.

Keywords: Sensor · Monitoring · Heart rate · Personalized · Working

1 Introduction

This paper is related with the measuring of physiological parameters of individuals while performing daily or labor activities in order to preserve or improve health and well-being.

The ability to measure the metabolic rate of people in daily activities, allows to improve their health and well-being, this is because it is formally established that the metabolic rate of a person can be estimated based on their effort [2].

The importance of estimating the physical effort of a person during labor activities, it has a particular interest in the workplace, given that the effort to perform an activity is different for each person. Misallocation of an activity can affect a person's welfare and health. Workers may have risks associated with the disparity between high physical work demands and capacity/labor skills. These risks include: musculoskeletal disorders, cardiovascular disease, prolonged absences, stress, burnout and early retirements from the labor market [9]. Furthermore, physical strength assessment in ergonomics has additional benefits as: worker selection and placement and job design [8].

Generic methods known to estimate the physical effort do not take into account important physiological characteristics of individuals [1,14,16].

C.R. García et al. (Eds.): UCAmI 2016, Part II, LNCS 10070, pp. 111–122, 2016.
DOI: 10.1007/978-3-319-48799-1_14

For many years, cardiac cost and metabolic expenditure from physical labor are calculated using formulas and generic tables [1]. Physical exertion is then set, based on standards, such as maximum heart rate (220-age). While in many cases this may be agile and convenient, it is not always true, as in the case of overweight or adapted people (acclimatized) to perform an activity. It is necessary to develop methods that can provide higher accuracy for predicting energy consumption for a wide range of physical activities. This would allow a greater chance of being accurate when to compare them to scientifically validated methods as doubly labeled water method [5].

In this sense, we show the advantages of a method that takes into account a personalized measurement to estimate workers' physical effort.

Most available solutions for health monitoring offer a generalized physiological measurement, that is, by reference to generic formulas or tables that are not customized to individuals [2,14]. Many others solutions are focused on predefined activities such as walking and running without considering physiological parameters of each person, giving results not clearly differentiated [5,6].

Therefore, it is needed to analyze how different are results when applying a generalized method compared with a method where a personalized maximum heart rate is used (instead a generic formula (220-age)). We use a customizable ergonomic method based on heart rate measurements to estimate physical efforts during work activities. Results were compared with those obtained with a method not allowing customization. The advantage of the method that can be customized is shown in this paper.

The purpose of this work is to establish that existing standards in effort estimation, do not allow continuous monitoring of the effort that people make in their daily activities. This is because standard methods do not consider the use of emerging technologies for real-time monitoring and they are not conveniently customized since based solely on age. The proposed solution is an extension to Chamoux method that allows continuous monitoring effort, taking into account the particular physical condition of each person through measuring the heart rate. We evaluate the goodness of this proposal through a comparative study with the other two methods (Original Chamoux and Borg) [2,7]. From these results, we can state that heart rate reflects health conditions (sick, tired, acclimatized) but to our knowledge, this has not been proven objectively and formally. The review of recently published results, related to the world of work, does not show a formula that reflects all involved factors.

2 State of Art

For many years, cardiac cost and metabolic expenditure from physical labor are calculated using formulas and generic tables [1].

The use of a custom method becomes more important when monitoring physical activities that require a lot of effort, such as heavy lifting. Since such activities are those that can compromise the welfare and health of workers [15].

As is established in the ISO 8996 standard [11] for estimating metabolic cost, the use of heart rate is an option that provides an estimation of effort with a margin of error is plus or minus 10 %. This method of analysis is surpassed only by custom measurements that require the use of specialized equipment commonly available in laboratories. The latter very precise methods are: equipment of indirect calorimetry (oxygen consumption test using a mask) and doubly labeled water (water consumption and urine analysis).

While measuring heart rate is a valid option to estimate the effort which represents a work activity for an individual, it is also important to consider that there are other factors influencing significantly, such as environmental conditions (temperature and humidity), weight, age, acclimation, mental stress, personality, etcetera [3].

Related studies have shown that for estimation of effort activities ranging from light to heavy may be more convenient to use simultaneously sensors of various types, for example, motion and heart rate sensors [3].

2.1 Related Work

Some studies have been carried using technology for energy expenditure (EE) and activity recognition in the workplace. Hwang et al. [10] proposed a measurement approach in energy estimation field. It is expected to provide in-depth understanding and continuous monitoring of workers physical demands from construction tasks. Their solution was to use heart rate (HR) to estimate EE according to a linear relationship between HR and EE. Their proposal was to achieve reliable field EE measurement through automatic action recognition using an embedded accelerometer, and applying HR-EE relationships for corresponding actions with acceptable HR monitoring accuracy.

In [4] is made a review of currently available monitors that are capable of measuring total physical activity as well as components of physical activity that play important roles in human health. The selection of wearable monitors for measuring physical activity will depend on the physical activity component of interest, study objectives, characteristics of the target population, and study feasibility in terms of cost and logistics. Six main categories of wearable monitors are currently available to investigators: pedometers, load transducers/foot-contact monitors, accelerometers, HR monitors, combined accelerometer and HR monitors, and multiple sensor systems. They mention that future development of sensors and analytical techniques for assessing physical activity should focus on the dynamic ranges of sensors, comparability for sensor output across manufacturers, and the application of advanced modeling techniques to predict energy expenditure and classify physical activities.

Migliaccio et al. [13] used sensors to monitor physical bends performed by construction workers, so, it is identified those physical activities that can be risky to health. In this experiment, a heart monitor was used to detect high heart rates which were directly associated with a subject carrying a load. Fusing heart rate data and posture data provided the capability of differentiating safe from unsafe material handling activities. The main objective of this research was to assist future decision makers in designing ergonomically safe and healthy work environments.

All works mentioned above try to estimate energy expenditure based on recognizing the activity, our proposal is that instead of recognizing the activity, we should estimate the physical effort, so heart rate is a good parameter.

2.2 Heart Rate Based Methods to Estimate Physical Effort

In this paper we use methods based on heart rate because this type of parameter has a 90 % accuracy in estimating physical efforts, as it is stated in safety and health standards at work (ISO 9886) [11,17].

There are several methods that rely on measuring heart rate to establish which is the physical effort that a work activity can represent for people [12]. We selected two of them: Borg rating scale of exertion [2] and Chamoux method [7].

The Borg scale is widely known and applied in sport and medical domains, it is generic and based on a table where, if a person has a certain value of heart rate, then it has a certain level of effort, it is called rating of perceived exertion. In Table 1 the Borg's scale shows 14 (6 to 20) values grouped in six categories.

Table 1. Borg's scale

Scale	Description
6	No exertion
7	
8	
9	
10	
11	Light
12	
13	Somewhat hard
14	
15	Hard (heavy)
16	
17	Very hard
18	
19	
20	Maximal exertion

In order to interpret Borg's scale the numbers in left column correspond to the number of beats of one person during physical activity, divided by 10 and the corresponding value in right column is the perceived exertion (level of effort), for example, if a worker has 110 beats per minute, the level on the scale is 11 and it belongs slight effort. In this method, it is assumed that the maximum heart rate of a person is 220 minus his/her age in years. It is not required a real effort test, therefore, it is a generic value.

Otherwise, Chamoux [7] proposes a lesser-known method and as far as we know not frequently used. This method requires to measure resting and maximum heart rate for each person, taking into account several physiological parameters.

The method consists of two steps to estimate physical effort. This first step is to obtain labor activity's absolute cardiac cost (ACC), which is obtained using the average cardiac frequency (ACF) and the resting cardiac frequency (RCF) for a person at every moment. ACF is obtained from the average value of the frequency of the worker during a day of conventional job. RCF is obtained after a person has slept (8 hours) and is resting.

ACC is obtained subtracting the resting cardiac frequency (RCF) to average cardiac frequency (ACF) as shown in formula 1 [7].

$$ACC = ACF - RCF \tag{1}$$

The second step is to compute the Relative Cardiac Cost (RCC). Therefore, we should get Theoretical Maximum Cardiac Frequency (TMCF). Conventionally, TMCF value is obtained subtracting person's age in years to 220. The formula for RCC is 2 [7].

$$RCC = \left(\frac{[ACC * 100]}{[TMCF - RCF]} \right) \tag{2}$$

Effort levels for a worker according to the method of Chamoux are shown in Table 2.

Table 2. Different levels of effort for RCC under Chamoux

RCC	Effort
0–9	Very light
10–19	Light
20–29	A little moderate
30–39	Moderate
40–49	A little heavy
50–59	Heavy
60–69	Intense

Additionally, we decided to customize the Chamoux method, that is obtaining the value of TMCF parameter for each person. To do this, we asked each user to perform a maximal exercise stress test using an electric treadmill and we took the value of heart rate as their TMCF. We refer to this as a personalized Chamoux method.

3 Experiments

The tests were conducted on a university campus, potential users were teachers, students, office staff (administrative clerks) and janitors. As janitors are who perform activities that require physical efforts that can range from light to intense, they were selected.

In the experiments, a group of 20 research participant (cleaning staff) conducted a series of work activities and heart rate measurements were taken during that activities. These data sets were collected using a population of 20 participants; 11 male (28.4 ± 8.5 years, 171.8 ±4.7 cm, 77.6 ± 13.09 kg, BMI 26.26 ± 3.77) and 9 female (28.7 ± 5.97 years, 161.1 ± 3.5 cm, 65.1 ± 11.4 kg, BMI 25.06 ± 4.45).

Three physical activities were defined for every research participants. These activities are described in Table 3.

Table 3. Activities in the experiments.

Activity	Description
Sweep the floor	One broom (1 Kg) was used in this activity. A hallway (42 m long × 0.5 m width) was the area to sweep. The volunteers started in one corner of hallway and sweep in overlapping strokes in towards the end of the hallway.
Washing windows	The total dimensions of the window were 110 cm × 90 cm. The research participants starting at the top and work down the window. This activity was executed in indoor environments.
Stacking chairs	Placing the entire stack of chairs had a short walk away (3 m). This activity was done using iron chairs (7 kg). During these activities were created several stacks, each stack with 8 chairs; all experiments were done in indoor hallway. Never were stacked more than ten chairs at a time.

Personal characteristics and physical conditions (such as age, sex, acclimation, physical condition, etc.) are attributes that are indirectly reflected when we measure maximal theoretical heart rate being their maximal personal effort for each user. Together with the heart rate at rest and individualized monitoring in real time during the execution of physical activities they allow customized estimations. During analysis, these characteristics results allow us to see that two people with similar characteristics do not necessarily perform the same effort to perform the same activity.

Heart rate was measured using a unobtrusive Basis B1 Fitness Tracker Band. Basis' precision is enough to know how many beats per minute has a user heart. Basis B1 measures our blood pressure, steps, intensity, and exertion of our workout, and sleep metrics. This device was placed on the hand of each worker. The first activity was to sweep a floor using a broom, the second activity was to clean glass windows with a rag and the last activity was stacking metal structure chairs.

Heart rate values used in all methods (Borg-Chamoux-Personalized chamoux) were the average heart rates during the activities.

Experiments related to three labor activities are shown in Fig. 1.

Fig. 1. Activities developed by workers: (a) sweeping floors, (b) cleaning windows and (c) stacking chairs

4 Results

In order to compare the resulting values of all methods tested, we made a mapping of the Borg's effort values (Table 1) with labels used in Chamoux method (Table 2). Scales 6–7 are No Exertion (NE), 8–9 are Very Light (VL), 10–11 are Light (L), 12 is A Little Moderate (ALM), 13 is Moderate (M), 14 is A Little Heavy (ALH), 15–16 are Heavy (H), and over 16 are Intense (I).

A frequencies analysis of results of physical effort of the participants obtained for each physical activity was included. In order to do this, we obtained some values describing the features of a collection of data from physical activities performed. For stacking chairs activity, Table 4 shows number of users for each effort level considering their BMI and Table 5 grouped by method and genre.

In both tables we can see that estimated efforts of people using Borg method are only two levels, Chamoux method classifies them into three levels, while our customized proposal classifies them into four levels. Borg method, classifies all people at levels very light (VL) and light (L), Chamoux classifies 20 % in ALM, as it only takes into account the age of the people, while the proposed method distributes 60 % of workers between ALM and ALH, this is because it takes into account personal maximum effort, in addition to the age of the individual.

Table 4. Number of users for each effort level during stacking chair activity, grouped by method and BMI.

Effort levels	Borg		Chamoux		Personalized Chamoux	
	BMI < 25	BMI ≥ 25	BMI < 25	BMI ≥ 25	BMI < 25	BMI ≥ 25
VL	6	5	1	3	0	0
L	5	4	7	5	4	4
ALM	0	0	3	1	3	3
M	0	0	0	0	2	2
ALH	0	0	0	0	2	0

Table 5. Number of users for each effort level during stacking chair activity, grouped by method and genre.

Effort levels	Borg		Chamoux		Personalized Chamoux	
	Male	Female	Male	Female	Male	Female
VL	6	5	3	1	0	0
L	5	4	7	5	6	2
ALM	0	0	1	3	3	3
M	0	0	0	0	2	2
ALH	0	0	0	0	0	2

This indicates that our proposal has a better effort discrimination because of the measuring of their personal maximum effort.

These results can be used in decisions making to preserve or improve health and quality of life of the worker. This can be done by adjusting their work environment or by measuring physical performance based on their effort for a better allocation of their workload.

Figure 2 shows how Personalized Chamoux method is more efficient for estimating individual efforts, which is appreciated particularly for the activity of stacking chairs (Fig. 2). Using Borg scale all studied activities were classified as light or minor effort, while Chamoux shows that participants had differentiated efforts. Even more, using personalized Chamoux method, where TMCF is derived from maximal exercise stress test performed to each participant, efforts for stacking chairs vary from Light (L) until A little Heavy (ALH).

As we can see in Fig. 2, when we apply Personalized Chamoux method to estimate physical efforts, results reflect different effort levels for individuals even though they perform the same activity (because of their particular physiology). While the Borg method fails to reflect the different efforts that can represent the same activity for different people.

We have designed a prototype for logging and informing to users about their effort levels and historical records during activities. Figure 3 shows prototype for Android devices.

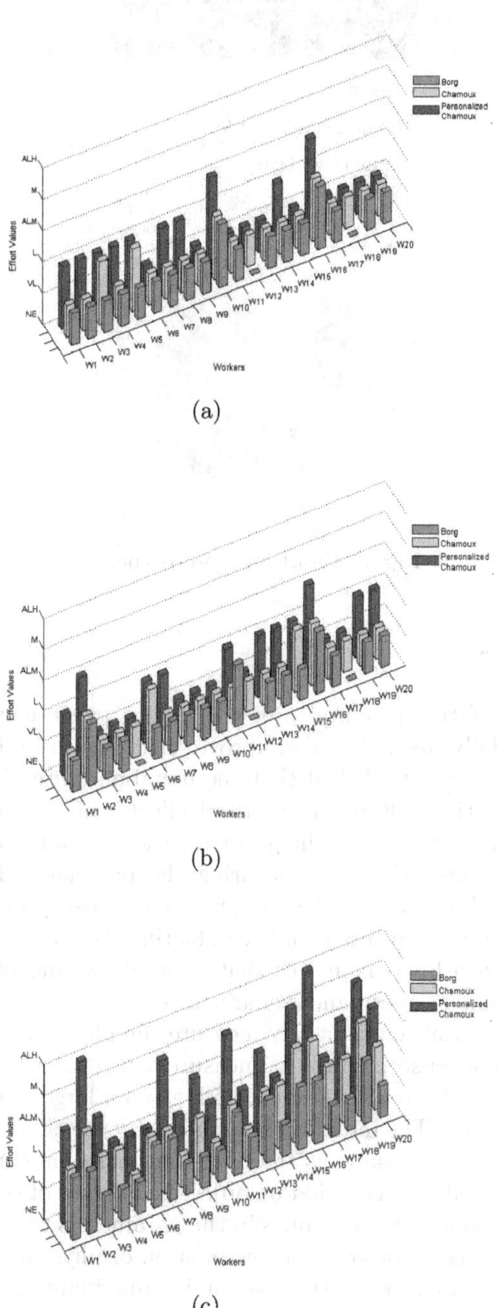

Fig. 2. Worker's Activities (a) sweeping, (b) cleaning windows and (c) stacking chairs

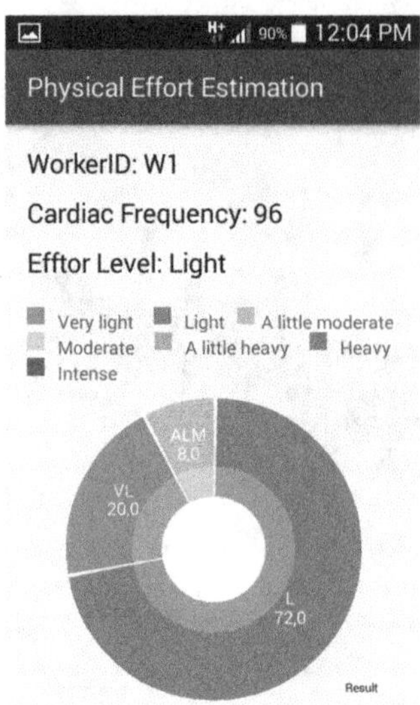

Fig. 3. Effort level prototype.

5 Conclusions

The contributions of this proposal are; the ability to measure the metabolic rate of people in daily activities, to improve their health and well-being, this is because it is formally established that the metabolic rate of a person can be estimated based on their effort. A standard effort can be estimated for each activity as a reference to analyze the gap with the individual effort to perform those activities; the usefulness of measuring the personalized productivity of workers in their work environment to improve enterprise productivity and the possibility to determine that a person is conducting its activities so appropriate i.e. in accordance with his personal capacities, abilities, and physical condition to improve performance, safety and welfare state.

This is not a proposal to accurately measure the physical effort, but emphasize the importance of customizing the measurement process and mention that it is hardly possible to have a generic method, given a large number of variables that must be considered. The intention is to show how the effort estimation varies when considering a custom value as the maximum personal cardiac frequency.

Analysis of our results reveals that an objective method of estimating individual effort should consider custom values in the parameters to capture the widest possible set of variables involved in the estimation of physical effort. Therefore, the decision to perform a stress test for obtaining maximum heart rate is important, because with this action, indirectly, we are including many factors as age, sex, BMI, acclimation, etc.

We consider as future work to evaluate branched equations techniques for combining data from these two types of sensors.

Acknowledgments. This paper was supported by CONACYT through FOMIX-TAB CONACYT - Gobierno del Estado de Tabasco, Grant Numbers: TAB-2014-C29-245876 and TAB-2014-C29-245877. We would also like to express our gratitude to the Juarez Autonomous University of Tabasco for supporting the academic resources needed for this research through Grant Number: UJAT-2014-IA-01.

References

1. Ergonomics guide to assessment of metabolic and cardiac costs of phys-ical work. Am. Ind. Hygiene Assoc. J. **32**(8), 560–564 (1971). http://www.tandfonline.com/doi/abs/10.1080/0002889718506506. pMID:5140430
2. Borg, G.A.: Psychophysical bases of perceived exertion. Med. Sci. Sports Exerc. **14**(5), 377–381 (1982)
3. Brage, S., Brage, N., Franks, P.W., Ekelund, U., Wong, M.Y., Andersen, L.B., Froberg, K., Wareham, N.J.: Branched equation modeling of simultaneous accelerometry and heart rate monitoring improves estimate of directly measured physical activity energy expenditure. J. Appl. Physiol. **96**(1), 343–351 (2003). http://jap.physiology.org/content/96/1/343
4. Butte, N.F., Ekelund, U., Westerterp, K.R.: Assessing physical activity using wearable monitors: measures of physical activity. Med. Sci. Sports Exerc. **44**(1 Suppl 1), S5–12 (2012)
5. Crouter, S.E., Churilla, J.R., Bassett, D.R.: Estimating energy expenditure using accelerometers. Euro. J. Appl. Physiol. **98**(6), 601–612 (2006). doi:10.1007/s00421-006-0307-5
6. Esliger, D.W., Rowlands, A.V., Hurst, T.L., Catt, M., Murray, P., Eston, R.G.: Validation of the genea accelerometer. Med. Sci. Sports Exerc. **43**(6), 1085–1093 (2011)
7. Frimat, P., Amphoux, M., Chamoux, A.: Interprétation et mesure de la fréquence cardiaque. Revue de Medicine du Travail **XV**(4), 147–165 (1988)
8. Gallagher, S., Moore, J.S., Stobbe, T.J.: Physical strength assessment in ergonomics. Am. Ind. Hyg. Assoc. **20000145**, 1–61 (1998)
9. Holtermann, A., Jørgensen, M.B., Gram, B., Christensen, J.R., Faber, A., Overgaard, K., Ektor-Andersen, J., Mortensen, O.S., Sjøgaard, G., Søgaard, K.: Worksite interventions for preventing physical deterioration among employees in job-groups with high physical work demands: background, design and conceptual model of finale. BMC Pub. Health **10**(1), 120 (2010)
10. Hwang, S., Seo, J., Ryu, J., Lee, S.: Challenges and opportunities of understanding construction worker's physical demands through field energy expenditure measurements using a wearable activity tracker. In: Proceedings of Construction Research Congress, pp. 2730–2739 (2016)
11. ISO, B.: 9886. 2004. Ergonomics-Evaluation of thermal strain by physiological (2004)
12. Laukkanen, R.M.T., Virtanen, P.K.: Heart rate monitors: state of the art. J. Sports Sci. **16**(supl), 3–7 (1998). doi:10.1080/026404198366920,pMID:22587712
13. Migliaccio, G.C., Teizer, J., Cheng, T., Gatti, U.C.: Automatic identification of unsafe bending behavior of construction workers using real-time location sensing and physiological status monitoring. In: Proceedings of the Construction Research Congress, West Lafayette, IN, USA. vol. 2123, pp. 633–642 (2012)

14. Nogareda-Cuixart, S., Luna-Mendaza, P.: Ntp. 323: determination of metabolic rate. Instituto Nacional de Seguridad e Higiene en el Trabajo. Ministerio de Trabajo y Asuntos Sociales, Espaa, pp. 1–11 (2005)
15. Organization, I.L.: Safety and health at work (2016). http://www.ilo.org
16. Parsons, K.: Occupational health impacts of climate change: current and future iso standards for the assessment of heat stress. Ind. Health **51**(1), 86–100 (2013)
17. Standard, I.: 9886, ergonomics-evaluation of thermal strain by physiological measurements, International Standard Organization, 2nd edn., pp. 1–21 (2004)

Ad-hoc and Sensors Networks

Have You Also Seen That? Collaborative Alert Assessment in Ad Hoc Participatory Sensing

Fátima Castro-Jul(✉), Rebeca P. Díaz-Redondo, and Ana Fernández-Vilas

Universidade de Vigo, Campus Universitario s/n, 36310 Vigo, Spain
{fatima,rebeca,avilas}@det.uvigo.es

Abstract. Due to their flexibility and immediacy, participatory sensing systems based on ad hoc networks have become a valuable source of proximity-based information about events and incidents in the city. However, easy contribution may result in the transmission of larges amount of data, some of them being duplicate or not relevant. We have proved that collaboratively filtering the information to be disseminated improves network efficiency while maintaining the system effectiveness.

Keywords: Ad hoc networks · Smart cities · Collaboration · Alert dissemination

1 Introduction

The proliferation of sensor-rich handheld devices has allowed users to constantly monitor their surroundings. The fact that they can easily share their findings with their peers has given rise to participatory sensing schemes [1], where their contributions form collective knowledge that can be used to retrieve any kind of local information. Thus, participatory sensing provides an opportunity to collaboratively detect and stay aware of what is going on anytime anywhere. This is specially interesting when it comes to alert about incidents in urban areas, where device density allows reliance on participatory strategies.

Once devices detect an event there are mainly two ways in which they can disseminate the information: social and ad hoc networks. Contribution to both is straightforward and available for any user ready to take part on them. On the one hand, this enriches and makes the detection process flexible. On the other hand, easy contribution can result in big amounts of irrelevant or duplicate data. As a result, it is necessary to establish mechanisms able to deal with user-generated information in order to filter received contributions.

Alert detection in social networks is performed using data mining techniques [2], such as *keyword burst* [3] or supervised classification [4]. Thus, it consists on a centralized system that processes large amounts of data and detects new events by finding trends or similarities between different messages. As a consequence, these systems benefit from receiving abundant data and do not worry about duplicate or irrelevant information, which is dealt with through data processing.

C.R. García et al. (Eds.): UCAmI 2016, Part II, LNCS 10070, pp. 125–130, 2016.
DOI: 10.1007/978-3-319-48799-1_15

However, in ad hoc alert systems the situation is quite different. There exist no central entity in charge of data processing and, as a result, there is no filter for user-generated alerts. This can result in a large amount of unnecessary transmissions that may provoke network congestion or even collapse. Research on network efficiency has been extensive but the attention has been aimed mainly at routing and dissemination techniques [5–7], instead of at the alert content.

There exist, however, proposals that assess message content for message dissemination. One possibility is to establish hierarchical structures, whose head is in charge of alert aggregation and transmission [8,9]. Nevertheless, this involves a setup cost that decreases network flexibility. An alternative consists on filtering on the receiver side. Nodes receive first metadata about available new messages in order to decide whether they want to receive them or not taking into account their interests and energy constraints [10,11]. Although this reduces processing overhead and energy expenditure, including a negotiation phase on every hop of the data dissemination process is much more resource-consuming than applying a starting filter, where the overhead falls only on the initial neighbor nodes.

In this paper, we introduce a collaboration strategy that involves neighbor nodes in alert assessment. Thus, we include a filtering step in order to reduce irrelevant or duplicate alert transmissions in ad hoc networks. And we do so in a distributed manner, without adding any centralized or hierarchical structure. Our evaluation of the strategy, using network simulations on urban scenarios, demonstrates the outcome of our approach.

The paper is organized as follows. In Sect. 2 we start by explaining the urban scenario we have considered and our collaborative assessment proposal. Then, we detail the simulation process (Sect. 3). Finally, we outline our conclusions and current line of research (Sect. 4).

2 Scenario and Collaborative Assement Proposal

We consider an urban scenario with a high density of pedestrians, equipped with sensor-rich handheld devices that allow them to monitor their surroundings and inform about their findings. Devices include short-range radio technologies, such as WiFi or Bluetooth, that allow them to communicate with each other directly. As a consequence, no dedicated infrastructure is required. Connections build a flat network, where no hierarchies or clusters are formed since the high pedestrian mobility does not make setup costs worth the effort. As a result, connections are flexible and proximity-based, which makes it simple for any device to join and contribute to the detection and dissemination process. Our system is targeted at general interest alerts, such as traffic incidents, public transport issues, crowds or unsafe situations, like robberies or fights. Thus, we ensure users' concern and ability to discern them.

We propose a collaboratively-triggered dissemination mechanism composed of three steps: user alert, collaborative assessment and alert dissemination.

The alert process may be triggered manually by users or automatically by devices. In the latter case, devices rely on their sensors data in order to start or assess an alert. For instance, a car accident or a big crowd can be detected using sound sensors. When the incident is detected, a broadcast notification is sent to neighbor nodes in order to be assessed and, if approved, disseminated.

Our contribution focuses on how to assess alert relevance and prevent alert duplication by using ad-hoc device cooperation. Neighbor nodes receiving the assessment request must decide whether to confirm the alert or not by sending an assessment reply to the requester, either positive or negative. This kind of assessment can be employed in scenarios where nodes' support requires users' intervention or where it is performed autonomously. Since we employ proximity-based communications, collaboration is restricted to physically close devices. Thus, only nodes with actual knowledge of the area, and therefore able to confirm or refute the alert, take part in the assessment process. This represents an advantage regarding social network approaches, where it is necessary to verify alert senders' location. Devices remember alerts they have been required to assess so they will not start a new dissemination if they detect the same event. However, if an alert has been received through flooding dissemination, instead of a direct request for assessment, the node will start its own assessment process as the alert has been originated outside its local area.

If the alert is backed up by neighbors, that is to say, most of the received replies in a certain time are confirmations; then it is disseminated through the whole network using simple flooding. Since we aim our attention to the assessment stage, developing an efficient strategy in the dissemination phase is out of the scope of this paper. Alert verification takes part exclusively in the first sender's neighborhood, no negotiation or agreement is required in its further dissemination. Negotiation on every hop is suitable for interest-based dissemination but not for alerts, which are considered of general interest and for whose verification we rely only on devices in the incident area.

Figure 1 details the alert process described in this paper. A pedestrian alerts about an event in its surroundings. The alert is first shared with its neighbors in order to be assessed (green arrows). Then, if they agree with the alert content, the alert is disseminated through the whole area using flooding (red arrows). In order to implement collaborative assessment, it is necessary to establish when several alerts can be considered the same. Alert description consists only on the incident code, which results in easier message processing. Categories must be narrow enough to be able to give significant information about certain incidents but broad enough not to make the detection process too complex. The list of possible categories can be adapted to different systems' purposes.

3 Simulation

In order to perform a simulation based on a real-life urban scenario, we have chosen the city center of Vigo (Spain). The chosen region, shown in Fig. 1, comprises an area of 1.46 km^2 and includes commercial streets and Vigo's old town. As a result, most of the streets are either pedestrian-only or include wide sidewalks, which makes the area suitable for pedestrian simulation.

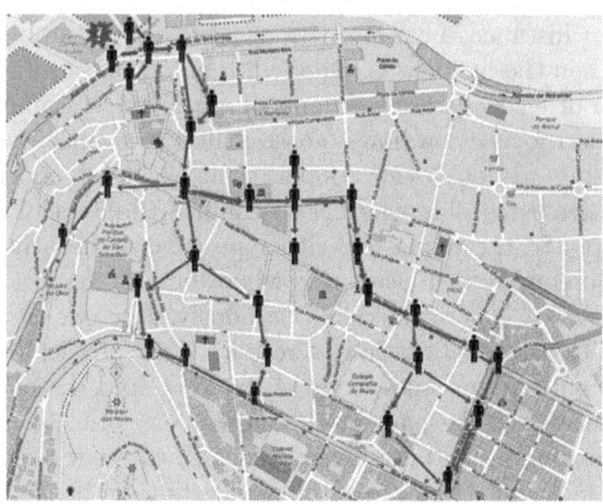

Fig. 1. Urban area used in simulation. (Color figure online)

We have exported the selected area from OpenStreetMap [12] and populated it with random pedestrian routes using SUMO urban mobility simulator [13]. Then, we have exported pedestrian traces to ns-3 network simulator [14], where we have implemented the assessment strategy and carried out the simulation. We have compared it with a simple flooding mechanism in situations where several neighbor devices detect the same incident and alert about it.

We have implemented the assessment strategy proposed in Sect. 2. We have set a time to wait for assessment replies of 100 ms. We have assumed that all the alerts are relevant and therefore, that they will be all backed up by neighbors. Besides, nodes reply automatically once they receive the assessment request, without users' intervention.

Transmission technology chosen for the implementation was ad-hoc WiFi. Reasons for this election include its availability in current smartphones and its transmission range ($\simeq$100 m), which makes it appropriate for urban communications.

We have carried out simulations with 100, 200, 500 and 1000 pedestrians in the area in order to assess the collaborative assessment behavior with different device density. In each one of those, we have simulated situations where 1, 2, 5, 10 or 20 nodes alert about the incident. Physically close nodes have been chosen as alert senders and time interval between their alerts has been set to one second. The following network parameters were considered as performance metrics:

- Message efficiency. We have measured the total number of messages that are necessary for an alert dissemination, including assessment requests, replies and disseminated alerts.
- Delivery ratio. We have measured the percentage of nodes in the area that receive the alert. Due to the randomness of the positioning and the characteristics of the urban area, some of the pedestrians are placed on the edges and cannot be reached. For this reason, delivery ratio never achieves 100 %.

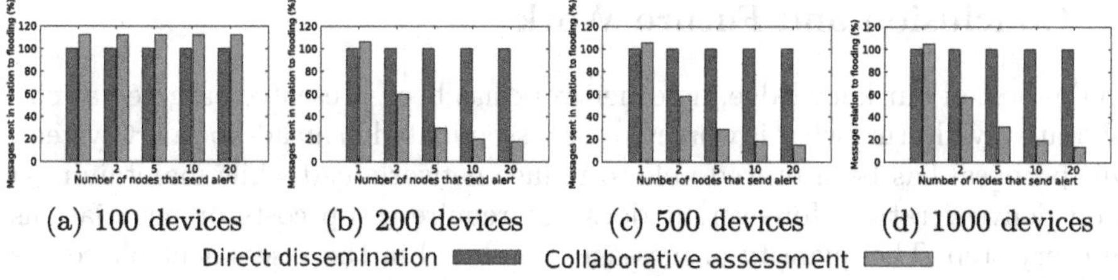

(a) 100 devices (b) 200 devices (c) 500 devices (d) 1000 devices

Direct dissemination Collaborative assessment

Fig. 2. Percentage of messages sent in relation to flooding.

3.1 Evaluation

We have concluded that our assessment mechanism outperforms direct flooding dissemination as long as more than one device alerts about the incident and there is enough device density. 100 devices have been proved to be too few to cover the considered area. As shown in Fig. 3(a), delivery ratio is always below 50 %. Distance between nodes prevents further dissemination while maintaining the quantity of messages sent constant. Moreover, assessment stage messages make the collaborative approach more inefficient than flooding, as shown in Fig. 2(a). From 200 devices on we can observe a clear trend on the system behavior. For one alert sender message efficiency of flooding outperforms the collaborative (Fig. 2) as it does not require any extra messages apart from the dissemination ones. For two alert messages, collaborative assessment requires about half of the messages flooding does. As the number of the nodes that send alert increases, so does the difference between flooding and collaborative assessment. With 20 alert senders, it requires less than 20 % of the messages flooding employs. And that happens with little difference in the delivery ratio, which is about 90 % with 200 and 500 devices and around 98 % for 1000 (Fig. 3). It could be argued that flooding is an inefficient dissemination technique that can easily be outperformed, but it has to be taken into account that flooding is also the dissemination mechanism used in the collaborative approach. As a result, comparison is made on equal terms.

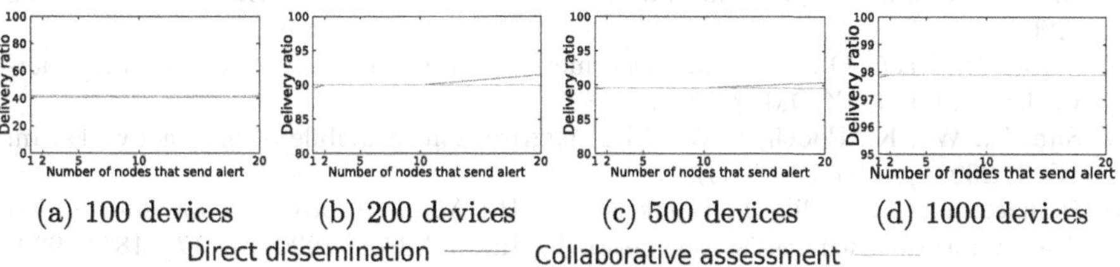

(a) 100 devices (b) 200 devices (c) 500 devices (d) 1000 devices

Direct dissemination Collaborative assessment

Fig. 3. Percentage of nodes in the area that receive the alert.

4 Conclusion and Future Work

To the best of our knowledge, no other work has been presented targeted at collaboratively filtering what is worthy to be disseminated in an ad-hoc alert system. Our proposal has been proved able to reduce network load while maintaining a good delivery ratio. Moreover, it does not require setup costs or negotiations on every step. The quantity of messages employed in the assessment phase has been shown to be small and therefore, the strategy cost is minor. However, we believe it could still be reduced. Replying to every alert proposal they receive may imply a significant overhead for mobile devices in crowded scenarios, where many alerts may be generated. Therefore, our current work focuses on developing a new collaborative assessment strategy that reduces this burden.

Acknowledgments. This work is funded by: the European Regional Development Fund (ERDF) and the Galician Regional Government under agreement for funding the Atlantic Research Center for Information and Communication Technologies (AtlantTIC) and the Spanish Ministry of Economy and Competitiveness under the National Science Program (TEC2014-54335-C4-3-R).

References

1. Campbell, A.T., Eisenman, S.B., Lane, N.D., Miluzzo, E., Peterson, R.A.: People-centric urban sensing. In: WICON 2006, pp. 18–31 (2006)
2. Imran, M., Castillo, C., Diaz, F., Vieweg, S.: Processing social media messages in mass emergency: a survey. ACM Comput. Surv. **47**(4), 67:1–67:38 (2015)
3. Mathioudakis, M., Koudas, N.: Twittermonitor: trend detection over the twitter stream. In: SIGMOD 2010, pp. 1155–1158 (2010)
4. Ritter, A., Mausam., Etzioni, O., Clark, S.: Open domain event extraction from twitter. In: SIGKDD 2012, p. 1104 (2012)
5. Goyal, D., Tripathy, M.R.: Routing protocols in wireless sensor networks: a survey. In: ACCT 20122, pp. 474–480 (2012)
6. Kokuti, A., Simon, V.: Location based data dissemination in mobile ad hoc networks. In: TSP 2012, pp. 57–61 (2012)
7. Tonguz, O., Wisitpongphan, N., Parikh, J., Bai, F., Mudalige, P., Sadekar, V.: On the broadcast storm problem in ad hoc wireless networks. In: BROADNETS 2006 (2006)
8. Saleet, H., Basir, O.: Location-based message aggregation in vehicular ad hoc networks. In: GLOBECOM, pp. 1–7 (2007)
9. Sun, B., Wu, K., Pooch, U.W.: Alert aggregation in mobile ad hoc networks. In: WiSE 2003, pp. 69–78 (2003)
10. Heinzelman, W., Kulik, J., Balakrishnan, H.: Adaptive protocols for information dissemination in wireless sensor networks. In: MobiCom 1999, pp. 174–185 (1999)
11. Rehena, Z., Roy, S., Mukherjee, N.: A modified SPIN for wireless sensor networks. In: COMSNETS, pp. 1–4 (2011)
12. OpenStreetMap (2015). http://wiki.openstreetmap.org/
13. Krajzewicz, D., Erdmann, J., Behrisch, M., Bieker, L.: Recent development and applications of SUMO simulation of urban mobility. Int. J. Adv. Syst. Meas. **5**(3&4), 128–138 (2012)
14. NS - 3 network simulator (2015). https://www.nsnam.org/

ZigBee Home Automation Localization System

Hector Rillo, Álvaro Marco, Rubén Blasco, and Roberto Casas(✉)

Aragon Institute of Engineering Research, University of Zaragoza, Campus Rio Ebro, María de Luna, 3, 50018 Zaragoza, Spain
hectorrillobautista@gmail.com,
{amarco,rblasco,rcasas}@unizar.es

Abstract. In this paper, a localization system of mobile nodes in a ZigBee Home Automation (ZHA) network has been developed. We used the ZigBee wireless protocol for networking due to its low cost, low power consumption, and acceptable data rate for most of smart home control systems, compared to other existing alternatives like Wi-Fi, Bluetooth or ZWave. Between the numerous localization techniques, we used the Received Signal Strength Indicator (RSSI), which can be obtained without the inclusion of additional hardware to the ZigBee nodes. Our system was implemented with three different Artificial Neural Networks (ANN), which results are compared and analysed; with a series of data treatments to avoid communications errors between the nodes and RSSI values fluctuations.

Keywords: RSSI · ZigBee Home Automation · RF fingerprint · Artificial Neural Network

1 Introduction

Nowadays, determining the location of sensor nodes in ZigBee [1] WSN is essential for many sensor applications, i.e. to track workers and underground locomotives in coal mines [2–4], to monitor hospital patients or to assist elderly care [5–7]. Some localizations techniques can be categorized as Time of Arrival (TOA), Time Difference of Arrival (TDOA), Angle of Arrival (AOA) and Received Signal Strength Indication (RSSI)-based, where RSSI-based techniques is the most commonly applied due to its good trade-off between hardware cost and positioning accuracy. Between the RSSI-based techniques, Artificial Neural Networks (ANN) are used very often. ANNs are powerful classifiers, which are computational models inspired in the natural neurons. In [8], it is used the technique of location fingerprint to create a Location Fingerprint Table (LFT) with sensor nodes' RSSI values and their positions inside the scenario. The LFT is used to train a Back Propagation Neural Network (BPNN), which performs the localization with a proposed method called Signal Index Pair (SIP). In [9], the authors employs a Probabilistic Neural Network (PNN) to perform the sensor localization. The PNN is trained with the received power between two nodes, obtained through RSSI values. In the last stage, the number of anchors nodes is reduced using Independent Component Analysis (ICA), to reduce the power consumption. In [10], a research work using the ZigBee Cluster Library (ZCL) based on localization fingerprint

C.R. García et al. (Eds.): UCAmI 2016, Part II, LNCS 10070, pp. 131–136, 2016.
DOI: 10.1007/978-3-319-48799-1_16

is developed. The method has two phases: an offline phase, where all the RSSI measurements across the scenario are registered; and an online phase, where the localization is performed by values comparison.

In this work, it is performed an RSSI-based indoor localization with room-level accuracy, in two ZigBee Home Automation (ZHA) WSN within two different scenarios. We have used two types of ANN: Multilayer Perceptron (MLP) and Self-Organizing Maps (SOM).

The remainder of the paper is organized as follows. In Sect. 2, we exposed the testbed. Section 3, describes the architecture of the proposed positioning algorithm. Test on the system are shown in Sect. 4 and Sect. 5 draws the conclusions.

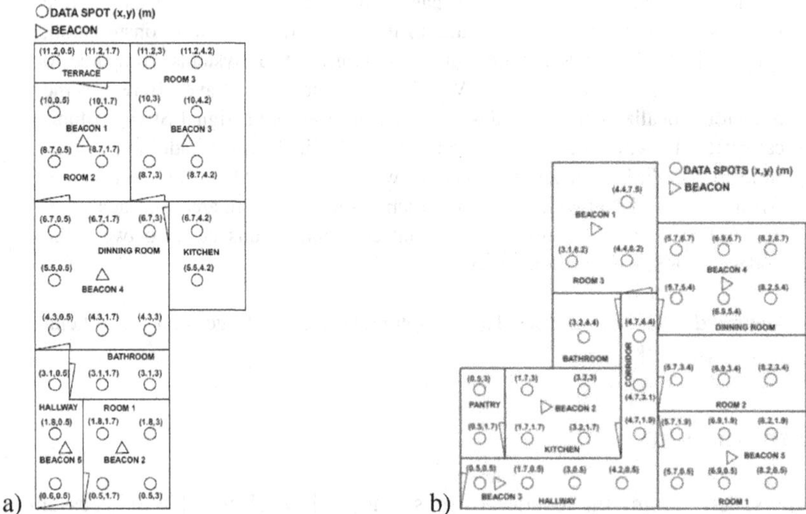

Fig. 1. Testbeds: (a) scenario 1, (b) scenario 2

2 Testbed

A ZHA network with 5 beacon nodes and 1 mobile node has been deployed. The ZigBee nodes are ETRX2 modules from Telegesis [11], which have an integrated ceramic antenna. The beacon nodes are expected to operate as light bulbs, so they are placed very close to the ceiling lamps, and all of them had the same orientation within a scenario. Each scenario has been divided in a grid, where the distance between two consecutive points is one relative unit, like in [12]. Figure 1 shows the two scenarios considered, were triangles represent the beacons' placements, and circles the different data spots. The mobile node is used as a panic button around the neck of the test subject. This way, the RSSI measurements are affected by the power loss due to the human body. In every spot, 25 RSSI measurements of each beacon have been registered for each cardinal orientation, and when a value between the mobile node and a beacon node is not received (holes), whether there has been communications errors or

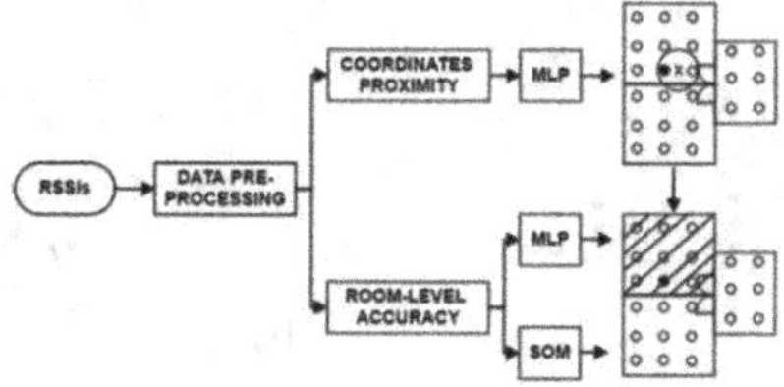

Fig. 2. General localization system design diagram

the scenario didn't allow it, we set its value to −105 dBm, which means out of range. In the first scenario, 3000 data samples have been obtained, while in the other one we have obtained 3200 data samples, all of them within a range of [−95,−32] dBm.

3 Algorithm Design

3.1 Data Pre-processing

Prior to the ANN design, we had to label each RSSI value according to the data spot relative coordinates and its room. We have also applied a window treatment to avoid the holes encountered during the gathering of RSSI values, and a feedforward filter to smooth the RSSI values fluctuation in each data spot [13]. The inputs had been standardized with mean 0 and standard deviation 1; and normalized within the range [−1,1].

3.2 System Architecture

We have developed three different neural networks with Matlab: two MultiLayer Perceptron (MLP), with a three layer architecture; and a Self-Organizing Map (SOM), as it is shown in Fig. 2. For the first MLP, we performed the location of the node using the coordinates of the data spots (MLP_GRID), and once we had the coordinates, we derive the room where the mobile node is located. The number of inputs match the number of beacons, and there are two outputs for x and y grid coordinates in the scenario; the hidden activation function is sigmoid within the range [−1,1], and the output activation function is linear. When the coordinates have been calculated, we round them to the closest integer in order to match a point on the grid and to decide in which room the mobile node is.

The other MLP is designed to obtain directly room-level accuracy (MLP_ROOMS). Like MLP_GRID, it has 5 input neurons, but the outputs neurons are 8 or 9, depending on whether it was used for the first scenario or the second scenario respectively; the activations functions of the hidden and output layers are sigmoid, within the range of [−1,1] and [0,1] respectively. Once the results has been obtained, the estimated room is designated by the output with the bigger value. Both MLP have been trained with different numbers of hidden neurons, in the range [0,25] with step of 5 units (Fig. 3).

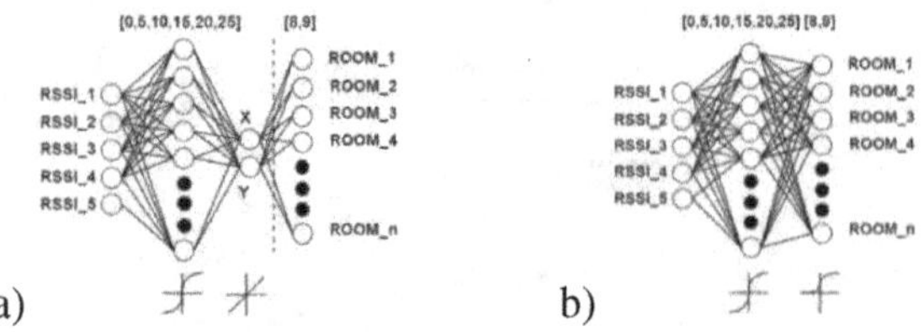

Fig. 3. MLP architectures: (a) MLP_GRID; (b) MLP_ROOMS

The last neural network implemented was the SOM. The map topology employed was hexagonal, and the dimensions were different for each scenario, because the number of measurements registered was different for each one. For the first scenario, the map size was 21 × 12 neurons, while for the other one, the map size was 26 × 10 neurons (Fig. 4).

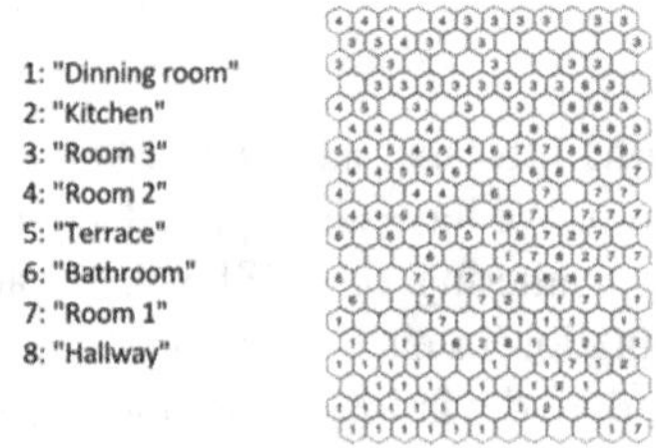

Fig. 4. SOM labelled with data samples of scenario 1

Before the ANNs were trained, all the RSSI measurements were divided into 3 groups: train (80 %), test (10 %) and validation (10 %). During the training stage, to avoid data overfitting, the method Early Stopping (ES) was applied to the training of both MLP, and for every configuration employed, a set of 10 pools of nets was designed, so the average error could be representative of how suitable the different architectures can be.

4 Results

After the training of all architectures, the best architectures for each ANN were obtained. For MLP_GRID, the architecture with less average error was a 5 × 20 × 2 for both scenarios. The validation average error is close to 1 m of distance between the data spot estimated and the original, with a 95 % confidence interval error of 3 m.

However, after the coordinates x and y were transformed into room-level classification, the kappa index of the ANN falls down to less than 0.70. due to the confidence interval error is higher than some of the rooms width, which measurements aren't correctly classified in the confusion matrix, like it is shown in Fig. 5.

	1	2	3	4	5	6	7	8
1: "Dinning room"	80	23	10	4	1	10	8	4
2: "Kitchen"	0	0	0	0	0	0	0	0
3: "Room 3"	0	0	60	1	0	0	0	0
4: "Room 2"	1	0	0	41	16	0	0	0
5: "Terrace"	0	0	0	1	7	0	0	0
6: "Bathroom"	2	0	2	0	0	10	14	12
7: "Room 1"	0	1	0	1	0	4	26	15
8: "Hallway"	1	0	0	0	0	0	0	5

Fig. 5. Average confusion matrix of MLP_GRID with 20 hidden neurons in scenario 1

For the other two ANN, the results were satisfactory, with a kappa index above 0.70 for all the selected architectures with the validation data. For MLP_ROOMS, the best architectures were 5 × 20 × 8 for the first scenario, and 5 × 20 × 9 for the second one. The highest value for the first scenario, was obtained with MLP_ROOMS, and for the second scenario with SOM (Table 1).

Table 1. Average Kappa of the most representative ANN architectures

		Scenario 1			Scenario 2		
ANN		Kappa train	Kappa test	Kappa validation	Kappa train	Kappa test	Kappa validation
MLP GRID	ARQ.15	0,5451	0,5374	0,5368	0,6569	0,5839	0,5967
	ARQ.20	0,5727	0,5345	**0,5594**	0,6824	0,6130	**0,6343**
	ARQ,25	0,5985	0,5891	0,5891	0,7009	0,6215	0,6379
MLP ROOMS	ARQ.15	0,8683	0,8423	0,8460	0,8158	0,7412	0,7674
	ARQ.20	0,8995	0,8690	**0,8687**	0,8450	0,7680	**0,8069**
	ARQ,25	0,9238	0,8752	0,8784	0,8669	0,7984	0,7889
SOM		0,7833	0,8350	**0,8576**	0,7515	0,7799	**0,8194**

5 Conclusions

In this paper, we have developed a localization system of mobile nodes for ZHA networks with 3 different approaches in two scenarios. The approximation method, MLP_GRID, obtained a result similar to [8], but after extrapolating the results to a room-level classification, this method has a very low accuracy, which means that the method couldn't transform the results correctly.

On the other hand, the other ANNs had obtained a very good results in room-level accuracy, with similar success rates for both ANNs. This means that whichever of them could be implemented for localization applications, and choosing among them should be based on practical criteria. In that sense, with the help of an ANSI C library named FANN [14], an ANN MLP_ROOMS has been implemented in ANSI C code. The results of this ANN were very close with MLP_ROOMS, when the ANNs were trained and executed with the same processor unit. So, in absence of more testing, it means that the implementation of the ANSI C ANN could be possible.

In future works, it would be wise to deploy as many beacons as rooms has the scenario, and design an algorithm which employs the beacons with less holes in communication. Also, we would implement the ANN in ANSI C in the mobile node and in the ZigBee Gateway, and compare the different results, while doing localization test in real time.

Acknowledgments. This work has been supported by the Spanish Ministry of Economy and Competitiveness, under project Memory Lane (TIN2013-45312-R).

References

1. The ZigBee Alliance | Control your World. http://www.zigbee.org
2. Hongju, L., Haifang, W., Nianxin, X., Chunxia, L., Panfeng, C.: Research on coal mine personnel positioning system based on Zigbee and CAN. In: 2009 International Conference on New Trends in Information and Service Science (2009)
3. Liu, Z., Li, C., Ding, Q., Wu, D.: A coal mine personnel global positioning system based on wireless sensor networks. In: 2010 8th World Congress on Intelligent Control and Automation (2010)
4. Bin, G., Kai, W., Jianghong, H.: Research of underground mine locomotive positioning algorithm based on RSSI. J. Softw. Eng. **9**, 598–609 (2015)
5. Zhao, H., Yin, K., Shao, J.: Design and implementation of the ZigBee-based pulse wave sensor position system. In: 2010 3rd International Conference on Biomedical Engineering and Informatics (2010)
6. Jihong, C.: Patient positioning system in hospital based on Zigbee. In: 2011 International Conference on Intelligent Computation and Bio-Medical Instrumentation (2011)
7. Lu, C.-H., Kuo, H.-H., Hsiao, C.-W., Ho, Y.-L., Lin, Y.-H., Ma, H.-P.: Localization with WLAN on smartphones in hospitals. In: 2013 IEEE 15th International Conference on e-Health Networking, Applications and Services (Healthcom 2013) (2013)
8. Hung, M.-H., Lin, S.-S., Cheng, J.-Y., Chien, W.-L.: A ZigBee indoor positioning scheme using signal-index-pair data preprocess method to enhance precision. In: 2010 IEEE International Conference on Robotics and Automation (2010)
9. Rajaee, S., Almodarresi, S., Sadeghi, M., Aghabozorgi, M.: Energy efficient localization in wireless ad-hoc sensor networks using probabilistic neural network and independent component analysis. In: 2008 International Symposium on Telecommunications (2008)
10. Kaemarungsi, K., Ranron, R., Pongsoon, P.: Study of received signal strength indication in ZigBee location cluster for indoor localization. In: 2013 10th International Conference on Electrical Engineering/Electronics, Computer, Telecommunications and Information Technology (2013)
11. Telegesis: ETRX2 Product Manual (TG-ETRX2-PM-001-109). http://www.telegesis.com/download/document-centre/user_guides_and_product_manuals/TG-ETRX2-PM-001-109.pdf
12. Blasco, R., Marco, Á., Casas, R., Ibarz, A., Coarasa, V., Asensio, Á.: Indoor localization based on neural networks for non-dedicated ZigBee networks in AAL. In: Cabestany, J., Sandoval, F., Prieto, A., Corchado, J.M. (eds.) IWANN 2009, Part I. LNCS, vol. 5517, pp. 1113–1120. Springer, Heidelberg (2009)
13. Aamodt, K.: Application Note AN042 (Rev. 1.0): CC2431 Location Engine. http://www.ti.com/
14. Nissen, S.: Implementation of a fast artificial neural network library (FANN). Department of Computer Science University of Copenhagen (DIKU), 31, 29 (2003)

Enhancing Smart Environments with Mobile Robots

Francisco-Angel Moreno(✉), Cipriano Galindo, and Javier Gonzalez-Jimenez

Machine Perception and Intelligent Robotics Group,
System Engineering and Automation Department, University of Málaga,
Campus de Teatinos, 29071 Málaga, Spain
{famoreno,cgalindo,javiergonzalez}@uma.es

Abstract. Sensor networks are becoming popular nowadays in the development of smart environments. Heavily relying on static sensor and actuators, though, such environments usually lacks of versatility regarding the provided services and interaction capabilities. Here we present a framework for smart environments where a service robot is included within the sensor network acting as a mobile sensor and/or actuator. Our framework integrates off-the-shelf technologies to ensure its adaptability to a variety of sensor technologies and robotic software. Two pilot cases are presented as evaluation of our proposal.

Keywords: Sensors networks · Smart environments · Mobile robotics

1 Introduction

The interest for sensor networks [7] is growing nowadays, opening new applications in different fields, like Ambient Assisted Living (AAL) [9,16], health monitoring [15], and smart homes [12]. Specially with the expansion of the so-called Internet of Things (IoT) [17], small devices have appeared in a number of scenarios, e.g. houses, workplaces, and warehouses, to provide assistance to the users' daily tasks.

Typical sensor networks operate controlled by a central computer that is in charge of receiving, processing and logging the information provided by the sensors, hence becoming the element where the *intelligence* of the system resides. In general, the interaction between the smart system and the user is limited to the exchange of basic information, either by voice or through a visual display as, for example, in the cases of commercial devices like Amazon Echo [10] or Google Home [1]. Moreover, home automation systems can also perform changes on the environment through a variety of *static* actuators (e.g. switching on/off or dimming the lights, lowering/rising the blinds, etc.). However, less attention

Work supported by the research projects TEP2012-530 and DPI2014-55826-R, funded by the Andalusia Regional Government and the Spanish Government, respectively, both financed by European Regional Development's funds (FEDER).

C.R. García et al. (Eds.): UCAmI 2016, Part II, LNCS 10070, pp. 137–143, 2016.
DOI: 10.1007/978-3-319-48799-1_17

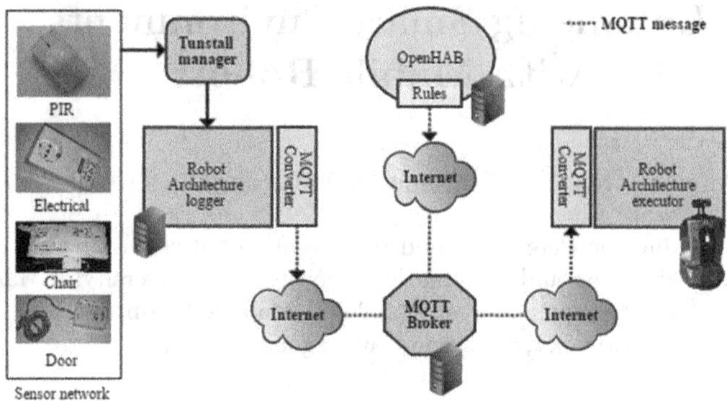

Fig. 1. Framework overview.

has been paid to the inclusion of a mobile robot in the environment, which can act as an additional, mobile, networked element, adopting the role of both a sensor and an actuator. This significantly enhances the interaction capabilities and provides the smart system with a variety of new interesting services. Robotic assistance ranges from companion for elder people at home, mitigating their loneliness and monitoring their health parameters, to helper in work environments by providing different services such as agenda management, reminders, pick & carry operations, etc.

The integration of the service robot within the system involves endowing the robot with the capabilities of being remotely controlled and providing feedback about the on-going tasks. For this, a communication scheme must be defined to interface the robot. Besides, as it will share its working space with humans, a considerable effort in terms of robustness, flexibility and safety must be done regarding its motion in a possibly dynamic environment.

This work describes a framework that conveniently integrates a service robot within a sensor network and presents different scenarios in an office-like environment that proves the suitability and the utility of the system. The presented system uses off-the-shelf technologies for (i) building a network based on wireless sensors, (ii) implementing the robot control architecture aimed at endowing the mobile robot with the needed abilities, and (iii) setting up a middleware that communicates the sensor network and the robotic architecture. By relying on a widely employed message protocol (MQTT) we ensure that the different elements of our framework can be easily replaced with other sensor technologies or robotic architectures.

2 Framework Overview

This section describes the four pillars of the proposed framework (see Fig. 1), namely: (i) the sensor network, (ii) the robotic architecture, (iii) the communication system and (iv) the rule manager.

Sensor network. A network of sensors provided by Tunstall [5] has been considered in this work. Tunstall provides solutions to the elderly and handicapped people based on wireless sensors and smart technologies.

From the variety of different sensors it provides, we have installed in our lab the following: 4 door contacts, 6 chair occupancy sensors, a power sensor and a presence sensor (PIR) (see Fig. 1). When triggered, these sensors send a wireless signal to the Tunstall manager device, which is in charge of collecting and sending the sensor ID and status to a computer through a standard USB port. The maximum number of sensor devices that can be linked simultaneously to the manager is 35.

Robotic Architecture. The mobile robot integrated in the framework is the robot SANCHO [11], built upon a Pionner base and endowed with two laser scanners, a RGB-D camera, and speakers. The robotic architecture considered is an instance of the OpenMORA architecture [2], based on MOOS [14]. Coded in C++, OpenMORA considers a centralized blackboard from which a number of modules that implement the robot capabilities can share information by publishing and subscribing to particular topics through TCP sockets. Some relevant robot capabilities implemented in Sancho are self-localization [8], reactive and global navigation [13], and Text-to-Speech. Note that ROS [4] could also be considered, albeit we prioritized the cross-platform feature of OpenMORA.

Communications. We rely on the MQTT (Message Queuing Telemetry Transport) protocol, which is a lightweight messaging protocol based on a publish-and-subscribe architecture. It implements a *star* topology with a central node called *broker* which broadcasts the incoming messages to the clients according to the topics they are subscribed to. Either encrypted and non-encrypted communications are supported and three levels of quality of service (QoS) are provided as additional features. Moreover, its small footprint and low-bandwidth requirements makes it ideal for wireless networks and devices with limited resources such as embedded systems or smartphones, becoming a popular protocol for Internet of Things (IoT) nowadays. Along the several MQTT brokers available, e.g. HiveMQ, CloudMQTT or Mosquitto, we have opted for the last one, given its compatibility and popularity.

Rule management. The *rule manager* is in charge of taking decisions about the robot operation according to the status of the sensor network. This has been tackled using OpenHAB [3], a Java-based, open source software that integrates different systems, sensors and technologies and provides the capability of creating rules to automatize domotic environments following the Xtend [6] syntax. For instance, a rule can be created to automatically switch on the lights and warm the stove up for dinner. The use of rules and the OpenHAB capability to be MQTT-compliant, make it an ideal element to become a part of our framework so that it can collect messages from all the different devices, analyze the state of the complete system and generate a certain command for the robot according

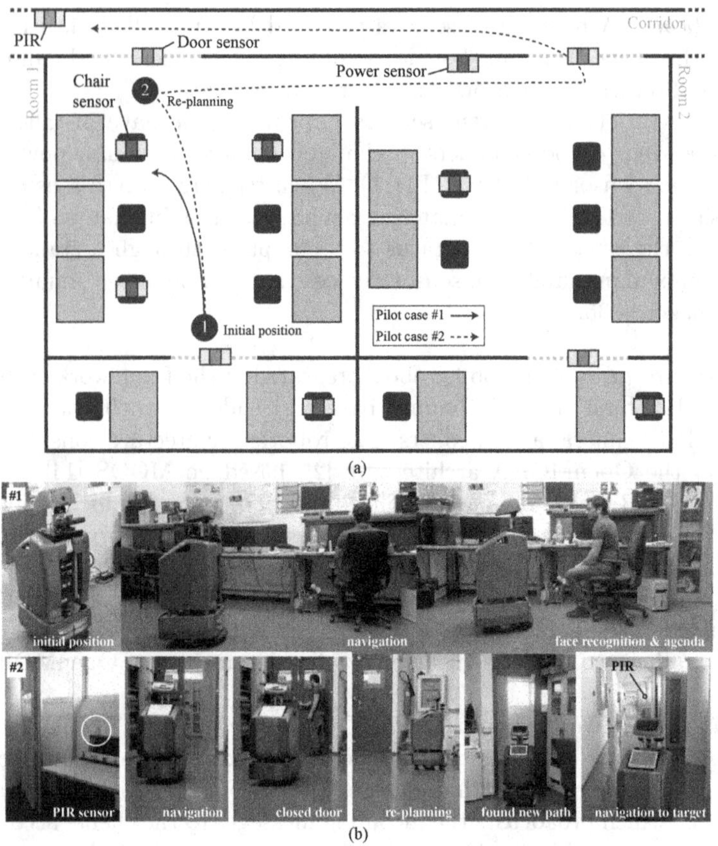

Fig. 2. (a) Environment floorplan and position of the sensors: PIR (orange), door sensor (blue), chair occupancy sensor (green) and power sensor (red). Robot trajectories for the pilot cases are also depicted. (b) Illustration of pilot case #1 (top) and #2 (bottom). (Color figure online)

to it. Besides, it provides a web interface that shows the status of all the involved sensors, hence becoming an interesting tool for monitoring an environment.

Framework operation. When a sensor is triggered, a radio signal is sent to the Tunstall manager device, connected to a PC running an OpenMORA module that converts the signal to MQTT messages associated to a specific topic. The broker broadcasts the message to the subscribers of the topic, including the rule manager, which operates in a different PC. The rule manager analyzes the status of both the sensor network and the robot, and decides a proper command that is sent to the robot through a MQTT topic. Finally, OpenMORA modules running on the robot's computer capture such command, and execute it. Note that we have chosen to distributedly run the described subsystems in different computers in order to balance the system's computational burden. However, it would be possible to run all the elements in the same computer.

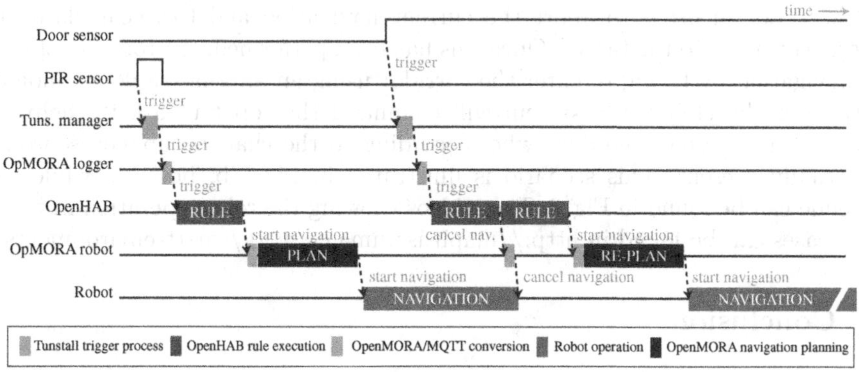

Fig. 3. Timeline for pilot case #2.

3 Pilot Cases

To evaluate our framework in real conditions, we have designed two pilot cases aiming to prove the potential of the combination of sensor networks and mobile robots to provide ambient intelligence services. Figure 2(a) sketches the chosen scenario composed of an office-like environment with two connected rooms and a near corridor.

Pilot case #1. In this case, when a chair occupancy sensor is triggered, the rule manager sends a navigation command to the robot ordering it to move to the sensor location. Then the robot uses its camera to detect the person on the chair and recognize his/her face. Subsequently, the rule manager retrieves from the user's agenda all the relevant information and informs about it to him/her by voice. Finally, the robot returns to its initial position and waits until a new sensor is triggered. If the person who triggers the sensor is not recognized by the robot, an alarm is raised informing the lab staff about the situation. A sequence of images illustrating this scenario is presented in Fig. 2(b, top).

Pilot case #2. This pilot case demonstrates the capabilities of combining real-time information from the networked sensors and the mobile robot in terms of flexibility and adaptability when performing some tasks. In this case, we have installed a PIR sensor in the corridor outside our lab, which is triggered each time a person walks along it. When activated, the system sends a command to the robot to inspect the corridor by launching a navigation command. This command is processed by the robot architecture by finding the shortest path from the current position to the target and elaborating a planned sequence of intermediate points. Once the robot starts navigating, we manually close one of the doors between the laboratory and the corridor, hence intercepting the planned path of the robot. Thus, the triggered door sensor activates a rule in the system that handles this *blocked-trajectory* situation by sending a signal to the robot in order to abort the current navigation and to re-calculate an alternative path to the target. Once this has been performed, the robot re-starts its navigation by trying to enter the corridor using an alternative door. Should both doors be closed, the system will command the robot to ask for help to the person closest to the door who, according to the chair occupancy sensors, is actually present. This scenario is illustrated in Fig. 2(b, bottom) while its timeline can be found in Fig. 3. Two videos showing the robot operation in both pilot cases can be found in http://mapir.isa.uma.es/work/smart-environments.

4 Conclusion

This work has presented a framework that enhances a sensor network with a mobile robot to create a versatile smart environment with increased capabilities in terms of provided services and interaction with the user. By using off-the-shelf technologies and the standard MQTT communications protocol we ensure the adaptability of the framework to different sensor technologies and robotic architectures. In particular, our proposal relies on Tunstall sensors, OpenMORA as robotic software and OpenHAB as rule manager. The capabilities of the complete system have been evaluated through two pilot cases.

References

1. Google Home website. https://home.google.com. Accessed 1 June 2016
2. MAPIR website. http://mapir.isa.uma.es. Accessed 1 June 2016
3. OpenHAB website. http://www.openhab.org. Accessed 1 June 2016
4. ROS website. http://www.ros.org. Accessed 1 June 2016
5. Tunstall website. http://www.tunstall.com. Accessed 1 June 2016
6. Xtend website. http://www.eclipse.org/xtend/ Accessed 5 Sept 2016
7. Akyildiz, I.F., Su, W., Sankarasubramaniam, Y., Cayirci, E.: Wireless sensor networks: a survey. Comput. Netw. **38**(4), 393–422 (2002)
8. Blanco, J., González, J., Fernández-Madrigal, J.A.: Optimal filtering for non-parametric observation models: applications to localization and slam. Int. J. Robot. Res. **29**, 1726–1742 (2010)
9. Coradeschi, S., Cesta, A., Cortellessa, G., Coraci, L., Galindo, C., Gonzalez, J., Karlsson, L., Forsberg, A., Frennert, S., Furfari, F., et al.: GiraffPlus: a system for monitoring activities and physiological parameters and promoting social interaction for elderly. In: Hippe, Z.S., Kulikowski, J.L., Mroczek, T., Wtorek, J. (eds.) Human-Computer Systems Interaction: Backgrounds and Applications 3. AISC, vol. 300, pp. 261–271. Springer, Heidelberg (2014)
10. Dempsey, P.: The teardown Amazon Echo digital personal assistant [Teardown Consumer Electronics]. Eng. Technol. **10**(2), 88–89 (2015)
11. Gonzalez, J., Galindo, C., Blanco, J., Fernandez-Madrigal, J., Arevalo, V., Moreno, F.: SANCHO, a fair host robot. A description. In: IEEE International Conference on Mechatronics, 2009, ICM 2009, pp. 1–6. IEEE (2009)
12. Han, D.M., Lim, J.H.: Design and implementation of smart home energy management systems based on ZigBee. IEEE Trans. Consum. Electron. **56**(3), 1417–1425 (2010)

13. Jaimez, M., Blanco, J.L., Gonzalez-Jimenez, J.: Efficient reactive navigation with exact collision determination for 3D robot shapes. Int. J. Adv. Rob. Syst. **12**, 1–12 (2015)
14. Newman, P.: MOOS — a mission oriented operating suite (technical report oe2003–07). Department of Ocean Engineering, MIT, Cambridge, MA, Technical report (2003)
15. Pantelopoulos, A., Bourbakis, N.G.: A survey on wearable sensor-based systems for health monitoring and prognosis. IEEE Trans. Syst. Man Cybern. Part C: Appl. Rev. **40**(1), 1–12 (2010)
16. Sun, H., Florio, V.D., Gui, N., Blondia, C.: Promises and challenges of ambient assisted living systems. In: Sixth International Conference on Information Technology: New Generations, 2009, ITNG 2009, pp. 1201–1207, April 2009
17. Xia, F., Yang, L.T., Wang, L., Vinel, A.: Internet of things. Int. J. Commun. Syst. **25**(9), 1101 (2012)

Reliable Publish/Subscribe in Dynamic Ubiquitous Systems

Ugaitz Amozarrain(✉) and Mikel Larrea

University of the Basque Country UPV/EHU, Paseo Manuel de Lardizabal 1, 20018 Donostia-San Sebastián, Spain
{ugaitz.amozarrain,mikel.larrea}@ehu.eus

Abstract. This work addresses content-based publish/subscribe in dynamic ubiquitous scenarios, composed of a variety of heterogeneous devices connected by wireless networks, mobility being an intrinsic characteristic of this kind of systems. We present an approach based on the simple routing strategy, which is incrementally extended in order to support client and broker mobility. We allow both client and broker migration without the need to flood the network to notify of this change.

1 Introduction

Publish/subscribe is a paradigm that allows a loosely coupled dissemination of events on a distributed system. The objective of such a system has been the distribution of messages over a wide area and static topology, e.g., the Internet [1].

The increase of mobile, wireless devices on recent years, be it wireless sensor networks, smart-phones or other mobile devices has created a need to adapt the initial publish/subscribe protocols designed for static systems. Indeed, in wireless sensor networks we lose the robustness of the Internet and focus more on challenges such as the mobility of the system [2,3].

Several approaches have been followed in order to create a more mobile publish/subscribe system, first by handling the mobility of clients and later by dealing with mobile brokers. A system like Jedi [4] expects the clients to proactively disconnect from the network in order to handle migrations, and inform the network when arriving to a new broker. This allows buffering the messages received while the client is migrating and delivering them when it reconnects. Broker mobility is more complicated to handle due to the changing network overlay [5].

Following a previous work [6] where client mobility for content based publish/subscribe systems was introduced, we expand it to include mobility also on the broker network.

Research supported by the Spanish Research Council, grant TIN2013-41123-P, and the University of the Basque Country UPV/EHU, grant UFI11/45.

C.R. García et al. (Eds.): UCAmI 2016, Part II, LNCS 10070, pp. 144–149, 2016.
DOI: 10.1007/978-3-319-48799-1_18

1.1 System Model

A publish/subscribe system is composed of two components: a set of *clients* that produce/consume events, and a *notification service* that handles the subscriptions issued by clients and the delivery of events to the corresponding clients.

There are two types of clients: *publishers* that produce events and send them to the system, and *subscribers* that register to one or more filters and consume matching events. We will use $p \in P$ to refer to a publisher belonging to the global set of publishers P. Similarly, we will use $s \in S$ to refer to a subscriber belonging to the global set of subscribers S. Finally, we will use $f \in F$ to refer to a filter belonging to the global set of filters F.

On the other hand the notification service is composed of a set of brokers B which we will refer to by using the notation $b \in B$. A broker will have at any moment a set of neighbor brokers it can communicate with, we will call this set N_i for broker b_i. Furthermore, a broker will also communicate directly with clients that are connected to it, for this reason we call I_i to the set of interfaces that broker b_i can communicate with, be it clients or other brokers.

1.2 Simple Routing

The Simple Routing [7] strategy assumes a static system where brokers are connected in an acyclic graph, and each client is permanently bound to a single broker. This routing strategy is based on the propagation of subscription (*SUB*) and unsubscription (*UNS*) messages to all of the brokers in the system.

The routing table R_i at every broker b_i contains, for every subscription in the system, a routing entry (f, z) where $f \in F$ and $z \in I_i$, to indicate that the publication of an event e matching f must either be forwarded towards broker z (if $z \in B$) or delivered to subscriber z (if $z \in S$).

2 Towards Dynamic Publish/Subscribe

In this section we first introduce Phoenix [6] as an extension to the Simple Routing protocol that is able to seamlessly handle subscriber migrations (publisher migration is inherently supported by Simple Routing). Then we explain the required changes in order to support broker mobility.

2.1 Supporting Dynamic Clients

Algorithm 1 presents the pseudo-code of Phoenix. Besides the *SUB*, *UNS* and *PUB* messages of Simple Routing, a new *MIG* message is used to notify the broker network when a subscriber has migrated. This message will follow the delivery path of a published message so there is no need to flood the network.

In order to adapt the Phoenix protocol for supporting broker migrations, some changes have been made. On the handling of *SUB* and *UNS* messages, due to possible inconsistencies on a converging network, now we check for the existence of the filter in the routing table, seen on lines 2 and 7.

```
1  when receive(SUB, f, s) from z ∈ I_i do
2      if ∄(f, _, s) ∈ R_i then
3          R_i ← R_i ∪ {(f, z, s)}
4      foreach b ∈ N_i where b ≠ z do
5          send(SUB, f, s) to b

6  when receive(UNS, f, s) from z ∈ I_i do
7      if ∃(f, _, s) ∈ R_i then
8          R_i ← R_i \ {(f, _, s)}
9      foreach b ∈ N_i where b ≠ z do
10         send(UNS, f, s) to b

11 when receive(MIG, s, b) from z ∈ I_i do
12     if z = s then
13         X ← ∅
14         foreach (f, _, s) ∈ R_i do
15             X ← X ∪ {f}
16         send(FILTERS, X) to s
17     if b ≠ b_i then
18         if ∃(_, _, s) ∈ R_i then
19             b_j ← y ∈ N_i where (_, y, s) ∈ R_i
20             send(MIG, s, b) to b_j
21     foreach (_, _, s) ∈ R_i do
22         replace (_, _, s) with (_, z, s) in R_i
```

Algorithm 1. Part of the algorithm for Simple Routing with dynamic clients in Phoenix. Highlighted parts are the additions made to the original algorithm.

Some changes were also made in the handling of a *MIG* message. The first broker that receives the message will send back to the subscriber a set containing all the subscriptions for that subscriber from its routing table, see lines 12–16. A new message type *FILTERS* was added to send this information. This is done in order to support the migration of the subscribers from one partition to another. Another change consists in the subscriber sending the identity of the previous broker it was connected to, which together with the check of line 17 allows us to handle reconnections as a particular case of migration. The inclusion of the check on line 18 is for the same reason *SUB* and *UNS* handling had to be changed, we need to check for consistency on the routing table. Finally, the entries of the routing table corresponding to the migrating subscriber are adjusted in order to correctly route future events.

2.2 Supporting Dynamic Brokers

In this section we introduce an extension to the Phoenix protocol for supporting broker mobility. Unlike subscriber mobility, when a broker migrates the physical change on the network might force a recalculation of the spanning tree that is used for routing the events. Using standard spanning tree algorithms this recalculation might end up changing several of the previous stable connections between brokers, thus potentially forcing the migration of more brokers than the one that is actually migrating.

In order to avoid this issue a leader election algorithm [8] was chosen for the broker network. Using the periodic heartbeat message sent by the leader we can create a spanning tree with the leader itself as the root node. Using this heartbeat message the brokers will realize when they have moved from their previous position on the network and migrate accordingly. The leader election algorithm in [8] is also able to handle small independent partitions on the network and once connectivity is restored between them, they come together forming a bigger network with a unique leader, chosen from one of the previous leaders. In other leader election algorithms, such as [9], the partitions are able to merge correctly but a new leader might be chosen, requiring bigger changes in the spanning tree. For all migrations we consider the partition with the final leader as the primary partition and the others as migrating partitions.

Each broker will keep stored the next hop to the leader, following the opposite path of the heartbeat message, and a set of brokers that are connected to itself. Using this information we can easily create a spanning tree. Every broker b_i keeps a set of connected subscribers, denoted C_i, which will change due to the mobility of both b_i and its subscribers.

We consider that a broker has migrated when its path to the leader changes. A migrating broker b_m will connect to a new broker b_{new} and send a *BMIG* message. This message, containing the set C_m of local subscribers connected to b_m, causes b_m to function as a proxy for subscriber migration and it will follow the delivery path for those subscribers as with single subscriber migrations.

Algorithm 2 shows on lines 23–32 how a broker will handle a *BMIG* message. As seen on lines 23–28 the behavior is similar to a *MIG* message for subscriber migration, we are just generalizing it for a set of subscribers, using a loop. After replacing all required values the broker will forward the same message it received to the previously stored brokers. Finally, on lines 31–32 we specify that if the broker from which the *BMIG* message has been received is the same as the originator of the message, the broker will reply with a *BTAB* message.

A *BTAB* message contains the routing table of the broker that sends the message. This message is used to update the table on b_i to the latest version on the primary partition. Broker b_i knows the latest subscriptions from its local subscribers but it cannot trust any other entry on its routing table, for this reason once it receives a *BTAB* message it will remove all entries from its table that do not belong to its local subscribers, lines 34–35, and it will store all entries, except the ones pertaining to b_i's subscribers, from the table it received, changing the next hop to the broker that sent the message, lines 36–37, so that

```
23 when receive(BMIG, C_m, b_m) from b_j ∈ N_i do
24     X ← ∅
25     foreach s ∈ C_m do
26         X ← X ∪ {b ∈ N_i where (_, b, s) ∈ R_i ∧ b ≠ b_j}
27         foreach (_, _, s) ∈ R_i do
28             replace (_, _, s) with (_, b_j, s) in R_i
29     foreach y ∈ X do
30         send(BMIG, C_m, b_m) to y
31     if b_j = b_m then
32         send(BTAB, R_i) to b_j
33 when receive(BTAB, R_j) from b_j ∈ N_i do
34     foreach (_, _, s) ∈ R_i where s ∉ C_i do
35         R_i ← R_i \ {(_, _, s)}
36     foreach (_, _, s) ∈ R_j where s ∉ C_i do
37         R_i ← R_i ∪ {(_, b_j, s)}
38     foreach (f, _, s) ∈ (R_i − R_j) do
39         send(SUB, f, s) to b_j
40     foreach (f, _, s) ∈ (R_j − R_i) do
41         send(UNS, f, s) to b_j
42     foreach b ∈ N_i where b ≠ b_j do
43         send(FMIG) to b
44 when receive(FMIG) from b_j ∈ N_i do
45     send(BMIG, C_i, b_i) to b_j
```

Algorithm 2. Simple Routing with dynamic brokers.

any *PUB* message can be routed correctly. Then b_i will check to see what new information it has on its table with respect to b_j, lines 38–41, this way b_i will know if the subscriptions of its subscribers in the primary network are the correct ones, if there are any inconsistencies it will fix them by sending a *SUB* or *UNS* message for the corresponding subscription propagating it to the network using the standard protocol.

At this point, the protocol works if a broker migrates alone, but if the broker that migrates has more brokers connected to it, b_i cannot know if there has been any change on that side of the network. For modularity we have decided to force a sequential migration of all the brokers that are hanging from the migrating broker in the spanning tree, using a new *FMIG* message. This way each broker will update in the primary partition the information corresponding to its local subscribers. This behavior can be seen on Algorithm 2, lines 42–45.

3 Conclusion

This work has presented an extension to the Phoenix publish/subscribe protocol that supports broker mobility, besides the already supported client mobility. The protocol has been verified to work correctly using the JBotSim [10] tool. We plan to also use other tools in order to evaluate its performance and compare it with similar works.

Acknowledgments. We thank the anonymous reviewers for their suggestions and comments.

References

1. Carzaniga, A., Rosenblum, D.S., Wolf, A.L.: Design and evaluation of a wide-area event notification service. ACM Trans. Comput. Syst. **19**(3), 332–383 (2001)
2. Mottola, L., Cugola, G., Picco, G.P.: A self-repairing tree topology enabling content-based routing in mobile ad hoc networks. IEEE Trans. Mob. Comput. **7**(8), 946–960 (2008)
3. Mühl, G., Ulbrich, A., Herrmann, K., Weis, T.: Disseminating information to mobile clients using publish-subscribe. IEEE Internet Comput. **8**(3), 46–53 (2004)
4. Cugola, G., Di Nitto, E., Fuggetta, A.: The Jedi event-based infrastructure and its application to the development of the opss wfms. IEEE Trans. Softw. Eng. **27**(9), 827–850 (2001)
5. Cugola, G., Murphy, A.L., Picco, G.P.: Content-based publishsubscribe in a mobile environment. P. Bellavista and A. Corradi, pp. 257–285 (2005)
6. Salvador, Z., Larrea, M., Lafuente, A.: Phoenix: a protocol for seamless client mobility in publish/subscribe. In: 11th IEEE International Symposium on Network Computing and Applications, NCA 2012, Cambridge, MA, USA, 23–25 August 2012, pp. 111–120. IEEE Computer Society (2012)
7. Banavar, G., Chandra, T.D., Mukherjee, B., Nagarajarao, J., Strom, R.E., Sturman, D.C.: An efficient multicast protocol for content-based publish-subscribe systems. In: Proceedings of the 19th International Conference on Distributed Computing Systems, Austin, TX, USA, 31 May - 4 June 1999, pp. 262–272. IEEE Computer Society (1999)
8. Gómez-Calzado, C., Lafuente, A., Larrea, M., Raynal, M.: Fault-tolerant leader election in mobile dynamic distributed systems. In: IEEE 19th Pacific Rim International Symposium on Dependable Computing, PRDC 2013, Vancouver, BC, Canada, 2–4 December 2013, pp. 78–87. IEEE (2013)
9. Melit, L., Badache, N.: An Ω-based leader election algorithm for mobile ad hoc networks. In: Benlamri, R. (ed.) NDT 2012. CCIS, vol. 293, pp. 483–490. Springer, Heidelberg (2012). doi:10.1007/978-3-642-30507-8_41
10. Casteigts, A.: JBotSim: a tool for fast prototyping of distributed algorithms in dynamic networks. In: Proceedings of the 8th International Conference on Simulation Tools and Techniques, pp. 290–292. ICST (Institute for Computer Sciences, Social-Informatics and Telecommunications Engineering) (2015)

Scheduling Real-Time Traffic in Underwater Acoustic Wireless Sensor Networks

Rodrigo Santos[1(✉)], Javier Orozco[1], Matías Micheletto[1], Sergio F. Ochoa[2], Roc Meseguer[3], Pere Millan[4], and Carlos Molina[4]

[1] Department of Electrical Engineering and Computers, IIIE, UNS-CONICET, Bahía Blanca, Argentina
ierms@criba.edu.ar, jadorozco@gmail.com, matiasmicheletto@gmail.com

[2] Computer Science Department, Universidad de Chile, Santiago, Chile
sochoa@dcc.uchile.cl

[3] Department of Computer Architecture, Universidad Politécnica de Catalunya, Barcelona, Spain
meseguer@ac.upc.edu

[4] Department of Computer Engineering, Universitat Rovira i Virgili, Tarragona, Spain
{pere.millan,carlos.molina}@urv.net

Abstract. Underwater sensor networks are an important field of research. Several applications require the use of this kind of networks like tsunami or oil spill alerts. The underwater medium is very harsh and only acoustic signals can be used for the transmission of information. The use of this kind of networks is still in a developing state far from reaching standard consensus on basic aspects like carrier frequency or modulation techniques. The use of these networks for real-time applications has not been analyzed previously. In this paper we present two solutions for the scheduling of real-time messages and we provide a time constraint analysis of the performance of the network.

Keywords: Underwater sensor networks · Environmental monitoring

1 Introduction

Underwater acoustic wireless sensor networks are becoming a hot research topic as they have turned into the primary tool to monitor and to act upon the well-being of marine environments [1,2]. Radio frequency electromagnetic signals do not propagate well underwater. Huge amount of power is required to transmit messages even for short distances. The presence of particles and moving obstacles, such as fishes or plants, prevents the use of optical carriers. For underwater transmissions, the best option is to use acoustic carriers. While wireless sensor networks based on radio frequency transmissions have been studied and several protocols have been proposed like ZigBee, Bluetooth or even Wi-Fi, the solutions achieved for them are not useful for acoustic underwater networks, since

C.R. García et al. (Eds.): UCAmI 2016, Part II, LNCS 10070, pp. 150–162, 2016.
DOI: 10.1007/978-3-319-48799-1_19

propagation delay is usually larger than transmission time. A message may be received well after its transmission has finished in the source node.

Tsunamis are generated by earthquakes in the ocean. Not every earthquake in the ocean produces a tsunami but the existence of an earthquake may end in a tragic tsunami, like the ones in Japan 2011 or Indonesia 2004. Detecting a tsunami is a hard task. Seismic sensors may be deployed in the area in which the earthquake may take place (geologic fault) and if one is detected, acording to its intensity a tsunami alert may be issued. The time available between the earthquake and the arrival of the wave to the beach depends on the distance to the earthquake epicenter. However, it is clear that there is a hard real-time restriction as the alert should be issued with enough time for people to move into a safe place.

The detection system may have some buoys anchored along the fault and linked to the seismic sensors, so once the earthquake is detected, the buoy connects through a satellite network to a disaster-management office reporting the event, intensity, and tsunami probability. However, buoys could be vandalized, jeopardizing the network operation. To avoid this, an underwater acoustic sensor network is proposed operating in real-time. The network deployment, nodes distribution and number of hops discussion is out of the scope of this paper. However, the real-time analysis and network performance modeling proposed here can be used to set-up the appropriate network.

Real-time (RT) communications require not only that messages are transmitted properly but also before a particular instant named deadline. If the deadline is missed, the message is not valid and may have serious consequences [3]. A feasible RT schedule is one in which all messages comply with their deadlines. RT message scheduling in multi-hop networks is a complex problem that requires the use of routing and queueing techniques. If all the nodes in the network have a direct link to the rest of the nodes, the problem may be solved using an integer linear programming approach, as presented later in the paper. However, when a message should go through intermediate nodes, it is not only a question of when a node should transmit (MAC problem) but also of selecting the appropriate path. In this case, the shortest path is not always the best one as a per-node scheduling should be incorporated in the analysis. In fact, a node holding more than one message has to schedule their transmission introducing additional delays.

Recently, we have proposed a simple distributed medium access control protocol (MAC) for the case of underwater wireless sensors networks [4]. The network was modeled as a tree with a sonobuoy as root and sensors as leafs. The information flow was from the leafs to the root using intermediate nodes for aggregating the information collected in the previous layer. The synchronization process was made in a hierarchical way from the root to the leafs. At each layer a synchronizing node was selected following certain rules and these nodes were in charged of aggregating the messages during the data transmission stage. The proposed algorithm considered the possibility of re-configuring the tree periodically. However, it was not designed to operate under RT constraints, power considerations were not incorporated in the analysis, and the possibility of transferring data between any pair of nodes was not evaluated. In this paper, we use the initialization phase in which the nodes are synchronized and the network topology is discovered. After this, messages may be sent between any pair of nodes.

As in standard wireless sensors networks (WSN), the most common MAC protocols can be grouped in two classes: Carrier Sense Multiple Access (CSMA) and Time Division Multiple Access (TDMA) oriented. In the first one, nodes transmit whenever they are able to lock the shared channel. For RT messages this approach is not useful as message delays may be unbounded. TDMA may introduce an important latency but the worst case delay may be computed and the timed behavior of the network is predictable. Moreover, the TDMA approach can be divided in two modes. The first one considers that each node sends a broadcast to every node within transmission range. In this case, if a node has several messages to transmit to different destinations, it has to wait for equal number of frames. In the second approach, a per-message TDMA is computed in such a way that the slot for sending a message from node a to node b is defined, and also the moment at which node b receives the message from node a. In this case, each message has a particular slot to be sent and received at destination, and the nodes may wait for the proper instants to become active.

Underwater sensor networks operate with acoustic carriers. Two basic approaches are followed in the medium access protocol: those based in CSMA [5,6] and those based in TDMA [7,8]. The first group can not guarantee a RT performance so we are not going to comment on them. The second group proposes different algorithms to allocate the nodes within the frame. In [9] the authors proposed an heuristic approach, however they are not considering RT constraints. In [7] the authors propose a dynamic slot-allocation. This approach provides an important feature as the network may change its topology so new allocations are necessary. However, the approach is not considering the routing and RT constraints involved in the node-to-node transmissions. Finally, in [8] the authors put the focus on energy aspects and the transmission power use. To this end, they optimize the node allocation mechanism. As in the previous cases, no RT analysis is performed.

Contribution: This paper extends the algorithm proposed in [10] to include RT constraints and message transfers between any pair of nodes in the system. A TDMA access protocol is proposed with an off-line allocation and scheduling algorithm. Feasibility conditions are given for the system to operate with hard RT constraints.

2 System Model

2.1 Physical Model

For the sake of simplicity, we assume the propagation delay between two nodes within transmission range is equal in both directions. That is, if a message originating in node a requires four time slots to reach node b, then a message originating in b also requires four time slots to reach a.

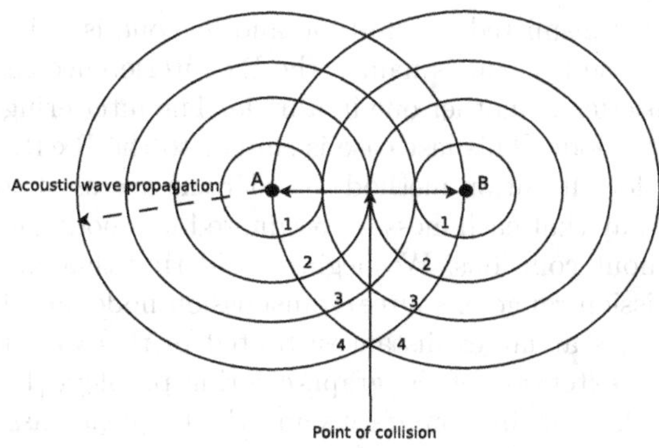

Fig. 1. Acoustic waves propagation and interference

In Fig. 1, lets suppose that both nodes begin their transmission simultaneously. Both messages propagate at the same speed and have the same duration: one slot time. Under the previous assumption, a collision happens exactly at two time slots. However, as these are longitudinal waves, there is a transitory composition of both waves at the point of collision, but both of them continue their propagation. If the transmission power is enough, both nodes receive each other message after four time slots. It is important to note that local collisions do not propagate and that nodes only detect a local collision.

2.2 Real-Time Message Model

We assume that any node may transmit a message to any other node in the network if there is a valid path between both nodes. We denote a message from node a to node b as m_{ab}. We also assume all messages require one time slot to be transmitted, and that they are sent periodically. Additionally, all messages should be received before the associated deadline. P_{ab} and D_{ab} denote the period and deadline, respectively. In general we define the set of messages as $Z = \{m_{ij}(P_{ij}, D_{ij})\}$.

2.3 Network Model

The network can be modeled as a directed graph $G = (V, E)$, in which V is the set of nodes in the network and E the set of edges. If two nodes u and v are within transmission range, there is an edge connecting them: $e = (u, v)$. Each edge has a label that represents the transmission delay between the nodes measured in *time slots*, τ_{uv}. The set of nodes which have a direct link with $i \in V$ is the neighbor set and is denoted $N(i)$. As collisions are important only if they are produced at the node, there are four different scenarios as stated in [9]. The first scenario is when two messages arrive simultaneously to a node: this case is named the Rx-Rx case. The second scenario is produced when two messages tried to be transmitted simultaneously in a node: Tx-Tx case. The third secenario is when a message is transmitted at the time another one is being received: this is the Tx-Rx case. The last one is named the Rx-Interference case and it arises when a message interferes another one in a node. The interfering message has a different destination node. This last case is similar to the Rx-Rx case.

We propose a slot allocation method to order the access of the nodes to the channel, in such a way that each message originated in a node may reach its destination node without collisions. We begin considering that destination nodes are within transmission range of source/transmission node, and later we extend the analysis for nodes at larger distances. Stated in this way, the slot assignment problem is an extension of the graph-coloring problem [11]. The problem is similar to the L(2,1) labeling on graphs and the frequency assignment [12].

We present an integer linear programming (ILP) model, to minimize the frame length measured in slots. If we note $m_i \in N$ the slot in which node i transmits, we have the following: `Minimize` $\sum_i m_i$ subject to:

$$
\begin{array}{lll}
m_i - m_j - M\delta_{ij} & \geq \tau_{ij} + 1 - M & \forall i \in V, \forall j \in N(i) \\
m_i - m_j - M\delta_{ij} & \leq \tau_{ij} - 1 & \forall i \in V, \forall j \in N(i) \\
m_j - m_k - M\omega_{ijk} & \geq \tau_{ik} - \tau_j + 1 - M & \forall i \in V \forall j, k \in N(i) \\
m_j - m_k - M\omega_{ijk} & \leq \tau_{ik} - \tau_{ij} - 1 & \forall i \in V \forall j, k \in N(i) \\
\delta_{ij} & \in \{0,1\} & \forall i \in V \forall j \in N(i) \\
\omega_{ijk} & \in \{0,1\} & \forall i \in V \forall j, k \in N(i)
\end{array}
$$

where M is a sufficiently large constant. The model is significantly more complex if a per-message slot allocation is performed. Further details in [9].

3 Scheduling

Path discovery is a well known problem in networking. Several algorithms have been proposed to compute the best path for a message to reach destination from a source. The most common solutions are based on Dijsktra algorithm to determine the shortest path from any node in the network to any other node (SPF, shortest path first) or the Bellman-Ford distance vector algorithm. In the case of communication networks, the cost associated to the edges may be related to the actual delay between the nodes, an economical cost for using that link (paying service to a third party company) or the power required to use the link. For real-time messages, the total delay in the path should be less or equal to the deadline of the message. If this condition is not guaranteed, the message is not schedulable and the network does not fulfill the real-time requirements.

$$
\forall a, b \qquad D_{ab} \geq \sum_{e \in \texttt{path}(ab)} \tau_e \tag{1}
$$

Equation (1) sets the basic condition for the network to be schedulable. This requires that the sum of the transmission delays in each hop of the path, plus the time needed in each intermediate node to gain access to the channel, should be less or equal to the deadline of the message. Besides, the transmission to the next hop should be scheduled in such a way that no collisions are produced at the destination or intermediate nodes.

When a node has several messages ready to be transmitted, a scheduling policy should be implemented to sort the transmission. Particularly we used the First-In First-Out policy (FIFO) that is easy to implement. However, messages do not have a priority associated, so an urgent message may wait for several frames before being transmitted. As messages are periodic, the waiting time in the queue is computed from the worst case arrival of the message to the queue and the frame length. Depending on the kind of TDMA computed (node or message allocation) the node should have one or more queues, depending on the amount of neighbors. In either case, the frame size T_f is used as the time needed to compute the delay in the waiting queue W_i in the node, Eq. 2. Q is the length of the queue at the instant of message arrival or generation.

$$W_i = (Q - 1)T_f + m_i \tag{2}$$

4 Example

In this section we present a simple example to show the different aspects discussed in the previous sections. Figure 2 shows a five node network with the labels in the edges denoting the transmission delay between adjacent nodes.

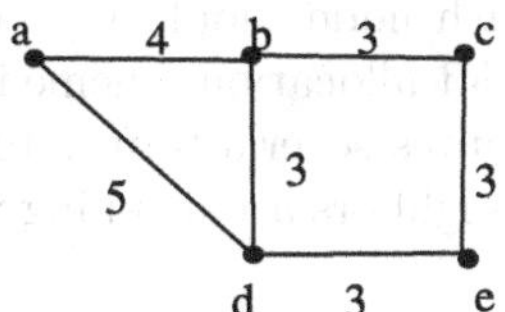

Fig. 2. Five nodes network example

The ILP model for this network has twelve messages for allocating in the frame. Each node transmits a message to all its neighbors. The transmission and reception scheme is shown in Table 1 where $T(ab)$ stands for a slot used by node a to send a message to node b and $R(ba)$ stands for a message received at node a from node b. The allocation was computed with GLPK 4.55 [13].

The schedule presented is minimum for transmitting a message from each node in the network to all its neighbors. The frame size has a duration of 13 slots. The empty slots consider the fact that messages should not interfere in the reception. Node a is active only in 4 out of 13 slots so it may save energy being kept off during the slots at which it has no activity.

The frame imposes a general upper bound for each hop. That is, in the worst case, for each hop in the path a whole time frame delay is introduced. Thus, transmitting a message from node a to node e, the SPF algorithm has a lower bound of 10 slots and an upper bound of 17 slots. In the analysis we are still not

Table 1. Message/Slot allocation for transmission and reception.

Node	Slots												
	1	2	3	4	5	6	7	8	9	10	11	12	13
a	$T(ab)$	$T(ad)$									$R(ba)$		$R(da)$
b	$T(bd)$		$T(bc)$		$R(ab)$		$T(ba)$			$R(cb)$		$R(db)$	
c			$T(ce)$			$R(bc)$	$T(cb)$				$R(ec)$		
d	$T(de)$			$R(bd)$	$R(ed)$		$R(ad)$	$T(da)$	$T(db)$				
c		$T(ed)$		$R(de)$		$R(ce)$		$T(ec)$					

Table 2. Node/Slot allocation for transmission of messages.

Node	Slots					
	1	2	3	4	5	6
a	$T(a)$				$R(b)$	$R(d)$
b	$T(b)$			$R(d)$	$R(a)$	$R(c)$
c			$T(c)$	$R(b)$	$R(e)$	
d	$T(d)$			$R(b)$	$R(e)$	$R(a)$
e		$T(e)$		$R(d)$		$R(c)$

considering queueing problems in the nodes. This means that in node a there is just one message that has to be sent to node d and in this last one, only one message (the one received from a) has to be forwarded to node e. If this is not the case, a scheduling policy in each node should be selected and the transmission delay increases. If a per-node slot allocation scheme is used, the frame is reduced to just 6 slots, but a node requires several frames to send consecutive messages to the neighbors, and all the neighbors are listening while they are transmitting. Table 2 shows this case.

As previously, node a is on in 3 out of 6 slots, being off in the rest (saving power). Let us consider a set of 8 messages.

$$Z = \{m_{ae}(20,30), m_{ac}(20,30), m_{ea}(20,30), m_{ca}(20,30), m_{de}(20,30), m_{db}(10,10), m_{bc}(10,10), m_{ae}(15,20)\} \quad (3)$$

A message from a to e has a transmission delay of 8 units and goes through 2 nodes a and d before reaching destination. For the case of node allocation, and considering a queue with one place for each connected neighbor, in the worst case the message has to wait for 1 frame ($Q = 2$) in node a to be transmitted at the next one, see (2). Once arrived to node d it may wait for 2 frames ($Q = 3$) before being transmitted to node e.

$$\tau_{ae} = W_a + W_d + \tau_{ad} + \tau_{de} = 6 + 1 + 5 + 12 + 1 + 3 = 26$$

In the described situation, considering the worst case, m_{ae} has an end-to-end delay of 26 slots. Computing in the same way for the rest of the messages, we found the worst-case delays for all messages as presented in Table 3. The

Table 3. Messages worst-case delays

m_{ij}	m_{ae}	m_{ac}	m_{ea}	m_{ca}	m_{de}	m_{db}	m_{bc}	m_{be}
r_{ij}	26	25	29	29	16	16	16	21

network scheduling of the proposed example shows that the system is stable and that messages will be transmitted through the network within their deadlines.

5 Heuristic Approach

In the proposed model, the variables that affect the communication speed and therefore the timing of the system are the frame duration, the order of transmission and reception of messages, and the route that each message follows within the network. In this section an heuristic algorithm is presented to optimize the message/slot allocation to minimize the frame size and meet the deadlines.

The minimum length frame is not necessarily the optimal to meet the system time requirements, and this impedes uncoupling the computation of the frame with respect to the computation of the routes. The heuristic presented in this section generates a fixed length frame and optimizes the paths of the messages to meet all system deadlines.

Let H denote the least common multiple between all message periods. If the frame is a time window of fixed length H, there is a number $H/P_{i,j}$ instances of the message $m_{i,j}$, so $m_{i,j,k}$ denotes the k-th instance of the message $m_{i,j}$.

Each instance $m_{i,j,k}$ has an associated path which is chosen from all possible paths between nodes i and j. The path is denoted $path_{i,j,k}$ and contains the nodes of the network which the message goes through. Optimal path for each instance must be computed to obtain the best solution, as will be explained later.

As messages require communication between nodes to propagate through the network, node allocation in the frame is performed following the corresponding route. Each node must be allocated to the minimum slot to ensure meeting all deadlines.

Each node is associated to a binary interference matrix which simplifies the collision avoidance scheduling. This matrix has dimensions n by τ_{max} where n is the number of nodes and τ_{max} is the delay between the transmitting node and its farthest neighbor. For the i-th node, the element $(i, 1)$ of the interference matrix is always 1, and the element (j, s) is 1 if and only if j-th node has a communication delay of s slots from i-th node. To perform allocability test of a transmitter node to a desired slot, interference matrix of the transmitter node is overlapped on the frame so that the first column of the interference matrix match the column of the frame correspondig to the allocation slot and finally an element by element product is computed. If the result is a null matrix, then the allocability test is positive, which means transmitter node is allocable to that slot. In Sect. 5.1 we present the allocation procedure for the example of Sect. 4.

Algorithm 1. Scheduling algorithm pseudocode.

```
frame:=zeros(N,H) // Frame matrix initialization.
forall the m_{i,j,k} sorted by increasing order of periods do
    slot:=(k − 1) · P_{i,j} // First slot of period.
    transmitter:=path_{i,j,k} (first) // First node of path.
    receiver:=path_{i,j,k} (second) // Second node of path.
    destination:=path_{i,j,k} (last) // Last node of path.
    while True do
        if allocable(frame, transmitter, slot) then
            allocate(frame, transmitter, slot)
            slot:=slot+τ_{transmitter,receiver}
            if receiver==destination then
                break
            end
            else
                transmitter:=receiver
                receiver:=path_{i,j,k} (next) // Next node of path.
            end
        end
        else
            slot:=slot+1
            if slot==H then
                return 'Non schedulable system with chosen paths'
            end
        end
    end
    margin_{i,j}:=j * P_i + D_i - slot
end
return margin_{i,j}, frame
```

Once all path nodes are allocated, the message has arrived to destination, and remaining time until deadline is computed and denoted by $margin_{i,j,k}$. Pseudocode 1 shows the scheduling procedure required to generate the communication frame.

5.1 Node Allocation Example

Based on the example of Sect. 4, Table 4 shows a slice of the frame where there are free and taken slots. It is desired to know if node d is allocable to slot 9. As it can be seen (Table 5), if node d transmits at slot 9, there is a Rx-Rx collision on node b at slot 12 and a Tx-Rx collision on node e at slot 12. Following the same procedure, node d is not allocable to slot 10 either. Finally, Table 6 shows that node d is allocable to slot 11.

Table 4. Slice of the communication frame.

		8	9	10	11	12	13	14	15	16	
a	...	T(a)	R(b)		T(a)	R(d)			R(b)		...
b				R(d)	T(b)	R(a)	R(c)		R(a)		
c		R(b)		T(c)		R(e)		R(b)	R(e)		
d		R(b)				R(e)	R(a)	R(b)	R(e)	R(a)	
e			T(e)	R(d)		T(e)	R(c)				

Table 5. Allocation test of node d to slot 9. Collision slots highlighted.

		8	9	10	11	12	13	14	15	16	
a	...	T(a)	R(b)		T(a)	R(d)			R(b)		...
b				R(d)	T(b)	R(a)	R(c)		R(a)		
c		R(b)		T(c)		R(e)		R(b)	R(e)		
d		R(b)				R(e)	R(a)	R(b)	R(e)	R(a)	
e			T(e)	R(d)		T(e)	R(c)				

Table 6. Allocation test of node d to slot 11.

		8	9	10	11	12	13	14	15	16	
a	...	T(a)	R(b)		T(a)	R(d)			R(b)		...
b				R(d)	T(b)	R(a)	R(c)		R(a)		
c		R(b)		T(c)		R(e)		R(b)	R(e)		
d		R(b)				R(e)	R(a)	R(b)	R(e)	R(a)	
e			T(e)	R(d)		T(e)	R(c)				

5.2 Optimization Algorithm

Towards obtaining optimal path for each message instance, different optimization algorithms can be implemented to solve the problem. Figure 3 shows a simplistic representation of the optimization model, that iterates over a loop in order to improve the solution's quality. As it is desired to find a frame where communication between nodes allows messages to reach their destination in the minimum number of slots as possible, it is considered the summation of all delay margins between the arrival time of messages and their deadlines as the quality of the solution. In the context of mathematical optimization, the objective function takes as input the set of paths for each message instance and returns a scalar quantity as output, which represents the quality of the proposed solution. The objective function computes the output following three basic steps: first, generates the communication frame following the Algorithm 1; second, determines the

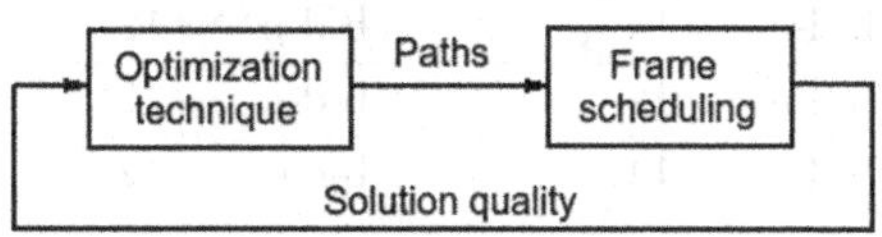

Fig. 3. Optimization model.

Table 7. SPF and Genetic Algorithm solutions evaluation

$m_{i,j,k}$	SPF		GA	
	$path_{i,j,k}$	delay margin	$path_{i,j,k}$	delay margin
$m_{a,e,1}$	a-d-e	21	a-d-e	21
$m_{a,e,2}$	a-d-e	22	a-d-e	22
$m_{a,e,3}$	a-d-e	22	a-d-e	22
$m_{a,c,1}$	a-b-c	19	a-b-c	21
$m_{a,c,2}$	a-b-c	22	a-b-c	22
$m_{a,c,3}$	a-b-c	19	a-b-c	19
$m_{e,a,1}$	e-d-a	21	e-d-a	21
$m_{e,a,2}$	e-d-a	19	e-d-a	21
$m_{e,a,3}$	e-d-a	19	e-d-a	21
$m_{c,a,1}$	c-b-a	17	c-b-a	18
$m_{c,a,2}$	c-b-a	18	c-b-a	18
$m_{c,a,3}$	c-b-a	14	c-b-a	17
$m_{d,e,1}$	d-e	16	d-e	19
$m_{d,e,2}$	d-e	19	d-e	19
$m_{d,e,3}$	d-e	15	d-e	16
$m_{d,b,1}$	d-b	7	d-b	7
$m_{d,b,2}$	d-b	7	d-b	7
$m_{d,b,3}$	d-b	7	d-b	7
$m_{d,b,4}$	d-b	7	d-b	7
$m_{d,b,5}$	d-b	7	d-b	7
$m_{d,b,6}$	d-b	7	d-b	7
$m_{b,c,1}$	b-c	7	b-c	7
$m_{b,c,2}$	b-c	7	b-c	7
$m_{b,c,3}$	b-c	7	b-c	7
$m_{b,c,4}$	b-c	7	b-c	7
$m_{b,c,5}$	b-c	7	b-c	7
$m_{b,c,6}$	b-c	7	b-c	7
$m_{b,e,1}$	b-d-e	12	b-c-e	12
$m_{b,e,2}$	b-d-e	14	b-d-e	12
$m_{b,e,3}$	b-d-e	12	b-d-e	12
$m_{b,e,4}$	b-d-e	14	b-c-e	12

delay margin for each instance; and finally computes the solution quality as the summation of all delay margins.

5.3 Analysis of Results

The proposed heuristic is better suited for complex problems where there are multiple paths for different messages. However, example of Sect. 4 is considered for better understanding of the situation. To begin with a simple case, the objective function was tested using shortest path for each message. Table 7 shows the delay margins of each message instance. This solution is feasible, has no message collisions, and no deadline is missed. Moreover, to improve the previous result, a genetic algorithm was used to find an optimal solution. Several instances of the optimization find the same solution which has a slight difference with the previous one. As it can be seen from the results in Table 7, message 8 alternates its path in the first and last instance, and this relieves the load of node d, so other messages reach their destination with greater delay margin.

6 Conclusions and Future Work

This paper presented a RT analysis for an underwater acoustic wireless network. We introduced two approaches. In the first one, the network is analyzed with ILP techniques. The shortest path is used as routing policy combined with a message or node slot allocation procedure in a TDMA frame. Based on this, we presented the schedulability condition for the case in which messages are transmitted following a First-In First-Out policy. This scheduling discipline is quite simple and requires little processing within the underwater nodes, reducing the computing complexity and demand on the processors. However, better results may be obtained if some RT priority policies are implemented, like fixed priorities or earliest deadline first. The performance of the network is left for future work. The second solution is based on a heuristic approach. In this case, messages are scheduled following a per-link approach and finding the route with shortest delay. The solution obtained improves the two step approach of finding the SPF in the first place, for allocating the slots within the frame later. As this heuristic only considers the messages actually being transmitted, unnecessary restrictions are avoided. We also presented a real application in which RT transmissions are necessary. Tsunami early alert problem is a very important issue for countries in the Pacific and Indic oceans and the routing proposal introduced here may help meet the RT requirements.

Acknowledgments. This work has been partially supported by the Spanish Ministry of Science and Innovation (MCI) and FEDER funds of the EU under contracts TIN2013-44375-R, TIN2013-47245-C2-1-R and TIN2013-47245-C2-2-R, and also CONFINE project: FP7-288535.

References

1. Açar, G., Adams, A.: Acmenet: an underwater acoustic sensor network protocol for real-time environmental monitoring in coastal areas. IEE Proc. Radar Sonar Navig. **153**(4), 365–380 (2006)
2. Akyildiz, I., Pompili, D., Melodia, T.: Underwater acoustic sensor networks: research challenges. Ad Hoc Netw. **3**(3), 257–279 (2005)
3. Liu, C.L., Layland, J.W.: Scheduling algorithms for multiprogramming in a hard real-time environment. J. Assoc. Comput. Mach. **20**(1), 46–61 (1973)
4. Santos, R., Orozco, J., Ochoa, S.F., Meseguer, R., Eggly, G., Pistonesi, M.F.: A MAC protocol to support monitoring of underwater spaces. Sensors **16**(7), 984 (2016)
5. Guo, X., Frater, M.R., Ryan, M.J.: A propagation-delay-tolerant collision avoidance protocol for underwater acoustic sensor networks. In: OCEANS 2006-Asia Pacific, pp. 1–6, May 2006
6. Pompili, D., Melodia, T., Akyildiz, I.: A CDMA-based medium access control for underwater acoustic sensor networks. IEEE Trans. Wirel. Commun. **8**(4), 1899–1909 (2009)
7. Chen, Y.D., Lien, C.Y., Chuang, S.W., Shih, K.P.: Dsss: A TDMA-based MAC protocol with dynamic slot scheduling strategy for underwater acoustic sensor networks. In: OCEANS 2011 IEEE-Spain, pp. 1–6 (2011)
8. Diamant, R., Lampe, L.: Spatial reuse time-division multiple access for broadcast ad hoc underwater acoustic comm. networks. IEEE J. Oceanic Eng. **36**(2), 172–185 (2011)
9. Guan, Y., Shen, C.C., Yackoski, J.: MAC scheduling for high throughput underwater acoustic networks. In: 2011 IEEE Wireless Comms and Networking Conference, pp. 197–202 (2011)
10. Santos, R., Orozco, J., Ochoa, S.F., Messeguer, R., Eggly, G.: A MAC protocol for underwater sensors networks. In: García-Chamizo, J.M., et al. (eds.) UCAmI 2015. LNCS, vol. 9454, pp. 394–406. Springer, Heidelberg (2015). doi:10.1007/978-3-319-26401-1_37
11. Lv, C., Wang, S., Tan, M., Chen, L.: UA-MAC: an underwater acoustic channel access method for dense mobile underwater sensor networks. Int. J. Distrib. Sens. Netw. (2014)
12. Shao, Z., Yeh, R.K., Zhang, D.: The L(2, 1)-labeling on graphs and the frequency assignment problem. Appl. Math. Lett. **21**(1), 37–41 (2008)
13. Makhorin, A.: GLPK (GNU) linear programming kit. https://www.gnu.org/software/glpk/. Accessed 10 Sep 2016

UAV-Based Rescue System for Emergency Situations

Moisés Lodeiro-Santiago(✉), Iván Santos-González, and Pino Caballero-Gil

Departamento de Ingeniería Informática y de Sistemas,
Universidad de La Laguna, San Cristóbal de La Laguna, Tenerife, Spain
{mlodeirs,jsantosg,pcaballe}@ull.edu.es

Abstract. This work describes a novel solution to face a civil security problem in the area of search and rescue of missing people. This proposal is based on the use of emerging technologies like unmanned aerial vehicles, also known as drones, and the use of simulated beacons in smartphones. In particular, the solution presented here which is focused on the use of several synchronized drones going over an area and scanning it to check whether they detect any Bluetooth Low Energy beacon signal emitted from the smartphone of a missing person and retrieve the exact GPS position. This paper also includes a preliminary study of possible attacks on the different elements and the security measures used to protect them.

Keywords: Drone · Unmanned aerial vehicle · Physical web · Rescue · Security

1 Introduction

The problem of missing people requires an urgent solution because nowadays when a person disappears, an emergency team has to search and locate him or her, involving a high economic and time costs. Furthermore, in the worst cases, unfortunately some missing people never could be found.

This paper describes a novel solution for this kind of emergencies, replacing the current emergency team with Unmanned Aerial Vehicles (UAV), also known as drones. Drones are used in the proposal for Search And Rescue (SAR) operations by detecting a wireless signal that is continuously emitted by a mobile application that simulates a beacon signal using Bluetooth Low Energy (BLE) technology. A drone that receives a Bluetooth signal can find out whether it corresponds to the searched beacon by reading the data that the signal contains. Drones used in the proposal can be controlled remotely by pilots or autonomously by on-board computers.

This work is structured as follows. Section 2 describes the beacon technology and introduces some basic concepts on UAVs. Section 3 presents the state of art and describes some examples of cases when the technology described in Sect. 2. Section 4 includes the main details of the implementation of the beacon

C.R. García et al. (Eds.): UCAmI 2016, Part II, LNCS 10070, pp. 163–173, 2016.
DOI: 10.1007/978-3-319-48799-1_20

signaling system in smartphones. Section 5 describes the steps followed in the proposal to successfully complete the SAR mission. Section 6 contains a study of some possible attacks that can affect the proposal. Finally, Sect. 7 describes the discussion with some conclusions and problems to solve in the future.

2 Preliminaries

Different technologies are combined in the proposal. The first one is beacon technology. A beacon is a low energy device that emits a broadcast signal thanks to BLE technology. Traditionally, beacons have been used in indoor positioning systems [1,2] for which they obtain accurate locations due to the short range that the beacons offer. Beacons have been also widely used in the commerce world. In this field, beacons are used as follows. When a client is approaching a certain commerce or product, he or she receives a beacon signal and automatically with it comes, an advertisement with discounts for this specific product/commerce.

The performance of beacons depends on a specific hardware, normally a BLE chip and a power battery. The use of BLE technology allows beacons to be used with minimum power consumption so the battery of a beacon usually resists for a long time, even for years [3].

A beacon device usually broadcasts its Universally Unique IDentifier (UUID), that identifies in a unique way the beacon and the application that uses it. The broadcast signal also includes some bytes that can be used to define the device position, send a URL, or automatically execute an action.

The performance of beacon devices is based on two main properties, independently of the used protocol, the Transmission Power (Tx Power) and the Advertising Interval. The Tx Power is the power the beacon signal is broadcasted with. This transmission power can be manually established. On one hand, it is known that a bigger Tx Power implies that the beacon can be discovered in a larger distance due to the properties of the signal intensity (which decreases with the distance, but implies a bigger battery consumption too). On the other hand, a lower Tx Power implies a minor range but also a lower battery consumption. The Advertising Interval is the frequency a beacon signal is emitted with. This frequency can be established, depending on the necessity of the developed system and its latency requisites. The Advertising Interval is established in milliseconds and bigger values imply bigger battery consumptions, while lower values involve lower battery consumptions. There are different protocols to send data in packets through the Advertising mode. These protocols establish a format in the advertising data so the applications can read this data in a proper way. The most extended protocols are: iBeacon [4], created by Apple; Eddystone [5], which is the open source project created by Google; and AltBeacon [6], which is the protocol developed by Radius Networks.

The other part of the proposed system corresponds to the UAV, which are unmanned aircraft vehicles controlled either remotely by pilots or autonomously by on-board computers with GPS technology. There are two different kinds of UAVs: gliders and multi-copters. On one hand, gliders are UAV that, as their name indicates, can glide, an important advantage over other type of drones because it supposes an important improvement on the energy consumption. On the other hand, multi-copters are UAVs that have more than one helix. Their main advantage is the capacity of being static in the air at the expense of higher power consumption.

The types of UAVs that are especially interesting for the proposal are autonomous UAVs. In this aspect, there are mainly two different systems that have been used to get an autonomous operation. The first one is known as Inertial Navigation System (INS) [7] and uses the output of the inertial sensors of the UAV to estimate the UAV position, speed and orientation. To use this kind of positioning system, the UAV uses a 3-axis accelerometer that measures the specific force acting on the platform and a 3-axis gyroscope that measures its rotation. An advantage of this kind of positioning systems is that it does not require the use of any other external signal to provide an external solution. On the other hand, this kind of systems produce positioning errors of the order of several hundreds of meters. The other kind of positioning system used by the UAVs is the GPS system. Since the GPS system needs an external signal to work and the navigation accuracy depends on the signal quality and the geometry of the satellite in view, depending on the used GPS, the error can vary between a meter and hundreds of meters. To solve the problems of these navigation systems in UAVs, it is normal to use a combination of INS and GPS to get a good precision from the GPS system and the frequency positioning data of the INS.

3 State of the Art

During the last years, different proposals have been presented in the field of SAR systems. Some of them are only communication systems but others include some rescue mechanisms. A lot of them have focused on the use of the so-called emergency call, included in all mobile devices some years ago. This mode allows the users to make an emergency call even when they have not coverage to make a phone call to any of their contacts. To make this system works, the European Union decided in 1991 that its member states had to use the 112 number to make emergency calls. Moreover mobile operators and mobile phone manufactures were forced to make the adaptation of all their products to, independently of the mobile operator, let the users use the network infrastructure of any other operator to make emergency calls. On this fact is based Alpify [8], a mobile application that allows the users not only to use the emergency call system when there is no Internet connection, but also to notify the emergency services and specific person (previously selected in the application in case of emergency) through an SMS with the georeferenced coordinates of their actual position. A problem of this proposal that derives from the use of the emergency call system, is the necessity of some network infrastructure because it requires coverage of at least of an operator.

In the situation analyzed in this work, the initial hypothesis is that there is no coverage of any mobile operator because the network infrastructures are unusable, collapsed, or do not exist because the users are in remote or difficult access places. In these cases, the use of any system based on communications using network infrastructures is not a feasible solution to the proposed problem. Moreover, the use of systems that need previous agreements between the company that develops the system and the different emergency services of every state of each country, implies difficulty to use them in places around the world.

Centralized systems like Alpify only notifies the emergency services and the contact person previously selected, and depending on where they are, they can delay to arrive to the position. The fact of not letting people who are near help in a faster way, supposes an important disadvantage of this kind of systems.

Other systems, like the one in [9], propose the use of a Wi-Fi Direct technology, so in the case where there is no Internet connection, people that are in the range of the Wi-Fi Direct technology are notified. The basis of this system consists on sending an emergency message that includes the geolocated position of the person, to other people in the range of Wi-Fi Direct. When the emergency message is received, if the user has Internet connection he/she notifies the warning automatically to the emergency services. If the user has not Internet connection, the message is re-sent through broadcast in a multi-hop system. This system involves an improvement compared to other systems than only use the emergency call, but it has problems when the number of users is not enough or they do not have the Wi-Fi Direct technology in their smartphones.

Other authors [10] try to solve this problem through the use of other devices like laptops carried by the emergency services. In that proposal, the goal is that the first units of the emergency services that arrive to the place deploy a Mobile Ad-hoc Network (MANET) based on Wi-Fi through laptops. After the network deployment, a group communication system based on Peer-to-Peer, that admits communications such as VoIP, Push-to-Talk, instant messaging, social networks, etc. is proposed. The main advantage of this kind of solutions is that the network is managed by specialized personnel preventing the access of other users to the network because the use is restricted only to emergency services. Its main disadvantage is that people who have suffered the catastrophe and is isolated, continue being isolated, both during the time that the emergency services take to arrive to the catastrophe place, and that the emergency services are acting.

Other systems, like the one in [11], use the Physical Web beacons to, once the emergency or rescue protocol is activated, the members of the SAR services find the injured people that carry the beacons. This kind of systems have the disadvantage that the search has to be done manually and the rescue or emergency service must have access to the emergency zone, which might not be possible in some situations.

Other proposals use UAVs for the SAR operations in emergency situations where the rescue system cannot access. This is the case in [12], where the use of the UAVs is proposed in combination with the use of Physical Web beacons, that the affected people must carry, to search people affected by an avalanche.

Moreover, there are systems, like the one in [13], that use aerial imaging processing to detect people in problems for post-disaster assessment. Their main disadvantage is that the use of image processing could be imprecise in situations where the visibility is not good, as can be in fires where smoke difficulties the visibility.

Other proposals, like the one in [14], help in the management and monitoring in emergency situations through the use of real-time aerial photos. The main advantage of this proposal is the use of real-time aerial photos to produce a Digital Elevation Model data of 5 m resolution that can be very useful, to see the latest terrain environment and provide reference for disaster recovery in the future.

Different to the aforementioned proposals, this work describes a practical system that combines the use of UAVs and BLE beacon to locate missing people in order to provide accurate location details to emergency services.

4 Beacon Implementation

The use of beacons creates an important advantage in the SAR operations concerning to speed and accuracy of locating missing people. In different systems the beacons have been applied in emergency situations to search people. The use of these devices involves also a disadvantage because if we want to use the system, we have to carry a device with us to allow being rescued if an emergency situation happens. We decided to use smartphones in this case because they are devices that people always carry with them.

In order to use the beacon system in the mobile platform, the solution is the use of BLE wireless technology to simulate the beacon. In Android this is possible in all devices with 5.0 and higher Android versions and a Bluetooth 4.1 compatible device. To implement the simulated beacon we use the Android BLE peripheral mode that allows us to run applications that detect the presence of other smartphones nearby with minimum battery consumption.

For the implementation we decided to use the AlteBeacon Android Beacon Library [6]. It is an open source project that allows us to detect beacons meeting the open AltBeacon standard by default, and it can be easily configured to work with the most popular beacon types like Eddystone or iBeacon formats. In the proposed system, we decide to implement the beacon using the Eddystone-URL format, a new variant of Google UriBeacon, also known as the Physical Web beacon. The main difference of the Eddystone-URL format is that it does not transmit an UID but a URL that can be automatically detected by the smartphone browser or an application and open the URL in the browser without user intervention. This system uses 17 bytes to store the URL, fact that makes the use of short URLs necessary, however this is not a problem because there are a lot of services, including one developed by Google, which allows shortened URL.

5 Proposed System

One of the main problems in emergency situations is to guarantee communication flow between all parts of the emergency team. Due to this, a one-way flow communication diagram has been used here focused on the search and rescue tasks. The proposed protocol in this work is schematically shown in the Fig. 1, where the numbers correspond to the steps described below.

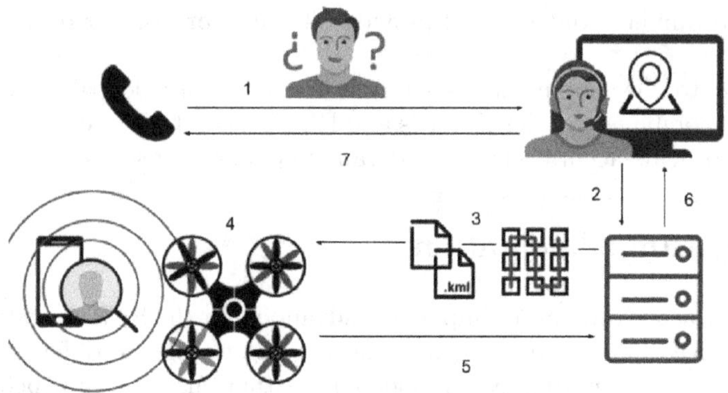

Fig. 1. Flow diagram of the emergency protocol

- **First Step:** The operator receives a call, that it is used to alert informing that a person has disappeared.
- **Second Step:** The operator launches a web application that contains a web control panel (shown in Fig. 2) to coordinate a new rescue mission. The panel contains a geographic map of the search area and a few options to configure the mission, such as for example the number of drones in flight, distance between searching points (grid), the grid size and a user list that contains a list of possible beacons related to users that were registered in the platform. The operator defines a search area on the map, which is represented with equidistant points in the plane.
- **Third Step:** When the operator completes the mission configuration, he/she clicks on a button that sends all the data to the backend server. The server gets the route and creates an optimal route (see Fig. 3) to minimize the distance between the first point and the last point, visiting previously the rest of those points. Apart of that, the server also generates a Keyhole Markup Language (KML) used to display geographic data in three-dimensional space. That file will be stored on the server (see Fig. 4) and loaded in the drone route planning system to visit all the waypoints in order.
- **Fourth and Fifth Steps:** These steps runs in parallel, being the most important ones in the emergency protocol because without them, using drones in the mission has not sense. The next step is to check the climatology conditions using the OpenWeatherMap API. If the system detects that wind (more than

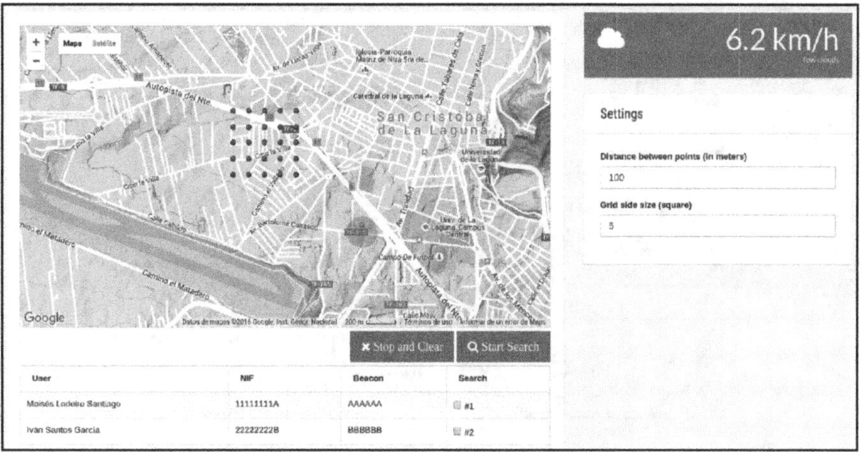

Fig. 2. Frontend control panel

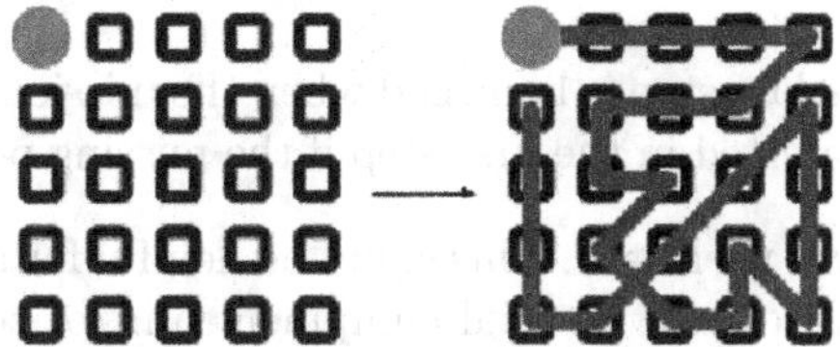

Fig. 3. Optimal drone route

10kmph) or rain can affect the flight, it shows an alert on the screen and the mission is not launched. The drone will fly over the waypoints while it tries to find a phone beacon signal (see Fig. 5). Meanwhile the drone will send the report to the server (step 5) when it arrives to each waypoint and after scanning that area. The phone beacon is constantly sending a broadcast signal in a 60 meters range using the Bluetooth Low Energy technology. This signal contains the next information:

- Physical address of the device: This data, that is a unique universal address, cannot be modified by the user.
- Web address: The smartphone broadcasts, within the beacon signal, a URL that the user can modify to include any chosen URL.

If the drone detects a beacon signal, it takes several cenital photos of the area while detecting the signal. These photos are also sent to the server (see Fig. 6). We assume that each drone has a smartphone on it with an Android application that is able to catch the signal emitted from the user mobile. The reason for using a smartphone is because it integrates a GSM/UMTS/LTE antenna, Bluetooth and GPS sensor, and people usually carry it with them.

- **Sixth step:** The server informs the operator of the web application with a refreshed map that contains the visited points, the found beacons and their GPS position.

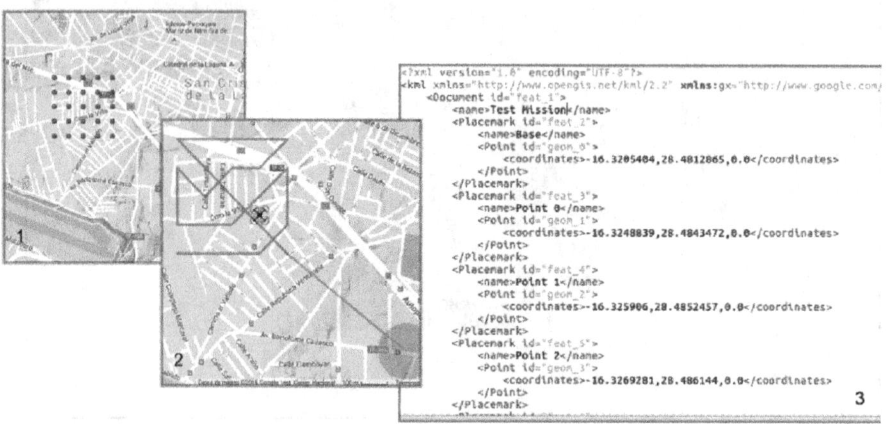

Fig. 4. Route waypoints, path and KML file

- **Seventh step:** This last step is launched when the mission ends. The operator informs the person alerted in the first step if the missing person has appeared.

The server also saves user data. This could be helpful for an emergency drone if the rescue team has to carry special equipment and/or to know how to act. This data could include personal information such as full name, address, phone number, allergies, blood type, etc.

6 Security

One of the most important aspects in this project is security. Sensitive user data managed to their protection is necessary. In particular, in the implementation of the proposal this data is stored encrypted with AES-256 CBC in the main data server. The communication between the different part of the project, like client, server and drone, is also encrypted using the same algorithm with pre-shared keys and we have to protect it as good as we can.

In this proposal, attacks have been focused on two aspects: attacks on the drones and attacks on the server.

6.1 Attacks on the Drones

- Physical attacks:
  - Net: If the drone is reached by a net (for example, a fishing net), the threads can roll up into the helices and the drone could fall to the floor. Also this technique works with any kind of clothes, for example a pair of jeans or a shirt.
  - Metallic dust: If an attacker throws any kind of metallic dust to a drone, the particles of dust can stick into the main motor bringing down the drone.

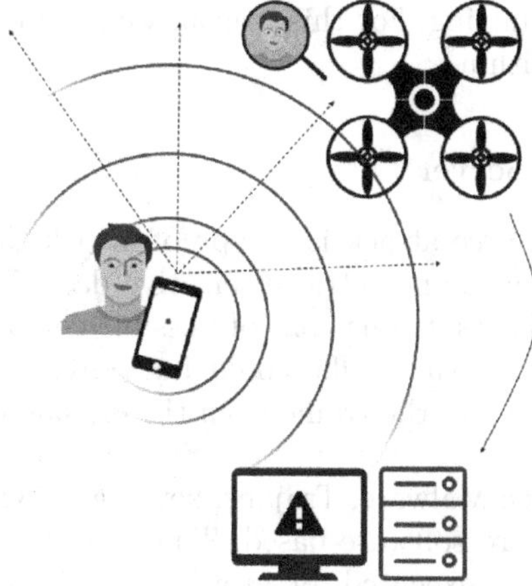

Fig. 5. Drone detecting a BLE signal from device

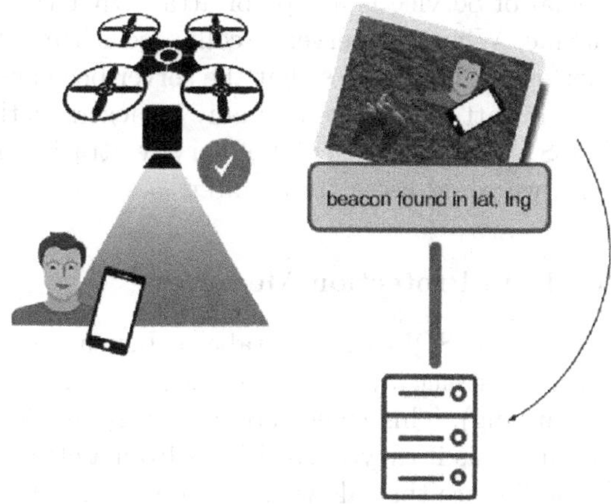

Fig. 6. Drone taking photo and sending information to server

- Electromagnetic methods:
  - Signal Jammer: A simple powerful signal jammer can nullify or create jamming into the phone signal or the phone sensors like Bluetooth, Wi-Fi, etc.
  - GPS Jamming: An attacker can send a fake GPS signal to change the drone route. This is possible when the attacker broadcasts interferences between the drone and the pilot so the drone thinks that it is in another place. Many security strategies have been proposed against jamming in wireless communications.
  - Data interception: When a drone is in flight and it emits a signal from the center of the Bluetooth or Wi-Fi sensor, the information travels through the air as a sphere (i.e. the signal is emitted in all directions). Anybody can intercept that signal using a kind of satellite dish and read the raw data

that the drone is emitting. For this reason, we need to cipher the sent data with a strong algorithm.

6.2 Attacks on the Server

- Brute force: A brute-force attack is a type of attack that is usually used to gain access to an account and retrieve sensitive data. The way to do that is by sending many packages, trying tons of possible combinations of usernames and passwords. Filtering the traffic could be a great solution to avoid this problem. Also, disabling all the traffic from the outside to the server could be useful.
- Software-based attacks: Malware, Trojans, keyloggers, virus, ramsonware, etc. All those techniques are software-based. They are normally used to control the machine where it is executed, or in a worst case, to control the drones. This could cause a sensitive data loss in our server. To face that problem, it is necessary an integrated server-protection like firewall, antivirus, etc.
- DoS/DDoS: A Denial of Service is a type of attack that tries to flood traffic on the server machine. When the server is collapsed it cannot answer all the requests from other users. This makes that the server becomes unavailable for the rest of users. If this attack is done by many attackers at the same time, it is considered a DDoS (Distributed Denial of Service attack). In order to avoid this kind of attacks, we could use a traffic filter.

6.3 Implemented Data Protection Measures

As database core we use an SQL-based database. Instead of querying over it directly, we use another abstract layer over the database motor known as ORM (Object-Relational Mapping). This layer allows a programmer to interact with the models of the database as if they were objects from a class. Also, this ORM is improved with a middleware that allows the raw stored data to be encrypted using an AES-256 CBC algorithm. With this method we avoid possible database intrusion using SQL injections, because the data will be safe. The AES-256 CBC is also the encryption system that is used in each package that the drone sends to the server, and on the BLE communication between the drone and the beacon.

7 Conclusions

This paper presents a novel and practical system to find missing people using technologies like BLE beacons and UAVs. Drones are used to scan the BLE signal that is emitted by the missing person's smartphone. In this way, the proposed system can be used to improve the SAR operations used in emergency situations because it allows the emergency team to scan an area in less time using drones instead of a human emergency squad (firemen, police, etc.) and without the need to use by part of the lost people any other device different from their smartphones. The way to coordinate all the parts that compose this proposal is by using a web platform that an operator uses to define a route before starting the mission. The data generated by the operator are processed in a backend server that traces the route to make it optimal. A beta version of the proposal has been developed using several security protocols to protect the system. As a future work, an optimized application will be developed to improve the system in order to make it more efficient in route tracing and drone interaction.

Acknowledgments. Research supported by projects RTC-2014-1648-8, TEC2014-54110-R and DIG02-INSITU.

References

1. Inoue, Y., Sashima, A., Kurumatani, K.: Indoor positioning system using beacon devices for practical pedestrian navigation on mobile phone. In: Zhang, D., Portmann, M., Tan, A.-H., Indulska, J. (eds.) UIC 2009. LNCS, vol. 5585, pp. 251–265. Springer, Heidelberg (2009)
2. Yim, J.: Introducing a decision tree-based indoor positioning technique. Expert Syst. Appl. **34**(2), 1296–1302 (2008)
3. The hitchhikers guide to ibeacon hardware: a comprehensive report by aislelabs. http://www.aislelabs.com/reports/beacon-guide/
4. ibeacon for developers. https://developer.apple.com/ibeacon/
5. Google beacons components. http://goo.gl/l6Js8p
6. Altbeacon protocol specification. https://github.com/AltBeacon/spec
7. Inertial navigation system. https://goo.gl/o7Pafi
8. Alpify. http://www.alpify.com/es/sistema-de-rescate/
9. Santos-González, I., Rivero-García, A., Caballero-Gil, P., Hernández-Goya, C.: Alternative communication system for emergency situations. WEBIST **2**, 397–402 (2014)
10. Jang, H.-C., Lien, Y.-N., Tsai, T.-C.: Rescue information system for earthquake disasters based on manet emergency communication platform. In: Proceedings of the 2009 International Conference on Wireless Communications, Mobile Computing: Connecting the World Wirelessly, pp. 623–627, ACM (2009). Observation of strains. Infect Dis Ther. 3(1), 35–43 (2011)
11. LaMarca, A., Chawathe, Y., Consolvo, S., Hightower, J., Smith, I., Scott, J., Sohn, T., Howard, J., Hughes, J., Potter, F., Tabert, J., Powledge, P.S., Borriello, G., Schilit, B.N.: Place lab: device positioning using radio beacons in the wild. In: Gellersen, H.-W., Want, R., Schmidt, A. (eds.) PERVASIVE 2005. LNCS, vol. 3468, pp. 116–133. Springer, Heidelberg (2005)
12. Dickensheets, B., Avadrone: an autonomous drone for avalanche victim recovery in Bachelor's thesis, Harvard College (2015)
13. Ezequiel, C.A.F., Cua, M., Libatique, N.C., Tangonan, G.L., Alampay, R., Labuguen, R.T., Favila, C.M., Honrado, J.L.E., Caos, V., Devaney, C., Loreto, A.B., Bacusmo, J., Palma, B.: UAV aerial imaging applications for post-disaster assessment, environmental management and infrastructure development. In: 2014 International Conference on Unmanned Aircraft Systems (ICUAS), pp. 274–283, May 2014
14. Chou, T.-Y., Yeh, M.-L., Chen, Y.-C., Chen, Y.-H.: Disaster monitoring and management by the unmanned aerial vehicle technology. Remote Sens. Spat. Inf. Sci. **38**, 137–142 (2010). cited By 8

A Network Performance Analysis of LoRa Modulation for LPWAN Sensor Devices

Carlos A. Trasviña-Moreno(✉), Rubén Blasco, Roberto Casas, and Ángel Asensio

Instituto de Investigación en Ingeniería de Aragón, Universidad de Zaragoza, Zaragoza, Spain
{trasvina, rblasco, rcasas, aasensio}@unizar.es

Abstract. The rise in low power devices has created a necessity for connectivity among systems, in some cases across great geographic lengths. Current wireless communication protocols for these devices cover only small areas or require several hops to communicate. LPWAN have surfaced to cover this necessity offering greater transmission range in energy efficient protocols. Among these can we find the LoRa technology, offering wide spread spectrum modulation for WSN. The most common implementations of LoRa work at 868 MHz frequency range, and there is few information for other frequency bands. Given the nature of this modulation, it is of great interest to analyse lower frequencies. In this article a direct comparison of LoRa in the 868 MHz and 433 MHz will be done. Additionally, several parameters will be modified to find the best configuration available. This will help validate the possibility of transmitting at longer distances than current 868 MHz implementations.

Keywords: Lora modulation · Long range communications · LPWAN · Wireless sensor networks · M2M · Low power communications · IoT

1 Introduction

A Wide Area Network (WAN) can be defined as a data communications network that covers a broad geographic area [1]. Usually these types of networks help interconnect different Local Area Networks (LAN), Metropolitan Area Networks (MAN) and other architectures. Within the WAN, a new paradigm is defined as Low-Power Wide Area Network (LPWAN) which aims to cover the necessity of long range transmissions, comparable to cellular technology, and low power wireless nodes [2] in Machine-to-Machine (M2M) communications. These LPWAN provide new possibilities for and Wireless Sensor Networks (WSN) and the Internet of Things (IoT), as its increased coverage allows for the interaction of low power devices across great geographic lengths. Yet, as no network architecture is ideal, to be able achieve these capabilities LPWAN provide lower data rates than that of standard WAN.

Among the LPWAN, there are several interesting proposals which use different transmission techniques such as ultra-narrow band modulations, for instance SigFox, Random Phase Multiple Access Direct Sequence Spread Spectrum (RPMA-DMSSS) technology used by Ingenu, or Weigthless which offers several different modulations

C.R. García et al. (Eds.): UCAmI 2016, Part II, LNCS 10070, pp. 174–181, 2016.
DOI: 10.1007/978-3-319-48799-1_21

[2–4]. Another proposal is the Long-Range (LoRa) modulation, which appears as one of the most promising technologies, offering a wide band spread-spectrum modulation with low-cost transceivers [2, 5]. In addition, it offers a high immunity to interference with a co-channel GMSK rejection of up to 20 dB. Its transmission frequency ranges from 137 MHz to 1020 MHz, granting worldwide functionality in free-band.

In WSN, application scenarios can be very diverse. It is common to find cases where devices communicate from near ground level to higher points and vice versa. Such is the case of this proposal where several slave wireless sensor nodes will be deployed near a shoreline, and will be communicating to a master node in a vantage point. Under such conditions, the theoretical calculations tend to diverge from the practical results as the deployment scenario presents a less than ideal characteristics for wireless communications.

Although there are many valid LPWAN implementations that could function for the application scenario of this proposal, the focus of this proposal will be the LoRa spread spectrum modulation. Within this modulation, several studies have been made regarding modulation at 868 MHz [6, 7], yet in other frequency bands little information can be found. The main objective of these analyses is usually to find the range limitations of LoRa modulation under given conditions. Although this is also of great interest for the application scenario, it is important to first compare with other frequency bands that could potentially increase the communication range.

With this in mind, the main objective of this article is to analyze the LoRa spectrum modulation at 433 MHz, making a direct comparison with 868 MHz under a similar scenario as the one described earlier. To demonstrate this, the current proposal is divided in various sections: hardware design, test environment & setup, test and results, discussion and conclusions. With this a full comprehension of the experimentation, as well as LoRa behavior, should be attainable granting the reader a clearer understanding of this modulation´s capabilities for IoT implementations.

2 Hardware Design

To benchmark the LoRa modulation, a RN2483 wireless module from Microchip was selected [8]. Internally, this unit integrates a PIC18LF45K22 and a SX1276 transceiver which enables the comparison between low and high frequencies [9]. Although LoRaWAN [10–12] is integrated by default in the wireless module, a custom firmware was created for this architecture with the capability of implementing a star network topology.

The wireless module was then mounted on a simple PCB, which enabled access to the module thru serial port communications. To properly configure the transceivers, there are three main configuration parameters that must be modified to achieve different transmission distance, data rate and noise immunity. These are the spreading factor, signal bandwidth and coding rate. The first two are the most significant as they influence the receiver sensitivity and the transmission data rate, albeit in different degree. The spreading factor parameter helps increase significantly the sensitivity of the receptor at the cost of bitrate. The higher the spreading factor, the further the transmissions and the lower the bitrate. Contrary to this, increasing the bandwidth allows for a higher data rate but slightly deters the sensibility of the receiver. Yet, as the theory explains, decreasing the bandwidth also increases the error in a channel [13]. Lastly, the coding rate grants different levels of redundancy to the transmission, helping improve immunity to noise of the signal. This parameter should be modified depending on the environment of the deployment, as increasing the coding rate will increase the transmission time due to additional overhead.

3 Test Environment and Setup

As the main objective of this study is to compare the LoRa modulation at 433 MHz and 868 MHz, and not the longest possible transmission range attainable, two sites where selected with a moderate distance between them. The objective is to have a separation between transmitter and receiver, which by theoretical calculations should be able to communication at both frequencies.

Even though the final deployment scenario of the nodes is to be at a shoreline, for practicality reasons it was thought better to test in a different scenario that maintained a similarity in height difference between the devices. Also, for the experimentation an environment with a direct line-of-sight was sought out, which is another of the key features of the deployment scenario.

All of the tests were done at the outskirts of Zaragoza, Spain. The receiver was located at ground level in coordinates 41.592466, −0.948032, and the transmitter was set at an elevated point in coordinates 41.530340, −0.954572. The separation between these two points is of approximately 7 km and the elevation differences is of roughly 300 m (Fig. 1).

In both cases, the modules where configured thru a serial port connection, which also served as a monitor for transmitted and received data. For the trials, a series of transmissions of sequential data and unique identifiers where sent in a systematic manner. This not only allowed verifying the reception of the data, but also viewing the Received Signal Strength Indicator (RSSI) of each package and the integrity of said transmissions.

4 Test and Results

Given that the LoRa is based on frequency spectrum modulation, one of the most defining of the three configuration parameters is the spreading factor. Thus several trials where made where the spreading factor was tested at different configurations. Additionally as the bandwidth also incurs in the sensitivity of the receiver, this parameter was modulated across the extent of its range. The coding rate was kept at its highest configuration value to minimize radio interference and to have a clearer understanding of the impact of the other parameters. For all the trials the RSSI, the successfully received packets, packets with errors, Packet Error Rate (PER) and Packet Error Loss Rate (PELR) was extracted, giving a better understanding of the channel activity. From here on, the different spreading factors will be referred to as SF12 (4096 chips/symbol), SF10 (1024 chips/symbol) and SF8 (256 chips/symbol).

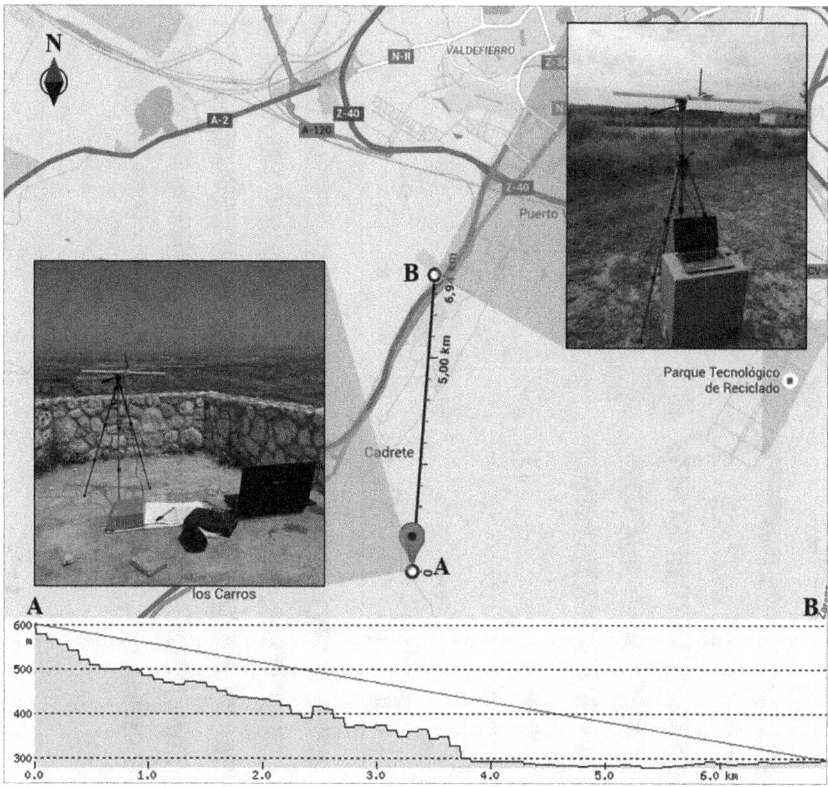

Fig. 1. Distance between both test points and its topographic profile. Point A represents the transmitter station at a vantage point and point B the receiver station at ground level.

In Fig. 2 and Tables 1–3 the different trials and comparison among the results for 433 MHz and 868 MHz can be viewed. A fourth experimentation was also done, with a spreading factor of 64 chips/symbol, yet the results were a complete packet loss in the grand majority of the trials in both frequencies, thus they are not shown due to the lack of comparability.

With the information provided by the experimentation, it can be noticed that at 433 MHz the RSSI is greater than that of 868 MHz, with the exception of the scenarios with complete packet loss, across the full extent of the experimentation. As the spreading factor is decreased, the average RSSI also diminishes. Additionally in the trials in which the bandwidth was lowest, the interference in the channel was very elevated causing an increase in the PER and PELR factors. In some cases, a complete packet loss was detected.

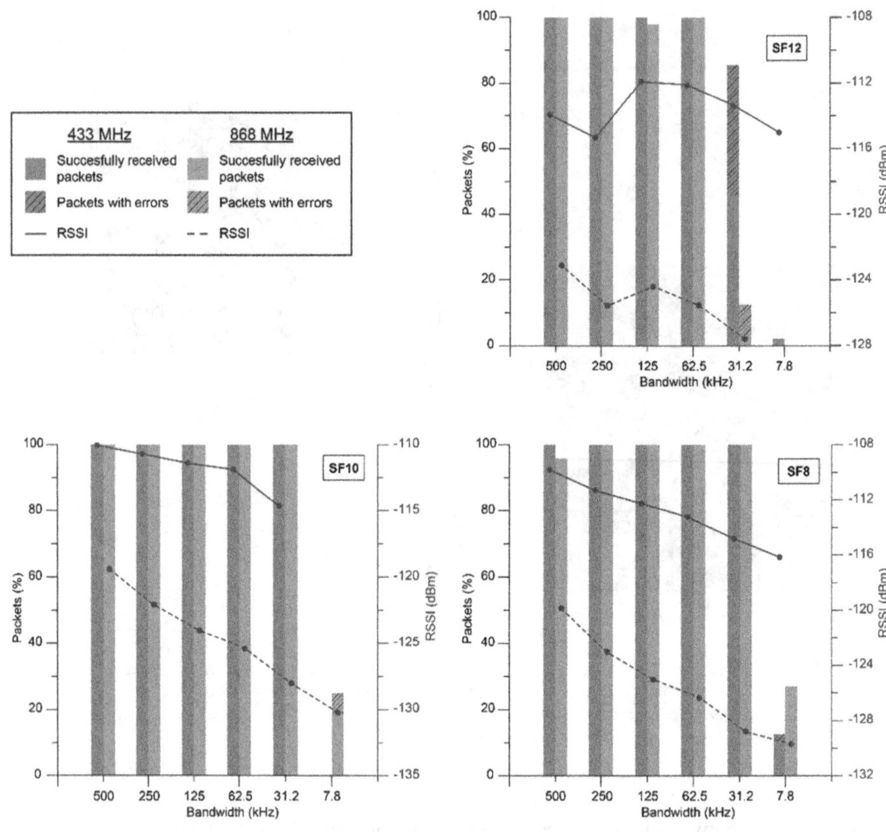

Fig. 2. Graphics for the different SF depicting the successfully received packets, packets with errors and the average RSSI per trial. Cases where there were complete packet loss show no RSSI.

Table 1. PER and PELR percentages for SF12 modulation.

BW (kHz)	Frequency (MHz)	RSSI	Received packages %	PER %	PELR %
500	433	−113,95	100,00 %	0,00 %	0,00 %
250	433	−115,34	100,00 %	0,00 %	0,00 %
125	433	−111,91	100,00 %	0,00 %	0,00 %
62,5	433	−112,10	100,00 %	0,00 %	0,00 %
31,2	433	−113,36	85,42 %	46,34 %	14,58 %
7,8	433	−115,00	2,08 %	0,00 %	97,92 %
500	868	−123,12	100,00 %	0,00 %	0,00 %
250	868	−125,58	100,00 %	0,00 %	0,00 %
125	868	−124,40	97,92 %	0,00 %	2,08 %
62,5	868	−125,54	100,00 %	0,00 %	0,00 %
31,2	868	−127,59	12,50 %	83,33 %	87,50 %
7,8	868	0,00	0,00 %	0,00 %	100,00 %

Table 2. PER and PELR percentages for SF10 modulation.

BW (kHz)	Frequency (MHz)	RSSI	Received packages %	PER %	PELR %
500	433	−110,06	100,00 %	0,00 %	0,00 %
250	433	−110,70	100,00 %	0,00 %	0,00 %
125	433	−111,39	100,00 %	0,00 %	0,00 %
62,5	433	−111,87	100,00 %	0,00 %	0,00 %
31,2	433	−114,63	100,00 %	0,00 %	0,00 %
7,8	433	0	0,00 %	0,00 %	100,00 %
500	868	−119,41	100,00 %	0,00 %	0,00 %
250	868	−122,1	100,00 %	0,00 %	0,00 %
125	868	−124,04	100,00 %	0,00 %	0,00 %
62,5	868	−125,39	100,00 %	0,00 %	0,00 %
31,2	868	−128,04	100,00 %	0,00 %	0,00 %
7,8	868	−130,25	25,00 %	25,00 %	75,00 %

Table 3. PER and PELR percentages for SF8 modulation.

BW (kHz)	Frequency (MHz)	RSSI	Received packages %	PER %	PELR %
500	433	−109,81	100,00 %	0,00 %	0,00 %
250	433	−111,31	100,00 %	0,00 %	0,00 %
125	433	−112,25	100,00 %	0,00 %	0,00 %
62,5	433	−113,25	100,00 %	0,00 %	0,00 %
31,2	433	−114,81	100,00 %	0,00 %	0,00 %
7,8	433	−116,16	12,50 %	16,67 %	87,50 %
500	868	−119,84	95,83 %	0,00 %	4,17 %
250	868	−123,06	100,00 %	0,00 %	0,00 %
125	868	−125,02	100,00 %	0,00 %	0,00 %
62,5	868	−126,31	100,00 %	0,00 %	0,00 %
31,2	868	−128,81	100,00 %	0,00 %	0,00 %
7,8	868	−129,69	27,08 %	0,00 %	72,92 %

5 Discussion

With the results shown in the previous section, several conclusions can be extracted. As seen in Fig. 2, by decreasing the operating frequency of the transceivers it is possible to achieve a greater sensitivity which, ideally, can be translated to data being transmitted over greater distances. Increasing the spreading factor helps achieve this goal, yet with the experimental results we can see that at SF12 greater error and packet loss percentage are displayed in lower bandwidths. It is in fact the SF10 configuration that has the best average RSSI of all with a low packet error/loss percentage.

In Tables 1–3 it is possible to see that at lower bandwidths there is an increased PER and PELR percentage. Not only is there a noticeable packet loss, but also the majority of the packets received present data corruption, which increased the PER. In this case, data corruption was recognized if the sequential string was not the one expected or if the unique identifiers were not present.

From the theory, it is possible to assume that by lowering the signal bandwidth it is conceivable to achieve a better, or at least the same, results as in higher bandwidths. Yet seeing as how a narrower bandwidth also incurs in channel noise, it was not possible to achieve a better result mainly because of the selected environment. Due to the nature of the physical location of the receiver end, it is possible that a certain degree of signal cancelling was afflicting the trials, either by the environment or by other variables. Ideally both the transmitter and receiver should be located at elevated points where Fresnel conditions are met [7]. Such a setup would greatly improve the outcome of the trials and, possibly, would have granted a better outcome with a SF of 64 chip/symbol.

Although 433 MHz presented a better response in the majority of the trials, there is one which stands out due to its poor results. In trial 6 of Table 2a complete packet loss is presented in 433 MHz, whilst in 868 MHz some data was still received. This could have been a due to a high occupancy of the channel at the time of the trial. This is one of the major issues of working in free-band frequencies, as it can present an elevated channel traffic which may impact the signal transmission. If a LoRa network is desired to be deployed and it does not have time or energy constraints, it is recommended that the highest CR is selected as it will grant the highest interference immunity. Ideally the selected environment should be analyzed for radio traffic so as to select the appropriate CR and reduce the on-air time of the data.

6 Conclusions

As seen in the tests, with a SF of 1024 chips/symbol it is possible to achieve some of the highest RSSI value. This configuration allows for a high sensitivity in the receiver, thus increasing the feasible transmission range. Although if the distance between the two transceivers is moderate, such as the one presented in this paper, a SF of 256 chips/symbol is also a viable configuration.

For both SF's the modulation of the bandwidth only slightly deterred the RSSI. Thus, it is best to use the 125 kHz configuration as it presents the best balance between receiver sensitivity and data rate. For scenarios where greater channel immunity or an increased data rate is required, due to energy or time constraints, it is recommendable to use a higher bandwidth.

Utilizing the 433 MHz frequency allows for an increased RSSI over the standard 868 MHz and a reliable signal channel. Having a greater sensitivity in the receiver also implies that a greater transmission distance could be achievable from those attained with 868 MHz. The usage of 433 MHz offers the possibility of creating a multi-purpose and multi-region enabled IoT network that may cover wide geographic areas with a just a few nodes.

Future Work. Given the results shown in this proposal, further tests were also done with the 433 MHz frequency band to test the transmission range. These measurements, in conjunction with node energy consumption and data-to-energy metrics, are to be compiled to be presented to the scientific community. Additionally, the deployment of the WSN at the shoreline application scenario, with its corresponding results, are also to be reported to the public.

Acknowledgments. Trasviña-Moreno would like to thank the Consejo Nacional de Ciencia y Tecnología (CONACYT) of México for providing the scholarship for his Ph.D. In addition, the authors would like to acknowledge the Centro de Investigación Científica de Educación Superior de Ensenada of México for project Sistema Multipropósito para Monitoreo del Medio Ambiente, and the Ministerio de Economía y Competitividad of Spain for projects Memory Lane (ref. TIN2013-45312-R) and Movilidad Verde Inteligente (ref. RTC-2014-2425-4) which this proposal is part of.

References

1. Internetworking technology handbook – DocWiki. http://docwiki.cisco.com/wiki/Internetworking_Technology_Handbook#WAN_Technologies
2. Sanchez-Iborra, R., Cano, M.-D.: State of the art in LP-WAN solutions for industrial IoT services. Sensors **16**, 708 (2016)
3. Margelis, G., Piechocki, R., Kaleshi, D., Thomas, P.: Low throughput networks for the IoT: lessons learned from industrial implementations. In: Proceedings of IEEE World Forum Internet Things, WF-IoT 2015, pp. 181–186 (2016)
4. Andreadou, N., Guardiola, M., Fulli, G.: Telecommunication technologies for smart grid projects with focus on smart metering applications. Energies **9**, 375 (2016)
5. Centenaro, M., Vangelista, L., Zanella, A., Zorzi, M.: Long-range communications in unlicensed bands: the rising stars in the IoT and smart city scenarios. IEEE Wirel. Commun. 17 (2015, Forthcoming)
6. Petäjäjärvi, J., Mikhaylov, K., Roivainen, A., Hänninen, T., Pettissalo, M.: On the coverage of LPWANs: range evaluation and channel attenuation model for LoRa technology. In: 2015 14th International Conference on ITS Telecommunication (ITST), pp. 55–59 (2015)
7. Aref, M., Sikora, A.: Free space range measurements with Semtech LoRa technology. In: 2014 2nd International Symposium on Wireless Systems within the Conferences on Intelligent Data Acquisition and Advanced Computing Systems, IDAACS-SWS 2014, pp. 19–23 (2014)
8. RN2483 - Wireless modules. http://www.microchip.com/wwwproducts/en/RN2483
9. SX1276 137 MHz to 1020 MHz low power long range transceiver|vsemtech. http://www.semtech.com/wireless-rf/rf-transceivers/sx1276/
10. Vazquez-gallego, F., Member, S.: Goodbye, ALOHA! pp. 2029–2044 (2016)
11. Stočes, M., Vaněk, J., Masner, J., Pavlík, J., Things, I., Agriculture, P., Agriculture, S.: Agris on-line papers in economics and informatics internet of things (IoT) in agriculture - selected aspects, vol. VIII, pp. 83–89 (2016)
12. Pham, C.: Deploying a pool of long-range wireless image sensor with shared activity time. In: 2015 IEEE 11th International Conference on Wireless & Mobile Networks Communication, WiMob 2015, pp. 667–674 (2015)
13. Semtech: LoRa™ modulation basics, pp. 1–26 (2015)

Electromagnetic Multi-frequency Model and Differential Measuring in Remote Sensing Applications

Francisco Javier Ferrández-Pastor(✉), Juan Manuel García-Chamizo, and Mario Nieto-Hidalgo

Department of Computing Technology, University of Alicante, P.O. Box 90, 03080 Alicante, Spain
{fjferran,juanma,mnieto}@dtic.ua.es

Abstract. The interaction between electromagnetic waves and matter has led to the development of applications to detect and characterise them. The conventional systems use the emission, transmission and reception of waves at a specific frequency range to detect medium parameters (constant dielectric, permittivity, conductivity or permeability) of an analysed area. The interaction between the electromagnetic wave and the analysed medium depends on the range of frequency used. This phenomenon is used in different disciplines and working environments, geoscience or medical disciplines are examples where the use of electromagnetic waves provides non-intrusive applications with clear benefits. Each frequency of signal transmitted and received is analysed to determine the interaction produced in absolute measurements. In this work a method based in differential measurement technique is proposed as a novel way of detecting and characterizing electromagnetic matter characteristics. The theoretical results show that it is possible to obtain benefits from the behaviour of the wave-medium interaction using differential measurement on reception of electromagnetic waves at different frequencies. Differential measures introduce advantages in detection processes and increase development possibilities of new non-intrusive applications.

Keywords: Dispersive media · Non-intrusive applications · Remote sensing · Multifrequency treatment

1 Introduction

The electromagnetic wave, throughout its emission-propagation-reception, interacts with the medium. The results of this interaction may be interpreted in the receiver and depend both on the parameters which characterise the signal (frequency, amplitude, polarisation) and those which define the medium through which it passes (permittivity, conductivity, permeability, etc.) [6]. In general, the frequency ranges of the applications are confined to those values which indicate the required mechanisms for study of the medium. Different disciplines

C.R. García et al. (Eds.): UCAmI 2016, Part II, LNCS 10070, pp. 182–192, 2016.
DOI: 10.1007/978-3-319-48799-1_22

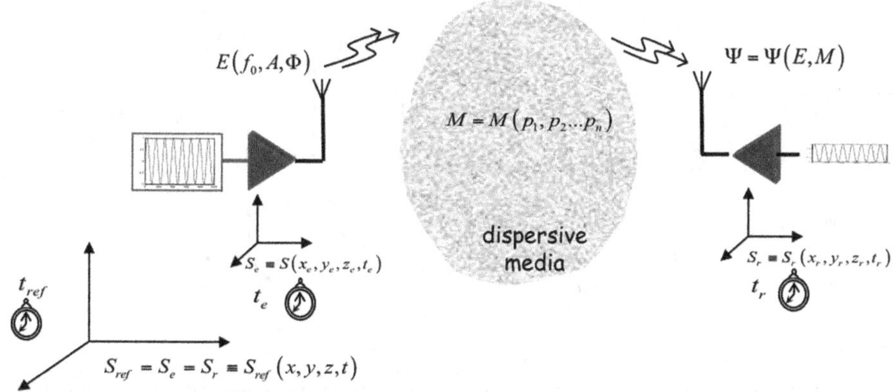

Fig. 1. Conventional treatment of the electromagnetic wave. Applications need to synchronise and/or calibrate the reference systems (time-space)

propose non-intrusive solutions that use remote sensing and detection of some element or characteristic which it is present in the analysed medium. This paper makes an approach to this phenomena and it intends to use it to characterize the medium. This paper is organized as follows: Sect. 2 reviews related works (electromagnetic waves and its interaction with the medium). Section 3 proposes a new method which uses multi-frequency waves. In Sect. 4, experiments including software simulation in biological medium are analysed and discussed to assess suitability of this method. Finally, Sect. 5 provides a discussion and conclusions.

2 Related Work

Speed, attenuation and phase of a electromagnetic wave in a transmission depends on the wave frequency and the electric and magnetic attributes of the medium crossed. This process is exploited in different disciplines in remote sensing and detection applications. In geoscience domain ground penetration radar [1] is an example, the composition and detection of materials in the first layers of soil are detected analysing its permittivity (ϵ). Permittivity in this work area depends on frequency [13] and this parameter characterise the analysed medium. Tests at different frequencies follow a procedure in which the emission, reception and subsequent analysis is carried out in an individual form for each of the frequencies used. As a working method effective permittivity of the material (ϵ_{eff}) is determined using the time of arrival (t_{arr}) of the electromagnetic wave in its reflection with the various layers which make up the subsoil. The arrival time of the signal depends on the frequency range (f) and the type of material represented by its permittivity in functional relations of the type $t_{arr} = t(f, \epsilon_{eff})$. In other domain as meteorological radars the conditions of the environment differ from the previous case, the composition and variation in time of the medium are two aspects to analyse. One of the applications of the meteorological radars is the

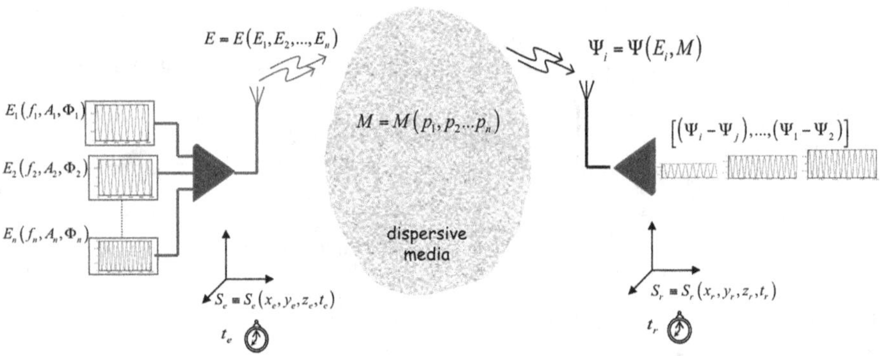

Fig. 2. Multifrequency treatment method. The differential measures in the receiver incorporate information which enables the devices to be calibrated and/or synchronised. As a result the management of the time-space reference system of the application is simplified.

measurement of rainfall. In this case the method used is based on measurement of the amount of energy reflected in the rain drops. Here the type of medium analysed is known (water) the goal is to determine its volumetric density and its size in the form of a drop [7]. Here also the frequency used is one of the main parameters to be taken into account. For this case there is a relation between the energy received by the radar echo, working frequency and the rate of rainfall to be estimated in relation to the type [8]. Weather radar [9], ionosphere [4] and atmosphere [12] use electromagnetic signals to monitor and detecting different components or conditions. Biological effects of electromagnetic waves are critical for understanding potential health and safety risks in order to set safe standards and developing and utilizing medical applications and therapies [5]. Biological medium has a large number of works [2,3,14] that use electromagnetic waves in different frequency ranges and applications.

3 Multifrequency Model

Conventional treatment of the electromagnetic wave (see Fig. 1) uses reference systems (normally positional and temporal ref $S_{ref} = S_e = S_r$) which are calibrated and/or synchronised as a preliminary step to establish the transmission to use in a specific application. Thus in GPS positioning systems, the position of the satellites and the synchronisation of the clocks is a necessary condition for addressing the task of determining the position of the receiver devices. In the case of radar in which the transmitter and receiver are not situated on the same device something similar occurs. In any case the referenced systems of all the devices should be related in order to enable the establishment of those initial values (time-distance) which the receiver should know in order to analyse the information received. Once the necessary relation has been established between the referenced systems a working frequency is used as magnitude which permits

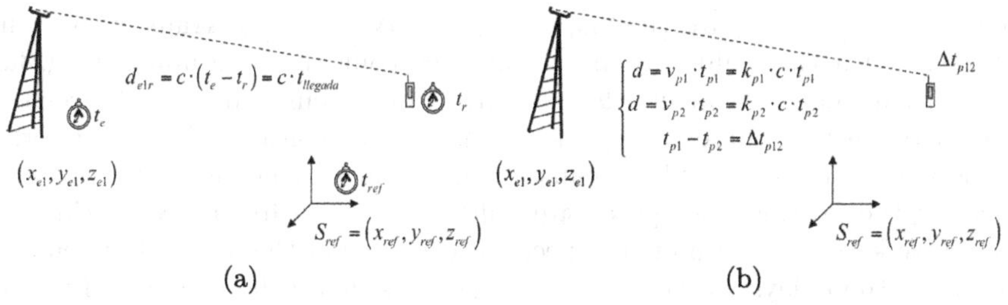

Fig. 3. Conventional and differential multi-frequency method to calculate distance between emitter and receiver devices. In (a) conventional method: arrival time measured and emitter-receiver synchronisation are necessary. In (b) the speed of propagation depends on the frequency (dispersive medium). The distance is calculated with equations based in differential time arrived: time synchronisation is not necessary. Time differences are measured

identification of the information in the receiver. Calibration or synchronisation of the system should be managed and maintained at all times.

The creation and maintenance of all these references has a cost which must be assumed when they are implemented. Electromagnetic wave emitted (E) is characterised by its frequency (f_0), Amplitude (A) and Polarisation (Φ). Signal received is a variable (Ψ) that depends of signal emitted (E) and the medium, expressed by its parameters ($M = M(p_1, \ldots, p_n)$). The variable analysed in receptor is $\Psi = \Psi(E, M)$ (see Fig. 1).

In contrast to the conventional signal model where a specific carrier frequency (f_0) and common time base is used, a multi-frequency differential model is proposed (see Fig. 2). The magnitudes measured in the receiver (arrival time, signal amplitude, etc.) are relative. This fact permits us to work with independent temporal references of the basis of common time and, in some scenarios, enables the application of solutions with independent positional reference systems.

In the differential multi-frequency model if the wave-medium interaction depends on the frequency and the medium, different frequencies will produce to different measures in the receiver for the same medium and for the same radio electric link. The working hypothesis uses these differences, measured in the receiver, to estimate the parameters of medium analysed. As has been mentioned this type of treatment of the signal introduces a series of operating advantages over the conventional treatment: it achieves some independence from the needs of the positional and temporal reference systems. Treatment with different frequencies take advantage from information obtained on the interaction with each frequency, useful in the systems where the medium is parametrised. In addition the fact of measuring difference would compensate undesirable interference such as common interference or noises to all working frequencies.

A establishing distances would measure time arrival on the receiver. If the system comprises various transmitters and receivers it would be necessary to maintain in all these the same temporal reference in order to be able to estimate the time of arrival in this way. Synchronisation between transmitter and receiver allows to measure the elapsed time between signal transmission and reception. With that information the distance could be determined (Fig. 3a). In multi-frequency treatment, the reference time is embedded in the relative delays between the different frequency signals. If we consider that the interaction between wave and medium causes delays and it depends on the working frequency, the propagation speeds are different for each frequency. In this scenario, if we know the ratio of the speed for each one of them, it will be enough to measure the delays in the receiver Δt_{p12} to estimate the distance (Fig. 3b). The equation system 2 is used to determine distance in this example. The wave propagation speed for frequency f_i is $v_{pi} = k_{pi} \cdot c$ known in the medium treated. A system of three unknown variables referred to distance (d) and time of arrival for two frequencies is used (t_{p1} *and* t_{p2}). The multi-frequency method is complementary to the application shown. In the case that the distance d between the transmitter and the receiver is known, the speeds of propagation can estimate the parameters of the medium (k_{pi}) through wave-medium interaction (equation system 1, included in Table 1). This case could be employed in applications where an unknown medium should be determined (biological components or geoscience medium are examples of potential applications).

$$\begin{cases} d = v_{p1} \cdot t_{p1} = k_{p1} \cdot c \cdot t_{p1} \\ d = v_{p2} \cdot t_{p2} = k_{p2} \cdot c \cdot t_{p2} \\ \Delta t_{p12} = t_{p1} - t_{p2} \end{cases} \tag{2}$$

Table 1. General equation system in media sensing applications to calculate medium parameters in multi-frequency method

Medium is represented by m parameters in $M = M(p_1, ..., p_m)$ functions

If Ψ is a measurable variable (speed propagation, time of arrival, amplitude of arrival) which represents the interaction: wave (E) - medium (M), and the medium M is function of $(p_1, ..., p_m)$ parameters $\Rightarrow \Psi = \Psi(E, M)$.
Then, if differences $(\Psi_i - \Psi_j)$ are measured in receiver, different equations can be combined to calculate media parameters $p_1, ..., p_m$:
$\Psi_i - \Psi_j = \Delta_{\Psi ij} = \Psi_i(E_i, p_1, ..., p_n) - \Psi_i(E_j, p_1, ..., p_m)$
$(p_1, ..., p_m) \rightarrow$ are the medium parameters
E_i and E_j $\rightarrow$ are waves at frequencies i and j
$\Delta_{\Psi ij} \rightarrow$ are de differential measure obtained in receiver
For $n+1$ frequencies there are n differential measures $\Delta_{\Psi ij}$ in receiver device:

$$\begin{cases} \Delta_{\Psi 12} = \Psi_1(E_1, p_1, ..., p_m) - \Psi_2(E_2, p_2, ..., p_m) \\ \Delta_{\Psi 23} = \Psi_2(E_2, p_1, ..., p_m) - \Psi_3(E_3, p_2, ..., p_n) \\ \cdots\cdots\cdots\cdots\cdots\cdots\cdots\cdots\cdots\cdots\cdots\cdots \\ \Delta_{\Psi(n)(n+1)} = \Psi_n(E_n, p_1, ..., p_m) - \Psi_{n+1}(E_{n+1}, p_2, ..., p_m) \end{cases} \tag{1}$$

The multi-frequency differential method proposed measure time differences between electromagnetic waves at different frequencies. These measures can be used in two kinds of application:

- Knowing the wave-medium interaction the distance of the link can be estimated.
- Knowing the distance emitter-receiver it is possible to estimate the medium using multi-frequency wave-medium interaction with differential measures.

The work, in this paper, examines the potential applications. The reference system is simplified with the possibility of using independent time references. This paper proposes this method to develop applications in remote sensing disciplines: detection in biological, ground, atmospheric and any dispersive medium.

4 Simulation of Wave Propagation in Frequency-Dependent Medium

The multi-frequency method depends on the medium in which it is used. As an example of its applicability a frequency-dependent medium is analysed to determine its conductivity and permittivity (dielectric constant). These mediums are dispersive media and correspond to environments in which parameters as dielectric constant, permittivity or conductivity become dependent on the frequency. As a result, mechanisms such as speed of propagation or reduction of the signal (abortion) depends on said value. Transmission of electromagnetic pulse in different materials are simulated using the numerical method Finite-Difference Time-Domain FDTD [11], by means of which the computational algorithms resolve the Maxwell equations in the time and the space. The FDTD formulation is a direct solution of Maxwell's time-dependent curl equations. In an isotropic medium, Maxwell's equations can be written as

$$\begin{aligned}\boldsymbol{\nabla} \times \boldsymbol{E} &= -\mu \frac{\partial \boldsymbol{H}}{\partial t} \\ \boldsymbol{\nabla} \times \boldsymbol{H} &= \sigma \boldsymbol{E} + \epsilon \frac{\partial \boldsymbol{E}}{\partial t}\end{aligned} \tag{3}$$

The medium is represented in Eq. 3 by its dielectric permittivity (ϵ), conductivity (ρ) and permeability (μ). This parameters represent the interaction of electric (E) and magnetic (H) fields. Using Finite Difference Algorithm electric and magnetic fields can be analysed in space-time domain. A simple 1D implementation of the Yee 1-D FDTD algorithm [15] using the MATLAB programming language. The fields E_x and H_y are simulated along the line $X = Y = 0$ and propagation along the z axis. Animations using MATLAB are produced to measure differences between electromagnetic waves when arrive to receiver, Fig. 4. In Yee algorithm the first order electric E and magnetic H equations are coupled via interlinked time and space grids. Because the underlying implementation of the Yee algorithm mimics the principle of a time varying electric field producing a time varying magnetic field and vice versa, solutions of more general class of problems can be handled robustly.

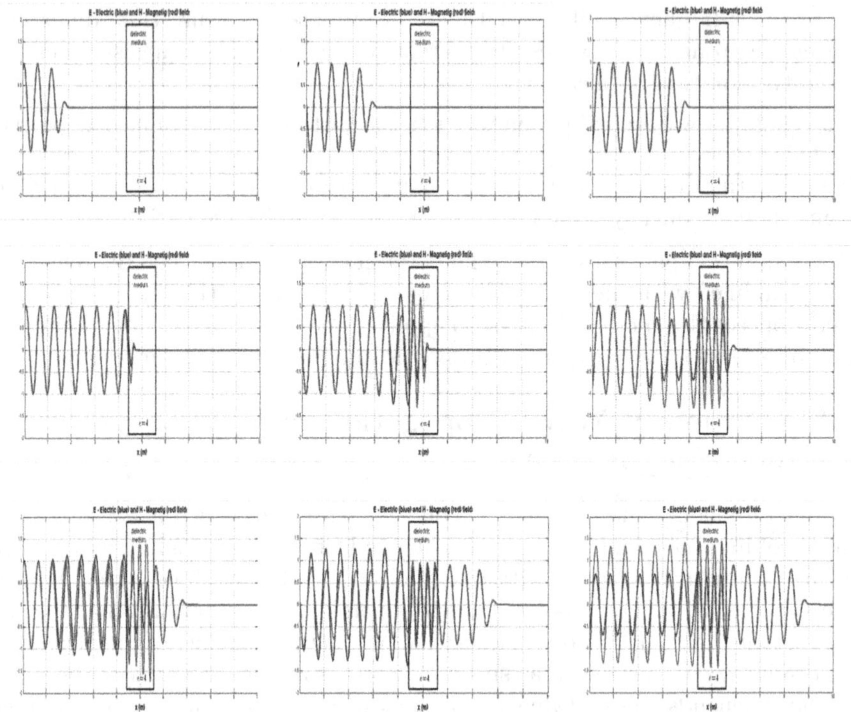

Fig. 4. Transmission and reflection of electromagnetic wave in dielectric medium

4.1 Dielectric Medium. Determining Dielectric Permittivity ϵ

Figure 5 shows the numeric simulation results of two waves transmission on a medium that has different dielectric constant (ϵ). It is assumed a medium with unknown dielectric permittivity (ϵ_r) which is constant in a range of frequencies $[\omega_m, \omega_n]$ and transparent in other ($\epsilon = 1$). In this simple case two frequencies are used to measure the time arrival differences (Δt_{12}) using an FDTD analysis. An equation system to calculate ϵ is proposed. Medium and wave speed are related by Eq. 4.

The results to different ϵ are shown in equation system (6) and Table 3.

$$\epsilon(\omega) = \epsilon_r \epsilon_0 \quad \epsilon = cte. \quad in \ \ \omega_m < \omega < \omega_n$$
$$v_p = \frac{1}{\sqrt{\mu\epsilon(\omega)}} \tag{4}$$

4.2 Dispersive Medium. Determining Dielectric Permittivity ϵ and Conductivity σ

Polymers, biopolymers, colloid systems (emulsions and microemulsions), biological cells, porous materials, and liquid crystals can all be considered as

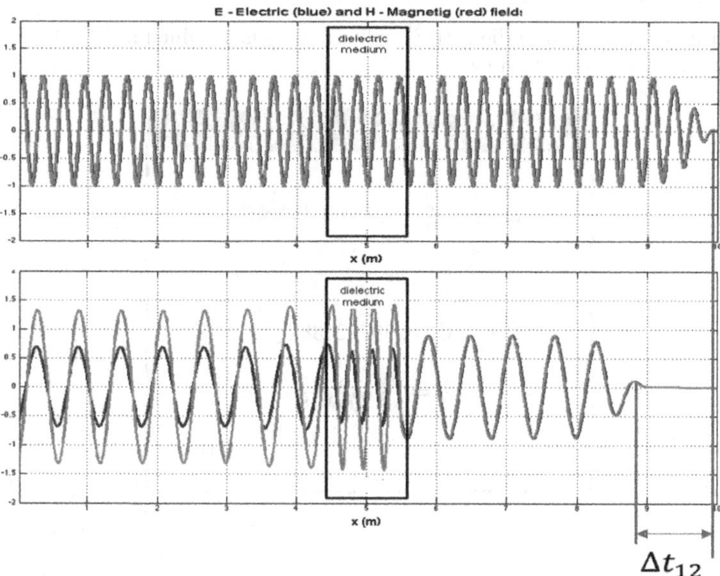

Fig. 5. Simulation of a wave propagation in free space crossing dielectric medium. Δt_{12} is the time difference of arrival between two waves at different speed propagation on constant dielectric medium $\epsilon = 1$ and $\epsilon = 4$

complex and dispersive systems. Dielectric polarization in static and time dependent fields, and the Dielectric Spectroscopy technique are used to characterise this materials. Dispersive medium can be identified with different models. In this case, It is assumed a Debye medium with de model shown in Eq. 6, where the conductivity (σ) and the susceptibility (χ) introduce frequency dependent interactions. Simulation in FDTD shows these interactions, difference in time of arrival and signal amplitude can be measured in the receiver. In Eq. 6 Debye medium model, propagation speed and attenuation frequency dependants for this model are shown [10] (Table 2).

$$\begin{gathered}\epsilon(\omega) = \epsilon_r + \frac{\sigma}{j\omega\epsilon_0} + \frac{\chi}{1+j\omega t_0} \\ \alpha = \omega\sqrt{\frac{\mu\epsilon}{2}\left[\sqrt{1+\left(\frac{\sigma}{\omega\epsilon}\right)^2} - 1\right]} \\ v_p = \frac{1}{\sqrt{\frac{\mu\epsilon}{2}\left[\sqrt{1+\left(\frac{\sigma}{\omega\epsilon}\right)^2}+1\right]}}\end{gathered} \tag{6}$$

where α represents the attenuation, v_p is the wave velocity, μ is the permeability, ρ is the conductivity, ω represents the wave frequency and χ the susceptibility. In this simulation differential amplitude ($\Delta\alpha_{ij}$) and time of arrival differences (Δt_{ij}) are measured in receiver. It is assumed that permittivity ϵ

Table 2. Equation system in dielectric medium. Δt_{12} is obtained in FDTD simulation. ϵ is calculated in this equation system

Medium is represented by ϵ

$$\Delta t_{12} = \frac{e}{t_1} - \frac{e}{t_2} = 0.333x10^{-8}$$

$$e = 1$$

$$10 = 299792458.t_1$$

$$\frac{1}{t_2} = \frac{1}{\sqrt{299792458\epsilon_r}} \tag{5}$$

Table 3. Dielectric permittivity calculated

Dielectric constant ϵ_r	
Determinated in system equation	Simulated in FDTD analysis
1.99	2
3.9	4
4.9	5

Table 4. Equation system in dispersive medium. $\Delta\alpha_{ij}$ and Δv_{pij} are obtained in FDTD simulation. ϵ is calculated in this equation system

Medium represented by ϵ and σ parameters

$$\begin{gathered}
\Delta\alpha_{12} = \omega_1\sqrt{\frac{\mu\epsilon}{2}\left[\sqrt{1+\left(\frac{\sigma}{\omega_1\epsilon}\right)^2}-1\right]} - \omega_2\sqrt{\frac{\mu\epsilon}{2}\left[\sqrt{1+\left(\frac{\sigma}{\omega_2\epsilon}\right)^2}-1\right]} \\
\Delta\alpha_{13} = \omega_1\sqrt{\frac{\mu\epsilon}{2}\left[\sqrt{1+\left(\frac{\sigma}{\omega_1\epsilon}\right)^2}-1\right]} - \omega_2\sqrt{\frac{\mu\epsilon}{2}\left[\sqrt{1+\left(\frac{\sigma}{\omega_3\epsilon}\right)^2}-1\right]} \\
\Delta v_{p12} = \frac{1}{\sqrt{\frac{\mu\epsilon}{2}\left[\sqrt{1+\left(\frac{\sigma}{\omega_1\epsilon}\right)^2}+1\right]}} - \frac{1}{\sqrt{\frac{\mu\epsilon}{2}\left[\sqrt{1+\left(\frac{\sigma}{\omega_3\epsilon}\right)^2}+1\right]}} \\
\Delta v_{p13} = \frac{1}{\sqrt{\frac{\mu\epsilon}{2}\left[\sqrt{1+\left(\frac{\sigma}{\omega_1\epsilon}\right)^2}+1\right]}} - \frac{1}{\sqrt{\frac{\mu\epsilon}{2}\left[\sqrt{1+\left(\frac{\sigma}{\omega_3\epsilon}\right)^2}+1\right]}}
\end{gathered} \tag{7}$$

and conductivity σ are constant in the range of frequencies analysed. Permittivity and conductivity produce different interaction wave-medium in different frequencies. The results to different ϵ and σ are shown in equation system 7 and Tables 4 and 5.

Table 5. Dielectric permittivity and conductivity calculated

Dielectric constant ϵ	
Calculated in system equation	Simulated in FDTD analysis
3.999	4
2.9	2
Conductivity σ	
Calculated in system equation	Simulated in FDTD analysis
0.011	0.01
0.019	0.03
0.049	0.05

5 Conclusions

The interaction between the electromagnetic wave and the medium depends strongly on the frequency range. This phenomenon is used in different disciplines and working environments. With this background a multi-frequency model has been presented based on the differential measurement in the reception of signals at different frequencies. The potentiality of the model formulated and its integration have been simulated in FDTD domain and equation systems resolution. The equation systems proposed in each case study depends on the type of differential measurement used (amplitude, speed) and on the model which characterises the analysed medium (dielectric constant, conductivity, etc.). The theoretical results obtained show that it is possible to obtain benefits from the behaviour of the wave-medium interaction by means of a differential measurement carried out in links to different frequencies. The relative measurement between two signals introduces advantages in relation to the absolute measurement of a signal. In the differential measurement, one of the signals could be used as a reference and therefore the need to synchronise the transmitter and receiver network is avoided. In addition, the common signals which introduce common noises and interference could more easily be eliminated using differential measurements of the receiver. Treatment based on multi-frequency links and the analysis of the differences obtained in the receiver is useful when measured differences are produced on the interaction wave-medium. Biological and other dispersive medium can be analysed using this method. In the near future, specific analysis in these kind of material and potential remote sensing applications are planned.

References

1. Davis, J.L., Annan, A.P.: Ground-penetrating radar for high-resolution mapping of soil and rock stratigraphy1. Geophys. Prospect. **37**(5), 531–551 (1989). doi:10.1111/j.1365-2478.1989.tb02221.x
2. Duke, S.: Basic Introduction to Bioelectromagnetics, 2nd edn. CRC Press, Boca Raton (1990). Colorado School of Mines, https://books.google.es/books?id=hRC4tgAACAAJ
3. Furse, C., Christensen, D.D.C.: Calibration of Ground Penetrating Radar and Calculation of Attenuation and Dielectric Permittivity Versus Depth. CRC Press, Boca Raton (2009)
4. Grima, C., Blankenship, D.D., Schroeder, D.M.: Radar signal propagation through the ionosphere of europa. Planet. Space Sci. **117**, 421–428 (2015). http://www.sciencedirect.com/science/article/pii/S0032063315002470
5. Guy, A.: History of biological effects and medical applications of microwave energy. IEEE Trans. Microw. Theory Tech. **32**(9), 1182–1200 (1984)
6. Kerle, N.: Electromagnetic radiation (EMR). In: Bobrowsky, P.T. (ed.) Encyclopedia of Natural Hazards, p. 250. Springer, Netherlands (2013). http://dx.doi.org/10.1007/978-1-4020-4399-4_111
7. Marshall, J.S., Palmer, W.M.: The distribution of raindrops with size. J. Atmos. Sci. **5**, 165–166 (1948)
8. Nanding, N., Rico-Ramirez, M.A., Han, D.: Comparison of different radar-raingauge rainfall merging techniques. J. Hydroinformatics **17**(3), 422–445 (2015). http://jh.iwaponline.com/content/17/3/422
9. Bhowmik, S.K.R., Roy, S.S., Srivastava, K., Mukhopadhay, B., Thampi, S.B., Reddy, Y.K., Singh, H., Venkateswarlu, S., Adhikary, S.: Processing of indian doppler weather radar data for mesoscale applications. Meteorol. Atmos. Phys. **111**(3), 133–147 (2011). http://dx.doi.org/10.1007/s00703-010-0120-x
10. Sullivan, D.: Electromagnetic Simulation using the FDTD method, 2nd edn. Wiley IEEE Press Series on RF and Microwave Technology (2013)
11. Taflove, A., Oskooi, A., Johnson, S.: Advances in FDTD Computational Electrodynamics: Photonics and Nanotechnology. Artech House, Norwood (2013)
12. Verma, A.K., Jha, K.K., Tewari, R.K.: Effect of the atmosphere on radio and radar performance. In: Fourth IEEE Region 10 International Conference TENCON 1989, pp. 844–847, November 1989
13. Vorst, A., Rosen, A., Kotsuka, Y.: RF and Microwave Interaction with Biological Tissues. Wiley, Hoboken (2006)
14. Williams, J.M.: Biological effects of microwaves: Thermal and nonthermal mechanisms. arXiv preprint physics/0102007 (2001)
15. Yee, K.: Numerical solution of initial boundary value problems involving maxwell's equations in isotropic media. IEEE Trans. Antennas Propag. **14**(3), 302–307 (1966)

Fine-Tuning the DARP Wireless Sensor Routing Protocol

Francisco J. Estévez[1,2(✉)], Jesús González[1,2], Peter Glösekötter[1,2], and Ignacio Rojas[1,2]

[1] University of Applied Sciences of Münster, Stegerweldstr. 39, 48565 Steinfurt, Germany
fjestevez@ieee.org, irojas@ugr.es

[2] Periodista Daniel Saucedo Aranda S/N, University of Granada, 18071 Granada, Spain

Abstract. This work presents an in-depth analysis of the influence of different configuration parameters of the wireless sensor network routing protocol, *DARP*. These parameters regulate the protocol performance in different scenarios. The analysis is based on an ANalysis Of VAriance (ANOVA) study of the effect on the performance of the configuration parameters of *DARP*. The objective of this work is to identify the most relevant configuration parameters, therefore finding the most effective values for a Smart City-type scenario.

Keywords: WSN · Routing protocol · ANOVA · Fine-tuning configuration

1 Introduction

Smart Metering [1], Smart Governance or even Smart Cities are becoming trendy. Smart City projects are rising not only as academic topic, but also as real projects in many countries around the world [2, 3]. This evolution in communications is pushing research groups to improve the actual WSN protocols or even to develop new specific ones.

The technology offers now a wide range of technologies to the Smart City development, but that does not mean that there are no different issues in this area. Formation time, reaction against dynamic events, messages overhead or energy consumption are some of the open questions in WSN. There are different approaches to answer to these questions, all of them based on the IEEE 802.15.4 standard [4] such as Ad-Hoc On demand Distance Vector (AODV) [5], IPv6 Routing Protocol for Low-Power and Lossy Networks (RPL) [6] or Dynamic and Adaptive Routing Protocol (*DARP*) [7]. These approaches differ in its base, facing the commented issues from different angles. Each one possesses interesting features, but they also present disadvantages when they are exposed to a scenario like the Smart City.

This work focuses on clustering-based protocols, due to their suitability for Smart City scenarios. Clustering-based routing protocols [8, 9] are usually based on the optimization of different parameters such as the quality of service (QoS), energy consumption reduction, traffic contention or range maximization [10], which are basic characteristics for this kind of scenarios. Clustering schemes are usually based on

C.R. García et al. (Eds.): UCAmI 2016, Part II, LNCS 10070, pp. 193–204, 2016.
DOI: 10.1007/978-3-319-48799-1_23

different node types, using the Full-Function Device (FFD) and the Reduced-Function Device (RFD) from the IEEE 802.15.4 standard. These node types basically define nodes with and without routing capabilities. Those with routing capabilities are used as cluster-heads, whereas the ones without routing capabilities are used like leafs or non-heads nodes.

A cluster is formed by a cluster-head and several non-head nodes, where the nodes of the cluster communicate between them (many-to-many) and mainly with their cluster-head (many-to-one), which also leads the inter-cluster communications (one-to-one).

In clustering schemes, one of the major interests is the process of choosing the cluster-head, as long as cluster-heads are responsible of the network management and message passing.

This work is based on Smart Cities as scenario and makes use of *DARP* as routing protocol due to the advantages presented in [7, 11] for Smart City-type scenarios. The present article focuses on an open issue in WSN. This issue is related to the search of an optimal configuration, which allows fitting an algorithm to a certain scenario and obtain an improved performance, representing a significant difference in terms of performance. Different articles such as the work of He et al. [12] the work of Bucur et al. [13] and the work of Xianghua et al. [14], deeply analyzes the impact of different configurations in the performance. This lack of research in the area of configuration leads us to carry out this study, focusing in the finding of an optimal configuration for *DARP*. This protocol is based on different configurable parameters, four thresholds and four timers, which are going to be fine-tuned among this work, describing the method to find the optimal configuration of *DARP* network protocol for a Smart City scenario under typical conditions.

The rest of the paper is organized as follows: Sect. 2 presents *DARP*, a novel routing protocol that has been chosen due to its fast set-up, low-overhead and reduced energy consumption. Section 3 presents the simulations, results and the methodology used in order to find the most relevant configuration parameters. The statistical analysis are commented and analyzed in Sect. 4. Finally, the most relevant conclusions of this paper are explained in Sect. 5.

2 *DARP* Overview

As the purpose of this paper is the development of a fine-tuning method for the protocol *DARP*. This section briefly presents the highlights of this protocol.

DARP has been designed for large-size scenarios under low-/medium-density conditions, like Smart Cities, focusing on infrastructure support. It is a clustering-based protocol that locates in the network layer over the IEEE 802.15.4 standard as Fig. 1 shows. *DARP* makes use of a pair of algorithms, the first one is a routing algorithm called Dynamical and Adaptive Routing Algorithm (*DARAL*) and the second one is Dynamical Role Selection Process (*DRSP*), which selects the cluster-head and forms a cluster.

Figure 2 shows how the clusters are configured like virtual sub-networks, with their own network identification (vID), working autonomously and in parallel. *DARP* makes

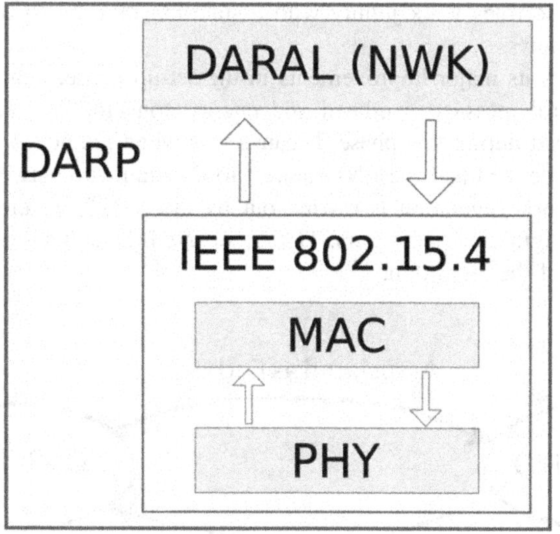

Fig. 1. DARP layer structure

use of the same type of node (IEEE 802.15.4 FFD) but using two different profiles or roles. A virtual coordinator (VC) develops the function of a cluster-head, managing its own virtual sub-network and carrying out inter-/intra-cluster communications. An end node (EN) develops the function of a non-cluster-head, a node that only communicates with its own VC, in an intra-cluster communication, reducing the duty cycle and the

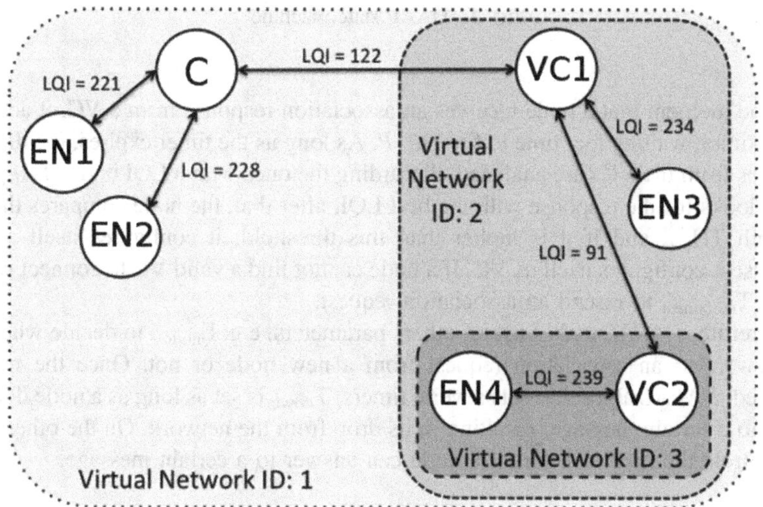

Fig. 2. DARP basic network overview

energy used. These roles work jointly with a state machine based on three different states as Fig. 3 shows.

DARP presents its major improvements in the set-up phase, reducing the convergence time, control message overhead and energy consumption. Thus, most of its parameters are used during this phase, because it is when the nodes adopt a role, the sub-networks are created and the ENs connect to a certain sub-network.

The sub-network generation is carried out by the *DRSP*, which is an algorithm based on two configuration parameters. $TH_{baselevel}$ and TH_{role}, that highly characterizes the performance of the algorithm.

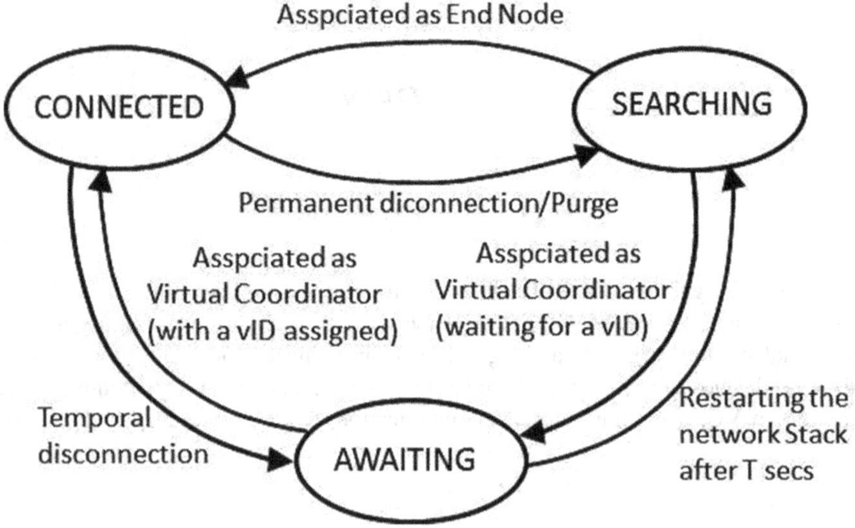

Fig. 3. DARP state machine

In the moment that a node receives an association response from a VC, it activates its T_{link} timer, waiting that time to fire *DRSP*. As long as the timer expires, the different responses from the VCs are analyzed, discarding the ones with a LQI under $TH_{baselevel}$. Then it looks for the response with the best LQI, after that, the node compares the best LQI with TH_{role} and if it is higher than this threshold, it configures itself as EN; Otherwise it configures itself as VC. If a node cannot find a valid VC to connect with it, it waits $T_{reconnect}$ to resend an association request.

Therefore, *DARAL* makes use of others parameters, e.g. L_{nodes}, to decide whether a VC answers to an association request from a new node or not. Once the node is connected, *DARAL* algorithm sets several timers, T_{down} is set as long as a node does not answer to a certain message, resulting in its drop from the network. On the other hand, T_{ack} controls the time slot during a node can answer to a certain message.

The different parameters with their specifically function are presented below.

- $TH_{baselevel}$: The base level threshold represents the minimum LQI that a link between nodes should have. If a link is not above this threshold, the node itself discards the connection and looks for another one.
- TH_{role}: The role threshold is used to determine the role of each node in the network. If LQI is above TH_{role}, a node connects to the network as EN, representing a good QoS and allowing that node to save energy adjusting its radio transceiver and reducing the interference with other nodes. If LQI is below TH_{role}, a node connects itself as VC, representing an extension for the coverage of the network.
- L_{nodes}: The node limit is a parameter that set the maximum number of nodes that a VC can handle. This limit balances the load between different sub-networks, creating areas with restricted traffic, due to the locality principle.
- T_{link}: The timer for link evaluation is fired when a node receives the first answer from a VC. T_{link} represents the time that a certain node awaits to receive more answers from different VCs. Once this timer is expired, the connection process starts.
- T_{down}: This timer is used by a VC to protect its sub-network from node drops. When a certain node surpasses T_{down} without responding messages from its VC, the VC proceeds to remove the node from the sub-network, informing to the topology about this drop.
- $T_{reconnect}$: This timer is used for two different tasks. First, it is used by a VC without vID, to resend the vID request to its VC. Secondly, it is used by non-connected nodes to restart the network stack, restarting also the connection process (sending a new broadcast asking for a valid link).
- T_{ack}: The timer for acknowledgement (ACK) measures the time that a certain message is valid. If an ACK is not received before the timer expiration, the packet should be resend. This kind of timer is typical in the network layer.

3 *DARP* Performance

This section presents the simulation environment and methodology used to find an optimal configuration of *DARP* in Smart City scenarios.

3.1 Simulations and Evaluation Scenarios

The simulations have been performed with *OMNeT++* [15], a well-known C++ discrete event simulator in the research community. As long as *OMNeT++* is not specifically designed for wireless networks, it is necessary to use an additional framework, which gives that compatibility. Inetmanet [16] has been used in order to support the implementation of *DARP* (publicly available in [17]) in *OMNeT++*.

Based on different studies as [2, 3, 11], the network is configured following a Smart City type, in terms of density, and using static nodes randomly distributed. As *DARP* is an *IEEE 802.15.4*-based routing protocol, the communication band used is the ISM

Table 1. Most relevant configuration parameters for the simulation

Configuration Parameter	Value
Carrier Frequency (GHz)	2.4
Carrier Sense Sensitivity (dBm)	−85
Transmit Power (mW)	1.0
Sensitivity (dBm)	−85
Thermal Noise (dBm)	−110
SNR Threshold (dB)	4
Path Loss Alpha	3
T_{alive} (s)	600
Payload Size (Bytes)	70
Maximum Simulation Time (s)	1200
CPU Active Drain (mA)	7.6
CPU Sleep Drain (mA)	0.237
CPU Radio Idle State (mA)	1.38
CPU Radio Detection (mA)	9.6
CPU Radio Sleep State (mA)	0.06
Battery Capacity (mA)	1500
Battery Voltage (v)	5.0

band of 2,4 GHz using the beaconless mode jointly with the carrier sense multiple access with collision avoidance (CSMA/CA) method.

Table 1 shows the most relevant parameters of the battery component and the physical, mac and application layers used in the simulations.

The scenarios considered in this work are based on a medium node density (ND=10), a measure previously defined in different works as [11, 18]. These works have analyzed how the Smart City infrastructure does not have a highly dense environment. Thus, it can be considered even lower, but, for the analytical purpose of this work, a scenario with a medium density is dense enough.

3.2 DARP Behaviour Analysis

Since the ANalysis Of Variance tool, often abbreviated to ANOVA, is a well known technique, we refer to the references [19, 20] for a detailed explanation of the ANOVA methodology. We recall that the factors considered in the analysis that are: the Base-level Threshold (TH_B), the Role Threshold (TH_R), the ACK Timer (T_ACK), the Reconnection Timer (T_REC), the Down Timer (T_DOWN) and the Link Timer (T_LINK). Thus for Smart City type scenarios with a fixed complexity as the presented in Sect. 3.1, some modification in the parameters are carried out a cording to the several levels of the factor presented in Table 2.

The suitability and validity of the ANOVA analysis performed in this paper is discussed now. In order to obtain a precise analysis, an enormous set of example would have to be considered, in order to take them randomly and analyze the performance of the system with the different levels of the factors. This means that a very high computational time is required if the number of factor is high (all possible combination of systems are exponentially increased with the number of levels of factor). This is obviously unmanageable, so a fixed/reduced set of levels of factor considered being significant enough has been used. These values are taken from [11], where a use recommending has been made. This way we consider that the results obtained will be at least very illustrative about the performance for Smart City type scenarios.

The next section presents the results that have been obtained in the ANOVA analysis.

4 Results of the Analysis

To carry out the statistical study, a selection is made from a set of alternatives that are representative of each of the factors being considered. By analyzing the different levels of each of these factors, it is possible to determine their influence on the performance of the analyzed *DARP* system. The response variable used to perform the statistical analysis are the followings: (a) Number of control messages sent during the set-up time; (b) Set-Up Energy. These variables are some of the most interesting in order to minimize time and energy consumption of the net as [11, 18] have shown. Table 2 gives the different levels considered in each factor for the multi-factorial ANOVA analysis.

Table 2. Variables used in the statistical study. All the possible configurations of factors levels (Baselevel threshold, role threshold, ACK timer, reconnection timer, down timer, link timer) are evaluated in *DARP*.

Factors	Levels of the factors		
Baselevel Threshold (TH_B)	TH_B1 / 1–10 (5)	TH_B2 / 11–50 (30)	TH_B3 / 51–150 (100)
Role Threshold (TH_R)	TH_R1 / 75–125 (100)	TH_R2 / 126–175 (150)	TH_R3 / 176–225 (200)
ACK Timer (T_ACK)	T_ACK1 / 0.1–1.0 (0.5)	T_ACK2 / 1.1–2.0 (1.5)	T_ACK3 / 2.1–10 (6.0)
ReconnectionTimer (T_REC)	T_REC1 / 0.1–4 (2)	T_REC2 / 4.1–10 (6)	T_REC3 / 11–50 (30)
Down Timer (T_DOWN),	T_DOWN1/ 0.1–10 (5)	T_DOWN2 / 11–100 (50)	T_DOWN3 / 101–200 (150)
Link Timer (T_LINK)	T_LINK1 / 0.1–2 (1)	T_LINK2 / 2.1–10 (6)	T_LINK3 / 11–20 (15)

Therefore, all the possible configurations of factors levels are evaluated 10 times in the *DARP* system, analyzing both the number of control message and the Energy.

4.1 Statistical Analysis of the Number of Control Message

Table 3 gives the six-way variance analysis for the whole set of examples of the DARP system methodology studied. For all the configurations of factors, the learning algorithm presented in Sect. 3 was used. The ANOVA table containing the sum of squares, degrees of freedom, mean square, test statistics, etc., represents the initial analysis in a compact form. This kind of tabular representation is customarily used to set out the results of the ANOVA calculations.

Table 3. Analysis of variance for message control. The main factors and interactions marked with (*) indicated that are statistically significant.

Source	Sum of squares	Df	Mean square	F-ratio	P-value
MAIN FACTORS					
A:Baselevel Threshold (TH_B)	81,70	2	40,85	2,91	0,0545
B:Role Threshold (TH_R)	31,61	2	15,80	1,13	0,3244
C:ACK Timer (T_ACK)*	16308	2	8154	580	0,0000
D:Reconnection Timer (T_REC)*	336269	2	168134	11974	0,0000
E:Down Timer (T_DOWN)	3,99	2	1,99	0,14	0,8675
F:Link Timer (T_LINK)*	4834	2	2417	172	0,0000
INTERACTIONS					
CD*	7093	4	1773	126	0,0000
CF*	4660	4	1165	82	0,0000
DF*	6751	4	1687	120	0,0000
RESIDUAL	285233	20314	14		
TOTAL (CORRECTED)	731196	20412			

Of all the information presented in the ANOVA table, the major interest of the researcher will most likely be focused on the value located in the “F-Ratio” and “Sig. Level” columns. If the numbers found in this column are less than the critical value set by the experimenter, then the effect is said to be significant. This value is usually set at 0.05 and any value less than this will result in significant effects, while any value greater than result in non-significant effects. If the effects are found to be significant using the above procedure, it implies that the means differ more than would be expected by chance alone. In terms of the above experiment, it would mean that the treatments were not equally effective. This table does not tell the researcher anything about what the effects were, just that there most likely were real effects. As can be seen from Table 3 three main factors are statistically significant (ACK Timer, Reconnection Timer, Link Timer), but it is important to note that the Reconnection Timer is a very important factor (that will be analyzed afterwards with the Multiple Range Test). In Table 3, for reason of space, only the statistically significant interactions are presented. Since 10 P-values are less than 0,05, these factors have a statistically significant effect on Message Control at the 95,0% confidence level, being all F-ratios are based on the residual mean square error. If the effects were found to be non-significant, then the differences between the means would not be great enough to allow the researcher to say that they are different.

In that case, no further interpretation would be attempted. When the effects are significant, the means must then be examined in order to determine the nature of the effects. There are procedures called "post-hoc tests" to assist the researcher in this task, but often the analysis is fairly evident simply by looking at the size of the various means.

Thus, a detailed analysis will be performed now for each of the factors examined, using the Multiple Range Test. Table 4 shows the Multiple Range Test for a relevant factor "Reconnection Timer" in which a multiple comparison procedure to determine which means are significantly different from which others is performed (in this case for the factor Reconnection Timer). The method currently being used to discriminate among the means is Fisher's least significant difference (LSD) procedure, and from Table 4 can be concluded that there exist three homogenous groups (identified using columns of X's, without intersection), therefore, the levels T_REC3, T_REC2 and T_REC1 are completely different and significant from an statistical point of view (analyzing the behaviour of the output variable Message Control), showing the factor T_REC1, with the highest mean value, the worst performance in terms of number of control messages (Fig. 4).

Table 4. Multiple range tests for message control by reconnection timer (T_REC)

Reconnection timer (T_REC)	LS mean	LS sigma	Homogeneous groups		
T_REC3	17,90	0,045	X		
T_REC2	19,83	0,046		X	
T_REC1	27,35	0,045			X
Limit to establish significant differences: 0,13					

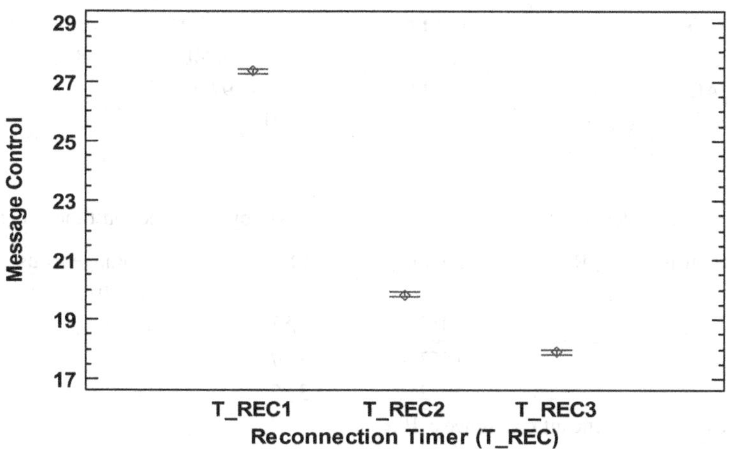

Fig. 4. Evolution of the output variable message control by modification of the levels of factor reconnection timer.

4.2 Statistical Analysis of the Energy

As previously presented in Sect. 4.1, a similar statistical analysis has been performed for the output variable Set-Up Energy (Energy), which shows the energy use by a node during the connection to a net. Modern network protocols [5, 6] usually rebuild the whole net, meaning that the set-up energy is regularly consumed.

From Table 5, it can be observed that again the three factors: ACK Timer, Reconnection Timer, Link Timer are the statistically significant in this case for the behaviour of the output variable Set-Up Energy. The main alteration in of the output variable is presented in Table 6, when modification of the levels of the factors Reconnection Timer are used (with a range in the mean between [1013,5032]).

Table 5. Analysis of Variance for Set-Up Energy (mWs). The main factors and interactions marked with (*) indicated that are statistically significant.

Source	Sum of squares	Df	Mean square	F-ratio	P-value
MAIN EFFECTS					
A:Baselevel Threshold (TH_B)	230297	2	115149	1,18	0,3080
B:Role Threshold (TH_R)	346247	2	173123	1,77	0,1702
C:ACK Timer (T_ACK) *	1,35E8	2	6,79E7	694	0,0000
D:Reconnection Timer (T_REC)*	6,39E10	2	3,19E10	327315	0,0000
E:Down Timer (T_DOWN)	162422	2	81210	0,83	0,4358
F:Link Timer (T_LINK)*	1,05E8	2	5,27E7	539	0,0000
INTERACTIONS					
AD*	8,24E6	4	2,06E6	21	0,0000
BC*	2,60E6	4	650738	6,66	0,0000
CD*	7,25E7	4	1,81E7	185	0,0000
CE*	988811	4	247203	2,53	0,0386
CF*	3,32E6	4	831602	8,51	0,0000
DE*	1,16E6	4	292385	2,99	0,0177
DF*	1,89E7	4	4,74E6	48	0,0000
RESIDUAL	1,98E9	20314	97762		
TOTAL (CORRECTED)	6,78E10	20412			

Table 6. Multiplerange tests for Set-Up Energy (mWs) by reconnection timer (T_REC)

Reconnection timer (T_REC)	LS mean	LS sigma	Homogeneous groups		
T_REC1	1013	3,81	X		
T_REC2	1557	3,87		X	
T_REC3	5032	3,82			X
Limit to establish significant differences: 10,6					

As can be observed from previous table, again the levels of factors Reconnection Timer are totally dissimilar, non-having intersections between them (Fig. 5).

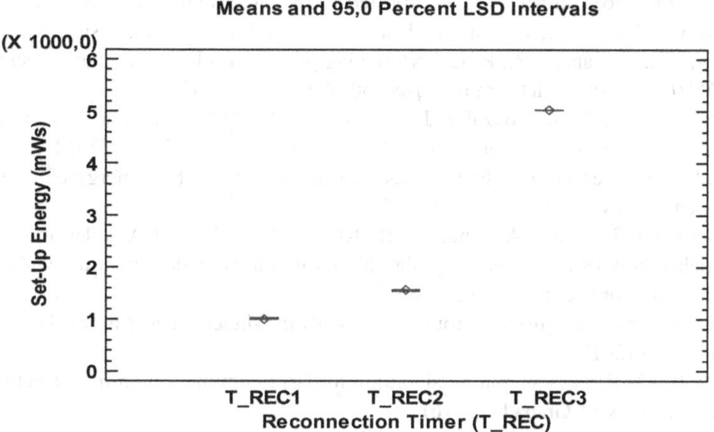

Fig. 5. Evolution of the output variable Set-Up Energy (mWs) by modification of the levels of factor Reconnection Timer

5 Conclusion

This work has presented the most relevant configuration parameters for the wireless network protocol *DARP*, which presents a large influence in Smart City type scenarios.

Among the different statistical analysis three parameters have emerged as the most relevant, $T_{reconnect}$, T_{link} and T_{ack}. In terms of configuration, the timers present an overall improvement in terms of energy and number of control messages sent during the set-up time for the highest time configurations.

Acknowledgements. This work was partially supported by projects TIC-2082 (Junta Andalucia) and TIN2015-71873-R (MINECO/FEDER).

References

1. Velasquez-Villada, C., Donoso, Y.: Delay disruption tolerant network-based message forwarding for a river pollution monitoring wireless sensor network application. Sensors **16** (4), 436 (2016)
2. Sanchez, L., Muñoz, L., Galache, J.A., Sotres, P., Santana, J.R., Gutierrez, V., Ramdhany, R., Gluhak, A., Krco, S., Theodoridis, E., Pfisterer, D.: SmartSantander: IoT experimentation over a smart city testbed. Comput. Netw. **61**, 217–238 (2014)
3. Kamouskos, S., Nass de Holanda, T., Simulation of a smart grid city with software agents. In: Third UKSim European Symposium on Computer Modeling and Simulation, pp. 424–429 (2009)

4. IEEE 802.15.4. IEEE standard for local and metropolitan area networks – part 15.4: low-rate wireless personal area networks (LR-WPANs). http://standards.ieee.org/getieee802/download/802.15.4-2011.pdf. Accessed 14 Feb 2016
5. Perkins, C., Belding-Royer, E., Das, S.: Ad-hoc on-demand distance vector (AODV) routing, RFC 3561. https://www.ietf.org/rfc/rfc3561. Accessed 14 Feb 2016
6. Winter, T., Thubert, P., Brandt, A., Hui, J., Kelsey, R., Levis, P., Pister, K., Struik, R., Vasseur, J.P., Alexander, R.: RPL: IPv6 routing protocol for low-power and lossy networks, RFC 6550. https://tools.ietf.org/html/rfc6550. Accessed 14 Feb 2016
7. Estevez, F.J., Rebel, G., González, J., Glösekötter, P.: DARP: dynamic and adaptive radio protocol for wireless sensor networks. Electron. Lett. **50**(2), 122–123 (2014)
8. Wang, D.J.: Clustering mesh-like wireless sensor networks with an energy-efficient scheme. Int. J. Sens. Netw. **7**, 199–206 (2010)
9. Shamshirband, S., Amini, A., Anuar, N.B., Klah, M.L.M.: D-FICCA: a density-based fuzzy impearialist competitive clustering algorithm for intrusion detection in wireless sensor networks. Measurements **55**, 212–216 (2014)
10. Llu, X.: A survey on clustering routing protocols in wireless sensor networks. Sensors **12**, 11113–11153 (2012)
11. Estevez, F.: DARP: a new routing algorithm for large communication infrastructures, Ph.D. thesis, University of Granada (2016)
12. He, W., Wang, J., Yang, X., Zhao, K., Zhou, M., Zhu, L., Zhang, S., Hua, X., Xie, C.: Wireless sensor network protocol performance testing system, has testing gateway provided with Ethernet communication module, and test group network protocol module connected with different sensor device through Du-Pont line, Shanghai Inst., Microsystem and Information (2015)
13. Bucur, D., Iacca, G., Squillero, G., Tonda, A.: Costs in wireless sensor networks: a multi-objective evolutionary framework for protocol analysis. In: GECCO, The 2014 Genetic and Evolutionary Computation Conference (2014)
14. Xianghua, X., Jian, W., Wei, Z., Chao, T., Changhua, W.: PMSW: a passive monitoring system in wireless sensor networks. Int. J. Netw. Manage. **21**, 300–325 (2011)
15. Varga, A.: The omnet++ discrete event simulation systems. In: Proceedings of the European Simulation Multiconference, Prague, Czech Republic, June 2001
16. Inetmanet framework for wireless sensor and ad-hoc networks using OMNeT++. https://github.com/aarizaq/inetmanet-2.0. Accessed June 2016
17. Estevez, F.J.: DARAL simulation code for OMNeT++. https://github.com/fjestevez/DARP. Accessed June 2016
18. Kermajani, H., Gomez, C.: On the network convergence process in RPL over IEEE 802.15.4 multihop networks: improvement and trade-offs. Sensors **14**, 11993–12022 (2014)
19. Fisher, R.A.: Contribution to Mathematical Statistics. Wiley, New York (1950)
20. Rutherford, A.: Introducing ANOVA and ANCOVA: A GLM Approach. Introducing Statistical Methods series. Sage Publications, London (2001)

Lightweight Multivariate Sensing in WSNs

João Marco C. Silva[1], Paulo Carvalho[1(✉)], Kalil Araujo Bispo[2], and Solange Rito Lima[1]

[1] Centro Algoritmi, Universidade do Minho, 4710-057 Braga, Portugal
{joaomarco,pmc,solange}@di.uminho.pt
[2] Dep. de Computação, Universidade Federal de Sergipe, São Cristóvão, SE 49100-000, Brazil
kalil@dcomp.ufs.br

Abstract. This paper proposes a self-adaptive sampling scheme for WSNs, which aims at capturing accurately the behavior of the physical parameters of interest in each specific WSN context yet reducing the overhead in terms of sensing events. The sampling scheme relies on a set of low-complexity rules capable of auto-regulate the sensing frequency in accordance with each parameter behavior. As proof-of-concept, based on real environmental datasets, we provide statistical indicators illustrating the added value of the proposed sampling scheme in reducing sensing events without compromising the estimation accuracy of physical phenomena.

Keywords: Sampling techniques · Data sensing · Network measurements · WSNs

1 Introduction

In Wireless Sensor Networks (WSNs), the energy consumed by the communication module is a key aspect to be addressed in the network and services design. As discussed in [1], the transmission of a bit throughout the network can consume more energy than processing thousands of instructions, as the communication subsystem has a much higher energy consumption than the computational subsystem. For this reason, communication can be improved through preprocessing the data (e.g., using aggregation schemes) before its dissemination. Other important WSNs characteristic is that the sensing subsystem can lead to a significant source of power consumption and, for this reason, sensing data should be acquired only when necessary, avoiding also unnecessary processing.

In this context, this paper proposes a new adaptive sampling scheme oriented to WSNs aiming at improving the trade off between capturing data accurately and saving energy to enhance operational sensors lifetime. The inherent self-adaptiveness of the sampling scheme provides the required flexibility to be adjusted to distinct sensing scenarios and multiple measuring parameters without human intervention. Through self-regulation of data readings and consequent transmissions, the present work demonstrates that adaptive sampling can be a

C.R. García et al. (Eds.): UCAmI 2016, Part II, LNCS 10070, pp. 205–211, 2016.
DOI: 10.1007/978-3-319-48799-1_24

solid approach to reduce significantly the number of sensing events, while maintaining an accurate view of WSN activity and behavior.

This paper is organized as follows: related work is discussed in Sect. 2; the sampling scheme rational is described in Sect. 3; the proof-of-concept and the corresponding evaluation results are discussed in Sect. 4; and the conclusions are summarized in Sect. 5.

2 Related Work

Although adaptive sampling has been successfully used in conventional computer networks [2,3], the available solutions can hardly be applied in resource constrained networks such as WSNs, due their computational requirements. In [4], the authors propose an optimal sensing scheduling policy for a power capture system equipped with a finite battery. The goal is to select sensing periods strategically so that the average sensing performance is optimized. As performance indicator, the analytical study only considers the battery level of sensors disregarding the variability of the observed parameter. In [5], the authors developed a recovering framework for big data sets through a small number of sensing readings based on space and time correlation characteristics from previous samples. The process lowers the number of transmissions and, consequently, the power consumption in sensor nodes. However, this study is mainly focused on reducing the rate of transmissions and not on the accuracy of the sensing process.

The complex relation between analysis and data acquiring in adaptive sensing paradigms can be extremely powerful, as many times it allows a reliable estimation and signal detection in situations where non-adaptive detection fails [6]. For this reason, the authors investigate a general signal estimation over the adaptive detection paradigm problem, however, they also recognize that the prior knowledge of some required parameters might not be available in a real-life setting. In [7], the authors establish a framework for collecting data from a WSN based on adaptive compressive sensing (as in [5]), taking into account the power consumption and the amount of information in sensing data. Thus, the paper proposes an algorithm to obtain a more precise approximation of the measurements by wasting as less energy as possible. This proposal is also limited to adapt the rate of the transmissions.

From the related literature, most of the studies on adaptive sensing assume either a theoretical approach limiting their applicability to real WSN scenarios or cover a partial set of variables to optimize, such as the rate of transmissions. This evinces the usefulness of studying and improving the trade-off between sensing events and measurements accuracy for distinct WSN contexts. This work is a contribution in this respect.

3 A Sampling Scheme for Environmental Sensing

This section describes the proposed sampling scheme taking into consideration the heterogeneity of WSN application scenarios and the self-adaptiveness as a mandatory property to assure. In this context, the adaptive sampling scheme uses the temporal variation in the observed scalar physical quantities (*e.g.*, temperature, humidity, etc.) in order to self-adjust the interval between two consecutive sensing events. Assuming the likely constraints on sensor devices where the proposed scheme is expected to be deployed, estimating the variation of sampled values resorts to efficient and simple operations, for instance, the lightweight method used in TCP control mechanisms.

Basically, when the sampled values of the observed parameter do not vary significantly, the interval between two sensing events is increased, reducing its frequency, which leads to less computational demand and consequent less energy consumption [1]. Conversely, if a significant variation in the sampled parameter is observed, the time scheduling for the next sensing event is decreased in order to improve the accuracy in identifying its temporal fluctuation.

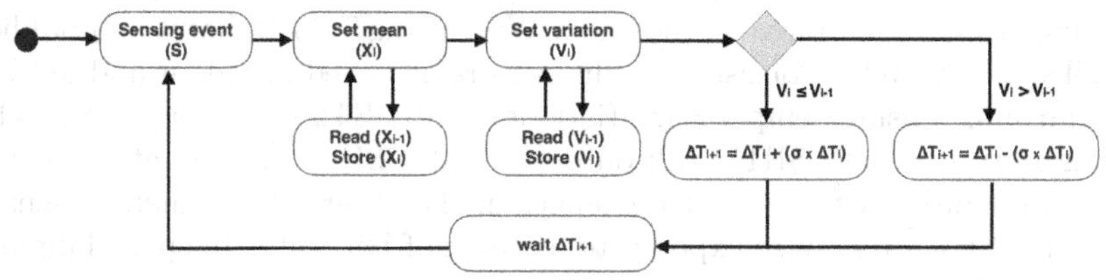

Fig. 1. Adaptive sampling - main steps

In this way, when a sensing event is performed, the mean of the observed variable is calculated using the moving average $\bar{X}_i = (1 - \eta)\bar{X}_{i-1} + \eta S$, where $\bar{X}_{i-1}$ is the mean calculated in the previous event and η is the weight of new observed value S. These actions correspond to the initial steps in the flowchart included as Fig. 1.

Although the standard deviation is the conventional choice for estimating the variance, it may involve expensive operations to constrained devices related to squaring $(\bar{X}_i - S)$. Alternatively, as discussed in [8], the mean deviation is a good approximation to the standard deviation, being easier to compute as it only resorts to integer arithmetics, even in expressions containing fractions. Therefore, using the current mean value $\bar{X}_i$, the variation in the observed values is calculated resorting to the mean deviation $V_i = (1-\eta)V_{i-1}+\eta|\bar{X}_i - S|$, where, V_{i-1} is the mean deviation identified in the last sensing event and η determines the weight of the current deviation $|\bar{X}_i - S|$.

As illustrated in Fig. 1, the adaptive mechanism compares the current estimated variation (V_i) with the variation calculated in the previous sensing event (V_{i-1}) in order to identify if the observed parameter has changed significantly, and then, the time interval used to schedule the next sensing event is adjusted accordingly. If V_i is lower or equal to V_{i-1}, the observed parameter did not change significantly from the last sensing events, which allows to reduce the sensing frequency by increasing ΔT. Otherwise, the observed parameter changed significantly since the last observation, which requires more frequent sensing events, obtained by reducing ΔT. An additional constraint is used to prevent ΔT from growing indefinitely (ΔT_{max}), thus guaranteeing a minimum number of samples per time unit. Conversely, the maximum frequency of sampling (ΔT_{min}) is also limited so that the interval between sensing events does not tend to zero, which would result in an overwhelming resource consumption.

4 Evaluation Results

The proof-of-concept evaluates the ability of the sampling scheme in: (i) reducing the number of sensing events; (ii) identifying the temporal variation of the observed parameters accurately; and (iii) self-adjusting the sensing frequency in accordance with the variability of environmental parameters.

The dataset used in the tests was previously collected during approximately six hours, at intervals of five seconds, in a WSN using TelosB motes and publicly available [9]. The WSN consists of eight sensors deployed in indoor and outdoor environments, sensing temperature (indoor - ST1, ST2; outdoor - ST3, ST4) and humidity (indoor - SH1, SH2; outdoor - SH3, SH4). Aiming at evaluating the accuracy in identifying sudden changes in the observed parameters, sensors (ST1, ST4; SH1, SH4) were exposed to a steam of hot water to spark humidity and temperature levels.

The adaptive scheme was set with $\eta = 0.7$ in order to stress the weight of the latest sensed value and corresponding variation. The rules mentioned above were set with $\sigma = 0.15$, meaning that the interval between samples (ΔT) is increased by a factor of 15 % when the observed temperature or humidity remain stable, and reduced by a factor of 15 % when the parameter changes significantly. This adjustment may also be indexed to the observed variation or to the current battery level. In this proof-of-concept, ΔT_{max} and ΔT_{min} were set to 30 and 5 s, respectively.

The performance of the sampling scheme is evaluated relating the number of sensing events along the monitoring period with the accuracy in identifying the temporal variation of the observed parameters (temperature and humidity). A reduction in the number of sensing events leads to less computational operations and, consequently, less energy consumption, however, this reduction should not compromise the accurate observation of physical parameters under monitoring.

As deterministic and adaptive sampling mechanisms yield distinct number of samples, the statistical analysis considers the mean estimated value per second from the resultant time series. The accuracy is then estimated resorting to the Mean Squared Error (MSE), which is commonly used to evaluate the accuracy of estimators, and to the correlation between the time series.

Regarding the ability to reduce the number of sensing events, Fig. 2 shows that, for all nodes and parameters, the adaptive scheme only performs around 20 % of the events observed through the deterministic scheme. Attending to the lightweight algorithm ruling the proposed scheme, this significant reduction will also contribute to reduce energy consumption in the sensors.

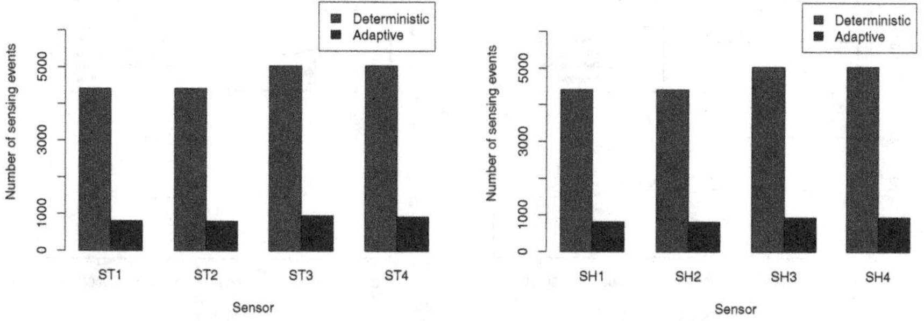

Fig. 2. Number of sensing events: temperature (left); Humidity (right) (Color figure online)

However, despite of reducing the number of sensing events significantly, proving the efficiency of the adaptive scheme requires verifying its ability in capturing the real distribution of the observed parameters. This is accomplished by estimating the statistical representativeness of adaptive time series against the deterministic behavior. In this way, Figs. 3 and 4 show the distribution of sampled values along the test period, for indoor and outdoor sensors. The almost complete overlap of adaptive and deterministic resultant series, highlighted during both smooth and unstable periods, demonstrates that, even reducing the sensing events in around 80 %, the adaptive scheme has the capability to catch up the real parameter pattern. Note that, even in presence of sudden environmental changes affecting sensors ST1, ST4, SH1 and SH4 (detailed above), the adaptive scheme adjusts the sensing schedule correctly, confirming the versatility of the self-adaptive scheme.

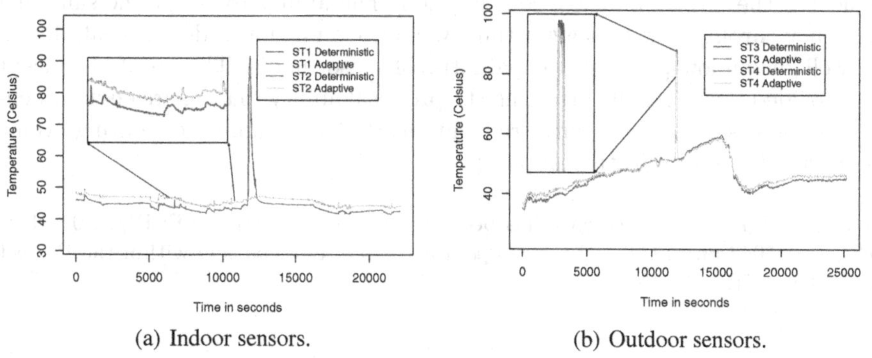

(a) Indoor sensors. (b) Outdoor sensors.

Fig. 3. Temperature observations.

These observations are corroborated through the high correlation (0.98 for all series) between the distributions of estimated parameters, and the low MSE

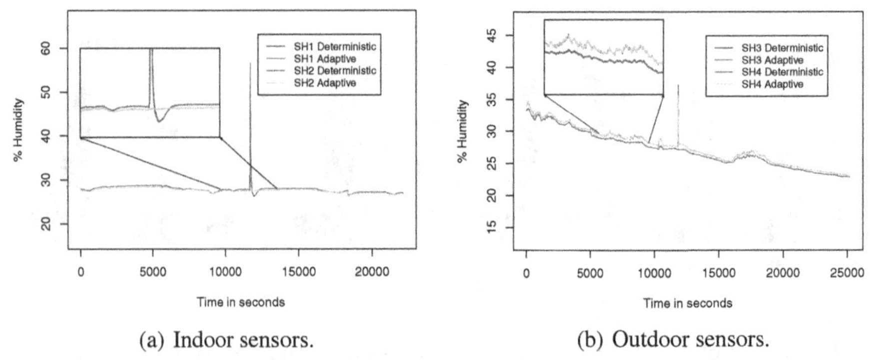

(a) Indoor sensors.

(b) Outdoor sensors.

Fig. 4. Humidity observations.

(approximately 0.5 for temperature and 0.03 for humidity). This means that, for the considered scenarios, the estimation of humidity levels was more accurate, however, as depicted in Fig. 3, the temperature was also accurately estimated. The differences in accuracy can however be explained with the use of a constant adjustment factor σ. In this regard, future work will focus on evolving the mechanism by indexing this factor to the estimated variation in observed parameter.

5 Conclusions

Attending to the inherent resource constraints of WSNs, this paper has proposed a self-adaptive sampling scheme able to capture the behavior of multiple physical parameters accurately while reducing the overhead of sensing events and, consequently, the levels of energy consumption. The ability to adapt the sampling frequency through low-cost algorithms was also defined as a design goal, due to the well known low-processing capabilities of sensor nodes. The proof-of-concept has provided initial results attesting the proposal ability to measure environmental parameters accurately, while reducing in 80 % the number of sensing events comparing to deterministic sampling.

Acknowledgments. This work has been supported by COMPETE: POCI-01-0145-FEDER-007043 and FCT - *Fundação para a Ciência e Tecnologia* within the Project Scope: UID/CEC/00319/2013.

References

1. Anastasi, G., Conti, M., Di Francesco, M., Passarella, A.: Energy conservation in wireless sensor networks: a survey. Ad Hoc Netw. **7**(3), 537–568 (2009)
2. Hernandez, E.A., Chidester, M.C., George, A.D.: Adaptive sampling for network management. J. Netw. Syst. Manag. **9**(4), 409–434 (2001)

3. Silva, J.M.C., Carvalho, P., Rito Lima, S.: A multiadaptive sampling technique for cost-effective network measurements. Comput. Netw. **57**(17), 3357–3369 (2013)
4. Yang, J., Wu, X., Wu, J.: Adaptive sensing scheduling for energy harvesting sensors with finite battery. In: IEEE International Conference on Communications (ICC), pp. 98–103, June 2015
5. Quer, G., Masiero, R., Pillonetto, G., Rossi, M., Zorzi, M.: Sensing, compression, and recovery for wsns: sparse signal modeling and monitoring framework. IEEE Trans. Wirel. Commun. **11**(10), 3447–3461 (2012)
6. Castro, R.M., Tanczos, E.: Adaptive sensing for estimation of structured sparse signals. IEEE Trans. Inf. Theory **61**(4), 2060–2080 (2015)
7. Chou, C.T., Rana, R., Hu, W.: Energy efficient information collection in wireless sensor networks using adaptive compressive sensing. In: 2009 IEEE 34th Conference on Local Computer Networks. 443–450, October 2009
8. Jacobson, V.: Congestion avoidance and control. In: Symposium Proceedings on Communications Architectures and Protocols, SIGCOMM 1988, pp. 314–329. ACM, New York (1988)
9. Suthaharan, S., Alzahrani, M., Rajasegarar, S., Leckie, C., Palaniswami, M.: Labelled data collection for anomaly detection in wireless sensor networks. In: 6th International Conference on Intelligent Sensors, Sensor Networks and Information Processing (ISSNIP), pp. 269–274. IEEE (2010)

WSN Related Requirement Analysis Towards Sustainable Building Automation Operations and Maintenance

Johanna Kallio(✉) and Jani Koivusaari

VTT Technical Research Centre of Finland, P.O. Box 1100 90571 Oulu, Finland
{Johanna.Kallio,Jani.Koivusaari}@vtt.fi

Abstract. New technologies, such as machine-to-machine networking, and a demand for energy-efficient buildings and security are driving the building automation market forward. The use of low cost wireless sensor networks (WSN) provides many advantages for sustainable building automation solutions. In this paper, we analyzed the WSN related requirements for sustainable building automation operations and maintenance. We used the three sustainability dimensions, economic, environment and social, to gather the requirements. The requirement analysis resulted in 10 requirements aiming at maximization of energy conservation, lowering of operation and maintenance costs while taking into accounts the users' or occupants' preferences, comfort, and safety.

Keywords: WSN · Building automation · Building maintenance · Sustainability

1 Introduction

Building automation is automatic centralized control of a building's heating, ventilation and air-conditioning (HVAC) systems, lighting, security, and other subsystems, through a single building control point [1]. Typically, building automation refers to an extensive category of control and communication technologies that link building systems, which are typically controlled separately. In the broadest sense, the concept of building automation is similar to the concept of a smart or intelligent building, which refers to a fully automated "digital" building targeting the demands of users while maintaining energy and cost-efficiency [2].

In this paper, sustainability refers to the three components of sustainability, namely environmental, social and economic sustainability. Environment sustainability is related to resource and ecosystem protection by means of renewable energy in buildings, the reduction of carbon dioxide emissions and energy efficiency [3]. Social sustainability targets to health and safety of people, whereas economic sustainability is related on investments and costs during the whole lifecycle of building. The interrelations of these three spheres of building automation sustainability are illustrated in Venn diagram in Fig. 1. Sustainable solutions are concurrently economically viable, environmentally bearable and equitable for the society [4].

C.R. García et al. (Eds.): UCAmI 2016, Part II, LNCS 10070, pp. 212–217, 2016.
DOI: 10.1007/978-3-319-48799-1_25

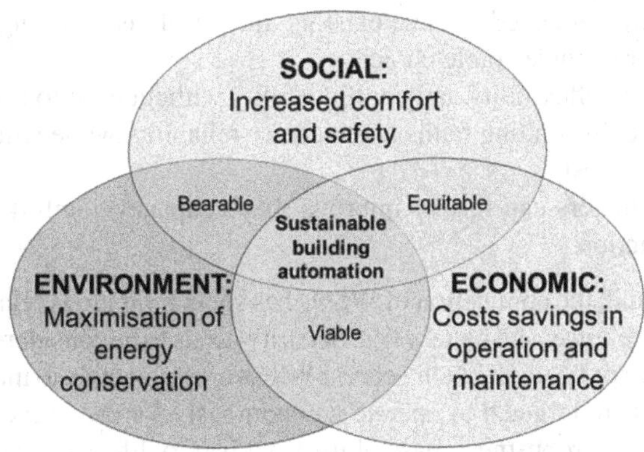

Fig. 1. Venn diagram of building automation sustainability. Adapted from [4].

Currently growing awareness, new technologies, and a demand for energy-efficient buildings and security are driving the building automation market forward. The energy consumption of buildings is approximately 40 % of the total world annual energy consumption and thus, performance of building automation systems (BAS) is critical to sustainability [5]. Nguyen and Aiello [6] have analysed several studies and found that occupancy-based control can result in up to 40 % energy savings for HVAC systems. By managing various building systems (HVAC, lighting, blinding, fire safety), building automation can ensure the sustainable performance of a building, aiming at maximization of energy conservation, lowering of operation and maintenance costs while taking into account the users' or occupants' preferences, comfort, and safety.

This paper focuses on analysing the requirements related to wireless sensor networks (WSN) to support sustainable building automation operations and maintenance. The aim is to ease the design, specification and implementation of interoperable building WSN solutions that can provide information about the conditions of the building and HVAC equipment to the decision making elements, such as building owners. The paper is organised as follows: In Sect. 2 WSN standards and solutions for building automation are discussed, Sect. 3 analyses the requirements towards sustainable building automation operations and management, and Sect. 4 summarises the results and discuss possible future development paths.

2 Sustainability Through Wireless Sensor Networks

Demand for more sustainable building automation solutions has resulted three open communications protocols - BACnet, KNX, and LonWorks [1]. These IP-compatible protocols cover building automation applications from sensor to management level, but are originally designed to be hardwired [7]. Technologically solutions are going towards being wireless, connected, and interoperable. Machine-to-Machine networking is driving every connected device to be Internet addressable, and low-cost and small-sized sensors with advanced sensing capabilities are a commodity [8]. Using low cost WSNs alongside with existing BAS provides many advantages for sustainability:

- WSNs can be implemented in new, existing and retrofitted buildings where wiring is a challenge or an undesirable choice,
- WSNs increase the flexibility and configurability without need to re-wire,
- WSNs can detect impending faults and increase reliability while reducing operation and maintenance costs,
- Sensors and actuators can further improve the occupancy comfort while reducing energy consumption.

On the other hand, the application of WSNs has some limitations related on security, performance, interference, and battery life. Security needs to be considered case-by-case depending on BAS application, but in general WSNs are vulnerable to malicious attacks. In addition, WSNs are targeted to operate autonomously for even several years, when performance (lifetime, robustness, ease of use) and battery life can constrain the use of WSNs [9].

Some of the wireless standards are already widely used in building automation applications, such as ZigBee [10], Wi-Fi [11], Bluetooth [12], and 6LoWPAN [13]. Bluetooth is based on IEEE 802.15.1 standard and targeted for exchange of data over short distance. The drawbacks of Bluetooth technology are high power consumption and very short range [14].

Wi-Fi refers to the IEEE 802.11 set of standards for wireless networks and has become the standard technology for wireless networking. Wi-Fi provides rather high bandwidth capacity, but is typically more expensive and consumes more power than for example ZigBee. ZigBee is based on based on 802.15.4 standard and is suitable for applications low data rate and long battery life. Compared to Wi-Fi and Bluetooth, ZigBee uses very little power and is more cost efficient [14].

6LoWPAN is targeted to applications that need wireless internet connectivity at low data rates. 6LoWPAN is typically used in sensoring and controlling indoor conditions, such as temperature, humidity and light. Comparison on ZigBee IP and 6LoWPAN is provided for example by [15].

Typical non-IP technologies for building automation WSNs are Z-wave and Insteon, which are originally designed for home automation. Moreover, the European wireless M-bus standard has gained a certain degree of importance for remote meter reading. M-bus can be used with different types of consumption meters and various types of valves and actuators [14, 1].

3 Requirement Analysis for Sustainable Solutions

We gathered the total of 40 requirements targeted especially for supporting building operation and maintenance. The requirements contained both functional and non-functional requirements and were categorized into three sets:

- WSN requirements for requirements that are directly related to the aimed WSN solution and its technical features;
- Monitoring requirements for requirements that are related to how the conditions and equipment are to be monitored and what technical properties are expected;

- Back-end requirements for requirements that contain requirements related to the back-end side and the utilization of the monitoring WSN and its data.

When sustainability as depicted in Fig. 1 was further elaborated, the analysis resulted in 10 requirements regarding the WSN solution for building automation operations and maintenance, described in the following subchapters.

3.1 WSN Requirements

WSN data format. The WSN data should be formatted with a standardized and widely used mark-up syntax and avoid proprietary descriptions to achieve interoperability with existing solutions and parallel. This also increases re-usability in other cases and domains.

WSN connection with building automation systems. The developed WSN solution should be able to communicate with current BASs. The facility owner may not want a separate control system or an interface for information. Thus, the developed WSN solution should have options to communicate with existing automation systems.

WSN battery life. The maintenance frequency of the developed WSN solution should not exceed the maintenance frequency of current SoA solutions in terms of battery life. To be a viable basis or input for a commercial WSN solution, the battery life must be at the same level as current SoA solutions and not cause dedicated battery exchange routines for the user.

WSN self-configuration. The WSN solution should be able to configure itself during installation procedures. The developed WSN solution needs to be re-deployable. Rationale: In order to reduce the installation time, a self-configuration procedure and/or tools to connect the nodes to gateways and the gateways to the next connection point or the internet is needed.

3.2 Monitoring Requirements

Dependable wireless communication. The WSN should be reliable and robust, the performance of radio link should be monitored. Dependability is a key component in the reduction of maintenance costs for WSN itself. The link quality should be monitored and possible transmission problems should be detected, identified and solved.

Indoor conditions measurement in nodes. The conditions monitoring nodes should be able to measure common indoor conditions parameters, which include temperature, relative humidity and CO_2. The nodes must be able to adapt and support common, commercially available measurement modules and indoor conditions monitoring parameters.

3.3 Back-End Requirements

Standardized data access. The conditions monitoring data should be accessible from an interface that is defined in a standardized format. To achieve interoperability with existing solutions and parallel solutions a standardized data format is necessary.

Collecting and storing of WSN monitoring data. The WSN data must be accessible for collection and storing into an external database. Storing monitoring data over long periods is essential for predicting system operation, and to determine the causality between building automation parameters and actual conditions within the facility.

Detect building automation system cross reference. In facilities with several separate automation systems, conflict conditions are possible. The back-end system needs to be able to detect these from the WSN monitoring data. For example, a facility may have local cooling system in addition to centralized heating systems. WSN monitoring data can be utilized to detect and optimize conflict conditions.

Alarm thresholds for monitoring data. The remote monitoring system must provide a feature to set alarm thresholds to conditions which the WSN is monitoring. To efficiently remotely monitor a specific facility, the user of the system must be able to set monitoring thresholds to the back-end system and/or the WSN system itself. This is especially relevant after some changes to the target facility's building automation are made and the causality of the changes is to be determined.

4 Conclusions

Most of the BASs are still closed types proprietary systems, but both customers and developers are starting to see the benefits of interoperable building solutions towards sustainability. This paper presented the WSN related requirement analysis for sustainable building automation operations and maintenance aiming at maximization of energy conservation, lowering of operation and maintenance costs while taking into accounts the users' or occupants' preferences, comfort, and safety. The requirement gathering resulted in 10 requirements, which were categorised as WSN, monitoring and back-end related requirements. From the sustainability point of view, operation and maintenance solutions must be economically viable, environmentally bearable and equitable for the society.

Many constrains remain, however, related the use of WSNs. The main challenges are security and the integration effort that is required to support the different systems and legacy protocols. In addition, wireless nature of WSNs may cause uncertainty, low reliability, and limited power, processing and memory resources of wireless nodes.

The next step for our research is setting up the WSN for building energy efficiency, operation and maintenance in real buildings. Further evaluation and quantitative measurements on how WSN can be utilised, especially in remote maintenance procedure, will be studied in the second phase of this research. Furthermore, user expectations drive the features of BASs and end-users should be taken as a part of the value chain, providing valuable feedback and information on indoor conditions or problems. Eventually, this will increase the quality of life, which should be one of the main priorities of sustainable building automation solutions along the energy efficiency and costs savings.

Acknowledgement. This work was funded by Tekes the Finnish Funding Agency for Technology and Innovation.

References

1. Kastner, W., Neugschwandtner, G., Sousek, S., Newman, H.M.: Communication systems for building automation and control. Proc. IEEE **93**(6), 1178–1203 (2005)
2. Wong, J.K.W., Li, H., Wang, S.W.: Intelligent building research: a review. Autom. Constr. **14**(1), 143–159 (2005)
3. Chappells, H., Shove, E.: Depating the future of comfort: environmental sustainability, energy consumption and the indoor environment. Build. Res. Inf. **33**(1), 32–40 (2005)
4. Lozano, R.: Envisioning sustainability three-dimensionally. J. Cleaner Prod. **16**(17), 1838–1846 (2008)
5. Wang, L., Laszewksi, G., Younge, A., He, X.: Cloud computing: a perspective study. Next Gener. Comput. **28**, 137–146 (2010)
6. Nguyen, T.A., Aiello, M.: Energy intelligent buildings based on user activity: a survey. Energy Build. **56**, 244–257 (2013)
7. Granzer, W., Kastner, W., Reinisch, C.: Gateway-free integration of BACnet and KNX using multi-protocol devices. In: 6th IEEE International Conference on Industrial Informatics (INDIN 2008), Daejeon, South Korea, 13–16 July 2008
8. Chen, M., Wan, J., Li, F.: Machine-to-machine communications: architectures, standards and applications. KSII Trans. Internet Inf. Syst. **6**(2), 480–497 (2012)
9. Sheng, Z., Yang, S., Yu, Y., Vasilakos, A., Mccann, J., Leung, K.: A survey on the IETF protocol suite for the internet of things: standards, challenges, and opportunities. IEEE Wirel. Commun. **20**(6), 91–98 (2014)
10. Egan, D.: The emergence of ZigBee in building automation and industrial control. Comput. Control Eng. J. **16**(2), 14–19 (2005)
11. ElShafee, A., Hamed, K.A.: Design and implementation of a WiFi based home automation system. Int. J. Comput. Electr. Autom. Control Inf. Eng. **6**(8), 1074–1080 (2012)
12. Callotta, M., Pau, G.A.: A solution based on bluetooth low energy for smart home energy management. Energies **8**(10), 11916–11938 (2015)
13. Shelby, Z., Bormann, C.: 6LoWPAN: The Wireless Embedded Internet. Wiley Series in Communications Networking and Distributed Systems. Wiley, Hoboken (2010)
14. Gomez, C., Paradells, J.: Wireless home automation networks: a survey of architectures and technologies. IEEE Commun. Mag. **48**(6), 92–101 (2010)
15. Rodrigues, J., Paulo, N.: A survey on IP-based wireless sensor networks solutions. Int. J. Commun. Syst. **23**, 963–981 (2010)

Leader-Based Routing in Mobile Wireless Sensor Networks

Unai Burgos[1,2(✉)], Carlos Gómez-Calzado[1,2], and Alberto Lafuente[1]

[1] University of the Basque Country (UPV/EHU), 20018 Donostia, Spain
{unai.burgos,carlos.gomez,alberto.lafuente}@ehu.eus
[2] Wimbi Technologies S.L. (WimbiTek), 20015 Donostia, Spain
{unai.burgos,carlos.gomez}@wimbitek.com

Abstract. In this paper we propose a routing algorithm for Mobile Wireless Sensor Network (MWSN) where all the nodes, sensors and sink, are mobile. We follow a leader election approach to build a spanning tree by using only information provided by neighbor nodes. The leader election approach allows automatic routing adaptation despite node mobility. The routing algorithm has been implemented and evaluated using the JBotSim simulator. We present some preliminary evaluations that show the impact of mobility in the message delivery rate.

Keywords: Mobile wireless sensor networks · Routing · Leader election

1 Introduction

Wireless Sensor Networks, WSN, have been successfully used in many applications, as environment monitoring, health care, transportation, ubiquitous home networks, and others. Nowadays, new application scenarios are arising for WSN. More specifically, WSNs are expanding from static to mobile deployments [1].

A WSN consists of one or more *sink nodes* that are in charge of collecting the information transmitted from a usually big number of *sensor nodes*, also called motes, which gather information of the environment. Sensor nodes are usually small devices with wireless communication and small computation capability. Sink nodes are in charge of processing the received data and making it available, usually by means of a Web service.

Since mote devices are small, work unattended in the real world, and are powered with limited batteries, energy constraints are usually severe and affect all the aspects in the system design. Therefore, instead of relaying on brute-force message forwarding (flooding), communication protocols should be designed carefully. More specifically, the design should consider a trade-off between transmission power and message retransmissions and forwarding. Additionally, a node

Research supported by the Spanish Research Council, grant TIN2013-41123-P, the Basque Government, grant IT395-10, and the University of the Basque Country UPV/EHU, grant UFI11/45.

C.R. García et al. (Eds.): UCAmI 2016, Part II, LNCS 10070, pp. 218–229, 2016.
DOI: 10.1007/978-3-319-48799-1_26

can crash, due to battery exhaustion or many other reasons. Therefore, a WSN needs an efficient routing protocol and a fault management mechanism that reacts by reconfiguring the network upon failures and ensure a sufficient quality of service [2].

In a static WSN routing can be initially configured to optimise communication and reduce latencies. However, some particular nodes, specifically the ones closer to a sink, must support more communication, which results in a reduction of their communication range due to the drop of the battery level, and henceforth in a higher probability of message loss. Maintaining an efficient level of operation in the network would require reconfiguring the routing on the basis of the information about the *quality of links* [3].

In WSN, the routing problem perspective changes when considering dynamic scenarios. In a Mobile WSN (MWSN), mobility can be introduced in two ways. On the one hand, sink nodes can be mobile while sensor nodes remain static, e.g., when using smartphones as sink devices to collect information about patients in a hospital. On the other hand, sensor nodes can be mobile, for example, when attached to animals for tracking purposes. In this scenario, one or more static sinks can be used to gather the tracking information of the sensor. Finally, mobile sinks and mobile sensors can be combined in many applications. For example, in residential environments for elderlies or dependable persons, RFID tags and other sensors attached to the persons can provide information to the mobile devices (e.g., smartphones) of the assistant personnel [4].

Despite the additional complexity of routing protocols for MWSN, mobility brings the opportunity of reducing the number of hops to the sink node. According to [5], the latency, or time until a mobile sink enters in the field of a sensor node, depends on the sink velocity, the communication radius of the sensor node, and the number of mobile sinks. In general, the higher the radius, the velocity and the number of sinks, the lower the latency. This is also basically true for the probability of having at least a sensor node in the range of a sink.

However, in a MWSN the time required to terminate the communication of a piece of data, i.e., to execute the wireless communication protocol, must also be considered. Extreme mobility could prevent many transmissions to successfully deliver messages [6]. Furthermore, the routing algorithm could require a minimum stability period to provide some guarantee for a sensor node to communicate with the sink. Therefore, in mobile scenarios, communication success is highly probabilistic[1]. The goal is to guarantee that communication succeed into a bounded time *with high probability* despite mobility.

In this paper we present a routing algorithm for Mobile Wireless Sensor Network. The algorithm uses a measure of the links quality to maintain a reconfigurable spanning tree in the network graph with the aim of minimising the communication cost from the mobile sensor nodes to the mobile sink. The algorithm is inspired on leader-election techniques for dynamic systems that we have explored previously [6,7]. We also present a preliminary evaluation of the

[1] Indeed, in static scenarios communication has a probabilistic component as well as communication ranges depend on environmental factors or battery level.

algorithm on the basis of the message delivery rate that the algorithm is able to provide under different levels of mobility, i.e., velocity of the nodes. The closest approach to ours in the literature is [8]. However, as far as we now, our proposal is the first routing algorithm for MWSN using leader election as a basis for the algorithm.

The rest of the paper is organised as follows. Section 2 introduces some background concepts on MWSN architectures, and performance parameters and metrics, as well as some related work. Section 3 describes the routing protocol. Section 4 presents the evaluation environment and the performance results. Finally, Sect. 5 is devoted to conclude the work and present future research directions.

2 Related Work

In this section we revise some routing techniques in MWSN, which have been developed in recent years. As mentioned in [9], a routing algorithm design can follow different approaches depending on the application scenario.

Despite that many works only address sink mobility, in this section we consider works that focus on node mobility in a general way. On the other hand, we have limited to works addressing algorithms in which routing is managed proactively, as it is the case of ours.

A cluster-based routing algorithm for MWSN, called ECBR-MWSN, is presented in [10]. As in our case, they consider that all the sensor nodes are mobile, however the sink is static. A cluster head is selected on the basis of a combination of the highest residual energy, lowest mobility and least distance from the sink. To face mobility ECBR-MWSN selects a new cluster head periodically. Consequently, new paths to the sink could be created. Our algorithm also uses a periodic cast of the topology, however we do not follow a cluster-based approach.

In [11] a protocol in which nodes cooperate to enhance the robustness of routing against path breakage is proposed. They use the Wireless Broadcast Advantage (WBA) [12], as we also do. In short, WBA refers to the fact that when a node sends a broadcast message all the nodes that are in it transmission range will receive the message. They also assume that every node in the network has a pre-established path between the node and the sink. In addition, they use special nodes, *guard nodes*, to support the routing.

Proactive routing, early used in static WSN (e.g., DSDV [13]), has been implemented in [10,11] for MWSN. A proactive routing protocol runs independently from the application to maintain and update routing tables. Following this approach the message delivery latency is reduced significantly which is a relevant QoS parameter. Our algorithm follows a proactive, two-layer approach as well.

As mentioned before, the closest approach to ours in the literature is [8], which differently to ours, proposes leader election as a complement for the algorithm to be apply in distributed systems.

3 An Algorithm for MWSN

In this section we propose a distributed spanning-tree-based routing protocol for mobile wireless sensor networks (MWSN). The protocol is based on a dynamic leader election approach, commonly studied in the field of fault tolerant distributed agreement [7,14,15], and uses heartbeat and timer mechanisms, very common in the literature [16].

3.1 Notation and Assumptions

We consider an architecture with an unknown set of resource constrained mobile sensor nodes and one more powerful mobile sink. We denote this set of sensor nodes as $V = \{p_1, p_2, \ldots, p_n\}$. For simplicity we will informally also refer to a node as p, q, etc. We will denote as s the sink node. Every node of the system has an unique identifier and a local clock to measure real-time intervals.

Every node, including the sink node, can move. For this reason, nodes can leave and join the system as they will. The mobility of a node is characterised according to two dimensions: speed and direction. At any time t a node p moves towards some direction $d(p,t)$ with a speed $s(p,t) \leq S_{\max}$, being $S_{\max}$ the maximum speed of every node p in the system.

At any time t, a node p can communicate directly (i.e., at one hop) with a subset $N_p(t) \subset V$, which are the nodes that are at time t into a radius r from p, also referred as the neighbourhood of p. The communication range r is a common parameter in V. Additionally, we use the parameter *link quality* (in dBm), since it is an information that can be extracted from the reception of a message by p from q. Therefore, we define link quality for a link (q,p) at time t, denoted $W_{p \leftarrow q}(t)$. For simplicity, we consider that message transmission delays are bounded and it is assumed that $W_{p \leftarrow q}(t) = W_{q \leftarrow p}(t)$.

When considering link quality, a graph $G(t)$ representing the connectivity conditions in V at time t is obtained. We are interested in representing a spanning tree $T(t) \subset G(t)$. Ideally, $T(t)$ will include only links with good link quality. Observe that partitions in $G(t)$ are possible, but we assume that $s \in T(t) \forall t$. A node p can be disconnected from $T(t)$ due to: (a) p is out or the radius of any node $q \in T(t)$, (b) $W_{p \leftarrow q}(t)$ in under a defined threshold for any $q \in T(t)$.

3.2 Algorithm Description

The main goal of our approach is to provide an efficient communication route from any process p to the root process s. To do so, the algorithm creates a spanning tree $T(t)$ with the root in the sink node s. The spanning tree is continuously maintained by the distributed algorithm in order to represent the best routing options at time t on the basis of the link quality information.

The algorithm uses a broadcast primitive to build the spanning tree. Note that, apart form providing energy-efficiency in the multi-hop information dissemination [12], broadcast is also useful to detect neighbourhood changes.

In the algorithm, every node $p_i \in V$ elects its leader, denoted $sinkBy_i$. Leader election is executed at every node p_i at time t such that $sinkBy_i \in N_{p_i}(t)$ and has the minimum distance to s in the te spanning tree $T(t)$. Ties are broken on the basis of the higher identifier.

The sink node s is in charge of generating new rounds in the spanning tree reconfiguration. The spanning tree is created from the sink node s, which is the root of the tree, to the rest of nodes. In this regard, s sends LEADER messages with refreshed round numbers each β time (see Fig. 2). Every node p_i is continuously listening to the communication channel. If no message is received (see Fig. 1, Lines 7, 15 and 23), p_i switches to inactive. The reception of a new round identifier from s by a node p_i enables a new election round in p_i, which will result in refreshing the spanning tree. Observe that no other node but s will send in its LEADER message a zero distance value. In this way, every $p_i \in N_s(t)$ will always become active and will have the variable $sinkBy_i$ pointing to s (Lines 19–21). Figure 3(a), (b) illustrate this situation.

To start a election round, every node p_i, by Line 10, sends the information of the previous round to every node $N_{p_i}(t)$. Thus, p_i sends its own LEADER message using the last distance known by p_i to the node s. These new LEADER message sent by p_i is essential for multi-hop scenarios. First, LEADER messages propagate the existence of a node sink in the system. Second, the periodic broadcast of LEADER message results in the activation of further nodes in multi-hop scenarios. And finally, LEADER messages provide the required information to its neighbourhood to create the spanning tree.

In order p_i to perform the next election, p_i stores the new distance from p_i to s[2], and the node which has received the message by, (i.e., the sender p_j) is denoted as $sinkBy_i$ (Lines 11–13).

Additionally, the periodic sending of information allows a timer-based monitorization of graph changes. The first time that a process p_i receives a LEADER message (let us say, at time t) from any $p_j \in N_{p_i}(t)$, p_i becomes active and will remain active during the time interval $(t, t + timeout]$[3] by setting the timer $timer\_connectivity_i$. The $timer\_connectivity_i$ determines whether p_i is still connected to the sink node s. Each time that an active node p_i receives a LEADER message at time t with a round identifier higher than the previously received, p_i resets the $timer\_connectivity_i$ variable (Line 15). This results in p_i to be active for *timeout* more time units. The $timer\_connectivity_i$ variable represents the uncertainty of p_i to be connected to the sink node. The expiration of $timer\_connectivity_i$ results in p_i inactive (Lines 22 and 23). If the non reception of a new round identifier is due to the distancing of p_i from s, p_i will shortly receive a new message and reconfigure again the spanning tree. Otherwise, if p_i is no longer connected to the spanning tree $T(t)$, then no new round identifier will be received in the disconnected subgraph, and eventually every node in $T(t)$ will become inactive forever.

[2] The distance is extracted from contextual information stored in the message.

[3] The *timeout* variable has a common value slightly higher than β in order to prevent premature time outs.

```
Initially:
actualRound_i ← −1;
sinkBy_i ← −1;
nextSinkBy_i ← −1;
sinkDistance_i ← ∞;
timeout ← v ~ β;
call(reset());

|| Task 1: when (j, LEADER, sender, round, distance) is received at time t such
that j ∈ N_i(t) and W_{i←j}(t) > −77                {When receiving a LEADER message}
  if round > actualRound_i then
    broadcast(LEADER, i, actualRound_i, sinkDistance_i + 1);
    sinkBy_i ← nextSinkBy_i;
    nextSinkBy_i ← sender;
    sinkDistance_i ← distance;
    actualRound ← round;
    set timer_connectivity_i to timeout;
  else if sinkDistance_i = distance and sender > sinkBy_i then
    nextSinkBy_i ← sender;
    sinkDistance_i ← distance;
  if not active_i then
    active_i ← True;
    sinkBy_i ← nextSinkBy_i;

|| Task 2: when timer_connectivity_i expires        {The node becomes not connected}
  call(reset());

|| Procedure reset:                                 {Initializes variables}
  timer_connectivity_i ← −1;
  active ← False;
  sinkBy ← −1;
  nextSinkBy_i ← −1;
  actualRound_i ← 0;
  sinkDistance ← ∞;
```

Fig. 1. Algorithm executed by any sensing node p_i.

```
roundId ← 0;
|| Task 1: each β time                              {Sends heartbeats}
  roundId ← roundId + 1;
  broadcast(LEADER, s, roundId, 0);
```

Fig. 2. Algorithm executed by the sink node s.

Observe that, while the round identifiers created by s lower-bounds the interval between two consecutive reconfigurations, $timer\_connectivity_i$ upper-bounds the interval between two consecutive reconfigurations.

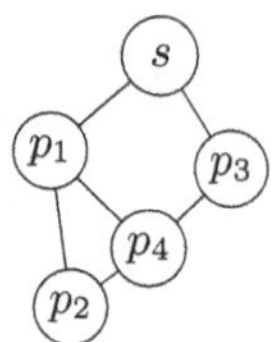

(a) The sink node starts executing the algorithm.

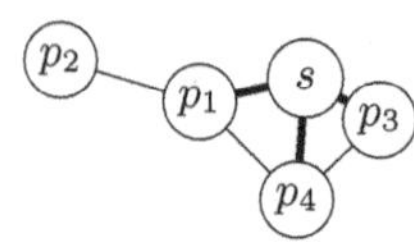

(b) The spanning tree is built from the sink.

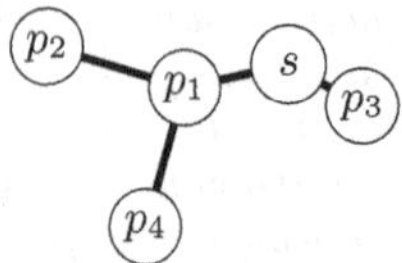

(c) The spanning tree is complete. Observe that it has been restructured in the meanwhile.

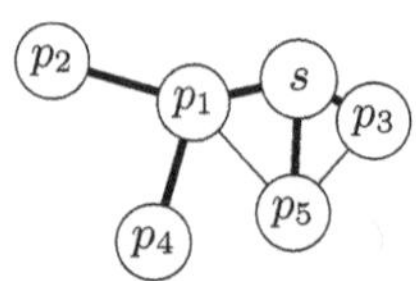

(d) A new node, p_5 joins the network.

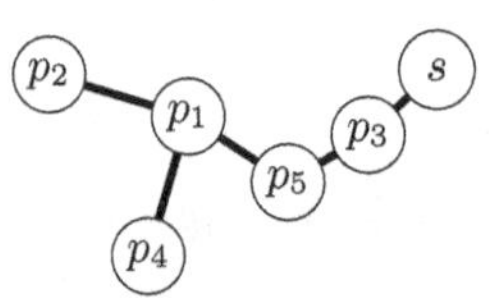

(e) A new reconfiguration due to mobility.

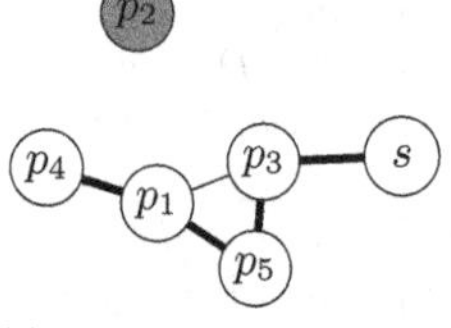

(f) Node p_2 becomes out of the range of any node in the spanning tree and considers itself as isolated.

Fig. 3. Sequence of rounds that shows how the algorithm builds the spanning tree.

Figure 3(a)–(f) illustrate how the algorithm builds up the distributed spanning tree despite node movements, new nodes arrivals or node disconnections.

Note that, the bigger is the β and *timeout* values the slower is the graph connectivity changes detection. This is the reason why there must be a compromise between the reaction time and the number of messages sent by the system in order to provide a good QoS and energy-efficiency at the same time.

Observe also that the number of messages sent by the system is linear with the number of nodes in the system, therefore, the algorithm is linearly scalable in terms of number of messages.

3.3 Data Routing Protocol

In contrast to the spanning-tree creation, where we use broadcast as the communication primitive, for data communication we use one-to-one communication primitives. Once an initial spanning-tree has been created, the following data routing protocol is executed. We have considered two different routing protocols for data communication.

The first one basically sends a single copy of the content to the current $sinkBy_i$ node without expecting any reception notification, i.e., not using ACK messages.

In the second protocol, nodes wait for an ACK message from the $sinkBy_i$ node. The non reception of that ACK from $sinkBy_i$ results in another sending attempt of that message. For this second communication protocol we introduce a parameter that represents the number of re-sending attempts allowed to perform in order to avoid life-locks.

In the following we denote the first protocol as no-*ACK* and the second protocol as *ACK-i* where i is the number of re-sending attempts performed by the protocol.

4 Evaluation

The algorithm has been implemented using JBotSim [17]. This Section presents a first evaluation of the algorithm, in terms of message delivery rate, under conditions of node mobility. Since the combination of possible configurations and conditions to evaluate is very high, in this work we focus on a limited set of experiments in order to gain a first insight of the algorithm performance and have the guidelines for a more complete future experimentation.

For the evaluation, we use periodic data messages which are generated at every sensor node with a period of 5 s, i.e., 25 times the period of heartbeat messages. Data message reception is checked at the sink node to compute the message delivery rate figures. Preliminary simulations on different conditions have been carried out to establish the most efficient configurations for the algorithm. In this regard, we have adjusted timeout values to be slightly higher than the heartbeat period, which is 0.2 s. Then, using these values, we have tested a number of configurations including the no-ACK version and three ack versions configured with respectively one, two and three resents, and denoted *ACK-1*, *ACK-2* and *ACK-3*.

In a set of 500 experiments with network sizes of 50, 100, 150, 200 and 250 nodes and node speeds from 0 to 4 m/s, we have found that, in terms of message delivery rates, the *No-ACK* protocol performs as least as well than the ack versions (Fig. 4). Furthermore, the no-ack configuration exhibits better scalabity, as summarized in Fig. 5(a). Note that these results have been obtained with modest node speeds. In sporadic simulations with high speeds we have observed that the negative consequences of extreme mobility, as it could be expected, are more evident when using the ack configurations, since these execute a heavier protocol. Additionally, avoiding ack messages reduces communication load, as reported in Fig. 5(b) and power consumption. Henceforth, further experimentation has been focussed to the no-ack configuration, as we describe next.

Specific experiments to evaluate the impact of mobility on the message delivery rate have been carried out with the no-ack configuration. Recall that the mobility of a node is characterised according to the speed and direction of the node. For each simulation run, a maximum speed $S_{\max}$ has been defined as a common magnitude for all the nodes so that a node p at time t will have a speed $s(p,t) \leq S_{\max}$. Rather than assigning absolute values, we made speed values relative to the communication radius of the nodes, r, which allows to

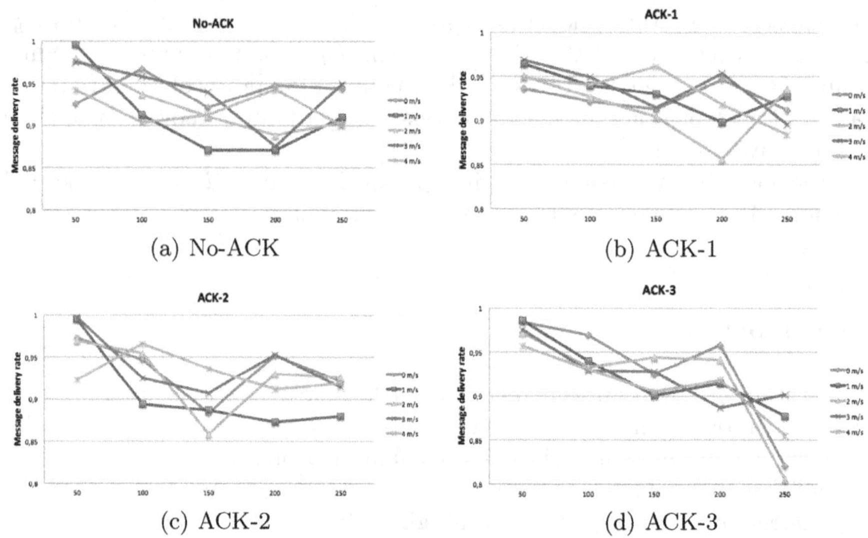

Fig. 4. Message delivery rate for different protocol versions and node speeds.

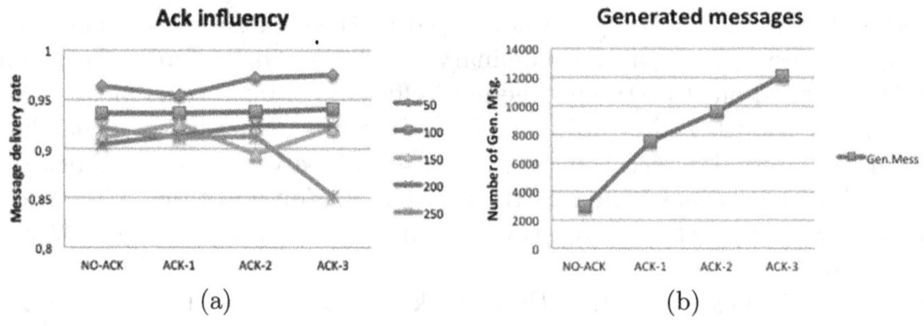

Fig. 5. (a) Message delivery rate for the tested protocol versions. (b) Message load for the tested protocol versions.

make the results independent of the communication radius. Henceforth, we fed the simulations with speeds (in m/s) from $0.01r$ to $0.32r$. For example, for a communication radius of 100 meters, these relative values correspond to speed values from 1 to 32 m/s. These mobility rules also apply to the sink node itself.

Speed and direction are generated in the simulator at random with a fixed frequency (each one second in our experiments). No bounds are defined for the position of a node. Note that this feature, combined with the fact that the frequency of changes in the direction do not increase with the speed, would penalise the behaviour of the system for high speeds, since some nodes could derive to remote and isolated positions. However, recall that our algorithm allows partitions and a node is able to be considered itself as isolated, thus communication from these nodes will not be computed for the final figures of the evaluation.

Table 1. Simulation parameters

Parameters	Values
Network size	50, 100, 150, 200, 250
Channel model	Free space loss model (FSL) [18]
Transmission range, r (m)	100
Maximum node speed (m/s)	$0.01r$, $0.02r$, $0.04r$, $0.08r$, $0.016r$, $0.32r$
Message generation interval (s)	[1, 900]
Heartbeats period (s)	0.2
Data messages period (s)	5

A summary of the configurations used for the experiments is shown in Table 1. We have run 10 times each configuration and obtained the results shown in Fig. 6. As seen in the Figure, the algorithm behaves uniformly with speeds up to $0.08r$ m/s, performing high delivery rates. For higher speeds, the delivery rate starts decreasing. This is due to the high volatility of links of the network, which prevents the protocol to effectively use the links decided by the spanning tree.

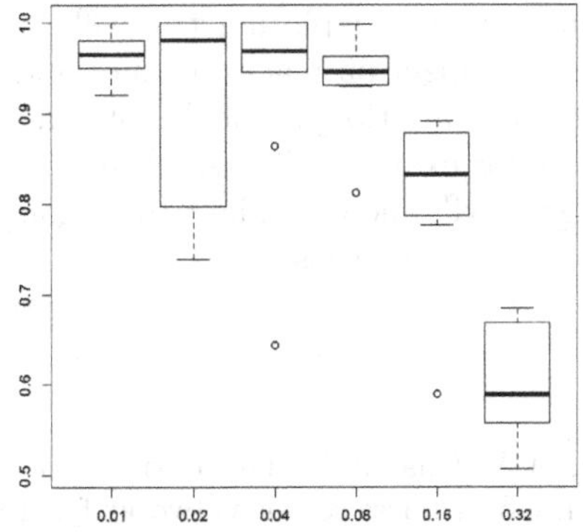

Fig. 6. Message delivery rate as a function of the speed.

To have a practical outlook of the significance of this figures, let us consider a communication radius of 100 meters. Note that a speed of about $0.08r$ m/s, i.e., 8 m/s, corresponds to the traffic speed in a city, indeed a more structured scenario than the one represented by the simulation conditions. For scenarios where nodes may have more mobility freedom, as for example in animal or person tracking, node speeds are expected to be usually in the ranges of the maximum performance of the algorithm.

5 Conclusions

We have presented a routing algorithm for mobile wireless sensor networks. The algorithm builds and maintains a spanning tree with the root in the sink node, which is mobile as well. The algorithm uses a heartbeat mechanism to react to node mobility. On the basis of local information about link quality, the algorithm executes leader elections in order to restructure the spanning tree so that message delivery rates could be optimised.

The algorithm can be configured to use ack and message resents. Nevertheless, experiments have shown that the no-ack configuration, apart of being the most energy efficient, exhibits better scalability.

We have carried out a preliminar evaluation to determine the behaviour of the algorithm with respect to the mobility level, measured as the maximum node velocity. The algorithm performs uniformly and produces high message delivery rates for velocities of up to 0.08 times the communication range, slowly decreasing for higher speeds. Considering current wireless technologies, these figures show that our approach has the potential for practical applications in many scenarios, for example in smart cities or person and animal tracking, among others.

In future experimentation we plan to introduce additional performance metrics, as latencies and reaction times, to complete the evaluation of the algorithm. Regarding algorithm configuration, exploring tradeoffs between heartbeat frequencies (which have a high impact on reaction times and henceforth on mobility resilience) and energy consumption would be of practical interest. Finally, testing new configurations, for example the use of multiple sinks, or combining static and dynamic elements, will allow to adapt the algorithm to the conditions provided by specific application scenarios.

References

1. Shakshuki, E.M., Kafi, M.A., Challal, Y., Djenouri, D., Doudou, M., Bouabdallah, A., Badache, N.: A study of wireless sensor networks for urban traffic monitoring: applications and architectures. Procedia Comput. Sci. **19**, 617–626 (2013)
2. Yu, M., Mokhtar, H., Merabti, M.: Fault management in wireless sensor networks. IEEE Wirel. Commun. **14**(6), 13–19 (2007)
3. Burgos, U., Soraluze, I., Lafuente, A.: Evaluation of a fault-tolerant wsn routing algorithm based on link quality. In: Proceedings of the 4th International Conference on Sensor Networks, pp. 97–102 (2015)
4. Ko, J., Lu, C., Srivastava, M.B., Stankovic, J.A., Terzis, A., Welsh, M.: Wireless sensor networks for healthcare. Proc. IEEE **98**(11), 1947–1960 (2010)
5. Munir, S.A., Ren, B., Jiao, W., Wang, B., Xie, D., Ma, J.: Mobile wireless sensor network: architecture and enabling technologies for ubiquitous computing. In: 21st International Conference on Advanced Information Networking and Applications Workshops, AINAW 2007, vol. 2, pp. 113–120, May 2007
6. Gómez-Calzado, C., Casteigts, A., Lafuente, A., Larrea, M.: A connectivity model for agreement in dynamic systems. In: Träff, J.L., Hunold, S., Versaci, F. (eds.) Euro-Par 2015. LNCS, vol. 9233, pp. 333–345. Springer, Heidelberg (2015)

7. Gómez-Calzado, C., Lafuente, A., Larrea, M., Raynal, M.: Fault-tolerant leader election in mobile dynamic distributed systems. In: 2013 IEEE 19th Pacific Rim International Symposium on Dependable Computing (PRDC), pp. 78–87, December 2013
8. Crowcroft, J., Segal, M., Levin, L.: Improved structures for data collection in wireless sensor networks. In: IEEE INFOCOM 2014 - IEEE Conference on Computer Communications, pp. 1375–1383, April 2014
9. Goyal, D., Tripathy, M.R.: Routing protocols in wireless sensor networks: a survey. In: 2012 Second International Conference on Advanced Computing Communication Technologies, pp. 474–480, January 2012
10. Anitha, R.U., Kamalakkannan, P.: Enhanced cluster based routing protocol for mobile nodes in wireless sensor network. In: 2013 International Conference on Pattern Recognition, Informatics and Mobile Engineering (PRIME), pp. 187–193, February 2013
11. Huang, X., Zhai, H., Fang, Y.: Robust cooperative routing protocol in mobile wireless sensor networks. IEEE Trans. Wirel. Commun. **7**(12), 5278–5285 (2008)
12. Wieselthier, J.E., Nguyen, G.D., Ephremides, A.: Algorithms for energy-efficient multicasting in static ad hoc wireless networks. Mob. Netw. Appl. **6**(3), 251–263 (2001)
13. Broch, J., Maltz, D.A., Johnson, D.B., Hu, Y.C., Jetcheva, J.: A performance comparison of multi-hop wireless ad hoc network routing protocols. In: Proceedings of the 4th Annual ACM/IEEE International Conference on Mobile Computing and Networking, MobiCom 1998, pp. 85–97. ACM, New York (1998)
14. Arantes, L., Greve, F., Sens, P., Simon, V.: Eventual leader election in evolving mobile networks. In: Baldoni, R., Nisse, N., van Steen, M. (eds.) OPODIS 2013. LNCS, vol. 8304, pp. 23–37. Springer, Heidelberg (2013)
15. Melit, L., Badache, N.: An Ω-based leader election algorithm for mobile ad hoc networks. In: Proceedings of the 4th International Conference on Networked Digital Technologies, NDT 2012, Dubai, UAE, 24-26 April 2012, vol. 293, pp. 483–490. Springer (2012)
16. Chandra, T.D., Hadzilacos, V., Toueg, S.: The weakest failure detector for solving consensus. J. ACM **43**(4), 685–722 (1996)
17. Casteigts, A.: JBotSim: a tool for fast prototyping of distributed algorithms in dynamic networks. In: Proceedings of the 8th International ICST Conference on Simulation Tools and Techniques, SIMUTools 2015, Athens, Greece (2015)
18. Rappaport, T.S., others.: Wireless Communications: Principles and Practice. vol. 2. Prentice Hall PTR, New Jersey (1996)

Self-organizing Connectivity for Mobile Agents in Dynamical Environments

Roberto G. Aldunate[1(✉)], Feniosky Pena-Mora[2], Miguel Nussbaum[3], Alfredo Valenzuela[4], and Cesar Navarro[4]

[1] College of Applied Health Sciences, University of Illinois at Urbana-Champaign, Champaign, IL, USA
aldunate@illinois.edu

[2] Fu Foundation School of Engineering and Applied Science, Columbia University, New York City, NY, USA
feniosky@columbia.edu

[3] Department of Computer Science, Catholic University of Chile, Santiago, Chile
mn@ing.puc.cl

[4] Independent Professionals, Temuco, Chile
alfredo.valenzuela.r@gmail.com, cnavarronm@gmail.com

Abstract. Field operations carried out by mobile users in inhospitable contexts like disaster relief or battlefield require that the communication between those mobile users is as effective and efficient as possible. To facilitate such communication, a highly available communication platform is required. This article envisions that Mobile Ad-hoc Networks (MANETs) could be feasible communication platforms for inhospitable contexts provided high connectivity is achievable. In this article, a proactive distributed mechanism, referred to as a self-organizing mechanism, to provide high connectivity for MANETs operating in inhospitable contexts is presented. This mechanism is based on the introduction of additional unmanned vehicles acting as communication bridges, where their demand is dynamically determined by the movement of the mobile users. By means of simulations it is demonstrated that the proactive distributed self-organizing mechanism proposed in this article allows MANETs to exhibit high connectivity under high values of link failure probability.

Keywords: MANETs · Connectivity · Simulations · Self-organizing

1 Introduction

Field operations carried out in inhospitable and sometimes chaotic environments, like disaster relief and battlefield, must be developed in an efficient and effective manner to mitigate as much as possible social and economic impact of such extreme events. In this context, a reliable communication platform is a must to achieve those goals. Nevertheless, much of current communication platforms utilized in inhospitable and chaotic contexts like disaster relief and battlefield are characterized by the use of voice channels [1, 2], which suffers from information overload and lacks the possibility of enabling a

C.R. García et al. (Eds.): UCAmI 2016, Part II, LNCS 10070, pp. 230–241, 2016.
DOI: 10.1007/978-3-319-48799-1_27

collective memory during operations, among other problems. A potential means to build such a communication platform is by using Mobile Ad Hoc Networks (MANET). This article introduces a mechanism to avoid connectivity problems between mobile users operating in inhospitable environments, like disaster relief or battlefield, where each mobile user wears or carry on a short-range wireless enabled communication device. The mechanism is based on the introduction of autonomous unmanned mobile devices, here referred to as Mobile Communication Bridges (MCB), which perform simple tasks as antennas or signal repeaters that proactively and dynamically aim to maintain high connectivity in a MANET involving mobile users. Each MCB is considered as being equipped with the same technology that mobile users may use; i.e., short-range wireless communication, battery, processing power. Hence, from a modeling perspective, the only distinction between the mobile users and the MCBs is their movement behaviors. The movement of the MCBs is triggered by connectivity problems generated by the mobile users move. For the design of a proactive movement behavior of the MCBs, in order to maintain connectivity in a MANET, one needs to evaluate fault tolerance, performance, and scalability, between centralized and distributed configurations of unmanned vehicles [3]. This research effort made a decision in favor of a distributed approach, because in general fault tolerance and scalability are more tractable under a distributed approach than under a centralized approach [4]. Specifically, as the key issue to deal with in this research is fault tolerance, using a centralized approach which centralizes the coordination of the MCBs on one or a few nodes of the system could make the whole system more vulnerable, especially under deliberate attack or non-random failures of nodes and/or communication links [5]. The objective of this research effort is to evaluate general conditions for the effectiveness of the proposed self-organizing mechanism.

2 Related Work

Research on coordination of mobile unmanned vehicles is a very active area. Various investigations have been made to improve the properties of wireless network connectivity [6]. Although traditionally one of the primary topics of research with unmanned vehicles has been avoidance of obstacles [7] using adequate sensing and localization awareness mechanisms [8, 9], in recent years several research efforts have focused on sensing, communication, and coordination issues in a community of unmanned vehicles (efficient multi-robot coordination), e.g., [3], as well as motion detection or using shared between them to avoid disconnections knowledge [10, 11]. It also has considerable importance on this, the use of mobility prediction [12]. While many current research efforts still consider a human making decisions and controlling a community of unmanned vehicles [13], the idea of mobile actuators has been increasing in the mobile sensor community [14–16] and some research efforts have focused on designing completely autonomous communities of unmanned vehicles. One of those efforts corresponds to Self-healing Minefield (SHM) project carried out at DARPA [17]. There are both strong similarities and differences between DARPA SHM initiative and the research presented in this article. Among the similarities between both research efforts are: the use of short-range wireless communication enabled mobile nodes and the existence of an autonomous distributed process in order to determine re-location of the nodes. On the other hand, the problem statement, and consequently the underlying approaches, between SHM and the research introduced in this article are different. First, SHM only considers a high probability of permanent failures of devices; i.e., devices are destroyed by the enemy. In our case, permanent failures could be as high as in the SHM context, for the case of battlefield where an enemy aimed to destroy nodes exists, or lower, as in the case of disaster relief contexts, where permanent failures may have not a significant impact [18]. Second, minefield healing is modeled as a statistical process [17], in opposition to the organizing process carried out by the MCBs, which is heuristic. Third, the objective of the research initiative presented in this article requires a proactive approach to dynamically avoid potential disconnections, while in SHM it is reactive; the healing process is activated once a breach is detected; i.e., once a communication link has been destroyed. For the purposes of improving connectivity in a MANET operating in inhospitable contexts, a proactive behavior of the nodes involved in supporting communication is better than a reactive one. This could be through a system capable of forming an autonomous network, forming connections with other members through a distributed architecture [19]. Finally, in SHM the problem to solve is how to distribute the mines in a determined area so that the area covered by the network of mines becomes maximized, while in the research shown in this paper the problem to solve is how the MCBs must proactively and collaboratively behave in order to maintain high level of connectivity. Several other research efforts have addressed the area-maximizing problem [20, 21], but no specific research has been found regarding the specific problem stated in this article. Another key issue related with distributed coordination in a community of autonomous mobile vehicles is message delivery. The research presented in this paper proposes the use of gossip-based multicast for MANETs comprised of a reduced number of nodes, e.g. 30 nodes, which is the case for teams responding to large scale disasters [22], extending the applicability of the results obtained by Haas et al. [23]. Haas and colleagues focused only on using gossip-based multicast for large MANETs. Similarly to Haas and colleagues our research on gossip-based multicast will focus on determining a link failure probability threshold above which it can be guaranteed message delivery becomes highly reliable. Other studies have proposed using unmanned vehicles to cover large areas and avoid obstacles, however they still use a reactive approach [24, 25]. Su et al.'s work [27] and the work presented in this document consider a space without obstacles in the trajectory of the mobile nodes, Su and colleagues assumes all the nodes have synchronized clocks, and based on this, the analysis of potential disconnections follows from the analytical-geometrical situation where the awareness of the network layout is shared among the nodes. In opposition, the disconnection detection mechanism introduced in this draft lies only on a heuristic, i.e.; the three-phase algorithm introduced in next section, individually followed by each unmanned node without either time synchronization or topological awareness. On the other hand, De Rosa and colleagues [26] research is characterized by the use of a probabilistic approach, based on a Markov chain model, to detect disconnections, using a centralized approach to predict disconnections, which we discarded due to the vulnerability of the system to failures of nodes centralizing some task, as mentioned previously in the introduction. Also, De Rosa and colleagues focus only on the problem of predicting disconnections without addressing what constitutes the core of the research presented in this article; i.e., network fragmentation avoidance or minimization to achieve high connectivity level in a MANET.

Research on autonomous dynamic networks is abundant and generally focused in data dissemination and communication issues, like UAVs collaborative communication systems [36]; urban surveillance operating on networks of vehicle sensors [33]; data spreading and availability [34]; or vehicle-to-vehicle information transmission [35], which is different to the connectivity problem approached in this article.

3 Self-organizing Communication Mechanism

Connectivity problems due to movement of mobile users are represented through the situation illustrated in Fig. 1. In that figure P1, P2, P3, and P4 represent mobile users who communicate with each other using short-range wire-less enabled devices, at a given time. Arrows represent the direction of movement for each mobile user. Thus, considering the direction of movement of each mobile user shown in Fig. 1, P2 will eventually leave the communication range of P1, and vice-versa. In addition, P3 and P4 will remain within the communication range of each other, and also within the communication range of P1. Depending on the movement of the nodes comprising the MANET, network fragmentation can be either permanent or temporary.

Fig. 1. MANET = {P1, P2, P3, P4} will become fragmented, Set1 = {P_1, P_3, P_4} Set2 = {P_2}

In developing a solution for the problem sketched in Fig. 1, based on introducing MCBs, this research aims to answer the following questions: What is the appropriate number of MCBs to be introduced in the system for a typical setting in operation areas? What is the mechanism to spread messages requesting support for possible disconnections? What is the effect of link failure probability on the self-organizing mechanism? What are the consequences regarding power consumption? What is the performance of the self-organizing mechanism? In order to address these questions, the three-phase algorithm presented below was developed. This algorithm relies on two principles: (a) an MCB never loses members (mobile nodes) in Supporting Communication mode, and (b) an MCB never rejects a mission (potential disconnection call), unless other MCB is closer to such mission (Fig. 2).

- Phase 1: Potential Disconnection Detection, this phase is always running on every device. At every time step t, each node monitors its 1-hop neighbors; i.e., the neighbors inside its communication range. For each 1-hop neighbor that is located at a distance greater than a certain threshold, given as a parameter, the monitoring node records such distance at that moment. At the next time step, the monitoring node will determine the new distance for each previously monitored 1-hop neighbor. For each 1-hop neighbor, if the distance has increased, the monitoring node will try to find out if at least one of its other 1-hop neighbors is closer to the neighbor under observation. To do this, the monitoring node will send a message, including its distance to the node under observation to each one of its 1-hop neighbors asking if their distances to the node under observation are shorter than the distance informed by the monitoring node. Each 1-hop neighbor receiving the message will send a yes or no message back, according to his or her own estimations of distance. If the monitoring node receives at least one yes message back, it will stop the process and start checking the other 1-hop neighbors, one neighbor at a time, to see if an eventual disconnection may be in progress with them. On the other hand, if the monitoring node did not receive a yes message back for a given period of time, it considers that the node under observation is leaving its communication range. Therefore, the monitoring node will propagate a message through the MANET to the monitored node searching if there is an alternative route to the monitored node.
- Phase 2: Correction, both mobile users and MCBs also implement this phase. Once a node detected a potential disconnection, it will propagate a message through the network, using gossip-based multicast. Any MCB receiving that message will wait a given period of time for the counterpart message; i.e., the message sent by the other node involved in the potential disconnection. If the counterpart message is received by the MCB, it will ignore the situation because it means that there is at least one alternative route connecting both nodes. But, if the counterpart message is not received by the MCB, it assumes a disconnection is in progress. Consequently, the MCB will set itself for this task; i.e., move toward the potential disconnection area (the point at the middle of the line between the nodes involved in the potential disconnection) where the wireless interface at the MCB is expected to receive similar signal strength from both supported nodes' wireless interfaces. When the MCB sets itself for a connectivity task, it sends a multicast message, which includes its estimation of distance to the disconnection area, to the community of MCBs. After sending the multicast message, the MCB starts moving toward the disconnection area.
- Phase 3; Maintenance, this phase of the algorithm is applicable only to MCBs; i.e., not applicable to devices used by mobile users. Once the MCB is placed at the potential disconnection area, it tries to detect the presence of the requesting nodes. If the MCB does not find the requesting nodes after a given period of time, it will set itself

back to Idle state. But, if the MCB detects the requesting nodes, it sets its state to supporting mode, adjusting its position.

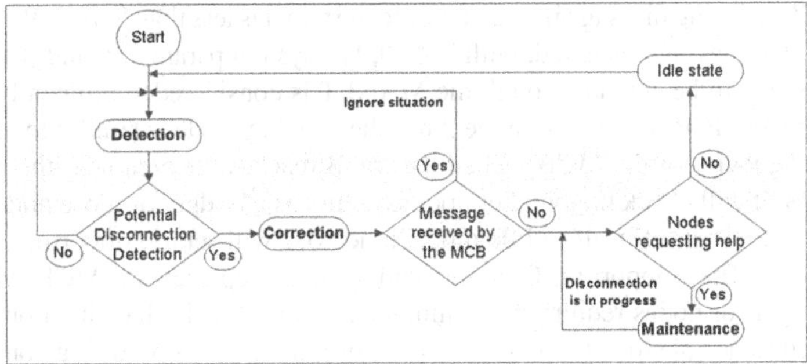

Fig. 2. Algorithm flowchart

4 Simulation

A discrete event simulation model was built, mainly due to the need of knowing the positions of mobile users, in this case, first responders, as well as of the MCBs at every time step. By knowing the position of each node in the area of operations, we are able to monitor and understand the movement behavior of MCBs. The area of operations is modeled as 2D square. The movement assigned to first responders is random and the movement behavior of MCBs must be accordingly implemented with the algorithm described in Sect. 2. The movement behavior of every node at the operations area is determined by the set of paths the node travels. Each path a node travels is determined by its position in the 2D square, its speed, the direction of its movement, and the time the node will travel on such path. Each node is modeled as being able to determine the distance to each one of its 1-hop neighbors by using some technique like signal strength propagation models or Global Positioning System (GPS). The time spent on each path for each node is variable as are the direction (between 0° and 360° with respect to its own reference frame assigned randomly) and the speed (between 0.0 and 3.0 m/s). During a simulation run MCBs are in one of three modes: (1) Idle, (2) Moving toward a required communication area or (3) Supporting Communication. The Idle mode represents a stationary MCB waiting for messages transmitted through the MANET, indicating a potential disconnection is in progress; some node sends a message searching an alternative route to some target node; or other MCB sends a message signaling that it is accepting a task; i.e., moving to avoid a disconnection. For the former case, the MCB will assume that connectivity support is required only when one message is heard by it during a period of time. On the contrary, when both messages are heard, one message from each one of the nodes detecting a potential disconnection, the MCB assumes there is at least one alternative route between the senders of gossip_search_alternative_path_to messages. For the latter case, if the MCB hears a gossip_MCB_moving from another MCB, it will evaluate if it is significantly closer to the target area than the other MCB, and then it will propagate a new gossip_MCB_moving message to inform others it is moving to the potential disconnection area. For this comparison process, two design characteristics are introduced: (a) the MCB will determine it is closer to the target mentioned in the received gossip_MCB_moving message if its distance to the target is less than S times the distance informed in the message received, with $S \in (0, 1)$ a system parameter, and (b) the time for any message to be spread through the MANET is considered significantly smaller than the time an MCB requires to move 2 m. The Moving mode is similar to idle mode in terms of behavior of the MCB. When the MCB reaches the area near the requiring pair of nodes, it will check if any other node is acting as a bridge for those nodes. If this is the situation it will set itself to Idle mode, otherwise will set to Supporting Communication mode. The Supporting Communication mode represents a MCB which has reached the pair of nodes requiring a communication bridge. In that situation, a MCB is considered to be able to determine the area between the nodes requiring connectivity by using some proximity or triangulation technique, like GPS. While in the Supporting Communication mode, the MCB will evaluate new positions of the pair of nodes for which it is providing connectivity. With that information, the MCB will re-determine its area of operation; towards the middle of the line representing the distance between the nodes supported.

4.1 Simulation Model and Metrics

The nodes' operations area is modeled as a square of side 400 m, because this represents a reasonable region of operation for a team of first responders in disaster relief operations. Usually, first responders are organized in groups of about 30 people, composed of firefighters, medical personnel, structural engineers, technicians, logistics, hazardous materials specialists and canine/handlers [22]. This study considers scenarios without obstacles, as the main goal of the research at this point is to determine general conditions for a proof of concept of the self-organizing mechanism. A more elaborate scenario with varied types of obstacles will be part of future developments (Table 1).

Table 1. Metrics to evaluate the self-organizing mechanism

Characteristic	Metric
Connectivity	# of disconnections depending on link failure probability
	# of disconnections depending on the # of MCBs for a given setting
	Disconnections detection prob., based on the prob. used in gossip-based multicast
Scalability	Number of messages used for self-organizing depending on the # of MCBs
Power	% of time in mechanical and communication stage based on # of MCBs
	% of time in mechanical and communication stage based on Link Prob. Failure

Every node in the system; i.e., mobile users and MCBs, are wearing or equipped with a wireless short-range communication device, e.g., Smartphones using IEEE802.11b/g/n, with a communication range of 100 m. On the other hand, speed, direction, and time associated to first responders are modeled as random uniformly distributed processes. The speed of each first responder can take a value between 0 and 3 m/s, within each time interval, where the duration of a time interval is variable and ∈ (0, Tmov). Such speed range represents a realistic average of movement speed for people and is also consistent with other similar simulation efforts [28, 29]. The probability for a first responder to stay stationary is also introduced in the model. For each new time interval, new speed, direction, and duration are calculated. The direction of movement ranges from 1° and 360°. Finally, the simulation clock runs on 5 s increments, consistent with routing protocols [30, 31].

4.2 Results

Simulation results highlight the relationship between the number of mobile users and connectivity, without including MCBs. It can be appreciated in Fig. 3(a) that connectivity positively correlates with the number of mobile users. Also, for a team of 30 mobile users operating in area of 400 × 400 m^2 the number of disconnections is approximately 12; i.e., the MANET becomes highly fragmented. Figure 3(a) also shows that to achieve high connectivity in the MANET, at least 70 mobile users should be present. A different way to understand Fig. 3(a) is that if MCBs have a pseudo-random movement pattern; at least 40 MCBs should be deployed to achieve high connectivity for a team of 30 mobile users in area of operations. Such strategy also means MCBs are always active; consuming valuable energy. This situation becomes the baseline to evaluate the self-organizing mechanism.

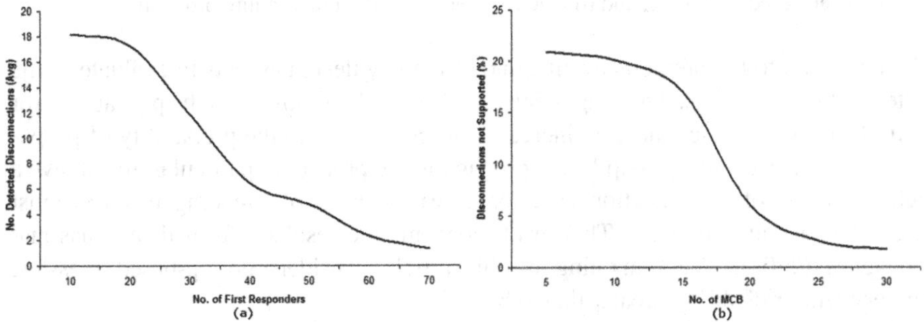

Fig. 3. Simulation results: (a) the number of disconnections decreases linearly as the number of first responders increase, without participation of MCBs; (b) the error % in supporting disconnections gets minimal near 25 MCBs for 30 first responders

Figure 3(b) shows that a small number of disconnections not detected was obtained for 25 or more MCBs. Increasing the number of MCBs above 25 has a minimal impact on connectivity. This outcome is supported by Fig. 4(a), where for approximately 25 MCBs, their utilization becomes the highest. Specifically, it is shown in Fig. 4(a) that for approximately 25 MCBs, the percentage of time that each MCB is on Supporting mode is maximal and the percentage of time in Idle mode is minimal.

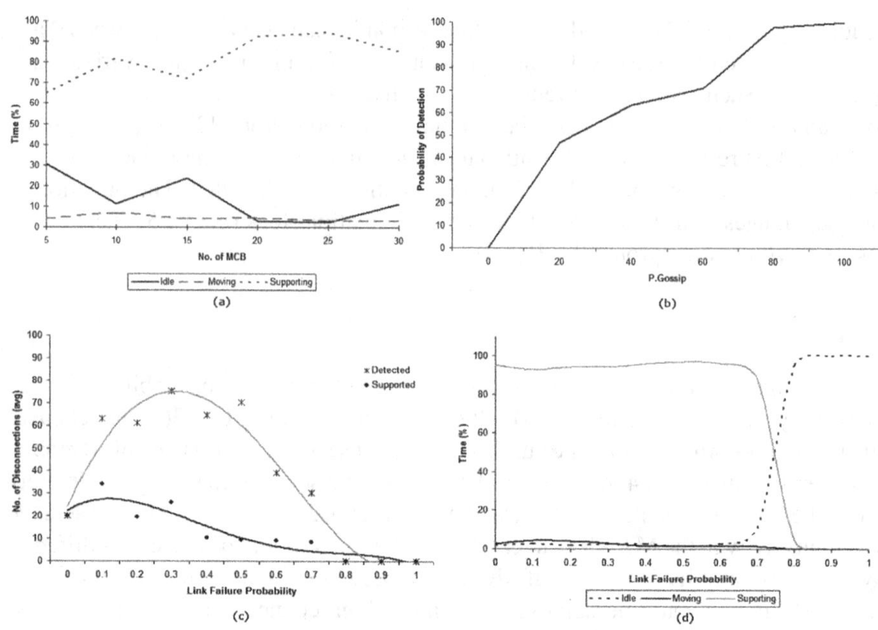

Fig. 4. Simulation results: (a) the maximum usability of MCBs occurs at the vicinity of 25 MCBs with 30 mobile users for 400 × 400 m^2; (b) detection probability of potential disconnections increases as probability of gossip-based multicast increases; (c) false potential disconnections (average) perceived by MCBs; and (d) MCBs' status based on link failure probability.

In addition to the previous results, one of the key design aspects to evaluate in the system is the gossip-based messages delivery. Figure 4(b) shows that the probability for a MCB to detect a disconnection increases proportionally to the probability of propagating messages using a gossip-based propagation approach. In particular, to achieve a high probability of disconnection detections, the probability of spreading messages must be greater or equal than 0.8. This result confirms the results informed by Haas and colleagues (2002). The remaining of this article considers gossip-based message delivery with probability greater than 0.8.

In order to determine a measure of performance of the system, the number of messages spread through the MANET was measured considering different number of MCBs in the system each time. Not surprisingly, the number of messages generated correlates linearly with the number of MCBs. Other important outcomes obtained through the simulation runs are those related to the impact of the link failure probability on the system. This impact is graphically presented in Fig. 4(c) and (d). Figure 4(c) shows the relationship between link failure probability and the number of disconnections perceived by the MCBs, true and false disconnections, and the number of disconnections supported by MCBs. False disconnection corresponds to a situation when an MCB receives a gossip_search_alternative_path from one node and does not receive the counterpart message from the other node involved in the potential disconnection due to loss of the message, though there exists an alternative route between the nodes searching for it. It can be appreciated in Fig. 4(c) that the average number of potential disconnections perceived by each MCB increases as LFP increases up to approximately a value of 0.5. For values of LFP greater than 0.7, the MCBs receive fewer messages and tend to stay more time in Idle state, as shown in Fig. 4(d).

Lastly, for a LFP lower than 0.7 the MCBs are mainly in Supporting mode, while for a LFP greater than 0.8 the MCBs are mainly in Idle mode. For a value of LFP between 0.7 and 0.8 the system suddenly experiences a phase transition. Put in other words, the self-organizing mechanism becomes useless for values of LFP greater than approximately 0.75.

5 Conclusions and Further Work

This article presents a completely distributed self-organizing mechanism to improve the connectivity in MANETs, where an infrastructure communication is not reliable or does not exist. Specifically, the self-organizing mechanism is based on deploying unmanned vehicles, enabled with short-range wireless communication technology, which perform a simple task; act proactively on demand of potential disconnections generated by the mobility of the mobile users. If the self-organizing mechanism is applied, high connectivity could be guaranteed for a smaller team of mobile users operating in the same area. This conclusion can also be stated from a different perspective: for a given fixed number of mobile users who comprise a team, who comprise a MANET, the self-organizing mechanism allows them to keep high connectivity in larger areas. In addition, from the perspective of the entire system, the use of the self-organizing mechanism represents an energy saving option if it is compared to the option of deploying unmanned vehicles in permanent pseudo-random movement.

Through simulations it is demonstrated that the self-organizing mechanism, and consequently the connectivity of the MANET, is resilient up to moderately high values of link failure probability. Nevertheless, the system experiences a clear phase transition, it suddenly switches from active to inactive; i.e., unmanned vehicles set themselves to Idle mode, for higher values of link failure probability.

Finally, further work will be oriented to increase the performance, and consequently the scalability, of the designed self-organizing mechanism, exploring the impact of different multicast strategies like tree-based multicast, e.g., [32], as well as to make the system even less vulnerable to link probability failures in more complex settings involving physical objects according to different inhospitable contexts. Different movement strategies for the MCBs will also be part of future work.

References

1. DHS S&T: Easing lines of communication, R-Tech newsletter, the newsletter of the first responder technologies program (2009)
2. Essid, C.: SAFECOM Guidance for Federal Grant Programs. Office of Emergency Communications, Federal Emergency Management Agency (2010)

3. Dias, B., Stentz, A.: Enhanced negotiation and opportunistic optimization for market-based mutirobot coordination. Technical report CMU-MI-TR-02-18, The Robotics Institute, Carnegie Mellon University, Pittsburg, Pennsylvania (2002)
4. Tanenbaum, A.S., Van Steen, M.: Distributed Systems. Prentice Hall, New Jersey (2006)
5. Allenby, B., Fink, J.: Toward inherently secure and resilient societies. Science **309**, 1034–1036 (2005)
6. Gupta, L., Jain, R., Vaszkun, G.: Survey of important issues in UAV communication networks. IEEE Commun. Surv. Tutor. Iss. **18**(2), 1123–1152 (2015)
7. Khatib, O.: Real-time obstacle avoidance for manipulators and mobile robots. In: Proceedings of the 1990 IEEE International Conference on Robotics and Automation, Cincinnati, Ohio, pp. 572–577 (1990)
8. Ladd, A., Bekris, K., Marceau, G., Rudys, A., Wallach, D., Kavraki L.: Using wireless ethernet for localization. In: IEEE/RSJ International Conference on Intelligent Robots and Systems (IROS), Lausanne, Switzerland, September 2002
9. Sibley, G., Rahimi, M., Sukhatme, G.: Robomote: a tiny mobile robot platform for large-scale sensor networks. In: Proceedings of the IEEE International Conference on Robotics and Automation, ICRA, Washington, DC (2002)
10. Reich, J., Misra, V., Rubenstein, D., Zussman, G.: Connectivity maintenance in mobile wireless networks via constrained mobility. JSAC Spec. Iss. Commun. Challenges Dyn. Unmanned Auton. Veh. **30**(5), 935–950 (2012)
11. Kumar, V., Arrichiello, F.: Connectivity maintenance by robotic mobile ad-hoc network (2013)
12. Jain, M., Chand, S.: Issues and challenges in node connectivity in mobile ad hoc networks: a holistic review. Division of Computer Engineering, Netaji Subhas Institute of Technology, NSIT, University of Delhi, New Delhi, India (2016)
13. Nourbakhsh, I.R., Sycara, K., Koes, M., Yong, M., Lewis, M., Burion, S.: Human-robot teaming for search and rescue. IEEE Pervasive Comput. **4**(1), 72–78 (2005)
14. Hu, L., Evans, D.: Localization for mobile sensor networks. In: Tenth Annual International Conference on Mobile Computing and Networking, Philadelphia, USA, pp. 45–57 (2004)
15. Wang, Z., Song, Z., Chen, P., Arora, A., Moore, K., Chen, Y.: A mobility node for MAS-net (Mobile actuator sensor networks). In: Proceedings of the IEEE International Conference on Robotics and Biomimetics, Shengyang, China, August 2004
16. Raissi-Dehkordi, M., Chandrashekar, K., Baras, J.S.: UAV placement for enhanced connectivity in wireless ad-hoc networks. CSHCN Technical Report 2004–2018 (2004)
17. Altshuler, T.: Opportunities in land mine warfare technologies. The self-healing minefield. In: Approved for Public Release, Distribution Limited, Defense Advanced Research Projects Agency (DARPA), Advanced Technology Office, Arlington, VA (2002)
18. Aldunate, R., Ochoa, S., Peña, F., Nussbaum, M.: Robust mobile ad-hoc space for collaboration to support disaster relief efforts involving critical physical infrastructure. J. Comput. Civil Eng. **20**, 13–27 (2006)
19. Sweeney, J.D., Grupen, R., Shenoy, P.: Active QoS flow maintenance in robotic, mobile, ad hoc networks. Laboratory for Perceptual Robotics, Department of Computer Science, University of Massachusetts, Amherst (2004)
20. Zou, Y., Chakrabarty, K.: Sensor deployment and target localization based on virtual forces. In: ACM Transactions on Embedded Computing Systems, vol. 3, pp. 61–91. IEEE INFOCOM (2003)

21. Howard, A., Mataric, M.J., Sukhatme, G.S.: Mobile sensor deployment using potential fields: a distributed, scalable solution to the area coverage problem. In: Proceedings of the 6th International Symposium on Distributed Autonomous Robotics Systems (DARS02), Fukuoja, Japan (2002)
22. U.S. Department of Homeland Security: National Incident Management System. Federal Emergency Management Agency Document (2008)
23. Haas, Z., Halpern, J., Li, L.: Gossip-based ad hoc routing. In: Proceedings IEEE INFOCOM 2002. The Annual Joint Conference of the IEEE Computer and Communications Societies. IEEE, New York (2002)
24. Kim, S., Oh, H., Suk, J., Tsourdos, A.: Coordinated trajectory planning for efficient communication relay using multiple UAVs. Control Eng. Prac. **29**, 42–49 (2014)
25. Rosati, S., Kruzelecki, K., Heitz, G., Floreano, D., Rimoldi, B.: Dynamic routing for flying ad hoc networks (2015)
26. De Rosa, F., Malizia, A., Mecella, M.: Disconnection prediction in mobile ad hoc networks for supporting cooperative work. IEEE Pervasive Comput. **4**, 62–70 (2005)
27. Su, W., Lee, S.J., Gerla, M.: Mobility prediction and routing in ad hoc wireless networks. Int. J. Netw. Manag. **11**, 3–30 (2001)
28. Broch, J., Maltz, D.A., Jonhson, D.B., Hu, Y.C., Jetcheva, J.: A performance comparison of multi-hop wireless ad hoc network routing protocols. In: Proceedings of the Fourth Annual ACM/IEEE International Conference on Mobile Computing and Networking, Dallas, TX, 25–30 October 1998, pp. 85–97. ACM, New York (1998)
29. Yasuda, K., Hagino, T.: Design and concept of ad hoc file system. IEICE Trans. Commun. **84**, 920–929 (2001)
30. Johnson, D.B., Maltz, D.A.: Dynamic source routing in ad hoc wireless networks. In: Imielinsky, T., Korth, H. (eds.) Mobile Computing, Chap. 5, vol. 353, pp. 153–181. Kluwer Academic Publishers, Boston (1996)
31. Perkins, C.E., Royer, E.M.: Ad hoc on demand distance vector routing. In: WMCSA 1999 Proceedings of the Second IEEE Workshop on Mobile Computer Systems and Applications, pp. 90–100. IEEE, Washington, DC, USA (1999)
32. Fang, Q., Liu, J., Guibas, L., Zhao, F.: RoamHBA: maintaining group connectivity in sensor networks. In: Proceedings of the Third International Symposium on Information Processing in Sensor Networks, pp. 151–160. ACM; Berkeley (2004)
33. Lee, U., Magistretti, E., Zhou, B., Gerla, M., Bellavista, P., Corradi, A.: MobEyes: smart mobs for urban monitoring with vehicular sensor networks. IEEE Wirel. Commun. **13**, 52–57 (2006)
34. Bellavista, P., Corradi, A., Magistretti, E.: REDMAN: a decentralized middleware solution for cooperative replication in Dense MANETs. In: IEEE PERCOM Workshop (2005)
35. Chadha, D, Reena.: Vehicular ad hoc network (VANETs): a review. Int. J. Innov. Res. Comput. Commun. Eng. **3**(3), 2339–2346 (2015)
36. Chauhan, A., Singla, M.R.: A detail review on unmanned aeronautical ad-hoc networks. Int. J. Sci. Eng. Technol. Res. **5**(5), 1351–1360 (2016)

Support Vector Machines for Inferring Distracted Behavior of Drivers Wearing Smart Glasses

Antonio Ordorica[1], Marcela D. Rodríguez[1(✉)], Luis A. Castro[2], and Jessica Beltran[2]

[1] Facultad de Ingeniería, Universidad Autónoma de Baja California, Mexicali, B.C., Mexico
{aordorica,marcerod}@uabc.edu.mx
[2] Sonora Institute of Technology, Ciudad Obregón, Mexico
luis.castro@acm.org, jessica.beltran@itson.edu.mx

Abstract. Driver distraction refers to the lack of attention to the driving tasks due to engagement in secondary tasks. Most methods reported in the literature are based on visual-features analysis of head pose, since it is a strong indication of driver distraction. In contrast, we propose to use the inertial sensors embedded in smart glasses. To this aim, we collected data from five participants and conducted experiments to assess the feasibility of using support vector machines (SVM) to generate drivers' models to infer their focus of attention. The results show that using the personalized training model renders an acceptable accuracy to identify particular car cabin's spots where drivers focus their attention (i.e. accuracy was greater than 50 % and less than 81.44 % for all subjects).

Keywords: Driving distraction · Support vector machines · Smart glasses

1 Introduction

Driver distraction or inattention refers to the lack of attention to the driving tasks due to engagement in other tasks while driving. These other tasks can be any diversion of attention like cognitive, physical, or visual distractions that lead to performance degradation [1]. It is estimated that distractions cause 23 % of crashes or near-crashes [2], and that could be reduced by 10–20 % by monitoring and predicting driving behaviors [3, 4]. Avoiding distracted driving has been of particular interest while using navigation artifacts [5]. Also, methods for detecting driver distraction and drowsiness have been explored, which are mainly based on the analysis of visual features of facial expressions and changes on head pose [4], and gaze behavior [6]. In particular, head pose (or head orientation) is a strong indicator of a driver's field of view and current focus of attention [7, 8]. Therefore, it has been considered as an integral process for monitoring driver awareness [8]. For deploying these methods so far, the vehicle's cabin needs to be instrumented with cameras [7–9]. For instance, faceLAB uses two cameras to determine the head pose and eye gaze direction [9]. On the other hand,

C.R. García et al. (Eds.): UCAmI 2016, Part II, LNCS 10070, pp. 242–247, 2016.
DOI: 10.1007/978-3-319-48799-1_28

smart glasses have emerged as an interesting research and product platform for a wide range of wearable assistive systems due their sensing capabilities. Drivers' safety and use of smart glasses while driving have been questioned as they allow users to send text messages or share on social media via spoken commands. However, research has shown that they could improve safety for operators who are at risk of fatigue (e.g. truck drivers), and that drivers using smartphones swerve longer and more frequently than those using Google Glass [10]. The abovementioned words motivated us to propose the use of the inertial sensors embedded in smart glasses for obtaining head pose features to infer drivers' current focus of attention. To this aim, we used Support Vector Machines (SVM), a supervised learning technique that searches for an optimal hyperplane to separate data between defined classes [11, 12]. In the following sections we explain the methods used for experimenting with the SVM (Sect. 2). In Sect. 3, we present our preliminary results, and finally, the conclusions are presented in Sect. 4.

2 Methods

2.1 Data Collection and Labeling

We collected data from 5 subjects (mean age M = 32; SD = 11.20 years) through controlled experiments in near naturalistic conditions. Each subject participated in a session in which they conducted a set of tasks (see Table 1) in a car while wearing Google Glass.

Table 1. Tasks conducted by the subjects, which are known to cause risks associated to distractions according to NHTS report [13]

Secondary Tasks	Tasks conducted during experiment
Using cell phone	Dialing (quick keys), talking/listening, texting
Interacting with object	Looking at object, Moving object in vehicle, Reaching for object
Drinking	Lid no straw, Open container
Using comfort and information console	Turn climate on/off, adjust temp, CD-Insert/remove, Radio Adjustment

First, participants performed the tasks while the car was parked (P), and then while the car was being driven (D). The former experiment lasted a mean time M = 5 m 34 s, SD = 1 m 29 s, and the later had mean time M = 8 m 34 s, SD = 2 m 55 s. The collected data consisted of 9-tuples vectors i.e., accelerometer, gyroscope, and orientation sensors (each along x, y, and z axes respectively). The accelerometer's sampling frequency was set to 15.5 Hz, the fastest through the Android API. All sessions were video recorded to obtain the ground truth by observing and labeling data. The objective of supervised learning techniques is to infer a function from labeled data [11, 12]. We labeled the data using two types of classes related to the car's cabin locations where participants centered their attention by changing their head pose. As presented in Fig. 1, these types of classes were: a) car's cabin spots and b) cabin's zones. Both of them are associated with tasks that drivers may conduct when their attention is focused on these spots and zones. For instance, a driver may focus his attention on the Comfort and Information zone (`C&I_Zone` which consisted of spot 5 and 6 according to Fig. 1) when changing the radio station (spot 5). Thus, we assessed the feasibility of identifying particular spots where drivers' focused their attention, which may help identify if she is conducting a secondary task.

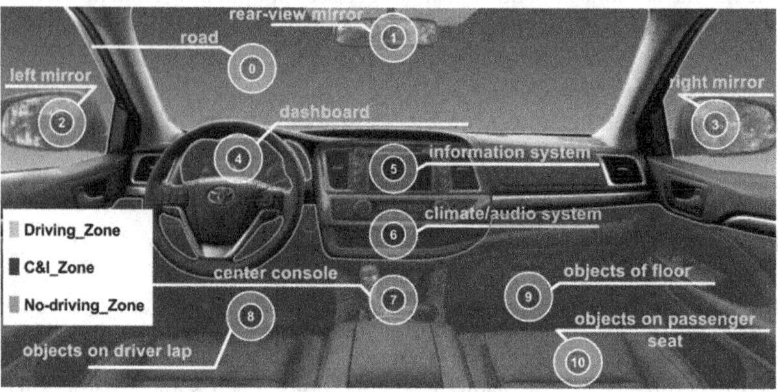

Fig. 1. Cabin's spots (numbered) and zones (colored) used as classifying classes.

2.2 Experiments

Two models were trained with the SVM, one using data from all participants (i.e., generalized model), and one using data of each participant (i.e., personalized model). For the generalized model, we used the leave-one out validation (i.e., data of four participants were used for training, and one for validation). And for the personalized model we used the 66–34 % modality (i.e. 66 % of data of each participant was used for training, and 34 % for validation). Finally, we compared how the classifier performs in real time by training the classifier with the collected raw data (9-tuple vectors) instead of using the vectors magnitude, which is a common feature computed to analyze data obtained from inertial sensors. Computing the vector magnitude may not take long using a PC, but on resource-constrained gadgets such as smart glasses, it may be desirable to avoid it for saving energy consumption. For each experiment, we report accuracy, precision and recall as classification performance measures [11, 12].

3 Results

We collected 21,621 data, i.e. 9-tuple vectors from the experiment, 12,337 were labeled (i.e., classes instances) for both, driving (D) and parked (P) setting conditions. As depicted in Table 2, approximately 90 % of the data belongs to one class (Driving_Zone) or a few number of classes (spots) located in the Driving_Zone. We resampled the dataset to even-up the classes used for generating training models by

Table 2. Data collected (DC) and data labeled (DL) for each subject (S) during corresponding to the driving condition.

			Spots on Driving_Zone						Spots on C&I_Zone			Spots on No_Driving_Zone				
S	Data	Inst	0	1	2	3	4	Total DL	5	6	Total DL	7	8	9	10	Total DL
S1	3,443	1,877	1,064	122	434	17	16	**1,653**	89	20	**109**	8	97	7	3	**115**
S2	3,138	1,203	466	281	238	87	7	**1,079**	51	49	**100**	8	6	5	5	**24**
S3	2,768	1,351	933	2	256	26	56	**1,273**	30	24	**54**	13	0	4	7	**24**
S4	2,000	898	463	14	308	23	33	**841**	15	17	**32**	7	8	3	7	**25**
S5	2,042	1,074	489	37	384	38	0	**948**	36	21	**57**	18	23	9	19	**69**
	13,391	6,403	3,415	456	1,620	191	112	**5,794**	221	131	**352**	54	134	28	41	**257**

Table 3. Confusion matrixes and classification accuracies by using personalized training models and the raw data obtained from S1 and S3.

	Subject 1						**Subject 3**					
	Spot0	**Spot3**	**Spot5**	**Spot7**	**Spot10**		**Spot0**	**Spot3**	**Spot5**	**Spot7**	**Spot10**	
Parked	305	27	38	0	2	**Spot0**	134	23	72	4	18	**Spot0**
	0	262	65	0	0	**Spot3**	63	167	29	0	0	**Spot3**
	86	114	140	0	0	**Spot5**	75	57	90	29	21	**Spot5**
	0	0	0	290	60	**Spot7**	0	0	42	223	22	**Spot7**
	0	4	4	118	231	**Spot10**	36	0	54	13	174	**Spot10**
	Precision = 0.70			**Recall = 0.70**			**Precision = 0.60**			**Recall = 0.59**		
	Spot0	**Spot3**	**Spot5**	**Spot7**	**Spot10**		**Spot0**	**Spot3**	**Spot5**	**Spot7**	**Spot10**	
Driving	176	5	54	15	125	**Spot0**	210	34	75	8	1	**Spot0**
	65	135	74	39	30	**Spot3**	92	187	30	0	0	**Spot3**
	108	14	153	11	76	**Spot5**	52	0	261	0	0	**Spot5**
	95	0	41	157	52	**Spot7**	0	0	0	313	0	**Spot7**
	0	0	0	0	366	**Spot10**	0	0	0	0	311	**Spot10**
	Precision = 0.60			**Recall = 0.55**			**Precision = 0.82**			**Recall = 0..81**		

using the over-sampling method, i.e., adding copies of instances from the under-represented classes.

In addition, we simplified the classifying classes by removing spots classes that tended to be incorrectly classified according to the confusion matrixes, e.g. we removed Spot 6, which was confused with Spot 5. Thus, the classification accuracy was improved, e.g. the instances classified correctly were 70.33 % in the P condition and 55.10 % in the D condition for subject 1 (S1); and 58.54 % and 81.44 % respectively for subject 3 (S3). By observing, Tables 3 and 4, we conclude that the accuracies obtained when using the 9-tuple vectors captured from the three sensors, are better than that obtained by using vectors magnitude.

Table 4. Confusion matrixes and classification accuracies by using personalized training models and vector magnitudes computed from raw data (9-tuple vectors) from S1 and S3

	Subject 1						Subject 3					
	Spot0	Spot3	Spot5	Spot7	Spot10		Spot0	Spot3	Spot5	Spot7	Spot10	
Parked	47	100	204	5	16	Spot0	119	84	12	18	18	Spot0
	0	192	135	0	0	Spot3	27	214	0	11	7	Spot3
	39	86	193	3	19	Spot5	73	141	16	38	4	Spot5
	32	67	79	127	45	Spot7	17	107	10	108	45	Spot7
	14	35	83	85	140	Spot10	60	83	28	37	69	Spot10
	Precision = 0.451			Recall = 0.40			Precision = 0.40			Recall = 0.39		
	Spot0	Spot3	Spot5	Spot7	Spot10		Spot0	Spot3	Spot5	Spot7	Spot10	
Driving	44	10	131	76	114	Spot0	181	7	134	4	2	Spot0
	0	158	41	29	115	Spot3	47	35	79	39	109	Spot3
	5	15	169	34	139	Spot5	60	20	225	0	8	Spot5
	0	0	0	245	100	Spot7	23	79	0	188	23	Spot7
	0	0	129	0	237	Spot10	0	139	39	0	133	Spot10
	Precision = 0.62			Recall = 0.48			Precision = 0.50			Recall = 0.48		

4 Conclusions

Our results show that inferring driving distraction based on data collected from the inertial sensors of smart glasses is a viable solution; and that using SVM for inferring the focus of attention renders acceptable accuracies measures. Additionally, we found that using raw data is an appropriate choice for enabling smart glasses to execute a process for inferring inattention in real time. However, there exists clearly trade-offs between accuracy, and the effort taken for collecting and training data in real time conditions. We realized that the drivers' habits contributed to obtaining unbalanced datasets. For instance, Table 2 shows that older subject S2 stared more times at the rear-view mirror (281 instances of Spot 1) and right mirror (instances of Spot 3) than the rest of the participants. Subject S1 reported that he is not used to interact with the mobile phone while driving, and when conducting the tasks related to mobile phone usage, a great quantity of instances of Spot 8 were obtained (i.e., he oriented his head more times to the `No_Driving Zone` than the rest of the subjects). Additionally, subjects interact with the comfort and information console (`C&I Zone`) as little as possible while driving. Further work is needed to efficiently infer visual distractions.

Acknowledgements. We thank all the volunteers of the study, and authors 3 & 4 for their comments to improve this work.

References

1. Sajan, S., Ray, G.G.: Human factors in safe driving - a review of literature on systems perspective, distractions and errors. In: Proceedings of IEEE Global Humanitarian Technology Conference, pp. 83–88. IEEE Press (2012)
2. Klauer, S.G., Dingus, T.A., Neale, V.L., Sudweeks, D., Ramsey, D.J.: The impact of driver inattention on near-crash/crash risk: an analysis using the 100-car naturalistic driving study data. Nat. Highw. Traffic Saf. Adm., USDOT (2006)
3. Bayly, M., Fildes, B., Regan, M., Young, K.: Review of crash effectiveness of intelligent transport system. Traffic Accident Causation in Europe (TRACE) (2007)
4. Kang, H.B.: Various approaches for driver and driving behavior monitoring: a review. In: Proceedings of the 2013 IEEE International Conference on Computer Vision Workshops (ICCVW 2013), pp. 616–623. IEEE Computer Society, Washington, DC (2013)
5. Tarqui, G., Castro, L.A., Favela, J.: Reducing drivers' distractions in phone-based navigation assistants using landmarks. In: Urzaiz, G., Ochoa, S.F., Bravo, J., Chen, L.L., Oliveira, J. (eds.) UCAmI 2013. LNCS, vol. 8276, pp. 342–349. Springer, Heidelberg (2013)
6. Chamberlin, J.: Smart glasses: driver distraction or safety tool? March 2014. vol. 45(3), 12. http://www.apa.org/monitor/2014/03/smart-glasses.aspx
7. Zhang, L., Liu, F., Tang, J.: Real-time system for driver fatigue detection by RGB-D camera. ACM Trans. Intell. Syst. Technol. 6, 2, Article 22 (2015)
8. Murphy-Chutorian, E., Manubhai, M.: Head pose estimation and augmented reality tracking: an integrated system and evaluation for monitoring driver awareness. IEEE Trans. Intell. Trans. Syst. **11**(2), 300–311 (2010). IEEE Press Piscataway, NJ, USA
9. Seeing machines Driver State Sensor. Report https://www.seeingmachines.com/solutions/
10. Zhang, Y.F., Gao, X.Y., Zhu, J.Y., Zheng, W.L., Lu, B.L.: A novel approach to driving fatigue detection using forehead EOG. In: 2015 7th International IEEE/EMBS Conference Neural Engineering (NER), pp. 707–710. IEEE (2015)
11. Mohri, M., Rostamizadeh, A., Talwalkar, A.: Foundations of Machine Learning. The MIT Press, Cambridge (2012)
12. Mitchell, T.M.: Machine Learning, 1st edn. Mc Graw Hill Higher Education, New York (1997)
13. NHTSA: National Motor Vehicle Crash Causation Study Report to Congress. DOT HS 811 059. National Highway Traffic Safety Administration, Washington, DC (2008)

Benchmarking Bluetooth SPP Communications for Ubiquitous Computing

Xabier Gardeazabal[1], Borja Gamecho[1,2(✉)], and Julio Abascal[1]

[1] Egokituz Lab, University of the Basque Country (UPV/EHU), Donostia, Spain
xgardeazabal@gmail.com, julio.abascal@ehu.eus
[2] Wimbi Technologies S.L. (WimbiTek), Donostia, Spain
borja.gamecho@wimbitek.com

Abstract. Seamless integration of devices in Ubiquitous Computing requires partaking nodes to perform periodic scans for new nodes in the area, and a set of protocols for interchanging information between devices, among them Bluetooth. In this paper we show an evaluation of the Bluetooth Serial Port Profile (SPP) to study how the communication performance behaves under the discovery process of Bluetooth for new nodes in the vicinity. The results so far show that the performance loss is not dramatic but that it can be improved using different strategies.

Keywords: Ubiquitous computing · Personal area networks · Bluetooth · Benchmarking

1 Introduction

Ubiquitous computing scenarios usually require the presence of a number of devices networked together to share information and interact with each other and the users. This property is frequently referred to as seamless integration [1]. However, these devices are often mobile and therefore ubiquitous environments suffer sudden discovery and loss of networked nodes while continuous data interchange is happening. Increasing the data exchange rates or discovery-scanning periodicity may improve the network's information richness, but at the expense of the scarce battery life of mobile devices. In order to solve problems related to these issues, several network protocols with their corresponding automatic discovery protocols have been proposed [2,3].

Notwithstanding, scenarios in which several devices are being discovered and used at the same time still require special attention. In such cases, sudden performance loss and battery life drops can be critical for the system. Moreover, even if Bluetooth Low Energy is becoming increasingly popular, the Bluetooth Classic protocol remains useful for creating context-aware applications due to the large number of sensor devices that still support it. We therefore designed a benchmarking framework for smartphones using Bluetooth SPP for ubiquitous computing with a set of tests for Bluetooth communications using Android and Arduino.

C.R. García et al. (Eds.): UCAmI 2016, Part II, LNCS 10070, pp. 248–253, 2016.
DOI: 10.1007/978-3-319-48799-1_29

2 Background and Related Work

Bluetooth's performance has been studied in numerous works focusing on different aspects. Cano et al. 2006 [4] concluded that the best power-saving option was to power-off the Bluetooth devices. However this would have an effect on performance since access time increases when booting the device. Bellavista et al. 2008 [5] performed extensive experiments testing Bluetooth's throughput when data was shared in to up to 5 nodes, and proved how throughput decreased and the packet delay increased with more nodes. However, they did not measure the communications' performance while new nodes were being discovered. Peterson et al. 2006 [6] claimed that the presence of a second inquiring device can significantly delay, and even preclude, the discovery of a discoverable node. Chakraborty et al. 2010 [7] concluded that the discovery-delay increases with the number of nearby devices in a logarithmic way. However, the works of Perruci et al. 2011 [8] indicate that energy consumption of discovery only depends on its duration time.

Our work has focused on the battery consumption of a smartphone when it is trying to connect with a set of generic Bluetooth devices. In particular, we want to ascertain if the duration and recurrence of the discovery process is really that detrimental for battery performance. We also want to know what the actual limits are of a mobile application connected to seven Bluetooth devices and what is the maximum bandwidth and throughput that can be achieved in such conditions using SPP.

3 Evaluation

Three Google Nexus smartphones have been used for the tests (Nexus 5, Galaxy Nexus and Nexus S). We also have used eight Arduino boards (four UNO and four MEGA) each with a DF-Robot Bluetooth module (compliant with the Bluetooth v2.1+EDR specification standard) in order to simulate the sensor nodes of the network. Each test was performed in isolation from any possible external interferences such as other Bluetooth antennas performing discovery actions. To avoid tampering the measurements, the smartphones have no processes other than the required. Three types of tests have been configured using the framework: (1) battery-tests, (2) ping-tests and (3) stress-tests.

3.1 Battery-Tests

In order to test the phone's battery drain rate under different situations, three test cases have been devised: (1) standby mode; (2) continuous discovery in isolation (the phone is isolated by placing it inside a metallic box to block interferences); (3) continuous discovery (regardless of the pairings' outcome).

Figures 1a and b show the obtained results for the Nexus S and Nexus 5 respectively. While in the standby mode the battery drain is minimal (as expected), the isolated continuous discovery shows a much larger drain rate.

Furthermore, continuous discovery with seven nearby Bluetooth nodes shows that the battery drain increases even further.

Table 1 summarizes the average battery drain rates for the three test cases and the three smartphones, and Table 2 shows the corresponding battery drain rate increase for the isolated and non-isolated discovery modes. The results show that the discovery process of Bluetooth causes the battery to be drained at about a rate of 5.34–8.5 % faster than when in standby mode. When nearby sensors are present, the battery drain rate is even higher (between 10.9 % and 31.06 %), but it seems to depend a lot on the specific smartphone used.

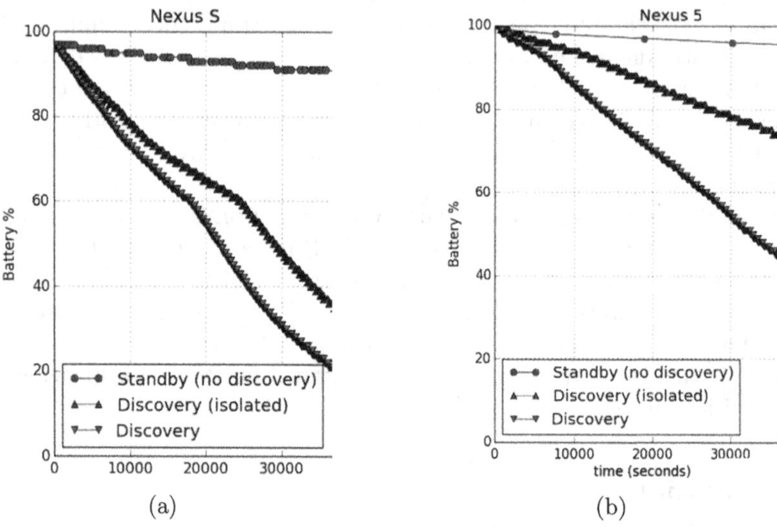

Fig. 1. Battery test for discovery modes: (a) Nexus S (b) Nexus 5.

Table 1. Battery drain rates (% per minute).

Device	Nexus S	Galaxy Nexus	Nexus 5
Standby	0.00844	0.00515	0.00523
Isolated cont. discovery	0.0451	0.04105	0.04454
Continuous discovery	0.092	0.16	0.06684

3.2 Ping-Tests

Ping tests let us measure the sensors' response time or ping (in milliseconds) and the throughput (in bytes per second) under several conditions and scenarios. (1) **Single-Initial**: one Arduino and a single initial discovery. (2) **Six-Initial**: six Arduinos and a single initial discovery plan. (3) **Single-Periodic**: one Arduino and a discovery every 30 seconds. (4) **Seven-Periodic**: seven Arduinos and a discovery every 30 seconds. Figure 2 shows the obtained results for the ping

Table 2. Battery drain increase rates (% per minute).

	Nexus S	Galaxy Nexus	Nexus 5
Isolated continuous discovery	5.34 %	7.97 %	8.5 %
Continuous discovery	10.9 %	31.06 %	12.78 %

tests. Comparing the Single-Initial with the Seven-Initial, a slight increase in the ping times (from a mean time of 50 ms to 75 ms) is seen, while the throughput increases considerably more (from around 125 B/s to 700 B/s). Thus, the mean throughput increases sixfold, while the mean ping time remains almost unchanged. The results for the Single-Periodic and Seven-Periodic tests clearly show the impact that a discovery process has on the ping and throughput values: the ping time increases and the throughput decreases.

3.3 Stress-Tests

With stress-tests we tried to find and measure the maximum usable throughput (without erroneous bytes) achievable with seven Bluetooth sensors transmitting

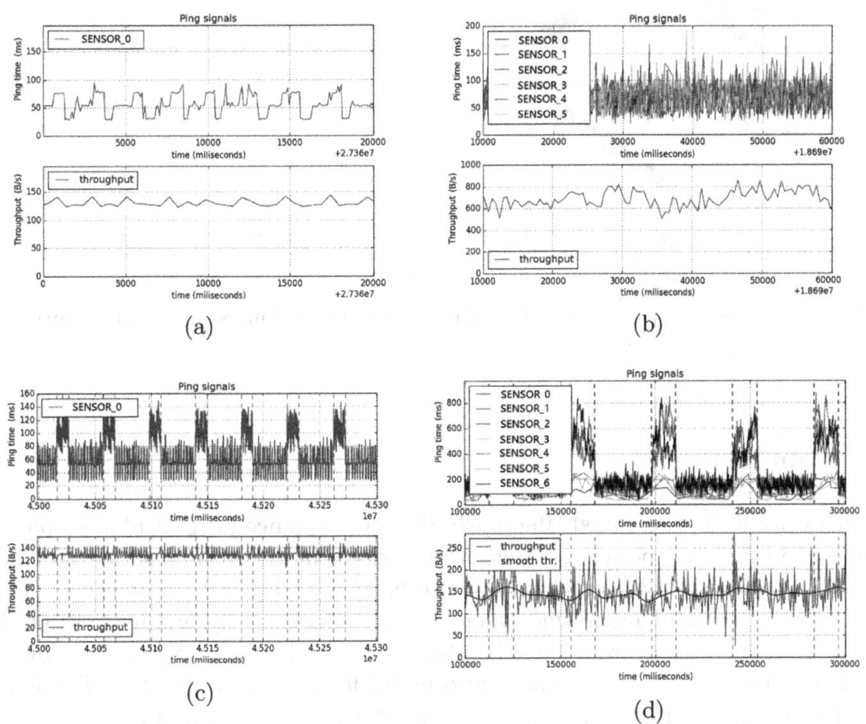

Fig. 2. (a) Single-Initial, (b) Six-Initial, (c) Single-Periodic, (d) Seven-Periodic.

data loads to a single smartphone. For this, we configured the sensors to continuously transmit random data increasingly over time (starting at 10 B/s and growing in 100 Bytes every 10 min). Figure 3 shows the results for a stress-test: the recorded ping times (top), the received useful throughput (middle), and the size of the received useful data-packages (bottom). During the first hour the throughput increases with acceptable ping times, but after around two hours, the number of erroneous packages overtake the number of useful packages. This is the point when the useful throughput begins to decline, until all of the received packages become erroneous. We concluded that the optimal data-package size should be limited to 400 bytes.

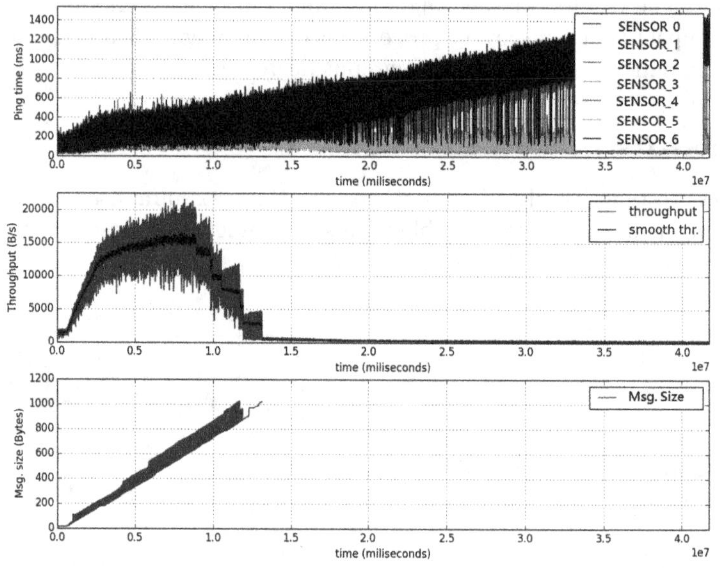

Fig. 3. Stress test: ping (top), throughput (middle) and message size (bottom).

4 Conclusion

In this work we have studied Bluetooth SPP performance using Android smartphones and Arduino powered Bluetooth sensors. The test results show that the discovery process of Bluetooth causes the battery to be drained at least 8.5 % faster than in standby mode when there are no sensors nearby, and up to 31.06 % faster when six sensors are within the phone's range. The prototype of the developed benchmarking environment is also useful for testing Android applications which make an exhaustive use of Bluetooth classic wireless sensors.

Acknowledgments. This work has been supported by the Ministry of Economy and Competitiveness of the Spanish Government and by the European Regional Development Fund (projects TIN2013-41123-P and TIN2014-52665-C2-1-R), and by the Department of Education, Universities and Research of the Basque Government under grant IT980-16. J. Abascal belongs to the Basque Advanced Informatics Laboratory (BAILab), grant UFI11/45, supported by the University of the Basque Country (UPV/EHU). B. Gamecho is backed by the "Convocatoria de contratación de doctores recientes hasta su integración en programas de formación postdoctoral en la UPV/EHU 2015".

References

1. da Costa, C.A., Yamin, A.C., Geyer, C.F.R.: Toward a general software infrastructure for ubiquitous computing. IEEE Pervasive Comput. **7**(1), 64–73 (2008)
2. Zhu, F., Mutka, M.W., Ni, L.M.: Service discovery in pervasive computing environments. IEEE Pervasive Comput. **4**(4), 81–90 (2005)
3. Ververidis, C.N., Polyzos, G.C.: Service discovery for mobile ad hoc networks: a survey of issues and techniques. IEEE Commun. Surv. Tutorials **10**(3), 30–45 (2008)
4. Cano, J.C., Cano, J.M., González, E., Calafate, C., Manzoni, P.: Power characterization of a bluetooth-based wireless node for ubiquitous computing. In: 2006 International Conference on Wireless and Mobile Communications, (ICWMC 2006), p. 13. IEEE (2006)
5. Bellavista, P., Stefanelli, C., Tortonesi, M.: Qos management middleware solutions for bluetooth audio distribution. Pervasive Mob. Comput. **4**(1), 117–138 (2008)
6. Peterson, B.S., Baldwin, R.O., Raines, R.A.: Bluetooth discovery time with multiple inquirers. In: Proceedings of the 39th Annual Hawaii International Conference on System Sciences, HICSS 2006, vol. 9, p. 232a. IEEE (2006)
7. Chakraborty, G., Naik, K., Chakraborty, D., Shiratori, N., Wei, D.: Analysis of the bluetooth device discovery protocol. Wirel. Netw. **16**(2), 421–436 (2010)
8. Perrucci, G.P., Fitzek, F.H., Widmer, J.: Survey on energy consumption entities on the smartphone platform. In: 2011 IEEE 73rd Vehicular Technology Conference (VTC Spring), pp. 1–6. IEEE (2011)

IoT

Physical Processes Control in Industry 4.0-Based Systems: A Focus on Cyber-Physical Systems

Borja Bordel(✉), Diego Sánchez de Rivera, Álvaro Sánchez-Picot, and Tomás Robles

Technical University of Madrid, Madrid, Spain
bbordel@dit.upm.es, diego.sanchezderiveracordoba@gmail.com,
alvaro.spicot@gmail.com, tomas.robles@upm.es

Abstract. Industry 4.0 or cyber-industry may employ Cyber-Physical Systems (CPS) profusely to organize production media in a new and more efficient way. Many processes might be defined in CPS and Industry 4.0, however, physical processes are probably the least studied. Therefore, in this paper we propose an architecture for Industry 4.0-based systems focused on the control of physical processes. The architecture follows the CPS paradigm. Moreover, a first evaluation of the performance of the proposed solution, using simulation tools, is provided. The results proved the proposed architecture is a valid solution for physical control processes.

Keywords: Cyber-Physical Systems · Industry 4.0 · Functional architectures · Physical processes

1 Introduction

Most authors agree Industry 4.0 is any solution for industry where information technologies belonging to the next technical revolution are used [1]. In particular, a new type of integrated systems has become really popular: the Cyber-Physical Systems (CPS). CPS are integrations of physical and computational processes [2].

The use of CPS technologies in order to create the Industry 4.0 has been analyzed in various works [3]. However, most works are focused in the deployment of CPS in manufacturing scenarios, where processes have the form of business processes (a collection of activities of tasks, making a workflow). Then, companies which work with physical processes (as pasteurization or chemical reactions) are not usually considered.

2 Processes in Industry 4.0 and CPS

Many types of process can be defined in CPS. In Fig. 1 we present a taxonomy for processes in CPS. Computational processes are described as a collection of activities, related by means of some transitions. Business processes may be orchestrated if a high-level entity controls the workflow and orders the execution of each task; or they may be choreographed if a collection of devices operating independently makes up the final high-level process. Finally, depending on the way in which the system is managed (if

C.R. García et al. (Eds.): UCAmI 2016, Part II, LNCS 10070, pp. 257–262, 2016.
DOI: 10.1007/978-3-319-48799-1_30

devices explicitly notify the changes or a supervisory module is deployed) the process might be event-driven, device-driven or human-driven. Physical processes (see Fig. 2) and processes mixing activities and physical processes (hybrid processes) are also present in CPS.

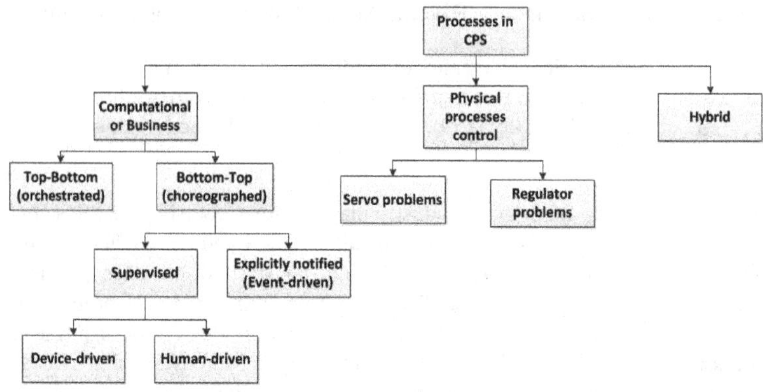

Fig. 1. Taxonomy of processes in CPS

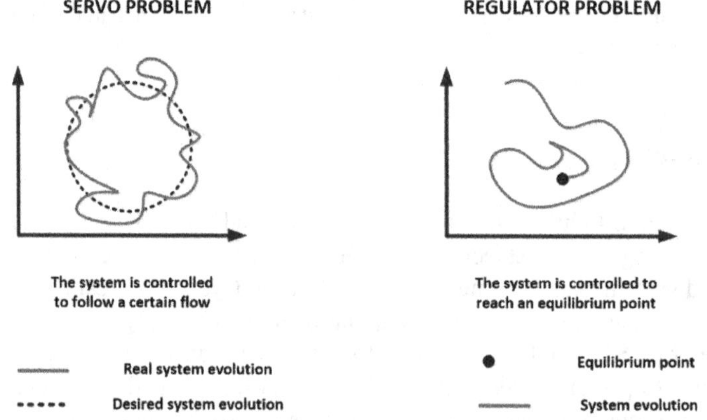

Fig. 2. Different physical processes in the state space

3 Requirements Analysis: Proposed Architectures

In this Section we are analyzing the specific requirements of CPS in industrial scenarios, as well as the needs of systems to perform physical processes control.

First, some specific requirements have to be considered in a CPS architecture for Industry 4.0.

- REQ#1: the architecture should support designed control systems for both, computational (including human-driven) and physical processes.

- REQ#2: high-level applications should be independent of the hardware platform, which may be heterogeneous
- REQ#3: the architecture should include elements to evaluate the system performing and determine if any result does not correspond to the expected one and/or some defined rules or tasks are not satisfied
- REQ#4: methods for informing domain experts and modules to allow them to define the processes, activities and/or rules to be executed in the system should be considered in the architecture
- REQ#5: the architecture should consider tools for self-management and automatic control of the hardware platform
- REQ#6: procedures to extract valuable information from the data generated by the hardware platform should be considered.

In the research literature, various architectures for CPS may be found [4]. Among all these proposals, two are especially interesting for this work. Namely: the 5C architecture [5] and the architecture created by National Institute of Standards and Technology (NIST) [6]. Taking into account these previous proposals, we present in Fig. 3 a general functional architecture for CPS in Industry 4.0 scenarios. Then, considering the general functional architecture for CPS presented in Fig. 3, and the requirements cited above, the detailed functional architecture showed in Fig. 4 for physical processes control may be deducted.

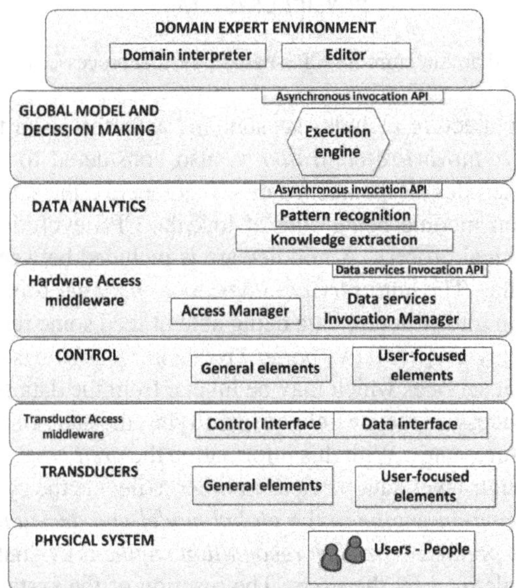

Fig. 3. Proposed architecture for CPS in Industry 4.0 scenarios

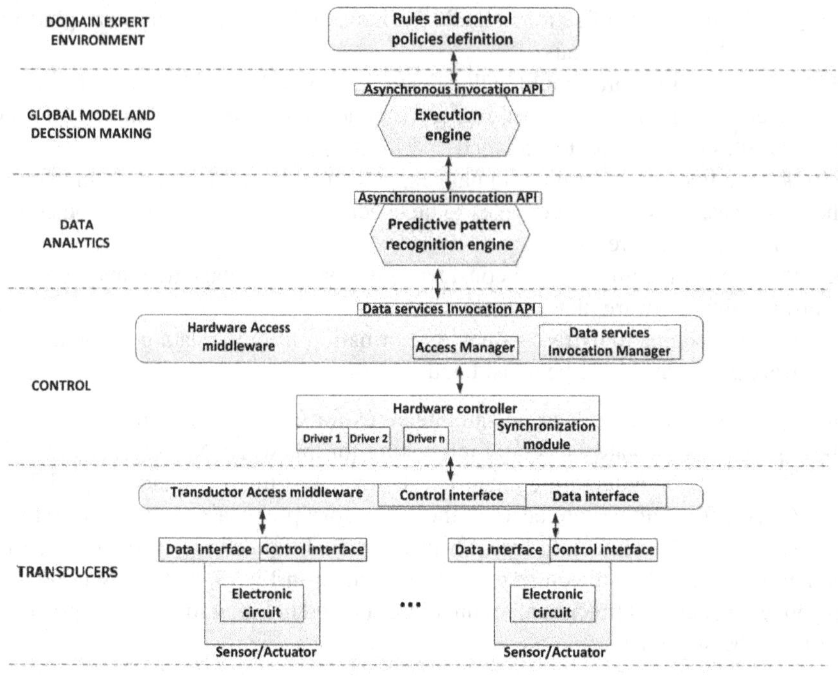

Fig. 4. Proposed architecture for CPS-based physical processes control systems

The proposed architecture includes sensors and actuators used for controlling the physical processes. A *hardware controller* is also considered to manage data from transducers. It also includes all the needed drivers to operate the sensors and actuators, and a synchronization module being able of link the CPS evolution to the temporal evolution of the physical process. A middleware is included between transducers and the hardware controller. The *data services invocation manager* transforms raw data in the hardware platform into structure data being able of feed some remote data services. In the *data analytics* layer a *predictive pattern recognition engine* is implemented. This engine offers different services which may be invoke from the data services invocation manager. These services are responsible of identifying the state of the physical world and/or predict the future states. With this information the *predictive pattern recognition engine* may invoke high-level data services in order to decide the system's reaction.

Finally, in an *execution engine* in the *global model and decision making* layer the information from the *predictive pattern recognition engine* is evaluated along the rules and control policies defined by the users. The reaction of the systems is immediately obtained and transmitted towards the *transducers* layer. At the same time, all the information about the physical world state and the system's reaction is showed in the domain expert environment (by means of which users can also define the rule or control policies to be applied).

4 Experimental Validation: System Simulation

In this Section we are simulating the performing of our proposal when used to control the cooling process in a steel factory.

The physical process of a piece of steel getting cooled was simulated using the three-dimensional heat equation. Actuators, represented by the additional term in the equation, along with a set of temperature sensors, made up the hardware platform of the *transducers* layer. The data is transmitted to a *hardware controller* in the *control* layer (Fig. 4), where a software phase-locked loop synchronizes the system behavior with the temporal evolution of the heat equation. The *hardware controller* sends data to the *data services invocation manager*, which invokes a REST service which represents the *predictive pattern recognition engine* at the *data analytics* layer. *Data analytics* elements process the information using a simplified model of the heat equation's solution to calculate the next states of the physical processes. In the *global model and decision making* layer an execution engine is deployed. Information about the current process state and the calculated future steps are sent to the *execution engine*, where the next value for the actuators in the *transducers* layer (represented by the control term in the heat equation) is calculated. In the *domain expert environment* the objective of the control system was to force the cooled process to follow a predefined temporal evolution, by default.

5 Results

The main problem in the proposed architecture is guaranteeing the stability of the control loop so that the physical process behaves as desired. Figure 5 shows the spatial media of the instantaneous error in the control loop in two different cases: (i) the sampling step is equal to the integration step and (ii) the sampling step is five times higher than the integration step. The media is presented normalized.

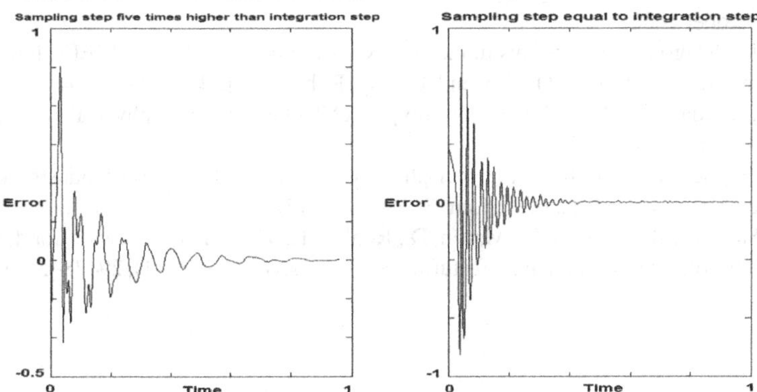

Fig. 5. Spatial media of the instantaneous error

As can be seen, in both cases the loop is stable and, finally the physical process behaves as desired (the error tends to zero). However, the time needed to reach the equilibrium goes up when the sampling period increases. Particularly, when the sampling step is five times higher than the integration step, the double time is necessary to reach the equilibrium. Moreover, the error varies faster when the sampling period is smaller, as can be seen in Fig. 5. Any case, Fig. 5 proves the proposed architecture is a valid solution for physical control processes.

6 Conclusions

In this paper we have investigated the use of CPS to control physical processes in the context of Industry 4.0. We have proposed a general architecture for CPS in Industry 4.0, and used that architecture to design a control system for physical processes. Moreover, we have proposed an experimental validation performed on a simulation environment. The results proved the proposed architecture is a valid solution for physical control processes. Besides, we discovered the importance of the sampling scheme in the system performance; thus, the use of advanced sampling schemes (such as on-demand sampling) will be another key to the success of CPS and Industry 4.0.

Acknowledgments. The research leading to these results has received funding from the Ministry of Economy and Competitiveness through SEMOLA project (TEC2015-68284-R).

References

1. Rüßmann, M., Lorenz, M., Gerbert, P., Waldner, M., Justus, J., Engel, P., Harnisch, M.: Industry 4.0: The Future of Productivity and Growth in Manufacturing Industries. Boston Consulting Group (2015)
2. Lee, E.A.: Cyber-physical systems-are computing foundations adequate. In: Position Paper for NSF Workshop On Cyber-Physical Systems: Research Motivation, Techniques and Roadmap, vol. 2, October 2006
3. Jazdi, N.: Cyber physical systems in the context of Industry 4.0. In: 2014 IEEE International Conference on Automation, Quality and Testing, Robotics, pp. 1–4, May 2014
4. Tan, Y., Goddard, S., Perez, L.C.: A prototype architecture for cyber-physical systems. ACM Sigbed Rev. **5**(1), 26 (2008)
5. Lee, J., Bagheri, B., Kao, H.A.: A cyber-physical systems architecture for industry 4.0-based manufacturing systems. Manufact. Lett. **3**, 18–23 (2015)
6. Bordel Sánchez, B., Alcarria, R., Martín, D., Robles, T.: TF4SM: a framework for developing traceability solutions in small manufacturing companies. Sensors **15**(11), 29478–29510 (2015)

Red Thread. An NFC Solution for Attracting Students and Engaging Customers

Irene Luque Ruiz, Gonzalo Cerruela García(✉), and Miguel Ángel Gómez-Nieto

Department of Computing and Numerical Analysis, University of Córdoba, Campus de Rabanales, Albert Einstein Building, 14071 Córdoba, Spain
{iluque,gcerruela,mangel}@uco.es

Abstract. In this paper we describe the advantages of using Near Field Communication technology (NFC) for engagement strategies carried out by companies or institutions. Augmented objects with NFC chips (gadgets) are given to potential targets having associated appropriate applications without requiring the installation of mobile applications. These gadgets and applications serve as bait for companies and institutions to be able to communicate with targets and spread any kind of multimedia aims for their engagement. We also describe the Red Thread application, a solution based on a romantic legend which is very suitable for young people whom universities want to attract every year for new enrolments.

Keywords: Near field communication · NFC · Engagement · Loyalty · Attracting · Red Thread · Marketing

1 Introduction

Currently the use of NFC technology in mobile applications has grown exponentially [1, 2]. The impulse in the spread of NFC technology is due to the growing visibility of NFC products in industries, increase in the use of NFC terminals such as point of sales (POS), the increasing penetration of NFC Smartphones in the market, increase in mobile commerce, and investments by several operators in the development of NFC infrastructures [3].

NFC has been widely used in payment and security applications [4, 5]. Moreover NFC has provided a wealth of applications in transport [6], advertising and promotion of tourism businesses [7, 8], ambient assisted living, authentication [9, 10], and oriented to a wide variety of scientific, as well as business areas [11]. NFC has been used in understanding customer behaviour in stores and other commercial centres and is essential for any business aiming to provide a more personal experience [12].

Different applications have considered the useful application of NFC to advertising, marketing or user loyalty [13, 14] purposes. Hence, objects or screens augmented with tags are used to provide users with information about products, sales or services. The secure element or SIM has been the main proposed way to support credit or loyalty card identification [14, 15]. In [14] a structure, called as Secure Common Domain Management System (SCDM), was proposed to maintain data interaction and data sharing

C.R. García et al. (Eds.): UCAmI 2016, Part II, LNCS 10070, pp. 263–274, 2016.
DOI: 10.1007/978-3-319-48799-1_31

among payment and loyalty applications. An integrated NFC mobile service solution for payment, ticketing loyalty and couponing was proposed in [16].

Some research [17] has demonstrated that the use of mobiles increases student engagement with other students as well as in learning activities. In the university environment NFC has been used in systems to track the attendance of a particular student [18], for improvement of students' self-organization as well as on the design and enhancement of specific learning scenarios [19], or the development of Smart university environments in compliance with European universities EHEA guidelines [20].

In [21] an ubiquitous game based on Near Field Communication technology was proposed to improve the students' motivation through solving challenges and for developing the right professional aptitudes. NFC technology has also been used to increase customer engagement, in [22] an NFC mobile application provides a complete end-to-end experience by allowing users to select food items, read micro-reviews of dishes, submit their order, and be alerted when the food is ready.

In this paper we propose a new approach based on NFC for the engagement of customers. A main application, the Red Thread, devoted to user engagement, associates gadgets to potential targets. Gadgets could also be associated to other applications in order for users to interact more frequently with them and the contents associated to the gadgets to be highly readable. Applications and contents associated to gadgets can be tailored for specific marketing campaigns without requiring users to install mobile applications.

This paper is organized as follows:

In Sect. 2, the materials and methods to develop the proposed solution are presented. Section 3 describes the system architecture, actors, principal process and communication technologies. In Sect. 4, a real application for attracting school students to the university is described. Finally, we summarise the principal conclusions of our approach.

2 Materials and Methods

2.1 Aims and Scope

The aim of the research described in this paper is to use NFC technology, wearables and a "legend" to serve as bait to attract students to the university and to provide the University of Córdoba a direct communication method to spread any kind of information.

The solution described in this paper can be extended to any other institution or company as a marketing method for customer engagement.

2.2 Materials

Materials used as bait are wristbands and hang tags equipped with a NFC chip (gadgets). These gadgets will be used as an interaction method to execute a set of applications associated with the chip by the services platform described in this paper. Applications are Web applications developed using pHp, JavaScript, Ajax, XML and MySql products. Users equipped with a NFC Smartphone interact with the gadgets and applications are executed in the Smartphone by means of any standard browser. In addition, a mobile application developed using Phone Gap and WebView software, can be installed by users, although not necessary, to interact with the gadgets.

2.3 The Main Application

Although many applications existing in our services platform can be associated with the gadgets, in this paper we describe the Red Thread application, because this product will be used to attract young students to the University of Córdoba in its yearly strategy of attracting school students.

This application reproduces the red string of the fate legend. The red string of fate, also referred to as the red thread of destiny, red thread of fate, and other variants, is an East Asian belief originating from Chinese and Japanese legend.

According to this myth, the gods tie a red cord around the ankles of those that are to meet one another in a certain situation or help each other in a certain way. The two people connected by the red thread are destined lovers, regardless of time, place, or circumstances. This magical cord may stretch or tangle, but never break [23].

3 Red Thread Architecture

Red Thread is a solution based on peer-to-peer communication between users having a NFC gadget. The gadget is used as a nexus and communication source between those users. Thus, Red Thread works as a point to point communication line. Gadgets act as the terminals of that communication line and these are in charge of initiating communication and ordering a NFC equipped device to send a message to the other side of the communication line, which is the matched gadget. In this section we explain the main actors and elements of this proposal.

3.1 Red Thread Actors

In Red Thread we can see the following elements:

- Gadgets. These are any augmented object containing a NFC chip. These chips have a unique identifier code (UID) that is used to identify them in the database.
- Users. These are people registered in the system. Users can possess one or many gadgets, but a gadget is only assigned to a unique user.
- NFC devices. Usually, these are Smart phones equipped with a NFC read/write capability. These devices are in charge of interacting with the gadget and establishing communication with another NFC device by means of Wi-Fi, GSM, GPRS, etc.

Gadgets are used with two aims. Firstly, gadgets mean a symbolic representation of the Red Thread legend. In the legend, couples are joined by an unbroken and invisible thread, and the gadgets represent the terminal or end of this thread in a visible way.

Thus gadgets can be used as a merchandising object. Companies can offer, sell or give these gadgets to their customers in order to attract and receive loyalty from them, as we will explain below.

Moreover, gadgets are in charge of initialising communication via the thread. When, a gadget is touched by the associated NFC device, a message is sent through the thread to the other side, that is, to the NFC device of the paired gadget.

Thus, gadgets are only recognized by the system in pairs. Each pair represents the visible terminals of an invisible thread. In addition, each gadget belongs to a unique user, so the pair of gadgets make the function of "eternally" joining two people by means of the legendary red thread. Users are the actors involved in the legend. As each gadget belongs to a unique user and the gadget is paired, users are joined in pairs by means of the gadgets. Gadget activation is initiated by assigning the user identification to the gadget information.

In this process, the identification of the NFC device is also assigned to the gadget information. In this way, we protect the sending of messages though the thread. Only the allowed NFC devices can establish communication with the associated gadget, so that if any other people touch the gadget with a NFC device it will not be activated.

3.2 Main Actions of the Red Thread

The main actions performed by the solution are as follows:

- Gadget activation. Gadget activation is carried out by a user the first time the gadget is touched by the NFC device of the user. In this moment, a flow of communication is created by the system and the user until the gadget activation is completed (see Fig. 1, left).
- Gadget pairing. In order to pair two gadgets, both gadgets should be activated (see Fig. 1, left). In the activation process the system asks each user for information about the other paired gadget; that is, the other user. Both users must accept the pairing. If any user rejects the pairing, gadgets are not activated.
- Gadget updating. This action consists in updating the information associated with a gadget. This information can be of any multimedia type: texts, images, videos, files, etc., and the gadget owner can update them as much as he/she wants.

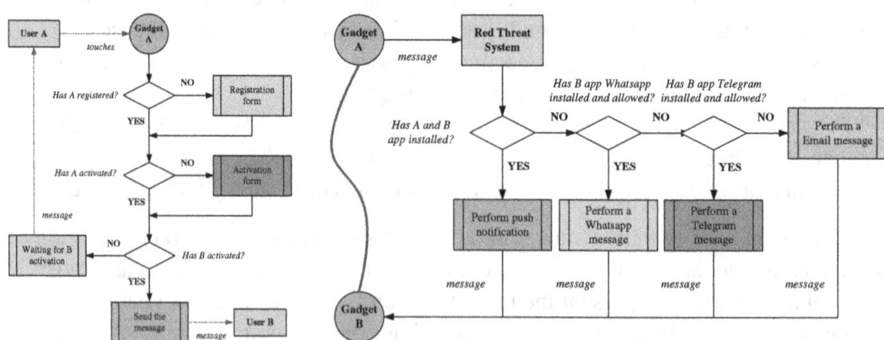

Fig. 1. Flow diagram of the activation process (left). Flow diagram of the notification message process (right)

- Message sending. When the owner's gadget touches with his/her authorized NFC device, the gadget automatically sends a message to the paired gadget. The message, as we will describe below, can be sent in different ways, the owners being the ones who determine how to send and receive the message in their profile.
- Message receiving. Users can also receive the notification of a message sent by the paired gadget in different ways. The message is visualized in the system interface by means of any standard browser or the Red Thread mobile application.

3.3 Communication Technologies

The Red Thread system uses different communication technologies in order to allow users to personalise the way of sending and receiving the notification of a new message that has been sent by the paired gadget.

As we mention above, many users are disappointed with the installation of a large number of specific mobile applications. Otherwise, users can download the Red Thread app (Mi Hilo Rojo, for Spanish language users) from Google Play Store.

However, the system does not require both owners of the paired gadgets to have the mobile application installed. So, we can find a diverse set of ways of communication through the thread as shown in Fig. 1 (right).

In the first, the system checks if both gadget owners have installed the mobile application. If so, when an owner touches his/her gadget, automatically a notification is sent to the other side of the thread. When the notification is checked by the receiver, the mobile application is launched automatically and the message is visualised.

When the mobile application is not installed for any of the gadget owners, then the notifications can be performed using Whatsapp, Telegram or email. Owners are in charge of selecting just one of these three ways of notifications and not necessarily both gadget owners have to select the same one. The system is in charge of sending the notifications and checking if the target receives and visualises the notification. Thus, when notification is visualized by the target, the system can inform the source of the message of this action.

For Whatsapp and Telegram notifications, the system uses the specific APIs for web services. These APIs are open to be used from Web applications and it is only necessary to register a phone number and user. This user is called "Red Thread", so the gadget owner will receive the messages from this contact. The messages sent when Whatsapp, Telegram or email notifications are used, contain information about the other side of the red thread (user data) and a link. When the link is made, the message is visualized by the default browser of the mobile device.

3.4 Pairing Process

There are two different procedures through which both sides of the thread can be paired, depending on how the gadgets have been identified by the systems. When gadgets are paired, the system generates a thread, which is defined by a unique identifier and the two unique identifiers of the gadgets.

Threads can be generated before the gadgets are given to the users, then each gadget can only be paired with its respective couple. In this case, the user does not need to identify the other gadget of the thread in the pairing process, thus the process is as follows:

- The user touches the gadget. If the user is not registered, he/she must register in the system. The registration process requires very little user data: name, phone number, email and the option of a user picture. After registering, an email message is sent to the user for registration confirmation. This registration process can also be performed through the Red Thread Web portal.
- If the gadget is not activated, the user must activate it. In the activation process, no data is required. A message is sent to the user in order to confirm the gadget activation. In this process, the user should fill in the form with the message content.
- Once the gadget is activated, users are informed if the thread is also activated or if the paired gadget is not activated yet.

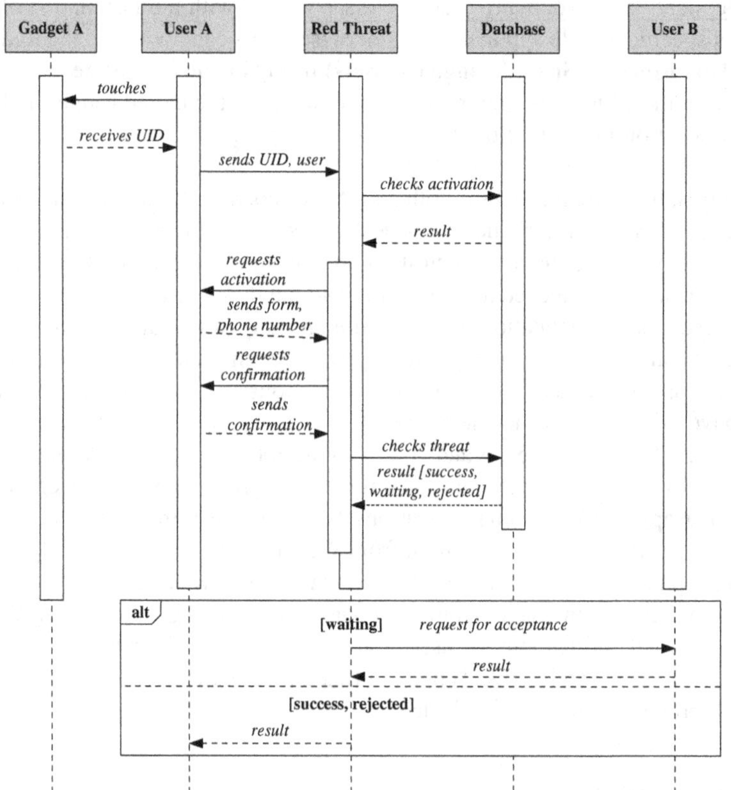

Fig. 2. Sequence diagram of the pairing process

In addition, gadgets do not have to be paired before they are given to users. In this case, the user needs to identify the other gadget of the thread. In this case, as a gadget can only have one assigned user and only accepts one mobile device for interactions, gadgets have a phone number assigned. Thus, the user in the activation process must enter the phone number assigned to the other gadget of the thread and optionally, an email.

As the sequence diagram of Fig. 2 shows, the system checks if both gadgets of the thread are activated and if each has entered the phone number of its corresponding pair. If the paired gadget is not activated, and the user has entered the email of the desired pair, the system sends an email to the user of gadget B requesting acceptance.

The result of the process is returned to the user informing of the success or rejection of the pairing process. Unless both users perform the activation and pairing process the thread is not activated by the system and therefore messages cannot be sent by means of the thread.

3.5 Updating User Profile

A registered user can update his/her profile data at any time. Profile data maintains user information such as the name, picture, email and phone number as well as the content of the message which will be sent by means of the thread. In addition, profile data maintains information about the configuration of the notifications. Thus, the user can decide how he/she wishes to receive notifications when a message is sent by the other gadget of the thread.

As commented above, if the mobile application is installed, the notifications are also received by means of a push message, the remaining options being disabled. If the mobile application is not installed, the user can decide if the notifications are received by just one of the allowed technologies: Whatsapp, Telegram or email.

Each user of the thread can personalize this option and it is not necessary for both users of the thread to use the same method.

3.6 Message Content

The content of the message can be changed by the gadget owners at any time. When the gadget is activated, users should enter a first message. The message can include any of the following data type:

- Text: This can have a maximum size of 256 characters. The text can contain any link.
- Image: A picture in .png or .jpg format. The size of this image should not be more than 2 Mb.
- Video: A URL or video file with a size less than 2 Mb.

The message is shown to the target as a screen with the picture of the sender (if it has been included in the user profile) and the text, image and video, if they are included in the message.

4 Attracting School Students to the University

Every year the University of Córdoba, as well as other universities around the world, devote many people and resources to attract new students.

Fig. 3. Pictures of tested NFC wearables (top). Some screenshots of the applications (bottom)

To do so, from January to May, staff from the university of Córdoba visit schools explaining to students and teachers the different advantages that the University of Córdoba offers: the courses, degrees, masters, sports utilities, colleges, residences, grants, etc. In addition, information about research centres and the level of research at the university are also shared with the students. Traditionally, in these visits to the schools, some books, flyers and pamphlets including university information is given to students, and usually this material is thrown away by the students.

With this traditional strategy, the university staff is unable to reach students or to maintain and update contact in order to understand students' intentions and wishes, etc.

In order to improve attracting students to the university, NFC gadgets will be used next time. The gadgets to be selected for this purpose (possibly wristbands, key folds or hang tags) will be given out to students of schools including the Red Thread application by default. It is well-known that young students like these kinds of applications and new technologies such as NFC and, even more so, wearables such as wristbands.

Moreover, legends such as the Red Thread legend could be a novelty use for young and romantic couples. In addition, these gifted gadgets will have the Business and Emergency card applications associated.

We have tested different types of wearables; some of them are shown in Fig. 3 (top). Fabric and silicone wristbands have been used for Red Thread applications, giving out gadgets that have previously been paired. Gadgets are given to users in a little box containing the wristbands and a flyer with the basic instructions for their use and the Red Thread legend.

We have also tested elastic wristbands, which are more comfortable, water proof and can be more easily personalized with different colours, pictures and logos. These wristbands also have the Red Thread application associated to them, although they are not paired before they are given to users.

The most accepted wearable was the elastic wristband followed by hang tags. They are very attractive and durable gadgets - very in tune with young fashion.

We observed that acceptance of the applications also depends on the type of wearable. This fact reveals the selection of wearables is not a trivial decision when a company establishes an engagement strategy.

The Red Thread application was well accepted for those wearables that were easy to interact with (wristbands) and better accepted (elastic and fabric). The acceptance diminishes for hang tags due to them being more difficult to interact with by making a natural gesture, as is the case of the wristband.

The installation of other applications by users was well accepted. Users installed the additional Business and Emergency Card applications which were highly evaluated, between 60 and 85 % using a specific questionnaire. Mobile applications were only installed by 62 % of the users.

To evaluate the usability and interface of the applications, the System Usability Scale questionnaire (SUS) was used. The participants of the test ranked each of the 10 questions from 1 to 5, based on their level of agreement. Finally, following the SUS methodology the scores can be obtained [24]. The average of SUS scores reported was equal to 73.7; suggesting that participants are very comfortable with this type of application and can recommend the experience to friends.

Figure 3 (bottom) shows some screenshots corresponding to Red Thread, Business and Emergency Card applications for two anonymous users (John and Jane Doe). As observed at the time, the institution provided gadgets to targets with some applications, which serve as bait, allowing the institution to send these targets any kind of information with the aim of attracting them to the institution.

All wristbands include a NTAG 213 NFC chip. This chip contains software and hardware protection, has a wide range of activity, data transfer speed and long reading durability.

In addition, we have tested hang tags and key folds, some of them shown in Fig. 3 (top). These gadgets are manufactured with different material such as plastic or epoxy, and can also be easily tailored. For these wearables we have tested the NTAG 203 chip. This chip does not admit software protection, but is cheaper and the hardware protection would be sufficient for our interests.

All wearables used in the testing also have the Business and Emergency Card associated, the gadget owners being the ones who decide whether or not to activate any or none of these applications. In the testing all users activated these applications.

Table 1 shows the results of the test performed in order to validate if it would be an acceptable strategy to use these or other wearables within the set of actions to attract school students to the university. To quantify the level of acceptance three levels were used: high (H) medium (M) and low (L).

Table 1. Results of the wearables and applications testing

Wearable	Pairing method	Pairs	Product			Red Thread			Business card			Emergency card		
			L	M	H	L	M	H	L	M	H	L	M	H
Fabric	Paired	10	10	15	75	10	25	65	15	15	70	5	10	85
Silicone	Paired	10	20	25	55	15	35	50	20	20	60	15	20	65
Elastic	Unpaired	10	10	5	85	15	10	75	5	10	85	10	5	85
Hang Tag	Unpaired	10	10	20	70	20	20	60	10	10	80	10	10	80

5 Conclusions

In this paper, we have shown the advantages that Near Field Communication technology might offer to companies and institutions for the engagement of customers or potential targets.

As NFC chips can be embedded to practically any object, these augmented objects or gadgets, could be used as bait for attracting these targets. Conveniently, selecting the gadgets and the associated applications according to the target characteristics (e.g age, students, customers, social network followers, etc.) and aims and strategy for that target engagement (e.g. enrolling, buying of offers, attending an event or place, etc.), gadget providers could use them to spread any kind of information to the users.

Red Thread is an application that is especially geared to young people. The sending of messages between a couple by simply touching the gadget is a type of game aimed at young lovers. Other applications such as those described in this paper are also well accepted by this kind of user. Our proposed solution based on a service platform, the simplicity of use, the capability of personalisation by the users of the execution mode of the applications and the fact that it is not necessary to install a mobile application, produced good results in the testing carried out.

Currently, the staff at the University of Córdoba is studying the strategy for applying this solution to improve attracting school students to the university for the next academic.

References

1. Coskun, V., Ozdenizci, B., Ok, K.: A survey on near field communication (NFC) technology. Wirel. Pers. Commun. **71**, 2259–2294 (2013)
2. Bravo, J., Hervas, R., Chavira, G., Nava, S.W., Villarreal, V.: From implicit to touching interaction: RFID and NFC approaches. In: Conference on Human System Interactions, pp. 743–748 (2008)
3. Arcese, G., Campagna, G., Flammini, S., Martucci, O.: Near field communication: technology and market trends. Technologies **2**, 143 (2014)

4. Pasquet, M., Reynaud, J., Rosenberger, C.: Secure payment with NFC mobile phone in the SmartTouch project. In: International Symposium on Collaborative Technologies and Systems, CTS 2008, pp. 121–126 (2008)
5. Halevi, T., Ma, D., Saxena, N., Xiang, T.: Secure proximity detection for NFC devices based on ambient sensor data. In: Foresti, S., Yung, M., Martinelli, F. (eds.) ESORICS 2012. LNCS, vol. 7459, pp. 379–396. Springer, Heidelberg (2012). doi:10.1007/978-3-642-33167-1_22
6. Chaumette, S., Dubernet, D., Ouoba, J., Siira, E., Tuikka, T.: Architecture and evaluation of a user-centric NFC-enabled ticketing system for small events. In: Zhang, J.Y., Wilkiewicz, J., Nahapetian, A. (eds.) MobiCASE 2011. LNICST, vol. 95, pp. 137–151. Springer, Heidelberg (2012)
7. García, O., Alonso, R.S., Guevara, F., Sancho, D., Sánchez, M., Bajo, J.: ARTIZT: applying ambient intelligence to a museum guide scenario. In: Novais, P., Preuveneers, D., Corchado, J.M. (eds.) ISAmI 2011. AISC, vol. 92, pp. 173–180. Springer, Heidelberg (2011)
8. Borrego-Jaraba, F., Ruiz, I.L., Gómez-Nieto, M.Á.: A NFC-based pervasive solution for city touristic surfing. Pers. Ubiquit. Comput. **15**, 731–742 (2011)
9. Chen, W.-D., Hancke, G., Mayes, K., Lien, Y., Chiu, J.-H.: Using 3G network components to enable NFC mobile transactions and authentication. In: 2010 IEEE International Conference on Progress in Informatics and Computing (PIC), pp. 441–448. IEEE (2010)
10. Mantoro, T., Milišić, A.: Smart card authentication for Internet applications using NFC enabled phone. In: 2010 International Conference on Information and Communication Technology for the Muslim World (ICT4M), pp. D13–D18. IEEE (2010)
11. Steffen, R., Preißinger, J., Schöllermann, T., Müller, A., Schnabel, I.: Near field communication (NFC) in an automotive environment. In: 2nd International Workshop on Near Field Communication, pp. 15–20. IEEE (2010)
12. Yaeli, A., Bak, P., Feigenblat, G., Nadler, S., Roitman, H., Saadoun, G., Ship, H.J., Cohen, D., Fuchs, O., Ofek-Koifman, S., Sandbank, T.: Understanding customer behavior using indoor location analysis and visualization. IBM J. Res. Dev. **58**, 3:1–3:12 (2014)
13. Murao, K., Terada, T., Ai, Y., Matsukura, R.: Evaluating gesture recognition by multiple-sensor-containing mobile devices. In: 2011 15th Annual International Symposium on Wearable Computers (ISWC), pp. 55–58 (2011)
14. Ozdenizci, B., Coskun, V., Aydin, M.N., Kerem, O.: NFC loyal: a beneficial model to promote loyalty on smart cards of mobile devices. In: International Conference for Internet Technology and Secured Transactions (ICITST), pp. 1–6 (2010)
15. Roduner, C., Langheinrich, M.: Publishing and discovering information and services for tagged products. In: Krogstie, J., Opdahl, A.L., Sindre, G. (eds.) CAiSE 2007 and WES 2007. LNCS, vol. 4495, pp. 501–515. Springer, Heidelberg (2007)
16. Ferreira, M.C., Cunha, J., José, R., Rodrigues, H., Monteiro, M.P., Ribeiro, C.: Evaluation of an integrated mobile payment, ticketing and couponing solution based on NFC. In: Rocha, Á., Correia, A.M., Tan, F., Stroetmann, K. (eds.) New Perspectives in Information Systems and Technologies, Volume 2. AISC, vol. 276, pp. 165–174. Springer, Heidelberg (2014)
17. Fabian, K., Topping, K., Barron, I.: Mobile technology and mathematics: effects on students' attitudes, engagement, and achievement. J. Comput. Educ. 1–28 (2015)
18. Chew, C.B., Mahinderjit-Singh, M., Wei, K.C., Sheng, T.W., Husin, M.H., Malim, N.H.A.H.: Sensors-enabled smart attendance systems using NFC and RFID technologies. Int. J. New Comput. Archit. Appl. **5**, 19–29 (2015)
19. Kiy, A., Geßner, H., Lucke, U., Grünewald, F.: A hybrid and modular framework for mobile campus applications. In: icom, pp. 63–73 (2015)

20. Miraz, G.M., Ruiz, I.L., Gómez-Nieto, M.Á.: How NFC can be used for the compliance of European higher education area guidelines in European universities. In: First International Workshop on Near Field Communication, NFC 2009, pp. 3–8 (2009)
21. Garrido, P.C., Miraz, G.M., Ruiz, I.L., Gomez-Nieto, M.A.: Use of NFC-based pervasive games for encouraging learning and student motivation. In: 3rd International Workshop on Near Field Communication (NFC), pp. 32–37. IEEE (2011)
22. Argueta, D., Lu, Y.-T., Ma, J., Rodriguez, D., Yang, Y.-H., Phan, T., Jeon, W.: Enhancing the restaurant dining experience with an NFC-enabled mobile user interface. In: Memmi, G., Blanke, U. (eds.) MobiCASE 2013. LNICST, vol. 130, pp. 314–321. Springer, Heidelberg (2014)
23. The red string of fate legend. https://en.wikipedia.org/wiki/Red_string_of_fate. Accessed November 2015
24. Brooke, J.: SUS - a quick and dirty usability scale. Usability Eval. Ind. **189**, 4–7 (1996)

A Rapid Deployment Solution Prototype for IoT Devices

Antti Iivari(✉), Jani Koivusaari, and Heikki Ailisto

VTT Technical Research Centre of Finland Ltd, Kaitoväylä 1, 90571 Oulu, Finland
{antti.iivari,jani.koivusaari,heikki.ailisto}@vtt.fi

Abstract. A typical application scenario related to the Internet of Things consists of smart sensing devices collecting and transmitting measurement data from their surroundings to a back-end. Efficiently deploying such devices on the field for the purposes of such applications is not a trivial task. Deployment of current IoT and sensor solutions on the field are often time consuming and inconvenient. Setup and configuration of both wireless and wired solutions require know-how, training and time from the person carrying out the deployment of the devices. In order for the rising amount of IoT-based solutions to break into wider usage, a solution for quick and easy deployment is needed that is both easy-to-understand and configuration free. In this work, a proposed solution for rapid deployment of IoT devices is prototyped and presented.

Keywords: Iot · Sensors · Deployment · Software · Mobile

1 Introduction

The Internet of Things (IoT) is the general term related to various technologies for connecting, monitoring and controlling devices such as sensors, home appliances, vehicles, industrial devices and even medical devices over a data network. A number of definitions and viewpoint to IoT have been presented. Atzori et al. [1] have categorized the viewpoints into "Things oriented", "Internet oriented" and "Semantics oriented" visions. The IoT based approach has been envisioned to provide substantial technical, social and economic benefits for the modern society and today's urbanized environments. Despite these promising visions, there are several technical challenges especially related to the deployment of such monitoring devices. The problem is certainly not an insignificant one, as a recent report by AT&T based on a survey [2] of more than 5,000 enterprises worldwide, found that 85 % of enterprises are in the process of or are planning to deploy IoT devices on a significant scale.

In this work, a prototyped technical solution is presented to tackle the issue of quickly and reliably deploying a number of IoT devices, or smart communication enabled sensors, on the field to begin their work of collecting measurements and transmitting that data towards a back-end for further processing, storage and analysis. The solution is based on the usage QR-codes, which are a type of matrix barcodes also referred to as Quick Response Codes. The QR-codes are scanned with a smartphone application, and based on the data extracted from the specific QR-code and other data available to the mobile application, the smartphone will contact the back-end and communicate all the

C.R. García et al. (Eds.): UCAmI 2016, Part II, LNCS 10070, pp. 275–283, 2016.
DOI: 10.1007/978-3-319-48799-1_32

necessary information and authorize the IoT device to begin transmitting measurement data to the back-end to be stored and processed. The QR-codes contain a globally unique identifier (GUID) that can be easily generated and physically attached to an individual device or piece of equipment. When the device has been deployed and activated within the back-end by using the mobile application, the IoT device can be simply turned on and the collection and transfer of sensor data can begin by using simple pre-defined configurations. Using the categorization presented by Atzori and co-workers mentioned previously, the issues discussed in this paper could be seen to stand on the intersection of "things oriented" and "internet oriented" visions.

2 Deploying Smart Connected Things

As the IoT concept relies on the use of large number of smart devices, objects and sensors, the easiness and sustainable cost of deploying these smart things becomes more and more critical. The lifetime costs of a local IoT installation ("a smart thing") can be divided into three main components as follows:

- the cost of the smart thing, both hardware and software
- the cost of connectivity
- the cost of deployment

The cost of smart things as such is decreasing with improving manufacturing technologies and scale benefits. Cost of connectivity is decreasing due to rapid development of wireless technology, both ISM and regulated cellular. The third important cost element is the installation and deployment cost. In many cases this may become more dominant when the two other costs are decreasing rapidly. The main component of the installation cost is human labor. This is even more of a problem, if professional technicians or other trained personnel are needed to carry out the various tasks related to the deployment, physical installation and configuration of the smart devices. This issue is mentioned in connection of a deployment of smart lighting system [3] and a smart home demonstrator where the fast installation of Wireless Sensor Nodes (WSN) is carried out by tapping a NFC smart phone to WSN node equipped appliances [4].

For the purposes of the work herein, we will use the term 'deployment' to refer to all the various steps and operations that must be carried out to bring a smart sensor node up and running to a fully functional state on the field. This encompasses everything from simply powering on the device to all the tasks related to the configuration, activation and setup of the device and all related software. After this phase has been carried out successfully, the device in question will begin its normal modes of operation, such as taking measurements and communicating its data.

Much of the recent related work [5, 6] concerning the deployment of wireless sensor nodes emphasizes the issues related to power efficiency, communication radius and the achieved coverage through specific placement patterns for wireless sensor networks and the optimization problems derived from such aspects. On the other hand, the work presented in this paper is more concerned with minimizing the time, effort and resources required to deploy and setup a smart sensor device on the field and enable it to begin collecting and transmitting measurement data as quickly and conveniently as possible for the benefit of the application at hand.

3 A Mobile QR-Code Based Approach

QR code (or Quick Response Code) [7] is a type of matrix barcode originally designed for purposes the automotive industry in Japan. It is essentially a machine-readable optical label that contains information about the physical item to which it is attached, using standardized encoding modes to efficiently store data. QR-code based approached in the context of ubiquitous applications and the Internet of Things are nothing new in and of themselves, as seen in some of the related work [8–10]. However, the exact manner in which QR-codes are employed in the proposed rapid deployment solution presented in this paper can be considered a novel one.

In the rapid deployment approach proposed herein, the QR-codes contain a globally unique identifier (GUID) that can be easily generated and physically attached to an individual device or piece of equipment. Globally unique identifiers (GUIDs) [11] are unique reference numbers used as an identifier in computer software and hardware. The term "GUID" typically refers to various implementations of the universally unique identifier (UUID) standard. A flowchart of the proposed approach is given in Fig. 1.

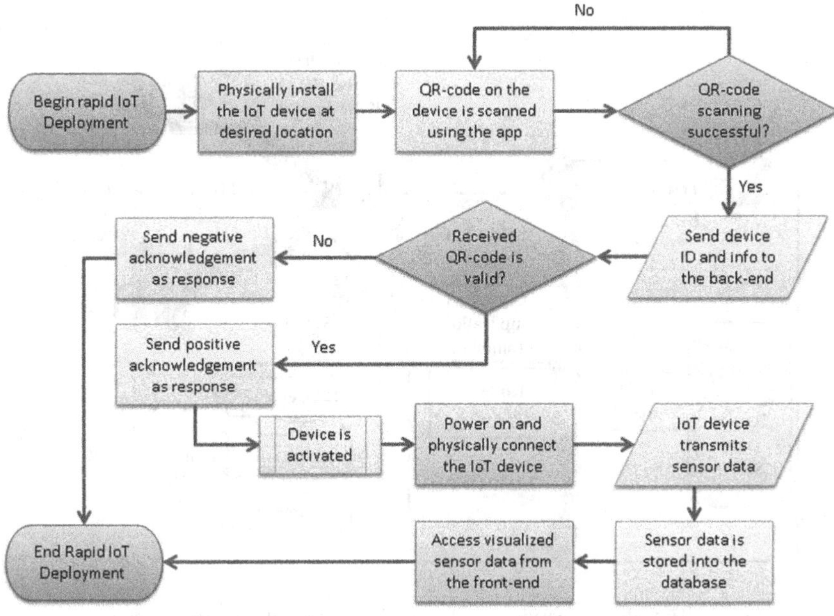

Fig. 1. A Flowchart of the whole rapid IoT device deployment process.

Essential to the presented rapid deployment solution is the smart phone application and the inherent capabilities of the smartphone as a device. When considering the person carrying out the deployment of IoT devices on the field with a smartphone or a handheld tablet computer, it is commonly safe to assume that the handheld device is equipped with data connectivity (towards the internet), GPS locator chip, a camera and sufficient memory and processing power to carry out the tasks of scanning a QR-code and sending a simple HTTP-message with a JSON-payload towards the activation back-end. While the IoT device itself might not even be turned on, the user of the handheld device (e.g. the technician deploying the IoT device) has easy access to a lot of information that is useful and relevant when carrying out the deployment of a IoT-enabled sensing device. This information could include things such as a GPS location, device ownership, security- and application context and so on. The proposed solution can be applied in most existing systems, thus increasing the value of already existing IoT technology without re-inventing the wheel or investing in costly upgrades.

4 Technical Details of the Prototype

The proposed approach for Rapid QR-code based IoT device deployment has been realized as a complete proof-of-concept pilot system, which enabled running experiments for the purpose of trialing and validating the solution. The overview of the whole system is visualized in Fig. 2, while technical details of the individual components are discussed further within the rest of this section of the paper.

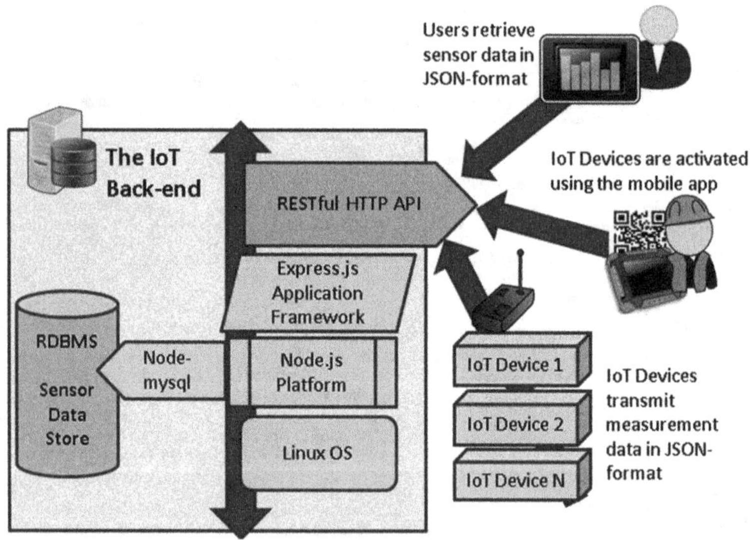

Fig. 2. High-level overview of the rapid deployment prototype system.

The implementation aims to trial and validate the proposed approach by running concrete tests and experiments with real-world devices. The key components of the prototype system are listed as follows:

- Android app for scanning and sending a QR code on a device to be activated
- Back-end for handling device activation and sensor data management
- Raspberry Pi – based IoT end-device emulating typical IoT application behaviour
- Interactive Web-based Front-end for sensor data visualization.

4.1 The Android Mobile Application

The purpose of the mobile application is to enable identifying and activating an IoT device on the field with a touch of a button by reading the physical QR-codes attached to a device on the field. The QR-codes are scanned by accessing the built-in camera functionalities present on most handheld devices on the market today. The mobile application prototype was developed for Android based devices, usable on both handheld smartphones and tablet-type devices. A series of screenshots from the Android application in action is provided in Fig. 3. After the QR-code has been successfully scanned by using the application, it is a trivial matter to send the extracted ID of the IoT device and other information (such as GPS-coordinates, timestamps, user information) to the back-end via the ubiquitous data communication capabilities of modern handheld devices.

Fig. 3. A series of screenshots from the Android mobile application.

The implemented mobile application for the rapid deployment prototype system is based on the Android SDK version 23.0.0. For accessing the Android camera capabilities for the purpose of scanning QR-codes, a library called ZXing [12] was employed. ZXing is an open-source, multi-format 1D/2D barcode image processing library implemented in Java, with ports to other languages. Version 3.2.0 of ZXing was utilized for the application developed in this work.

4.2 The IoT Back-End

In a typical IoT scenario, in addition to the embedded intercommunicating smart objects (the "things"), there exists the server-side functionalities where the actual application specific logic and data processing takes place. This is referred to as the back-end, which usually consists of three main parts: a server, an application, and a database. In order to make the server, application, and database communicate with each other, one or more server-side languages are used. The functionalities related to the IoT back-end discussed here were implemented on top of the open source Node.js [13] platform. The Node.js platform enables the server side application developer to discard the traditional and somewhat cumbersome, LAMP-stack altogether while still providing excellent modules and built-in capabilities for development and interacting with various database technologies such as MySQL. A REST – interface was programmed for storing and retrieving JSON-based sensor data payloads sent through standard HTTP GET and POST – messages. All the information on the IoT devices and the sensor data itself is stored into a relational MySQL database. In the case of the prototype system for rapid deployment described in this paper, the back-end functionalities include a device id database table for the activation and authentication of the IoT sensor nodes and the data coming from them. Once the back-end receives the activation message from the mobile app through the REST-interface, it validates the ID and stores all necessary information into the database for the system to start collecting data from any activated IoT devices. The back-end also sends response messages with a status code to the mobile app on the field, allowing the person carrying out the deployment to check whether the attempted activation has been successful or not. When the successful acknowledgement-message is received on the smart phone, the deployed device can be turned on and sensor data transmission toward the back-end can begin thus finalizing the rapid deployment process.

Node.js is an open source JavaScript-based platform built on top of Google Chrome's JavaScript V8 Engine. As it provides an event-driven architecture and a non-blocking I/O API making it very lightweight and efficient it is especially suitable for building data-intensive real-time applications that are scalable and run across distributed devices [13]. Node.js facilitates the creation of highly scalable servers without using threading by using a simplified model of event-driven programming.

The REST interfaces implemented in the context of the prototype also include support for HTTP Basic authentication as a relatively simple access control technique to ensure an elementary level of security in the exchange of measurement information and message exchange related to the rapid device activation.

4.3 IoT Devices

The actual end-devices used in the context of the prototype and the experimental work were Raspberry Pi – based single-board computers with Debian GNU/Linux as operating systems and a QR-code sticker added to the outer casing. A simple Python client program was developed for the IoT end-devices based on the Requests Apache2 Licensed HTTP library. The client program emulates the behavior of typical IoT applications, where several communications enabled sensing devices collect measurement data at specific intervals and transmit this data as JSON payloads over HTTP towards the back-end. This also allows for some basic stress testing of the HTTP/REST – functionalities specifically concerning the back-end. It is important to note, however, that the rapid deployment mechanism presented here can be utilized with all kinds of IoT devices to which a physical QR-code can be attached.

4.4 Cross-Platform Visualization Front-End

In addition to the Android mobile application, the implemented prototype system also includes a web-based front-end for accessing and visualizing the gathered sensor data. The time-series data may be viewed by a specific sensor device and by a desired time period. Viewing measurement data simultaneously from multiple sensors is also supported by the system. Furthermore, the specific graphs may be viewed in more detail on a separate dynamically zoomed view, as can be seen on the screenshot of the front-end presented in Fig. 4.

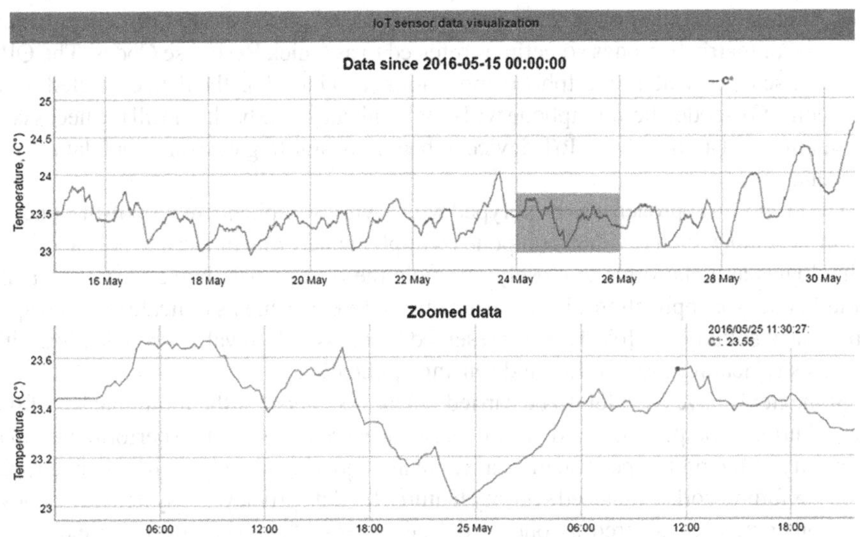

Fig. 4. A Screenshot of the web-based sensor data visualization front-end.

As the front-end may be accessed by the Android device used for the device activation as well as with any browser on a PC, the front-end should be designed to support both. The front-end utilizes single page design principles and is built mainly on AngularJS [14] open-source client-side web application framework. AngularJS together with UI Bootstrap directives provide impressive look and feel, responsiveness and support for both mobile and desktop browsers, with short implementation time. The graphs are generated by utilizing the digraph.js library, which is capable of presenting up to millions of points of data without any noticeable performance issues.

5 Conclusions

As the IoT concept relies on the use of large number of smart devices, objects and sensors, the easiness and sustainable cost of deploying these smart things becomes critical. A typical application scenario for the technologies related to the Internet of Things consists of smart monitoring sensors collecting and transmitting measurement data to a back-end. Efficiently deploying such devices on the field for the purposes of such applications is not a trivial task as deployment of current IoT and sensor solutions are often time consuming and inconvenient.

In this work, a prototype solution is presented, in addition to a complete proof-of-concept implementation, to tackle the issue of quickly and reliably deploying a number of IoT devices, or smart communication enabled sensors, on the field to begin their work of taking measurements and transmitting that data towards a back-end for further processing, storage and analysis. The solution is based on the usage QR-codes, which are a type of matrix barcodes sometimes referred to as Quick Response Codes. The QR-codes are scanned with a smartphone application, and based on the data extracted from the specific QR-code; the smartphone will communicate to the back-end all the necessary information and authorize the IoT device to begin transmitting measurement data to the back-end.

The proposed approach was prototyped with a wholly implemented proof-of-concept piloting system, with individual components implemented with modern widely accepted technologies and platforms to closely resemble the operational characteristics of real-world IoT sensor applications. Initial results from the experiments indicate that the rapid deployment solution for IoT devices presented herein is indeed valid when dealing with scenarios typical for modern IoT and sensing applications.

Some items have been left to be carried out as next steps for the future phases of the work. Further comparisons and quantitative measurements on the performance and scalability of the prototype system as a whole and individual components are one topic of left for future work. Enhanced security features for data privacy and system robustness are another item considered as one of the next steps. Also, running more extensive experiments with various real-world devices, environments and communication technologies is another topic that was left for future work and publications.

Acknowledgements. The research work presented in this paper was supported by the VTT program Productivity with Internet of Things.

References

1. Atzori, L., Iera, A., Morabito, G.: The internet of things: a survey. Comput. Netw. **54**(15), 2787–2805 (2010)
2. AT&T Cybersecurity Insights, https://www.corp.att.com/cybersecurity/
3. Magno, M., Polonelli, T., Benini, L., Popovici, E.: A low cost, highly scalable wireless sensor network solution to achieve smart LED light control for green buildings. IEEE Sens. J. **15**(5), 2963–2973 (2015)

4. Jonjic, A., Grosinger, J., Herndl, T., Holweg, G., Beer, G., Bosch, W.: A secure miniaturized wireless sensor node for a smart home demonstrator. In: 2015 IEEE MTT-S International Microwave Symposium (IMS), pp. 1–4. IEEE (2015)
5. Beutel, J., Römer, K., Ringwald, M., Woehrle, M.: Deployment techniques for sensor networks. In: Sensor Networks, pp. 219–248. Springer, Heidelberg (2010)
6. Liu, X., Mahapatra, P.: On the deployment of wireless sensor nodes. In: Proceedings of the 3rd International Workshop on Measurement, Modeling, and Performance Analysis of Wireless Sensor Networks, in Conjunction with the 2nd Annual International Conference on Mobile and Ubiquitous Systems (2005)
7. Pandya, K.H., Galiyawala, H.J.: A survey on QR codes: in context of research and application. Int. J. Emerg. Technol. Adv. Eng. **4**(3) (2014). Website: www. ijetae. com (ISSN 2250-2459, ISO 9001: 2008) Certified Journal
8. Want, R., Schilit, B.N., Jenson, S.: Enabling the internet of things. Computer **48**(1), 28–35 (2015)
9. Narayanan, A.S.: QR codes and security solutions. Int. J. Comput. Sci. Telecommun. **3**(7), 69–71 (2012)
10. Bologna Airport chooses Connecthings' Internet of Things Platform. https://www.connecthings.com/2016/01/25/bologna-airport-chooses-connecthings-internet-of-things-platform/
11. A Universally Unique IDentifier (UUID) URN Namespace. https://www.ietf.org/rfc/rfc4122.txt
12. ZXing, an open-source, multi-format 1D/2D barcode image processing library implemented in Java. https://github.com/zxing/zxing
13. About Node.js. https://nodejs.org/en/about/
14. AngularJS. https://angularjs.org/

The Advanced Network of Things: A Middleware to Provide Enhanced Performance and Functionality in IoT

Gabriel Urzaiz[1](✉), Ramon Hervas[2], Jesus Fontecha[2], and Jose Bravo[2]

[1] Universidad Anahuac Mayab, Merida, Yucatan, Mexico
gabriel.urzaiz@anahuac.mx
[2] Universidad de Castilla-La Mancha, Ciudad Real, Spain
{ramon.hlucas,jesus.fontecha,jose.bravo}@uclm.es

Abstract. The Internet of Things (IoT) imposes several challenges and opportunities. Most of the existing and ongoing network solutions are limited in scope and technology, ignoring important IoT aspects and using traditional protocols and technologies that are not necessarily suitable for things. The proposal is named the Advanced Network of Things (ANT) which constitutes an alternate solution to provide network enhanced services in IoT. In this paper the ANT model design is presented.

Keywords: Internet of things (IoT) · Middleware · Enhanced services

1 Introduction

From a technological point of view, there have been several challenges since the beginning of the Internet, such as the limitation of the addressing scheme, routing, management, multiservice and QoS, semantic web, heterogeinity, security, mobility and recently, the IoT.

Most of these challenges have already been addressed, but many efforts are now focused to meet the needs posed by IoT. The features and functionality of the current Internet may not be the best to meet the needs imposed by the interconnection of things to the Internet.

IoT has essential differences compared to the Internet of humans. Among the major IoT challenges [1, 2] are the following.

IoT implies that a huge number of sensors will be deployed, and therefore a large volume of information will be generated and collected. The type of information generated in IoT is different to that produced by humans. Most of the information in IoT is of real-time nature, reliability or accuracy is unpredictable, and spatial and temporal information redundancy should be taken into consideration. There is a need for generating exact and timely responses. The purpose of data processing in IoT may not only be a response but also an action of a machine or a human. There should also be a place for understanding the context and providing smart services.

C.R. García et al. (Eds.): UCAmI 2016, Part II, LNCS 10070, pp. 284–294, 2016.
DOI: 10.1007/978-3-319-48799-1_33

Table 1. IoT challenges and activities

	Challenge	Activity
1	Huge number of sensors will be deployed	Deployment and maintenance
2	Large volume of information will be generated and collected	Communication of the collected information
3	Real-time nature of information	
4	Spatial and temporal information redundancy	Measurements collection
5	Need for robustness to unpredictable reliability or accuracy	
6	Need for exact and timely responses or actions.	Response and/or action generation
7	Usability features (context-aware, mobile services)	

A list of seven major IoT challenges is proposed in Table 1. This list will be used later in the article as a model design basis.

The rest of the article is organized as follows. Section 2 includes a revision of the models and technologies preceding IoT. The solution design is presented in Sect. 3, starting from the motivation, approach, and design goals, and describing the model structure and main components. This section also includes a positioning analysis of ANT when compared to other selected architectures. ANT implementation is presented in Sect. 4, including the implementation scenarios and describing the proof of concept that was performed to verify feasibility. Conclusion and work in progress are discussed in Sect. 5.

2 Revision

The traditional architecture models (OSI, TCP/IP) may not be directly applicable for current needs of the connection of things.

It is difficult to achieve a single architecture capable of satisfying all the requirements for IoT, due to the wide variety of application areas, and therefore there are also some efforts for establishing a standard [3].

In the current scenario there are at least two major initiatives that guide the development of the Internet. On one side is the Future Internet Architecture project, and on the other, specific architectures for IoT.

One of the best sources where to find the most adequate architectures for IoT, is probably the Future Internet Architecture (FIA) NSF project, which has financed the development of several approaches such as Name Data Networking (NDN) [4], MobilityFirst (MF) [5], NEBULA [6], eXpressive Internet Architecture (XIA) [7], and Choicenet [8]. Among these projects, probably the most relevant for IoT are MF which establishes an important framework for the development of IoT services [9, 10], and NDN which is also an important reference to be considered for the development of new architectures for IoT [11].

There are also another approaches based on traditional paradigms, such as services-based architectures [12, 13], distributed architectures [14], architectures based on semantic models [15], etc.

There are also some effort focused on specific problems, such as an architecture for the development of Intelligent Traffic Management Systems (ITMS) called Nova Genesis [16], architectures for Quality of Service (QoS), and also those that tries to solve the consistency problem [17], etc.

Some middleware was developed for IoT, such as VIRTUS [18] which is based on XMPP for a secure communication.

There are some architectures which development is focused specifically for IoT, such as the following:

- ITU-T (IoT Global Standards Initiative, IoT reference model, Y.2060) [19]
- IEEE (Architectural framework for IoT, draft 2413) [20]
- IETF (Architectural considerations in smart object networking, RFC7452) [21].

3 Solution Design

3.1 Motivation and Approach

Most of the solutions currently offered to connect things to the Internet, are limited in scope and technology.

They are limited in scope because they focus only on solving access and processing, ignoring other important aspects such as the volume of information, the nature of it, the need for action and response, etc.

They are limited in technology, because they use available protocols and technologies that are not necessarily suitable for things. Access protocols are often the same ones used for interactive traffic. Processing is often achieved by traditional local and/or cloud and/or remote processing solutions, or any combination thereof (Fig. 1), but this is not exactly a solution of IoT.

The concept of IoT goes beyond, is something new, it is a new version of the Internet, but designed specifically for the interconnection of things. It involves changes in structure and operation.

In this paper, the ITU-T Y.2060 model is taken as a reference to develop a middleware to provide enhanced functionality and performance (Fig. 2).

3.2 The Advanced Network of Things (ANT)

We named our proposal as the Advanced Network of Things (ANT). The idea is to provide enhanced services in the existing Internet, by adding some code to be executed either externally or as part of the network components, either as an overlay or as a middleware. The proposal takes into consideration the requirements for IoT. These requirements have a significant impact on the model architecture.

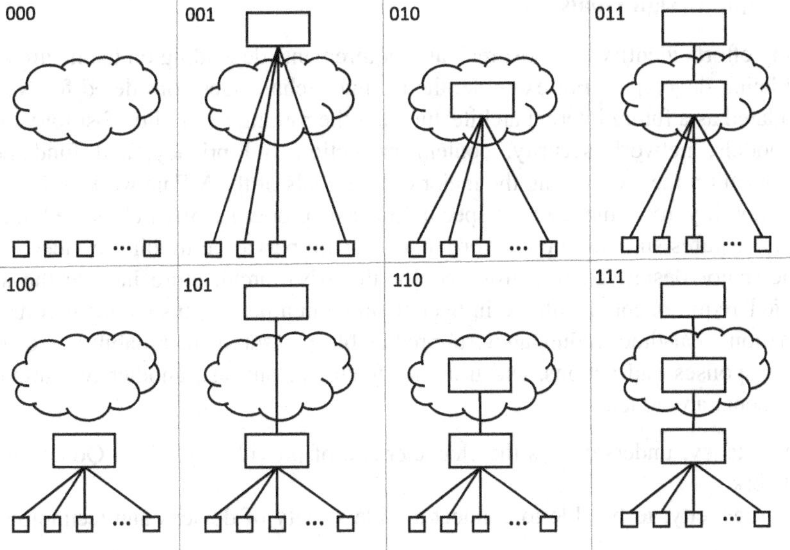

Fig. 1. IoT by using local and/or cloud and/or remote processing.

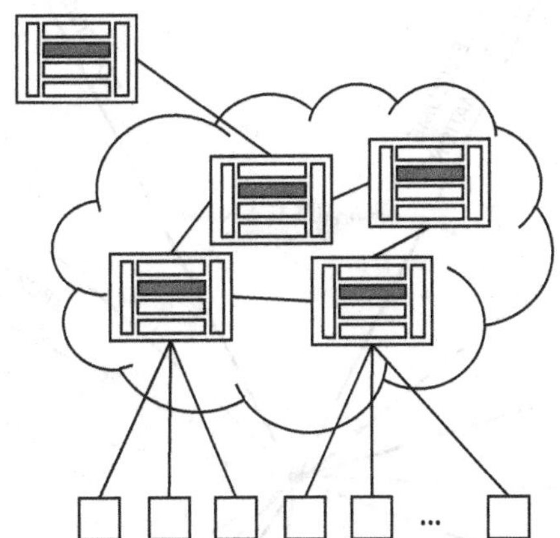

Fig. 2. Middleware with ITU-T Y.2060 as a reference

ANT considers not only the network requirements for the communication of humans but also the network requirements to communicate things.

ANT could be considered as an external network enhancement tool. This is important because it offers a way to provide enhanced services in an existing network without the need of modifying its internal components. This means that ANT could be used today with the existing Internet to provide consistent services for IoT.

3.3 Major Design Goals

Ongoing efforts identify the most relevant requirements depending on the nature of the model being developed. For example, the technical challenges considered for NDN to be validated as a future internet architecture, are the routing scalability, fast forwarding, trust models, network security, content protection and privacy, and fundamental communication theory. Among the major design goals of the MF network architecture, are the mobility, robustness with respect to intrinsic properties of wireless medium, and usability features such as support for context-aware pervasive mobile services.

The major design goals considered for the ANT architecture include the seven major IoT requirements identified in Sect. 1 (huge number of sensors, large volume of information, real-time, redundancy, unpredictable measurement reliability, exact and timely responses and actions, and usability features), but also another two important requirements are added:

- Consistency, understood as the characteristic of providing uniform QoS along the network
- Heterogeneity, to be able to connect a wide variety of devices and technologies.

ANT major design goals are summarized and graphically represented in Fig. 3, which also shows the positioning of ANT and other selected architectures.

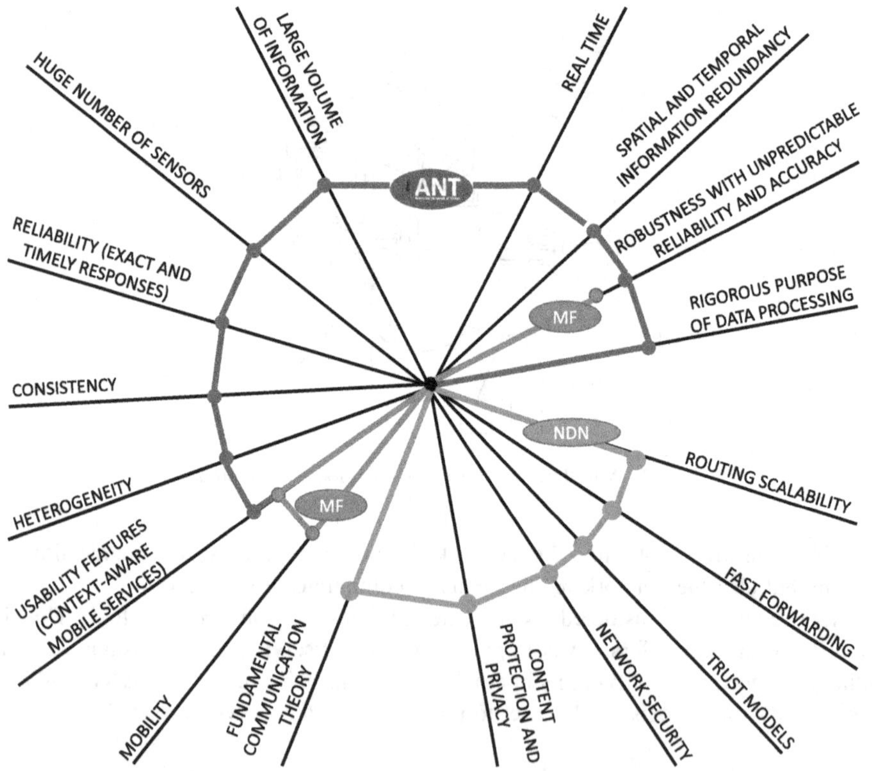

Fig. 3. ANT positioning

3.4 ANT Architecture and Components

The ANT architecture includes four components: Configuration Management (CM), Network Functionality (NF), Measurement Functionality (MF) and Semantic Functionality (SF). The relationship between these components is represented in Fig. 4.

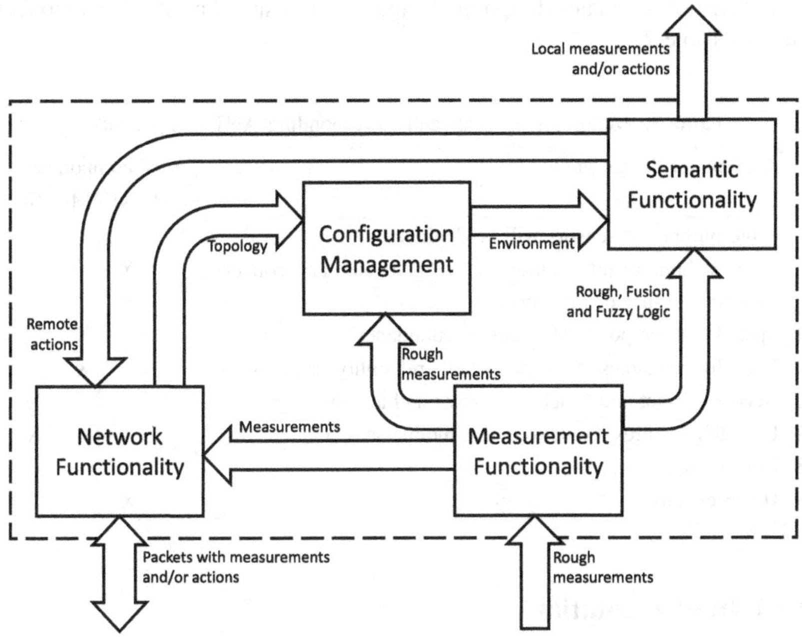

Fig. 4. Relationship between ANT components

The Configuration Management component includes the following features:

- Learns position and other characteristics of every sensor since the first time it sends information;
- Builds a topology table, and
- Keeps track of every sensor in the network.

The Network Functionality component includes the following features:

- Routing with network capacity optimization (similar to link state)
- Heterogeneity to connect a wide variety of devices and technologies, and
- Overlay virtual mesh topology for Quality-of-Service (QoS) and consistency.

The Measurement Functionality component includes the following features:

- Collect rough measurement;
- Fusion techniques for information enrichment, and
- Fuzzy Logic to provide robustness in sensor measurements.

The Semantic Functionality component includes the following features:

- Expert system and other Artificial Intelligence (AI) techniques to analyze, understand and interpret the context, in order to take the appropriate action;
- Continuous feedback to make sure that response is exact and adequate; and
- Application Program Interface (API) with ant_get and ant_send commands.

A summary of the major design goals and the corresponding ANT components is presented in Table 2.

Table 2. Major design goals and corresponding ANT components

	ANT major design goal	ANT component			
		CM	NF	MF	SF
1	Huge number of sensors will be deployed	X			
2	Large volume of information will be generated and collected		X		
3	Real-time nature of information		X		
4	Spatial and temporal information redundancy			X	
5	Need for robustness to unpredictable reliability or accuracy			X	
6	Need for exact and timely responses and actions				X
7	Usability features (context-aware, mobile services)				X
8	Consistency		X		
9	Heterogeneity		X		

4 ANT Implementation

4.1 Implementation Scenarios

ANT was implemented in three ways:

1. As an overlay;
2. As a middleware, with traditional TCP/IP stack;
3. As a middleware, with the ITU-T Y.2060 IoT reference model.

The three-layer architecture implemented as an overlay network is presented in Fig. 5a.

ANT was also implemented as a middleware by using the traditional TCP/IP stack (Fig. 5b). The user application uses ANT to communicate with any other device in the network, instead of using sockets as usual. The ANT semantic layer is connected to the TCP/IP application layer by means of the above described API, and the ANT network layer is connected to UDP running at the TCP/IP transport layer by using traditional UDP sockets and UDP ports.

ANT was also implemented as a Generic Support Capability at the Service Support and Application Support Layer of the ITU-T Y.2060 IoT reference model (Fig. 5c).

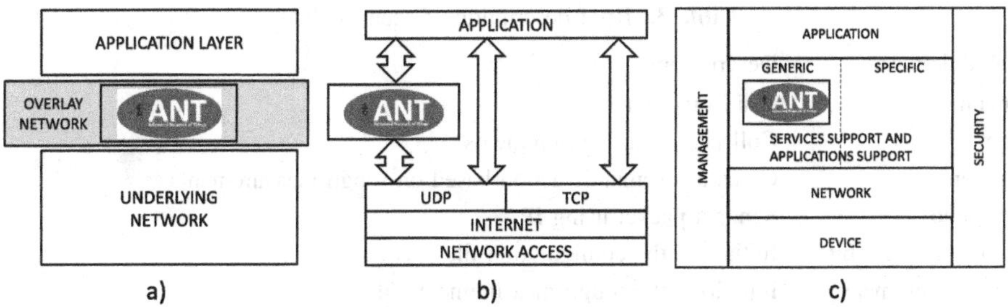

Fig. 5. ANT implementation. (a) as an overlay, (b) as a middleware with traditional TCP/IP stack, and (c) as a middleware with the ITU-T Y.2060 IoT reference model

4.2 Proof of Concept

A proof of concept was performed to verify ANT feasibility. A piece of software was developed to implement the four model components. The software was developed in the C++ programming language. The general structure of the software is represented in Fig. 6, and a brief description of each module is presented in Table 3.

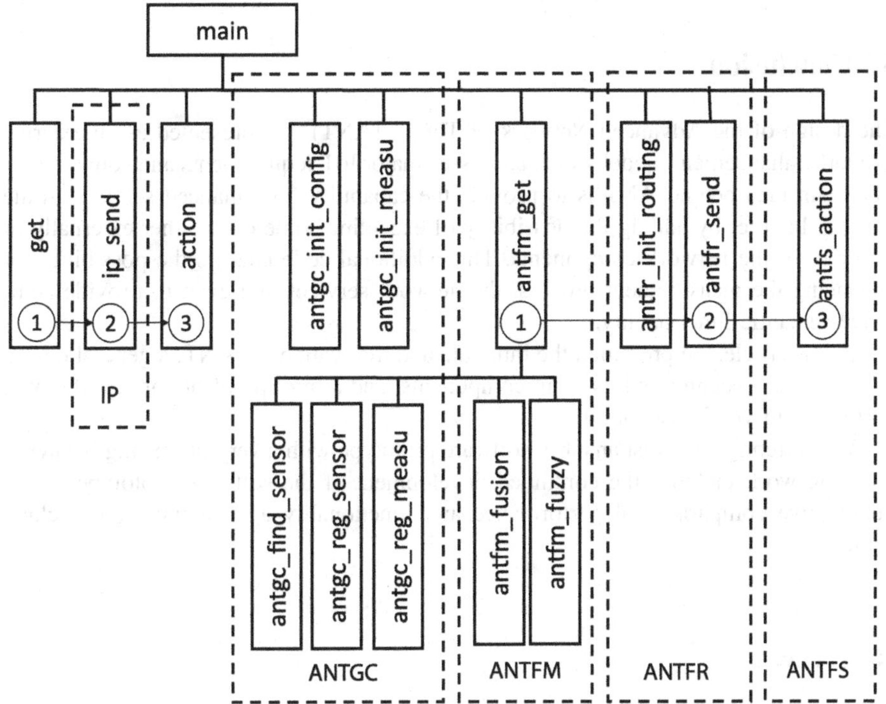

Fig. 6. General structure of the ANT proof of concept software

Table 3. Brief description of each module

Module name	Description
main	Main function
get	Collects rough measurements
action	Generates semantic action based on rough measurements
ip_send	Sends a packet using IP
antgc_init_config	Initializes the configuration file
antgc_init_measu	Initializes the rough measurements file
antgc_find_sensor	Verifies the existence of a specific sensor in the configuration file
antgc_reg_sensor	Learns position and other characteristics related to each sensor since the first measurement that the sensor sends
antgc_reg_measu	Keeps track of all measurements of each sensor
antfm_get	Collects measurements using ANT
antfm_fusion	Calculates measurement by using information fusion techniques for information enhancement
antfm_fuzzy	Calculates measurement by applying Fuzzy Logic to enhance robustness
antfr_init_routing	Initializes routing table
antfr_send	Sends a packet using ANT
antfs_action	Based on context analysis, generates a semantic action based on ANT measurements

5 Conclusion

The design of the Advanced Network of Things (ANT) was presented as an external network enhancement model which addresses major IoT requirements and some others. The main idea behind ANT is to provide the capability for enhanced services in the existing Internet by adding the possibility of executing some code either externally or as a part of the network components. This additional code enables the possibility for enhancing the measurement process, the network services and even to provide additional semantic functionality.

In this article, we presented the rationale and motivation for ANT, a general design of the model structure and its main components, and a brief proof of concept that was performed to verify feasibility.

We currently have just an early software prototype with a very promising behavior. Ongoing work includes the continued development of the software prototype, and a quantitative comparison of performance and functionality against typical IoT cloud solutions.

References

1. Chen, Y.-K.: Challenges and opportunities of internet of things. In: 2012 17th Asia and South Pacific, pp. 383–388, 30 January 2012–2 February 2012. doi:10.1109/ASPDAC.2012.6164978

2. Khan, R., Khan, S.U., Zaheer, R., Khan, S.: Future internet: the internet of things architecture, possible applications and key challenges. In: 2012 10th International Conference on Frontiers of Information Technology (FIT), pp. 257–260, 17–19 December 2012. doi:10.1109/FIT.2012.53
3. Krco, S., Pokric, B., Carrez, F.: Designing IoT architecture(s): a european perspective. In: 2014 IEEE World Forum on Internet of Things (WF-IoT), pp. 79–84, 6–8 March 2014. doi:10.1109/WF-IoT.2014.6803124
4. Name Data Networking project overview. http://named-data.net/project/, date consulted October 06, 2015
5. Mobility First Future Internet Architecture project overview. http://mobilityfirst.winlab.rutgers.edu/, date consulted October 06, 2015
6. NEBULA: a trustworthy, secure and evolvable Future Internet Architecture. http://nebula-fia.org/, date consulted October 06, 2015
7. eXpressive Internet Architecture. http://www.cs.cmu.edu/~xia/, date consulted October 06, 2015
8. Choicenet: network innovation through choice. https://code.renci.org/gf/project/choicenet/. Date consulted October 06, 2015
9. Li, J., Shvartzshnaider, Y., Francisco, J., Martin, R.P., Nagaraja, K., Raychaudhuri, D.: Delivering internet-of-things services in mobility first future internet architecture. In: 2012 3rd International Conference on the Internet of Things (IOT), pp. 31–38, 24–26 October 2012. doi:10.1109/IOT.2012.6402301
10. Li, J., Shvartzshnaider, Y., Francisco, J., Martin, R.P., Raychaudhuri, D.: Enabling internet-of-things services in the mobility first future internet architecture. In: 2012 IEEE International Symposium on a World of Wireless, Mobile and Multimedia Networks (WoWMoM), pp. 1–6, 25–28 June 2012. doi:10.1109/WoWMoM.2012.6263787
11. Li, S., Zhang, Y., Raychaudhuri, D., Ravindran, R.: A comparative study of MobilityFirst and NDN based ICN-IoT architectures. In: 2014 10th International Conference on Heterogeneous Networking for Quality, Reliability, Security and Robustness (QShine), pp. 158–163, 18–20 August 2014. doi:10.1109/QSHINE.2014.6928680
12. Evdokimov, S.; Fabian, B.; Kunz, S.; Schoenemann, N., "Comparison of Discovery Service Architectures for the Internet of Things. In: 2010 IEEE International Conference on Sensor Networks, Ubiquitous, and Trustworthy Computing (SUTC), pp. 237–244, 7–9 June 2010. doi:10.1109/SUTC.2010.22
13. Lan, L., Li, F., Wang, B., Zhang, L., Shi, R.: An Event-Driven Service-Oriented Architecture for the Internet of Things. In: Services Computing Conference (APSCC), 2014 Asia-Pacific, pp. 68–73, 4–6 December 2014. doi:10.1109/APSCC.2014.34
14. Sarkar, C., Nambi, A.U.S.N., Prasad, R.V., Rahim, A., Neisse, R., Baldini, G.: DIAT: a scalable distributed architecture for IoT. IEEE Internet Things J. **2**(3), 230–239 (2015). doi:10.1109/JIOT.2014.2387155
15. Singh, D., Tripathi, G., Jara, A.J.: A survey of internet-of-things: future vision, architecture, challenges and services. In: 2014 IEEE World Forum on Internet of Things (WF-IoT), pp. 287–292, 6–8 March 2014. doi:10.1109/WF-IoT.2014.6803174
16. Singh, D., Alberti, A.M.: Developing nova genesis architecture for internet of things services: observation, challenges and ITMS application. In: 2014 International Conference on Information and Communication Technology Convergence (ICTC), pp. 1009–1014, 22–24 October 2014. doi:10.1109/ICTC.2014.6983361
17. Duan, R., Chen, X., Xing, T.: A QoS architecture for IOT. In: 2011 International Conference on and 4th International Conference on Cyber, Physical and Social Computing Internet of Things (iThings/CPSCom), pp. 717–720, 19–22 October 2011. doi:10.1109/iThings/CPSCom.2011.125

18. Conzon, D., Bolognesi, T., Brizzi, P., Lotito, A., Tomasi, R., Spirito, M.A.: The VIRTUS middleware: an XMPP based architecture for secure IoT communications. In: 2012 21st International Conference on Computer Communications and Networks (ICCCN), pp. 1–6, 30 July 2012–2 August 2012. doi:10.1109/ICCCN.2012.6289309
19. ITU-T, IoT Global Standards Initiative, IoT reference model. Y.2060). http://www.itu.int/itu-t/recommendations/rec.aspx?rec=Y.2060. Date consulted 07 June 2016
20. P2413 - Standard for an Architectural Framework for the Internet of Things (IoT). IEEE Standards Association. https://standards.ieee.org/develop/project/2413.html. Date consulted 07 June 2016
21. IETF RFC7452: Architectural considerations in Smart Object Networking. https://tools.ietf.org/html/rfc7452. Date consulted 07 June 2016

Using Beacons for Creating Comprehensive Virtual Profiles

Angela Barriga Rodriguez[1](✉), Alejandro Rodriguez Tena[1], Jose Garcia-Alonso[1], Javier Berrocal[1], Ricardo Flores Rosco[2], and Juan M. Murillo[1]

[1] University of Extremadura, Escuela Politecnica, Avda de la Universidad s/n, 10003 Caceres, Spain
{abarrigaj,arodriguysf}@alumnos.unex.es, {jgaralo,jberolm,juanmamu}@unex.es

[2] Gloin S.L., Las Ocas 2, 10004 Caceres, Spain
rflores@gloin.es

Abstract. The number of Internet of Things systems in which the general population is involved keeps increasing. At the same time, the configuration and adaptation of these systems to their users' preferences are still mostly manual. To achieve a better personalization of these systems comprehensive virtual profiles of their users, including as much information as possible, is needed. One of the most relevant information of a user virtual profile is his location. With the rise of the bluetooth low energy protocol and the appearance of the beacon technology, indoor positioning of smartphone owners can be added to these virtual profiles. However, the lack of a beacon standard and the low level information provided by these devices is hindering its adoption. To solve this, this paper presents a Beacon Management System that abstracts applications developers from the low level details of the different beacons protocols and allows the management of unregistered beacons. The proposed system has been integrated into the People as a Service computation model and in the commercial platform nimBees to improve the creation of virtual profiles in IoT applications.

Keywords: Internet of Things · People as a Service · Beacons · Bluetooth low energy

1 Introduction

The current ubiquitous Internet presence has led to the creation and deployment of all kinds of devices equipped with a network interface. Connecting those and other everyday physical objects to the Internet is getting ever easier. This has enhanced the popularity of the Internet of Things (IoT). However, the current integration between humans and IoT technologies still leaves much room for improvement [7,17]. Currently, final users must manually configure most of the devices, indicating what are their preferences and how they should behave. In a foreseeable situation in which millions of devices will be connected [27], their

C.R. García et al. (Eds.): UCAmI 2016, Part II, LNCS 10070, pp. 295–306, 2016.
DOI: 10.1007/978-3-319-48799-1_34

configuration and reconfiguration when users' preferences change will entail a great effort and will difficult obtaining the full benefits proposed by this technology.

In a desirable IoT scenario, technology would take the context of its users into account, learning from it, and taking proactive actions according to their needs and expectations, avoiding user intervention as much as possible. The users' contextual information plays a key role in achieving this scenario. This information can be used to infer complex data and create virtual profiles of the users [9,28]. This representation can then be used to control the IoT systems without direct human interaction. Currently, there are different approaches for creating these virtual profiles [15,23,26]. In particular, the authors of this paper proposed the People as a Service (PeaaS) computing model. This model uses the smartphones as the key element for gathering all the needed information to construct a virtual profile of their owners [18].

One of the core elements of these profiles is the user location. Currently, the precise location of a smartphone is calculated using its GPS sensor. However, its precision decreases drastically when the user is inside a building. Other techniques, such as Wi-Fi or 4G networks, could be used indoors. Nevertheless, these techniques do not have a great precision. So that, they have a limited use when a person should be located with an error range of less than a meter [20].

To improve indoor location, several companies, including Apple and Google, had recently developed new protocols and sensors typically called *Beacons*. These beacons are Bluetooth Low Energy based devices that broadcast information to nearby devices in order to allow them to trigger location-based actions or to get a fine-grained indoor position.

By integrating the information provided by these devices into the users virtual profile the indoor location problem would be solved. However, this integration has some issues: on the one hand, there is a lack of standardization of the protocols used by these devices. Different companies have defined proprietary formats for the data packets transmitted by using them [5,6,14]. This leads to some problems for mobile applications developers, since they have to specifically implement the required decoders and listeners for each protocol, and vendor lock-in problems for clients, hampering the change from one manufacturer to another.

On the other hand, beacons do not send the location of a user. They send specific information that have to be processed by the final application. For that, this application should have registered all beacons from which to receive information. This hinder the generic approaches building the users' virtual profile to make use of any detected beacon to infer the indoor location of the user. They are normally limited to infer this information only from the registered beacons. To build a more complete virtual profile, ideally, these proposals should be able to get and interpret the information transmitted by any of these devices.

This paper presents a Beacon Management System. This system, first, abstracts applications developers from the low level details of the different beacon protocols. Secondly, it allows the management of unregistered beacons. For that, if a beacon is not registered in the system, when it is detected, the system searches it in different public databases, like Wikibeacon [1], in order to get information on how to interpret the information transmitted and, thus, to know the indoor location of the user. Therefore, this system allows the developer to focus further on modelling the users' virtual profile with higher quality and precision, as they can forget about beacon specifications. In addition, it has been integrated into the PeaaS computation model and in the commercial platform supporting it, nimBees [13], so that it can create more comprehensive virtual profiles.

To present the Beacon Management System the rest of the paper is organized as follows. Section 2 details the background of this work. In Sect. 3 the Beacon Management System is presented focusing on its architecture. In Sect. 4 the integration of the Beacon Management System with nimBees is described. Section 5 lists the most relevant related work. And finally, in Sect. 6 the conclusions of this work are detailed.

2 Background

As was indicated by Dey and Abowd in [3], if we can fully understand context in a given environment, we would be better able to include context-aware behaviour in our applications.

Many research efforts have been dedicated to gather this contextual information in order to create more complete virtual profiles of the users. In [21], Liang and Cao review the most relevant context middleware tools for collecting sociological information from the user. They focus on the information acquisition through multiple sources, including users smartphones and other sensors, and providing it to different software solutions.

The authors of this paper have also been working on the PeaaS and the Internet of People (IoP) approaches. PeaaS [18] is a mobile-centric computing model to infer the context of smartphones' owners and generate their virtual profiles. IoP [24] propose an infrastructure and a manifesto for IoT systems that support proactive adaptations of the systems to the users' profile. This manifesto indicates that the interactions between things and people must *be social*, must *be personalized* with the users' profile and context, must *be predictable* from the users' context, and must *be proactive* and automatically triggered depending on the context.

These two approaches have been implemented in a commercial platform called nimBees [13]. This platform, between other elements that will be explained further, defines a library that can be imported by almost any mobile application. This library is responsible for reading the different information gathered from the smartphone sensors in order to create the users' virtual profile. One of the basic data that it has into account is the users' location.

As a running example, we are going to consider a supermarket mobile application. The nimBees library could be incorporated to the supermarket app in order to send users ads adapted to their profile. For example, if a user is taking a walk nearby one of the supermarket establishments, the system would send him an ad with the discounts of the day and, thus, encourage him to go inside.

While these approaches simplify the complexity of obtaining and processing the contextual information, there is still an open challenge regarding the user location data in indoor areas [21]. The GPS sensor loses precision inside buildings. However, the indoor location of users is very valuable for constructing more complete virtual profiles [29]. In the running example, the supermarket would also be interested in knowing if a user is inside its establishment and what sections he visits. This information would be very valuable to better know the users' preferences and to send ads suited to them, leading into a higher human-ambient interaction. Counting with such detailed data, would permit to create a new business model, opening a wide horizon of new marketing strategies. In addition, it would make the client feel as if the supermarket is adapting to himself, creating a personalized experience and reinforcing his trust in that particular establishment.

As detailed above, currently beacons can be used to obtain this fine-grained location of users in indoor places. These devices are based on one of the protocols defined by large companies, such as iBeacon [6], Eddystone [14] or AltBeacon [5]. These protocols define the format of the transmitted information. This implies that the final mobile applications should implement specific decoders for the protocols used by the beacons with which will interact. This is a burden for developers, but also difficult clients to change the type of beacons deployed in their establishment.

Therefore, to use beacons in contextual-aware inference systems, it would be necessary to register the different beacons from which receive information and how to interpret it. This is suitable for final applications in order to identify if a user is in specific locations, but it is not valid to obtain location information of a user regardless of whether the beacon is registered or not. This functionality would be quite interesting for the supermarket running example, since the application would be able to detect if a user is in a certain section of a rival supermarket and, thus, sends him an ad indicating that its prices are more competitive.

Currently, there are public beacons databases, like Wikibeacon [1], containing information on their location and the transmitted data. These databases could be used to interpret the data of unknown beacons.

In order to explain the details of the Beacon Management System deeply, the next section states its main features. This system abstracts developers and clients from specific beacon protocols and, by means of public databases, can manage unknown devices.

3 Beacon Management System

As stated above, the use of beacons would enrich the contextual information that can be gathered from IoT users by including accurate indoor positioning information to their virtual profiles. However, the lack of a standard beacon protocol, the low abstraction level of the beacon packets and the ad-hoc way in which beacons are included in most applications hinder their adoption.

To improve this situation, in this work we present a Beacon Management System that abstracts application developers from the low level details of working with these beacons and that can be used to enrich the contextual information of the users of IoT systems. Figure 1 shows the architecture of the proposed system.

All beacons protocols are based on the Bluetooth Low Energy (BLE) technology [16]. This technology provides a low-power solution for controlling and monitoring applications. In the case of beacons, it can be summarized as advertising devices that broadcast connectionless data and scanning devices listening from advertisers [22]. Once a scanning device found an advertising device a connection can be established. Advertising devices regularly transmit packets of data.

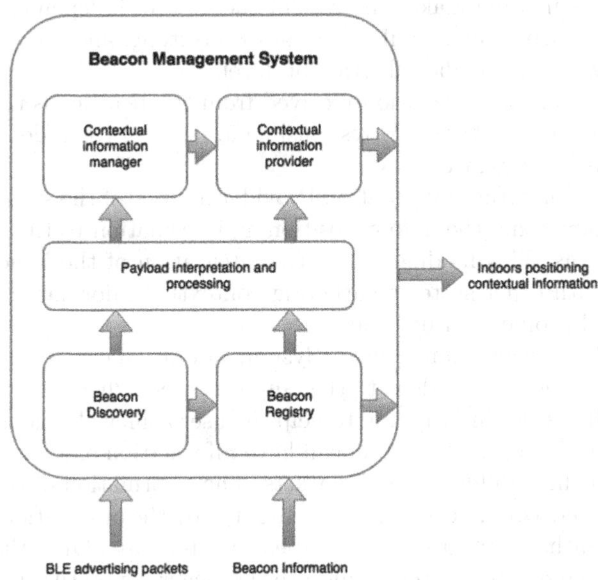

Fig. 1. Architecture of the Beacon management system.

The Beacon Management System acts as a scanning device as defined in the BLE protocol. Most current beacons applications are configured to scan only in search of specific set of beacons that are associated with the application. The Beacon Discovery module (integrated in the management system), however, listens to any advertising packet sent from any BLE device.

Once an advertising packet is received, the information of the beacon which sent it, regardless if it is an iBeacon or an Eddystone device, is sent to the Beacon Registry module of the architecture. This module contains the information of any beacon that has been found by the system. Additionally, the Beacon Registry contains information about how the beacon payload should be processed. This information defines the specific geographical position of each beacon, so accurate indoor positioning can be calculated, and if the emitting device is an iBeacon device or an Eddystone one. This information can be provided to the system as Beacon Information. By using this module and providing the specific information about the corresponding beacons, the Beacon Management System can replicate the behaviour of the supermarket application example. Moreover, when a beacon with no specific information is detected, its basic data is stored in the Beacon Registry and a default behaviour is applied to this information.

The payload of the advertising packet and the specific information about the emitting beacon contained in the Beacon Registry is then transferred to the Payload Interpretation and Processing module of the system. This module extracts the raw fields from the different types of beacons, as detailed in Sect. 2, and process them. Then, the processed information is provided to the rest of the system. This module makes the rest of the system independent of the different types of beacons, namely iBeacon and Eddystone, and allows application developers to work at a higher abstraction level.

Then the processed information received from the beacons is treated by the Contextual Information Manager, responsible for storing the indoor positioning of the system in an organized way.

Finally, the Contextual Information Provider module of the system is responsible for communicating the indoor positioning information to the user or other interested systems. This module allows the integration of the Beacon Management System with other systems gathering contextual information of the user, so richer virtual profiles can be collected.

By using the Beacon Management System in our supermarket example, an application could be used to detect other supermarkets where the user has been and then use this richer information to help the user achieve his goals. For example, the Beacon Management System can have information of a user going to the same section of three different supermarkets. The information of the beacons of these supermarkets could be added to the registry by the application owner or be automatically gathered from an external beacons database. Once the user enters a fourth supermarket, the system could use the richer contextual information to directly guide the user to the appropriate section.

3.1 Case Studies

To assess the viability and performance of the Beacon Management System it was deployed in two cases studies. Next, these are detailed.

European Researchers' Night. The first case study was designed to be part of the 2015 European Researcher's Night. The European Researchers' Night is an annual event promoted by the European Commission dedicated to popular science and fun learning [11].

For this event, an activity revolving around a mobile application was designed using the Beacon Management System. The purpose of the activity was to familiarize participants with beacon technology and indoor location. To achieve that several beacons were placed in different parts of the university buildings and participants had to locate them in a specific order.

The model of beacons used in this activity were ibks 105 beacons following the iBeacon protocol. These beacons are based on the chipset Nordic Semiconductors nrf51822 and use a CR2477 coin cell battery. More information about these specific beacons can be found on [4]

The Beacon Management System was used to develop an Android application. Participants of the activity installed this application on their mobile devices and used it to locate the beacons placed in different buildings of the university. To do that, the application received the packets emitted by the beacons and showed the users the distance in meters to the next beacon they had to find. By the variations in distance to the beacon as they moved around, the participants were able to find the beacons. Once a user was close enough to a beacon, less than 2 meters, the app marked it as found and started guiding the users to the next beacon in the activity.

By developing this case study we evaluated the viability of the Beacon Management System to perform as a traditional beacon application. In this case all the beacons in the activity were known beforehand and their information was provided to the system by the developers. Nowadays, most beacon applications work in this way and the system presented in this work was able to replicate their behaviour.

Beacons Monitoring App. The second case study focus on a more general usage of the Beacon Management System. In this case, the case study consists of an Android application to monitor any beacon.

Unlike the previous case study, and most modern beacon applications, this application process advertising packets emitted by any BLE device. The purpose of the application is very simple, to process and show the user the information provided by any nearby beacon.

Figure 2 shows a screenshot of the beacons monitoring app. In the figure, the information of three different BLE advertising devices, near which the user has passed, is shown. This information can be used by the user to know the devices that are deployed on a specific place. This application can be downloaded, and more information about it can be found, on [12].

By developing this case study and using the information obtained by its use for external users, we evaluated the viability of the Bluetooth Beacon management system in a more general situation than in the first case study. In this case, information provided by unknown beacons, both following the iBeacon and Eddystone protocols, were processed. The application has been downloaded by more than 100 users which has allowed us to test the Beacon Management System in a wide variety of situations.

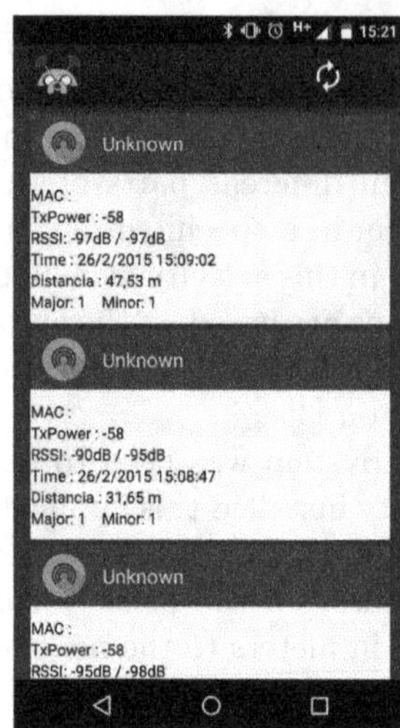

Fig. 2. Screenshot of the Beacons monitoring app.

4 Indoor Positioning as Part of a Complex Virtual Profile

Both case studies presented in the previous section allowed us to asses the viability and performance of the Beacon Management System by itself. However, the system is designed to be used as a part of a greater system in which the indoor positioning information could be used to enrich other contextual information about the users.

To verify its benefits it has been integrated with nimBees [13,25], a commercial push notification system based on the PeaaS paradigm [18]. nimBees, is an API that can be incorporated to any mobile application to provide the capabilities of creating virtual profiles of their users. These profiles are then used to send them segmented push notifications. Currently, nimBees is being used in more than 100 apps, and more than 560.000 notifications have been sent from it.

The nimBees architecture is divided into two main components, the nimBees Server and the nimBees Mobile Application. Figure 3 shows the nimBees architecture and how the Beacon Management System has been integrated with it.

The integration of the proposed system with nimBees has taken place in the nimBees Mobile Application. Once its API is integrated in an application it manages the reception of segmented push notifications. Again, by following the PeaaS paradigm the contextual information used to perform this segmentation is kept on the users devices.

With the integration of the Beacon Management System new information is added to the virtual profile of nimBees users. In particular BLE advertising packets are received by the devices and delegated to the Beacon Management System. This system provides two types of information to nimBees virtual profiles. First, the raw information received from the beacons. This information

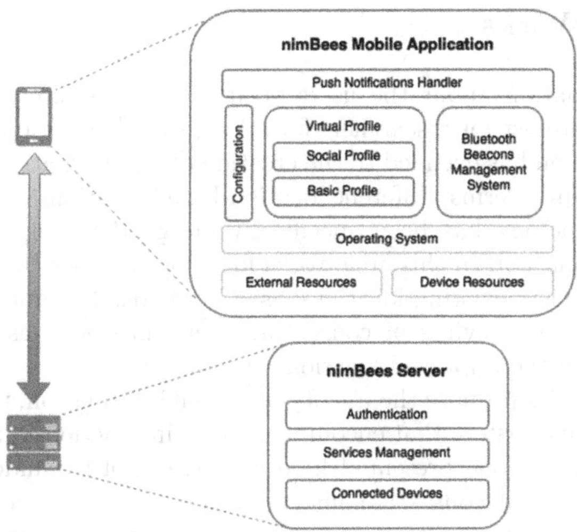

Fig. 3. Integration of the Bluetooth Beacons management system with nimBees.

is then stored in the Basic profile of the users which is later used to perform basic segmentation and to infer more complex social information. Secondly, the processed information of the beacons is provided. This information is integrated into the Social profile of the user in a timeline that contains all the complex information that has been obtained from the raw data gathered by the device.

How the data is gathered and stored in the virtual profile and how is treated can be defined at development time as usual, but it can also be modified on run-time through the nimBees server or by specific configuration push notifications which allows a more flexible management of beacons.

Finally, when a push notification is received the Push Notification Handler decides, based on the users' virtual profile, if the notification is directed to the device owner or if it should be ignored. With the inclusion of the Beacon management system new segmentation capabilities have been added to the notification handler, in particular those related to the indoor positioning of the users. For example, coming back to the supermarket scenario, an application would be able to know the indoor positioning of the user being able to recommend the user different products in relation with his profile, like a gift for his mother if his profile indicates he is going to visit her later, and directly guide him to them through the supermarket.

Since its integration, the beacons capabilities of nimBees have attracted the attention of several important customers including a Spanish supermarket chain who is piloting the use of BLE beacons in some of its more relevant supermarkets.

5 Related Works

Gathering information about the users positioning in different situations has been a topic of interest for researchers for a long time [19]. The need for precise location information has even led to the creation of an international competition to evaluate, on equal terms, different location-based solutions [8].

Beacons technology has been specifically designed to improve the indoor positioning information. In this area works like [30] proposes the use of beacons to improve previously existing location-based methods. The authors propose to transform the mobile devices of consenting users into beacons so other users could benefit from the improved location information.

In [2], the authors propose the use of contextual information, indoor positioning data, to create a system that encourages social interactions among strangers. This proposal, as the one presented here, makes use of the indoor location to improve the quality of contextual information gathered. However, unlike the work presented here, the system is designed for a particular use and it is not prepared to be used in other contextual information based systems.

Finally, in [10] the authors propose the use of beacons to improve the recognition of daily activities performed by users of ambient-assisted living systems. In this work a combination of the user's smartphone plus other wearable devices and the information emitted from a set of beacons, allow the researchers to identify more daily activities than previous works in the area. The inclusion of the indoor positioning provided by the beacons helped to improve the performance of the proposal, as in many of the previous ones. However, again the beacon inclusion was developed ad-hoc and is not transferable to other systems.

Summarizing, the use of contextual information is relevant in many systems and research areas. Also, these systems benefit from having richer contextual information. At the same time, the use of beacons allows contextual information based systems to improve the indoor positioning of users using pervasive devices such as mobile phones. However, as far as the authors know, there are no works proposing a generic solution to include the indoor positioning information provided by beacons to other contextual information based systems.

6 Conclusions

Current IoT applications can be implemented to have a specific behaviour depending on the preferences and the context of the user. This adaptation is limited to the contextual information that can be gathered from the users. The rise of the beacon technology has simplified the inclusion of indoor positioning data to the contextual information of users.

In this paper, we present a Beacon Management System which purpose is to be included in IoT systems, gathering contextual information from their users. The proposed system allows the use of beacons under different protocols, namely iBeacon and Eddystone, and allows applications developers to work at a higher abstraction level without having to deal with the technical details of the BLE protocol. The presented system has been integrated into two case studies whose success lead to its integration in a commercial push notification platform.

The next steps on this system focus on the inclusion of alternative beacons protocols to increment the number of devices supported and on provisioning higher level contextual information based on the indoor positioning provided by the beacons.

Acknowledgments. This work was partially supported by the projects TIN2014-53986-REDT, TIN2015-67083-R and TIN2015-69957-R (MINECO/FEDER), by the Department of Economy and Infrastructure of the Government of Extremadura (GR15098), and by the European Regional Development Fund.

References

1. Wikibeacon. http://wikibeacon.org/
2. Abouzied, A., Chen, J.: Commonties: a context-aware nudge towards social interaction. In: Proceedings of the Companion Publication of the 17th ACM Conference on Computer Supported Cooperative Work & Social Computing, CSCW Companion 2014, pp. 1–4. ACM, New York (2014)
3. Abowd, G.D., Dey, A.K., Brown, P.J., Davies, N., Smith, M., Steggles, P.: Towards a better understanding of context and context-awareness. In: Gellersen, H.-W. (ed.) HUC 1999. LNCS, vol. 1707, pp. 304–307. Springer, Heidelberg (1999). doi:10.1007/3-540-48157-5_29
4. Accent System: ibks 105 datasheet. http://accent-systems.com/wp-content/uploads/2015/11/iBKS-105-Datasheet.pdf
5. AltBeacon: Altbeacon. the open and interoperable proximity beacon specification. http://altbeacon.org
6. Apple Inc.: ibeacon for developers. https://developer.apple.com/ibeacon/
7. Atzori, L., Iera, A., Morabito, G.: From "smart objects" to "social objects": the next evolutionary step of the internet of things. IEEE Commun. Mag. **52**(1), 97–105 (2014)
8. Barsocchi, P., Chessa, S., Furfari, F., Potorti, F.: Evaluating ambient assisted living solutions: the localization competition. IEEE Pervasive Comput. **12**(4), 72–79 (2013)
9. Bellavista, P., Corradi, A., Fanelli, M., Foschini, L.: A survey of context data distribution for mobile ubiquitous systems. ACM Comput. Surv. **44**(4), 1–45 (2012)
10. De, D., Bharti, P., Das, S.K., Chellappan, S.: Multimodal wearable sensing for fine-grained activity recognition in healthcare. IEEE Internet Comput. **19**(5), 26–35 (2015)
11. Europe Commission - Marie Sklodowska-Curie Actions: European researchers night. http://ec.europa.eu/research/mariecurieactions/about-msca/actions/researcher-night/index_en.htm
12. Flores Rosco, R.: Beacons monitoring application. https://play.google.com/store/apps/details?id=com.campeador.bluetooth
13. Gloin: nimbees push notification platform. http://nimbees.com
14. Google: Google's beacon platform. https://developers.google.com/beacons/overview

15. Gronli, T.M., Ghinea, G., Younas, M.: Context-aware and automatic configuration of mobile devices in cloud-enabled ubiquitous computing. Personal Ubiquitous Comput. **18**(4), 883–894 (2014)
16. Group, B.S.I.: Bluetooth 4.0. core specification. https://www.bluetooth.com/specifications/adopted-specifications
17. Gubbi, J., Buyya, R., Marusic, S., Palaniswami, M.: Internet of Things (IoT): a vision, architectural elements, and future directions. Future Gener. Comput. Syst. **29**(7), 1645–1660 (2013)
18. Guillen, J., Miranda, J., Berrocal, J., Garcia-Alonso, J., Murillo, J.M., Canal, C.: People as a service: a mobile-centric model for providing collective sociological profiles. IEEE Softw. **31**(2), 48–53 (2014)
19. Hightower, J., Borriello, G.: Location systems for ubiquitous computing. Computer **34**(8), 57–66 (2001). http://dx.doi.org/10.1109/2.940014
20. Kashevnik, A., Shchekotov, M.: Comparative analysis of indoor positioning systems based on communications supported by smartphones. In: 12th Conference of Fruct Association (2014)
21. Liang, G., Cao, J.: Social context-aware middleware: a survey. Pervasive Mob. Comput. **17**(Part B(0)), 207–219 (2015)
22. Mackensen, E., Lai, M., Wendt, T.: Bluetooth low energy (ble) based wireless sensors. In: Sensors, 2012 IEEE. pp. 1–4, October 2012
23. Makris, P., Skoutas, D.N., Skianis, C.: A survey on context-aware mobile and wireless networking: on networking and computing environments' integration. IEEE Commun. Surv. Tutorials **15**(1), 362–386 (2013)
24. Miranda, J., Makitalo, N., Garcia-Alonso, J., Berrocal, J., Mikkonen, T., Canal, C., Murillo, J.: From the internet of things to the internet of people. IEEE Internet Comput. **19**(2), 40–47 (2015)
25. Miranda, J., Guillén, J., Berrocal, J., Garcia-Alonso, J., Murillo, J.M., Canal, C.: Architecting infrastructures for cloud-enabled mobile devices. In: Canal, C., Villari, M. (eds.) ESOCC 2013. CCIS, vol. 393, pp. 277–287. Springer, Heidelberg (2013). doi:10.1007/978-3-642-45364-9_23
26. Park, H.S., Oh, K., Cho, S.B.: Bayesian network-based high-level context recognition for mobile context sharing in cyber-physical system. Int. J. Distrib. Sens. Netw. **2011**, 1–10 (2011)
27. Perera, C., Liu, C.H., Jayawardena, S., Chen, M.: Context-aware computing in the internet of things: a survey on internet of things from industrial market perspective. CoRR (2015)
28. Raskino, M., Fenn, J., Linden, A.: Extracting value from the massively connected world of 2015 (2015)
29. Sykes, E.R., Pentland, S., Nardi, S.: Context-aware mobile apps using ibeacons: towards smarter interactions. In: Proceedings of the 25th Annual International Conference on Computer Science and Software Engineering, CASCON 2015, pp. 120–129. IBM Corp., Riverton, NJ, USA (2015)
30. Zhu, J., Zeng, K., Kim, K.H., Mohapatra, P.: Improving crowd-sourced wi-fi localization systems using bluetooth beacons. In: 2012 9th Annual IEEE Communications Society Conference on Sensor, Mesh and Ad Hoc Communications and Networks (SECON), pp. 290–298, June 2012

RoboCAM: Robot-Based Video Surveillance Application

Jonay Suárez-Armas(✉), Pino Caballero-Gil, and Cándido Caballero-Gil

Department of Computer Engineering, University of La Laguna, La Laguna, Tenerife, Spain
{alu0100600674,pcaballe,ccabgil}@ull.edu.es

Abstract. The use of automated surveillance systems has become essential in different application fields, from the domestic to the military. Current surveillance systems used in controlled environments can be easily complemented through the use of robots to improve their functionality. This paper describes RoboCAM, a secure video surveillance application for Android devices based on robots. The proposal uses a smartphone placed on a Lego Mindstorms EV3 robot and connected via Bluetooth to it. The smartphone runs in background a motion detection application with its camera. If motion is detected, it begins to capture images that are sent to a streaming server, in order to see them live from a web application. Remotely via the web application and the smartphone connected via Bluetooth it is possible to move the robot in order to find out more information about what is happening in the monitored location.

Keywords: Video surveillance · Streaming · Motion detection · Robot

1 Introduction

The burglary of houses and businesses is nowadays a problem that requires an urgent solution. Domestic burglary increased by 14 % between 2007 and 2012 in Europe [1]. Among the EU countries, the highest increases in the number of domestic burglary cases occurred in Greece, Spain, Italy, Romania and Croatia. Furthermore, Spain is the third EU country that suffers more shoplifting, and more than 310 home burglaries a day are recorded [2].

Therefore, more and more alarms are being installed in businesses and houses, which automatically contact the police in case of intrusion. In addition, many of these alarms consist of video surveillance systems based on IP cameras that allow viewing images in real time from a centralized monitor and/or remotely from another location via the Internet. Apart from all this, there are applications Android for motion detection such as Android Motion Detector [3] and video surveillance application like Home Security Camera [4]. Furthermore, there are robots capable to monitor an area and make the corresponding functions according with the situation.

This work aims to upgrade to a higher-level current video surveillance systems, by adding the ability to move the video surveillance cameras through the

C.R. García et al. (Eds.): UCAmI 2016, Part II, LNCS 10070, pp. 307–312, 2016.
DOI: 10.1007/978-3-319-48799-1_35

protected room. In order to take advantage of current smartphones, the proposal does not tend the use of conventional video surveillance cameras, but of Android smartphones, because they are much more than simple cameras and they are widely available.

The next section briefly describes the proposed Android application, including some aspects of one of its principal features: video streaming. Section 3 comments some properties of the two main functionalities of the proposal: motion detection and robot control. Section 4 sketches the used architecture and technologies while Sect. 5 describes the communication between the two applications. Finally, a brief conclusion closes the paper.

2 Android Application

The most basic function of the proposal is to send a video captured in real time to a streaming server in order to display images on another device through a web application.

The proposal also takes advantage of using a smartphone to detect motion so that if motion is detected, it sends a notification and a video recorded in real time via streaming.

In addition, the smartphone is connected via Bluetooth with a robot Lego Mindstorms EV3 [5], so that the user can move the smartphone through the room as he/she wishes. To this end, at the web application, while the images are captured in real time, it is possible to control the robot.

Given the high degree of sensitivity of sent information, the security of the connection is protected with encryption and authentication methods.

The three main functions of the proposal are:

1. Sending video and audio streaming: The main function of this proposal is to captured audio and image by a mobile device and send them to a streaming server, so that with the client application it is possible to display this video in real time and perform other functions. See Figs. 1 and 2.
2. Motion detection: The application, while is capturing images around, is constantly checking if there is movement in front of the camera. If so, send a text message to recipients that have been added to the notification list. See Fig. 3. This functionality is carried out thanks to Android Motion Detector library [6], which updates the reference frame every few time to avoid false alarms in motion detection.
3. Robot control: Through the client application, while the images captured by the main application are being displayed, it is possible to move the robot in order to analyse the different areas of the monitored site. See Fig. 4. The application uses Lego Mindstorms EV3 Android API [7] to connect with the robot via Bluetooth and to send him the commands of movement.

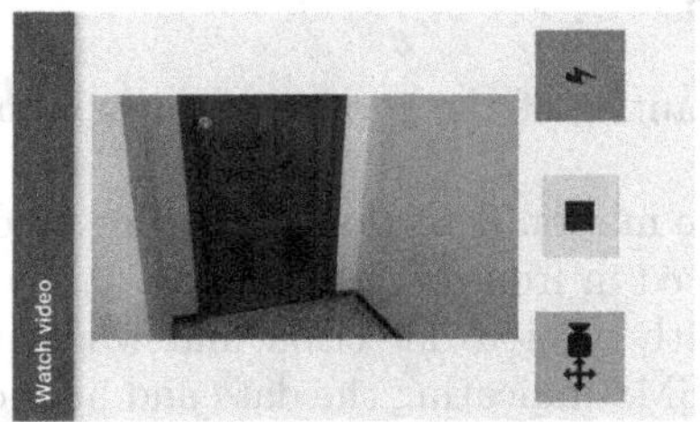

Fig. 1. Captured video

Fig. 2. Video received at a streaming server

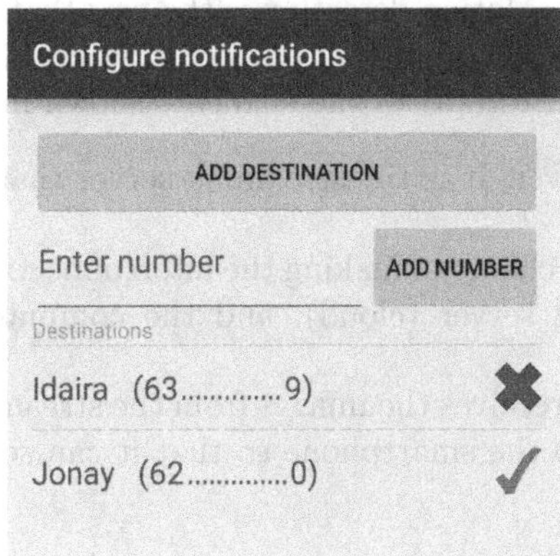

Fig. 3. Notification list

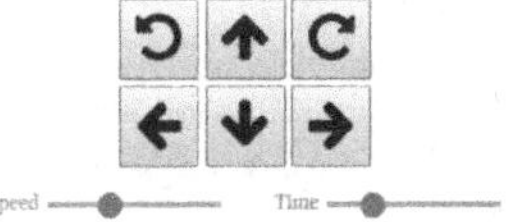

Fig. 4. Robot control

3 Functionalities

The two main functionalities of the proposal are motion detection and robot control.

On the one hand, the motion detection is used in video surveillance cameras to detect motion produced in front of the cameras.

RoboCAM starts with motion detection and when motion is produced it sends a notification via SMS indicating the date and hour of the detection. Then it begins to send the video through streaming and it allows robot control.

On the other hand, the robot control comes into operation when the Android application starts to send the video to the streaming server. In that moment, a communication is established between the Android application and the web application for sending movement commands to the Lego Mindstorms EV3 robot.

The movement commands are sent from the web application to the Android application through a socket. Then, the mobile application sends these commands to the robot via Bluetooth.

4 Architecture

RoboCAM combines motion detection, sending video via streaming, and control robot in one application. Motion detection is the first that comes into operation, and then the video streaming and the robot control begin to function.

The complete system comprises the elements shown in Fig. 5.

- Wowza streaming server: It is the streaming server that stores and sends the images [8].
- WLAN router: It is in charge of making the interconnection between the smartphone, the streaming server (cloud), and the computer running the client application.
- Client application: It receives the images from the streaming server, and allows sending commands to the smartphone so that it can send them to the robot via Bluetooth.

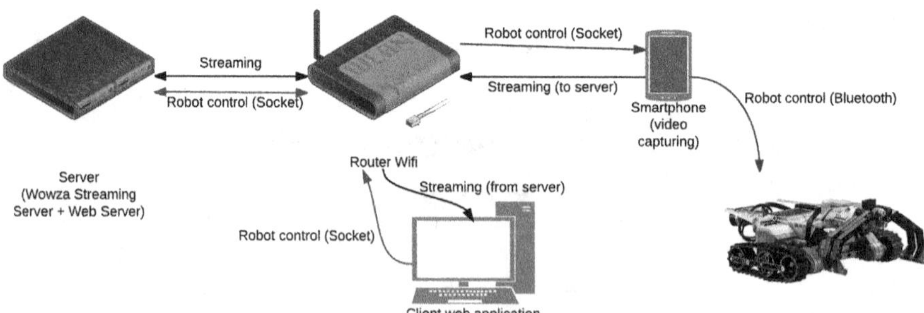

Fig. 5. Architecture

- Smartphone: It is one of the two essential elements of the proposal because it runs the main application, which sends the video recording to the streaming server, and allows the robot to move according to commands received from the client application.
- Lego Mindstorms EV3 robot: It is the other essential element of the proposal because it carries the smartphone with the main application connected via Bluetooth, so that it moves according to the signals it receives from the smartphone.

The main technologies used by the system are:

- Main application: The main application, which runs the smartphone, is developed on Android. It connects to the network via Wi-Fi or 4G (LTE) and also connects to the Lego Mindstorms robot via Bluetooth.
- Client application: The client application is a web application, allowing run on any computer without the need to pre-install it. To run it requires only a browser. For the development of this client application it has been made use of HTML5, CSS, JavaScript and NodeJS.

5 Communication Between the Two Applications

Communication between the two applications, for robot control, is established through sockets. See Fig. 6.

- The principal Android application has a server socket that is constantly listening on port 1234 to receive robot commands. Depending of the received command, the robot moves in a direction with a certain speed during a determined time.
- The client web application connects to the mobile application through a client socket thanks to the IP address of the smartphone. Once connected, sends the corresponding command to move the robot and close the connection.

The information exchanged between the two applications is encrypted via AES with 256 bit key size in CBC mode. The key used in AES is previously agreed between the two parts with Elliptic Curve Diffie-Hellman algorithm. Moreover, the information is signed and verified with Elliptic Curve Digital Signature Algorithm.

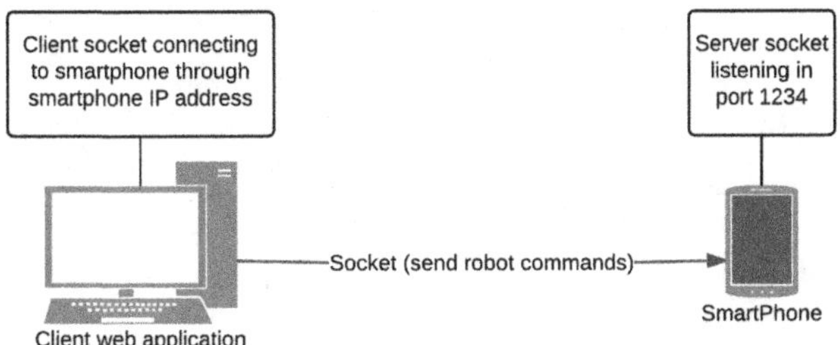

Fig. 6. Communication between mobile and web application

6 Conclusions

The proposal here described allows enjoying a cheap system that is superior to the traditional video surveillance systems, thanks to the innovative ability of remotely browsing the monitored environment. In particular, it is based on an Android smartphone and a Lego Mindstorms EV3 robot. The principal novelty over conventional video surveillance systems is we have more than cameras, we have intelligent devices that it will allow us to add more functionalities in the future. Moreover, the use of old smartphones and Lego robot allow us to save in costs. A beta version of this application has been developed. As part of work in progress, a future version of this paper will include an experimental evaluation of the real time performances of the system.

Acknowledgments. Research supported by Binter-Sistemas grant and RTC-2014-1648-8 and TEC2014-54110-R projects.

References

1. Eurostats Statistics Explained. Crime statistics. http://ec.europa.eu/eurostat/statistics-explained/index.php/Crime_statistics#Robbery
2. La Nueva España. En España se registran más de 310 robos en casas al día. http://www.lne.es/sociedad/2016/02/10/espana-registran-310-robos-viviendas/1881035.html
3. Motion Detector Pro. https://play.google.com/store/apps/details?id=dk.mvainformatics.android.motiondetectorpro.activity&hl=es
4. Home Security Camera. https://play.google.com/store/apps/details?id=com.ivuu&hl=en
5. Lego. Lego Mindstorms EV3. http://www.lego.com/es-es/mindstorms/about-ev3
6. Android Motion Detector library. https://github.com/jkwiecien/android-motion-detector
7. Lego Mindstorms EV3 Android API. https://github.com/cqjjjzr/LEGO-MINDSTORMS-EV3-Android-API
8. Wowza. Wowza Streaming Engine. https://www.wowza.com/products/streaming-engine

Real-Time Streaming: A Comparative Study Between RTSP and WebRTC

Iván Santos-González(✉), Alexandra Rivero-García, Tomás González-Barroso, Jezabel Molina-Gil, and Pino Caballero-Gil

Departamento de Ingeniería Informática y de Sistemas, Universidad de La Laguna, 38271 La Laguna, Tenerife, Spain
{jsantosg,ariverog,bicacaro,jmmolina,pcaballe}@ull.edu.es

Abstract. This work presents a comparative study between two of the most used streaming protocols, RTSP and WebRTC. It describes a system designed to evaluate times at live streaming: establishment time and stream reception time from a single source to a large quantity of receivers with the use of smartphones. Two systems that use the commented protocols have been implemented, specifically, two Android applications that use these protocols in the scope of video surveillance at airports. Both systems are composed of a mobile application and a web service. The design of the systems has been done avoiding differences between these protocols for P2P communication in the same local network. Several simulations have been performed to compare them and the obtained results have been used for a comparative study between streaming establishment and sending package times of each protocol.

Keywords: Streaming video · RTSP · WebRTC · Android

1 Introduction

In the last years the high penetration of streaming video through Internet has suffered a huge increase of use. In [3] the company Cisco predicts that the Internet video traffic will be 80 % of all consumer Internet traffic in 2019, up from 64 % in 2014, without taking into account the Peer-to-Peer (P2P) communication. The video traffic will be from 80 to 90 % of global consumer traffic by 2019. For this reason, some of the most important companies of multimedia content have tried to develop different strategies to improve the Quality of Experience (QoE) of their services. The fast evolution of performances and the low cost of mobile devices make them excellent candidates to provide new streaming features for different proposals.

Video streaming is the process where a video is transmitted from a point to one or multiple destinations. Video on Demand (VoD) is defined as a service in which high-speed of data services are used to provide customers with streaming content [9]. In this paper we analyse two of the most used protocols in streaming based on mobile phones. The objective is the evaluation of the speed in both systems using Android applications and similar contexts.

C.R. García et al. (Eds.): UCAmI 2016, Part II, LNCS 10070, pp. 313–325, 2016.
DOI: 10.1007/978-3-319-48799-1_36

On the one hand, Real Time Streaming Protocol (RTSP) [16], based on Real-time Transport Protocol (RTP) [17] is analysed. This protocol is not based on the establishment of connection Instead, the server has a session associated to an identifier.

On the other hand, Web Real-Time Communications (WebRTC), a project maintained by Google based on RTP is analysed. This system allows real-time communications through some Application Programming Interfaces (API) with a high quality, low latency and low bandwidth consumption.

We are interested in the problem of live streaming establishment time, response time and delay time from a single source to a large quantity of receivers with the use of these protocols. The aim of this work is to know which protocol is better to be used in the mobile platforms and specifically in the Android platform. Moreover, we are interested in having quantitative measurements to know how much an protocol is better than the other to use in our future implementations.

The paper is organized as follows. In Sect. 3, we analyse different solutions used currently. In Sect. 4 we describe the system based on RSTP in detail. Section 5 defines a similar system based on WebRTC. Finally, we present an in-depth comparison between theses systems in Sect. 6. Conclusions and future works close the paper in Sect. 7.

2 Preliminaries

Sharing information in a network between nodes can be done in different ways. The kind of the information that the system shares usually determines the method for the chosen communication. In this proposal, sharing audio and video media is the main objective For this reason, the most important point is the guarantee of a low latency, low jitter and efficient transmissions, but occasional losses could be tolerated.

The media streaming protocol is defined taking into account the structure of the packets and the algorithms used to send real-time media on a network. Different media streaming protocols are available today, which differ in a few implementation details. Two communication categories are: push-based and pull-based protocols [1].

- Push-Based Media Streaming Protocols: In these protocols, when a server and a client establish a connection, the server starts to stream packets to the client until the client stops or interrupts the session.
- Pull-Based Media Streaming Protocols: In these protocols, the media client is the active entity that requests content from the media server. Therefore, the server's response depends on the client requests when the server is idle or blocked for that client.

In Table 1, some examples of different streaming protocols and their characteristics are shown. This information is based on [19], where there is an analysis of the transmission protocols for the H.265 encoder.

In [1] there is an analysis where the efficient, overhead-wise, of push-based protocol over pull-based streaming is explained. For this reason, in this paper we analyse the efficiency of two protocols based on RTP.

3 Related Work

There are some analysis based on the comparison between different streaming protocols. In [20] there is a study of HTTP, RTSP and Dynamic Adaptive Streaming over HTTP (DASH) [18] protocols on a smartphone. That paper is based on the calculation of switch delay or the time between a user sends a command and the screen of the client suffers theses changes. They analyse these protocols and the response when the user switches the mode. In [12] HTTP, RTSP, and IMS are compared. That work describes some approaches promising the synthesis of IMS, HTTP, and RTSP based networks.

Table 1. Comparison between push-based and pull-based streaming protocols.

Characteristic	Push-based	Pull-based
Source	Broadcasters and servers like Windows media, QuickTime, RealNetworks Helix Cisco CDS/DCM	Web servers such as LAMP, RealNetworks Helix, Microsoft BS, Cisco CDS
Protocols	RTSP, RTP, UDP	HTTP
Bandwidth usage	Likely more efficient	Likely less efficient
Video monitoring	RTCP (RTP transport)	Currently propietary
Multicast support	Yes	No

Authors of [7] describe measurements collected from DASH and WebRTC implementations while moving at walking speeds through an 802.16e WiMAX network. They collected data from an application, the network and physical layers under different wireless environments. The characteristics that directly impact the quality of video service in mobile data network were also identified. Finally, they conclude that to adapt the channel conditions, these services did not achieve acceptable service quality for the mobile users under different network conditions.

In the proposal [11], a QoE instrumentation for video streaming on smartphone, called VLQoE, has been presented. They use VLC media player to record a set of metrics from the user interface, application-level, network-level and from the available sensors of the device. They present two state models based on the time to the HTTP and RTSP protocols via streaming 3.5G.

4 Video Streaming Protocols

In this Section, the analysed streaming protocols are explained. On the one hand, the RTSP scheme is described. On the other hand, WebRTC system based on API calls is analysed.

4.1 RTSP Protocol

The Real Time Streaming Protocol (RTSP) [16] is a non-connection oriented application layer protocol that uses a session associated to an identifier. RTSP usually uses the UDP protocol to share the video and audio data and TCP for the control (TCP is used just if it is necessary). The syntax of the RTSP protocol is similar to the syntax of HTTP protocol and supports the next operations:

- **Retrieval of media from media server:** The client can request a presentation description via HTTP or some other method. If the presentation is being multicast, the presentation description contains the multicast addresses and ports to be used for the continuous media. If the presentation is to be sent only to the client via unicast, the client provides the destination for security reasons.
- **Invitation of a media server to a conference:** A media server can be "invited" to join an existing conference, either to play back media into the presentation or to record all or a subset of the media in a presentation. This mode is useful for distributing teaching applications. Several parties in the conference may take turns "pushing the remote control buttons".
- **Addition of media to an existing presentation:** Particularly for live presentations, it is useful if the server can tell the client about additional media becoming available.

The structure of an URL for RTSP is very similar to the URL in HTTP, with the only difference in the used scheme *rtsp://* in RTSP instead of *http://* in the HTTP protocol but adds new request methods such as DESCRIBE, SETUP, PLAY, PAUSE and TEARDOWN. The DESCRIBE method is used to obtain a description of the presentation or object appointed by the URL RTSP. The server responds to this request with a description of the requested resource. This response corresponds to the initialization phase of RTSP and contains the list of the necessary multimedia streams. On the other hand, the SETUP method is used to establish how is the stream transported, the request contains the URL of the multimedia stream and a transport specification that usually includes the port to receive RTP data (video and audio) and another one to the RTCP [10] data (metadata). The server responds confirming the selected parameters and fill the other parts, as they are the ports selected by the server. Every stream has to be configured before sending a PLAY request. The PLAY request is used to start the data stream shipment by part of the server using the ports configured with the SETUP request method. Moreover, the PAUSE method stops one or all streams temporarily to resume it later with a PLAY request. Finally, the

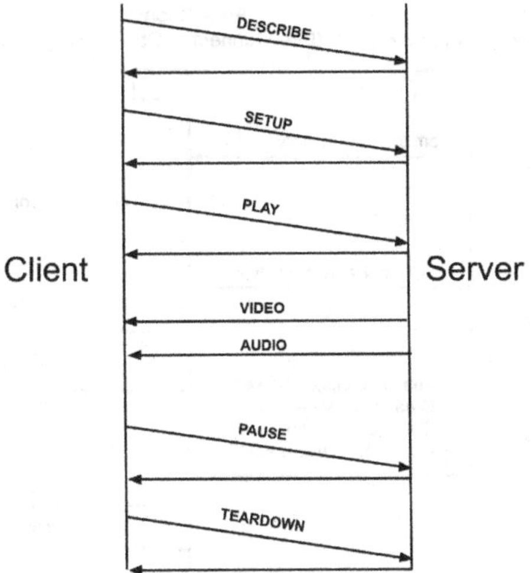

Fig. 1. RTSP request order

use of the TEARDOWN request method stops the shipment of data releasing all resources. Note that first of all a TCP connection is established between the client and the server, started by the client and typically over the well-known port of TCP, the 554 port.

The exact performance and request order of the RSTP protocol is shown in Fig. 1.

4.2 WebRTC Protocol

WebRTC [2] is an API created by the World Wide Web Consortium (W3C) that allows the browser apps to make calls, video chats and the use of P2P files without any plugin. The first implementation of WebRTC was created by Google and released as Open Source. Different organism as the Internet Engineering Task Force (IETF) to standardize the used protocols and the W3C with the browser APIs have been working on this implementation.

The main components of WebRTC are the next:

- **getUserMedia:** It allows obtaining video or audio streams from the hardware (microphone or camera). This API call allows us to get a screenshot or share our screen with other users too.
- **RTCPeerConnection:** It allows us to set up the audio/video stream. This consists in a lot of different tasks like the signal processing, the codec execution, the bandwidth administration, the security of the streaming, etc. This API call allows implementing this different task without the intervention of the programmer.
- **RTCDataChannel:** It allows sharing video or audio data between connected users. RTCDataChannel uses a bidirectional communication between peers

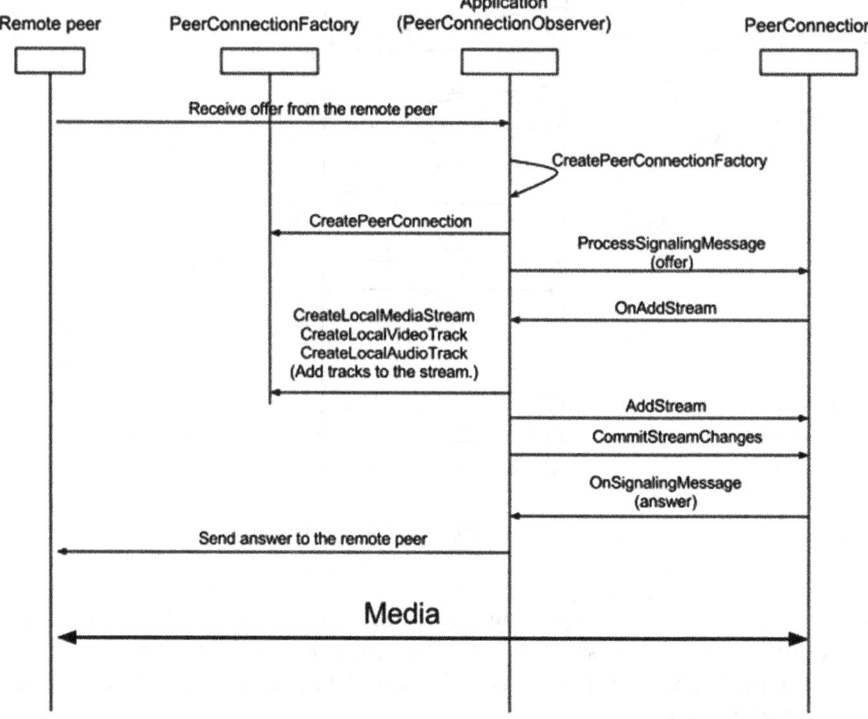

Fig. 2. WebRTC request order

and allows the exchange of any data type. To do this, RTCDataChannel uses Websockets, which allows us to get a bidirectional communication between the client and the server and allows using a slower and reliable communication over TCP or a faster and non-reliable communication over UDP.
- **geoStats:** API call that allows getting different statistics about a WebRTC session.

The performance of the WebRTC protocol used to make a call with the API calls commented before is shown in Fig. 2.

5 Implemented Systems

The implemented system consists in an Android application that covers the use case of the video surveillance at an airport environment. This application has been developed on an Android platform and uses the RTSP protocol in the application called "A" and the WebRTC protocol in the application called "B". It makes it possible that every airport employee can take videos at the airport from their smartphones. Furthermore, all these videos can be viewed by others in real time or by the security personnel in the control room. The developed

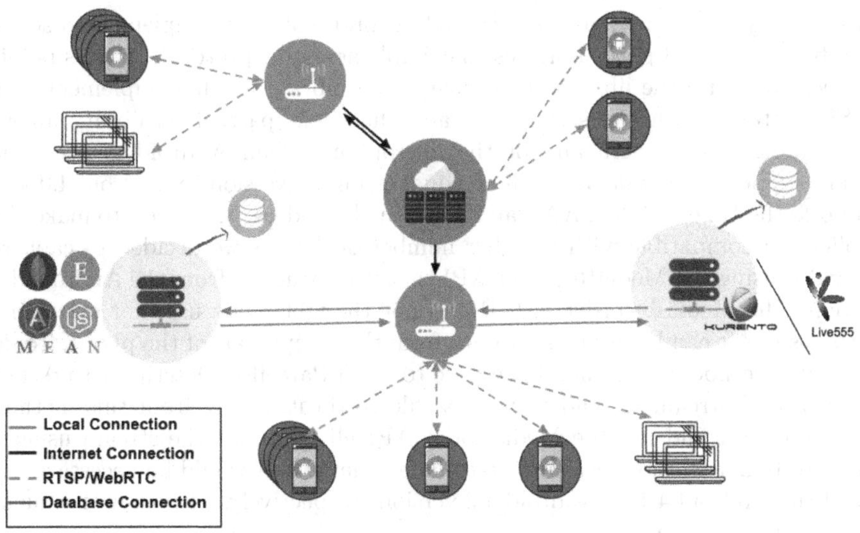

Fig. 3. System global view

application supposes a huge improvement on the security of the airport because, in combination with the previously installed video surveillance cams, the system allows the airport personnel to record every strange situation in the airport and inform other co-workers or the security personnel of the airport in real time in order to be helped or assisted by them. In Fig. 3 we can see few screenshots of the developed application. Note that both media servers have been released in a Windows 10×64 machine, with an Intel core i7-3612QM CPU, 8 GB of RAM memory and a 240 GB Intel SSD.

5.1 RTSP Scheme

The architecture of the application "A" consists in the use of P2P communications through the RTSP protocol in places where the two users are in the same network, and through the use of a Live555 media server in cases where we have not a dedicated network and we have to use the Internet connection. Live555 media server [14] is a complete open source RTSP server that supports the most common kinds of media files. Moreover, this server can stream multiple streams from the same or different files concurrently, using by default the UDP protocol to transmit the streams, but we can transmit over the TCP protocol if we decide it.

The Android application we developed acts as the server and/or the client depending on the situation. This application allows us to connect with multiple users and send their real time stream. In the implementation of this system we decided to use the last version of Android available, which was Android 6.0 that corresponds to the API 23 of the Android SDK. In this version of Android and consequently in no previous ones, the RTSP protocol is not implemented so we have to use to third party libraries that implement this protocol. At this point, we decided to use the libstreaming open source library [8] that implements the RTSP protocol both the server part and the client part. This library allows us to stream the camera and/or the microphone of an Android device. The library supports every device with an equal or higher version to Android 4.0 and supports the H.264, H.263, AAC and AMR media codecs. Moreover, to make the application compatible with a higher number of devices we decided to capture the video using the MediaRecorder API that it is available from the Android 4.0 version. The MediaRecorder API [15] is not thought to be used for streaming purposes but it can be used to get data from the peripherals of the phone. To do that, this method works fine, so we have to use a ParcelFileDescriptor to record the captured stream instead of using a file to do it. Apart from this method to record, we could use the MediaCodec API [4] to record the stream using a buffer-to-buffer method or a surface-to-buffer method. It would be necessary the use of the Android 4.1 or Android 4.3 versions respectively, with the consequent loss of potential users.

5.2 WebRTC Scheme

The architecture of the application "B" consists in the use of P2P communications through the WebRTSP protocol in places where the two users are in the same network, and through the use of a Kurento media server [13] in cases where we have not a dedicated network and we have to use the Internet connection. Kurento is a WebRTC media server and it has a set of client APIs that simplifies the development of advanced video applications for web and smartphone platforms. Kurento Media Server features include a group of communications, transcoding, recording, mixing, broadcasting and routing of audio-visual flows and it also provides advanced media processing capabilities involving computer vision, video indexing, augmented reality and speech analysis.

The developed application acts as client and/or server depending on the situation. It allows us to connect with one or multiple users and send their real time stream. We decided to use the last version of Android available that was Android 6.0 that corresponds to the API 23 of the Android SDK. In this version of Android and consequently in no previous ones, the WebRTC protocol is not implemented at the core of Android and so we have to use to third party libraries that implement this protocol. At this point, we decided to use the Libjingle library [6] that it is an open source library written in C++ language by Google and that allows to establish P2P connections and to develop P2P applications. To use this library in Android we had to compile the source code to generate the JNI API that lets the Java implementation reuse the C++ implementation of the same API. This library allows us to stream the camera and/or the microphone of an Android device. The library supports every device with a equal or higher version to Android 4.1 and supports the H.264, H.265, VP8 and VP9 media codecs. Moreover, we decided to use the Socket.io library too. This library allows us to establish communications through the Websocket protocol, for this reason it is used in the initial communications between the Android App and the SIP (Session Initiation Protocol) server. The developed application acts as client and/or server depending on the situation.

6 Comparative Study

In this section the results of the different measurements taken about the connection establishment time and stream reception time in the implementations of two stream protocols are analysed. The measurements have been taken using the system time that is implemented in Java programming language, and therefore

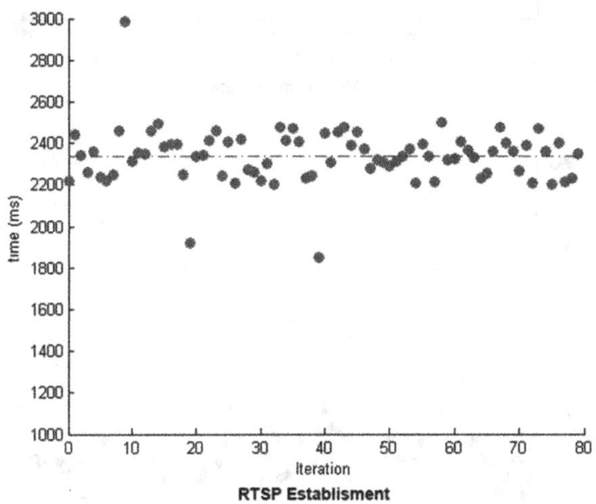

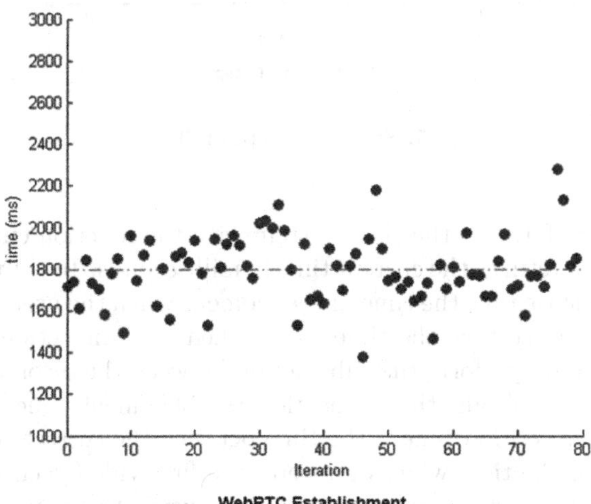

Fig. 4. Connection establishment time

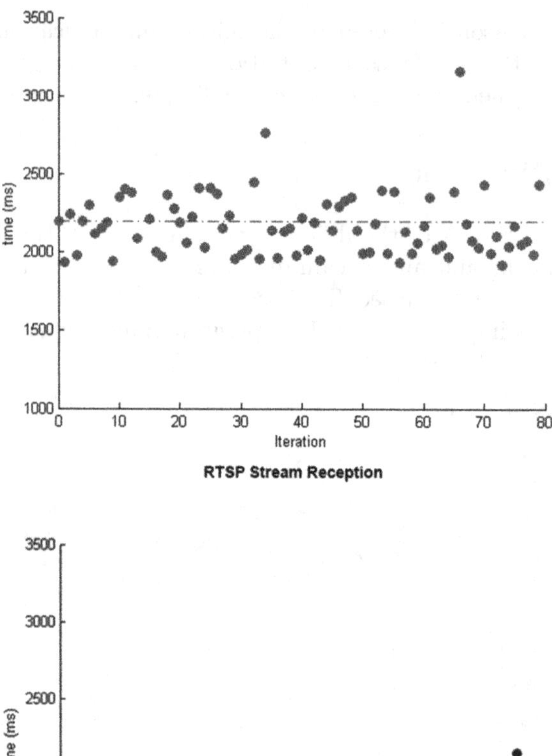

Fig. 5. Stream Reception Time

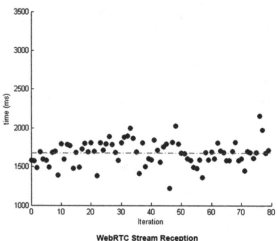

in the Android platform, in the class System with the function currentTimeMillis(). This function returns the current time in milliseconds. To get the connection establishment time we take the time in the moment when the user A launches the streaming and then we take the time again when the connection is completely established. Then, we perform the subtraction between the second measurement and the first one to obtain the connection establishment time. On the other hand, the stream reception time is the time between the correct communication establishment and the time when we receive the first video packet.

The different measurements have been done using the same smartphone, a LG L9 with 1 GB of RAM memory, CPU 1 GHz Dual Core and 4 GB of storage

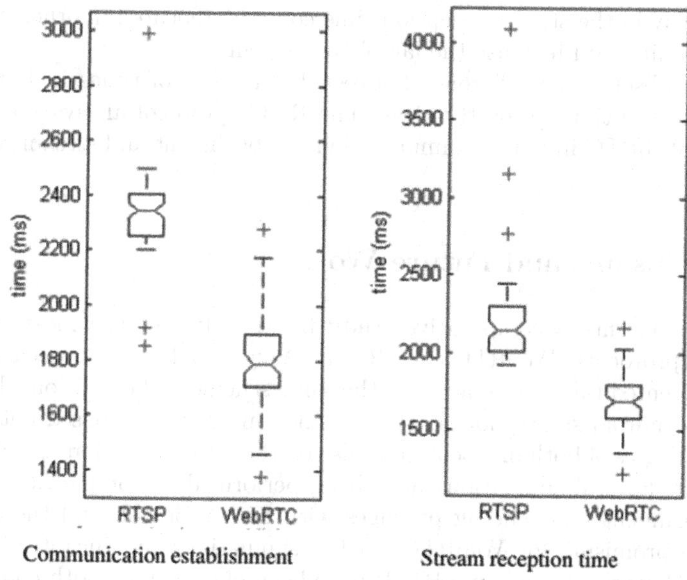

Fig. 6. Comparative Between Times of RTSP and WebRTC

memory and the 4.4.4 Android version. To perform these measurements, we implemented a series of tests using Expresso tests [5] that simulate the exact behaviour of using the application. To get a significant number of measurements we performed the same test for 80 iterations for each measurement. Figure 4 shows the comparative analysis between the two systems: RTSP in 4a and WebRTC in 4b.

We can see how the system that uses the RTSP protocol is slower than the WebRTC protocol having an average of connection establishment time of 2,304 s in the case of the RTSP protocol and an average of 1,835 s in the case of the WebRTC protocol. The difference between the two implemented protocols in the connection establishment time average is 0,469. In spite of having some outlier points in the graphs of the two systems, we can say that WebRTC protocol is more efficient in the connection establishment time than the RTSP protocol.

On the other hand, we have the stream reception time comparison that can be seen in Fig. 5, RTSP in 5a and WebRTC in 5b.

There, we appreciate a similar behaviour to that in case of the connection establishment time and we can see an average of 2,161 s in the case of RTSP and an average of 1,709 in the case of the WebRTC protocol being the average difference of 0.452. If we add the two difference, we obtain a total difference between the two protocols of almost 1 s favourable to the WebRTC protocol. This improvement can be viewed easily when we use the two implemented systems having a lag of about 1 s that sometimes is incremented due to delays in the packet sending in the case of the RTSP implemented system and having almost no lag in the case of the WebRTC implemented system. Moreover, we suppose that the delay in the stream reception time could be repeated in other moments of the streaming and increase the lag of the system.

We can observe the difference between both protocol times in Fig. 6. The difference in the times is pretty clear. The RSTP protocol always spend more time than WebRTC in both communication establishment and stream reception time.

7 Conclusions and Future Work

This work presents a comparative study between two of the most used live streaming protocols, WebRTC and RTSP. A system based on each protocol was implemented taking into account the same scheme and conditions, based on the use of Android smartphones. The obtained measures are based not only on sending packages of both protocols, but also on the communication establishment of each one. Several simulations have been performed to compare the streaming establishment and sending packages with each protocol, and the obtained results are promising for WebRTC. In the simulations, significant advantages in WebRTC protocol time over RTSP have been obtained for both communication establishment and sending packages. As future work, several possible future tasks can be mentioned, such as the creation of comparatives taking into account more protocols such as DASH streaming, Adobe HTTP Dynamic Streaming or Microsoft Smooth Streaming in the same environment with smartphones.

Acknowledgments. Research partially supported by TESIS2015010102, TESIS2015010106, RTC-2014-1648-8, TEC2014-54110-R, MTM-2015-69138-REDT and DIG02-INSITU.

References

1. Begen, A.C., Akgul, T., Baugher, M.: Watching video over the web: Part 1: streaming protocols. IEEE Internet Comput. **15**(2), 54–63 (2011)
2. Bergkvist, A., Burnett, D., Jennings, C., Narayanan, A.: Webrtc 1.0: real-time communication between browsers. World Wide Web Consortium WD WD-webrtc-20120821 (2012)
3. Cisco: Consumer internet traffic report (2015). http://www.cisco.com
4. Codec, A.M.: Mediacodec API. https://developer.android.com/reference/android/media/MediaCodec.html?hl=es
5. Developers, A.: Testing with expresso. https://developer.android.com/training/testing/uitesting/espressotesting.html?hl=es
6. Developers, G.: Libjingle library. https://developers.google.com/talk/libjingle/developer_guide
7. Fund, F., Wang, C., Liu, Y., Korakis, T., Zink, M., Panwar, S.S: Performance of dash and webrtc video services for mobile users. In: 2013 20th International, Packet Video Workshop (PV), pp. 1–8. IEEE (2013)
8. Fyhertz: Libstreaming library. https://github.com/fyhertz/libstreaming
9. Garfinkle, N.: Video on demand (Jun 25 1996), uS Patent 5,530,754

10. Schulzrinne, H.: RTP: a transport protocol for real-time applications. https://www.ietf.org/rfc/rfc3550.txt
11. Ickin, S., Fiedler, M., Wac, K., Arlos, P., Temiz, C., Mkocha, K.: Vlqoe: video qoe instrumentation on the smartphone. Multimedia Tools Appl. **74**(2), 381–411 (2015)
12. Khan, S.Q., Gaglianello, R., Luna, M.: Experiences with blending http, rtsp, and ims [ip multimedia systems (ims) infrastructure and services]. IEEE Commun. Mag. **45**(3), 122–128 (2007)
13. Kurento: Official web page. https://www.kurento.org/
14. Live555: Official web page. http://www.live555.com/
15. Recorder, A.M.: Mediarecorder API. https://developer.android.com/reference/android/media/MediaRecorder.html
16. Schulzrinne, H.: Real time streaming protocol (rtsp) (1998)
17. Schulzrinne, H., Casner, S., Frederick, R., Jacobson, V.: Real-time transport protocol. RFC1899 (2003)
18. Stockhammer, T.: Dynamic adaptive streaming over http-: standards and design principles. In: Proceedings of the Second Annual ACM Conference on Multimedia Systems, pp. 133–144. ACM (2011)
19. Umesh, A.: Performance analysis of transmission protocols for h. 265 encoder (2015)
20. Zhang, H., Al-Nuaimi, A., Gu, X., Fahrmair, M., Ishibashi, R.: Seamless and efficient stream switching of multi-perspective videos. In: 2012 19th International Packet Video Workshop (PV), pp. 31–36. IEEE (2012)

Developing a Context Aware System for Energy Management in Urban Areas

Francisco-Javier Ferrández-Pastor(✉), Sergio Gómez-Trillo, Juan-Manuel García-Chamizo, and Rafael Valdivieso-Sarabia

University of Alicante, Ctra San Vicente del Raspeig, s/n, 03690 San Vicente Del Raspeig, Alicante, Spain
{fjferran,juanma,mnieto}@dtic.ua.es, dukysgt@hotmail.com

Abstract. To achieve energy self-sufficiency in housing, it is necessary to know the capacity of microgeneration of systems and the real needs of consumption of the users. Each house includes a microgeneration system based on the use of sustainable energy. In theoretical conditions, the design is capable of satisfying entirely its energy needs. However in real conditions there are situations in which it is necessary more energy, and others on the contrary, it produces more energy than necessary. This paper proposes the use of context-aware paradigm that integrate ubiquitous sensor network for the optimization of the energy resource available. The goal is to achieve the maximum energy efficiency during the distribution, in real time and according to energy demand in housings and community equipments. Using context-aware paradigm the system obtains environmental information, determines the profile of consumption of the users and calculates the instantaneous energy needs. This information is obtained from ubiquitous networks and will be used by systems of distribution of the electrical grid of the group of housings. Different paradigms of communication are used that provides the necessary support to achieve near real time. These paradigms are based on the protocols used in the development of the Internet of things.

Keywords: Context awareness · Smart buildings · Energy efficiency

1 Introduction

Microgeneration system based on the use of sustainable energy facilitate the design of housing and architectural volumes capable of achieve an optimum energy balance and environmentally responsible. This technology is observing the increasing investment in recent years and the implementation of actions such as the Strategy 2020 in the European Union or the Microgeneration Strategy promoted in the United Kingdom. Context-aware paradigm seek to deal with linking changes in the environment with computer systems, which are otherwise static. Information, communication and control technologies using context-awareness and microgenetration systems are integrated in this work to develop systems that can manage energy generation-consumption information to decide, in real time

C.R. García et al. (Eds.): UCAmI 2016, Part II, LNCS 10070, pp. 326–331, 2016.
DOI: 10.1007/978-3-319-48799-1_37

how the energy can be distributed in an local smartgrid. This paper is organized as follows: Sect. 2 reviews related works. Information Technologies applied are revised. Section 3, platform specifications and requirements in local microgeneration and local smartgrids scenarios are analysed. A design method is proposed to develop a platform which uses USN architecture and IoT technologies for the development of effective services. Section 4, experiments including a simulation prototype development are analysed and discussed to assess suitability of this method. Finally, Sect. 5 provides results and conclusions.

2 Related Works

In [7] the environmental problematic is treated as an urban problem, however currently almost half of the population lives in rural areas. Despite the increasing urbanization of the planet, in 2050 will be more than 3,000 million people who live in these areas, without forgetting the numerous buildings with different use that is located in not urban areas. There are many valid urbanized areas for the implementation of efficient local production and energy distribution networks. Context-aware systems ([1,2,6]) are useful for achieving efficient management of the produced energy and its distribution in the local network. These systems allow to represent the environment using information received in real time on smart devices, and perform your treatment to achieve certain purposes.

Monitoring user activity inside the housing allows the definition of standards of behaviour. Based on this information, systems capable of achieving important energy savings can be developed. The context-aware system incorporated in a building is treated in [5]. A system that decreases up to a 20 % in heating and air conditioning is the result of this work. A similar result obtained during the experimentation the intelligent system of energetic saving developed in reaching between 16–24 % of saving depending on the number of systems installed in the home ([3,4]).

3 Context-Aware System Design

Context-aware computing, Internet of Things and smart-mobile devices (phones, embedded systems, tablets and wearable) are paradigms and technologies that can be integrate to develop new solutions. Context-aware proposes systems based in information that can be used to characterize the situation of persons and devices. Internet of Things offers ecosystems to access information and content anywhere at any time, and finally mobile devices or connected wearables are used by nearly everybody when they are at work, in their home or during the holidays. In this work an ubiquitous sensor network is proposed as communication paradigm between metering sensor, actuator devices and IoT processing. Ubiquitous networks allows an *n-to-m nodes* information (Fig. 1) dissemination model where besides being able to query and be queried by other nodes as well as exchange its data, any node of the network may play the role of a base station (skin node)

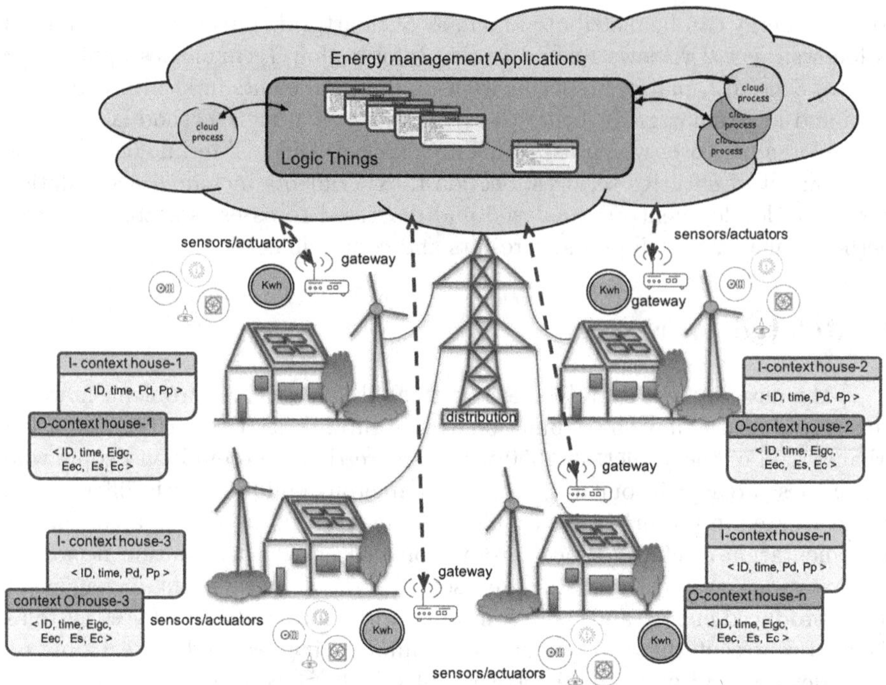

Fig. 1. Context-aware focused by houses using IoT communication (REST and MQTT protocols)

capable of transmitting its information to remote processing places using gateway device. USN local nodes can use and process local data, with a gateway these nodes have a global accessibility and they can offer extended services on an IoT scenario. Local and global access over the same node (sensor/device/actuator) has different possibilities and benefits. Whereas a local data processing is necessary in basic process control (security, system start-stop, etc.), global processing (analytic) can be used in pattern detection and information generation. In this sense, the proposed platform uses both technologies combined: USN and IoT.

In Table 1 specifications of context-aware input model are showed. Every 10 s energy demanded and energy produced are obtained by sensor meters. In each house, patterns of consumption, production and others parameters are processed to determine the energy that will be consumed and produced in the next time-frame. Next-time frame is configured in all houses. System implementation uses 15 min following time-frame used by energy distributors, it can be more o less. Process in cloud has management algorithms that optimize distribution energy. The aim is:

- Distribute energy that is generated in their own houses and the nearby buildings.
- Manage power demand or supply to the Electricity Company.
- Obtain power consumption patterns.

Table 1. Vector data input generated for each house and communicate to cloud processes

Context: INPUT Requirements Specification
$CTI_i = \{ID, time, Pd, Pp\}$
$ID \rightarrow$ context identification
$time \rightarrow$ date and time
$Pd \rightarrow$ Power consumption/10s
$Pp \rightarrow$ Power produced/10s

In Table 2 specifications of context-aware output model are showed. Every 15 min cloud process calculate distribution of energy for each house and planned energy to supply or demand depending on the current circumstances. This information is provided to automation system that control power distribution.

Table 2. Vector data output generated by cloud processes. Information is used by distribution system

Context: OUTPUT Requirements Specification
$CTO_i = \{ID, time, Eigc, Eec, Es, Ec\}$
$ID \rightarrow$ context identification
$time \rightarrow$ date and time
$Eigc \rightarrow$ Internal Energy generated and consumed/15 min
$Eec \rightarrow$ External Energy consumed/15 min
$Es \rightarrow$ Energy supplied /15 min
$Ec \rightarrow$ Electric Company Energy demanded (-) or supplied (+)/15 min

4 Experimental Work

Demand estimated and consumption patterns for profiles associated with different users and the energetic available resource have been considered. For its calculation have been defined a set of criteria such as the number and profile of users, hours of stay in housing, equipment, daily activities and the measures stored by sensor meter installed in a prototype (Fig. 2). The following figure shows the profiles of the users, which has taken the vector calculation power.

This vector details the electricity consumption in a selected day, January 14, 2016 at 14:00 o'clock, during a period of 10 s. With the sampling time chosen connections and disconnections of devices can be detected near real time. This time Such data are shown in Table 3.

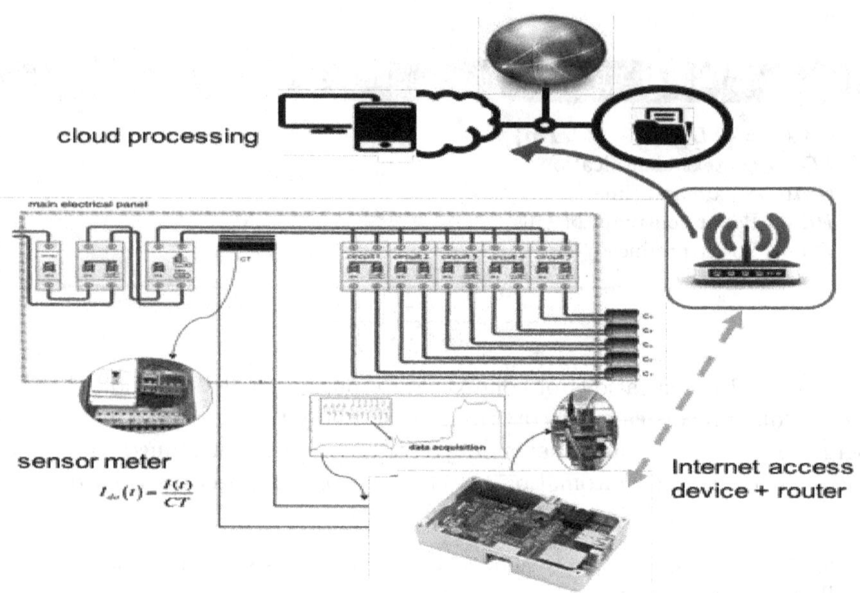

Fig. 2. House hardware prototype

Table 3. Vector data input sample obtained/10 s

ID	Date-time	User profile	Equipment	Pd (W)	Pp (W)	Users are at home
A 1	14/01/2016, 14:00	P(2A)	Basic	0,52876	0,81331	Yes
B 1	14/01/2016, 14:00	P(2A+2N)	Basic	0,81283	0,72385	Yes
C 1	14/01/2016, 14:00	P(2A)	Medium	0,95973	0,76207	Yes
D 1	14/01/2016, 14:00	P(4A OCA)	Basic	0,12762	0,73117	No

Table 4. Vector data Output generated in cloud-process /15 min

ID	Date-time	Eigc			Eec	Es	Ec
		Consumed (W)	Produced (W)	+/−	(W)	(W)	(W)
A 1	14/01/2016, 14:00	47,589	73,198	25,609	0,000	25,609	12,710
B 1	14/01/2016, 14:00	73,154	65,146	−8,008	8,008	0,000	0,000
C 1	14/01/2016, 14:00	86,376	68,586	−17,789	17,789	0,000	0,000
D 1	14/01/2016, 14:00	11,486	65,805	54,319	0,000	54,319	41,420
	Total	218,605	272,735	54,130	25,798	79,928	54,130

Wind and solar energy in all houses have been considered. Small turbines are installed in the surroundings of the housing, with a performance that is limited because of the turbulent nature of surface breezes. Cloud output context calculated for next 15 min. on the cloud processes is shown in Table 4.

5 Results and Conclusions

In this work a new context-aware system is proposed to distribute energy in urban areas. A simulation using real consumption patterns shows that the use of this system optimize the distribution of sustainable energy generated. Hardware embedded system is developed to install in housing. Cloud processing are being developed. In the next work, test in real scenarios will be showed.

References

1. Adomavicius, G., Tuzhilin, A.: Context-aware recommender systems. In: Ricci, F., Rokach, L., Shapira, B., Kantor, P.B. (eds.) Recommender Systems Handbook, pp. 217–253. Springer, USA (2011)
2. Baldauf, M., Dustdar, S., Rosenberg, F.: A survey on context-aware systems. Int. J. Ad Hoc Ubiquitous Comput. **2**(4), 263–277 (2007)
3. Byun, J., Hong, I., Kang, B., Park, S.: A smart energy distribution and management system for renewable energy distribution and context-aware services based on user patterns and load forecasting. IEEE Trans. Consum. Electr. **57**(2), 436–444 (2011)
4. Byun, J., Park, S.: Development of a self-adapting intelligent system for building energy saving and context-aware smart services. IEEE Trans. Consum. Electr. **57**(1), 90–98 (2011)
5. Moreno Cano, M.V., Santa, J., Zamora, M.A., Skarmeta Gómez, A.F.: Context-aware energy efficiency in smart buildings. In: Urzaiz, G., Ochoa, S.F., Bravo, J., Chen, L.L., Oliveira, J. (eds.) UCAmI 2013. LNCS, vol. 8276, pp. 1–8. Springer, Heidelberg (2013)
6. Perera, C., Zaslavsky, A., Christen, P., Georgakopoulos, D.: Context aware computing for the internet of things: a survey. IEEE Commun. Surv. Tutorials **16**(1), 414–454 (2014)
7. Vanolo, A.: Smartmentality: the smart city as disciplinary strategy. Urban Stud. 0042098013494427 (2013)

Efficient Management of Data Models in Constrained Systems by Using Templates and Context Based Compression

Jorge Berzosa[1(✉)], Luis Gardeazabal[2], and Roberto Cortiñas[2]

[1] IK4-Tekniker, Eibar, Spain
jorge.berzosa@tekniker.es
[2] University of the Basque Country UPV/EHU, San Sebastián, Spain
{pedrojoseluis.gardeazabal,roberto.cortinas}@ehu.eus

Abstract. Data communication is at the heart of any distributed system. The adoption of generic data formats such as XML or JSON eases the exchange of information and interoperability among heterogeneous systems. However, the verbosity of those generic data formats usually requires system resources that might not be available in resource-constrained systems, e.g., embedded systems and those devices which are being integrated into the so-called IoT. In this work we present a method to reduce the cost of managing data models like XML or JSON by using templates and context based compression. We also provide a brief evaluation and comparison as a benchmark with current implementations of W3C's Efficient XML Interchange (EXI) processor. Although the method described in this paper is still at its initial stage, it outperforms the EXI implementations in terms of memory usage and speed, while keeping similar compression rates. As a consequence, we believe that our approach fits better for constrained systems.

Keywords: IoT · XML · JSON · Template · Context · Compression · EXI

1 Introduction

The current trend to integrate heterogeneous systems into a big network like the Internet of Things (IoT) demands interoperable communication and data models. Since many systems are composed of resource-constrained devices, a big effort is being done to provide those systems with protocols and tools adapted to their limitations. The general approach is to tackle the challenge at different layers. For example, we can find IEEE 802.15.4 [6] for the media access control layer, 6LoWPAN [10] in the case of the network layer and the Constrained Application Protocol (CoAP) [11] at the application layer.

This work considers the representation of data, which could be located at the presentation layer. Data can be represented by using many different formats. In this work we will focus on semi-structured data models and, more precisely,

C.R. García et al. (Eds.): UCAmI 2016, Part II, LNCS 10070, pp. 332–343, 2016.
DOI: 10.1007/978-3-319-48799-1_38

W3C's XML (Extensible Markup Language) as a main reference, even though we could also consider other options such as JSON (JavaScript Object Notation). XML is widely extended and is the basis for many web services and related protocols, e.g., SOAP [5]. Roughly speaking, XML has been designed to be human readable, with tokens and attributes codified as strings. Nevertheless, this makes XML too large to be efficiently managed by resource-constrained devices like embedded systems. Additionally, parsers need to deal with large amount of string data, thus involving too much processing for energy and processor constrained devices.

The efficient management of formatted data models would ease the native use of Web Services and high level protocols and data models in resource-limited IoT devices. This would enhance the application of self-* services family (self-discovery, self-configuring, etc.) as well as overall interoperability. The benefits for all IoT domains in general are clear but they are specially important for consumer electronics targeted domains (domotics, entertainment, etc.) where improved interoperability across services/vendors and increasing complexity and richness of the interactions with the "smart" devices/environment would enhance user experience.

Efficient XML Interchange, EXI [9], adopted as a recommendation by the World Wide Web Consortium (W3C), relies on a binary representation of XML Information Set. It is designed to provide a considerable reduction on the size of the information in XML format (70–80 % as shown in [12]) and a high performance when encoding/decoding (6.7 times faster decoding and 2.4 times faster encoding according to [4]). In EXI a XML document is represented by an EXI stream, which is composed of a header (containing encoding information) and a body (representing the data). Data are represented based on formal grammars to model redundancy. Interestingly, when the schema of the XML is available, EXI achieves better results.

In this work we propose an approach based on templates. Roughly speaking, templates are extracted from managed data model schema documents so that their representation can be replaced in the data model instance documents with a minimum number of references. The documents are then compressed (by using lossless compression) following a context based grammar. The templates are registered at running time and made available to the rest of the system. In order to manage the data model documents, nodes will go through a preliminary discovery phase, where required templates and identifiers are downloaded from its location.

Outline. The paper is structured as follows; Sect. 2 presents the basis for template based compression. Then, Sect. 3 discuss about the dissemination of the templates in the system. A brief performance study compared to EXI is presented in Sect. 4. Finally, Sect. 5 presents the conclusions of the paper and future work.

2 Template Based Compression

Formatted data models can be represented by a tree graph encapsulating the links between the elements and the attributes of those links (such as the cardinality of the children showed in Fig. 1). In this work we define a grammar that is able to describe the links between the elements and templates that compose a formatted data model as well as the rules to follow in order to apply the grammar for efficient encoding and decoding. The proposed method is intended to be generic and not tied to a specific data description format (such as XML or JSON).

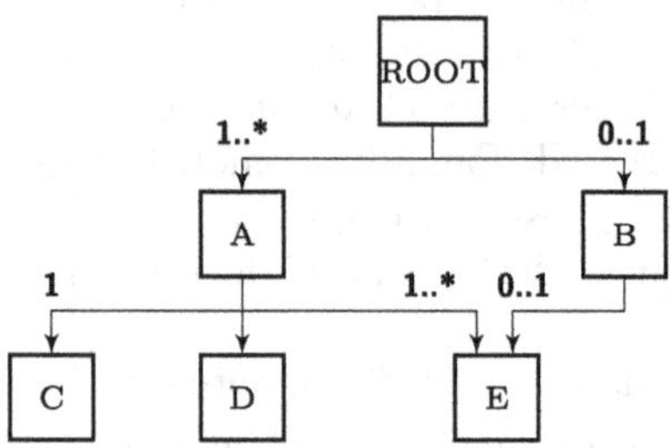

Fig. 1. Formatted data model tree example. The numbers in the links denote the cardinality: "1" one child, "1..*" one to many children, "0..1" none or one child (optional).

Each data model is described by a specific schema. This schema is used to extract the generic tree graph that is independent of the schema's original representation format. The tree graph is represented by a *Schema Context* that contains all the relevant schema information including elements and links. The generic grammar is used to process the *Schema Context* and execute the encoding and decoding processes. A set of generic rules is defined to map a schema into a *Schema Context*. However, these rules have to be specifically implemented for each data format type as the mapping of the schema to a *Schema Context* is data format specific.

2.1 Context Table and Schema Context

A *Context Table* contains all the information of the data model schemas known to the node. Each entry of the *Context Table* is a *Schema Context* that contains the information related to the elements and templates used in the schema, links between elements and, in summary, all the information needed to process a data model described by the schema. Figure 2 shows a detail of the Context Table of the example shown in Fig. 1.

A *Schema Context* is identified by the *URI* and *SchemaId* attributes. The *URI* attribute must be unique and is used to globally identify the *Schema Context*. The *SchemaId* attribute is assigned in the node bootstrapping phase (as

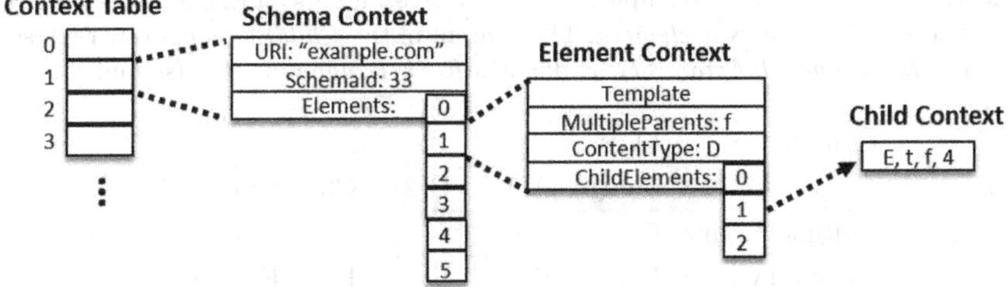

Fig. 2. Example context table detail.

described later) and must be unique within the (sub-)network the *Schema Context* is used.

A *Schema Context* contains the list of *Element Contexts* that describe the elements of the schema. An *Element Context* has the following attributes:

- *Id*: the identifier of the element in the schema, which is denoted by its index in the *Schema Context* element list.
- *Template*: a reference to the entry in the *Template Table* that contains the template for this element.
- *MultipleParents*: *true* if the element is a child of more than one parent. *false* otherwise.
- *ContentType*: the value of this attribute depends on the order the children may appear in a data model instance. If the order of the children is fixed and coincides with the order in which they are defined in the schema, the value is *fixed*. If the order is random, the value is *dynamic*. Finally, if only one single children can appear (among all the ones defined in the schema), the value is *choice*.
- *ChildElements*: it contains the *Child Context* list.

Finally, *Child Context* is a tuple composed of the following attributes:

- *Type*: data type of the element. The data type can be either a basic type or an *element* type. For the basic data type case the following types (inherited from the EXI [9] specification) are supported: *binary*, *boolean*, *decimal*, *float*, *integer*, *date-time* and *string*.
- *IsOptional*: *true* in case the cardinality of the child is $0..m$, where $m > 0$, and *false* otherwise.
- *IsArray*: *true* in case the child is an array, i.e., those children which have cardinality $n..m$, where $m > n \geq 0$.
- *ElementId*: if the *Type* attribute is *element*, *ElementId* contains the *Id* (i.e., the index) of this child's *Element Context*.

Table 1 shows the Element Contexts associated to the data model of the example in Fig. 1.

Table 1. *Element Contexts* example. Each column represents an Element Context. The Type of all *Child Contexts* is *element*. The content of the *ChildElements* row represents the tuple (*IsOptional*, *IsArray*, *Id*). *F* denotes *fixed*, *D dynamic*, *f false* and *t true*.

Atribute	Id					
	root(0)	A(1)	B(2)	C(3)	D(4)	E(5)
MultipleParents	f	f	f	f	f	t
ContentType	F	D	F	F	F	F
ChildElements	(f,t,1) (t,f,2)	(f,f,3) (t,f,4) (f,t,5)	(t,f,5)	()	()	()

2.2 Template Table

The *Template Table* contains the list of templates known by the node. Basically, templates are represented by using a custom format. They are strings which use the @ symbol to denote place-holders. Each place-holder represents a child of the element represented by the template.

In addition to the information about the template, each row also contains context information in order to ease the matching between the original format and the template, thus, improving and optimizing the searching and codification processes.

2.3 Template Grammar

The *Template Grammar* allows processing data model elements by using the information available in the *Context Table*.

Figure 3 shows the grammar, where $\text{Child}_0 \ldots \text{Child}_{k-1} \in C$, being C the group of children of an element and k the number of children of the element. The index i, $0 \leqslant i < k$, denotes any children of C.

```
Element ::= FixedChildren
  | DynamicChildren
  | ChoiceChildren

FixedChildren ::= Child_0 ... Child_k-1

DynamicChildren ::= ε
  | Child_i DynamicChilds

ChoiceChildren ::= Child_0
  | ...
  | Child_k-1

Child ::= ε
  | ChildElement Child

ChildElement ::= binary
  | boolean
  | decimal
  | float
  | integer
  | date-time
  | string
  | Element
```

Fig. 3. Template grammar. k denotes the number of children ($0 \leqslant i < k$).

The production used for the left-hand *Element* depends on the value of the attribute *ContentType*. If the value is *fixed*, the right-hand production *Fixed-Children* is used. If instead the value is *dynamic*, the right-hand production used will be *DynamicChildren*. Finally, if the value of *ContentType* is *choice*, the right-hand production *ChoiceChildren* will be used.

The production for left-hand *Child* depends on the value of *IsOptional* and *IsArray* attributes. In case both are *false*, only "ChildElement ϵ" is accepted. The *root* element always should have *IsOptional* and *isArray* attributes to *false*.

Finally, the left-hand *ChildElement* contains the terminal symbols of the basic types as well as the non-terminal symbol *Element*.

2.4 Context Table and Template Table Creation

As explained before, the *Context Table* contains the list of all the *Schema Context* structures known by the node. Each *Schema Context* is created by processing the data model schema. Also, as the schema is processed, each *Element Context* is created strictly following the order in which the elements are defined.

When processing an element, the process checks whether it already exists in the *Schema Context*. In case it does not exist, a new *Element Context* is created, together with an unique *Id* identifier, and *MultipleParents* attribute is set to *false*. In case the element already exists, *MultipleParents* is set to *true*. Then, its attribute *Template* is assigned with the identifier of the associated template in the *Template Table*.

In case (1) the order of appearance of children is fixed and (2) the appearance matches the order defined in the schema, *ContentType* attribute is set to *fixed*. If the appearance order of the children can be different, *ContentType* attribute is set to *dynamic*. Finally, in case only one of the children can appear, *ContentType* attribute is set to *choice*.

Once *Element Context* attributes have been set, children links are processed. If the cardinality related to the child is *1*, *IsOptional* and *IsArray* attributes are set to *false*. If the child has cardinality $n..m$, where $n = 0$, *isOptional* is set to *true*. If $m > 1$ then *isArray* is also set to *true*. Finally, the child type is added to *Type* attribute. In case the child type is *element*, *ElementId* attribute is set with the *Id* identifier of the associated Element Context.

Once all the schema has been processed and the *Schema Context* has been created, a process called *Context Collapsing* is performed in order to reduce the number of *Element Contexts* and *Child Contexts* without any loss of information. Starting from the root node, if two or more siblings (nodes that share the same parent) (1) are neither optional nor arrays (i.e., *IsOptional=false* and *IsArray = false*), (2) they only have one parent (i.e., *MultipleParents = false*) and (3) the order of the siblings is fixed (i.e., *ElementContent* attribute of the parent is *fixed*), then the *Element Contexts* of the children are merged together. In a similar way, if a parent and a child fulfill those same conditions, then the *Element Context* of the child is merged with the *Element Context* of the parent.

Context Table and Template Table Example. We present an example of an *Element Context* and *Template Table* generated from an XML Schema. To this end, we use the *Notebook* XML Document example proposed by Peintner et al. [8]. Figure 4 shows the original XML Schema of *Notebook* example.

```
<?xml version="1.0" encoding="UTF-8"?>
<xs:schema xmlns:xs="http://www.w3.org/2001/XMLSchema"
                        elementFormDefault="qualified">
  <xs:element name="notebook">
    <xs:complexType>
      <xs:sequence maxOccurs="unbounded">
        <xs:element name="note" type="Note"/>
      </xs:sequence>
      <xs:attribute ref="date"/>
    </xs:complexType>
  </xs:element>
  <xs:complexType name="Note">
    <xs:sequence>
      <xs:element name="subject" type="xs:string"/>
      <xs:element name="body" type="xs:string"/>
    </xs:sequence>
    <xs:attribute ref="date" use="required"/>
    <xs:attribute name="category" type="xs:string"/>
  </xs:complexType>
  <xs:attribute name="date" type="xs:date"/>
</xs:schema>
```

Fig. 4. *Notebook* XML document schema.

Figure 5 shows the Template Table generated before *collapsing* (see Fig. 5a) and after *collapsing* (see Fig. 5b). Also, Table 2 shows the Context table generated after collapsing[1].

Table 2. *Element Context* example, after collapsing. The *ContentType* attribute of all the elements is *fixed*. The content of the ChildElements row corresponds with the tupla (*Type*, *IsOptional*, *IsArray*, *ElementId*). S denotes *string*, E *element*, D *date-time*, t *true* and f *false*.

Atribute	Id				
	root(0)	notebook(1)	date(2)	note (3)	category (4)
Template	-	0	1	2	3
MultipleParents	f	f	t	f	f
ChildElements	(E,f,f,1)	(E,t,f,2) (E,f,t,3)	(D,f,f,-)	(E,t,f,4) (E,f,f,2) (S,f,f,-) (S,f,f,-)	(S,f,f,-)

[1] Context table before *collapsing* is available at [3].

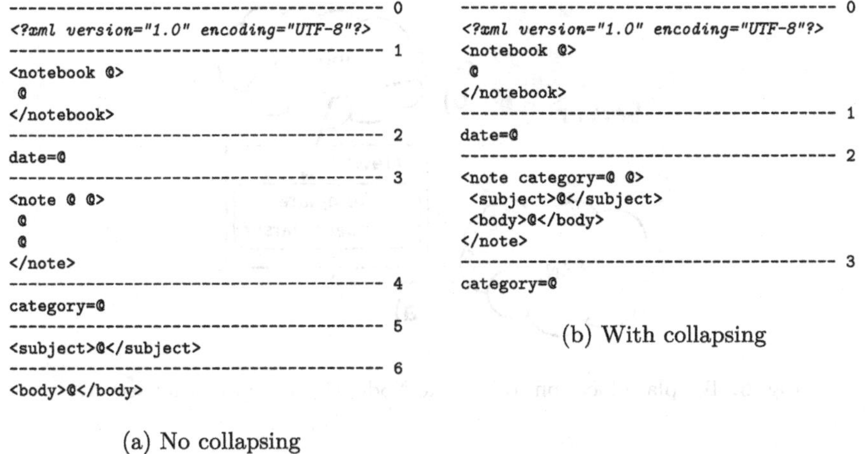

Fig. 5. Schema example template table.

3 Template Management Configuration

3.1 Schema Register

Nodes need to know the templates (and their identifiers) associated with the data models they are using. This information is made available in an initial dissemination phase, in which *Template Tables* and *Context Tables* of the data models are distributed.

When a node joins the network for the first time, it can start a schema registration process. Schemas are registered in a centralized schema repository, usually located at the gateway. Nodes use the URI of the data model schema to register. When the gateway receives a registration request, it first checks whether that schema is already registered. In that case, the associated *SchemaId* is returned. If the URI is not registered yet, the gateway generates a new *schemaId.*

When registering a schema, an associated URL is provided so that its data model schema can be accessed and downloaded. Schemas can be stored at a node (see Fig. 6a) or at an external server (Fig. 6b). Once the gateway has downloaded a schema, it generates the *Context Table* and *Template Table.* As an efficiency improvement, the schema repository could also pre-load a set of standard schemas or download already pre-compiled *Context Tables.*

Note that constrained nodes only need to store the schemas of the data models they actually use. Moreover, if the schemas can be accessed from an external server, they can be totally stripped from the node.

In case a central schema repository were not available, nodes could select proper identifiers based on point-to-point agreement. Optionally, distributed system convergent algorithms could be used.

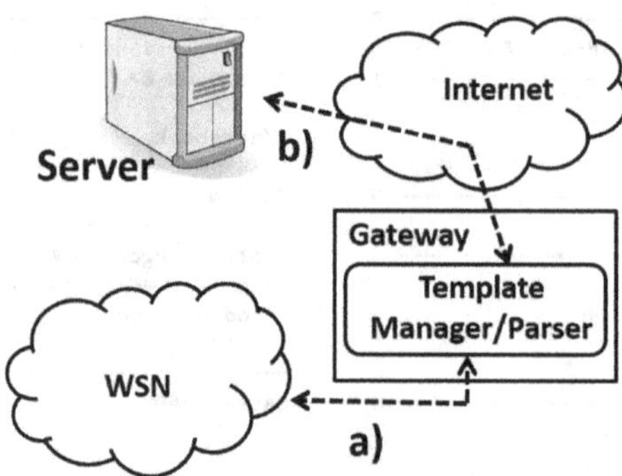

Fig. 6. Template location. (a) at the Node, (b) at an external server.

After the registration process, the *schemaId* and *Context Table* are available in the schema repository so that nodes can access them in their bootstrapping phase.

4 Performance Evaluation

In this section we present two performance tests in order to compare context based compression and EXI. In the first test, a set of XML instances are compressed by using (a) EXIficient [2], an implementation of EXI, and (b) a preliminary implementation of the templates and context based compression approach. In the second test, we study the performance of the decoding process using as input the streams obtained from the previous test. In order to decode EXI streams, another EXI implementation, EXIP [7], is used.

The set of XML documents used in the tests is composed of the *netconf* and *SenML* instances (three documents each) used in the EXIP evaluation paper [7], as well as the notebook XML instance used as an example in the EXI Primer web page [8].

4.1 First Test: Encoding

In this test we compressed the XML instances using the EXIficient [2] implementation of EXI. In order to ensure fairness in the comparison, the encoding was performed setting the *schema strict* option to *true* and all the *preserve* options to *false*. The options were not included in the header of the encoded stream. For the Context Based compression we created the Context and Template Tables from the schemas and performed the encoding using the grammar presented in this work. The results in terms of size are shown in Table 3.

Observe that results are very similar. It is interesting to note that in the case of the *SenML-01* document, EXI shows better compression results. The reason lies in the fact that our proposal is not able to compress occurrences of strings outside the schema, while EXI does not differentiate between strings belonging to data and schema space.

Table 3. XML document compression comparative. Numbers are in bytes.

XML	original	EXIP	CB
notebook	297	59	60
netconf-01	395	21	20
netconf-02	660	51	49
netconf-03	423	3	2
SenML-01	448	97	129
SenML-02	219	61	59
SenML-03	173	45	43

4.2 Second Test: Decoding

For the second test we decoded the EXI streams produced in the previous encoding test using the EXIP v5.4 [1] implementation of EXI. Only decoding time has been measured (grammar generation time has not been considered). In the case of the context based approach, we used a preliminary implementation of the Templates and Context Based compression to decode the same streams compressed in the previous test.

We performed 1000 runs for each stream encoding in similar system load conditions. Table 4 shows the results. Two columns are presented for each case. The first one contains the non-optimized program (compiled with -O0) measurements while the second one is the optimized program (compiled with -O3).

Table 4. XML document compression time comparative. Numbers are in milliseconds.

XML	EXIP		CB	
notebook	25.3	23.1	15.0	13.8
netconf-01	28.6	24.4	7.9	6.8
netconf-02	38.4	32.0	15.4	13.1
netconf-03	30.1	25.7	7.5	6.4
SenML-01	38.7	33.6	23.7	19.7
SenML-02	25.6	22.2	16.1	14.3
SenML-03	20.5	18.3	14.0	12.5

Observe that decoding compressed streams is significantly faster[2] in the case of Context Based Compression. This is a direct result from using the simpler grammar and structure of the Context and Template Tables compared to the EXI specification.

[2] This is very relevant for resource-constrained devices as sorter processing cycles imply lower energy consumption.

Regarding memory requirements, performed tests showed that RAM usage by EXIP [7] was 23KB. In the case of Context Based Compression, the RAM allocations of the Context and Template Tables for the *notebook.xsd*, *senml.xsd* and *netconf.xsd* schemas were 565, 969 y 3611 bytes respectively. Also note that the Context and Template tables are constant data so, for the most resource-constrained devices, they could be stored and accessed from flash in order to save RAM. Finally, the programming memory used by the core Context based implementation was 7KB, while EXIP reported 79KB.

Results from the tests show that Context Based Compression performed better in terms of processing time (31.3 %-75.2 % time reduction) and memory usage (78.2 % less RAM and 89.9 % less program memory).

5 Conclusions

In this paper we have presented a context based compression technique that can be applied to formatted data models. Context based compression allows a better performance in the representation of data model structures, keeping independence from the original format. Additionally, since templates are used, different *Template Tables* can be applied to the same *Context Table* in order to manage different representations, such as XML or JSON or even the same XML document with different extensions (e.g. with or without comments).

We have shown that Templates and Context based compression provides good performance results compared to EXI implementations. Context Based Compression achieves better performance than EXI implementations in terms of speed and memory usage, while keeping a similar efficiency in terms of space in its better case (*Schema Strict*). Additionally, since templates are used, the binding between the *Schema Table* and the original document is also achieved in an speed efficient way.

On the other hand, the preliminary version of Templates and Context based compression does not offer support for deviations from the data model schema. As a consequence, data models can not be extended (for instance, for nesting multiple data models) and extensibility attributes of the native formats (e.g., `<any>` and `<anyAttribute>` XML elements) are not currently supported, so they are ignored in the parsing process.

As a future work, we are considering to improve Context based compression in order to enable Schema Context extensions and nested data models. This mechanism would also allow assigning templates to dynamic parameters, improving the compression of repeated values in the data space. We are also studying the representation in the Context Table of constraints described in the schema. This would improve the compression and the addition of partial validations of the coded streams. Finally, one of our main objectives is to develop a modular library which allows to be configured and customized to the resources of a given system. This library will provide an API and required functions to manage the formatted data in an efficient way. Additionally, we are also planning to develop a toolbox which will automatically generate Context Tables and *Template tables* from standard schema formats (such as XML and JSON schemas).

Acknowledgements. Research partially supported by the European Union Horizon 2020 Programme under grant 680708/HIT2GAP, by the Spanish Research Council, grant TIN2013-41123-P, and the University of the Basque Country UPV/EHU, grant UFI11/45.

References

1. Embeddable EXI processor in C (2016). http://exip.sourceforge.net/. Accessed June 2016
2. Exificient (EXI procesor) (2016). http://exificient.github.io/. Accessed June 2016
3. Berzosa, J., Cortiñas, R., Gardeazabal, L.: Efficient management of data models in constrained systems by using templates and context based compression. Technical report, University of the Basque Country UPV/EHU, Computer Science Faculty (Donostia, San-Sebastian) (2016). http://go.ehu.eus/BerzosaGC16-TR-05-16.pdf
4. Bournez, C.: Efficient XML interchange evaluation. Technical report, W3C (2009). http://www.w3.org/TR/exi-evaluations/. Accessed June 2016
5. Gudgin, M., Hadley, M., Mendelsohn, N., Moreau, J.J., Frystyk Nielsen, H.: SOAP version 1.2 part 1: messaging framework. Recommendation, W3C, June 2003. http://www.w3.org/TR/2003/REC-soap12-part1-20030624
6. Gutierrez, J.A., Callaway, E.H., Barrett, R.: IEEE 802.15.4 Low-rate wireless personal area networks: enabling wireless sensor networks. IEEE Standards Office, New York, NY, USA (2003)
7. Kyusakov, R., Punal Pereira, P., Eliasson, J., Delsing, J.: EXIP: a framework for embedded web development. TWEB **8**(4), 23:1–23:29 (2014). doi:10.1145/2665068
8. Peintner, D., Pericas-Geertsen, S.: Efficient XML interchange (EXI) primer (2014). https://www.w3.org/TR/exi-primer/. Accessed June 2016
9. Schneider, J., Kamiya, T., Peintner, D., Kyusakov, R.: Efficient XML interchange (EXI) Format 1.0 (2nd edn.). Technical report, W3C (2014). http://www.w3.org/XML/EXI. Accessed June 2016
10. Shelby, Z., Bormann, C.: 6LoWPAN: The Wireless Embedded Internet. Wiley Publishing, Hoboken (2010)
11. Shelby, Z., Hartke, K., Bormann, C.: The constrained application protocol (CoAP). Technical report 7252, RFC Editor, Fremont, CA, USA, June 2014. http://www.rfc-editor.org/rfc/rfc7252.txt
12. White, G., Kangasharju, J., Brutzman, D., Williams., S.: Efficient XML interchange measurements note. Technical report, W3C (2007). http://www.w3.org/TR/exi-measurements/. Accessed June 2016

A QoC-Aware Discovery Service for the Internet of Things

Porfírio Gomes[1], Everton Cavalcante[1], Thais Batista[1], Chantal Taconet[2], Sophie Chabridon[2(✉)], Denis Conan[2], Flavia C. Delicato[3], and Paulo F. Pires[3]

[1] DIMAp, Federal University of Rio Grande do Norte, Natal, Brazil
porfiriodantas@gmail.com, everton@dimap.ufrn.br, thais@ufrnet.br
[2] SAMOVAR, Télécom SudParis, CNRS, Université Paris-Saclay, Télécom SudParis, Évry, France
{chantal.taconet,sophie.chabridon,denis.conan}@telecom-sudparis.eu
[3] PPGI/DCC, Federal University of Rio de Janeiro, Rio de Janeiro, Brazil
fdelicato@gmail.com, paulo.f.pires@gmail.com

Abstract. The Internet of Things (IoT) is an emergent paradigm characterized by a plethora of smart objects connected to the Internet. An inherent characteristic of IoT is the high heterogeneity and the wide distribution of objects, thereby calling for ways to describe in an unambiguous and machine-interpretable way the resources provided by objects, their properties, and the services they offer. In this context, discovery services play a significant role as they allow clients (middleware platforms, end-users, applications) to retrieve available resources based on appropriate search criteria, such as resource type, capabilities, location, and Quality of Context (QoC) parameters. To cope with these concerns, we introduce *QoDisco*, a QoC-aware discovery service relying on multiple-attribute searches, range queries, and synchronous/asynchronous operations. *QoDisco* also comprises an ontology-based information model for semantically describing resources, services, and QoC-related information. In this paper, we describe the *QoDisco* architecture and information model as well as an evaluation of the search procedure in an urban air pollution monitoring scenario.

1 Introduction

The *Internet of Things* (IoT) [5] is an emergent paradigm that has rapidly evolved in recent years as an extension of the current Internet with seamlessly interconnected physical entities (a.k.a. *things*) towards providing value-added information and functionalities for end-users and/or applications. Devices can be attached to or embedded into these things or be deployed to monitor the surrounding environment. Two types of devices are of particular relevance in IoT, namely *sensors* and *actuators* [16]. Sensors typically obtain data from entities while actuators are capable of actuating on an entity or its environment. Both sensors and actuators comprise *resources* often hosted in these devices, allowing clients (middleware platforms, users, applications) to interact with them through

C.R. García et al. (Eds.): UCAmI 2016, Part II, LNCS 10070, pp. 344–355, 2016.
DOI: 10.1007/978-3-319-48799-1_39

the Internet. Since implementations of resources can be highly dependent on the underlying device hardware, *services* provide high-level interfaces exposing the functionalities of these resources. Resources can be described in terms of metadata such as resource type, capabilities, location, etc. [7], as well as the information required to interact with the exposed services.

An inherent characteristic of IoT is the high heterogeneity of available resources, a consequence of the widely distributed plethora of smart things with different capabilities/functionalities and network protocols. This makes finding, selecting, and using smart things in a fast, user-friendly way a hard task for both machines and human users [22]. In this context, *discovery services* play a significant role because they enable clients to retrieve unknown available resources based on given search criteria. These mechanisms also allow obtaining up-to-date information about functional capabilities offered by devices in the environment and/or the *observations* obtained by them [23]. Although discovery services represent a well-studied topic in distributed systems, traditional approaches are not suitable to this context mainly due to the high dynamicity of IoT resources.

A discovery process in the IoT can highly benefit from considering *Quality of Context* (QoC) information associated with data provided by devices, e.g. precision, accuracy, up-to-dateness, etc. [9]. Using such an additional information is relevant because it can augment the richness of the discovery procedure and better support decision-making actions, besides dealing with the inherently imperfect, inconsistent, and noisy nature of data provided by devices [19]. Therefore, QoC arises as way of filtering out these data and ranking which information should be used [10].

Aiming to tackle the aforementioned concerns, this paper presents *QoDisco*, a QoC-aware discovery service structured upon a set of repositories storing resource descriptions and QoC-related information. *QoDisco* complies with important requirements for discovering resources in the IoT context, e.g. multi-attribute and range queries [23], and support to both synchronous and asynchronous searches. Furthermore, our proposal encompasses an ontology-based information model with concepts related to resources and services, relationships among them, and QoC information. This information model takes advantage of well-established, standardized ontologies to semantically describe resources and services, namely the Semantic Actuator Network (SAN) ontology [28], the Semantic Sensor Network (SSN) ontology [6], and the Ontology Web Language for Services (OWL-S) [21]. In addition, we have incorporated part of the Quality of Context Information Meta-model (QoCIM) [20] to our information model aiming at dealing with QoC criteria in the search procedure.

The remainder of this paper is organized as follows. Section 2 elicits important requirements to be addressed by a discovery service in IoT. Section 3 describes *QoDisco*, its architecture, and the information model used to describe resources, services, and QoC information. Section 4 presents an evaluation of the search procedure performed by *QoDisco* in an urban pollution monitoring scenario. Section 5 briefly discusses related works. Finally, Sect. 6 contains some concluding remarks and directions for future work.

2 Requirements for a Discovery Service in IoT

There are some important concerns to be considered by discovery services targeting IoT. Paganelli and Parlanti [23] highlight five of these requirements, in particular the identification of resources, the ability to perform multi-attribute and range queries, dealing with the existence of multiple providers for publishing information about resources, and APIs for managing resources. In addition to those requirements, we have considered three other important concerns, namely (i) semantic description of resources, (ii) modeling of QoC criteria, and (iii) support for both synchronous and asynchronous interactions. Table 1 outlines these requirements.

Table 1. Important requirements for a discovery service in IoT

Requirement	Description
Flexible identification schema	Transparency regarding the adopted identification schema (e.g. URIs, IP addresses, etc.) used to address resources, services, and observation data
Multi-attribute query	Capability of finding resources by performing queries based on an exact matching of one or more attributes
Range query	Capability of finding resources based on queries specifying bounds on single or multiple attributes
Dealing with multiple publishers	Several entities can produce and publish information about a given resource
Management APIs	Capability of managing information associated with a given resource
Semantic description of resources and services	Use of ontologies to semantically model resources and exposed services
Modeling QoC criteria	Modeling QoC indicators associated with context data
Synchronous and asynchronous interactions	Capability of handling both synchronous and asynchronous interactions with clients

Chun et al. [12] argue that an information model should be semantically modeled in terms of ontologies defining common terms used in IoT to model resources and exposed services. Adding semantics to an information model can promote interoperability among resources, information models, data providers, and service consumers, as well as it can make data access, service integration, semantic interpretation, and knowledge extraction easier. In addition, we argue

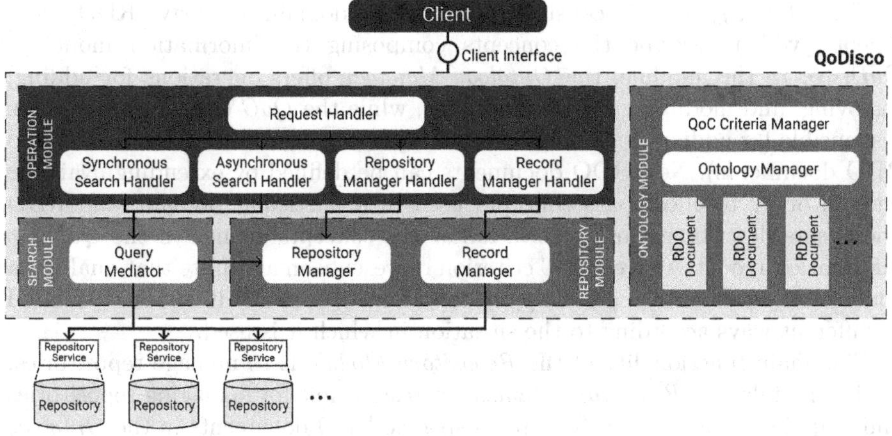

Fig. 1. *QoDisco* architecture

that the imperfect and uncertain nature of data in IoT requires considering associated QoC indicators.

Due to the dynamicity of resources, a discovery service in IoT should also be able to handle both synchronous and asynchronous interactions. When receiving a synchronous request, the discovery service sends a unique response to the client. When registering asynchronous searches, clients of the discovery service are notified in case of removal, insertion or update of resources.

3 *QoDisco*

This section presents *QoDisco*, our QoC-aware discovery service for IoT. Section 3.1 details the *QoDisco* architecture whereas Sect. 3.2 describes the information model used to describe IoT resources, services, and QoC information.

3.1 Architecture

QoDisco relies on a collection of repositories to perform data and service discovery tasks. This approach provides several advantages over a single repository approach, in particular high scalability, fault-tolerance, independent control of repositories, and data distribution among repositories [27]. In the context of this work, we envision clients such as IoT middleware platforms, applications, and users storing resource descriptions (a.k.a. records) in repositories and registering them in *QoDisco*. When receiving a discovery request, *QoDisco* performs a search for resource descriptions and/or data stored in the available repositories.

The *QoDisco* architecture comprises four modules, each one responsible for a set of functionalities provided by the platform. Figure 1 illustrates these modules, which are briefly described in the following. The current prototype of *QoDisco* is available at http://consiste.dimap.ufrn.br/projects/qodisco.

The *Ontology Module* consists of repository domain ontology (RDO) documents, which describe the concepts composing the information model of *QoDisco*. In this module, the *Ontology Manager* offers operations for adding, removing, and modifying RDO documents, while the *QoC Criteria Manager* is responsible for adding, removing, and modifying QoC criteria (also defined into RDO documents). New RDO documents can be defined by extending available ones in order to encompass concepts used in a particular domain, and RDO documents describing QoC criteria follow the concepts defined in the *QoDisco* information model. A given QoC criterion represents an attribute that qualifies a context information (e.g. accuracy, up-to-dateness, etc.) and it can be calculated in different ways according to the situation in which it is used.

The main functionality of the *Repository Module* is to manage repositories. In this module, the *Repository Manager* is responsible for managing repositories and mapping each one to a (group of) specific RDO documents in the *Ontology Module*. This implies that a repository joining *QoDisco* has to be mapped to at least one domain specified by a RDO document. In turn, the *Record Manager* is responsible for adding, removing, and modifying records in repositories.

The *Search Module* encompasses the *Query Mediator*, which forwards queries to the repositories belonging to *QoDisco*. To perform the search, this component specifies an RDO document name (i.e. domain name) to the *Repository Manager*, which provides the IP addresses and port numbers of the repositories mapped to such a domain. For instance, if the *Query Mediator* makes a request for repositories belonging to the health care domain, the *Repository Manager* returns the respective addresses and port numbers of these repositories.

The *Operation Module* is composed of the five following components:

Request Handler: It is the entry point of the *Operation Module*, and receives both synchronous and asynchronous requests for searching and managing repositories and records.

Synchronous Search Handler: It performs synchronous queries by querying the *Query Mediator*.

Asynchronous Search Handler: Using the publish-subscribe paradigm [13], it notifies clients (i) about the discovery of a new resource matching the search query and (ii) about the modification or removal of a resource description.

Repository Manager Handler: It interacts with the *Repository Manager* to add or remove repositories.

Record Manager Handler: It interacts with the *Repository Manager* to add, remove or modify records.

The functionalities of the *Operation Module* and the *Ontology Module* are provided through the *Client Interface*, which complies with the Representational State Transfer (REST) architectural style [15]. The operations of the *Client Interface* are related to both synchronous and asynchronous search, as well as to the management (insertion, removal, update) of records, repositories, RDO documents, and QoC criteria. More information about the *Client Interface* is available at http://consiste.dimap.ufrn.br/projects/qodisco.

3.2 Information Model

Figure 2 depicts the information model adopted by *QoDisco*. As previously mentioned, this information model comprises an ontology-based vocabulary of concepts related to IoT resources and services, relationships among them, and QoC-related information. In order to semantically describe resources, the *QoDisco* information model takes advantage of the SAN ontology [28], an extension of the W3C's SSN ontology [6] that provides concepts, attributes, and properties to model both sensors and actuators. Additionally, we have incorporated part of the SOUPA ontology [11] in order to include location-related concepts to describe spatial locations of entities (*PhysicalStructure*) in terms of latitude, longitude, altitude, distance, and surface, as well as symbolic representations of space and spatial relationships, e.g. a room situated at a given floor of a building. In our information model, location-related information can be associated with both resources and context data (observations).

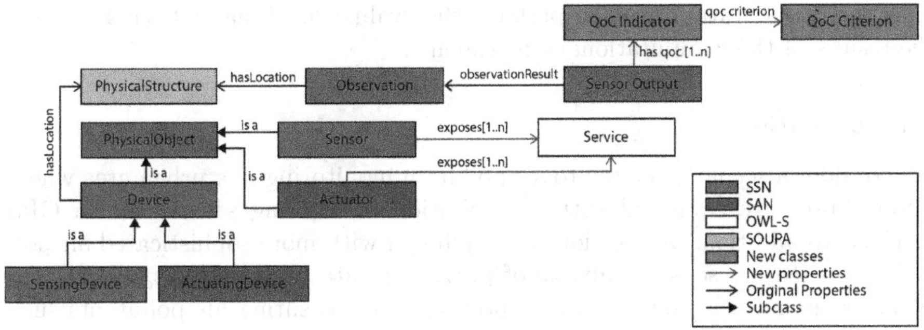

Fig. 2. Information model adopted by *QoDisco*

In spite of their comprehensiveness for describing sensors and actuators, both SSN and SAN ontologies do not provide elements for modeling services exposed by resources. For this reason, the *QoDisco* information model also comprises the OWL-S ontology [21], which has been used to semantically model Web services. In OWL-S, a service is described in terms of three sub-ontologies, namely *ServiceProfile*, *ServiceModel*, and *ServiceGrounding*. A *ServiceProfile* describes a service in terms of its inputs, outputs, preconditions, and effects. A *ServiceModel* describes the operations performed by a service and allows invoking, composing, and monitoring it. A *ServiceGrounding* describes how a service is invoked and provides information about data types used in its operations. In order to represent the relationship between resources and services, we have created the *exposes* property, which links the *Sensor* and *Actuator* concepts (representing resources) to the *Service* concept (representing services), as shown in Fig. 2.

To cope with QoC-related concerns, we have incorporated part of the QoCIM meta-model [20] by describing its concepts as an ontology. The *QoC Criterion* concept can be used to represent a QoC parameter associated with context data, e.g. accuracy, precision, completeness, up-to-dateness. In turn, the *QoC Indicator* expresses the QoC level of an observation (measured data) made by a resource. In the *QoDisco* information model, the *has_qoc* property associates a QoC level (*QoC Indicator* concept) to an observation made by a resource (*SensorOutput* concept) while the *qoc_criterion* property indicates that a QoC indicator must be associated with a QoC criterion. Our information model follows the same flexible ideology of QoCIM, i.e. defining a basis to design and represent any QoC criterion instead of providing a predefined list of supported QoC criteria. A given QoC criterion can be built upon other primitive or composed QoC criteria.

4 Evaluation

This section presents an evaluation of the scalability of *QoDisco* by assessing the performance of the search for resources and observations. Such an assessment was carried out to evaluate both synchronous and asynchronous search processes. Section 4.1 describes the scenario considered in our evaluation. Section 4.2 outlines the configuration used to perform the evaluation. Finally, Sect. 4.3 shows the results of the computational experiments.

4.1 Scenario

We consider a scenario related to air pollution monitoring in a urban area where public buses are equipped with air pollution monitoring sensors and a GPS receiver. In addition, bus stations are equipped with more sophisticated air pollution monitoring sensors capable of providing data with better QoC. The air pollution monitoring sensors are responsible for measuring air pollutants such as ozone, carbon monoxide, sulfur dioxide, and nitrous oxide. Four QoC criteria are used to qualify pollution measurements as well as the GPS location: (i) *margin of error*, which quantifies doubt about the result of a measurement and is expressed in the same unit of the measurement; (ii) *freshness*, the time elapsed from the collect of observations and its delivery to a requester; (iii) *precision*, which qualifies how close or how repeatable the results from a measurement are and is typically expressed as a percentage; and (iv) spatial *resolution*, which measures the precision with which a physical area is expressed.

The location of the buses and bus stations is qualified with spatial resolution. Pollution measurements provided by buses are qualified with both precision and freshness, while the ones provided by sensors are qualified with margin of error and freshness. In this scenario, *QoDisco* can be used by clients to search for and select sensors and respective measurements according to their capabilities, location, QoC indicator parameters, etc. All of this information is described in conformance with the *QoDisco* information model.

4.2 Experimental Setup

Aiming at minimizing network influence, all experiments were performed using a single computational node with Intel® Core^{TM} i5 processor, 8 GB of RAM, and Mac OS 10.11.3 64-bit operating system. This computational node was used to deploy the *QoDisco* repositories in a virtual machine with 1 GB of RAM and running Linux Ubuntu 14.04.3 Server OS 64-bit. Each repository was deployed at a Linux container using the Docker technology [2]. In order to ensure the reliability of the results, the experiments were run 20 times.

To discover resources and observations by using their location, type, or any of their properties in *QoDisco*, queries can be created using the SPARQL Protocol and RDF Query Language [4], a W3C standard for performing semantic searches, or using the Web interface of the platform. In all experiments, we have calculated the time spent by *QoDisco* for a SPARQL query[1] that searches for all the observations related with ozone pollution levels registered in *QoDisco* with a QoC indicator of precision greater than or equal to 95 %.

```
SELECT * WHERE {
?observation a ssn:Observation ;
    ssn:observedProperty pol:Ozone ;
    ssn:observationResult ?observationResult .
    ?observationResult qodisco:has_qoc ?qoc .
    ?qoc qodisco:has_qoc_criterion context:Precision .
    ?qoc qodisco:has_qoc_value ?value
FILTER (?value >= 95)
}
```

This query returns a response in the XML format containing (i) an URI to the observation itself, (ii) an URI referring to the sensor output, (iii) a reference to the QoC indicator, and (iv) the QoC value regarding the observation. It is worth mentioning that additional attributes could be considered in addition to the ozone pollution levels by adding other observed properties (`observedProperty` element). Other QoC criteria can be also considered by including logical operators in the `FILTER` clause of the SPARQL query.

4.3 Results

Synchronous search. To assess the performance of *QoDisco* when performing a synchronous search, we have inserted a set of dummy observations on ozone pollution level in five repositories associated to the air pollution domain. Next, we have measured the time spent by *QoDisco* to respond to a client query as the number of observations increases. Figure 3 (left) shows the average time (in milliseconds) to respond to the synchronous search query with an increasing number of observations. Such a response time is directly influenced by the sequential search performed by *QoDisco* on the available repositories. Improvements might be achieved by parallelizing the search procedure when it is performed on multiple repositories. Nonetheless, different SPARQL queries could influence the obtained assessments.

Asynchronous search. To assess the performance of *QoDisco* when performing an asynchronous search, we have considered five repositories associated to

[1] Due to space constraints, prefixes referring to the *QoDisco* ontologies were omitted.

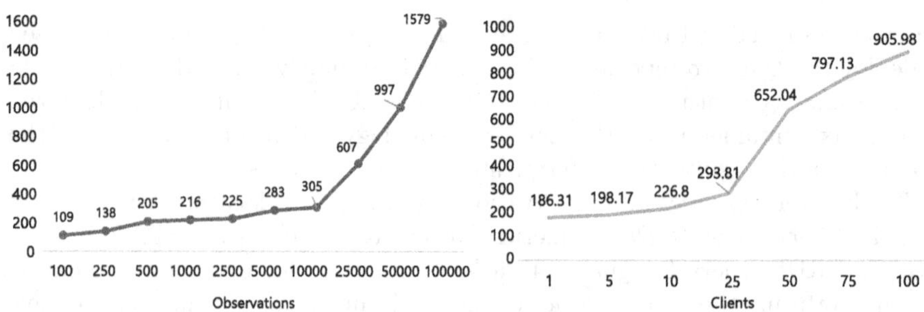

Fig. 3. Average response time to respond to synchronous (left) and asynchronous (right) searches

the air pollution domain, each one with 1,000 dummy observations on ozone pollution level. Next, we have measured the time spent by *QoDisco* to respond to searches performed by an increasing number of clients interested on notifications upon new ozone pollution level measures with precision greater than or equal to 95 %. Such simultaneous requests were simulated by making use of Apache JMeter [1], a Java-based open-source tool for analyzing and measuring the performance of Web services. Figure 3 (right) shows the average time (in milliseconds) to notify clients upon an asynchronous search, with an increasing number of client requests. It is important to highlight that such a response time highly depends on the publish-subscribe broker responsible for the management of the exchanged messages. In the current prototype of *QoDisco*, we use Mosquitto [3], a lightweight publish-subscribe message broker service for IoT. *QoDisco* only sends a message to Mosquitto, which handles the requests and responses from/to clients (subscribers) interested on the notifications.

5 Related Work

Bellavista et al. [8] review context distribution solutions for ubiquitous computing and investigate in particular how they perform context source selection. Some solutions take into account QoC, but with some restrictions. COSINE [17] and CMF [29] perform automatic context source selection depending on the QoC ensured by context sources, but selection criteria are limited and are not reconfigurable which limits their dynamicity. MiddleWhere [26] adopts a dynamic approach and let services apply QoC constraints on the received context data, but it is dedicated to location data.

Focusing on IoT, Perera et al. [25] analyze fifty context-aware projects and identifies context discovery as one of the six challenges where new solutions are required. Context discovery encompasses understanding sensor data produced by context sources, and relating them to high-level context information automatically. This might require to annotate context data, but in an automated way in order to tackle the scale and the dynamicity of the IoT. According to the authors, semantic technology shows promising ways to encode domain knowledge. In this direction, not much effort has been dedicated to resource discovery based on QoC-related information. One of the few existing proposals is CASSARAM [24], a framework that uses sensor characteristics and context information such as reliability, accuracy, and battery life registered at a single, centralized registry to automatically search for, select, and rank appropriate sensors among a large set of available devices according to user-defined criteria and priorities. Similarly to *QoDisco*, CASSARAM is built upon an ontology-based information model comprising the SSN ontology and the SPARQL language is used in the search process. In turn, the discovery mechanism of the LOCA framework [18] relies on a distributed peer-to-peer architecture and considers context information modeled by means of a lightweight and completely novel ontology.

An important aspect to be considered with respect to the aforementioned works regards the use of centralized and decentralized approaches. A significant limitation of CASSARAM is the use of a single centralized registry, which is not suitable for IoT due to well-known drawbacks related to scalability, fault-tolerance, and security threats. As stated in the comparative study conducted by Evdokimov et al. [14], decentralized architectures such as the ones used in LOCA are more suitable to IoT since they well fulfill important requirements such as fault-tolerance and scalability. *QoDisco* benefits from these requirements as it is structured upon a collection of repositories, each one mapped to one or more domains. Despite these works take into account context information, they do not consider in addition QoC criteria in the discovery process, which is valuable towards providing more accurate results according to application/user requirements. Indeed, we have not found any proposal in the literature addressing the use of QoC criteria for discovery services in IoT, thereby constituting a significant contribution of our work.

6 Conclusion

The discovery of suitable resources among the plethora of existing available entities connected to the Internet poses an important challenge to the development of IoT systems as these resources are highly dynamic and heterogeneous. Therefore, it is important to provide clients (e.g. middleware platforms, end-users, and applications) with means of easily retrieving available resources and describing them in an unambiguous way. Due to the imperfect nature of data provided by IoT devices, it is valuable complementing observations with QoC criteria to augment the richness of the search procedure and the support of decision-making.

In this paper, we address these concerns by proposing *QoDisco*, a QoC-aware discovery service for IoT. *QoDisco* supports resource discovery based on multiple attributes, range queries, synchronous/asynchronous interactions, and QoC criteria. Additionally, *QoDisco* encompasses an information model that takes advantage of well-established, standardized ontologies to semantically describe resources (sensors and actuators), the services that they expose, and QoC-related information. Unlike the approaches commonly found in the literature, the collection of repositories of *QoDisco* allows coping with important requirements in the IoT scenario. Moreover, the definition of a consistent information model is highly relevant as semantic annotations can be used to describe resources and specify search queries for discovering resources. Obtained experimental results have shown that *QoDisco* is able to handle discovery requests quite efficiently, even with a significant number of registered data and simultaneous clients.

This work can be continued in several ways. As ongoing work, we are carrying out additional experiments considering network environments closer to the ones observed in IoT, with low bandwidth, delays, package losses, etc. We also need to consider other important facets in discovery services for IoT, such as dynamism and security/privacy concerns regarding resources and their metadata. Finally, we intend to implement strategies aimed to reduce response times, in particular by parallelizing the search on repositories (instead of the current sequential search) and using optimized semantic search algorithms.

References

1. Apache JMeter. http://jmeter.apache.org/
2. Docker. https://www.docker.com/
3. Mosquitto: an open source MQTT Broker. http://mosquitto.org/
4. SPARQL Query Language for RDF. http://www.w3.org/TR/rdf-sparql-query/
5. Atzori, L., Iera, A., Morabito, G.: The Internet of Things: a survey. Comput. Netw. **54**(15), 2787–2805 (2010)
6. Barnaghi, P., et al.: Semantic sensor network XG final report, June 2011. http://www.w3.org/2005/Incubator/ssn/XGR-ssn-20110628/
7. Bassi, A., et al. (eds.): Enabling Things to Talk: Designing IoT Solutions with the IoT Architectural Reference Model. Springer, Berlin (2013)
8. Bellavista, P., Corradi, A., Fanelli, M., Foschini, L.: A survey of context data distribution for mobile ubiquitous systems. ACM Comput. Surv. **44**(4), 24:1–24:45 (2012)
9. Buchholz, T., Küpper, A., Schiffers, M.: Quality of context: what it is and why we need it. In: Proceedings of the 10th International Workshop of the OpenView University Association (2003)
10. Chabridon, S., Laborde, R., Desprats, T., Oglaza, A., Marie, P., Marquez, S.M.: A survey on addressing privacy together with quality of context for context management in the Internet of Things. Ann. Telecommun. **69**(1), 47–62 (2014)
11. Chen, H., Finin, T., Joshi, A.: The SOUPA ontology for pervasive computing. In: Tamma, V., Cranefield, S., Finin, T.W., Willmott, S. (eds.) Ontologies for Agents: Theory and Experiences. Whitestein Series in Software Agent Technologies, pp. 233–258. Birkhäuser, Basel (2005)
12. Chun, S., Seo, S., Oh, B., Lee, K.H.: Semantic description, discovery and integration for the Internet of Things. In: Proceedings of the 2015 IEEE International Conference on Semantic Computing, pp. 272–275. IEEE, USA (2015)
13. Eugster, P.T., Felber, P.A., Guerraoui, R., Kermarrec, A.M.: The many faces of publish/subscribe. ACM Comput. Surv. **35**(2), 114–131 (2003)
14. Evdokimov, S., Fabian, B., Kunz, S., Schoenemann, N.: Comparison of discovery service architectures for the Internet of Things. In: Proceedings of the 2010 IEEE International Sensor Networks. Ubiquitous, and Trustworthy Computing, pp. 237–244. IEEE, USA (2010)

15. Fielding, R.T.: Architectural styles and the design of network-based software architectures. Ph.D. Dissertation, University of California-Irvine, USA (2000)
16. Holler, J., Tsiatsis, V., Mulligan, C., Avesand, S., Karnouskos, S., Boyle, D.: From Machine-to-Machine to the Internet of Things: Introduction to a New Age of Intelligence. Academic Press, Oxford (2014)
17. Juszczyk, L., Psaier, H., Manzoor, A., Dustdar, S.: Adaptive query routing on distributed context - the COSINE framework. In: Proceedings of the 10th International Conference on Mobile Data Management: Systems, Services and Middleware, pp. 588–593. IEEE Computer Society, USA (2009)
18. Li, J., Zaman, N., Li, H.: A decentralized locality-preserving context-aware service discovery framework for the Internet of Things. In: Proceedings of the 2015 IEEE International Conference on Services Computing, pp. 317–323. IEEE Computer Society, USA (2015)
19. Marie, P., Desprats, T., Chabridon, S., Sibilla, M.: Extending ambient intelligence to the Internet of Things: new challenges for QoC management. In: Hervás, R., Lee, S., Nugent, C., Bravo, J. (eds.) UCAmI 2014. LNCS, vol. 8867, pp. 224–231. Springer, Heidelberg (2014). doi:10.1007/978-3-319-13102-3_37
20. Marie, P., Desprats, T., Chabridon, S., Sibilla, M.: The QoCIM framework: concepts and tools for quality of context management. In: Brézillon, P., Gonzalez, A.J. (eds.) Context in Computing: A Cross-disciplinary Approach for Modeling the Real World, pp. 155–172. Springer, New York (2014)
21. Martin, D., et al.: Bringing semantics to web services: the OWL-S approach. In: Cardoso, J., Sheth, A. (eds.) SWSWPC 2004. LNCS, vol. 3387, pp. 26–42. Springer, Heidelberg (2005). doi:10.1007/978-3-540-30581-1_4
22. Mayer, S., Guinard, D.: An extensible discovery service for smart things. In: Proceedings of the Second International Workshop on Web of Things. ACM, USA (2011)
23. Paganelli, F., Parlanti, D.: A DHT-based discovery service for the Internet of Things. J. Comput. Netw. Commun. **2012**, 1–11 (2012)
24. Perera, C., Zaslavsky, A., Christen, P., Compton, M., Georgakopoulos, D.: Context-aware sensor search, selection and ranking model for Internet of Things middleware. In: Proceedings of the 14th IEEE International Conference on Mobile Data Management (2013)
25. Perera, C., Zaslavsky, A., Christen, P., Georgakopoulos, D.: Context aware computing for the Internet of Things: a survey. IEEE Commun. Surv. Tutorials **16**(1), 414–454 (2014)
26. Ranganathan, A., Al-Muhtadi, J., Chetan, S., Campbell, R., Mickunas, M.D.: MiddleWhere: a middleware for location awareness in ubiquitous computing applications. In: Jacobsen, H.-A. (ed.) Middleware 2004. LNCS, vol. 3231, pp. 397–416. Springer, Heidelberg (2004). doi:10.1007/978-3-540-30229-2_21
27. Schmidt, C., Parashar, M.: A peer-to-peer approach to Web service discovery. World Wide Web **7**(2), 211–229 (2004)
28. Spalazzi, L., Taccari, G., Bernardini, A.: An Internet of Things ontology for earthquake emergency evaluation and response. In: Proceedings of the 2014 International Conference on Collaboration Technologies and Systems, pp. 528–534. IEEE, USA (2014)
29. van Kranenburg, H., Bargh, M.S., Iacob, S., Peddemors, A.: A context management framework for supporting context-aware distributed applications. IEEE Commun. Mag. **44**(8), 67–74 (2006)

Are Supercaps Ready for Ubiquitous Computing?

Andre Loechte(✉), Ludwig Horsthemke, Thomas Brinkmann, Michael Leuker, Andreas Heller, and Peter Gloesekoetter

Department of Electrical Engineering and CS,
University of Applied Sciences Muenster, 48565 Steinfurt, Germany
a.loechte@fh-muenster.de

Abstract. A lot of devices for ubiquitous computing are portable and can be used in any location. Therefore energy storage systems become increasingly important to power mobile devices. Supercaps provide a high power density, hence they are, for example, suited for driving high current peaks that occur during wireless transmissions. However, an analysis of first generation devices revealed that permanent application of the nominal voltage stressed the supercap to such an extent that the life cycle was unexpectedly short. Now a further analysis of second generation supercaps regarding reliability and life cycle will try to find out if the overall performance has improved.

1 Introduction

Electrolytic capacitors in general are used for smoothing signals, filtering and storing energy. So the application range of these components are widely spread. The supercaps by IOXUS for example are used for uninterrupted power supply (UPS) [1]. The main advantage of these components is their high energy density compared to other capacitor types and their high power density compared to batteries. Electrolytic capacitors are poled components whose anode is made of metal which is layered with a dielectric by electrolysis. The cathode of the capacitor can be made of a solid or non solid electrolyte, which is brought on surface of the dielectric. If the capacitor gets charged the electrical energy is stored within the electric field between the anode and cathode. To achieve a high capacity, i.e. a large layer-surface on small construction volume, these layers are rolled to a cylinder.

This paper is going to analyse the supercaps with eyesight on the following questions:

- What are the advantages and/or disadvantages of the 2nd generation supercaps compared to the previous generation?
- Has the performance of the supercaps improved well enough to use them as energy storage for ubiquitous computing?

The compared examples are shown in Fig. 1. Both capacitors are manufactured by IOXUS. Main differences are the volume ($55.8\,cm^3$ vs. $17.1\,cm^3$), the capacity (350 F vs. 300 F) and the nominal voltage (2.7 V vs. 2.3 V) [1,2].

C.R. García et al. (Eds.): UCAmI 2016, Part II, LNCS 10070, pp. 356–361, 2016.
DOI: 10.1007/978-3-319-48799-1_40

Fig. 1. Tested capacitor samples, left: old generation, right: new generation

2 Stress Methods

In order to make reliable conclusions about the capacitors degradation after a rather short period of usage, the capacitors were exposed to increased stress. Therefore three main factors of degradation are used: high operating voltage, high temperatures and a high amount of charge and discharge cycles [3]. From an electrical point of view, the aging of the hybrid capacitor causes a decrease of the capacity and a higher equivalent series resistance. There are different reasons for these effects. For example the carbon surface oxidates and the pores closes which results in a worser access. Moreover starving of the electrolyte leads to ionic depletion in the electrode. These effects are accentuated with voltage and temperature. High temperatures accelerate the aging because of the higher reactivity of the chemical components. When a high voltage is applied to the capacitor the decomposition of the electrolyte on the active surface of carbon substrate is accelerated [4,5]. The influence of temperature and voltage on degradation can be described by the Arrhenius equation which will be in the focus of our later analysis. The latter mentioned factor, the amount of charge cycles, represents the lifespan of the capacitors since the datasheet limits them by a fixed number. Thus, increasing the frequency of charging and discharging will directly accelerate the degradation over time [3].

3 Measuring Setup

The discharging curve of a capacitor with the initial voltage U_0 which is discharged through a resistor R is given by the equation

$$U(t) = U_0 \cdot \mathrm{e}^{-\frac{t}{R \cdot C}} \tag{1}$$

While discharging, the voltage across the capacitor is measured at two different points in time. Using the natural logarithm and subtracting both voltages lead to

$$C = \frac{t_2 - t_1}{R \cdot \ln\left(\frac{U_1}{U_2}\right)} \tag{2}$$

With $t_1 = 0s$, U_1 equals the initial voltage U_0. So the capacitance can be obtained by measuring the initial voltage U_0, discharging the capacitor over the resistor with known value R over fixed period of time t_2(360 s) and finally measuring the voltage U_2. R was chosen to be 1 Ω. Boards with several channels allow that multiple capacitors can be controlled and monitored by one microcontroller. The respective ambient temperatures were held constant by climatic chambers. The capacity was measured every 4 h over a timespan of 56 d. One sample was used for each parameter combination of the following table:

Stress parameter	Tested values
Voltage	2.43 V, 2.70 V, 2.97 V
Temperature	25°C, 45°C, 65°C

Moreover three capacitors, one capacitor for each temperature, were measured at nominal voltage but with a shorter cycletime of 1 h.

4 Measurement and Experimental Results

Figure 2 shows the measured capacity values over time at nominal voltage. Higher ambient temperatures of 45°C and 65°C significantly lead to a faster capacity drop.

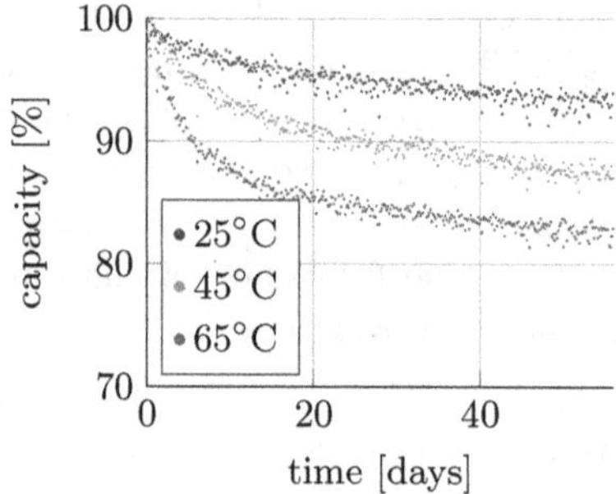

Fig. 2. Measured capacity of new capacitors at nominal voltage

As seen in Fig. 3 reducing the voltage to 2.43 V tends to an increased lifespan. Nevertheless high temperatures still harm the capacitors. In return the operation at higher voltages (2.97 V) leads to a faster degradation of the capacitor. Nevertheless the 90 % line is never reached at an ambient temperature of 25°C. So the operating temperature is a more determining factor for aging of a capacitor than the voltage (Fig. 4).

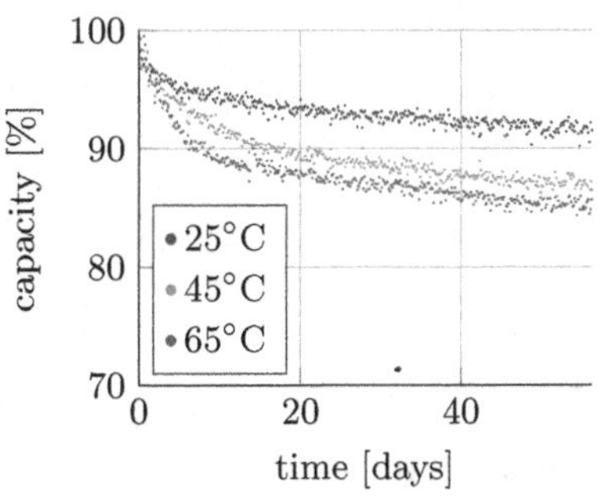

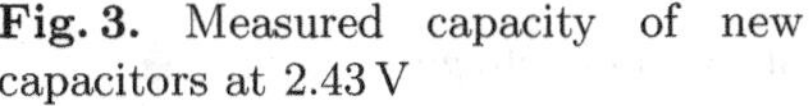

Fig. 3. Measured capacity of new capacitors at 2.43 V

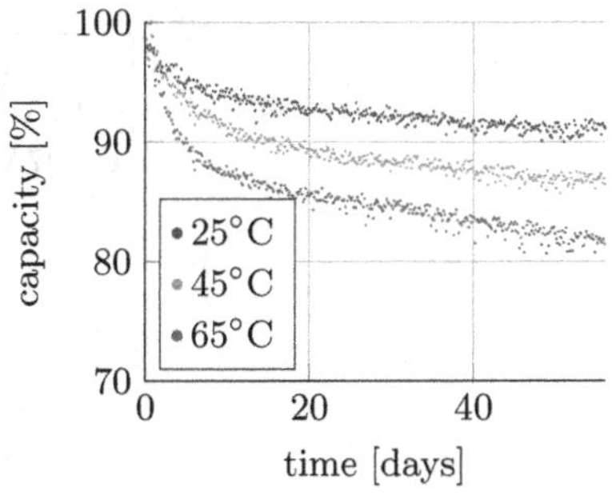

Fig. 4. Measured capacity of new capacitors at 2.97 V

5 Analysis

According to DIN EN 62391-2-1 an electrolytic capacitor is usable until its capacity has dropped 30 % below the nominal value specified by the manufacturer [6]. The stress test was extended by 16 d compared to the previous test of the first generation supercaps [5] to a total test time of 56 d. As seen in Chap. 4, the test time did not suffice to reach the 30 % limit. Therefore the criteria of defect was redefined to 10 % capacity drop of the starting value, in order to analyze the influence of the different stressing parameters. The redefined criteria results in lifetime values shown in the following table:

Temperature	25°C			45°C			65°C		
Voltage	2.43 V	2.70 V	2.97 V	2.43 V	2.70 V	2.97 V	2.43 V	2.70 V	2.97 V
Lifetime	n.r	n.r	n.r	25 d	16.5 d	14.5 d	7.25 d	5.5 d	4.5 d

At 25°C even the new criteria is not reached without voltage stressing. The lifetime at 25°C can be approximated through the Arrhenius equation. According to Arrhenius the reaction rate is proportional to $\exp(-E_a/(RT))$ in which E_a is the activation energy and T the absolute temperature. This proportionality can be seen by using logarithmic axis of ordinate to show the lifetime and an abscissa that present the inverse of the absolute temperature. Figure 5 shows the Arrhenius plot at different voltage levels. The higher the voltage, the lower the lifetime. Though, the difference between 2.97 V and 2.7 V is bigger than the difference between 2.7 V and 2.43 V. The actual lifetime at room temperature are the intersections with the 25°C line:

Voltage	2.43 V	2.70 V	2.97 V
Lifetime	101.8 d	57.4 d	51.4 d

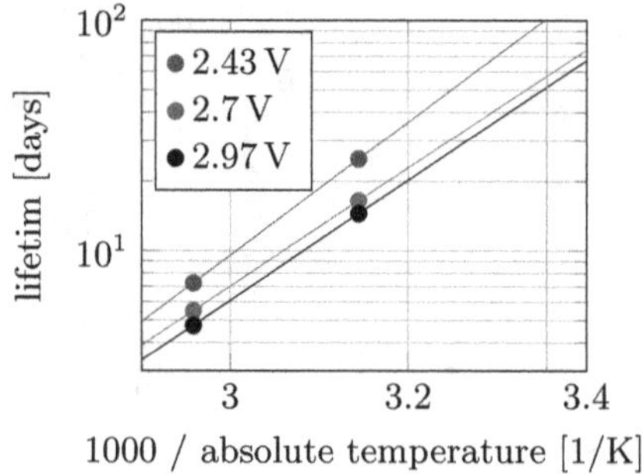

Fig. 5. Arrhenius plots as a function of voltage

Decreasing the voltage by 10 % nearly doubles the lifetime. The first generation supercaps showed this strong voltage dependence, too [5].

5.1 Comparison with First Generation Supercaps

Figure 6 presents the measurement results of the first generation supercaps [5]. Compared to the results of the new generation, they aged faster. Even at 40°C the capacitor nearly lost 30 % of its starting capacity within 40 d. In order to compare the lifetime at room temperature and nominal voltage, the data is again plotted in an Arrhenius plot (Fig. 7). The lifetime of the new generation is more than 5 times higher than the old generation at room temperature, but the temperature dependence is also higher. This results to closer values at higher temperatures.

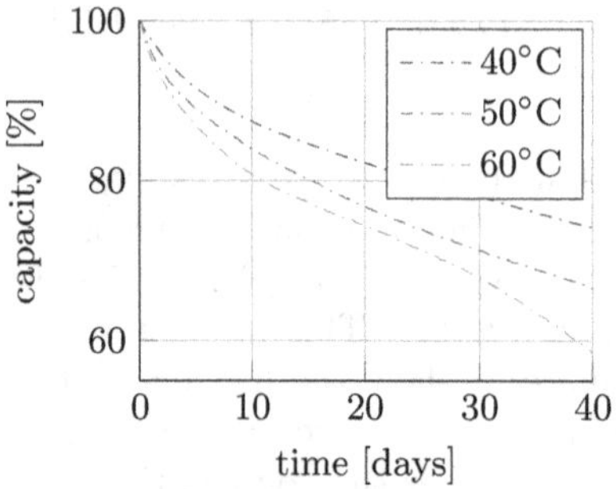

Fig. 6. Measured capacity of old gen capacitors at nominal voltage

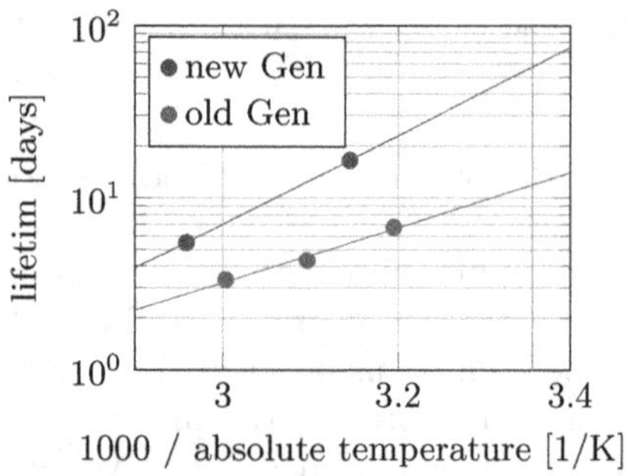

Fig. 7. Arrhenius-plot comparing lifetime of both generations

The new generation supercaps have a higher nominal voltage and capacity than the old generation. This increases the storable energy within the capacitor to

$$E_{\text{new}} = \frac{1}{2} \cdot C \cdot U^2 = \frac{1}{2} \cdot 350\,\text{F} \cdot (2.7\,\text{V})^2 = 1275.75\,\text{J} \tag{3}$$

compared to

$$E_{\text{old}} = \frac{1}{2} \cdot C \cdot U^2 = \frac{1}{2} \cdot 300\,\text{F} \cdot (2.3\,\text{V})^2 = 793.5\,\text{J}. \tag{4}$$

However, the volume is also increased compared to the older generation as seen in Fig. 1. For most mobile devices, volume is limited. Therefore it is important to know, whether the energy density could also be increased. The energy density of the new supercaps is

$$w_{\text{new}} = \frac{E_{\text{new}}}{V_{\text{new}}} = \frac{1275.75\,\text{J}}{55.8\,\text{cm}^3} = 22.9\,\text{J cm}^{-3}. \tag{5}$$

The energy density of the old generation is

$$w_{\text{old}} = \frac{E_{\text{old}}}{V_{\text{old}}} = \frac{793.5\,\text{J}}{17.1\,\text{cm}^3} = 46.4\,\text{cm}^{-3}. \tag{6}$$

The volume increased by a factor of 3.3 while the storable engergy increased by a factor of 1.6. So the improvement of the lifetime has the disadvantage of a lower energy density.

6 Conclusion

The new results show that the new generation of supercaps made a big step forward. On the one hand the nominal voltage is increased and thus comparable with battery cells. One the other hand the lifetime reliability has grown, too. The old generation capacitors showed a highly reduced lifetime at 2.3 V. The new generation extends the lifetime to a factor of 5 at a higher voltage (2.7 V). Even at 65°C and an overvoltage of 10 % did not yield to a defect (30 % drop) within the test time. Though, these improvements bring a lower energy density. Therefore the new generation supercaps are ready to power ubiquitous computing devices if there is enough space to place them. The new generation also has a strong dependence on the voltage. So the lifetime can be extended by using a smaller value than the nominal voltage.

References

1. IOXUS Inc., datasheet RSC2R7357SR (2010)
2. IOXUS Inc., datasheet Series: Snap In (2011)
3. Kreczanik, P., Venet, P., Hijazi, A., Clerc, G.: Study of supercapacitor aging and lifetime estimation according to voltage, temperature, and RMS current. IEEE Trans. Ind. Electron. **61** (2013)
4. Alcicek, G., Gualous, H., Venet, P., Gallay, R., Miraoui, A.: Experimental study of temperature effect on ultracapacitor ageing. In: European Conference on Power Electronics and Applications (2007)
5. Hoffmann, F., Loechte, A., Rebel, G., Krimphove, C., Gloesekoetter, P.: Degradation aware energy storage using hybrid capacitors. In: 2nd IEEE ENERGYCON (2012)
6. Din, E.N.: 62391-2-1: Part 2–1: Blank detail specification-Electric-double layer capacitors for power application-Assessment level EZ (IEC 62391-2-1:2006) (2007)

Design of an Architecture of Communication Oriented to Medical and Sports Applications in IoT

Freddy Feria[1], Octavio J. Salcedo Parra[1,2(✉)], and Brayan S. Reyes Daza[2]

[1] Universidad Nacional de Colombia, Bogotá, Colombia
{faferiab,ojsalcedop}@unal.edu.co
[2] Internet Inteligente Research Group, Universidad Distrital Francisco José de Caldas, Bogotá, Colombia
osalcedo@udistrital.edu.co, bsreyesd@correo.udistrital.edu.co

Abstract. The design of an architecture of communication oriented to medical and sports applications is presented, with the goal to get a series of information collected from a network of portable sensors, those sensors are arranged in the body of the person in order to gather vital constants of the user and then transmit them to a web service on the internet, as well as to monitor the state of health and user's physical performance.

Keywords: Bluetooth low energy · Internet of things · WSN · Web services

1 Introduction

Nowadays the growth of sources of information and interconnection represents great challenges in terms of the volume of data handled by the network and the inherent security that should have that data; however, it presents opportunities in a field that will impact education, communication, business, science, Government and humanity, the Internet of things (IoT). The concept was simple but powerful: If all the objects of our daily lives were equipped with identifiers and wireless connectivity, these objects could communicate with others and be managed by computers, thus is could follow and tell all, and greatly reduce waste, losses and costs. Provide computers to perceive the world and get all the information we need to make decisions. This paradigm of approaching the people, and not just to the Internet devices, needs underlying technologies that facilitate the transition from the real world to the web world and more precisely the use of personal data, that will allow the collection of data from a person, the treatment of the such information and making decisions based on the information collected.

At this point technologies such as personal area networks (PAN) or body (BAN), can contribute significantly to the development and conception of an IoT more closer to the user so that allow a user from satisfy a lifestyle, to meet a need or solve a disability. The constant Monitoring of the health of a person with any condition is only possible with portable devices that non-invasive and that allow to carry out a comfortable and secure life by alerting and providing information about the development of the State of health to the medical authorities in case of emergency.

C.R. García et al. (Eds.): UCAmI 2016, Part II, LNCS 10070, pp. 362–367, 2016.
DOI: 10.1007/978-3-319-48799-1_41

2 Related Work

Some of the significant advances aiming at defining exactly what IoT is, many of these works propose features that a system must meet to be able to accomplish this paradigm and they assign names to the constituent parts of the system (nodes, gateways, devices, layers, modules, etc.) [3, 9], and based on these definitions propose a number of architectures most of them using Gateways that facilitate the interconnection of a series of sensors and interactions with the web world as well as the design of protocols that allow these devices to comply with specifications of power, speed, reliability, loyalty and security [2, 7]. Besides, the two large existing communication links are explored: one, between portable devices of the user, and two, between these devices and the internet [5, 6]. There is also related research specifically to medical applications and health systems, monitoring of patients both in hospitals [8, 10], as well as in sports activities [1], refining the previously proposed architectures in some cases and generating new architectures in others, depending on the context and strongly oriented to the final application.

3 Description of the Proposed Architecture

The main goal of he proposed architecture is to use the fundamental aspects of both PAN and IoT technologies and achieve interoperability between them. To bring an object to the Internet it is necessary to meet a series of requirements proposed by the Internet Engineering Task Force (IETF): unique identifiers for each object or service, management of ID for the object (security, authentication, privacy), presence of people and devices, geographical location, modeling of objects for search and discovery, follow-up and support of mobility for moving objects, interoperability and interconnection, global connectivity, scalability, autonomy, restrictions of the object (power, energy), web services and data traffic. Unique identifiers will correspond to the web service that is implemented for the analysis and collection of data, as well as the modeling of objects, global connectivity and web services. The control device will be responsible for the Administration of IDs, geographic location, interconnection, scalability and autonomy, restrictions of the object and data traffic.

The Fig. 1 show the architecture which consists of three parts, remote portable devices, Portable Control device and the Web service application. The remote portable devices (RPD) are sensors and actuators that interact with the user. Each device is comprised of a sensor or actuator, a microcontroller, a means of communication and a battery. These devices perform the data collection and the shipping of instructions to a Gateway through the Portable Control Device. Such devices must be auto-configurable, autonomous, light and with a very low power consumption.

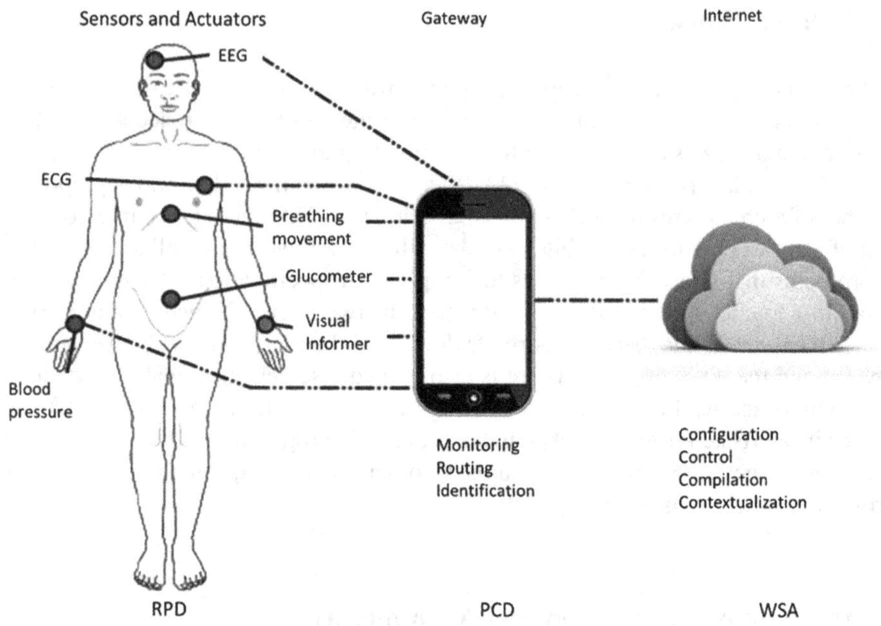

Fig. 1. Proposed network architecture

The responsible for the administration of devices and data from the system is the Portable Control Device (PCD), which also manages the connection with the RPDs through Bluetooth low energy technology. On one hand, the device must be capable of performing operations of addiction, reading, updating, and removal of devices on the network, on the other hand, it must carry out the exchange of information between remote devices and web services. It must temporarily save the collected data for later transmission to the internet, as well as having the ability to handle events of importance at local scale.

The PCD is the object that will be taken to the Internet and the RPD are the properties and characteristics of that object, which will be consulted and informed according to the user's requirements. The data processing will be at PCD level and RPD reducing traffic to Internet and simplifying the system. Finally the Web service application (WSA) is responsible for contextualizing the received data, store it and present it in such a way that the user can make decisions based on that information. It has in addition domain rules to filter relevant data and generate events and alerts when necessary.

3.1 Remote Portable Devices

The remote portable devices are deployed in the body or around a person, must not be invasive, must have a low power consumption and tolerate environmental conditions. Each of these devices must have an own identification number and one assigned by the network so it can be addressed and managed, it should distinguish the type of device and the characteristics of the product, and be able to inform the operational status of itself, and report damage and breakdowns. To achieve interoperability, and the modeling of them, they possess a series of common features that allow its configuration and the obtaining of data in a generic way implementing a protocol designed for the collection of data of web objects, the common things protocol CTP.

Such devices are divided into two groups Personal sensing devices and Personal Action Devices.

The function of these remote devices is shown in Fig. 2, where the units will sense or will act according to its type, once they have finished they will inform to the central unit the outcomes and will go to a waiting period. Where there is an important event this must be reported immediately to the control unit. The communication will be through Bluetooth low energy, which allows the transmission of data reliably at high speed, with low energy consumption and has the advantage of the use of different profiles according to the designed application.

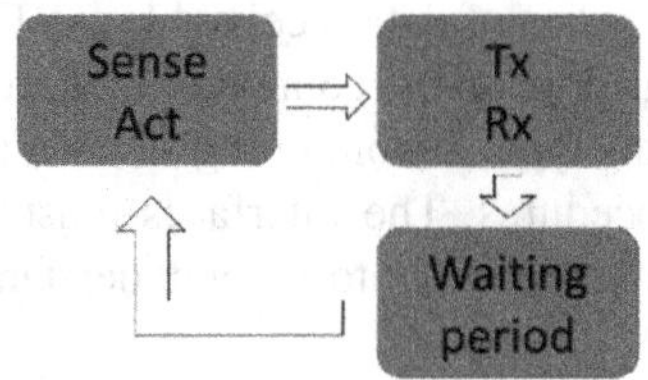

Fig. 2. Operation of the RPD scheme

3.2 Common Things Protocol

This Protocol provides a specification that enables interoperability across different standards of communication and the coexistence of IoT protocols, but giving priority to simplicity, efficiency, and functionality to build specific systems of IoT. CTP takes into account existing standard specifications and the needs of the final applications that are required by the objects. This integrates the strategies, concepts, and terms of some alternatives, such as the concept of TEDs in IEEE1451 to provide information from the devices, working modes in sensors and actuators, and concepts of Zigbee as clusters and endpoints.

3.3 Bluetooth Low Energy

It is a technology for wireless personal area networks oriented to applications in the field of health, fitness, safety and domestic automation among others. Bluetooth technology offers advantages over other technologies used in the market, with transfer rates of 1 Mb/s, 128-bit AES encryption, 6 ms latency and shipping time of 3 ms, the number of slave devices is dependent on the implementation, the power consumption is 0. 01 W having devices that can run a whole year with a CR 2032 battery, also includes profiles of work oriented to applications including medical and fitness applications. In comparison with other technologies it has an improved performance, lower power consumption and higher relationship of power vs transfer rate.

3.4 Portable Control Devices

This is not properly a device, but rather, an application used for the administration of the RPD. This application must add, read, edit, update, and remove peripheral devices on the network. It is deployed using Bluetooth Low Energy technology, where the app will connect from time to time depending on the number of RPDs, in such way the application serves as a gateway between the data collected and the service web, thus simplifying the given architecture by reducing the amount of equipment required and taking advantage of existing technologies.

3.5 Web Service Application

Finally the data are entered in a web service and it becomes information usable by the application. This application must take into account the context in which the data is located, it is not the same, a series of data received by an ECG of a person in medical treatment and a person doing sport, so the context of the information is important when developing applications of this type. Secondly registration and data storage is vital for tracking and traceability procedures. The Interfaces must be clear and should easily expose the information so that it is obvious to a user understand what you want to convey.

3.6 Service Oriented Architecture (SOA)

Since we want to implement a web service that manages the data collected, the best design for system architecture corresponds to a service-oriented type. Through this architecture is sought that the system is distributed heterogeneously to achieve greater interoperation with the existing solutions on the market, and low coupling so that you can scale according to the growth of the platform.

4 Conclusions and Further Work

Once the architecture is deployed, it is necessary to carry out the implementation of it in a way so that it can evaluate performance and make the necessary settings that allow to define factors such as efficiency, quality, QoS, the user experience, etc.

As a platform for the transmission of data, it is important to count with a Smartphone that allows to monitor the data received and sent, in addition it must have Bluetooth technology. For the web service, there are platforms for collection of data with SOA architectures in the market that would be worth exploring.

The proposed design takes the best of different proposed architectures, in such way that it meets the specified objective. The use of Bluetooth in wireless sensing networks is widely documented in the medical field, the technology as well as the proposed architecture have cast out that the system can acquire, transmit, store and display in real time, reliably and accurately, vital signs of a person [4].

References

1. Altini, M., Penders, J., Roebbers, H.: An android-based body area network gateway for mobile health applications. In: Holst Centre / IMEC the Netherlands, Eindhoven (2010)
2. Asensio, A., Marco, A., Blasco, R., Casas, R.: Protocol and Architecture to Bring Things into Internet of Things. Aragon Institute of Research, University Zaragoza, 50018 Zaragoza, Spain (2014)
3. Bassi, A., Bauer, M., Fiedler, M., Kramp, T., van Kranenburg, R., Lange, S., Meissner, S.: Enabling Things to Talk: Designing IoT solutions with the IoT Architectural Reference Model, pp. 1–349. Springer, Heidelberg (2013)
4. Yu, B., Xu, L., Li, Y.: Bluetooth Low Energy (BLE) based mobile electrocardiogram monitoring system. Sina-Dutch Biomedical and Information Engineering School, Northeastern University, Shenyang, China, pp. 763–767. IEEE, Shenyang (2012)
5. Castellani, P., Bui, N., Casari, P., Rossi, M., Shelby, Z., Zorzi, M.: Architecture and Protocols for the Internet of Things: A Case Study. Department of Information Engineering, University of Padova, Padova, Italy. Consorzio Ferrara Ricerche (CFR), Ferrara, Italy (2010)
6. Singh, K.K., Sing, M.P., Singh, D.K.: Routing protocols in wireless sensor networks –A survey. In: IJCSES, vol. 1(20) (2010)
7. Patel, M., Wang, J.: Applications, challenges, and prospective in emerging body area networking technologies. Wireless Commun. **17**(1), 80–88 (2010)
8. Poorter, E., Moerman, I., Demeester, P.: Enabling direct connectivity between heterogeneous objects in the internet of things through a network-service-oriented architecture. J. Wireless Commun. Netw. **2011**, 1–14 (2011)
9. Rashwand, S., Misic, J.: Bridging Between IEEE 802.15.6 and IEEE 802.11e for Wireless Healthcare Networks. University of Manitoba, Department of Computer Science. Ryerson University, Department of Computer Science, pp. 303–337 (2012)
10. WSO: A Reference Architecture for the Internet of Things (2015). www.wso2.com

A Computationally Inexpensive Classifier Merging Cellular Automata and MCP-Neurons

Niklas Karvonen(✉), Basel Kikhia, Lara Lorna Jiménez, Miguel Gómez Simón, and Josef Hallberg

Department of Computer Science, Electrical and Space Engineering, Luleå University of Technology, 971 87 Luleå, Sweden
niklas.karvonen@ltu.se

Abstract. There is an increasing need for personalised and context-aware services in our everyday lives and we rely on mobile and wearable devices to provide such services. Context-aware applications often make use of machine-learning algorithms, but many of these are too complex or resource-consuming for implementation on some devices that are common in pervasive and mobile computing. The algorithm presented in this paper, named CAMP, has been developed to obtain a classifier that is suitable for resource-constrained devices such as FPGA:s, ASIC:s or microcontrollers. The algorithm uses a combination of the McCulloch-Pitts neuron model and Cellular Automata in order to produce a computationally inexpensive classifier with a small memory footprint. The algorithm consists of a sparse binary neural network where neurons are updated using a Cellular Automata rule as the activation function. Output of the classifier is depending on the selected rule and the interconnections between the neurons. Since solving the input-output mapping mathematically can not be performed using traditional optimization algorithms, the classifier is trained using a genetic algorithm. The results of the study show that CAMP, despite its minimalistic structure, has a comparable accuracy to that of more advanced algorithms for the datasets tested containing few classes, while performing poorly on the datasets with a higher amount of classes. CAMP could thus be a viable choice for solving classification problems in environments with extreme demands on low resource consumption.

1 Introduction

Neural networks are algorithms that have proven to perform with great accuracy in a wide variety of applications [16,20,23]. They have important and useful characteristics, such as the ability to approximate nonlinear functions, to use different activation functions, to perform both regression and classification, and to be executed in parallel. Neural networks, however, require that all weights between the layers are stored in memory. In addition, these weights are floating point values that need to be multiplied and summed together for being used in a discretization of a continuous function. This makes Neural Networks challenging to implement in hardware or in resource-constrained devices such as FPGA:s.

C.R. García et al. (Eds.): UCAmI 2016, Part II, LNCS 10070, pp. 368–379, 2016.
DOI: 10.1007/978-3-319-48799-1_42

Even for more sophisticated devices like microcontrollers, this can pose problems if there are hard constraints on memory or real-time response.

In order to implement a neural network in such resource-constrained devices, memory consumption, computational complexity and the use of floating point values must be addressed. This could, for example, be achieved by simplifying the neural network by using integer or even binary values and reducing the interconnectivity between neurons. The complexity of implementing the activation function in hardware is of course depending on the function used, but the common sigmoid and hyperbolic tangent functions are not easily implemented in devices such as FPGA:s [27]. This paper aims to find a simplified model addressing all these problems in order to produce a neural network that is suitable for hardware implementation, or for use on devices with limited resources.

1.1 The McCulloch-Pitts Neuron Model

The neuron model introduced by McCulloch-Pitts in 1943 is an interesting choice for our problem, since it uses only binary values for both neuron output and network weights. Inputs, that are of either inhibitory or excitatory type, are summed together and compared to a threshold value, which determines the output of the neuron. Inhibitory inputs override excitatory inputs, meaning that if there are any inhibitory inputs active, the neuron will always output zero.

Due to its binary-only values, the architecture of the MCP-network is much easier to implement in hardware than a traditional neural network. Although being structurally well-suited to run on primitive devices, there are two problems using the MCP-network for resource constrained classification:

1. It can only model linearly separable problems [21].
2. The computational complexity of three layered MCP-networks is quadratic when using an equal amount of neurons in each layer.

The first problem can be overcome by replacing the activation function with a non-linear one, while the second problem requires to reduce the number of connections between neurons. While there are many ways to solve these problems, this paper examines how principles of binary Cellular Automata could be used for doing so. Binary Cellular Automata has several interesting properties that fit our problem domain, such as having a low computational complexity, being parallelizable and having been proven to be useful in pattern recognition [8,18].

1.2 Cellular Automata

Cellular Automata (CA) is known to work at the edge of chaos and can show complex behaviour emerging from seemingly simple rules [19]. A binary one-dimensional CA consists of binary cells on a lattice. The cells' states are updated in timesteps in the following way: the next state for each cell is calculated by looking at the cell's own state together with its left and right neighbourhood, called a *configuration*. This configuration, whose size is denoted by $\mathbf{r}$, is used for

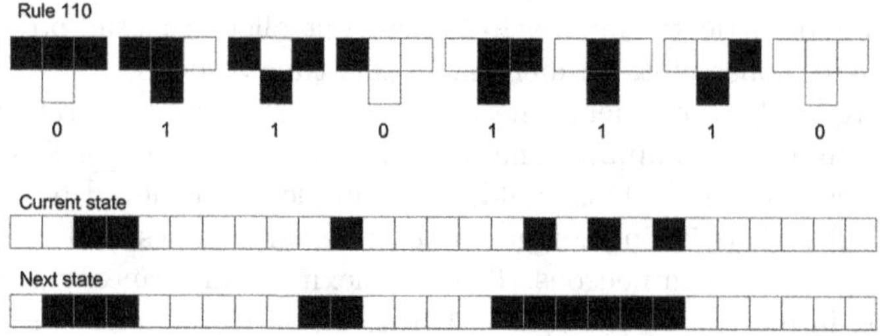

Fig. 1. Rule 110 for a 1-dimensional binary cellular automata. The rule is named by translating the output pattern to an integer (0b01101110 = 110). At the bottom is an example of a CA using the rule to evolve one time step.

looking up the cell's next state in a rule table that holds all possible combinations of configurations. In the case of, for example, 3-neighborhood binary CA, one can construct 256 possible rules. Rules are commonly named by first permuting the possible configurations in an orderly fashion and then constructing a bit pattern from the according next states that is translated to an integer number [26].

Despite its deceitful simplicity, CA has been shown to be turing complete even for a 3-neighbourhood binary cellular automata using rule 110 [10], making it interesting to study this setup and its applications further (Fig. 1).

1.3 Research Questions

The hypothesis assumed in this paper, is that using a CA with rule 110 as an activation function could increase the performance of the McCulloch-Pitts model while reducing the number of needed interconnections between neurons (Fig. 2). The research questions addressed are:

1. Can a 3-neighbourhood binary cellular automata using rule 110 be used as an activation function in a simplified MCP-network to create a computationally inexpensive classifier?
2. What is the accuracy of such an algorithm compared to common machine learning algorithms?

The paper is structured as follows: Sect. 2 reviews related work, Sect. 3 describes the CAMP classifier, Sect. 4 explains how CAMP is trained using a Genetic Algorithm, Sect. 5 explains the testing setup, Sect. 6 shows the performance of the classifier, Sect. 7 discusses the results, and Sect. 8 proposes future work and concludes the paper.

2 Related Work

3-neighbourhood binary cellular automata has shown promising results in pattern recognition. Chaudhuri et al. have done extensive work on additive cellular

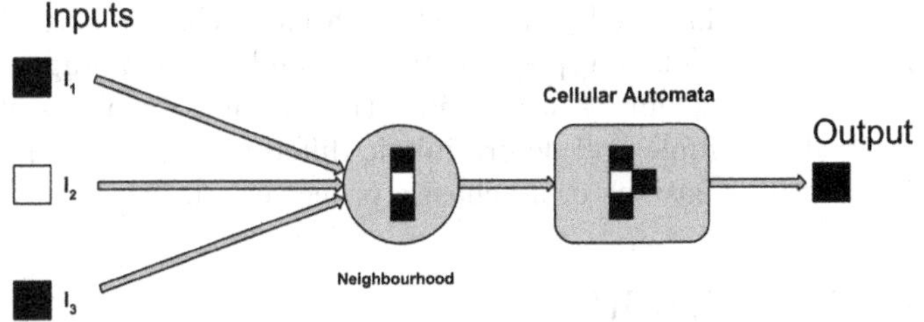

Fig. 2. The CAMP neuron. Each neuron has 3 incoming connections. Both inputs and outputs are binary-valued.

automata [9]. Among their work we find a multi-class pattern classifier using Multiple Attractor Cellular Automata (MACA). This classifier saved on average 34 % of computer memory using pseudo-exhaustive patterns compared to the straight-forward approach of storing the class of each pattern directly [8]. Maji et al. performed pattern recognition with CA:s using General Multiple Attractor Cellular Automata (GMACA). They proposed an associative memory using CA that was found to be 33 % more effective than a hopfield network [18].

The pattern recognition algorithms using (G)MACA:s are highly computationally efficient, but they only act as content-addressable memories and do not create generalised models over data. They also require that the learnt patterns are close to each other in Hamming Distance [15], which is problematic since data from e.g. sensors and such need to be encoded into binary patterns in a suitable way (e.g. gray code [6], thermometer encoding [12] or scatter code [22]). The CAMP algorithm, however, does not require such binary encoding of input data due to its non-constant neighborhood configuration inspired by traditional feedforward neural networks.

Combining principles from Neural Networks with Cellular Automata is not in itself a novel approach. Cellular Automata Neural Networks (CNN:s, note this is not to be confused with Convolutional Neural Networks), for example, are also neural networks using principles from CA. The focus of CNN research has however mainly been to improve the accuracy of classification and regression. In a CNN, decimal values are used for weights and neuron outputs like in a traditional neural network. Cells are often connected in a 2-dimensional grid with an 8-neighbor configuration, and are updated using their neighbors values as inputs to an output function. Cells' outputs are connected to other cells and/or the output of the algorithm. CNN:s are promising and have shown to be successful in, for example, image processing [5], fluid dynamics [17] and statistical physics [14]. The CAMP algorithm differs from a CNN in the way that each cell can connect to any $\mathbf{r}$ cells in the CA, not just adjacent ones, and it uses only binary values and relies on binary logic operations instead of floating point value computations.

Another field of research related to the work in this paper is chaotic neural networks. There is research showing that chaotic dynamics may exist in biological neurons [2–4,13] which have led to research with using chaotic activation functions in neural networks. These types of networks can have advantages regarding computational time and memory usage, since the complex dynamics of the neurons are described by simple and deterministic difference equations rather than models of differential equations or stochastic processes [1].

3 The CAMP Algorithm

This work tries to utilize the fact that CA works at the edge of chaos, and is turing complete even for a binary neighborhood of three cells, in order to create a simplistic neural network. In traditional Cellular Automata, a configuration consists of adjacent cells, but in order to create the proposed algorithm, this principle is loosened to allowing cells to get their neighbourhood from *any* 3 cells, not just adjacent ones. Another way of looking at the algorithm, is considering it to be a MCP-neural network, where each neuron has 3 connections to neurons in the previous layer and all connections are of excitatory types (unit weight) only.

A CAMP neuron gets updated in the following two steps:

1. Determination of its neighbourhood configuration.
2. Calculation of the next state using the CA rule for that configuration.

In essence, the CAMP algorithm works in the same manner as a feed-forward neural network. Since the aim of this paper is to keep resource consumptions at a minimum, a three layered network structure was used (input, hidden, output). All layers were chosen to have equal size. To perform the classification, the output layer's pattern is compared to chosen output patterns for the different classes.

The memory M and time T required by the CAMP algorithm for a number of neurons n in "Big O" notation evaluates to (assuming n neurons in each layer):

$$\begin{aligned} M(n) &= \Theta(n) \\ T(n) &= \Theta(n) \end{aligned} \tag{1}$$

This can be compared to a "traditional" feed-forward Neural Network (assuming n neurons in each layer):

$$\begin{aligned} M(n) &= \Theta(n^2) \\ T(n) &= O(n^2) \end{aligned} \tag{2}$$

It should be noted though, that CAMP requires we create a neuron *for each bit* in an input variable. This means that the number of neurons n is always higher for CAMP than it is for a Neural Network by a multiplier that has the size of the input variables bit-resolution. This number is however constant, so the Big-O notation comparison still holds.

The CPU operations required to update each CAMP neuron can easily be calculated due to the simplistic structure of the classifier (assuming AND, OR and NOT are part of the CPU instruction set and are atomic). The operations consists of evaluating the boolean expression that is the activation function. For rule 110 this expression is:

$$q = (\neg a \wedge b) \vee (b \wedge \neg c) \vee (\neg b \wedge c) \tag{3}$$

Where q is the next state for a neuron with incoming connections a, b, c. In the case of rule 110, each such update requires 8 instructions which means that in order to calculate the activation functions of n neurons we must perform 8n CPU instructions.

As we can see, the CAMP algorithm holds several interesting properties that are important for machine learning algorithms running in resource-constrained environments:

1. It has a small memory footprint.
2. It is computationally inexpensive.
3. It does not make use of floating point values, making it faster to compute on less sophisticated processors [11].
4. Updates of neurons are done locally, i.e. does not need access to a global state making parallel computations possible.
5. It has a simple structure and logic making it suitable for FPGA or ASIC implementation.

4 Training of the Classifier

The output of the classifier depends solely on the set of connections between the cells, and training the classifier consists of finding the best set of connections among the nodes that will map an input set to an desired output set. The chaotic behaviour of the CA, however, makes it problematic to solve this mapping mathematically. Exhaustive search is not an option either, since there are C possible combinations of connections for a three layer network with I, J, K number of nodes in each layer:

$$C = \left(\frac{I!}{r!(I-r)!}\right)^{J} \left(\frac{J!}{r!(J-r)!}\right)^{K} \tag{4}$$

This means that even for a limited neighbourhood of $\mathbf{r} = 3$, the number of permutations of connections escalates quickly. In order to find a connection set, we instead rely on a genetic algorithm to converge towards a solution. This is unfortunate, since this does not guarantee finding the optimal solution. The following sections describes the genetic algorithm's four steps:

1. Chromosome encoding.
2. Fitness calculation.
3. Selection.
4. Crossover and mutation.

4.1 Chromosome Encoding

The input connections to a neuron from the previous layer, is represented using a bit string, or a connection-vector, where each bit corresponds to a neuron in the previous layer. A set bit indicates there's a connection to the corresponding neuron. Each connection-vector becomes a gene, and chromosomes are created by concatenating all the connection-vectors (genes) into one binary string using a lexicographical order.

4.2 Fitness Calculation

The fitness F for each chromosome is simply calculated by running the algorithm with the chromosomes connections and counting the amount of correct classifications among the q training examples.

$$F = \sum_{1}^{q} (classifierOutput_q \wedge correctClassPattern_q). \tag{5}$$

4.3 Selection of Individuals

Roulette wheel selection was used to select mating individuals from the current population based on their fitness results. The 10 most fit individuals were added to the next generation unmodified (elitism).

4.4 Crossover and Mutation

Uniform crossover was used where both parents' connection vectors for each cell was equally probable to be used in the offspring chromosome. Mutation rate was set to 5 percent and mutation was performed by randomly changing one of the offspring connections. Each offspring could only mutate once.

5 Test Setup

In order to evaluate the CAMP algorithm the WEKA 3.7.12 platform was used [25]. WEKA is an open source tool for machine learning and data mining, that supports several standard machine learning algorithms of various types along with other useful tools such as validation methods, pre-processing, visualization, and feature selection. The CAMP algorithm was implemented as a classifier in WEKA since that allowed for the algorithm to be benchmarked against validated implementations of other machine learning algorithms. This also makes it easier for other researchers to put the results presented here into perspective.

5.1 Datasets and Feature Selection

Six different classification datasets with numerical features were used in order to evaluate the algorithms performance (see Table 1). These datasets are all included with the WEKA distribution and are thus publically available. Further, they have all been part of published scientific work, making it possible for researchers to compare our results with other work on the same datasets.

For each dataset, the three highest ranked features were selected using InfoGain [7] to avoid overfitting. All results were obtained using 10-fold cross validation.

5.2 CAMP Setup

Dataset instances' binary representations were used to setup the input layer (each bit corresponding to a CAMP-neuron). Both the hidden layer and the output layer were chosen to have the same size as the input layer. Each output neuron corresponds to a choice of a class. For example, a three class dataset would have the output configurations; "100...." = class A, "010...." = class B, "001...." = class C. Classification is then performed by evaluating the Hamming Distance between the CAMP output and these output configurations. Training was performed by running the genetic algorithm for 1000 generations with a population size of 100 and with a 10 individual elite.

5.3 Comparative Algorithms Setup

To put the CAMP performance in perspective, five of WEKAs standard machine learning algorithms of different types (Bayesian, Tree, Neural Networks, Ensemble) were used as a comparison. Since this was performed only to have an indicative comparison of CAMPs performance, all the comparative algorithms used their default settings in WEKA in order for the experiments to be easily repeated. This means that neither CAMP nor the comparative algorithms were adapted in any way to fit the datasets and it is therefore important to note that the results presented here are not to be considered the best performance possible for neither CAMP nor the comparative algorithms. The results from the different classifiers are shown in Table 2.

6 Results

The results in Table 2 show that CAMP works as a classifier. In 2 out of 6 datasets CAMP shows less than 4 percent worse accuracy compared to a Multilayer Perceptron which, while in half the tests this figure is less than 10 percent. Also, for 2 out of the 6 datasets, the CAMP algorithm even performs marginally better than 3 of the other comparative algorithms. This is promising and shows that the algorithm could prove beneficial, at least for certain kinds of classification problems. The datasets for which the algorithm has the highest performance have in common a low number of classes. Similarly, the algorithm seems to perform poorly on datasets with a higher amount of classes.

Table 1. Description of the tested datasets.

Dataset	Classes	Instances	Features selected	Description	Creator
Glass	7	214	Mg, Al, K	Dataset for classification of types of glass motivated by criminological investigation	B. German – Central Research Establishment Home Office Forensic Science Service Aldermaston, Reading, Berkshire RG7 4PN
Ionosphere	2	351	a05, a06, a33	Radar data classifying good or bad radar returns. Good radar returns are those showing evidence of some type of structure in the ionosphere. Bad returns are those that do not; their signals pass through the ionosphere	Space Physics Group Applied Physics Laboratory Johns Hopkins University Sigillito, V. G., Wing, S. P., Hutton, L. V., and Baker, K. B. (1989)
Segment-Challenge	7	1500	Intensity-mean, rawred-mean, rawgreen-mean	The instances were drawn randomly from a database of 7 outdoor images. The images were hand segmented to create a classification for every pixel. Each instance is a 3 × 3 region	Vision Group, University of Massachusetts
Labour	2	57	Wage-increase-first-year, wage-increase-second-year, statutoru-holidays	Data includes all collective agreements reached in the business and personal services sector for locals with at least 500 members (teachers, nurses, university staff, police, etc.) in Canada in 87 and first quarter of 88	Collective Barganing Review, monthly publication, Labour Canada, Industrial Relations Information Service, Ottawa, Ontario, K1A 0J2, Canada
Diabetes	2	768	Plas, mass, age	A diagnostic, binary-valued variable is investigated to show whether the patient shows signs of diabetes according to World Health Organization criteria	National Institute of Diabetes and Digestive and Kidney Diseases, Vincent Sigillito (vgs@aplcen.apl.jhu.edu) Research Center, RMI Group Leader Applied Physics Laboratory The Johns Hopkins University

Table 2. The classification results for the algorithms on the different datasets.

	CAMP	Naive Bayes	Bayes Net	Multi-layered perceptron	K-star	J48	Random forest
Glass	**43.45 %**	49.06 %	63.55 %	63.08 %	64.49 %	64.49 %	67.29 %
Ionosphere	**80.34 %**	86.32 %	89.46 %	87.46 %	89.17 %	90.60 %	90.03 %
Segment-challenge	**41.80 %**	60.60 %	70.53 %	78.47 %	76.20 %	81.00 %	86.00 %
Labour	**64.91 %**	84.21 %	78.90 %	84.20 %	80.70 %	80.70 %	84.20 %
Unbalanced	**98.60 %**	98.60 %	98.60 %	98.60 %	98.60 %	98.60 %	97.90 %
Diabetes	**72.91 %**	76.43 %	74.22 %	76.43 %	72.40 %	74.61 %	72.53 %

7 Discussion

It is important to look at the CAMP results with its computational complexity and simple structure in mind. In this light, the performance of the algorithm is impressive. Also, results could most likely be improved since there were no efforts made to adjust the algorithm to fit each dataset. By using different feature selections and feature scaling or changing parameters such as bit resolution, the algorithm could be better matched against a certain dataset.

Results suggest that the algorithm performs better on binary classification problems. In Cellular Automata there can exist states that can't be reached from some previous state given restrictions of rules and timesteps. Therefore, increasing the number of output patterns (states) in a classification problem will reduce the solution space for the CAMP input-output mapping. It is therefore possible that reducing the single multiclass classification problems into multiple binary classification problems (similar to e.g. multiclass Support Vector Machines [24]), could improve the accuracy of the algorithm. In the same way, increasing the number of output patterns per class could improve the accuracy by increasing the input-output mapping solution space. Both these solutions, however, could impose a much higher level of implementation complexity for ASIC:s and FPGA:s.

Another possible way of increasing the accuracy of CAMP would be to use an expanded neighbourhood size in order to allow for more complex computations. This would, however, result in both a larger memory footprint and a higher computational complexity, since the number of connections between neurons would increase. Using a deeper network, with two or more hidden layers, could also allow for a higher complexity of computations, but with the same tradeoff as an expanded neighborhood.

A final way that could improve the classification performance, would be to use different rules. The CA rule 110 was chosen for this work based on its ability of universal computation, but further studies of the algorithm should include the use of other rules as well. Another interesting study would be to expand the algorithm to use non-uniform cellular automata. Each neuron would then have its own update rule, thereby drastically expanding the solution space for the input-output mapping. This would, however, increase the memory usage of the algorithm and could increase the number of atomic operations needed to update the neurons.

8 Conclusions and Future Work

This paper proposes a binary-valued classifier based on a combination of Cellular Automata and the McCulloch-Pitts neuron model. The classifier is designed to be computationally inexpensive and highly suitable for microcontrollers, FPGA:s and ASIC:s. Evaluation was performed using six different datasets with their three highest ranked features selected using InfoGain. Results show that the classifier is a viable choice for certain problems where resource constraints are high.

Future work should include studying how reducing the single multiclass classification problems into multiple binary classification problems affect the accuracy of the algorithm. Another study would be to allow a higher amount of connections between neurons, as this allows for more complex input-output computations. Furthermore, the use of hybrid CA's (each neuron/cell having its own update rule) could also be studied, but both these studies would make the algorithm itself more complex and thus less suited for the initial purpose.

References

1. Adachi, M., Aihara, K.: Associative dynamics in a chaotic neural network. Neural Netw. **10**(1), 83–98 (1997)
2. Aihara, K., Matsumoto, G.: Forced oscillations and routes to chaos in the Hodgkin-Huxley axons and squid giant axons. In: Degn, H., Holden, A.V., Olsen, L.F. (eds.) Chaos in Biological Systems, pp. 121–131. Springer, New York (1987)
3. Aihara, K., Matsumoto, G.: Chaotic oscillations and bifurcations in squid giant axons. Chaos **12**, 257–269 (1986)
4. Basar, E.: Chaos in Brain Function: Containing Original Chapters by E. Basar and T.H. Bullock and Topical Articles Reprinted from the Springer Series in Brain Dynamics. Springer Science & Business Media, Heidelberg (2012)
5. Batrk, A., Gnay, E.: Efficient edge detection in digital images using a cellular neural network optimized by differential evolution algorithm. Expert Syst. Appl. **36**(2), 2645–2650 (2009). http://linkinghub.elsevier.com/retrieve/pii/S0957417408000420
6. Bitner, J.R., Ehrlich, G., Reingold, E.M.: Efficient generation of the binary reflected gray code and its applications. Commun. ACM **19**(9), 517–521 (1976). http://portal.acm.org/citation.cfm?doid=360336.360343
7. Bolon-Canedo, V., Sanchez-Marono, N., Alonso-Betanzos, A.: A review of feature selection methods on synthetic data. Knowl. Inf. Syst. **34**(3), 483–519 (2013)
8. Chattopadhyay, S., Adhikari, S., Sengupta, S., Pal, M.: Highly regular, modular, and cascadable design of cellular automata-based pattern classifier. IEEE Trans. Very Large Scale Integr. (VLSI) Syst. **8**(6), 724–735 (2000)
9. Chaudhuri, P.P.: Additive Cellular Automata: Theory and Applications, vol. 1. Wiley, California (1997)
10. Cook, M.: Universality in elementary cellular automata. Complex Syst. **15**(1), 1–40 (2004)
11. Cotton, N.J., Wilamowski, B.M., Dundar, G.: A neural network implementation on an inexpensive eight bit microcontroller, pp. 109–114. IEEE, February 2008. http://ieeexplore.ieee.org/lpdocs/epic03/wrapper.htm?arnumber=4481278
12. Crook, P., Marsland, S., Hayes, G., Nehmzow, U., et al.: A tale of two filters-on-line novelty detection. In: Proceedings of the IEEE International Conference on Robotics and Automation, ICRA 2002, vol. 4, pp. 3894–3899. IEEE (2002)
13. Duke, D.W., Pritchard, W.S.: Proceedings of the Conference on Measuring Chaos in the Human Brain, 3–5 April 1991, at the Supercomputer Computations Research Institute, Florida State University, Tallahassee, FL. World Scientific (1991)
14. Ercsey-Ravasz, M., Roska, T., Nda, Z.: Statistical physics on cellular neural network computers. Phys. D Nonlinear Phenom. **237**(9), 1226–1234 (2008). http://linkinghub.elsevier.com/retrieve/pii/S016727890800122X

15. Ganguly, N., Maji, P., Sikdar, B., Chaudhuri, P.: Design and characterization of cellular automata based associative memory for pattern recognition. IEEE Trans. Syst. Man Cybern. Part B (Cybern.) **34**(1), 672–678 (2004). http://ieeexplore.ieee.org/lpdocs/epic03/wrapper.htm?arnumber=1262538
16. Hunt, K.J.: Neural networks for control systems - a survey. Automatica **28**, 1083–1112 (1992)
17. Kocsrdi, S., Nagy, Z., Csk, Á., Szolgay, P.: Simulation of 2d inviscid, adiabatic, compressible flows on emulated digital cnn-um. Int. J. Circ. Theory Appl. **37**(4), 569–585 (2009). http://doi.wiley.com/10.1002/cta.565
18. Maji, P., Ganguly, N., Saha, S., Roy, A.K., Chaudhuri, P.P.: Cellular automata machine for pattern recognition. In: Bandini, S., Chopard, B., Tomassini, M. (eds.) ACRI 2002. LNCS, vol. 2493, pp. 270–281. Springer, Heidelberg (2002). doi:10.1007/3-540-45830-1_26
19. Sarkar, P.: A brief history of cellular automata. ACM Comput. Surv. **32**(1), 80–107 (2000). http://portal.acm.org/citation.cfm?doid=349194.349202
20. Schaffer, J.D., Whitley, D., Eshelman, L.J.: Combinations of genetic algorithms and neural networks: a survey of the state of the art. In: International Workshop on Combinations of Genetic Algorithms and Neural Networks, COGANN-1992, pp. 1–37. IEEE (1992)
21. Schmitt, M.: On the size of weights for mcculloch-pitts neurons. In: Proceedings of the Sixth Italian Workshop on Neural Nets WIRN VIETRI-1993, pp. 241–246. Citeseer (1994)
22. Smith, D., Stanford, P.: A random walk in hamming space, vol. 2, pp. 465–470. IEEE (1990). http://ieeexplore.ieee.org/lpdocs/epic03/wrapper.htm?arnumber=5726715
23. Vellido, A., Lisboa, P.J.G., Vaughan, J.: Neural networks in business: a survey of applications (1992–1998). Expert Syst. Appl. **17**, 51–70 (1999)
24. Weston, J., Watkins, C.: Multi-class support vector machines. Technical report. Citeseer (1998)
25. Witten, I.H., Frank, E.: Data Mining: Practical Machine Learning Tools and Techniques. Morgan Kaufmann, San Francisco (2005)
26. Wolfram, S.: A New Kind of Science, vol. 5. Wolfram Media, Champaign (2002)
27. Zhen-zhen, X., Su-yu, Z.: A non-linear approximation of the sigmoid function based FPGA. In: Jiang, L. (ed.) ICCE 2011. AISC, vol. 111, pp. 125–132. Springer, Heidelberg (2012)

Smart Cities

A GIS Water Management System Using Free and Open Source Software

Pablo Fernández[1(✉)], Jaisiel Santana[1], Alejandro Sánchez[1], Agustín Trujillo[2], Conrado Domínguez[3], and Jose Pablo Suárez[1]

[1] IUMA Information and Communications System, Division of Mathematics, Graphics and Computation (MAGiC), University of Las Palmas de Gran Canaria, 35017 Las Palmas de Gran Canaria, Canary Islands, Spain
pablo.fernandez@ulpgc.es

[2] Imaging Technology Center (CTIM), University of Las Palmas de Gran Canaria, 35017 Las Palmas de Gran Canaria, Canary Islands, Spain
agustin.trujillo@ulpgc.es

[3] University of Las Palmas de Gran Canaria, Juan de Quesada, 35001 Las Palmas de Gran Canaria, Spain
conradodt@gmail.com

Abstract. Water management systems are having an increasing impact for sustainable development on all types of urban infrastructures. This paper describes the framework of a water management system, as a project of transformation from a traditional commercial software approach to a new, open source flexible system, capable to afford new demanding requirements. Among these new demanding requirements we cover analysis and implementation issues for: an open source GIS for water management, the challenge to big data management, reusing existing data, and network integrity and robustness. A real case scenario is thoroughly described. The integration of a powerful data model and spatial process model into a water modeling framework is proved to enhance the software capabilities for water management system.

Keywords: Water management · FOSS · Data base · GIS · Data model

1 Introduction

Water distribution systems are complex networks of elements that transport water directly to consumers. The companies responsible for managing these systems must keep large datasets of interlinked spatial elements: hydraulic controls, pipes, valves, hydrants, water tanks, etc. All these elements are usually stored using big spatial databases. These databases are used by technicians for analysis, management, planning and monitoring tasks. All those software components taking part in this complex system, where also geographical information are integrated, can be viewed as a GIS application applied to water management (GIS-WM).

C.R. García et al. (Eds.): UCAmI 2016, Part II, LNCS 10070, pp. 383–394, 2016.
DOI: 10.1007/978-3-319-48799-1_43

These big systems are usually composed of a data model, a systematic description, an user interface, and several data management, reporting and visualization capabilities. The data model also allows to run water management mathematical models to be used in water resource decision support systems, such as the work of Harou et al. [4] in several cities of USA, Schenk [11] in Birmingham, Saikrishna et al. [10] in India, and Schmitt et al. [12] in Germany. This data model can be also interlinked with other models from different research areas (urban development, smart cities, socio-economy), as proposed by Mair et al. [5]. That work proposed a web based platform for improving urban water cycle modelling in Austria.

In the field of Ambient Intelligence (AmI), some authors like Mikulecky [7] have incorporated intelligence in sensor nodes within a sensor network, providing more benefits as early warning possibilities or better logistical planning. More recent methodologies employ heuristic optimization techniques, as indicated in Ostfled [8].

Many local/regional governments in Spain are enforcing to the companies responsible of the water management to efficiently provide with the information involved in the supply water network. Besides, all the customer issues, as infrastructure, counting, etc. must be provided in a fast and easy way by means of instant reports. In this paper, an open source platform is proposed for the city of Las Palmas de Gran Canaria. This system is composed of different modules, allowing the water management company in this city to analyze and manage the whole water distribution system.

Main requirements of the proposed system are:

1. having a high level of functional robustness and usability,
2. providing with fast and coherent responses when water related queries are demanded,
3. being adapted to local features of the region and citizens,
4. being capable of holding up an increasing load of the management (new customers, increasing water supply to the city, etc.),
5. Completely developed using software technologies that are multi-platform and open source.

In the Sect. 2, we present an insight into the older system that the company was previously using, and the benefits of migrating to open source software. In Sect. 3, the proposed system architecture is explained in detail. In Sect. 4, thematic validations to guarantee the robustness of the network are introduced. Finally in Sect. 5, we present a historic information management, allowing officers to manage with all the modifications and updates to the water distribution network at different times of the past.

2 Analysis of the Previous System and Requirements

Water management companies require different kinds of software ecosystems to manage a huge variety of information. This means that several Information

Systems (IS) are usually involved in the storage, recovery, processing and publication of data. The presented case is not an exception, where different data warehouses and technologies deployed can be found, such as Oracle or AS/400.

The first aspect that must be improved is the data model. In its previous GIS, the data model was generic, and it lacked the flexibility to be adapted to their specific needs. This is one basic pillar of the entire system, since the data model is the most important asset in an information system.

The deficiency of control over the data model is also reflected in the difficulties faced developing new analytical tasks to aid with their maintenance work. Instead of allowing the user to control the information directly, a middleware proprietary software manages the database to implement the data model and the interactions with it. Therefore, the front-end software lacks some desired features such as loading raster layers or publishing directly to a Web Map Service (WMS). In this case, every specific requirement must be requested to the vendor, adding important costs to the expenses in the license.

A common deficiency in traditional GIS-WM is the loss of flexibility regarding the interoperability of the database implementation. In this case, the front end software was proprietary, making it difficult to use other GIS front end software solutions for specific problems to solve. The system also lacks of advanced analysis queries at the database level, limiting them to the available tasks implemented at the client level. It also limits the connections to other subsystems, which are needed to feed the GIS with relevant information from other departments. At the user level, an important limitation encountered is the restricted number of usage licenses available at a reasonable cost.

Another important point to be covered by the new system is increasing the system assistance in the digitizing process. The previous system had a posteriori validations, which lead to inefficiencies in the validation process since all the errors were detected when all data were already saved. Therefore, a desired feature for the new GIS is the ability to display important errors as soon as possible, preventing the digitizers to save critically inconsistent states into the system.

Finally, with the previous system, the company was unable to easily query previous valid states of the system. The GIS-WM to be developed should provide the administrators with tools to navigate to previous important events of the system and, if needed, recover any chosen state to become the current one in the production database.

2.1 Benefits of Migrating to FOSS

Free and Open Source Software (FOSS) allows the possibility to use, study, modify, copy and redistribute the source code. This freedom brings several benefits like avoiding technology locking due to restrictive licensing and improving software reusability. Companies can also benefit from FOSS by decreasing their license expenses and having the opportunity to customize their software.

A very famous and successful FOSS project in the field of GIS is QGIS [9]. It is licensed under the GNU General Public License and runs on Linux, Unix,

Mac OSX, Windows and Android systems; for this reason, it is a great candidate for the ecosystem of a custom GIS-WM.

After taking into account all the requirements, the DBMS chosen to implement the GIS-WM was PostgreSQL with its spatial extension PostGIS. PostGIS is considered one of the most powerful and mature geographic data management software in the geospatial market, as commented in [1]. Furthermore, PostgreSQL allows to connect with other information systems through Foreign Data Wrappers (FDW) thanks to a specification called SQL/MED (SQL Management of External Data) (see [2]). Currently there are a huge variety of FDW to connect with different data stores.

3 GIS-WM Architecture

3.1 Designing the New Data Model

Designing the data model is one of the first steps to create the GIS-WM. It is considered one of the most important parts of any IS (see [3]). Technologies change over time, but a well designed data model remains unalterable. This is the reason to focus and use the necessary resources to create the new data model.

The steps followed to obtain the first draft of the data model are the following:

1. Identify unused entities and attributes: here we process all the unused elements in the data model.
2. Remodel entities and attributes: remodeling process implies a search for consistency in the actual data model.
3. Add new entities and attributes: new entities are added to the data model.
4. Verify with technicians: we confirm the status of the data model with the technicians.

Table 1 shows the first draft of the new data model. This achieves a significant reduction of the number of attributes used in the entity representations. Therefore, it results in a much lighter and efficient model tailored to the real needs of the company.

Table 1. Compression rate in the new data model

Table	Prev. attributes	New attributes	Compression rate %
Filter	44	25	56,82
Connection	47	26	55,32
Pipe	53	32	60,38
Enclosure	55	27	49,01
Valve	62	33	53,23

In Fig. 1, the customized data model can be seen being used to display a fragment of the overall water management network. The layers are loaded from a PostgreSQL database with PostGIS extension.

Fig. 1. Sample network displayed in QGIS client using the customized data model.

3.2 Editing Workspace and Production System

Taking into consideration both the day-to-day digitizers work and the necessity of a trustful and verified network to query about the state of the WMS, we decided to atomize the system in two subsystems:

1. An editing workspace where digitizers should make the database changes in their daily work. In the editing subsystem, data only persists if it passes the set of critical restrictions defined as level 1.
2. A production system where the official state of the company water management network is stored and direct modifications are not allowed. All elements in this system must satisfy all the restrictions and validations defined for the network.

Figure 2 shows the scheme of the general architecture, where digitizers are able to work on the editing workspace until an administrator validates the changes and imports them to the production system. In order to update the database, an administrator should execute the import process on a specific zone from the editing subsystem. This import process checks all the restrictions and validations on all the elements located in the defined zone. If all of them are accomplished, the production subsystem is updated with these data. In the case that all validations can not be accomplished, the import process is revoked. Every subsystem tracks the network changes in their respective history databases.

The main benefit of having the GIS-WM divided into two subsystems is that digitizers can work with enough flexibility. However, at the moment of publishing the information to the production system, all data must be validated, enforcing a robust and coherent dataset.

It is important to note that each of these subsystems are connected to an additional database that stores their respective history of changes, which are used by the GIS-WM history management implementation.

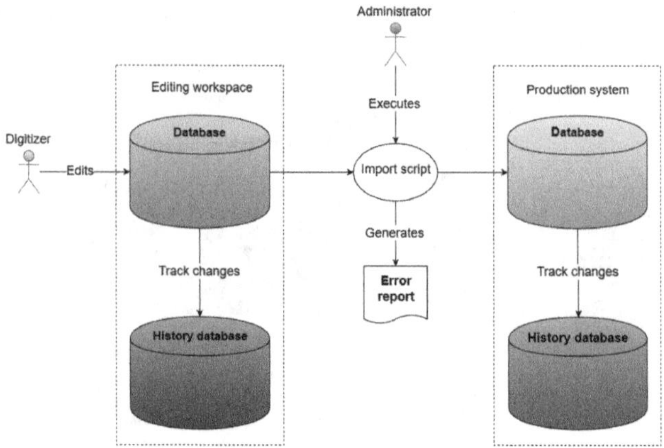

Fig. 2. Overview of the general architecture of the presented GIS-WM.

3.3 Connecting the Subsystems

Two important systems playing a central role in the WMS are the asset management and commercial management. Asset management allows to have an active management and inventory of the company assets (including plants production, infrastructures and facilities) whereas commercial management allows to the company to manage all the information related to their clients.

In our case of study, the asset management system is implemented on an Oracle 11g database, and the commercial management system data is implemented in an IBM AS/400 server. It is important for the company to connect their different systems together, and SQL/MED provides a solution for this problem, as commented in [6]. As can be seen in Fig. 3, the new GIS uses FDW to connect to the different subsystems, although all of them are implemented using different technologies.

The process to achieve the connections are simple. First, it is needed to install the proper FDW extension for PostgreSQL. In the case of Oracle, an Oracle FDW is already available. However, to do the same with AS/400 databases, a generic Open Database Connectivity (ODBC) FDW has to be installed. After that, a foreign data server has to be defined, and users existing in PostgreSQL database have to be mapped to the target storage systems. Once the mapping is done, all the desired datasets from the target systems have to be defined as foreign tables in PostgreSQL with their respective data conversions.

4 Thematic Validations

In the GIS-WM presented, a set of defined rules is available to guarantee the integrity and robustness of the network. These are known as thematic validations. In an ideal scenario, all the database modifications should be fully correct, but this case is not always possible. Sometimes, the digitizers do not have all

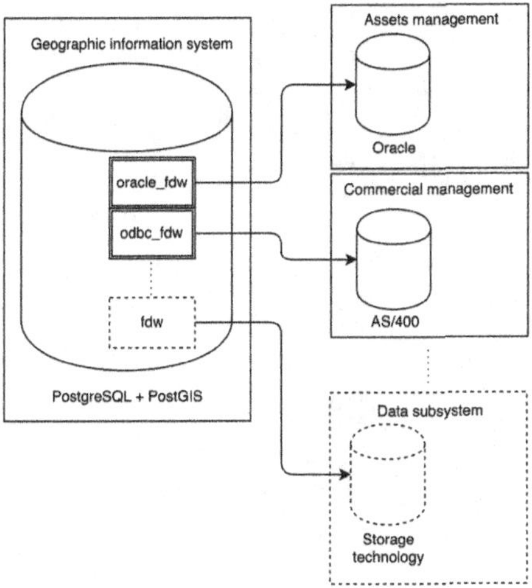

Fig. 3. Database connections of the GIS with the asset management (Oracle) and the commercial management (AS/400).

the information about the network elements, or they need to save a partial network state to continue their work later. Furthermore, the system should provide enough information for the digitizers to fix an invalid digitization.

We want digitizers to do their work with great agility. For this reason, early detection of critical errors must be achieved, avoiding excessive delay of the network validation. To do this, two different types of validations can be distinguished in our proposed system:

- Level 1 validations are the more critical, and they can be detected at the insertion moment. Some examples of these kind of restrictions are geometry overlapping (two water tanks overlapped, as can be seen in Fig. 4) or invalid combination of attributes (a network element that is private and also belongs to the transport network).
- Level 2 validations are non critical restrictions and they cannot be performed at insertion time. They are encapsulated in a generic validation function that executes them sequentially. An example of this kind of validation is the verification of the connections between elements, for instance by checking disconnected pipes as can be seen in Fig. 5.

With the purpose of optimizing the validation process, verifications are only performed against the elements that can cause errors. To be able to implement this optimization, the $ValidationState$ field has been added to all the entities, which can have the following values:

- $Modified$: The element has been modified directly or by another element connected to it.
- $Validated$: The element has already passed all validations.
- $NotValidated$: The element has not passed the last validation process.

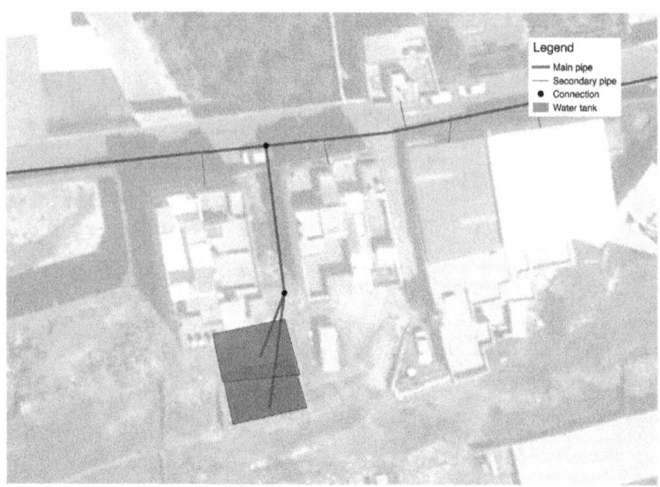

Fig. 4. Example of overlapped water tanks.

It is worth noting that an element is modified when it is updated directly, or when a second element connected to it is also modified. Thus, if a pipe is connected to two elements, and one of them is deleted or moved, the pipe is also considered as modified.

With the adoption of the proposed model, the digitizers can perform their work without worrying about having to digitize the network correctly from the beginning. The validation process provides useful hints if they have any doubt about how to draw an element. Therefore, even new digitizers can easily be adapted to the system. Since all the validations are implemented at database level, users can use them with any GIS program that supports PostgreSQL, and the model restrictions can not be avoided. This is very important to bring mobility to the company, because it reduces the computational load and logic on mobile devices.

5 Simplifying Access to Historic Information

One of the main requirements is to provide reports, based in the system status at specific dates, to facilitate information exchange internally, or even to external institutions. Traditionally, this information can be obtained from regular queries, but the historic information was not contemplated in regular reports. Therefore, they could not be retrieved. In these cases, technicians should search through the system backups in order to restore previous data, making the process complex and time consuming for the administrators.

In Sect. 3, the database distribution for the developed GIS-WM was introduced. There we could see that the editing workspace and production system have a history database associated to each one, where data changes are stored.

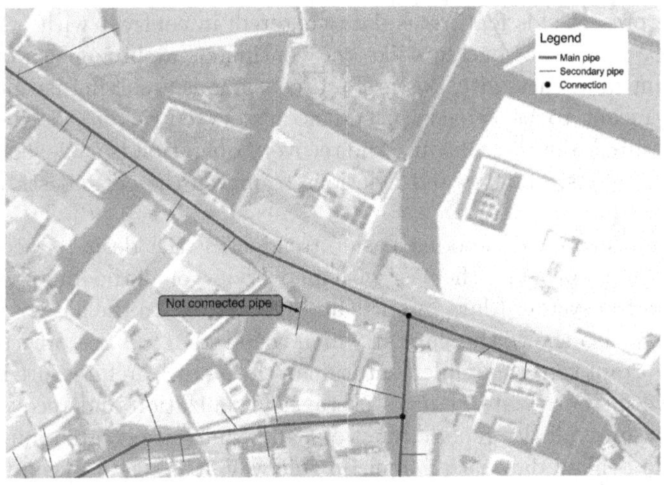

Fig. 5. Example of disconnected pipe.

These history databases keep the entities information, the type of operation performed (update, insertion or deletion) and the time range at which this registry was up-to-date every time they are modified. Table 2 represents a simplified example of a history table.

Table 2. Simplified example of a history table. Note the use of date ranges to determine at which period of time the row is valid

Id	Attribute 1	Attribute 2	Valid-date-range	Operation
20031	True	5	["2016-04-11 21:43:07.507211+01", "2016-04-11 21:47:53.5493+01")	UPDATE
20034	False	3	["2016-04-11 21:47:53.5493+01", infinity)	INSERT
45374	True	2	["2016-04-11 21:43:07.507211+01", "2016-04-11 21:47:53.5493+01")	UPDATE
33407	True	7	["2016-04-11 21:47:53.5493+01", infinity)	UPDATE

Based on this table structure, the history databases provide two useful functionalities to the user of the GIS-WM: visualization of historical data and data-centered Point-In-Time Recovery (PITR). The history visualization feature defines a set of table views that use a timestamp specified by the user. Once the user has specified the desired date to examine, the views will display all the entities as they were at that specific point in time.

If the administrators of the GIS-WM are not satisfied with the evolution of the network digitizing after a certain point in time, they can use the PITR feature. We present this feature as data-centered, in contrast with other strategies designed as system backups like the continuous archiving in PostgreSQL. An important difference with PostgreSQL continuous archiving is that this feature is not meant to be a backup, and no history entries are deleted when a PITR is executed. On the contrary, the recovery operation is achieved by issuing the required inserts, updates and deletions to match the current state with the target state.

With the purpose of making easier to identify the desired recovery time stamp, the system provides the user with an overview of all the important actions performed in the system (data imports and recoveries). In the case of recoveries, this summary also shows the date at which the system was restored to.

It is important that the implementation of the history architecture be efficient and effective for both data changes storage, visualization and recovery. In the developed system, all the generic functions and tables are created automatically based on the defined database model. In this way, it is easy to keep the history system synchronized with the base tables, since the administrators will just need to re-execute the automated scripts to generate all the history tables, triggers and functions in charge of tracking the data changes.

Furthermore, we should consider that the system recovery is a critical operation, as it modifies the system status by reverting the effect of past transactions, and must also ensure a valid state. In order to decrease the time needed to perform a PITR, we disabled some triggers that are executed for each operation. These triggers compare the entity with many others (like geometry overlaps). These validations are still needed to avoid a possible incorrect system status. Therefore, we have developed a set of functions that check the restrictions for all the elements at once at the end of the recovery process. Figure 6 shows the performance comparison to recover 500 entities as the number of history entries increases. We can observe how the optimized system stays with a constant recovery time, achieving a maximum optimization of 96.

6 Final Remarks

In this paper we have presented a GIS water management system using FOSS. The target situation started with the need to migrate from a traditional commercial software approach to a new, open source flexible system, capable to afford new demanding requirements. We have emphasized several critical features needed for the success of a water management system. We have also pointed out the difficulties when facing new analytical tasks and developing maintenance work. Instead of allowing the user to control the information directly, a middleware proprietary software manages the database to implement the data model and the interactions with it.

An important feature in the water management system is the thematic and geometric validation to guarantee the integrity and robustness of the network. We have presented a validation workflow structured in two levels that permits reliable and consistent edition tasks made by operators and digitizers, so they

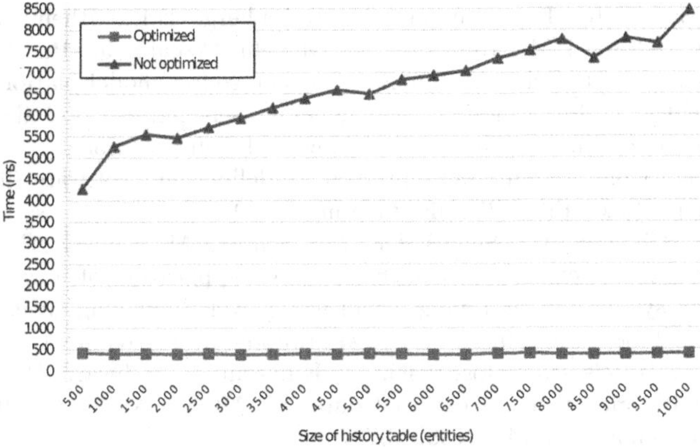

Fig. 6. PITR time comparison between optimized and not optimized systems. The number of entities retrieved in every iteration is 500.

can perform their work without worrying about having to digitize the network correctly from the beginning. For example to avoid subsequent validations, which lead to inefficiencies in the validation process, since all the errors are detected at the end of tasks. Instead we introduce a new feature to properly send warning and error messages to the user to prevent a final collapse of the system validations.

From the point of view of water management companies, it is extremely important to keep track of the changes made into their networks. Storing the history of changes improves the transparency towards users and institutions, but it also enables and facilitates more complex research aiming to improve the services provided. The GIS-WM provides to the administrators with tools to navigate to previous important events of the system and, if needed, recover any chosen state to become the current one in the production database.

In summary, the paper contributes with the integration of a powerful data model and spatial process model into a water modeling framework with new software capabilities for water management systems, which has been proved in the context of Gran Canaria island, Spain.

References

1. Akbari, M., Peikar, S.R.H.: Evaluation of free/open source software using osmm model case study: webgis and spatial database. Adv. Comput. Sci. Int. J. **3**(5), 34–43 (2014). http://www.acsij.org/acsij/article/view/159
2. Chacko, A.M., Basheer, A.M., Kumar, S.D.M.: Capturing provenance for big data analytics done using sql interface. In: 2015 IEEE UP Section Conference on Electrical Computer and Electronics (UPCON), pp. 1–6, December 2015
3. Codd, E.F.: A relational model of data for large shared data banks. Commun. ACM **13**(6), 377–387 (1970). http://doi.acm.org/10.1145/362384.362685

4. Harou, J.J., Pinte, D., Tilmant, A., Rosenberg, D.E., Rheinheimer, D.E., Hansen, K., Reed, P.M., Reynaud, A., Medellin-Azuara, J., Pulido-Velazquez, M., Matrosov, E., Padula, S., Zhu, T.: An open-source model platform for water management that links models to a generic user-interface and data-manager. In: International Environmental Modelling and Software Society (iEMSs) 2010 International Congress on Environmental Modelling and Software Modelling for Environments Sake, Fifth Biennial Meeting (2010)
5. Mair, M., Mikovits, C., Sengthaler, M., Schöpf, M., Kinzel, H., Urich, C., Kleidorfer, M., Sitzenfrei, R., Rauch, W.: The application of a web-geographic information system for improving urban water cycle modelling. Water Sci. Technol. **70**(11), 1838–1846 (2014). http://wst.iwaponline.com/content/70/11/1838
6. Melton, J., Michels, J.E., Josifovski, V., Kulkarni, K., Schwarz, P., Zeidenstein, K.: Sql and management of external data. SIGMOD Rec. **30**(1), 70–77 (2001). http://doi.acm.org/10.1145/373626.373709
7. Mikulecký, P.: Ambient intelligence in water management. In: 2011 7th International Conference on Intelligent Environments (IE), pp. 302–305, July 2011
8. Ostfeld, A.: Water distribution networks. In: Kyriakides, E., Polycarpou, M. (eds.) Intelligent Monitoring, Control, and Security of Critical Infrastructure Systems. SCI, vol. 565, pp. 101–124. Springer, Heidelberg (2015). doi:10.1007/978-3-662-44160-2_4
9. QGIS: Qgis project (2016). http://qgis.org. Accessed 24 May 2016
10. Saikrishna, V., Pandey, K., Bharath, B.D., Karnatak, H.: Urban water information system (uwis): a web based spatial decision support system for management and monitoring of water utility assets. In: FOSS4G 2015 - Second National Conference Open Source Geospatial Tools in Climate Change Research and Natural Resources Management (2015)
11. Schenk, C.: A systems-based generic decision support system application to urban water management. Ph.D. thesis, Technical University of Lausanne (EPFL) (2010)
12. Schmitt, T.G., Worreschk, S., Kaufmann, I.A., Herold, F., Thielen, C.: An optimization and decision support tool for long-term strategies in the transformation of urban water infrastructure. In: 11th International Conference on Hydroinformatics HIC 2014. Cuny Academic Works, New York City, USA (2014)

Arrival Time Estimation System Based on Massive Positioning Data of Public Transport Vehicles

Gabino Padrón, Francisco Alayón, Teresa Cristóbal, Alexis Quesada-Arencibia, and Carmelo R. García(✉)

Institute for Cybernetic Science and Technology, Department of Computing and Systems, University of Las Palmas de Gran Canaria, Las Palmas, Spain
{gpadron,falayon,aquesada,rgarcia}@dis.ulpgc.es, teresa.cristobaln@gmail.com

Abstract. Nowadays the public transport systems play a main role in the advanced societies. How to evaluate the quality of the public transport is a critic task of the transport regulatory agencies. One indicator used to measure this quality is the fulfilment of the scheduled operation by the transport operators, specially scheduled arrival times and frequencies at stops. In this paper, an automatic system to estimate arrival times in the context of road public transport is proposed. The system works autonomously, acquiring massive vehicle position readings, registering and processing them automatically in order to estimate arrival times. This autonomous behaviour is achieved using pattern recognition and statistical techniques. To illustrate the application of the system, the estimation of arrival times at a bus stop is presented.

Keywords: Intelligent transport systems · Float car data · Pattern recognition

1 Introduction

In the context of regular public passenger transport by road, the knowledge of arrival times at bus stops is crucial for transport companies and agencies since punctuality is an important parameter to measure the quality of service [1]. Therefore, this information is necessary to make the operations scheduling and to provide reliable information to the public transport user. This paper describes a system that allows regulatory agencies or transport companies to predict the arrival times at bus stops over the public transports network. Additionally, this information can be used by the transport agencies to evaluate the quality of service and predict the routes duration in the context of private transport by road. The system is based on the massive data acquisition done by the positioning system of the public transport buses.

The verification of the quality of service provided by the public transport companies is a responsibility of the transport regulation agencies. To perform this task, these agencies request data from transport companies. This task is not easy to perform due to three main reasons: the duration of travels is a dynamic value that depends on different factors, the amount of required data and the required technology to obtain these data [2]. The proposed system is a case of float car data system; the public transport buses travel

C.R. García et al. (Eds.): UCAmI 2016, Part II, LNCS 10070, pp. 395–406, 2016.
DOI: 10.1007/978-3-319-48799-1_44

through the main roads of the transport network periodically at a high frequency. To manage the massive data provided by vehicles, the system performs an intelligent management of the communication infrastructure. Finally, to provide automatically reliable and dynamic information about the travel times the system uses pattern recognition and statistic techniques.

The paper is structured as follows: in the next section related works is presented, preliminary concepts to facilitate the understanding of the working principles of the system are explained in Sect. 3, the Sect. 4 is dedicated to explain the proposed system, illustrating it through a case of application and finally, the main conclusions and future works are presented in the Sect. 5.

2 Related Works

The acquisition of the required information to verify and improve the operations scheduling is an important challenge for transport operator and agencies. According to Furth [3], this information is obtained from four different data sources: surveys from travellers, use rates records obtained from vehicles, automatic passenger counting (APC) systems and automatic vehicle location (AVL) systems.

APC systems are based on the use of different types of sensors, such as infrared light [4] and acoustic [5], optical [6] and even Bluetooth technology [7] to detect the presence of travellers in the vehicle. These sensors are usually installed at the entry and exit points of the vehicle.

AVL systems are used to locate the position of the vehicle or to detect the presence of the vehicle at a specific point in the transport network. The arrival time at bus stops can be obtained using the position or the presence of vehicles at bus stops and the time when the position is calculated or when the presence is signalled. Different technologies are used to obtain the measurement of the position in AVL systems, for example, Mazloumi [8] proposes the use of GPS while Song [9] proposes the use of cellular communication systems. In this system, when the vehicle is traveling through a cellular territory, the on board device receives those signals and calculates the attenuation of those signals to locate the current vehicle position. Zhou [10] uses RFID technology to detect the presence of public transport buses at stops.

From the point of view of the computing methods used to predict the travel or arrival time, these methods can be classified in three categories: Kalman filter, Yu [11], non-parametric regression techniques, Chang [12], and neuronal networks Jeong [13].

3 Preliminary

The positioning system used is the GPS. The data provided by the GPS receptor are the geodesic vehicle's position (latitude, longitude and elevation), velocity, the quality of readings and the instant, expressed in Universal Time Coordinates (UTC). It is important to note that GPS units provide geographical position readings with an error that is a function of different factors: climate conditions, terrestrial curvature radius and the presence of random selective error. In general, assuming there is no random selective error, the maximum positioning error for GPS is 100 m. In the proposed system, the latitude, longitude, elevation, horizontal velocity and vertical velocity are coded by a 4 bytes float value for each of them, the UTC of each measurement is coded by a 4 bytes integer value, the source of reading specifying the number of satellites used for measurement and the age of the measurement are coded by a 1 byte chart value for each of them. Strictly speaking, to calculate the distance between two GPS positions, geodesic distance should be used, considering the flattening factor of the Earth's surface, but in order to simplify the calculations, the system uses the Euclidean distance, assuming that the error is minimal and therefore it can be neglected.

The conceptual model used by the system is based on standard specifications for public transport. This includes all the concepts related to public transport activity, being represented these concepts by entities, attributes and relationships that are finally implemented by a database that represents all the planned and performed operations (PTDB). The topological transport network is represented by points and links. The points can be one of three different types: stop points, timing points and route points, reflecting the different roles. The attributes of a Point entity are: a unique identifier, point type (stop, timing and route) and geographical position (latitude, longitude and height). The Link is an entity the represents the line that joins two points. The attributes of a Link entity are a unique identifier, the two points joined and an identifier of the road or street. The Line is an entity used to represent the different routes in the transport network for transporting passengers. The attributes of a Line entity are: a unique identifier and a sequence of links arranged in the order of the route, being at least two stop points. The entity Trip is used to represent a scheduled line that must be periodically performed on a given time, for example: every day at 08:00, every weekend at 12:00, every day in summer at 07:45, etc. The Trip attributes include: a unique identifier, line, period specification and time. Each bus of the fleet of the public transport is represented by the Vehicle entity and among its attributes; there is a unique vehicle identifier. All the scheduled trips performed by a bus on a given day, starting at a given time, is represented by the Service entity which has different attributes: a unique identifier, bus and start time of the service. Finally, in order to register the vehicles activities and to verify the fulfilment of the vehicle scheduling, all the relevant events produced in the vehicles are recorded in PTDB.

To formalize the previously defined concepts, a network of road public transport can be describe as a directed graph G = {P, A}, where P is the set of nodes, representing each node a point of the transport network, and A is the set of arcs (link) which connect pairs of nodes, representing each arc a direct connection by road or by walking trail.

- P is the set of points of the transport network, P = {Pi}, Pi represents a given point of the transport network, i is an integer such that $0 \leq i < Np$, being Np the number of points of the transport network. A complete definition of a network point must include at least the geographical position (latitude, longitude and elevation) and the point type (stop, timing and route).
- A is the set of arcs (direct connections) of the transport network, A = {Ai}, i is an integer such that $0 \leq i < Na$, being Na the number of arcs of the transport network. A complete definition of arc Ai must include at least: the pair of nodes connected and the road or walking trail used to connect the pair of nodes.

- L is the set of the lines defined in the transport network, L = {Li}, Li represents a route such that $0 \leq i < Nl$, being Nl the number of different routes defined in the transport network. A route Li is defined by an ordered sequence of arcs which must be travelled by a vehicle, that is, Li = (Ah, Aj, …, Az), being Ah the first arc to be travelled in the route, Aj the second arc to be travelled and so on. A complete definition of Li line must include at least the ordered sequence of arcs.

The above formal notation represents the network of regular passenger transport by road, but to complete the formal notation of the public transport activity it is necessary to represent the operations scheduled in the transport network. For the purposes of this work, this is performed using the concepts of Service and Trip explained above. Formally:

- A Trip is a route that should be performed at a given date and time. The set of all the scheduled trips that should be performed at a given date and time is represented by T, T = {Tt}, Tt represents a scheduled expedition such that $0 <= t < Nt$. Nt is the number of trip scheduled in the transport network. The notation T_{Li} is used for representing a subset of trips of the line Li in different days and time.
- A service is a set of expeditions that should be performed by a vehicle at a given date and time. A set of all the scheduled services is represented by S, S = {Ss}, Ss represents a scheduled service such that $0 <= s < Ns$, being Ns the number of scheduled services to perform through the transport network. A service Ss is defined by the vehicle, the starting date of the service, starting time of the service, end time of the service and the sequence of expeditions ordered by the starting time of each expedition.

Assuming this formalization, the goal of the proposed system is to estimate the arrival times of each bus to each stop for each scheduled trip through the transport network. Additionally, this estimation can be used to evaluate the quality of service expressed as fulfilment of these arrival times. It is important to note that for a given stop node of a line, their arrival times, for the different trips that contain this stop node, could vary due to traffic conditions and the demand conditions, being both dynamic aspects. More specifically, the aim is to estimate the time spent on travelling each arc that defines the route of an expedition. This time is calculated by the sum of the passengers loading and unloading time at the origin node of the arc and the travel time between the two nodes that define the arc of the expedition. The loading and unloading time at the origin node is the time spent by travellers to get on and off the bus in this node. This time depends on the payment system used by passengers and the demand, which also varies depending on the day (working day, holiday day, weekend, season, etc.) and the time slot of the day (start time of a working day, end time of a working day, start time of a school day, end time of a school day, etc.). The travel time between the two nodes that define the arc of the trip depends on the traffic conditions and it also depends on the type of day and the slot time of the day.

To validate the proposed system, it has been applied to estimate the arrival times at bus stops of a line of the Company of Public Transport of Passengers Global Salcai-Utinsa. This company operates on the island of Gran Canaria (Canary Islands, Spain) covering the intercity transport of this island. The chosen route is a line that connects the cities of Las Palmas de Gran Canaria and Arucas, being 210 the identifier code of the route. This line has 28 bus stops and the distance covered by the line is 23 kilometres, crossing urban and non-urban zones during the route. To illustrate the system description, the results obtained in each module of the system will be presented for this practical case. The selected line for testing the system is represented by L_{210}. Figure 1 shows an aerial vision of the selected route.

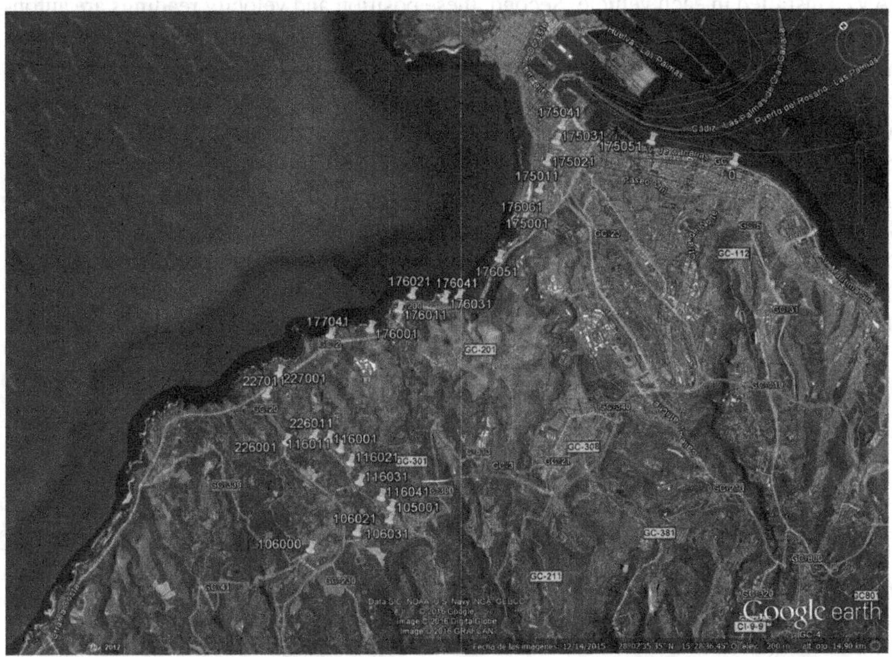

Fig. 1. Aerial vision of the analysed route. The pushpin icons represent the route bus stops

Taking into account that the trip times are dynamic values because they depend on variable factors, such as the type of day and the time slot of the day, we considered the trip times following the operations scheduling of the lab vehicle during the test period. They were trips of the L_{210} route performed every two hours, from Monday to Friday, from 6 am until 22 pm. This set of trips of the L_{210} line studied is called T_{L210}.

4 System Description

As it was mentioned in the introduction section, the verification of the quality of service of public transport, using the fulfilment of the arrival times as an indicator, is not easy to perform due to the amount of required data and the dynamic property of this variable.

The proposed system works autonomously, acquiring vehicle position readings, registering and transferring these readings automatically to remote data processing centre of the regulatory authorities or companies, where the arrival times estimation is performed using pattern recognition and statistical techniques. This system is a case of float data system, being the used vehicles the buses of the public transport.

The execution of the system is performed by 5 phases. First, the buses of public transport acquire and record continuously their positions and velocity provided by their positioning systems. This task is performed by the Automatic Vehicle Location System (AVL) installed in each vehicle. Second, these position and velocity readings are autonomously and periodically transferred to the data repositories of the transport regulation agencies using the vehicle mobile communication systems. The next processing step consists of selecting the relevant and reliable readings for the estimation of arrival times; a module called Filter performs this task. Each reliable and relevant position reading is processed to find out which scheduled trip was obtained, this step is performed using the transport database and the system element responsible is named Tracker. The Classifier is the next module to run and its goal is to identify each position reading with a bus stop of the line analysed. The last processing phase consist of performing the estimation of the arrival times for each bus stops of the set of line trips in different type of days and time slots of the day. Figure 2 shows a general representation of the system.

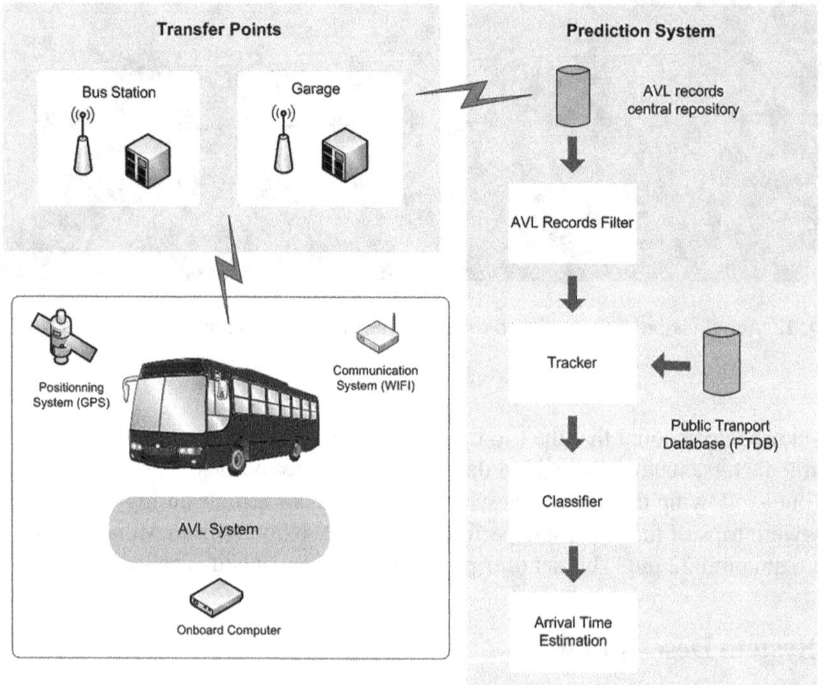

Fig. 2. General vision of the system

4.1 The AVL System

The vehicles are equipped with an AVL system. This element gets the vehicle position provided by the GPS receiver, recording the measurement in a positions file stored on the onboard computer. The positions file is automatically transferred to the data processing centre using a Wifi infrastructure available in the vehicles in specific points of the transport network (stations and garages). Each position recorded has the following data:

- F1: Vehicle identifier.
- F2: UTC of the vehicle position measurement.
- F3: Vehicle geodesic position (latitude, longitude, elevation).
- F4: Source of the measurement.
- F5: Age of the measurement.

The period of reading the GPS position of the vehicle is configurable. In the tests performed by the system this period was set to one second. Therefore, the sizes of the positions files are large, requiring an intelligent management of Wifi communications when these files are transferred. This intelligent management is performed considering the vehicle operations planning; specifically, the files transferences are made when the vehicles are stopped and the intelligent management system evaluates that the data transfer can be completed. The position reading acquired in a vehicle is represented by Mv, representing v the vehicle where the readings were acquired. For the case of lab vehicle (LV), this set is named M_{LV}.

To analyse the chosen line, the line 210 of the Company Salcai-Utinsa, the AVL system was installed and configured in a vehicle, lab vehicle (LV), to get periodically the position and velocity each second, during a period about 3 months, getting 7.948.800 of position readings in this period; that is the number of readings of M_{LV}.

4.2 Filter

The GPS receptor does not always provide a reliable positioning measurement, for this reason it is necessary to filter M_V records that contain erroneous position readings. The detection of unreliable GPS readings is based on the use of F4 and F5 fields of the AVL records. The F4 field informs whether the positioning measurement has been properly calculated using the minimum number of satellites that must be four to obtain a tri-dimensional coordinates. The F5 field tells if the measurement is available and if so, the time elapsed since the last positioning measurement was calculated.

Whereas a vehicle comes to a stop its speed is zero, then a second goal of this step is to remove irrelevant positioning measurements for the estimation of the arrival times. In this context the measurements indicating that the vehicle is moving are filtered. To carry out this second filtering, the F3 field of the M_V is used. The result of this step is a set of all the reliable positioning readings with zero velocity of the vehicle V; this set is named Zv, representing V the vehicle where the readings were acquired.

Applying this filtering method to the set of position readings of LV, that is M_{LV} set, yields a set of 1.987.688 of reliable position reading of the lab vehicle with velocity of zero, which is Z_{LV} set. Observing Z_{LV} set on an aerial photograph of the geographic area containing the L_{210} line, one can see that the majority of the readings are grouped. These groups are associated with the locations of bus stops and the locations of unscheduled stops related to points where LV had to stop due to traffic signals. When interpreting this graphical representation, note that a conventional non-differential GPS unit provides readings with a maximum margin of error of 100 m and that the stops in the transportation network have variable lengths. For the case of the L_{210} line, the average length of stops is 15 m.

4.3 Tracker

This module of the system assigns each observation of the Z_V sets, in both space and time, to an operation of trip performed by the vehicle. To make this assignation, the tracker queries the PTDB using as a search input data the number of vehicle (F1) and the time when the search was performed (F2). If the vehicle location was recorded when the vehicle was performing a scheduled operation, then the output of the query will be the attributes that describe the operation (service, line, trip, driver, date and time of the start of the trip, etc.). Specifically, the registers recovered from the PTDB are the start trip register and the end trip register that specify the date and time of these events. With this data the system can know the instant in which an expedition started and when it ends.

- $Z_{V,Li.}$ is the set of reliable position readings with velocity of zero of the V vehicle performing any trip of the Li line, being $Z_{V,Li.}$ a subset of $Z_{V.}$
- The set of reliable position readings of a given vehicle, V, with velocity of zero assigned to a given trip, t, is named $Z_{V,L,t}$, being $Z_{V,L,t}$ a subset of. $Z_{V,Li.}$

The number of position readings, assigned to a given trip of the T_{210} set, depends on the type of day and time slot of the trip. For example, the duration of the trips of the L_{210} route varies from 43 min to 32 min depending on the type of day (weekday, holiday, school day, etc.) and time slot (starting time of a working day, ending time of a working day, starting time of a scholar day, etc.). The number of trips of the L_{210} line performed during the test period by LV was 213.

4.4 Classifier

The goal of the classifier is to identify each position reading of the $Z_{V,Li}$ set as a point of scheduled stop (bus stops) or points of unscheduled stop (traffic conditions, traffic signals, incidents, etc.). For this purpose, the method is based on the following hypothesis: "If we consider the $Z_{V,Li}$ set, the reliable readings obtained for points where the vehicle V systematically stops, that include the bus stops and stop points due to traffic signalling, during a trip of the line Li, will have a high frequency compared with those points at which the vehicle stops sporadically, for example due to traffic incidents. In addition, applying patterns automatic recognition techniques based on classifying methods, such as K-means, the readings obtained at points of systematic stops must be grouped, with the number of groups being equal to the number of existing systematic stops along the route".

To verify the previous hypothesis, the frequency histogram of the $Z_{V,Li}$ is calculated, observing the following behaviour: there should be a high frequency measurements at the points of the route at which the vehicle stops systematically, whereas the readings associated with the positions around points at which the stop is not systematic should have a lower frequency. In addition, the elements of the $Z_{V,Li}$ will tend to form concentrated clusters when the vehicle is at one of the stops scheduled along the route. Considering this behaviour, the method used to identify the points on the Li line is based on the detection of these groups and subsequent classification into two categories: scheduled stop points of the Li route, $B_{V,Li}$ set, and singular points, $C_{V,Li}$ set associated to stop points due to traffic signalling. The used technique is a recursive one in which the K-means classification algorithm is applied in each step to a subset of readings of the Z_V,L_i. In the first iteration, the K-means algorithm is applied to the entire $Z_{V,Li}$, using as the initial solution the set of scheduled stops, that is B_V,L_i, that have been identified by their positions.

Executing the classifier for the $Z_{LV,\ L210}$ set; the results converge on a solution with a number of clusters equal to 28 that is the number of bus stops. There are 28 clusters represented by their centroids and 28 scheduled stops. The positions of the majority of the centroids are close to the positions of the points representing scheduled stops. Figure 3 shows the centroid, circle icon, and the initial position, pushpin icon, of the analysed bus stop.

Fig. 3. Aerial vision of the analysed bus stop. Pushpin icons represent bus stops of the L_{210}, the 175031 bus stops is the bus stops studied. The circular icons are the centroids representation obtained by the Classifier

4.5 Arrival Time Estimation

To estimate the arrival times of each bus stops of a Li line, the following procedure is executed:

1. For each trip, t, of Ti set, to get the $Z_{V,Li,t}$ set.
2. For each $Z_{V},_{Li,t}$ set, to get the $Bv,_{Li,}t$ and $Cv,_{Li,}t$ sets.
3. For each point of each $Bv,_{Li,t}$, set to get the associated bus stop. This relationship is made computing the distance of the point to the centroid which represents each bus stop, selecting the bus stop with minimum distance. As a result of this step, the $Bv,_{Li,}t$, set will be partitioned into N subset, being N the number of bus stops of the expedition t. To represent each of these subsets, the following notation is use $Bv,_{Li},t,j$,such that Li represent the studied line, t a trip of Li route and j a bus stop, such that if j = 0 represents the first bus stop, j = 1 the second and so on. For a given j, if $Bv,_{Li,t,}j = \{\Phi\}$, then it means that the vehicle did not stop at j bus stop when the t trip of the Li line was performed.
4. For each $Bv,_{Li,t,}j$ such that $Bv,_{Li,t,j} \neq \{\Phi\}$, to select the positioning measurement whose time coordinate, F2 field, is the lower. This measurement is the arrival time of the j bus stop, for the t trip of the Li line. This value of time is represented by $A_{Li,t,j}$.
5. For each bus stop of Li and different types of day and time slots, that is types of trips of the Li line, the statistical parameters required for the timetable estimation is calculated. In this study the mean, variance, maximum, minimum values of the arrival times.

Finally, we will show the results for a bus stop of the L_{210} line. The chosen bus stop is the fourth stop of the L_{210} route, being located in the city of Las Palmas de Gran

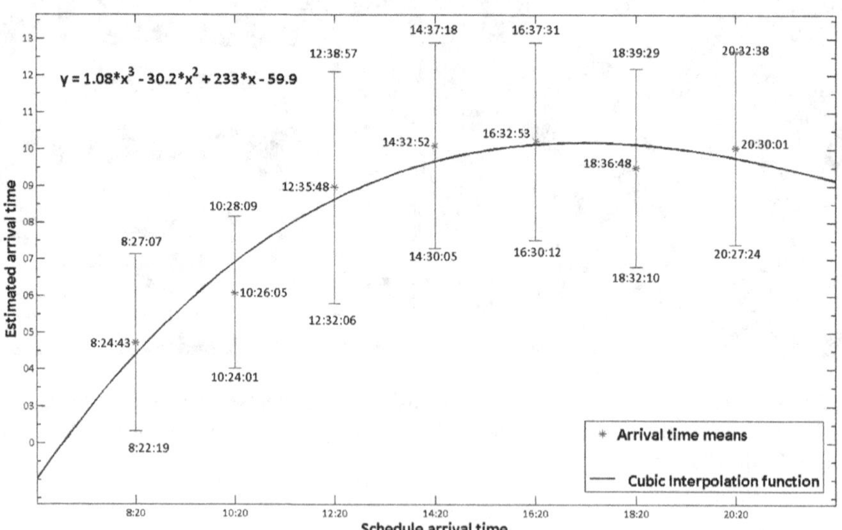

Fig. 4. Estimated arrival time at the analysed bus stop. The cubic interpolated function is the arrival time for different times. The variance is a metric of punctuality

Canaria, so this is located in an urban area. This bus stop appears in Fig. 3, labelled with the 175031 code and its centroid is NL. For the set of trips selected for this study, T_{210}, and following the timetable scheduled for this bus stop, the bus must arrive at 08:20, 10:20, 12:20, 16:20, 18:20 and 20:20 following the scheduled arrival time. The mean, variance, maximum and minimum values calculated are presented in Fig. 4. Interpolating the mean values, the mean arrival time function can be calculated and the values of this function can be used to estimate the arrival time and the variance can be used to evaluate the level of punctuality at this bus stop.

5 Conclusions

Nowadays the public transport systems play a main role in the advanced societies. How to evaluate the quality of public transport is a critic task of the transport regulatory agencies. One indicator used to measure this quality is the fulfilment of the scheduled operation by the transport operators, especially timetables and frequencies. In this paper we have described a system for automatic estimation of travel time in the context for public transport on roads. The system can be used by transport regulatory agencies to achieve their objectives related to the control and improvement of public transportation. The system works autonomously, acquiring vehicle position readings, registering and transferring these readings automatically to remote data processing centre of regulatory authorities where the travel time estimation is performed using pattern recognition and statistical techniques. The pattern recognition technique used is the K-means method which is executed to identify the vehicle position readings in relevant point of the transport network. The statistical methods are used to estimate the timetable for each stop. This estimation can be used to evaluate the fulfilment of the timetable in each stop for different types of day and time slots. To illustrate the application of the system, a case study has been presented. This practical application consists of the timetable estimation at a stop on a route performed by the buses of a public transport company.

As a future works, the research team intends to apply the system for the main routes of public transport network of the Gran Canaria Island. A second future research line consist of applying the system to identify and estimate the different times involved in the total time of the journeys, that are load/unload time and travel time for the routes performed in different types of day and in different time slots of the day.

References

1. Muller, T.H.J., Furth, P.G.: Trip time analyzers: key to transportation service quality. Transp. Res. Rec. **1760**, 10–19 (2001)
2. Tyrinopoulos, Y.: A complete conceptual model for the integrated management of the transportation work. J. Public Transp. **7**(4), 101–121 (2004). University of South Florida
3. Furth, P.G., Muller, T.H.J., Strathman, J.G., Hemily, B.: Uses of Archived AVL-APC Data to Improve Transportation Management and Performance: Review and Potential. Report 113, pp. 1–12. Transportation Research Board (2003)
4. Lindholm, U.: Apparatus for the Automatic Counting of Passengers. http://www.google.com/patents/US4009389 Accessed 15 May 2016. Patent US 4009389 A (1977)

5. Frielinghaus, K.H., Shahbaz, Z.: Automatic Counting System for Passages. http://www.google.com/patents/US4528679. Accessed 15 May 2015. Patent US 4528679 A (1985)
6. Chen, C., Chang, Y., Chen, T., Wang, D.: People counting system for getting in/out of a bus based on video processing. In: Proceedings of the Eighth International Conference on Intelligent Systems Design and Applications (ISDA 2008), pp. 565–569, Kaohsiung, Taiwan, 26–28 November 2008
7. Camacho, T., Mantero, C.: Wireless detection of end-to-end passenger trips on public transport buses. In: Proceedings of the 13th IEEE Conference on Intelligent Transportation Systems, pp. 1795–1800, Madeira Island, Portugal, 19–22 September 2010
8. Mazloumi, E., Currie, G., Rose, G.: Using GPS data to gain insight into public transport travel time variability. J. Transp. Eng. **136**(7), 623–631 (2010)
9. Han-Lee, S.: Automatic vehicle location in cellular communications systems. IEEE Trans. Veh. Technol. **43**(4), 902–908 (1994). IEEE
10. Zhou, H., Hou, K.M., Zuo, D., Li, J.: Intelligent urban public transportation for accessibility dedicated to people with disabilities. Sensors **12**(8), 10679–10692 (2012). MDPI
11. Yu, B., Lam, W.H.K., Tam, M.L.: Bus arrival time prediction at bus stop with multiple routes. Transp. Res. Part C **19**(6), 1157–1170 (2011). Elsevier
12. Chang, H., Park, D., Lee, S., Lee, H., Baek, S.: Dynamic multi-interval bus travel time prediction using bus transit data. Transportmetrica **6**(1), 19–38 (2010). Taylor and Francis
13. Jeong, R., Rilett, L.R.: Bus arrival time prediction using artificial neural network model. In: 7th International IEEE Conference on Intelligent Transportation Systems: (ITSC 2004), Washington DC, pp. 988 – 993 (2004)

Evaluating Reorientation Strategies for Accelerometer Data from Smartphones for ITS Applications

M. Ricardo Carlos[1], Luis C. González[1(✉)], Fernando Martínez[1], and Raymundo Cornejo[2]

[1] Facultad de Ingeniería, Universidad Autónoma de Chihuahua, 31125 Chihuahua, Mexico
ricardo.carlos@gmail.com, {lcgonzalez,fmartine}@uach.mx

[2] CONACYT – Universidad Autónoma de Chihuahua, Chihuahua, Mexico
rcornejoga@conacyt.mx

Abstract. Given their ubiquity and sensing capabilities, current smartphones have been used to explore different real-life tracking and monitoring scenarios. Particularly, in the domain of Intelligent Transportation Systems (ITS), the exact orientation of the smartphone must be known to gain full advantage of the data provided by its internal accelerometers. From here, rich contextual information could be inferred. Nonetheless, in real-life scenarios, smartphones are freely placed within vehicles, so a reorientation strategy needs to be applied. The usage of several algorithms to reorient acceleration readings has been mentioned for ITS applications, but very little evaluation of their efficacy has been performed. In this work, we study the effectiveness of four algorithms for vertical reorientation, and two for triaxial reorientation of acceleration readings. Results suggest that all methods for the vertical case are equivalent, however, in the case where triaxial reorientation is needed, current strategies are far from acceptable results. We expect these findings could promote further research to alleviate these issues.

Keywords: Accelerometer · Reorientation · Smart cities · Mobile sensing · Smartphones

1 Introduction

Smartphones are everywhere. According to the International Data Corporation (IDC), 1432.9 million units were shipped during 2015 (10.1 % up from 2014).[1] These devices usually offer high resolution video cameras, microphones, and a variety of sensors such as accelerometers, gyroscopes, magnetometers, temperature, light, and GPS. Their availability, sensing capabilities and computing power, enable them to collect environmental data, as well as the current location, becoming an attractive platform to support context-aware and ubiquitous

[1] https://www.idc.com/getdoc.jsp?containerId=prUS40980416.

C.R. García et al. (Eds.): UCAmI 2016, Part II, LNCS 10070, pp. 407–418, 2016.
DOI: 10.1007/978-3-319-48799-1_45

computing [1]. In the domain of Intelligent Transportation Systems (ITS), acceleration data is used to track and monitor road conditions, score driver maneuvers and identify faulty-style driving, among other possibilities [2].

The processing of accelerometer data is helpful for ITS applications because it allows identifying contextual information. It is possible to know the direction and orientation of a vehicle, if it suddenly stops, whether it made a swerve, or passed over a bump. The processing of acceleration data might however not be straightforward, specially in uncontrolled application scenarios, for instance, when the mobile phone is used to collect data in the background, while the user performs everyday activities. In a controlled scenario, the axes of the smartphone are aligned with the moving vehicle, but this is not always true for normal smartphone usage, so in many cases the axes will not correspond to the frames of reference that reflect the experience of the devices' users. In such a situation, a series of rotations of the accelerometer's cartesian axes is required in order to align this to a specific frame of reference. For example, when the smartphone is lying laterally inside a vehicle and we are interested in capturing events from shock absorbers associated to anomalies in the road, we can apply a reorientation to the accelerometer samples so that the readings can be correctly displayed in the Z axis, instead of the X axis.

Although different approaches for acceleration data reorientation have been proposed in the literature [3–7] there are signs that suggest that this problem may still be open. For example, details on the implementation of the methods are left out, or the information provided may be confusing. Another issue is that there has not been a direct comparison among methods using the same data, so we don't know which strategy is better. Or even worse, some proposals suggest how to infer the angles of rotation, but no complete procedures are shown. Overall, no clear conclusion has been *carved in stone* about this problem, and technological proposals that assume that this problem is solved need to be warned about possible issues.

In this paper we aim to evaluate two scenarios where reorientation of accelerometer data from smartphones is required. In the first one, there is a need to extract vertical acceleration (in the axis perpendicular to the road), a typical use for this would be to detect road anomalies. Results from the comparison of four methods suggest that this problem can be considered as solved, since all of them perform similarly. In the second scenario, there is a need for the reorientation of triaxial acceleration in order to get richer contextual information, an application for this would be detecting bad driving behavior. The two methods compared here don't perform as expected. There is a considerable error and large heterogeneity in the computation of angles of rotation. We expect this contribution will motivate further discussion on current challenges and novel strategies that could eventually be applied to solve this problem.

The rest of this paper is structured as follows: next section presents related work. Section 3 introduces the data collection process that was performed to obtain acceleration samples. Section 4 deals with the evaluation of vertical acceleration reorientation. In Sect. 5, we elaborate on the azimuth[2] estimation, and triaxial reorientation. Finally, conclusions and future work are stated in Sect. 6.

2 Related Work

The orientation of accelerometer data is important for ITS applications because of the information that can be extracted from each of the vehicle's axes of movement: vertical acceleration (along the Z axis, pointing to the roof of the vehicle) mostly reflects the conditions of the road, while the other two axes reflect steering (on the X axis, pointing to the right side of the vehicle), acceleration, breaking and gear shifting (on Y axis, pointing to the front of the vehicle).

The simplest approach presented in the literature relies on placing the sensors in a known (and fixed) orientation with respect to the vehicle. Variations of this include attaching a dedicated accelerometer to the vehicle [8], fixing a smartphone to a surface using a holster [9] or adhesive tape [10], and placing a mobile device on the floor of the vehicle with its screen pointing to the roof to get vertical acceleration [11]. There are two main paths where the smartphone could be freely located within the vehicle. In the first one, the magnitude of the resulting tridimensional acceleration vector has been used as an estimate of vertical acceleration. This calculated value has been used for the detection of road anomalies because vertical acceleration, including gravity, contributes the most to this vector [5]. In the second path, a series of rotation matrices can be constructed with trigonometric functions, evaluated over the angles between the axes of the original and the desired frames of reference. The product of these matrices and a disoriented acceleration vector yields a reoriented vector. Euler angles are a way to represent tridimensional rotations by using three angles [12], and several different conventions are frequently described. Quaternions are an extension of complex numbers frequently used in many fields to deal with rotations [13], they can be used in conjunction with Euler angles and rotation matrices. Mathematical rotations have been used to either reorient only vertical acceleration, leaving the other two axes disoriented, or to fully reorient acceleration in three axes. Among the works performing vertical reorientation we find [4], where the authors calculate two angles from acceleration readings by means of trigonometric equations, and use Euler angles with the X-Y-Z formulation to extract vertical acceleration for the detection of speed bumps and potholes. An alternative based on quaternions is presented in [6] to extract vertical acceleration from a smartphone located at the user's waist, using the average of ten seconds of acceleration readings to calculate the required rotations.

A strategy for triaxial reorientation of data captured with smartphones was proposed in [3]. The two angles required for vertical reorientation are determined from median values of acceleration, by means of trigonometric equations. GPS is used to get an estimation of the vehicle's speed and detect moments of deceleration. Knowing when sharp deceleration occurs, an equation is solved to find

[2] An azimuth is a horizontal angle measured from a north base line.

the angle that maximizes the effect of deceleration in the forward-backward axis. A different way to estimate the last angle required for triaxial reorientation in smartphones is the usage of an electronic compass. In [7], the authors argue that this angle can be estimated as the difference between the bearing angle reported by the GPS and an azimuth estimated from magnetometer data. However, they do not address the dynamic determination of this angle in their experiments, of great relevance in real-life scenarios given that the user could alter smartphone orientation several times during a ride.

3 Data Collection

Two Android applications were developed to collect acceleration samples for our experiments. The first, *Log acceleration*, is run in up to six smartphones, which are in turn used as sensing devices to capture accelerometer, magnetometer, and GPS data while driving a car. The second, *Tag events*, is run in a tablet, and serves as a remote control to start and stop data capture without manipulating the sensing devices that run *Log acceleration*. One smartphone was used as a hotspot, and all the devices running our applications were connected to a Wi-Fi network. For the sensing smartphones, the sampling frequency was set to 50 Hz for both accelerometer and magnetometer (*middle of the road* of what is reported in the literature), GPS data was sampled at 1 Hz (the highest frequency available in these devices). Two datasets were collected using these applications.

3.1 Dataset A

A car was driven for about 25 min. In that period, data was captured and it was marked when the vehicle passed over speed bumps. Two smartphones (LG Nexus 4, and Samsung Grand Prime) were oriented with respect to the car's axes and fixed in the dashboard holder and the center console between the frontal seats, respectively. The data logged by the Samsung Grand Prime served as ground truth (LG Nexus 4 served as a control). Four more smartphones (first generation Motorola Moto G) were placed in the left door compartment (Loc. 2), in a dashboard compartment (Loc. 3), in the driver's right trouser pocket (Loc. 4), and inside a pocket in a jacket tossed over the copilot's seat (Loc. 6). Each of these smartphones had at least one axis unaligned with respect to the vehicle.

Twelve short acceleration time series were selected from these 25 minutes of collected data, each corresponding to the data logged when the vehicle passed over a speed bump. These were chosen because the waveform recorded when passing over this type of road anomaly is rather distinctive. In total, 60 time series were used (12 considered ground truth, with oriented data, and 48 with disoriented data), with an average of 270 acceleration data points per time series (equivalent to 5.4 s). The time series for the complete session were also kept. This dataset was used to evaluate reorientation algorithms in Sects. 4 and 5.2.

3.2 Dataset B

A predefined route (4.8 km, usually completed in 13 min) was driven five times. Five smartphones (from a pool of four first generation Motorola Moto G, one Samsung Grand Prime, and one LG Nexus 4) were placed in different locations inside the vehicle: attached to a dashboard holder (Loc. 1), in the left door compartment (Loc. 2), in a dashboard compartment (Loc. 3), in the driver's right trouser pocket (Loc. 4), and on the copilot seat (Loc. 5). The smartphones were placed so that the device's azimuth was aligned with the front of the car. In total, 25 time series formed this dataset, used to evaluate azimuth calculation in Sect. 5.1.

4 Extraction of Vertical Acceleration Values

The methods described in [4–7] were used to extract vertical acceleration values from the disoriented data sequences in each event of Dataset A. Except for the equations described by Tundo et al. [6], which were reformulated to match the conventions used here for the smartphone axes, we performed the calculations as described in the original papers. Median values of the times series were used as baseline for the methods to calculate angles for the rotation operations[3].

To evaluate the results of the selected methods, we use Normalized Cross-Correlation (NCC) and Dynamic Time Warping (DTW) as metrics of similarity between the output of each method, for each smartphone, and the ground truth (acceleration readings obtained from an oriented smartphone). A NCC score of 1 or −1 indicates maximum correlation, whereas values closer to (and including) zero indicate no correlation. Low DTW coefficients indicate high similarity between time series.

4.1 Data Pre-processing

Prior to the calculation of NCC and DTW, both oriented and reoriented data were filtered with a simple moving average filter (with a sliding window of ten elements) and a low-pass filter ($\alpha = 0.4$) to remove noise and extract the low frequency components (significant for road anomaly detection). Each time series was centered and scaled[4] to reduce the effects of the different placements of the smartphones and the possible variations between the uncalibrated accelerometers. To reduce the effect of temporal shifting on NCC, the filtered and normalized time series pairs were aligned, before calculating the similarity metrics, by using a manually selected prominent peak as reference.

---

[3] The equations used in our experiments are summarized in http://accelerometer.xyz/reorientations/equations.pdf.

[4] As $Z_i = (z_i - \overline{z})/s_z$, where z_i represents the ith datapoint in the time series of axis Z, $\overline{z}$ is the mean, and s_z is the standard deviation on the same axis.

4.2 Results

Figure 1 shows a scatter plot of NCC and DTW values calculated to compare reoriented signals with the ground truth, by method. In general, we can observe that all methods have minimal differences when vertical reorientation is applied. In most of the cases, the works of Astarita et al. [4], Tundo et al. [6], and Promwongsa et al. [7] perfectly agree.

All methods yielded good results. Even for the cases with the poorest NCC or DTW scores (NCC ≈ -0.3, DTW ≈ 0.16), the reorientations of the time series by the four methods present an acceptable agreement with respect to ground truth, as shown in Fig. 2.[5]

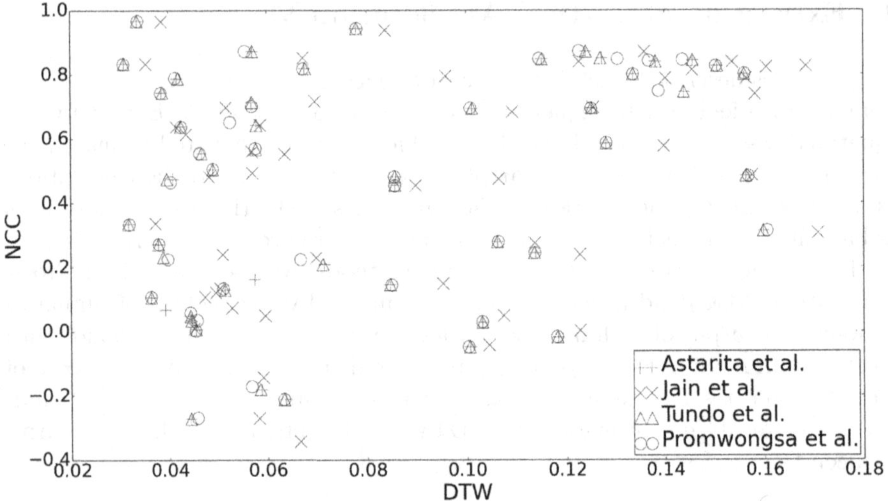

Fig. 1. NCC and DTW by method for vertical reorientation.

To validate our conclusions, we applied a one-way ANOVA test with $p = 0.01$ to the vectors of NCC and DTW scores for each of the four methods, resulting in no statistically significant differences between them.

5 Triaxial Reorientation of Acceleration Data

Once vertical acceleration has been achieved, the other two axes can be reoriented by performing one more rotation over the Z axis. In this section we evaluate two strategies to find the angle (ϕ) required to perform this rotation. The first strategy uses GPS and magnetometer data to find the rotation angle, the second one uses GPS and acceleration data.

[5] Some of the series are not visible because their values are very similar, and only one line is displayed.

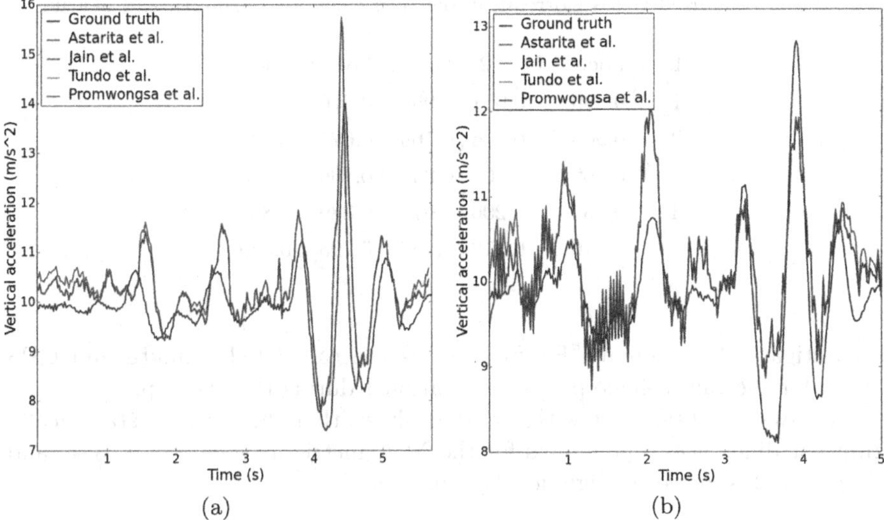

Fig. 2. (A) Reorientation results with NCC ≈ -0.3 and DTW ≈ 0.042. (B) Reorientation results with NCC ≈ 0.25 and DTW ≈ 0.16. Raw reoriented data for both.

5.1 Smartphone Azimuth Calculation

It is possible to fuse a magnetometer and an accelerometer to create a tilt-compensated electronic compass and calculate the angle between a device and the magnetic north [14]. In Android smartphones, this sensor fusion can be performed by using the API method *SensorManager.getOrientation()*, which takes as an input a rotation matrix calculated from acceleration and magnetometer data. This method returns three angles that describe the device's orientation on each axis with respect to gravity and the magnetic north. An azimuth from true north is obtained if the magnetic declination, reported by the API method *GeomagneticField.getDeclination()*, is taken into account. Promwongsa et al. proposed in [7] that, by comparing the vehicle's heading (calculated by the GPS) with the smartphone's (reported by the sensor fusion compass), the angle of rotation around the Z axis could be found and triaxial reorientation could be performed.

We obtained the smartphone's azimuth (twice per second) from the data in Dataset B, using the Android API methods described above. Both accelerometer and magnetometer readings were stabilized with a lowpass filter ($\alpha = 0.3$). We considered the direction of travel (bearing) reported by the GPS as ground truth (since the smartphones' azimuths were aligned with the vehicle's, they should match the vehicle's bearing), and calculated the NCC between azimuth and bearing as a metric of similarity between the two time series. Table 1 presents these results. In general, bearing and azimuth show similarity, although location 2 shows particularly low NCC scores. No further experiments were done

Table 1. Normalized Cross-Correlation between calculated azimuth and bearing.

Lap	Loc. 1	Loc. 2	Loc. 3	Loc. 4	Loc. 5
1	0.980	0.051	0.966	0.876	0.737
2	0.965	0.206	0.766	0.627	0.721
3	0.969	0.504	0.948	0.896	0.453
4	0.965	0.206	0.972	0.889	0.864
5	0.946	−0.619	0.460	0.795	0.846

to investigate this anomaly. Figure 3 shows the calculated azimuth and GPS bearing for the smartphone placed in location 1 during the first lap.

A one-way ANOVA test with $p = 0.01$ shows that there are no statistically significant differences among laps for the NCC metric for locations 1, 3, 4, and 5. Location 2 is, however, significantly different.

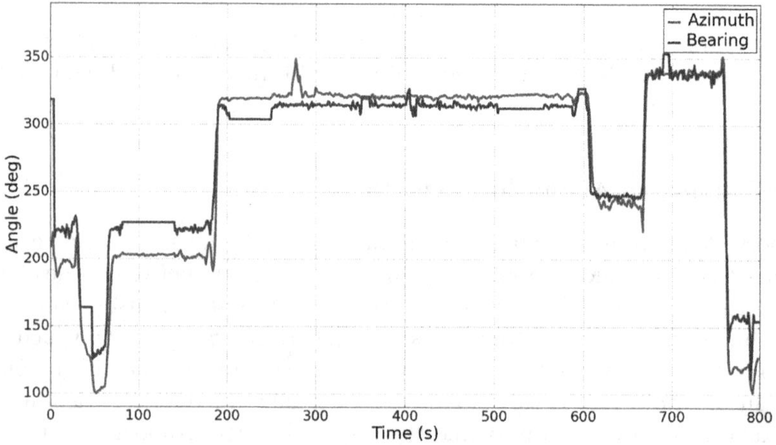

Fig. 3. Calculated azimuth and GPS reported bearing for Lap 1 in Loc. 1.

5.2 Comparison of Triaxial Reorientation Results

We compared the results of triaxial reorientation of acceleration data with ϕ obtained with a compass-GPS method, using the azimuth calculation described above, and an accelerometer-GPS strategy.

In the compass-GPS strategy, rotation angles were obtained by calculating two times per second the difference between azimuth and bearing, during one minute intervals. These long periods of time were considered to mitigate the instability in azimuth calculation. We then generated a histogram with 15°-wide bins for the calculated angles, and chose the center of the bin with the highest count as an estimate of ϕ for that period of time.

To implement the accelerometer-GPS strategy, we solved $\frac{dY}{d\phi} = 0$ (where Y is the equation that gives us reoriented values in the forward-backward axis), and then rearranged the equation to obtain ϕ, as indicated in Appendix B of Mohan et al. [3][6] The angle ϕ was calculated from acceleration values during a period of sharp deceleration, these periods were found by analyzing GPS reported speed values.

We calculated ϕ thirty times with each of these two methods, for each disoriented smartphone, from the complete time series of Dataset A. Each angle was used with the rotation matrices presented by Promwongsa et al. [7] to reorient in three axes the disoriented time series for the twelve individual events in Dataset A. We performed the same signal processing and used the same metrics from Sect. 4.

Figures 4 and 5 show the differences between reoriented time series and the ground truth, for compass-GPS and accelerometer-GPS based reorientation, respectively. It is remarkable that metrics for axes X and Y are very disperse when compared with the results for vertical acceleration, which suggests that triaxial reorientation in smartphones is not yet solved with the two evaluated methods.

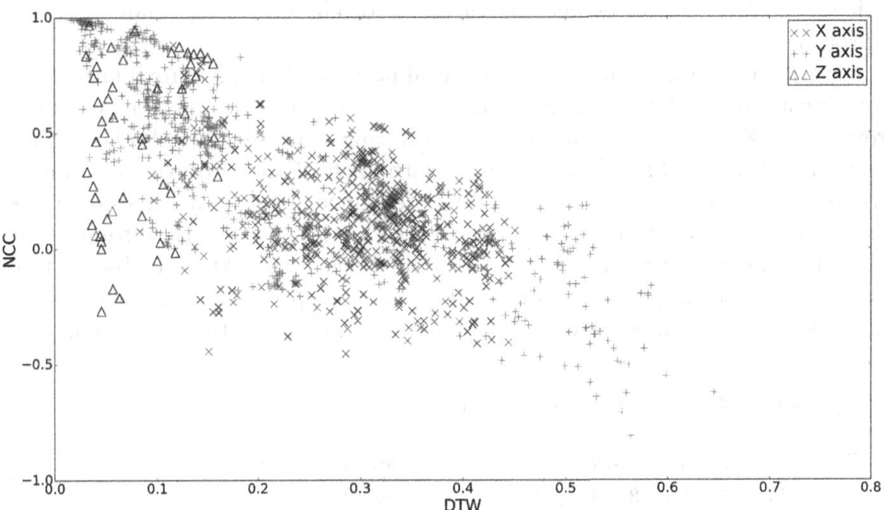

Fig. 4. NCC and DTW by axis for compass-GPS based reorientation.

If none of the compared methods accurately solves this problem, how do they compare in error? For a side by side comparison between both methods for the reorientation of the Y axis, Fig. 6 shows histograms for the distributions of DTW and NCC values. Compass-GPS based reorientation shows better performance,

[6] In their article, the authors use a different convention for axes. Their X axis corresponds to our Y, and vice versa.

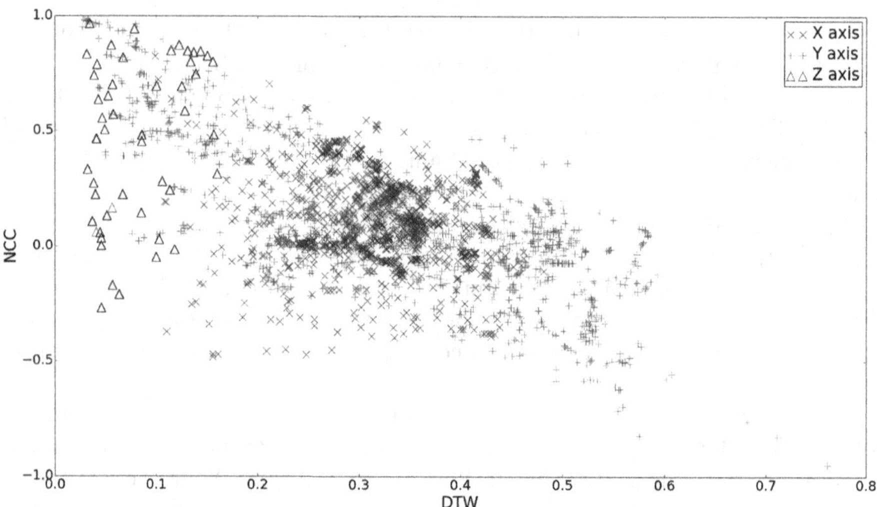

Fig. 5. NCC and DTW by axis for accelerometer-GPS based reorientation.

with lower DTW distances and higher cross-correlation values, than the other approach.

We tried to estimate the error in the evaluated methods. Approximate values of ϕ for each smartphone were manually determined by performing the rotations around the Z axis and comparing the resulting time series with the ground truth. The thirty values for ϕ obtained with each of the two evaluated methods were compared with this manually-determined angle. Table 2 summarizes the accumulated distribution of the error (the angle between the automatically calculated values and the manually determined one) up to 90°. We observe that the error for calculated values for ϕ is far from acceptable. For instance, when the tolerance is set to ±20° very few predictions fall below this threshold.

Table 2. Accumulated distribution of ϕ estimates for each method.

Error	Accelerometer-GPS				Compass-GPS			
	Loc. 2	Loc. 3	Loc. 4	Loc. 6	Loc. 2	Loc. 3	Loc. 4	Loc. 6
±5°	0.00 %	3.33 %	0.00 %	0.00 %	10.00 %	0.00 %	0.00 %	3.33 %
±10°	0.00 %	10.00 %	0.00 %	0.00 %	10.00 %	10.00 %	40.00 %	3.33 %
±20°	0.00 %	33.33 %	0.00 %	3.33 %	20.00 %	10.00 %	40.00 %	13.33 %
±30°	16.66 %	36.66 %	0.00 %	3.33 %	23.33 %	16.66 %	43.33 %	16.66 %
±45°	20.00 %	53.33 %	0.00 %	6.66 %	40.00 %	20.00 %	43.33 %	26.66 %
±60°	20.00 %	60.00 %	0.00 %	26.66 %	60.00 %	40.00 %	56.66 %	60.00 %
±90°	50.00 %	70.00 %	30.00 %	40.00 %	60.00 %	50.00 %	70.00 %	86.66 %

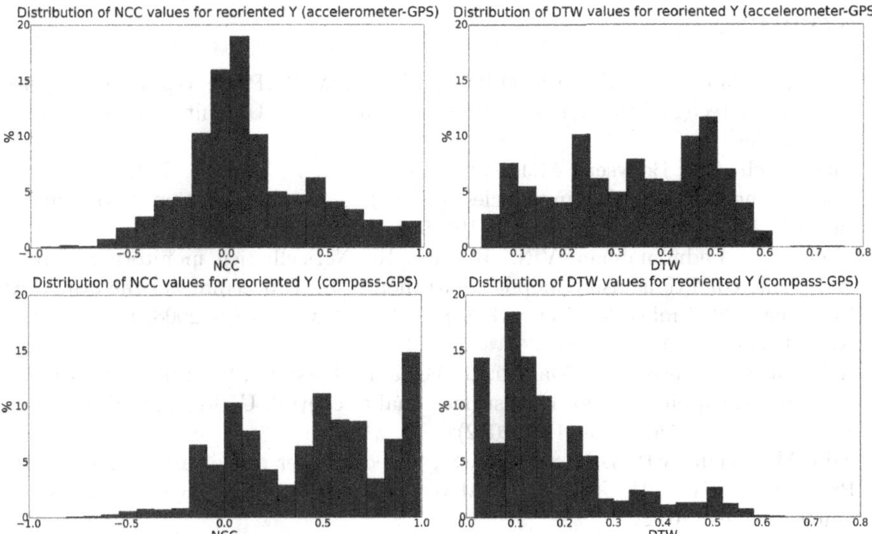

Fig. 6. Distribution of NCC and DTW in the Y axis for accelerometer-GPS and compass-GPS based reorientation.

6 Conclusions and Future Work

Although different reorientation strategies for accelerometer data from smartphones had been presented in the literature, no evaluation or comparison between them had been performed previously. In the case of vertical reorientation, results suggest that any of the evaluated methods could be used to successfully extract data from the Z axis, although, given its simplicity, the use of the magnitude vector as an approximation for this axis should be considered if no information from the other axes is required. On the other hand, when triaxial reorientation is needed in smartphones, results suggest that the evaluated methods show considerable discrepancies in axes X and Y, possibly leading to erroneous contextual information. The exact source from the errors in the estimation of ϕ is yet to be determined. Possible explanations for it include magnetic interference caused by the vehicle, influence of vibration in accelerometer readings when calculating the device's azimuth, and hardware limitations. Future work should include the analysis of these factors' influence, the usage of more sophisticated filters, and the inclusion of gyroscope data.

References

1. Figo, D., Diniz, P.C., Ferreira, D.R., Cardoso, J.M.P.: Preprocessing techniques for context recognition from accelerometer data. Pers. Ubiquit. Comput. **14**(7), 645–662 (2010)
2. Engelbrecht, J., Booysen, M.J., van Rooyen, G.-J., Bruwer, F.J.: Survey of smartphone-based sensing in vehicles for intelligent transportation system applications. IET Intell. Transp. Syst. **9**(10), 924–935 (2015)
3. Mohan, P., Padmanabhan, V.N., Ramjee, R.: Nericell: rich monitoring of road and traffic conditions using mobile smartphones. In: Proceedings of the 6th ACM Conference on Embedded Network Sensor Systems - SenSys 2008, pp. 323–336. ACM Press (2008)
4. Astarita, V., Caruso, M.V., Danieli, G., Festa, D.C., Giofrè, V.P., Iuele, T., Vaiana, R.: A mobile application for road surface quality control: UNIquALroad. Procedia Soc. Behav. Sci. **54**, 1135–1144 (2012)
5. Jain, M., Singh, A.P., Bali, S., Kaul, S.: Speed-breaker early warning system. In: Proceedings of the 6th USENIX/ACM Workshop on Networked Systems for Developing Regions (2012)
6. Tundo, M.D., Lemaire, E., Baddour, N.: Correcting smartphone orientation for accelerometer-based analysis. In: 2013 IEEE International Symposium on Medical Measurements and Applications (MeMeA), pp. 58–62. IEEE, May 2013
7. Promwongsa, N., Chaisatsilp, P., Supakwong, S.: Automatic accelerometer reorientation for driving event detection using smartphone. In: 13th ITS Asia Pacific Forum, Auckland, New Zealand (2014)
8. Eriksson, J., Girod, L., Hull, B., Newton, R., Madden, S., Balakrishnan, H.: The pothole patrol: using a mobile sensor network for road surface monitoring. In: Proceeding of the 6th International Conference on Mobile Systems, Applications, and Services - MobiSys 2008, pp. 29–39. ACM Press (2008)
9. Fazeen, M., Gozick, B., Dantu, R., Bhukhiya, M., González, M.C.: Safe driving using mobile phones. IEEE Trans. Intell. Trans. Syst. **13**(3), 1462–1468 (2012)
10. Douangphachanh, V., Oneyama, H.: A study on the use of smartphones for road roughness condition estimation. In: Proceedings of the Eastern Asia Society for Transportation Studies (10), 1551–1564 (2013)
11. González, L.C., Martínez, F., Carlos, M.R.: Identifying roadway surface disruptions based on accelerometer patterns. Latin Am. Trans. IEEE (Revista IEEE America Latina) **12**(3), 455–461 (2014)
12. Goldstein, H., Poole, C.P., Safko, J.L.: Classical Mechanics, 3rd edn. Addison Wesley, Boston (2001)
13. Kuipers, J.B.: Quaternions and Rotation Sequences: A Primer with Applications to Orbits, Aerospace and Virtual Reality. Princeton University Press, Princeton (1999)
14. Ozyagcilar, T.: Implementing a Tilt-Compensated eCompass using Accelerometer and Magnetometer Sensors. Freescale Semiconductor (2015)

Preparing for OCR of Books Handled by Visually Impaired

César Crovato[1(✉)], Delfim Torok[1], Regina Heidrich[2], Bernardo Cerqueira[3], and Eduardo Velho[3]

[1] Institute of Technology and Exact Sciences at Feevale University, Novo Hamburgo, Brazil
{cesarc,delfimlt}@feevale.br

[2] Feevale University, Novo Hamburgo, Brazil
rheidrich@feevale.br

[3] Scientific Improvement Researcher, Feevale University, Novo Hamburgo, Brazil
{bcerqueira,velho}@feevale.br

Abstract. The objective of this work is to synthesize the difficulties an algorithm must handle in book digitization for subsequent OCR application, such as angle correction, image distortion and words segmentation in addition to being operated by blind or visually impaired people real-time by video stream without further assistance. The developed method seems reliable, and provides good OCR results on a page by page basis. The results show improvements above 99,3 % in OCR performance in some cases, although execution time has increased. "The Vocalizer Project" emerged from a demand from the Brazilian Ministry of Culture and Education for application in schools and public libraries. It aims to create more inclusive smart cities. Furthermore, it is destined for the inclusion of visually impaired and blind people to the vast bibliographic material existent.

Keywords: OCR · Visually impaired · Voice scanner for blind people · Book flipping · Angle correction · Image correction · Image distortion · Real-time processing · Book video stream · Image streaming

1 Introduction

The current scientific literature comprises a wide range of works related to image pattern recognition for scanned documents [1]. Scanning a document or book is the mechanical stage of the recognition process, which usually requires human interference to ensure correct handling and framing of the subsequent steps [2]. Among the various methods used for scanning, the most common are by using a flatbed scanner or a handheld camera [3]. Each of these methods has a significant impact on the required preprocessing and the final quality of the scanned document. Subsequently, the automated reading of scanned images of characters is done through a technique known as optical character recognition (OCR), in which adequate handling and precise preprocessing provide improved results [1, 3, 4].

The main objective of this paper is to develop an algorithm for an adequate preparation of documents, aimed at obtaining a low error rate through correct digitization, considering these documents would be handled by blind or visually impaired people

C.R. García et al. (Eds.): UCAmI 2016, Part II, LNCS 10070, pp. 419–430, 2016.
DOI: 10.1007/978-3-319-48799-1_46

without any help or supervision [5]. Hence, the user will be able to have experience reading books in real time, while using his hands only to flip the pages, guided by the program. A developed algorithm for a camera-based device capable of recognizing and, afterwards, aurally assisting the user during the handling and digitization stage in real time is also discussed in this study.

Likewise, this paper presents an assistive technology which enables blind and visually impaired people having access to books. Raising their horizon of consciousness, increasing their social inclusiveness and action area in diverse fields, opening possibilities for oneself as well for the wider community [6].

Digitizing whole books is known to raise the character recognition rate, due the fact that all converted pages can be post-processed following statistic criteria [2]. However, works that focus on the process of digitizing whole books while the pages are being browsed in real time [3] are very rare. This would allow visually impaired and blind people the experience of reading a book.

The handling of a book by blind people makes the automatic character recognition system more difficult as a whole. This is due to the fact that blind people cannot notice their hands or fingers overlapping any text in the book. In addition, the way the book is held also impacts in page distortion [5]. During the handling process, the book may change position and angle at each turned page, which could compromise the OCR results. Ways of overcoming these obstacles are discussed in the following sections.

This paper is organized as follows: Sect. 2 describes works that are related to this topic. Section 3 presents the necessary specifications for making this work functional. Section 4 includes the algorithm description and necessary explanations for its proper functioning. Section 5 presents the experimental results and discussion. Section 6 brings the conclusion and suggests future related works.

2 Literature Review

Several researches focus on the OCR technology for scanning documents and its inherent difficulties [1]. Compared to scanned images, pictures taken by cameras suffer from major distortions due to perspective and image warping [3]. These distortions are more common for pictures of open books and bound documents, and require page by page rectification [7]. Currently, two categories of techniques are able to perform this task: 3-D document shape reconstruction [2, 8, 9], which reconstructs digitally the shape of the document through existing information in the obtained image, but requires a larger computational effort; and 2-D document image processing [2, 10], which does not depend on previous information and works only with current document information for processing it, without the need of auxiliary hardware [5, 11]. Technically, skew is the deviation of text lines from its horizontal orientation in some degrees on a document [12, 13]. Projection profiles is one of several methods that can be used for the detection of this deviation [13] Although the results are considered effective, the accepted limits for deviation angles proposed by this method ought to be considered low for the purpose of this study. As visual impairment is unpredictable in this matter, the accepted angle along with the computational effort increase widely at the same time [13]. The angles used in the proposed method are larger than in real life, having in mind that the operational process will be done using the Vocalizer platform, depicted in Fig. 1, preventing wider angle discrepancy.

Fig. 1. Red arrows indicate the limit of the stage, where the user must lean the top of the book.

The Vocalizer Platform prototype consists in a USB ELP 75° Camera 8Mpx HD (no distortion lens) for taking the book images, and the lighting conditions properly leveled using a 22 W circular lamp, color temperature 6400 K, standard model. Figure 1 illustraste how these elements are set. Although not used for the tests presented in this paper, the algorithm was created to simulate the usage of the book with this platform and most difficulties aroused by utilizing it.

Methods based in Hough Transform find the better orientation of straight lines in text [14], but require a large computational effort. On the other hand, another group of methods utilizes nearest neighbors (neighbor clustering) in connected components to find a more accurate direction between them and their neighbor components [13].

A few methods can be employed to straighten up curved text line due to image distortion along with bound-document distortion. Ulges [15] utilizes a mapping of each letter into a rectangular cell of a given size and position, extracting information of each pixel in the page. The region segmentation of words, on the other hand, is done to detect the integrity of words within a page, so that each word detected as a "text area" corresponds to their respective row and column [5, 13, 16]. Text quality degradation [4, 17] can result from irregular illumination, which impairs letter recognition as a whole in uncontrolled environments. This can be contoured on a semi-controlled ambient light. In the method proposed in this study, this happens through a directional light attached to the camera support for the book digitization [5].

Based on the pioneering work of Chakraborty [3], this paper focuses on processing a video stream at a low velocity rate and high resolution, in order to aid visually impaired or blind people to handle books adequately, and digitize them with a higher hit rate. There are very few scientific researches related to real-time book digitization. The proposed method by Chakraborty, which utilizes video streaming for digitization purposes, is the most relevant research to the scope of this work.

The proposed function for the algorithm in this paper consists in a 1 frame per second high resolution video (13Mpx), which represents an average of 14 images under a semi-controlled 8Mpx ambient light, which is expanded to 13Mpx. Chakraborty [3] uses, instead, a 50 frame per second video in 2Mpx (1920 × 1080) on the video stream, in uncontrolled ambient. This frame stream is then utilized to verify if the page is entirely open or being turned, when only parts of the page appear. In order to verify the moment the user is not turning the page, Chakraborty [3] uses statistical stability of candidate lines as basis, in which the region of interest of the book is captured first and compared to its edges, using a straight line searching algorithm. Once the candidate lines are set, if there are any lines within the region of interest, the algorithm detects that the book page is being turned, signaling that it is a bad frame. If the candidate lines are not affected, it is considered as a good frame [3]. Nevertheless, this operation requires the book to be properly arranged. Moreover, due to the constant moving hands of the visually impaired or blind person during the process, any of the edge lines could be slightly modified in any direction in each frame, as well as the book, without being noticed.

A challenge is set: how can frames be stabilized when not only rotation, but also translation could occur?

In order to overcome this instability, the proposed method utilizes a video stabilization algorithm known as Point Feature Matching [18]. To stabilize the frames, both frame 1 and 2 of the same page are translated and rotated in the view to correspond one another. The user's fingers represent approximately 5 % of the book area. Therefore, the difference in image 1 and 2 should be around 10 % in a threshold operation. If the result of the operation is above 10 % between these 2 frames, it means that the base of the book was moved. The algorithm must search and locate the regions that suffered wider energy change, in order to determine whether the fingers are or not present in the image. This process is based on the differential power stability between frames [19]. The difference between candidate lines statistical stability [3] and differential power stability is that the first must elect one over all the frames considered good, temporally, when the book pages are wide open and do not present obstacles, which means that warping may occur. A larger computational effort is required. On the other hand, in the latter technique, only the frames with low energy variation with the book wide open are processed, along with the book being stretched out, meaning that warping is naturally reduced. This technique requires a lower computational effort, and fits the needs of this work overall.

3 The Specification

The hands removal algorithm and the respective text substitution necessarily need two images to be taken. The pages must be stretched with the hands of the individual. However, the hands cannot be placed in the same area in each image. The purpose of the algorithm is to replace the regions covered by the hands with the corresponding text area, as depicted in Fig. 2.

Fig. 2. Illustration of the regions that could be blocked by the hands during the process.

In order to accomplish this substitution, an image difference algorithm is applied. This algorithm compares two images and generates a new one, composed by the sum of those two. For instance, the algorithm compares two images by pixel – the images A and B (mold), the elements (pixels) are compared between Axy and Bxy, where A and B are any element, and x and y are defined according to the position of a determined element (line and column). In case there are different pixels in the same position, these pixels are highlighted, as shown in the following images:

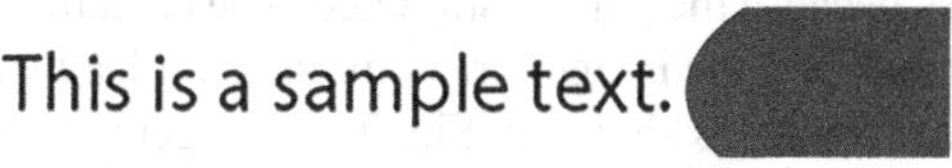

Fig. 3. Exemplification of hands blocking the text (grey color).

This is a sample text. Testing

Fig. 4. Exemplification of the next frame, when hands are not present and the text appears.

Testing

Fig. 5. Difference detected by the algorithm.

In other words, only different pixels are maintained in the composed image. Figure 5 is the result of application of the difference algorithm in Figs. 3 and 4. To maintain the text in both versions of the document, the regions where there are differences are composed in a way to maintain the images united at a transparency level, instead of being entirely removed (Fig. 10).

However, before applying this algorithm, text alignment is needed. In order to do so, a rotation correction algorithm (deskew) is applied. The algorithm finds the existing text lines in the page and calculate its angles. This angle is found by using the rotation as parameter. Figure 6 illustrate this process:

Fig. 6. Angle detection and deskew operated by the algorithm.

In synthesis, the hand removal algorithm is processed as follows:

(a) Adaptive threshold;
(b) Rotation algorithm;
(c) Image difference algorithm;

4 The Algorithm

Overall, the algorithm consists in taking one frame in high resolution per second. The captured image is then utilized to verify if the page is entirely open or being turned, when only parts of the page appear. If the page is entirely open, a beep is emitted and the book page should be stretched with the user's hands. Once the image of the page is taken, another beep sounds and the user should reposition their hands. Another frame is then captured. The algorithm then deskews the images for a proper alignment. No dewarping is necessary because the page is stretched. The detection of areas covered by the user's hands is done. Then, the images are combined, replacing the covered areas in a new image. In the first frame, as shown in Fig. 7, the finger region is marked red, and the algorithm defines this as "Finger_Region1" and cuts off the image in this region, discarding its contents. In the second frame, shown in Fig. 8, the process is repeated, and the red region is defined as "Finger_Region2". The result is a new image of each one, respectively "CleanImage1" and "CleanImage2", in which the finger regions are empty (Fig. 10).

In frame 1, the coordinates from "Finger_Region2" are copied into "CleanImage1". In frame 2, the coordinates from "Finger_Region1" are copied into "CleanImage2". Then "CleanImage2" is copied to "Finger_Region1" coordinates on the first frame, and on the second frame "CleanImage1" is copied into "Finger_Region2" coordinates. The resulting image is then binarized through a threshold process, so that the OCR might be more accurate in real-time detection.

To evaluate the process, page 32 from the book "Tolstoi, The Biography" was used. The book has been digitized using a flatbed scanner Plustek BookReader V200 [20]. The objective of this study is to evaluate the performance changes that the process causes in a character recognition precision level by OCR. Thus, images obtained by the process were utilized as OCR entry and the precision of the identified text was quantified. The text angle was the altered variable in the tests.

The book "Tolstoi, The Biography" was chosen for possessing plain and justified text, in a way to isolate any text segmentation questions that may affect the OCR performance. The flatbed scanner Plustek BookReader V200 was chosen as it is designed to be used by visually impaired and blind people. Since its functionalities include OCR and text-to-speech, the images obtained provide a favorable format for the OCR application.

No images were taken beforehand for the tests. In other words, images of documents being obstructed by hands on text regions were not utilized. There are many factors such as lighting, document position and other deformations that are still not predicted to be treated by this process. Hence, specially prepared images were used. To simulate the hands over the document, visual obstructions were added to the image via software. These obstructions consist in red circular areas of 999 × 999 pixels. The areas were added randomly so as to simulate hands, generating thus pairs of images to be utilized as a parameter by the image difference algorithm.

Fig. 7. Example of red areas inserted in the original image to test the algorithm.

Fig. 8. Example of angle inserted in the original image to test the algorithm.

In addition, the software ImageMagick [21] was used to rotate the images in order to test the angle correction process. Pairs of images were generated, in which the first possessed a positive angle and the other, the same angle, but negative.

Fig. 9. Example of image that will be run through the algorithm.

After the process is complete, the resulting images of the algorithm were submitted to an OCR software, Tesseract [22]. To measure the accuracy of the OCR performance in terms of character recognition, Google Diff [23] was used as a comparison algorithm. This algorithm can compare two text documents and measure differences between them. For example, considering text A and B as parameters for Google Diff, the following differences are evidenced: a) characters that exist in A but not in B, b) characters that are present in B but not in A. Thus, text images that were recognized by OCR were compared with the same exact respective to that image – which is known as ground truth. Ground truth of the images was obtained by applying OCR with Tesseract in each image and correcting the resulting text manually (twice), so that any possible identified errors could be eliminated. The text obtained by OCR was then compared with ground truth. The error percentage (performance) was obtained through the character quantity of the given text identified by the OCR that did not match its respective ground truth characters. In other words, if ground truth has 10 characters, and the text obtained by OCR presented 2 wrong characters, error percentage is 20 %. The images were all 96 DPI, converted from TIFF to PNG.

5 Results

The results reveal, as depicted in Table 1, that there are no significant alterations of OCR performance by the application of the suggested process, as all steps occurred properly.

Table 1. Test results showing different angles used in the tests and correspondent performance.

Process Applied	Image Size (MB)	Text Obstruction	Rotation Angle (degrees)	Execution Time (seconds)	Performance (error rate in %)
OCR	8	No	0 (no rotation)	25.911	1.9
ID and OCR	6	Yes	0 (no rotation)	67.537	0.6
AC, ID and OCR	11	Yes	45 and -45	98.643	0.8
AC, ID and OCR	11	Yes	30 and -30	94.338	1.1
AC, ID and OCR	11	Yes	15 and -15	72.729	0.6
AC, ID and OCR	10	Yes	7,5 and -7,5	98.352	100

(Acronyms taken as parameters used in the table as follows. OCR-Optical Character Recognition. ID-Image Difference. AC-Angle correction.)

For instance, the OCR error rate in the unprocessed image is 1.9 %, in a total of 2432 characters. With the application of image difference, the error rate changed to 0.6 %. With angle correction and image difference, the error rate increased to 0.8 %, at an angle of 45 degrees. That is, the process may even improve performance compared to the unprocessed image accuracy. This probably is due to the fact that the images are limiarized through the process (Fig. 10).

Thus, the process is at a great risk if one of the steps fail. Figure 11 shows that at an angle variation of 7.5 degrees, there is an error rate of 100 % on character recognition due to a failure in the angle correction process.

In terms of comparison in the best scenario, Chakraborty [3] utilizing Tesseract OCR reaches 70 % character recognition accuracy through their process, while the presented algorithm in this paper the OCR accuracy reaches around 99,4 %. Although, the conditions that the experiments went through vary as the first experiment utilizes whole books

Fig. 10. Resulting image after the steps of the algorithm succeeded.

and uncontrolled environment as parameters, while the second utilizes a single frame under a virtually controlled ambient.

The experiments were done utilizing a Intel Core Duo T2400 1,83 GHz processor, having 3 GB RAM DDR2, while Chakraborty [3] utilizes a 1.87 GHz CPU and 2 GB RAM.

Fig. 11. Resulting image after the angle correction failed in the algorithm.

6 Conclusion

This work proposed an algorithm capable of solving difficulties aroused by visually impaired and blind people handling books for digitization. The objectives were successfully reached, as shown in Table 1. Although a few improvements are needed, the results are promising. The rotation angles used in the tests are largely wider than the ones in real life, having in mind that the tendency is to obtain good results in practice due to guidance from the Vocalizer platform, in which the top of the book must be matched, preventing further angle discrepancy.

For future research, the difference algorithm should be applied only to hand-covered areas. This can be accomplished by applying the algorithm only in regions where the pixel is greatly different. The rotation algorithm needs to be further developed in order to be more accurate. The next tests should be done in real cases, with the subject's hands instead of being simulated by a software, and in which ambient illumination is also considered. Moreover, the quality of the composed image must be improved, considering that the text image will be recognized by OCR afterwards.

Acknowledgements. We would like to thank FINEP and CNPq for the financial support. And a special acknowledgment to the company Pináculo.

References

1. Singh, S.: Optical character recognition techniques: a survey. J. Emerg. Trends Comput. Inf. Sci. **4**(6), 545–550 (2013)
2. Xiu, P., Baird, H.S.: Whole-Book recognition. IEEE Trans. Pattern Anal. Mach. Intell. **34**(12), 2467–2480 (2012)
3. Chakraborty, D., Roy, P.P., Alvarez, J.M., Pal, U.: OCR from video stream of book flip-ping. In: 2013 2nd IAPR Asian Conference on Pattern Recognition, pp. 130–134. IEEE, Okinawa (2013)
4. Sarkar, P., Baird, H.S., Zhang, X.: Training on severely degraded text-line images. In: Proceedings of the Seventh International Conference on Document Analysis and Recognition, pp. 38–43. IEEE (2003)
5. Crovato, C.D.P., et al.: A preprocessing algorithm to increase OCR performance on application processor-centric FPGA architectures. In: 14th International Conference on Smart Homes and Health Telematics. ICOST 2016 - Inclusive Smart Cities and Digital Health, Wuhan, China (2016)
6. Hersh, M., Johnson, M.A. (eds.): Assistive technology for visually impaired and blind people. Springer Science & Business Media, London (2010)
7. Liang, J., DeMenthon, D., Doermann, D.: flattening curved documents in images. In: IEEE Computer Society Conference on Computer Vision and Pattern Recognition, vol. 2, pp. 338–345. IEEE, San Diego (2005)
8. Shamqoli, M., Khosravi, H.: Warped document restoration by recovering shape of the surface. In: 8th Iranian Conference on Machine Vision and Image Processing, pp. 262–265. IEEE Press, Zanjan (2013)
9. Song, L., Wu, Y., Sun, B.: A robust and fast dewarping method of document images. In: International Conference on E-Product E-Service and E-Entertainment, pp. 1–4. IEEE Press, Henan (2010)
10. Stamatopoulos, N. Gatos, B., Pratikakis, I., Perantonis, S.: A two-step dewarping of camera document images. In: The 8th IAPR International Workshop on Document Analysis Systems, pp. 209–216. IEEE Press, Nara (2008)
11. Stamatopoulos, N., Gatos, B., Pratikakis, I., Perantonis, S.J.: Goal-oriented rectification of camera-based document images. IEEE Trans. Image Process. **20**(4), 910–920 (2011). IEEE
12. Mitchell, P.E., Yan, H.: Document page segmentation and layout analysis using soft ordering. In: 15th International Conference on Proceedings Pattern Recognition, vol. 1, pp. 458–461. IEEE (2000)
13. Sadri, J., Cheriet, M.: A new approach for skew correction of documents based on particle swarm optimization. In: 10th International Conference on Document Analysis and Recognition, pp. 1066–1070. IEEE (2009)
14. Shivakumar, P., Kumar, G.H., Guru, D.S., Nagabhushan, P.: A new boundary growing and hough transform based approach for accurate skew detection in binary document images. In: International Conference on Proceedings of Intelligent Sensing and Information Processing, pp. 140–146. IEEE (2005)
15. Ulges, A., Lampert, C.H., Breuel, T.M.: Document image dewarping using robust estimation of curled text lines. In: Eighth International Conference on Document Analysis and Recognition, pp. 1001–1005. IEEE (2005)
16. Gatos, B., Pratikakis, I., Ntirogiannis, K.: Segmentation based recovery of arbitrarily warped document images. In: Ninth International Conference on In Document Analysis and Recognition, vol. 2, pp. 989–993. IEEE (2007)

17. Peng, X., Cao, H., Subramanian, K., Prasad, R., Natarajan, P.: Automated image quality assessment for camera-captured OCR. In: 18th IEEE International Con-ference on Image Processing, pp. 2621–2624. IEEE (2011)
18. Video Stabilization Using Point Feature Matching. http://www.mathworks.com/help/vision/examples/video-stabilization-using-point-feature-matching.html. Last Access: 1 June 2016
19. Lee, K.Y., Chuang, Y.Y., Chen, B.Y., Ouhyoung, M.: Video stabilization using robust feature trajectories. In: 12th International Conference on Computer Vision, pp. 1397–1404. IEEE (2009)
20. Plustek BookReader V200. Plustek Inc., Taipei, Taiwan
21. Image Magick, version 7.0.2, Computer Software, ImageMagick Studio LLC (2016)
22. Tesseract, version 3.03 (rc1), Computer Software, Google Inc., Mountain View, California (2014)
23. DiffMatch, version 20121119, Computer Software, Google Inc., Mountain View, California (2012)

Toolkits for Smarter Cities: A Brief Assessment

Auriol Degbelo[1(✉)], Devanjan Bhattacharya[2], Carlos Granell[3], and Sergio Trilles[3]

[1] Institute for Geoinformatics, University of Muenster, Münster, Germany
degbelo@uni-muenster.de
[2] NOVA Information Management School (NOVAIMS), Universidade Nova de Lisboa, Lisbon, Portugal
[3] Institute of New Imaging Technologies, Universitat Jaume I, Castelló, Spain

Abstract. The literature has offered a number of surveys regarding the concept of smart city, but few assessments of toolkits. This paper presents a short analysis of existing smart city toolkits. The analysis yields some general observations about existing toolkits. The article closes with a brief introduction of the Open City Toolkit, a toolkit currently under development which aims at addressing some of the gaps of existing toolkits.

1 Introduction

A review of smart cities documentation and literature reveals two distinct ways of using the term "toolkit". While some documents (e.g., [1]) evaluate smart cities services based on social parameters such as efficacy of the smart solutions on improving living conditions or the social benefits, many other smart cities reports (e.g., [2]) have propped up the definition of toolkit technically as a generic collection of utilities, applications and guidelines for citizens to wield these tools and smart city facilities. Additionally there are descriptions for citizens, administrators and industries about smart cities such as [3] to create further utilities, share developments and products, and maintain their own city in a smart way. Mostly toolkits are not reported in literature as they are software packages available online for access and use: for instance a search for "toolkits for smarter cities" returns no relevant publication about toolkits in Google Scholar and Microsoft Academic Search as of August 2016. Hence a comparative study of existing toolkits for smart cities is needed, as well as an evaluation of their pros and cons in order to propose a more effective solution that could be used and shared by citizens towards an engaged development of their cities. Though some reviews exist in the literature regarding smart cities (e.g., [4]), few so far, if any, have specifically looked at toolkits. This article is a preliminary work addressing this gap.

Existing toolkits are briefly assessed in Sect. 2 along different dimensions such as topical coverages, institutions developing them, user-centeredness, the degree of integration (i.e., interconnectedness) of the toolkit's components, openness of the toolkit's components, deployment in a city (i.e., whether or not the toolkit

C.R. García et al. (Eds.): UCAmI 2016, Part II, LNCS 10070, pp. 431–436, 2016.
DOI: 10.1007/978-3-319-48799-1_47

or its components have been used in any city), maintenance, publication format and publication year. We also shortly introduce the early development of the Open City Toolkit (OCT) in Sect. 3.

2 Toolkits for Smarter Cities: A Brief Assessment

The concept of smart cities has been changing from a top-down and mostly technological-driven approach, towards a bottom-up process that facilitates participation and collaboration among city stakeholders [5]. In this latter respect, the city is an ecosystem in which smart applications, open government data, and new modes of participation are fostering innovation [6]. As van der Graaf [7] pointed out, toolkits play an important role in this context and have two possible benefits: (a) they assist in systematically outsourcing certain design tasks from public institutions to users (i.e., citizens); and (b) toolkits tend to reduce the threshold for engagement by enabling and facilitating user participation in product or service development corresponding to their individual needs.

Table 1 summarizes the features of the toolkits analysed. The inclusion criterion was that toolkits' authors/publishers specifically mention the goal of making cities smarter in the toolkit's scope. The mention "n/a" in a column means "not applicable"; the mention "INA" means "information not available"; the mention "partly" in the column 'Open Source?' indicates that *only some* toolkit components are freely accessible for re-use; "partly" in the column 'Deployed?' means that *only some* toolkit components have been deployed in a city. Some toolkits were considered during the analysis but do not appear in Table 1, either because they do not specifically address smart cities, or because they are still at a very preliminary stage of development. These are: the Downtown Developer Toolkit (http://bit.ly/1OSeOcH), the City of Pittsburgh's Vacant Lot Toolkit (http://bit.ly/28zKez9), the GeoSmartCity cross-platform toolkit (http://bit.ly/1S2TyPX), the Data driven Interactive Smart City decision support toolkit (http://bit.ly/28zKbmV), the Farming Concrete data collection toolkit (http://bit.ly/1Yo4EGI), the Green City Development toolkit (http://bit.ly/1YmHEHT) and the Mixities Toolkit (http://bit.ly/1Om6TIv). All urls mentioned in this paper were last accessed on August 23, 2016. Table 1 was compiled based on information available about the toolkits on that date.

The CLAIRE toolkit (http://bit.ly/1WM0usF) is a visual analytics toolkit which aims to create and implement roadmaps, stakeholder management and engagement, model-based scenario planning, as well as a smart energy system evaluation. According to the toolkit's brochure, CLAIRE is currently used in the EU FP7 City-zen project (http://bit.ly/1xERnfY).

The Citadel toolkit was developed within the EU Citadel on the Move research project. According to [1], Citadel has helped more than 120 cities across Europe to open up their data and create over 600 basic applications.

CitySDK is a "service development kit" for cities and developers that aims at harmonizing application programming interfaces (APIs) across cities. CitySDK APIs enable new services and applications to be rapidly developed, scaled and

Table 1. Current toolkits for smarter cities and their characteristics.

Name	Topical coverage	Developer	User-centered?	Integrated?	Open Source?	Deployed?	Maintained?	Format	Year
CLAIRE toolkit	visual analytics	DNV GL	INA	INA	✗	✓	INA	INA	INA
Citadel toolkit	mobile apps development	Citadel Consortium	✓	✓	✓	✓	INA	Web templates	2012-2015
CitySDK Toolkit	participation, mobility, tourism	EU Consortium	✗	✗	✓	✓	✓	apps, maps, utilities	2012-onwards
EPIC IBM	relocation, urban planning	IBM for EU	✗	✓	✗	✓	✗	Website	2011-onwards
ESD Toolkit	tools for city governance	UK Govt	INA	INA	partly	partly	✓	Website	2012-onwards
Hackable City Toolkit	digital media, urban planning	One Architecture, Mobile City	n/a	n/a	n/a	n/a	n/a	PDF	2015
ICOS URENIO	tourism, sensing parking, etc.	EU Group	✗	✗	partly	partly	✗	Website	2013-onwards
Organicity EU	health, safety, parking, etc.	EU Consortium	✗	✗	✗	✗	✗	tools	2015-onwards
Smart Citizen Kit and Platform	citizen participation	Univ. Coll. London and others	✗	✓	✓	✗	✓	Mobile, Arduino, IDE and Web	2015-onwards

reused through providing a range of tools and information for both cities and developers [8]. CitySDK (www.citysdk.eu/citysdk-toolkit) concentrates on "participation", "mobility" and "tourism" as three of the most common interactions that citizens have with their municipality.

The European Platform for Intelligent Cities (EPIC) has been a flagship project for creating the base for smart cities (www.epic-cities.eu). A project developed by IBM for the EU, EPIC provides solutions to city managers and citizens about better managing their city using information and communication technology (ICT).

The ESD-toolkit framework (Effective Service Delivery Toolkit, http://bit.ly/237a5KO) is a set of tested tools, models, case studies and guidance, many of which are freely available to support national and local agendas for pubic services. It helps local authorities develop a logical approach to "achieving more with less", improving productivity, delivering value for money, targeting socially excluded citizens and protecting vulnerable communities. At the moment of writing, the ESD Toolkit has been upgraded to become LG Inform Plus.

The Hackable City Toolkit (http://bit.ly/1PpBGz5) was jointly developed by One Architecture and the Mobile City Foundation. It is a series of seven phases and eight strategies useful to deal with urban issues. The toolkit was developed based on an analysis of 84 projects which used digital media to improve urban life.

The Urban and Regional Innovation Research (URENIO, http://bit.ly/1toa9cC) is a university laboratory for the promotion of research and supply of scientific and technological services in the field of innovation systems and intelligent cities. URENIO Research has created the ICOS Community in order to promote the adoption of open source solutions for smart cities. The ICOS platform enables developers to upload five types of open source applications for smart cities: generic applications, applications related to the innovation economy of cities; applications related to the quality of life in cities; applications related to city infrastructure and utilities; as well as applications related to city governance.

The OrganiCity experimenter portal (http://bit.ly/1VX7nXa) is a hub where registered stakeholders can log in, and interact with tools they need to create and manage their city experiments in one place. These tools share and utilise data which has been made available across Aarhus, London and Santander. The OrganiCity experimenter portal is an ongoing work that will enable the creation and modification of 'citizen experiments', the monitoring of progress and the analysis of results in a user friendly way.

Smart Citizen (http://bit.ly/1JLYx7H) is a platform to ease participatory processes in cities. By connecting data, people, knowledge, and technology, Smart Citizen enables the creation of productive and open indicators, as well as tools for data capture and analysis or for social and educational experiments. Its goal is the collective construction of the city by, and for its own inhabitants. The Smart Citizen platform combines software and hardware, fostering co-creation processes so that people can create real deployments (e.g., crowd sensing initiatives in local neighbourhood, local maps of air quality or sound problems).

This brief assessment of toolkits leads to the following observations:

- the topical coverage of current toolkits is relatively broad (o1);
- the EU consortium (through research projects), and private companies are currently the main drivers of toolkit development for smarter cities (o2);
- few toolkits follow a user-centered approach during their development (o3);
- few toolkits provide an integrated solution for smart cities; instead many offer a plethora of independent software components to choose from (o4);
- only few toolkits make all their components freely accessible for re-use (o5);
- information about the maintenance of the toolkits is, in most cases, not available (o6);
- many toolkits analyzed have deployed their components, i.e., they provided examples of use of (at least some of) their components in cities (o7);
- existing toolkits are mainly published as software components (o8);
- toolkits for smarter cities are, by and large, at an early stage of their development (o9).

(o1) suggests an interest for toolkits in a broad number of smart city domains, and augurs (along with o9) an explosion of tools dealing with smart city problems in the coming years; (o6) may have its roots in (o9). In addition, truly empowering citizens to add value to existing open data is still an open issue as there is currently no open source community driving toolkit development for citizens (o2). Also, more open source toolkits are needed to catalyse knowledge sharing as fully open source toolkits are currently the exception rather than the rule (o5). These observations are a snapshot of current toolkits' characteristics. As a result, they are necessarily limited in scope and need continuous update to keep pace with the rapid changes of the toolkit landscape. Despite these limitations, they are still valuable as they provide a useful complement the recent review of the smart city research landscape presented in [4].

3 The Open City Toolkit

The OCT [9] is envisioned as an integrated, open source software empowering citizens, providing them with analytical tools and citizen-centric services in the context of a smart city. With reference to the previous section, it mainly addresses gaps (o4) and (o5). The OCT is incorporating the results of the various research lines within the GEO-C project. It is designed to keep all the resulting resources (i.e., data, processes, services, guidelines, ontologies, and models) along with utilities, tools and applications that make use of these resources.

By a set of tools, utilities, and applications, we mean all the complementary but much-needed functionality to support the discovery, browsing, access, edition, and visualization of OCT resources. A CKAN-based implementation is a step towards our purpose since CKAN comes with built-in facilities for managing, browsing, and exploring resources. We have used existing CKAN extensions, customised them, and integrated them into the live instance of the OCT portal (http://giv-oct.uni-muenster.de:5000). Examples are search facilities to retrieve resources according to specific purposes and needs. Nevertheless, our interest lies in extensions which are helpful to manage and handle geospatial data and resources. Currently, OCT uses the *spatialUI* and *spatial_metadata*, and *spatial_query* for retrieving spatial data, and *geo_view* and *geojson_view* for visualising it. Besides, other extensions have been installed to cover extra functionalities, such as data viewers (pdf, image and text), charts using different visualizations, RDF vocabularies, local storage, API for reading, connect with google analytics, usage statistics, and the creation of documentation pages. Also, we have developed a CKAN template in order to customize the way to visualize the different resources that the OCT offers.

In order to facilitate the use of the OCT, a collection of tutorials is provided. These snippets are offered using an associated website, called Open City Toolkit Developer Corner (http://giv-oct.uni-muenster.de/dev-corner). It includes short installation instructions for different development environments (e.g., node, bower, mkdocs), as well as different code snippets, in different languages, useful for data collection, storage, retrieval, analysis and visualization using the OCT. All components that form the OCT use open source software such as CKAN and Mkdocs, and all new developments are continually published as open source software components on GitHub (https://github.com/geo-c).

Looking at the toolkit review (Sect. 2), there are quite a lot of toolkits that share the overall vision of the OCT in making cities more efficient and a better place through ICT by making available a collection of city applications and APIs. The OCT goes one step further and offers a collection of datasets, services, apps, and guidelines. Indeed, a distinguishing and novel feature of the OCT is the concept of guidelines or city stories, as a way to deliver successful (or not) experiences of smart city initiatives addressing the second main objective of the OCT: educate people and democratise Smart City initiatives to any city. For this reason, the OCT is taking into account different user profiles, in order to provide helpful guidelines and solutions to citizens, developers and city councils.

4 Conclusion

Though the current literature has provided a passel of surveys and reviews about concepts of smart cities, there are still few assessments of toolkits, and their role in enabling smart cities. The current work is a first step towards closing this gap. The work looked at nine toolkits, summarized their features, and pointed at preliminary insights from their assessments. Future work along these lines could investigate the actual usage of toolkits in the smart city context and their impact (e.g., through user surveys). The work also briefly introduced the OCT which is an ongoing work aiming at providing an integrated open source platform which will empower citizens to add value to existing open data. Currently the OCT features a Developer Corner, as well as a CKAN platform which catalogs all its resources. The OCT aims to be a set of best practices which can be replicated in other sites with similar requirements.

Acknowledgments. The authors gratefully acknowledge funding from the European Union through the GEO-C project (H2020-MSCA-ITN-2014, Grant Agreement Number 642332, http://www.geo-c.eu/). Carlos Granell has been funded by the Ramón y Cajal Programme (grant number RYC-2014-16913).

References

1. Veeckman, C., Graaf, S.V.D.: The city as living laboratory: empowering citizens with the Citadel toolkit. Technol. Innov. Manage. Rev. **5**, 6–17 (2015)
2. Lee, J., Lee, H.: Developing and validating a citizen-centric typology for smart city services. Gov. Inf. Q. **31**(Supplement 1), S93–S105 (2014)
3. Vanolo, A.: Smartmentality: the smart city as disciplinary strategy. Urban Stud. Early View **1**(1), 1–16 (2013)
4. Ojo, A., Dzhusupova, Z., Curry, E.: Exploring the nature of the smart cities research landscape. In: Gil-Garcia, J.R., Pardo, T.A., Nam, T. (eds.) Smarter as the New Urban Agenda. Public Administration and Information Technology, pp. 23–47. Springer International Publishing, Switzerland (2016)
5. Townsend, A.M.: Smart Cities: Big Data, Civic Hackers, and the Quest for a New Utopia. Norton & Company, New York (2013)
6. Eskelinen, J., García Robles, A., Lindy, I., Marsh, J., Muente-Kunigami, A.: Citizen-Driven Innovation - A Guidebook for City Mayors and Public Administrators, Technical report, World Bank and European Network of Living Labs (2015)
7. der Graaf, S.: Smarten up! open data, toolkits and participation in the social city. Commun. Strat. **96**(4), 35–52 (2014)
8. Pereira, R.L., Sousa, P.C., Barata, R., Oliveira, A., Monsieur, G.: CitySDK tourism API - building value around open data. J. Internet Serv. Appl. **6**(1), 1–13 (2015)
9. Degbelo, A., Granell, C., Trilles, S., Bhattacharya, D., Casteleyn, S., Kray, C.: Opening up smart cities: citizen-centric challenges and opportunities from giscience. Int. J. Geo-Inf. **5**(2), 16 (2016)

Playability Index, Built Environment and Geo-Games Technology to Promoting Physical Activity in Urban Areas

Ignacio Miralles(✉), Carlos Granell, and Joaquín Huerta

Universitat Jaume I, Castellón, Spain
{mirallei,carlos.granell,huerta}@uji.es

Abstract. The natural and built environment has an impact on the amount of daily physical activity that people do, being less than the minimum recommended by international organizations. However, some characteristics of the environment may incentive physical activity more than others. While technological advances in geospatial information can be regarded as powerful enablers to identify and analyse these main features of the built environment, there is still a large gap between health-related professionals and the proper use of such technologies to address the prevalence of physical inactivity. This paper presents the research plan being conducted for a doctoral thesis with two major objectives: to identify a Playability Index that gives insights about how friendly is a city from the perspective of physical activity, and to develop a technological framework that eases the development of software-driven, effective interventions for promoting physical activity for young people in urban areas.

Keywords: Physical activity · Built environment · Playability index · Technological framework · Playable cities · Geogames

1 Introduction

Physical activity along with a moderate and healthy diet is one of the main components of a healthy lifestyle. However, current physical inactivity rates do not seem to be altered by this evidence, remaining below the recommendations of international health organizations [1, 2]. Nevertheless, the deficiency of physical activity is not only the result of people's lifestyle. Other factors may be equally important such as the lack of access to open spaces and sports facilities, and the absence of knowledge about the influence of the natural and build environment in physical activity [3].

Several reviews have identified multiple strategies to increase and improve levels of physical activity. Among others, aspects related to designing the streets resulting in more comfortable to walk, or improving the access to areas like parks or open environments are commonly included [4]. In fact there is recent evidence suggesting that people living in neighborhoods or environments more conducive to physical activity show a lower level of sedentary lifestyle [5], which is directly related to a lower prevalence of overweight [6].

A crucial aspect of this research is thus to identify the attributes or characteristics that make a public space more or less friendly for physical activity [7]. In order to

C.R. García et al. (Eds.): UCAmI 2016, Part II, LNCS 10070, pp. 437–444, 2016.
DOI: 10.1007/978-3-319-48799-1_48

characterize a friendly physical activity area, different variables or factors such as the type of activities that can be developed in public areas, the quality of the green areas of the environment, the available equipment or safety will be gathered and assessed. Taking as input such a list of attributes and variables, together with other relevant data and indexes (e.g. walkability index) for the case study, i.e. promoting physical activity for young people in urban areas, it will be possible to spatially analyse all these data sets together covering the same geographical area (e.g. city, neighborhood), and to determine and assign a Play Value [8] to contained public zones within the study area.

Some studies have also identified the impact of features of the urban environment centering on the use of public transport in access to school, concluding that the actual design of the city and not only the distance is important when promoting active travel and commuting behavior [9]. However, the vast majority of these studies are limited to analysis of the urban environment applied to commuting routes (for example, moving from home to work, or home to school), whereas the objective of this research aims to determine a methodology for calculating the Playability Index for an urban environment, so that it can be applied in a great variety of use cases and scenarios other than those limited to mobility through specific routes.

Using the Playability Index as a general framework to determine favorable zones to physical activity in a given urban area, existing applications in the literature that include GIS (Geographic Information Science) components and/or geospatial technologies will be discussed, generally called "Context-Aware" or more specifically "Geo Games" technology [10]. The latter is a novel and dynamic alternative to classic table games or videogames. As widely-recognized in the literature, geo games are also games, and so they are a useful tool to improve the motivation and engagement of users [11]. The social aspect of (video-)games complements and most likely reinforces user's motivation and engagement, because people often do not exercise only by the exercise itself, but by the social relationship with others [12].

In addition to the use of sensors, web-based and mobile-based methodologies for fostering physical activity, there are, for example, studies using these technologies to helping with depression [13] or motivating behavioral activation, which also influence a healthy life. It also cannot be forgotten that gamification techniques can be applied to varied demographic and social profiles, and not just adolescent population. To this regard, a recent study [14] shows that adding a linear navigation component to applications based in gamification, elderly population was able to solve tasks and become more involved with technology (a Web application, in this case study).

Despite all the above evidence, we conducted a literature search in both specific databases (Scopus) and search engines for scholarly literature, (Google Scholar), and found a few studies directly linking healthy characteristics of the natural and built environment in a city with applications that can exploit them for promoting physical activity. This undoubtedly opens a door to the expected contributions of the thesis.

When it comes to developing "Geo games" applications, a typical limitation or barrier is the complexity of the application itself, the software development process, and the handling of the interaction with other devices in the environment. This often requires the development of the application from scratch [15]. Some prototypes have been presented [16], although targeting developers as end users rather than health professionals with no-tech skills. Furthermore, there is a clear gap between developers and professionals of without advanced technical skills.

Overcoming such a technology barrier has been proven to show positive results. Two remarkable examples are worth to note. In Beat The Street [17], a cohort of children and adolescents was encouraged to make the way to and from school by placing a card at different points along the route followed. The second example refers to an international competition in collaboration with NGOs [18] where the social aspect of the Web was used to motivate and encourage children the same attitude. In both examples gamification and motivation techniques were closely used to create mobile (geo) games applications to increase physical activity.

From this perspective it seems prudent to hypothesize that if more accessible platforms for health professionals were developed, focused on promoting the increase in physical activity, maximizing the use of healthy attributes of urban environments, more effective interventions would be available to attack the problem of physical inactivity, and hence might ultimately lead to a direct decrease in sedentary life-style of the adolescent population.

After this motivating introduction to the overall context, problem, and main goals of the research, we describe in detail the research questions that drive our research work. Next, we present the expected contributions that address these research questions, followed by the methodology, research plan and activities to achieve the expected outcomes.

2 Research Questions

Recent studies show that there is a widespread problem of physical inactivity in urban settings: dedication to physical activity is much lower than recommended by international organizations (i.e. WHO). This problem is especially suffered by teenagers. Some of the factors that may explain this circumstance is the geography of the built environment itself which characterizes cities and neighborhoods [19]. The term "built environment" refers to the artificial elements that are part of everyday human activity in neighborhoods and cities, such as buildings, types of streets, parks and green spaces. The (spatial) configuration and organization of such artificial elements of the built environment helps determining that some neighborhoods or cities are more attractive to physical activity than others. Such cities tend to be considered healthier, and expose lesser sedentary lifestyle rates. In this sense, the geography of the built environment affects not only the health of people, but it can also bring positive economic and environmental impact, reducing pollution and facilitating mobility in neighborhoods and cities.

There are different groups of professionals (psychology, medicine, etc.) that are interested in taking advantage of healthy characteristics of cities to deal with physical inactivity in adolescents. However, the design and development of specific interventions, i.e. experiments, to address the problem of sedentary lifestyles often requires a far from negligible technological component. This can a priori be perceived as a positive aspect, because the technology can be seen as a magnetic pole to easily attract teens to get involved and participate in interventions. But at the same time, as introduced earlier, technology acts as an entry barrier, preventing health professionals from focusing its efforts on the strategies, methodologies, and techniques to promoting physical activity rather than unnecessarily struggling in technological aspects.

With the ultimate aim of promoting physical activity for young people in urban environments, the intention of this thesis is to give some insights to the following research questions:

1. Are spatial characteristics of the natural and built environment invariant, i.e. are the observed differences on the levels of physical activity in adolescents in an area (e.g. city) due to random fluctuations?
2. Are all types of spatial characteristics of the environment equally strong across all levels of physical activity, i.e., are such levels affected more or less by certain types of characteristics of the environment?
3. Do highly correlated characteristics of the environment make an impact in real interventions to incentive physical activity for young people?

In particular, the first research question refers to the null hypothesis. We will try to reject this null hypothesis during the course of our research project.

The second research question is concerned with the identification of strong, moderate or steady correlation between certain characteristics of the environment and variations of physical activity.

The third research question attempts to explore how highly correlated characteristics of the environment can be leveraged for supporting technology-based interventions to incentive physical activity for young people.

3 Expected Contributions

Based on the brief overview of the literature, on the identification of problems and needs, and the research questions introduced in previous sections, the present doctoral thesis aims to make three substantial contributions to the current state of the art.

- The first contribution, in response to research questions 1 and 2, is the creation of a Playability Index based on the natural and environment characteristics of urban spaces;
- The second contribution, related to research question 3, is the technological framework to support the creation of interventions with an important technological base; and
- The third contribution is the experimental validation of the last two research question (as the research question 1 is the null hypothesis) by developing proof-of-concept applications for promoting and encouraging physical activation of adolescents with prevalence of sedentary lifestyle.

The first contribution will encompass the identification and analysis of the characteristics of the environment, both built and natural, that potentially have implications for physical activity in adolescents. This means the creation of a Playability Index. In short, the Playability Index will comprise various research steps or activities, being detailed in Sect. 5, resulting in the assignment of values to different administrative units or sectors of the city of study with respect to the influence of natural and built environment characteristics on physical activity.

The second contribution is the development of a technological framework that facilitates and guides health-related professionals in other fields (psychology, medicine or physical education, for example) to create applications that offer activities and content for their patients, students or users. For doing so, it relies on the characteristics analysed in the first contribution. This framework will add the novelty of being based on the latest GIS and geo games technologies together with the reactive programming paradigm and actor-based models.

The third contribution is aimed at consolidating the two previous ones by developing two applications capable of promoting physical activity in adolescents. For this it relies on the framework developed in the second contribution while serving as feed-back for it. Applications will aim to provide information, reminders and specific tasks that bring the city gameplay features to users. These applications will be evaluated with prototype experiments to demonstrate proper operation.

Despite being clearly defined and delimited, the three contributions follow a sequential order to cover different aspects of the study in order to provide relevant in-sights and solutions to help improving rates of physical activity in a particular sector of society such as teenagers.

4 Work Planning

The proposed work plan covers the traditional stages in a PhD research, which can be grouped in two large blocks with differentiated methodologies.

In the first group, typical stages include the research plan, literature review and analysis, dissemination (paper writing, etc.), and writing up the thesis manuscript. In this case the methodology requires a direct relationship (discussions, meetings, etc.) with thesis advisors or experts from other areas who will offer iteratively and incrementally orientation in each of the tasks performed.

The second group comprises stages related directly to the very research activities, which involve both social and technical/coding aspects. Social-oriented techniques will include for instance focus groups to collect relevant factors and assess them during the realization of the Playability Index. On contrast, recent software engineering methodologies and best practices on software development, combining classic waterfall development scheme with agile software development, will be employed for developing the technical framework. Although some stages will be carried out traditionally, as the collection of specific requirements, the analysis and implementation phases will be developed using an agile methodology based on CodeSprints, with concrete objectives to be met and evaluated in each sprint. This will generate frequent feedback on a sprint basis to quickly meet key requirements.

The stages (in a tentative chronological order) of the proposed work plan are described below. We omit literature review and dissemination (papers writing) because they will run continuously during the course of the research.

- Research Plan: It is the initial stage to frame the entire research project. It includes an initial but deep analysis of the literature, the identification of the research questions, the establishment of methodologies, and the breakdown of individual tasks.
- Development of Playability Index: At this stage, specific literature that can provide and justify the attributes or characteristics of the environment that may qualify a neighborhood as healthy or playable will be analysed. Besides methods and techniques as focus group will be used too, along with GIS analysis to model the Playability Index and provide pertinent visualizations. Finally, the index must be validated with actual data on physical inactivity. Although the main output of this stage is the Playability Index, the assessment of the characteristics analysed will be an equally relevant output.
- Creation and Validation of the Framework: At this stage the technological framework is developed. It includes aspects such as analysis of available technologies, specific requirements, design, development and deployment. The output of this stage should be a functional version of the Framework.
- Creation and Validation of the Applications: This stage focuses on the development of two applications that promote physical activity. Again it includes identification of requirements, analysis, design, development and publishing. It also includes pilot tests to confirm proper operation. The outputs of this stage are the two generated applications.
- Writing Thesis: Unlike the previous stages, which are sequential, this stage starts off with the research plan and will be running until the end of the research. Taking research notes and documenting research activities on a regular basis are key habits to excel academic writing skills, in order to facilitate dissemination tasks (papers, blog posts) and the final writing of the PhD thesis manuscript.

5 Next Steps: Playability Index

We detail here the methodological approach of the immediate step in the course of the PhD: the development of the Playability Index. We will use different methods to define, design, create, and validate the proposed Playability Index. For example, focus groups with health specialists will be conducted to determining the relative influence of the spatial characteristics of the natural and built environment on the prevalence of insufficient physical activity. Data in this case will be collected by running semi-structured questionnaires or from direct interviews. Field experiments will be conducted, if required, for validating in situ spatial characteristic of the environment in the city of study or for geocoding clinical data on levels of sedentary lifestyle. Several GIS analytical methods will be used to implement the Playability Index in the form of a map or other types of visualizations.

The proposed activities for building up the Playability Index are:

- Finding of environmental variables influencing insufficient physical activity, in order to this different steps will be followed:
  - Depth review of the literature.
  - Health care professionals consulting.

  - Focus groups and questionnaires.
- Weighting of variables and theoretical generation of Playability Index.
- Acquiring clinical data of levels of sedentary lifestyle and geocoding it if required. The aim is to validate the attributes and weight selected with real data.
- Performing GIS analysis:
  - Identification and collection of GIS data and sources.
  - GIS data ground, data preparation and integration.
  - Generating Playability Index map and/or other types of visualizations.
  - Model testing/validation.

All in all, we expect that the contributions of the present thesis help stakeholders to build up better and efficient interventions to help mitigate the insufficient level of physical activity of young people in urban areas.

Acknowledgements. Ignacio Miralles was funded by the Spanish Ministry of Education, Culture and Sports (FPU grant reference FPU14/00020). Carlos Granell has been partly funded by the Spanish Ministry of Economy and Competitiveness "Ramon y Cajal" Programme (grant number RYC-2014-16913).

References

1. Pate, R.R., Pratt, M., Blair, S.N., Haskell, W.L., Macera, C.A., Bouchard, C., Kriska, A.: Physical activity and public health: a recommendation from the Centers for Disease Control and Prevention and the American College of Sports Medicine. JAMA **273**(5), 402–407 (1995)
2. Haskell, W.L., Lee, I.M., Pate, R.R., Powell, K.E., Blair, S.N., Franklin, B.A., Bauman, A.: Physical activity and public health: updated recommendation for adults from the American College of Sports Medicine and the American Heart Association. Circulation **116**(9), 1081 (2007)
3. Witten, K., Hiscock, R., Pearce, J., Blakely, T.: Neighbourhood access to open spaces and the physical activity of residents: a national study. Prev. Med. **47**(3), 299–303 (2008)
4. Buchner, D.M., Gobster, P.H.: Promoting active visits to parks: models and strategies for transdisciplinary collaboration. J. Phys. Act. Health **4**, S36–S49 (2007)
5. Sallis, J.F., Cerin, E., Conway, T.L., Adams, M.A., Frank, L.D., Pratt, M., Davey, R.: Physical activity in relation to urban environments in 14 cities worldwide: a cross-sectional study. Lancet **387**(10034), 2207–2217 (2016)
6. Saelens, B.E., Sallis, J.F., Black, J.B., Chen, D.: Neighborhood-based differences in physical activity: an environment scale evaluation. Am. J. Public Health **93**(9), 1552–1558 (2003)
7. Badland, H.M., Keam, R., Witten, K., Kearns, R.: Examining public open spaces by neighborhood-level walkability and deprivation. J. Phys. Act. Health **7**(6), 818–824 (2010)
8. Jenkins, G.R., Yuen, H.K., Rose, E.J., Maher, A.I., Gregory, K.C., Cotton, M.E.: Disparities in quality of park play spaces between two cities with diverse income and race/ethnicity composition: a pilot study. Int. J. Environ. Res. Public Health **12**(7), 8009–8022 (2015). http://doi.org/10.3390/ijerph120708009
9. Helbich, M., van Emmichoven, M.J.Z., Dijst, M.J., Kwan, M.P., Pierik, F.H., de Vries, S.I.: Natural and built environmental exposures on children's active school travel: a Dutch global positioning system-based cross-sectional study. Health Place **39**, 101–109 (2016). doi: 10.1016/j.healthplace.2016.03.003

10. Schlieder, C., Kiefer, P., Matyas, S.: Geogames: a conceptual framework and tool for the design of location-based games from classic board games. In: Maybury, M., Stock, O., Wahlster, W. (eds.) INTETAIN 2005. LNCS (LNAI), vol. 3814, pp. 164–173. Springer, Heidelberg (2005). doi:10.1007/11590323_17
11. Garris, R., Ahlers, R., Driskell, J.E.: Games, motivation, and learning: a research and practice model. Simul. Gaming **33**(4), 441–467 (2002)
12. Mueller, F., Agamanolis, S., Picard, R.: Exertion interfaces: sports over a distance for social bonding and fun. In: Proceedings of the Conference on Human Factors in Computing Systems - CHI 2003, (5), pp. 561–568 (2003). http://doi.org/10.1145/642611.642709
13. Botella, C., Mira, A., Moragrega, I., García-Palacios, A., Bretón-López, J., Castilla, D., Guillén-Botella, V.: An internet-based program for depression using activity and physiological sensors: efficacy, expectations, satisfaction, and ease of use. Neuropsychiatric Dis. Treat. **12**, 393 (2016)
14. Castilla, D., Garcia-Palacios, A., Miralles, I., Breton-Lopez, J., Parra, E., Rodriguez-Berges, S., Botella, C.: Effect of Web navigation style in elderly users. Comput. Hum. Behav. **55**, 909–920 (2016)
15. Dey, A.K., Sohn, T.: Supporting end user programming of context-aware applications. IST PROGRAMME, 23 (2003)
16. Biegel, G., Cahill, V.: A framework for developing mobile, context-aware applications. In: Proceedings of the Second IEEE Annual Conference on Pervasive Computing and Communications, PerCom 2004, pp. 361–365. IEEE, March 2004
17. Coombes, E., Jones, A.: Gamification of active travel to school: a pilot evaluation of the Beat the Street physical activity intervention. Health Place **39**, 62–69 (2016). doi:10.1016/j.healthplace.2016.03.001
18. Hunter, R.F., de Silva, D., Reynolds, V., Bird, W., Fox, K.R.: International inter-school competition to encourage children to walk to school: a mixed methods feasibility study. BMC Res. Notes **8**(1), 19 (2015). doi:10.1186/s13104-014-0959-x
19. Lopez, R.: The Built Environment and Public Health, vol. 16. Wiley, New York (2012)

Ubiquitous Signaling System for Public Road Transport Network

Gabriel de Blasio[1(✉)], Alexis Quesada-Arencibia[1], Carmelo Rubén García-Rodríguez[1], Jezabel Miriam Molina-Gil[2], and Cándido Caballero-Gil[2]

[1] Instituto Universitario de Ciencias y Tecnologías Cibernéticas, ULPGC, Las Palmas de Gran Canaria, Spain
{gabriel.deblasio,alexis.quesada,ruben.garcia}@ulpgc.es

[2] Department of Computer Engineering and Systems, University of La Laguna, San Cristóbal de La Laguna, Spain
jmmolina@ull.edu.es, ccabgil@ull.es

Abstract. Mobility is a basic need for people, therefore the authorities in advanced societies pay special attention to systems and initiatives that improve or facilitate it. In this work, a ubiquitous signaling system for visually impaired people, using a combination of WiFi and Bluetooth Low Energy (BLE) technology with Smart Mobile Devices, is proposed. The system is conceived as a solution to help and support these users in places of public road transportation with travellers massive transit, such as bus stations, interchangers or preferred stops. In addition, once the user is positioned in the desired location, the system would offer advanced services: information on lines schedules, tickets sale, etc.

Keywords: Ubiquitous computing · Intelligent transport system · Indoor positioning system

1 Introduction

A Smart City is an urban space committed to the environment, providing advanced architectonic and technological elements in order to facilitate the citizen interaction with the urban elements, with the goal of improving the life quality. The environment refers to both, environmental issues as well as the cultural and historical elements. Smart Cities are spaces that integrate different areas: mobility and logistic, human resources and human capital, economy and competitively, urbanism and sustainable housing, ecosystem and sustainable environment, e-democracy and e-government, etc. [31].

The availability of user-adapted information is an essential aspect of public transportation systems, since it helps to improve the quality of service and constitutes a basic resource in complex and dynamic transport systems [10]. According to the studies conducted by different local, regional, national and even international organizations, such as the University of Michigan Transport

C.R. García et al. (Eds.): UCAmI 2016, Part II, LNCS 10070, pp. 445–457, 2016.
DOI: 10.1007/978-3-319-48799-1_49

Research Institute [26] and the European Conference of Ministers of Transport (ECMT) [6], the information should be adapted as needs vary according to the type of person using the service. Indeed, for the information to be effective for the traveller, it must be comprehensible and coherent. Thus it is vital to know what travellers really need; this knowledge involves identifying the different groups of travellers and their specific requirements. For people with specific needs, accessing a public transportation system can be a source of concern, from the moment they access the service, because of the physical difficulties experienced in accessing the stations or vehicles, or the uncertainty of unexpected situations during the trip. Following Stradling [27], these feelings discourage them from using the public transportation.

The proposed work is part of two specific policy areas:

- Using Ubiquitous Systems in the field of mobility: as we indicated before, mobility is a basic need for people and therefore the authorities in advanced societies pay special attention to systems and initiatives that improve or facilitate it.
- Using Ubiquitous Systems as tools to help visually impaired people: one of the most important learnings for people with blindness and visual impairment is personal autonomy. Without the sense of sight, is more difficult to collect, process, store and retrieve information from the environment, causing problems to move and a cognitive development delay, related to spatial and figurative aspects. For these individuals, their displacement in any environment, familiar or not, should be carried out in a safe, efficient and independent manner.

The technological solution provided in this work basically consists of three integrated subsystems:

- An application for Smart Mobile Devices adapted to visually impaired people, that will be the element of the system with which the user interacts directly.
- A network of WiFi Access Points (AP) and Bluetooth Low Energy (BLE) beacons deployed in the area of interest: in our case, places of public road transportation with travellers massive transit, such as bus stations, interchangers or preferred stops.
- An information system in The Cloud to provide users with information and advanced services, directly related to the transport system: bus lines of interest scheduling, ticketing, etc.

As indicated above, the system relies on a network of devices based on two basic technologies and widely used in indoor positioning systems, such as WiFi and BLE. In addition, the proposed system model, where two redundant information channels (WiFi and BLE) with different accuracy and information detail level are used, proposes an architecture inspired by the natural sensory systems, so that there is an overall redundancy of information that makes it more robust against possible "damages" that could occur in some of its subsystems [23]. Both features, the existence of different computing subsystems and layers, are very present in living beings sensory systems, for example, in the visual system of many species including humans [24].

2 Related Works

Indoor Positioning Systems (IPS) use different technologies, such as WiFi, Bluetooth, RFID, Ultra Wide Band (UWB), ZigBee, Ultrasound, Infrared, Sensor Networks, Magnetic Signals, Visible Light, etc. where each system takes advantage of these technologies in particular or the combination of them, also inheriting their limitations [13]. The most popular technologies for these systems are WiFi and Bluetooth and specifically BLE, because among other factors, WiFi uses existing infrastructures which makes it very cheap to implement, and in the case of BLE, for its high accuracy, energy efficiency, low cost, being able to receive background notifications and it is also more accurate than WiFi, so beacons can be relatively easy deployed in indoor environments [8].

In the case of systems using WiFi, there are different approaches: those based on Received Signal Strength Indicator (RSSI) [9], Fingerprint [34], Angle of Arrival [33] or Time [12]. Each approach uses its own techniques and algorithms, with corresponding advantages and disadvantages, being the accuracy of positioning affected by different factors such as the presence of walls, AP overlapping signals, etc. and with values ranging from a few meters, in the case of RSSI-based solutions [21] or under a meter for other solutions [34] in the best environment conditions.

There are also different approaches to systems using Bluetooth [32], but for conciseness reasons and factors mentioned above, we will focus on the BLE technology. For this technology there is a growing literature, but being implanted recently (2010), there is not as much as in the case of WiFi. We can list a few: RSSI-based [20] or Fingerprint-based [7]. In all these approaches an accuracy to the meter with a high precision is achieved, sufficient to facilitate the positioning in indoor environments. For the particular case of Eddystone beacons (Google BLE beacons), as an emerging project, there is not much literature, although some recent works may be mentioned: in [19] it is stated the problem that each service requires its own beacons producing interference between them and hence a decrease in service accessibility is detected. As a solution, it is proposed to accurately identify the RSSI of the beacons applying a low-pass filter. In [15], a prototype application that helps users navigate inside a building was developed using signals from Eddystone beacons as reference. The application is also capable of providing information to the users related to their location using additional data attachments associated to the beacons. Infsoft company [16] has developed an indoor navigation mobile application for Swiss Federal Railways: using BLE beacons it helps passengers to find their way through Zurich main station, using ca. 1,200 beacons in an area of ca. 370.000 square meters, obtaining an accuracy of 2–3 m.

In the case of hybrid systems, that combine WiFi and Bluetooth, there are works like [2] in which an algorithm that identifies locations to deploy a limited number of Bluetooth hotspots in order to achieve the best positioning is proposed, also presenting several architectures for a hybrid indoor positioning system that serve different user needs and user hardware constraints, and works like [28] in which wireless signals intensity values are combined (WiFi-RSSI as principal and Bluetooth as secondary) obtaining better results than only with WiFi signals.

In relation to specific systems for the visually impaired, there are some works based on WiFi: in [1], an indoor tracking and navigation system is implemented on a Personal Digital Assistant (PDA) with limited resources. Experimental results suggest that the proposed system can be used to guide visually impaired subjects to their desired destinations, being the main limitation of the system in its low sampling rate of the RSS signal, due to limitations imposed by the hardware that was used for the implementation of the prototype device. In [25], an indoor positioning system that runs on a smartphone or tablet and takes advantage of WiFi signals is proposed. It comprises a calibration and a navigation stage: at the calibration stage, a WiFi fingerprint is created in each room of a building minimizing the calibration time through the use of waypoints, and the navigation stage matches WiFi signals to the fingerprints to determine the user's most likely location. In the case of Bluetooth-based works: in [11] two indoor positioning systems and a specific interface are implemented. The first system uses beacon selection and pseudo-intersection as pre-processing, and uses triangulation and fingerprinting as the main algorithms. It achieves a positioning accuracy of 1.83 meters. The second system uses a proximity algorithm, and a specific user interface was tailor-made for blind and visually impaired users for these two systems. In [5], a prototype of an indoor mobility assistant for visual impaired users is presented. The system uses the RSSI provided by beacons BLE strategically placed to identify different areas of a building, using also the pedometer and gyroscope of a smartphone.

3 Definition of Scenarios: Bus Stations

Mobility is a basic need for people, therefore the authorities in advanced societies pay special attention to systems and initiatives that improve or facilitate it. A fundamental aspect of transit systems is its accessibility, existing standards and recommendations to ensure their accessibility to all people, including those with special needs [6]. According to the United Nations, currently the percentage of the world population with disabilities is about 15 % [29], this percentage is expected to increase due to the increased life expectancy of people in developing countries. In advanced countries, transit systems offer services designed to improve accessibility and safety of transport networks. However, these services are often designed for people with full physical and cognitive abilities. This work describes a positioning system in places of public road transport with travellers massive transit, such as bus stations, interchangers or preferred stops for visually impaired people. With this system, the user could move through transport network places in order to locate the points where a service of interest is provided, such to a bus stop, an information point, etc.

Positioning systems play a key role in systems that provide ubiquitous services based on location. With technological advances in mobile telephony, wireless local area networks and positioning systems, ubiquitous services systems providers based on location are becoming more frequent, both in urban contexts with a large number of potential users, like in confined spaces contexts with a limited number of users. This work presents a location system for physically bounded spaces where there may be a large number of potential users, specifically it is a location system for public road transport with a travellers massive transit, such as bus stations, interchangers or preferred stops. These places are points where several services are provided to the transport user, such as: ticket sales, information points, cafeterias, where at any given time, there may be several public transportation vehicles parked in platforms, where travellers can board and unboard, which in the case of large stations or interchangers can be dozens of vehicles in this situation. Therefore, those are places where there are different locations of interest to the transport user, these places being normally marked by signposts. The proposed system is a location assistant for people with special needs who have difficulty locating such points of interest in these places of massive transit. From the technological point of view, an important feature of the proposed system is that it doesn't requires a special and costly infrastructure, as it is based on elements widely used, easily deployable and have minimal impact on other infrastructure elements.

Different studies have shown that public transportation is safer than private transport [30]. In the context of transport safety, and for the people with special needs collective, several studies examining aspects to be considered and recommended means to guarantee it for this type of people are developed. We should cite the work of Mitchell [22] identifying situations that require special attention, namely: boarding and unboarding vehicles, the use of payment systems, the occupation of a free seat and resuming the march of the vehicle (see Table 1). Location systems are elements that are needed in several of the required services for people with special needs. These required services depending on user types are presented in Table 1.

Table 1. Services for users with special needs

User types according to special needs	Required service
Reduced mobility user	Vehicle board and unboard assistant. Alert systems. Traveller's information systems with adapted terminals. Adapted pay systems
Reduced vision user	Vehicle board and unboard assistant. On route assistant. Adapted pay systems
Hearing loss user	Traveller's information systems based on mobile terminals and visual information based
Cognitive impairment user	User friendly traveller's assistantproviding easy to understand information

In the specific context of location systems for users with special needs in public transportation, it can be mentioned the works of Ivanov [17], proposing a GPS navigation system for visually impaired users, and Baudoin [3], describing aspects to consider to make accessible the services in public transportation, considering different points of view: technical (information, communication, location, energetic), ergonomic, economic and legal.

4 Used Technologies

In this paper a dual channel indoor positioning system is proposed using the combination of WiFi and BLE technologies and Smart Mobile Devices. The system will have two levels of accuracy provided by a WiFi channel used for positioning in a first approximation and a second channel BLE more accurately. The combination of both channels allow to offer the user advanced services: bus routes and schedules, tickets sale, etc.

Indoors mobility for visually impaired people has usually been a concern due to accuracy problems in indoor location systems. Therefore, this work proposes a new location system that allows greater freedom of movement in previously unthinkable environments for people with visual disabilities. As indicated above the proposal makes use of a location system based on the combination of WiFi and BLE technologies. This system takes advantage of the features of both technologies providing a new location system without deploying a large infrastructure and using technology that is currently available to any user, such as smartphones.

On one hand, the channel that uses the WiFi technology is commonly used to provide RF connectivity, locally reaching a device that sends Ethernet data from its location to a fixed network connection data. This point provides access to the data network through copper or fiber. Operation is defined in IEEE 802.11. It is a very popular technology, and has become the dominant standard for this type of connections. One advantage of using this technology is that it is very often found deployed in the scenario for which we propose our system, and furthermore, the deployment of such infrastructure is continuously growing. BLE devices operate in a bandwidth of 2.4 GHz with a range between 10 and 15 mts. It has a very low power consumption, providing a lifetime of several years, thus reducing maintenance. It has two modes of operation, as a receiver or as transmitter or beacon. In beacon-mode, the BLE emits a signal which provides some information allowing other devices in receive-mode to be located with respect to this beacon based on the RSSI and the information provided.

5 Proposed Positioning System

In this section a new two channels multi-layer scheme to help indoor positioning is described. On one hand, it is a generic location mechanism with a lower level of accuracy to roughly provide information of the existing environment and location (WiFi channel). This will be a first mental map of what can be found in the environment in which the user wants to move. On the other hand, we have a more accurate positioning system that provides a more detailed environmental information and allows to locate and reach the exact site (BLE channel). This second channel, in addition to assist the user in locating, also allows to access to advanced information services (schedule information, etc.) using the first channel. Therefore, it is proposed a multi-layer two-channel system that provides a initial level of abstraction, allowing later to concrete to reach the user desired target. The system abstraction levels have been created in order to look like as much as possible to the spatial perception of human beings.

5.1 Precision Levels: Definition of Zones

This first level of abstraction has been created to provide knowledge or first awareness of the environment and its surroundings. The aim is to provide the users with some awareness of their situation in the surrounding space, environment and the objects in it.

Having a good space perception allows the users to locate, move in this space, orient, taking multiple directions, analyze situations and represent them. The zones are a key concept in this proposal. When people are confronted to a new environment, it is very useful to have a generic view of what is around, and then, specifying the information to reach the target point. For example, approaching a station, in many cases it makes no sense to start to give a person instructions without providing information on the surrounding environment. Therefore, in this proposal, two levels of accuracy depending on how close or how far users are from their goal are defined. In particular, different parts of the protocol run depending on the zone where the user is compared to its final goal. As shown in Fig. 1, three zones are defined in a real scenario (schematic view of a local bus station), depending on the user's location relative to his ultimate goal:

- First abstraction level: in this zone, users does not have direct contact with their target so they will be provided with a generic visualization of environment, emphasizing the location of their target.
- Second abstraction level: users are not exactly in their destination point but receive information from both their target and the environment.
- Third abstraction level: users are in their target location where it can detect the target signal directly.

The size of the radius where the different technologies come into play will depend on the environment where the users are using the system, taking into account factors such as coverage, complexity of the environment in which to move, distance to the target, etc. In Sect. 6 a use case is proposed in which the system of this work is deployed in a bus station.

5.2 Positioning System

When a user arrives, in this case, to a bus station, the system has to define its ultimate goal. At the first level of abstraction, it will come into play WiFi

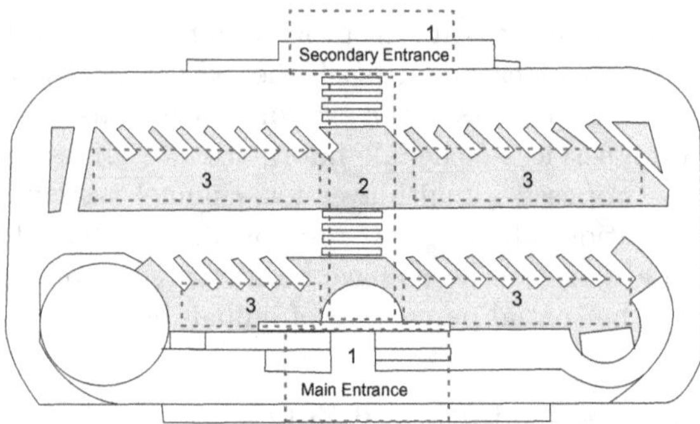

Fig. 1. Schematic view of abstraction zones in a real scenario

technology, which depending on the user's location and with respect to AP, will prompt the user the roughly distribution of its environment. For example, "stairs to the right", "cafeteria 200 meters left", "platforms 300 meters ahead", etc. Thus, the user can make itself a mental map of where is and where everything in their environment is and the system will provide a first level of information that may be useful for a user who has never been to the station. On the contrary, if the user had been before, will know where is are compared to previous situations. At this time, and given that the user will use an application on the mobile phone, it will indicate where he must go, and immediately receive the first indications.

Obviously this first positioning system, as discussed above, works relatively well when little precision is required, since it is affected on the one hand, by the wide range of sensors that current devices handle since the received signal strength depends on them, and on the other hand, by the number of people who are in place, since up to 60 % of the human adult body is water, and water absorbs radiation, so the signal will be affected. Therefore, and as already mentioned, this unique system does not solve the problem. Once the user receives a first approximation, will start walking following the initial instructions. As he moves, will not only receive WiFi signals but also BLE signals, so his route will be refined. Once the second level of abstraction is reached, the BLE devices, along with WiFi AP, will provide more information, reducing limitations of each separate technology and complementing each other.

However, there will come a point where all signals overlap and will be almost impossible to determine where the exact spot is, the bus platform required for the user, in this case. In this case it will be necessary to decrease the intensity of the signal so that the user can only receive it when he is exactly where it is expected. This can be achieved by configuring the transmission power of the beacons.

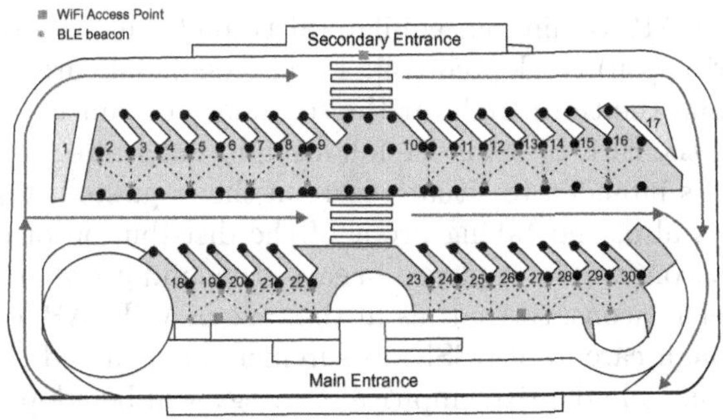

Fig. 2. Schematic view of bus station important elements, such as WiFi AP and BLE beacons distribution

6 Use Cases

The scenario where the positioning system will be tested is a local bus station, whose shape can roughly be approximated by a 150×62 meters rectangle. The schematic map of the station is shown in Fig. 2. In that schematic view it is shown, as important elements, the two boarding areas or areas of interest (gray filled), the distribution of WiFi AP and BLE beacons, buses paths (red lines) and stops (numbers), columns (black circles) and, finally, crosswalks.

Users will access the station by two entrances (main and secondary) and then move to areas of interest, directly (no stairs or ramps) or using disabled-accessible ramps or stairs. Note that when entering to the station the system must place users in one of the two zones of interest and then provide them with a service (information of a bus line, etc.).

Regarding to the deployment of WiFi and Beacons BLE, it is important to consider their number and position, because an incorrect deployment can produce coverage failures or interferences, in addition to the consequent increase in the installation cost. A possible approach to find best placement is based on the study of the intensity and quality of the signal, in addition of the noise level in various positions of the deployment area. Another approach not based on "fixed strategies" (uniform distributions and very dense distributions) may be an adaptive one [4] in which, given a location algorithm, an initial set of beacons is deployed, and then extend the set if it proves insufficient. Finally, a more theoretical approach is to use optimization techniques [18].

From the above scenario, it is necessary to deploy WiFi AP and BLE beacons optimally to meet two objectives: (a) The signals reaches with sufficient intensity to all areas, particularly to areas of interest, (b) The positioning in that zones is correct, avoiding positioning errors that lead users to danger zones, and gives the user the desired advanced services. The chosen model balances the objectives (a) and (b) but considering especially the safety and convenience of users.

Due to the particular distribution of architectural elements of the bus station (columns, etc.) and to avoid positioning errors of mobile devices, a strategy of deploying 3 WiFi AP forming an equilateral triangle (instead of a random or square-grid distribution) is adopted [14]. Two access points are located near the main entrance, and the third, right at the secondary entrance.

In the case of the BLE beacons the following initial strategy will be adopted: since the system is intended to situate users in the requested stop, giving them advanced services also, and taking profit of the distribution of columns in the enclosure, the beacons will be deployed in each stop, and just in front of alternate stops, some other beacons, so that, as in the case of WiFi AP, form equilateral triangles. If through careful of RSSI measurements it is noted that the deployment is insufficient, an adaptive empirical strategy will be adopted [4] in which the quality of the location would be improved by adjusting the beacons placement or increase their number.

Because the WiFi AP and BLE beacons share the same frequency range (2.4 GHz) there might be interference problems but: (1) interference problems usually occur when the number of access points is very large, something that does not happen in our case, (2) possible interference problems could be overcome by avoiding certain channels and taking into account that Bluetooth automatically uses FHSS (Frequency Hoping Spread Spectrum).

7 Conclusions and Future Work

The positioning and navigation systems are a key element in many of the ubiquitous information services available today. Currently the positioning and navigation in outdoor environments is determined reliably and accurately by using different solutions based on technologies widely used, as in the case of GPS and mobile telephony. However, positioning and navigation in indoor environments pose a number of challenges, such as optimal infrastructure, precision, most appropriate navigation route, etc., which make today still a subject of interest to researchers. This works presents an indoor location system proposal located in places of public road transportation with travellers massive transit, such as bus stations, interchangers or preferred stops. This system has the peculiarity that uses two types of basic technologies for indoor positioning, specifically WiFi and Bluetooth Low Energy. The reason for this choice is that, in this way, the problems that the spread of Bluetooth signal has, are solved, when used for positioning purposes in environments with physical elements acting as obstacles to this type of signal. In the proposed solution the Bluetooth Low Energy beacons have a dual mission: first, to provide the signal used to obtain the position by triangulation and second, to provide users with personalized information of interest. The proposed system is designed to road transportation users with special needs, such as visually impaired.

A navigation system, through the user's position knowledge, might tell the user the route to follow to reach his target, for example a bus platform, or a ticketing sale point. Once the point of interest is reached, the BLE device associated to that point will provide information, according to user preferences. In order to make the system attractive from the economic point of view, a combined strategy deploying sensors in a fixed distribution with an iterative refinement is contemplated. Some aspects to be considered in a future work would be: add to the current system a navigation system and an online ticketing sale service.

References

1. Au, A.W.S., Feng, C., Valaee, S., Reyes, S., Sorour, S., Markowitz, S.N., Gold, D., Gordon, K., Eizenman, M.: Indoor tracking and navigation using received signal strength and compressive sensing on a mobile device. IEEE Trans. Mob. Comput. **12**(10), 2050–2062 (2013)
2. Baniukevic, A., Jensen, C.S., Lu, H.: Hybrid indoor positioning with wi-fi and bluetooth: Architecture and performance. In: MDM, vol. 1, pp. 207–216. IEEE Computer Society (2013)
3. Baudoin, G., Venard, O.: Information, communication and localization environment for travelers with sensory disabilities in public transports. In: 2010 5th International ICST Conference on Communications and Networking in China (CHINACOM), pp. 1–7, August 2010
4. Bulusu, N., Estrin, D., Heidemann, J.S.: Adaptive beacon placement. In: ICDCS, pp. 489–498. IEEE Computer Society (2001)
5. Castillo-Cara, M., Huaranga-Junco, E., Mondragón-Ruiz, G., Salazar, A., Barbosa, L.O., Antúnez, E.A.: Ray: smart indoor/outdoor routes for the blind using bluetooth 4.0 ble. Procedia Comput. Sci. **83**, 690–694 (2016)
6. European Conference of Ministers of Transport: Improving Transport Accessibility for All. Guide to Good Practice. OECD Publications Service, Paris, France, pp. 41–71 (2006)
7. Faragher, R., Harle, R.: Location fingerprinting with bluetooth low energy beacons. IEEE J. Sel. Areas Commun. **33**(11), 2418–2428 (2015)
8. Faragher, R., Harle, R.: An analysis of the accuracy of bluetooth low energy for indoor positioning applications. In: Proceedings of the 27th International Technical Meeting of The Satellite Division of the Institute of Navigation, pp. 201–210 (2014)
9. Feng, C., Au, W.S.A., Valaee, S., Tan, Z.: Received-signal-strength-based indoor positioning using compressive sensing. IEEE Trans. Mob. Comput. **11**(12), 1983–1993 (2012)
10. García, C.R., Pérez, R., Alayón, F., Quesada-Arencibia, A., Padrón, G.: Provision of ubiquitous tourist information in public transport networks. Sensors **12**(9), 11451–11476 (2012). (Basel, Switzerland)
11. Ge, T.: Indoor positioning system based on bluetooth low energy for blind or visuallyimpaired users. Master's thesis, KTH Royal Institute of Technology, School of Information and Communication Technology (ICT), Department of Communication Systems, October 2015
12. Golden, S.A., Bateman, S.S.: Sensor measurements for wi-fi location with emphasis on time-of-arrival ranging. IEEE Trans. Mob. Comput. **6**(10), 1185–1198 (2007)
13. Gu, Y., Lo, A.C.C., Niemegeers, I.G.: A survey of indoor positioning systems for wireless personal networks. IEEE Commun. Surv. Tutor. **11**(1), 13–32 (2009)
14. Han, G., Choi, D., Lim, W.: Reference node placement and selection algorithm based on trilateration for indoor sensor networks. Wirel. Commun. Mob. Comput. **9**(8), 1017–1027 (2009)

15. Herrera-Vargas, M.: Indoor navigation using bluetooth low energy (BLE) beacons. Master's thesis, Turku University of Applied Sciences, June 2014
16. Infsoft: Sbb - my station. http://www.infsoft.com/industries/railway-stations/success-story/utm_source/website/utm_medium/link/utm_campaign/indoornavigation. Accessed 14 June 2016
17. Ivanov, R.: Mobile gps navigation application, adapted to visually impaired people. In: Proceedings of International Conference Automatics and Informatics, Sofia, Bulgaria, pp. 1–4 (2008)
18. Kouhbor, S., Ugon, J., Kruger, A., Rubinov, A., Branch, P.: A new algorithm for the placement of WLAN access points based on nonsmooth optimization technique. In: The 7th International Conference on Advanced Communication Technology, ICACT 2005, vol. 1, pp. 352–357 (2005)
19. Lee, B., Im, S., Lee, S., Kim, B., Roh, B., Ko, Y.: The beacon identification using low pass filter for physical web based IoT services. In: 2015 IEEE Pacific Rim Conference on Communications, Computers and Signal Processing (PACRIM), pp. 354–358, August 2015
20. Li, H.: Low-cost 3D bluetooth indoor positioning with least square. Wirel. Pers. Commun. **78**(2), 1331–1344 (2014)
21. Liu, H., Darabi, H., Banerjee, P.P., Liu, J.: Survey of wireless indoor positioning techniques and systems. IEEE Trans. Syst. Man Cybern. Part C **37**(6), 1067–1080 (2007)
22. Mitchell, C., Suen, S.L.: Urban travel, intelligent transportation systems, and the safety of elderly and disabled travelers. J. Urban Technol. **5**(1), 17–43 (1998)
23. Moreno-Díaz, R., Quesada-Arencibia, A., Rodríguez-Rodríguez, J.C., de Blasio, G.: Mechanism for retinal motion description suggested by a bio-inspired artificial vision system. Sci. Math. Japonicae **64**(2), 395–403 (2006)
24. Nakayama, K.: Biological image motion processing: a review. Vis. Res. **25**(5), 625–660 (1985)
25. Pritt, N.: Indoor location with wi-fi fingerprinting. In: IEEE Applied Imagery Pattern Recognition Workshop: Sensing for Control and Augmentation (AIPR 2013), pp. 1–8 (2013)
26. Richardson, B.C., Huang, H.C., Ebarvia, B.N., Kearney, O.P.: Toward estimating intelligent transportation system benefits based on user needs. Technical report. ITSRCE 939424, The University of Michigan Transportation Research Institute, The Buhr Building, 837 Greene Street, Suite 1210, Ann Arbor, Michigan 48104-3213, December 2000
27. Stradling, S.G.: Moving around: some aspects of the psychology of transport. Commissioned Science Review for Intelligent Infrastructure Systems project, Foresight, Department of Trade and Industry, London (2006)
28. Su, H.K., Liao, Z.X., Lin, C.H., Lin, T.M.: A hybrid indoor-position mechanism based on bluetooth and WiFi communications for smart mobile devices. In: 2015 International Symposium on Bioelectronics and Bioinformatics (ISBB), pp. 188–191, October 2015
29. United Nations: United nations enable. https://www.un.org/development/desa/disabilities/. Accessed 1 June 2016
30. U.S. Department of transportation: older road users. http://safety.fhwa.dot.gov/older_users/. Accessed 14 June 2016
31. Vera-Gomez, J.A., Quesada-Arencibia, A., García, C.R., Suárez-Moreno, R., Guerra-Hernández, F.: Intelligent management of parking lots in urban contexts. In: García-Chamizo, J.M., Fortino, G., Ochoa, S.F. (eds.) UCAmI 2015. LNCS, vol. 9454, pp. 499–504. Springer, Heidelberg (2015). doi:10.1007/978-3-319-26401-1_47

32. Wang, Y., Yang, X., Zhao, Y., Liu, Y., Cuthbert, L.: Bluetooth positioning using RSSI and triangulation methods. In: 2013 IEEE 10th Consumer Communications and Networking Conference (CCNC), pp. 837–842, January 2013
33. Youssef, M., Agrawala, A.K.: Small-scale compensation for WLAN location determination systems. In: 2003 IEEE Wireless Communications and Networking, WCNC 2003, New Orleans, LA, USA, 16–20 March 2003, pp. 1974–1978 (2003)
34. Youssef, M., Agrawala, A.K.: The horus WLAN location determination system. In: Proceedings of the 3rd International Conference on Mobile Systems, Applications, and Services, MobiSys 2005, Seattle, Washington, USA, 6–8 June 2005, pp. 205–218 (2005)

Development of Smart Inner City Recreational Facilities to Encourage Active Living

Leon Foster[1(✉)], Ben Heller[1], Alan Williams[2], Marcus Dunn[1], David Curtis[1], and Simon Goodwill[1]

[1] Centre for Sports Engineering Research, Sheffield Hallam University, Broomgrove Teaching Block, 11 Broomgrove Road, Sheffield, S10 2LX, UK
{l.i.foster,b.heller,m.dunn,d.curtis,s.r.goodwill}@shu.ac.uk
[2] The Parks and Countryside Service, Moorfoot, Level 3, West Wing, Sheffield, S1 4PL, UK
alan.williams@sheffield.gov.uk

Abstract. Lowfield Park in Sheffield, UK is a green recreational space maintained by the City Council. Lowfield Park was selected as the primary Sheffield FieldLab for the ProFit project which ended in 2015. The ProFit project was European Interreg IVbNWE funded with the aim of encouraging physical activity through innovations in products, services and ICT systems. In 2014 the Sheffield Hallam University City Athletics Stadium (SHUCAS) was introduced as a secondary FieldLab. A number of innovative systems have been installed into the FieldLabs, these include: Pan Tilt Zoom cameras, automatically timed sprint and running tracks, outdoor displays/touchscreen and a gait analyser. This paper describes the hardware, software and cloud infrastructure created to enable these systems. Pilot testing has been carried out over the last year and has found a positive effect on both sites. The systems created will be taken forward to Sheffield's Olympic Legacy Park, which is currently under development.

Keywords: Smart public monitoring · Participant tracking · RFID running lap · ProFit FieldLab · SHUCAS · Smart Park

1 Introduction

ProFit was a collaborative European Union Interreg IVbNWE funded project that aimed to support product innovation and novel ICT system development in sport, exercise and play. Public recreational spaces in five European cities are now hosts to FieldLabs, which serve as end-user locations for research and development of product and ICT innovations. The cities that currently host FieldLabs are: Sheffield and Ulster in the UK, Delft and Eindhoven in the Netherlands and Kortrijk in Belgium [1]. Sheffield's first FieldLab is located in a City Council controlled recreational green space called Lowfield Park [2] and houses a children's playground, 3G football pitch, fitness zone and a community building called the U-MIX Centre run by the charity, Football Unites Racism Divides (FURD). An overview of the Lowfield site is shown in Fig. 1a/d. As a spin off from the ProFit project a second Sheffield FieldLab was created within the Sheffield Hallam University City Athletics Stadium (SHUCAS) on Woodburn Road [3] shown in Fig. 1b/c.

C.R. García et al. (Eds.): UCAmI 2016, Part II, LNCS 10070, pp. 458–468, 2016.
DOI: 10.1007/978-3-319-48799-1_50

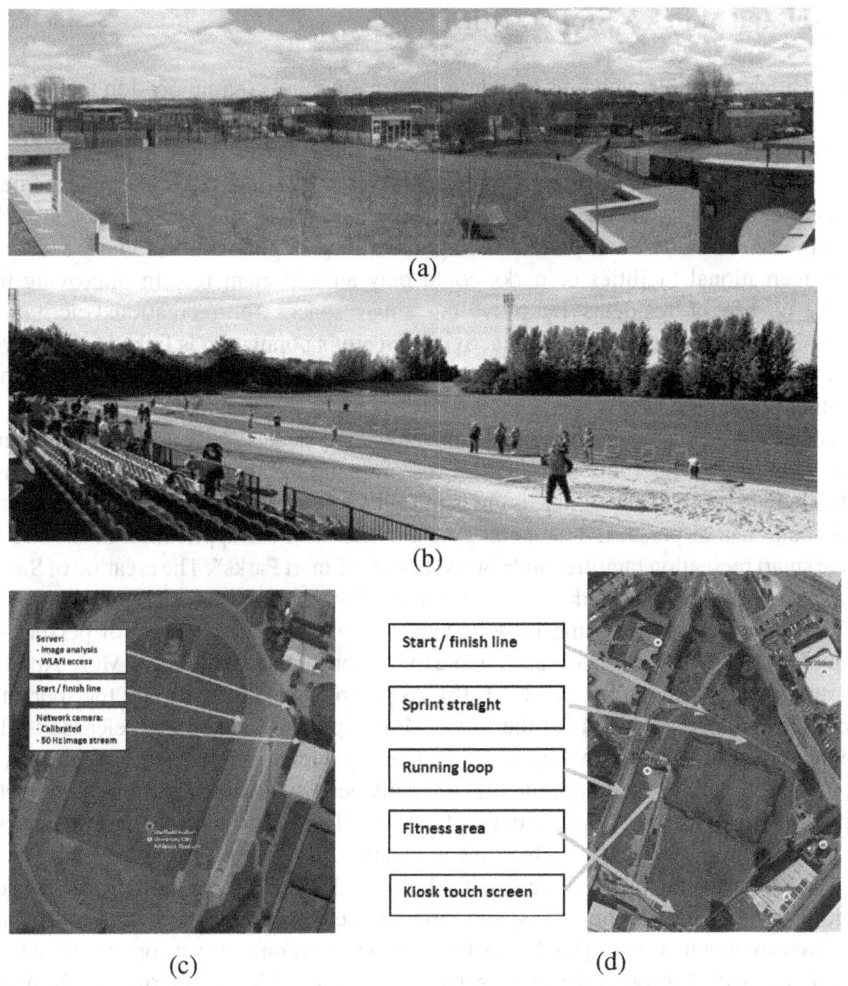

Fig. 1. Overview of the: (a) Lowfield Park (b) Sheffield Hallam University City Athletic Stadium SHUCAS and aerial view of (c) Lowfield park and (d) SHUCAS.

Over the lifetime of the ProFit project a number of innovative ICT systems were installed at both Sheffield FieldLab sites, creating a "Smart park" and a "Smart track". These recreational spaces were utilized by the Centre for Sports Engineering Research to under-take various research and development projects for these systems. Both sites act as demonstrator and prototyping hubs for the research centre and external partners.

2 Related Work – Smart Cities

Smart Cities are cities which use modern information and communication technology (ICT) as well as the Internet of Things (IoT) to function more efficiently and provide an improved quality of life for residents and visitors. Smart Cities aim to manage and integrate various city services such as transportation, water supplies, waste management law enforcement and other community services in order to function more efficiently. As part of the Smart City concept, and falling under the category of community services, smart recreational facilities or parks could play an important role in improving the quality of life of residents by providing smart spaces for recreational activities. Increasing recreational and physical activity of a city's population is linked to improvements in health and well-being, and a potential reduction in health care costs, due to a healthier population [4, 5].

The use of persuasive technology to encourage physical activity as part of a preventative healthcare model is a new field of research and the most effective ways to use technology to motivate healthier living is not fully known [6, 7]. One effective method could be to use of persuasive technology combined with the application of the IoT to create smart recreation facilities and open spaces or "Smart Parks". The creation of Smart Parks" has not been as abundant as other Smart City concepts and is potentially due to the benefits of smart not being fully documented as yet. One example of persuasive technology being used to encourage people to be more active is the Move More App for smartphones deployed in Sheffield, UK [8]. As part of the National Centre for Sport and Exercise Medicine, NCSEM [9] the Move More App was created and released to the general public in Sheffield in August 2016. The app intention is to encourage the city's population to be active through the logging daily activity and the creation of competitions between individuals and groups of people. The effectiveness and competitive nature of the app is currently undergoing evaluation.

The use of IoT within Smart cities has been used widely in other applications such as traffic monitoring, lamppost systems, smartphone detection, patient monitoring and waste management systems [10, 11]. All systems have in common sensor systems which are interconnected through the latest standards in Bluetooth, the internet, LAN/WAN as well as Wi-Fi. These sensor units usually communicate to a central server where data is stored and processed to produce reports. Some of these sensors units are stationary such as traffic monitoring sensors mounted on traffic signs [12] and other are mobile such as air pollution sensors mounted on refuse vehicles and have other issues such as power provision [13, 14].

The use of a variety of sensor systems and other IoT technologies have been deployed in the two Sheffield FieldLabs as a novel "Smart park" concept, for ongoing evaluation as to the effectiveness of these technologies in promoting physical activity. As the most effective method to encourage physical activity through technology is not fully understood the concept of monitoring and reporting activity performance was considered, following on from the Move More App. For the benefit of future Smart Park and FieldLab sites, this paper gives an overview of the IoT systems installed at both Sheffield field labs, the benefits of the systems and pitfalls of creating and running Smart Park sites.

3 Technology Systems Overview

3.1 Server, Centralised SQL Research Database and Cloud Database

Given the collaborative nature of FieldLab sites, an agent software model was considered to be appropriate. An agent model allows the separate development of software applications that communicate with each other through a central data storage medium. This enables software to be developed independently at different sites by developers using any development environment. Within the ProFit project all software created for use on FieldLab sites followed a standardised database structure. In this way each FieldLab site has its own individual database based on this standard structure.

A Microsoft™ SQL database was created on a central high specification Windows based server and managed through Microsoft™ SQL Server Management Studio 2012. Microsoft™ SQL was chosen as this is widely used, and universal connection strings can be used by most agent applications. The database is accessible by any device or agent software, providing that the correct permissions have been granted and a local area network link has been obtained. For applications that are used by the public an additional layer of security was implemented, whereby web services were used to communicate with the database. Additionally, the server hosting the database was encrypted with Microsoft BitLocker.

A cloud database was created to store public accessible data which was later utilised in a running lap system. This was initially hosted in a Parse backend, but has been moved to the Microsoft Azure hosting services. The Parse backend system was initially used because it was free platform system which was envisaged to be sustainable with little operating costs. However, the system had to be migrated to an SQL database on the Microsoft Azure cloud platform due to cost constraints and available IT resources provided by the Sheffield Hallam University IT team.

3.2 Connectivity of the Server and Technology Systems

The Sheffield FieldLabs central server was connected to a local area network, and local Wi-Fi. This allowed for the interconnection of other devices at the site and communication to the central SQL database. The main server had an internet connection to allow remote access of the server system for maintenance and monitoring. Additionally, this allowed for a connection to a cloud database. A schematic of the LAN system is shown in Fig. 2.

3.3 Pan-Tilt-Zoom and Fixed Camera System

At all FieldLabs a number of high definition pan-tilt-zoom and fixed camera systems were installed. These systems were used to gain quantitative/qualitative information about participants using the sites. Additionally, these cameras are used to directly measure the interaction of participants within the FieldLab. All cameras communicate via the LAN and were accessible from the central server. The camera systems were not directly accessible remotely due to security concerns.

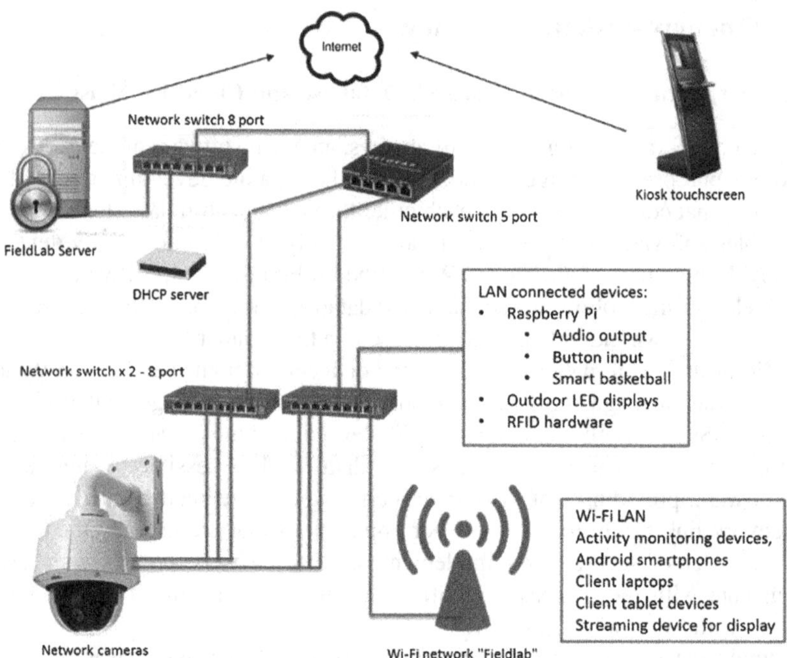

Fig. 2. Overview of the basic local area network infrastructure at each FieldLab site.

3.4 LED Display and Outdoor Screen Systems

To feedback information to park and track users, two outdoor screens were created. At Lowfield a permanent LED display Fig. 3a was installed that feedback lap and sprint times to participants. Communication with the LED screen was over a serial port emulator on the Ethernet network. A 42″ outdoor display screen system was implemented for the SHUCAS site, Fig. 3b. This was a standard screen with multiple HDMI inputs. A Chromecast device was used to stream a second screen from the server PC

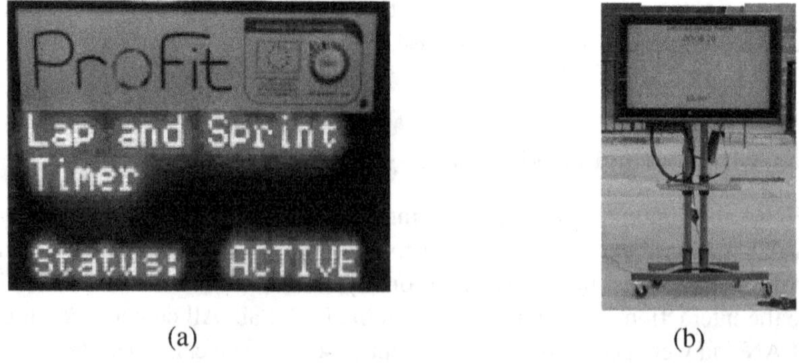

(a) (b)

Fig. 3. Outdoor displays at the field lab sites (a) SHUCAS (b) Lowfield

which allowed the use displaying of information from software applications around the track. This system could be wire-less through the use of a battery.

3.5 Kiosk Feedback System

Touch-screen kiosk PCs were installed at the Lowfield and Delft FieldLab. These consisted of internet connected low power PC with a large touchscreen. A high screen was created for adults and a lower screen for children and wheelchair users. These kiosks were used to give out information of the FieldLab site but also capture verbal/visual feedback from users through a webcam and microphone. The kiosk is also used as a platform for results from the RFID lap timing system to be presented.

3.6 Smartphone Activity Monitoring System and Tracking

An activity monitoring system was created to enable live monitoring of participants for research studies investigating participant interaction with pieces of installed equipment [15]. This system includes: Android smartphones with a custom application, Wi-Fi access points for beacons and various server based applications. An overview of this system is shown in Fig. 4.

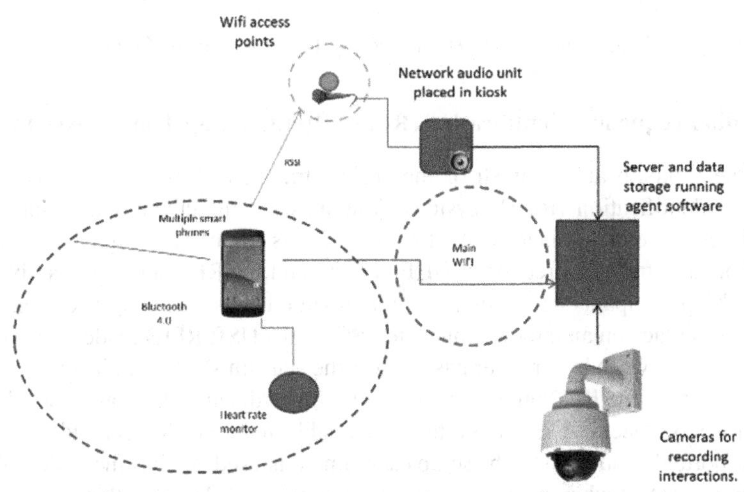

Fig. 4. Overview of the sprint track system components and agents

3.7 Interactive Sprint Track System

An automatically timed interactive sprint track was created on a perimeter footpath at Lowfield Park FieldLab. The system is started by a participant pressing a button at the start of a 50 m marked out running track. The button is linked to a Raspberry Pi model

A running a script to monitor button-push. The system then outputs a start sound through a speaker and sends a signal to image processing software running on the main server. The software on the main server uses on of the pan-tilt-zoom camera pointed at the finish line to monitor two participants crossing the finish line in two lanes. A time is calculated based on the start trigger and the crossing of the participants over the line. When a time is calculated, these are posted to an LED display. An overview of this system is shown in Fig. 5.

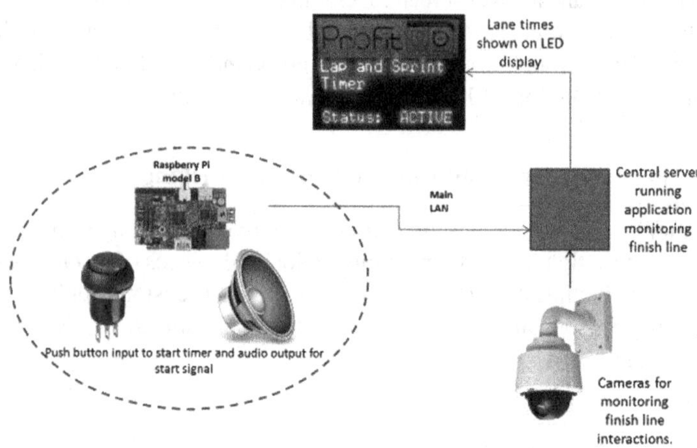

Fig. 5. Overview of the sprint track system components and agents

3.8 Radio Frequency Identification (RFID) Running Lap Timing System

Within the footpath at the finish of the sprint straight at Lowfield park is a Radio frequency identification (RFID) system. Antennas are directly mounted underneath composite non-metal drainage covers to allow the passing of radio signals. The system is based on an ultra-high-frequency UHF system, and the RFID tags are passive. Tags are worn by participants and registered on a cloud database. The tag-user registration process takes place on an internet connected PC with a USB RFID reader within the U-Mix. When a tag worn by a runner passes over the start finish straight it is registered on the system and time/lap logging is initiated. Times/distance/laps are posted to the outdoor display system. A similar system is available at the SHUCAS FieldLab, but this system is portable and needs to be setup each time it is used and has the option of using a split timing system whereby distance run can be specified. To make this second system portable it was connected via a Wi-Fi link.

3.9 Gait Analyser

The Gait Analyser is an example of an agent application which has been deployed at the SHUCAS FieldLab site. The software analyses the gait of a participant in view on the running track. To perform analyses, users need only identify the running lane and capture duration (typically 3 s); no markers or sensors are applied to the athlete or running track. Software is operated using a graphical user-interface (shown in Fig. 6 on Wi-Fi enabled devices, minimising restrictions to the system's use (i.e. portability).

Fig. 6. Graphical-user-interface for the Gait Anlyser agent software

When performing live running analyses, a fixed network camera, viewing the final 10 m of the 100 m straight (perpendicular to running direction), streams RGB colour images (1280 × 720 pixels) to a server computer at 50 Hz. The Gait Analyser – developed using the.NET framework (C#) – automatically analyses images to identify foot contacts observed during running; multithreading allows parallel image capture and processing. Camera calibration parameters are retrieved from a database, allowing the calculation of real-world, spatio-temporal gait parameters. It has been reported that the system identified 100 % of foot contacts (optimised setup) during sprint running; root-mean-square error was 108.9 mm and 0.03 s for foot contact position and time respectively [16]. Further, numeric and video results were provided to athletes within 2–3 s of capture.

3.10 Justification for the Selection of IoT Technology Systems

An overview of the IoT systems used, alternatives and the justification behind each of the choices for the FieldLab Smart Park systems are shown in Table 1.

Table 1. IoT system deployed in both the Sheffield FieldLab Smart Parks, their alternatives and justification for their use.

System type	System used	Alternatives	Original justification
Central database	Microsoft™ SQL	MYSQL or NoSQL alternatives	Widespread use of Microsoft SQL, in existing systems and data validation could be undertaken.
Cloud database	Parse™	Microsoft Azure, AWS + other cloud providers	Parse™ free to setup and had a host of featured to help development. Moved to Microsoft Azure due to Parse shutting down in Jan 2017.
LAN cameras	Axis Network cameras	Various other network camera systems	Development team had experience with Axis products
Health care sensors for live streaming of data	Smartphone with bespoke software	No available at the time of development	No cost effective alternatives at the time
Input system, network enabled switch	Raspberry Pi	Off the shelf solutions such as the Axis P88221 input output module	Raspberry Pi, low cost and quick to develop. Provided option for customization and includes audio output
Identification system	RFID, UHF passive system	Near field RFID, active RFID	RFID UHF tags are cheaper and do require battery power. Range can be greater for UHF system over alternative frequency ranges. Range gained by an active system not required.
Permanent display	Bright LED 4 line	Outdoor HD display	LED display less likely to be stolen and vandalised compared to the alternatives.
Portable display	Weatherproof outdoor display	Bright LED display	Flexibility to show video and custom display information
Interactive kiosk system	Windows based website touchscreen	Tablet based	Off-the-shelf outdoor system were available and website development could be outsourced easily.

4 Conclusions and Future Work

Overall the creation of the Smart Parks or FieldLabs in Sheffield and the other European cities was deemed a success. The technology systems developed and deployed at both sites in Sheffield have generated a lot of interest from the general public and researchers. The technology has also been welcomed by elite athletes and coaches who use the video capture system and gait analyser at the SHUCAS site. The running lap system and sprint track at the Lowfield site has been well received and the user base is growing daily. The running lap has now been included as one of the official 'Run Route' which are being promoted around the city of Sheffield. The number of users of the Lowfield site has been monitored and qualitative feedback has been collected from the Kiosk touchscreen PCs, which have been positive. The majority of systems deployed at the SHUCAS site have also been utilized in school events where events have been automatically timed and results displayed on the outdoor screen.

There have been some issues with implementing the IoT systems at both the FieldLab sites. The first issue is that both sites are remote which meant that general maintenance and upkeep of the technology was difficult. Remote access was carried out with Teamviewer™, but supporting users of the system proved difficult remotely. Additionally, simple things such as a reliable internet connection was difficult to secure at both sites. This meant the stability of the RFID running lap system which used a cloud database was affected when the internet connection was down. One of the problems of the Lowfield site specifically was environmental issues, where some of the systems were affected by water ingress and extreme cold temperatures. This meant some of the hardware on the site had to be replaced and some of the systems have been down for periods of time since the end of the ProFit project. Finally, it has been found that some of the systems at the SHUCAS site have suffered from reduced usage due to the potential complexity of the system and lack of training of staff at each site to use the systems to their full potential.

In conclusion the prototype systems showed that people will utilize the IoT systems to enhance their experience in using the facilities and the numbers of users at the Sheffield Smart Parks are increasing. If there are any technical issues users will get frustrated and cease to use the system. Therefore, any system being deployed needs to be simple and robust. Longitudinal data is currently being collated to see whether these systems can sustain their usage in the long term.

The systems developed in the Sheffield FieldLabs are going to be transferred to the Olympic Legacy Park [17] which encompasses the Advance Well-being Research Centre (AWRC) [18]. The systems will be developed to fit in with the new recreation space available within this park and incorporate new features to make the systems more user-friendly, robust and easy to deploy. This will hopefully increase the usability of the systems and increase numbers using the systems.

The vision of the AWRC is to encourage healthy living through increases in physical activity levels in the general population. Technology and systems like that explained in this paper allow for the creation of "smart" recreational facilities which could help facility the AWRCs goals in the future.

References

1. ProFit 2013. FieldLAB: an opportunity for internation cooperation in sports innovation. http://www.fieldlabs.eu/. Accessed 01 Nov 2013
2. Lowfield Park. https://www.sheffield.gov.uk/out–about/parks-woodlands–countryside/parks/city-district-local-parks/lowfield-park.html. Accessed 01 June 2013
3. Sheffield Hallam University City Athletics Stadium. https://www.shu.ac.uk/shucas. Accessed 01 June 2016
4. Godbey, G.: Outdoor recreation, health, and wellness: Understanding and enhancing the relationship (2009)
5. Lachowycz, K., Jones, A.P.: Towards a better understanding of the relationship between greenspace and health: development of a theoretical framework. Landscape Urban Plan. **118**, 62–69 (2013)
6. Arnrich, B., Mayora, O., Bardram, J., Tröster, G.: Pervasive healthcare. Method Inf. Med. **49**(1), 67–73 (2010)
7. Intille, S.S.: A new research challenge: persuasive technology to motivate healthy aging. IEEE Trans. Inf Technol. Biomed. **8**(3), 235–237 (2004)
8. Move More App #EveryMinuteCounts. https://www.movemoresheffield.com/app. Accessed 31 Aug 2016
9. Sheffield NCSEM up and running. http://www.iseh.co.uk/news/latest-news/sheffield-ncsem-up-and-running. Accessed 31 Aug 2016
10. Gluhak, A., Krco, S., Nati, M., Pfisterer, D., Mitton, N., Razafindralambo, T.: A survey on facilities for experimental internet of things research. IEEE Commun. Mag. **49**(11), 58–67 (2011)
11. Nati, M., Gluhak, A., Abangar, H., Headley, W.: Smartcampus: a user-centric testbed for internet of things experimentation. In: 2013 16th International Symposium on Wireless Personal Multimedia Communications (WPMC), pp. 1–6). IEEE, June 2013
12. Sánchez, L., Gutiérrez, V., Galache, J.A., Sotres, P., Santana, J.R., Casanueva, J., Muñoz, L.: SmartSantander: experimentation and service provision in the smart city. In: 2013 16th International Symposium on Wireless Personal Multimedia Communications (WPMC), pp. 1–6). IEEE, June 2013
13. Perera, C., Zaslavsky, A., Christen, P., Georgakopoulos, D.: Sensing as a service model for smart cities supported by internet of things. Trans. Emerg. Telecommun. Technol. **25**(1), 81–93 (2014)
14. Kotsev, A., Schade, S., Craglia, M., Gerboles, M., Spinelle, L., Signorini, M.: Next generation air quality platform: openness and interoperability for the internet of things. Sensors **16**(3), 403 (2016)
15. Foster, L., Gielen, M., Beattie, M., Goodwill, S: Real-time monitoring of user physical activity and position in an outdoor public space. In: Hervás, R., Lee, S., Nugent, C., Bravo, J. (eds.) UCAmI 2014. LNCS, vol. 8867, pp. 100–107. Springer, Heidelberg (2014)
16. Dunn, M., Kelley, J.: Non-invasive, spatio-temporal gait analysis for sprint running using a single camera. Procedia Eng. **112**, 528–533 (2015)
17. Olympic Legacy Park. http://olympiclegacypark.co.uk/. Accessed 01 June 2016
18. Advanced Wellbeing Research Centre (AWRC). www.shu.ac.uk/research/awrc. Accessed 01 June 2016

Towards Citizen Co-created Public Service Apps

Diego López-de-Ipiña[1(✉)], Mikel Emaldi[1], Unai Aguilera[1], and Jorge Pérez-Velasco[2]

[1] DeustoTech-Deusto Foundation, University of Deusto,
Av. Universidades 24, 48007 Bilbao, Spain
{dipina,m.emaldi,unai.aguilera}@deusto.es
[2] TECNALIA, eServices, Madrid, Spain
jorge.perez@tecnalia.es

Abstract. This paper describes the WeLive framework, a set of tools to enable co-created urban apps by means of bringing together Open Innovation, Open Data and Open Services paradigms. It proposes a more holistic involvement of stakeholders across service ideation, creation and exploitation. The WeLive co-creation process applied to three new urban apps in the city of Bilbao is described. The two-phase evaluation methodology designed and the evaluation results of pre-pilot sub-phase are also presented. As a result, an early user experience evaluation for WeLive has been obtained.

Keywords: Open government · Open data · Open services · Open innovation

1 Introduction

The 2010 edition of the EU eGovernment Benchmark Report [1] states that currently public services are built following an administration-centric approach, driving to a low usage, rather than according to the citizens´ need (user-centric approach). Therefore, there is a clear need to move towards a more open model of design, production and delivery of public services involving citizens, entrepreneurs and civil society.

Public administrations are facing key socioeconomic challenges such as demographic change, employment, mobility, security, environment and many others. The squeeze on public finances has created renewed momentum for the modernisation of public administration. The fact is that in the EU, according to data of 2013 [2], public expenditure accounted for almost 50% of GDP and the public sector represents about 17% of total employment. Besides, citizens' expectations, in terms of burden reduction, efficiency, and personalization, are growing. Citizens want to transit from being mere consumers of public services to providers of those services, i.e. prosumers of the open government ecosystem.

ICT-enabled Open and Collaborative Government is the recipe to deliver "more from less", i.e. meeting public needs in times of tighter budgets, improving the business environment by providing better services to business and citizens, and adapting service provision to the needs of a more digital economy [3].

The WeLive project is devised to transform the current e-government approach by facilitating a more open model of design, production and delivery of public services

C.R. García et al. (Eds.): UCAmI 2016, Part II, LNCS 10070, pp. 469–481, 2016.
DOI: 10.1007/978-3-319-48799-1_51

based on the collaboration among public administrations (PAs), citizens and entrepreneurs. WeLive comprises a novel ecosystem of tools built on the Open Data, Open Services and Open Innovation paradigms, easily deployable in different public administrations. It aims to promote co-innovation and co-creation of personalised public services through a bottom-up approach that leverages active participation of different stakeholders. As shown in Fig. 1, WeLive's Open & Collaborative Government ICT infrastructure resembles an assembly line for e-government services. It offers tools to transform the needs into ideas, then tools to select the best ideas and create the building blocks necessary to build the envisioned solutions, and finally a way to compose the building blocks into mass market apps which can be exploited through a marketplace.

This paper has the following structure. Section 2 reviews related work. Section 3 describes the WeLive platform and its key components. Section 4 outlines the WeLive co-creation approach. Section 5 describes the evaluation methodology designed and its application to the pilot in Bilbao. Finally, Sect. 6 draws some conclusions.

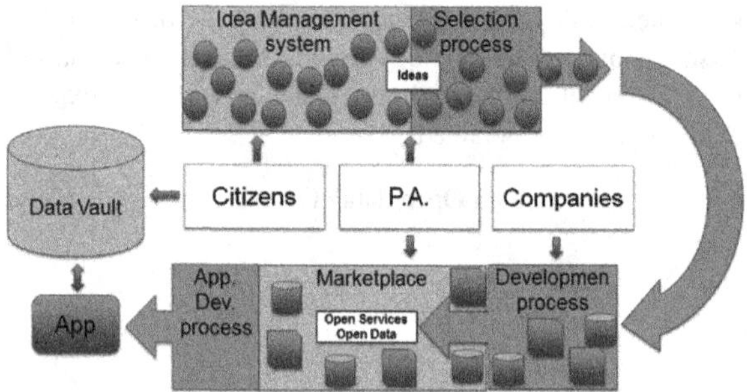

Fig. 1. WeLive concept: IDEAS >> APPLICATIONS >> MARKETPLACE

2 Related Work

To enable a user-centric collaborative public service ecosystem, new types of infrastructure are needed where public value is created by the ability to share, interact and collaborate between actors. Novel processes and approaches are required with a decentralised, cross-government and multi-actor architecture, coupled with the integration of Big Data and the role of social tools [4]. Potential problems related to security, privacy and data protection issues have also to be tackled. An open government framework, as intended by WeLive, also requires interoperability (both at the organisational and technological level), open standards, adoption of Linked Data principles and Cloud Computing. In terms of web evolution, a solution like WeLive has to embrace 3.0 development, i.e. machine integration of data. Research demonstrates the potential of mobile apps to transform governments and to provide access to public information; m-Government is therefore emerging as the next big wave for ICT use in public sector [5].

Open Innovation [6] provides a framework for involving actual customers in the service and product innovation process. It is a co-creational process that facilitates stakeholder engagement, where companies and governments should use external ideas to develop their services in a collaborative Public Private Partnership setting. With the increased focus on sustainability and development of Smart Cities, a more inclusive public administration is enabled, i.e. one that incorporates citizens into the planning of development activities through different channels enabling their engagement on various matters. This has resulted in Living Labs [7], e.g. cities used as places where new services can be deployed and tested in a real environment, capturing the feedback and contributions crowdsourced by the citizens.

Since the first public administrations started sharing their data as Open Data, the idea of Open Government has been disseminated around the world rapidly. As described by the Open Data Barometer [8], Europe leads the region ranking, with widely known initiatives like data.gov.uk (UK), opengov.se (Sweden) or Helsinki Region Infoshare. However, most of countries which have started adopting Open Government policies have serious lacks on exploiting the potential of Open Data. Many of them are focused only on implementing open data portals, placing little efforts on bringing open data closer to entrepreneurs and citizens through APIs, consumable by application developers [9], targeted by WeLive.

3 The WeLive Platform

WeLive encompasses a suite of tools that provides companies, governments, researchers and citizens with the capability to collaborate in order to promote innovation. WeLive supports innovation from the co-creation of innovative ideas (through the *Open Innovation Area* component) and their implementation, to the publication of artefacts (i.e. datasets, building blocks (BBs) and public service applications) in the WeLive *Marketplace*. Furthermore, developers who want to create services or building blocks for the WeLive ecosystem can freely choose diverse technologies (such as programming language, operating system, third party libraries) which they find reasonable, as long as they host the service/BB by themselves. Still, WeLive also provides hosting environments for those who do not want to set up and maintain their own servers.

The WeLive platform architecture is structured into four layers, see Fig. 2, where a central component, WeLive Controller, orchestrates requests issued through the WeLive web UI[1] or the WeLive RESTful API[2], see Fig. 3, to other components:

1. The *Open Innovation layer* is dedicated to boost collaborative research and development as a mechanism to fuel innovative discovery of novel public services.
2. The *Open Data Layer* handles data managed by the public administration which may have been contributed directly by the administration but also provided by the end-users through their smartphones' apps or extracted from social networks.
3. The *Open Service Layer* helps public administrations, companies and citizens to realize new added value services on top of the Open Data layer. It includes the Marketplace component where WeLive artefacts are published.

[1] https://dev.welive.eu/.

[2] https://dev.welive.eu/dev/swagger/.

4. The *Intelligence Layer: Personalization & Analytics* provides mechanisms to customize public services using users' personal information. Personalized services use a variety of data related to the users (memorized in the Citizen Data Vault component) to adapt their behaviour and to provide significant user benefits thanks to services that better support them (recommended by the Decision Engine component). At the same time, this layer is used by the WeLive stakeholders to monitor and evaluate the available artefacts (both in the form of ideas and as actual applications) in the WeLive ecosystem through the Analytics Dashboard component.

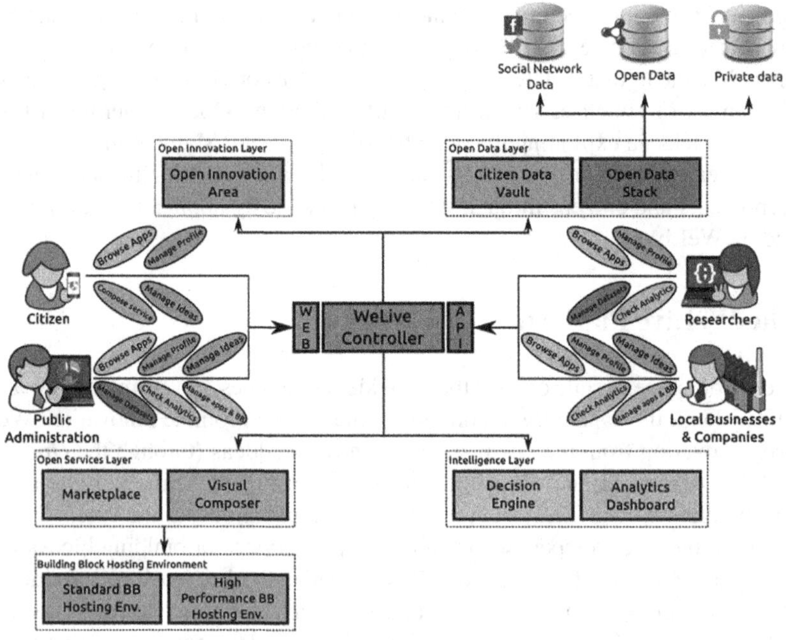

Fig. 2. WeLive platform architecture.

3.1 Open Innovation Layer

This layer is embodied by the Open Innovation Area component. Such component is a social co-creation environment where needs, ideas and possible "solutions" can be matched and asked to Public Administrations for implementation. This is the place where requests meet possible offers. Needs are made public and so highlighted to the community. Several ideas are suggested to satisfy a specific need (e.g. coming from citizens or directly from PAs). It offers tools for: (a) eliciting, analysing and improving ideas; (b) to vote and select the 'best' ideas for a need, (c) to allow companies to offer technical solutions to selected ideas and be funded by interested citizens or the P.A.

It implements the following procedural steps to carry out Open Innovation within a city: (a) suggest or report common needs to the Authorities, for the "development" of the territory; (b) co-define, through social and collaboration features, new ideas; (c) evaluate and select the best ideas through voting and commenting; (d) monitor the status of ideas consisting of co-experience, co-definition, co-development and co-delivery phases: (e) contribute to the idea implementation through the interaction with the Visual composer, a future WeLive component which will enable non-technical people to mash-up building blocks; and (f) associate ideas with artefacts published into the Marketplace, to track the relationship between ideas and datasets, BBs and public services.

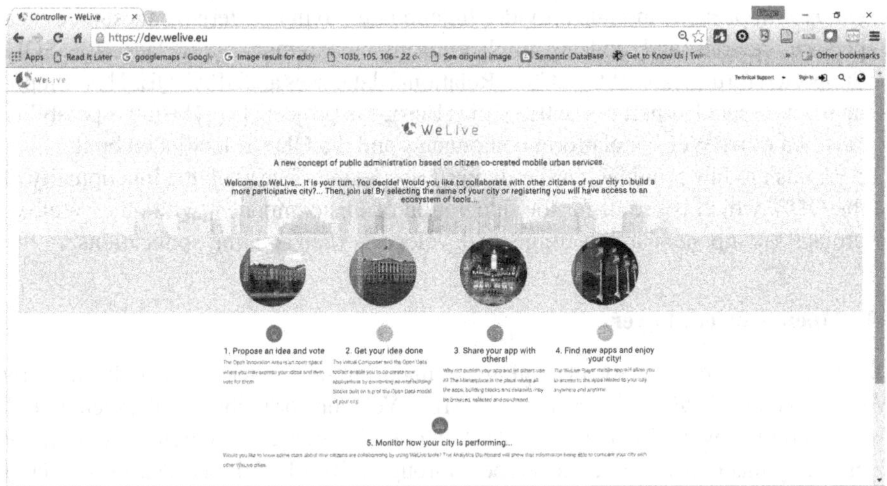

Fig. 3. WeLive Web front-end.

3.2 Open Data Layer

This layer is responsible for managing Broad Data [10] gathered within a city, coming from different heterogeneous sources such as Open Government Data repositories, user-supplied data through social networks or apps, public private sector data or end-user personal data (which can be used to filter and recommend the contents and services most relevant to them). For that, it provides the Open Data Stack and the Citizen Data Vault components. The former serves to address the whole lifecycle of broad data management: data discovery, capture, curation, storage, linkage, publication, exploitation and even visualization. The latter one is used to keep a safety vault where the user's personal data, preferences and profile details are accessed only under user control. The ODS functionality consists of the following internal modules:

- *Data source management*: provides the functionality to perform CRUD operations with heterogeneous datasets and its associated resources. It provides a user interface to facilitate the management of this data.
- *Rating system*: manages the ratings of datasets and its associated resources provided by Open Data Stack users. They can provide a rating for a dataset and the system will compute the aggregated rating for all the users.

- *Validator*: this module checks the data associated with a dataset/resource and validates it applying a set of rules, e.g. JSON schema, which can be defined and extended by the users. The results of the validation process is shown through the data source management component to provide a seamless experience to the users.
- *Harvester*: the harvesting module manages all the information and functionality related with automatic data extraction from external sources. User can configure the existing harvesters, i.e. web scrapper and twitter harvester, or create new ones to extract and process data from non-structured data sources.
- *Query Mapper*: this module provides functionality to map external data sources and perform queries and updates to them using a common query language SQL. Supported formats are: JSON, CSV, Relational databases and SPARQL. This component was created as part of the IES Cities European project [11]. The interoperability between other WeLive platform components and the ODS is facilitated by it.
- *API*: this module provides a programmatic access interface to all the functionality of the ODS, which is useful for the integration of this component with other WeLive project's component and its usage by developers when creating applications.

3.3 Open Services Layer

This layer is responsible for managing the main public service artefacts handled by WeLive, namely *public service apps* –HTML5 Web apps or mobile apps executable in diverse mobile devices by final users, *building blocks* – represent a digital capability of a smart city made available to developers through a REST API, and *dataset* – data of interest to create a new building block or app. This layer comprises the components:

- *WeLive Marketplace*. It represents the repository where to look at in order to identify available apps/building blocks/datasets, i.e. WeLive artefacts. It is the core component to exploit the economic potential brought forward by WeLive. There, WeLive artefacts can be browsed, selected, purchased (not implemented yet) by different stakeholders following SaaS and DaaS [11] approaches.
- *Hosting environments*. They host WeLive artefacts' business logic back-end. Such hosting might be done in one of the environments provided by WeLive or, alternatively, at a third party, Cloud-based IaaS or PaaS, as long as artefacts hosted there are WeLive Open Services framework compliant. The project currently offers: (a) a CloudFoundry-based hosting environment as a general-purpose solution to host web apps in the cloud; and (b) a hosting environment operated within Cloud'N'Sci.fi marketplace for hosting computationally complex and/or commercialized BBs.
- *WeLive Player*. An app (see Fig. 4 leftmost screenshot) to access the city service ecosystem. It permits to search and discover the public service apps of the city, filtered through user's context, profile, and preferences.

Artefacts deployed in a hosting environments must provide standard descriptions depicting both general-purpose information (e.g., providers and authors, license info, classification) and technical information (e.g., the supported protocols and formats, security constraints). The specification, which relies on the Linked USDL [13] notation, a formal semantic specification language, aims at representing the following elements of the building block life-cycle: (a) BB definition (name, description, publisher, etc.); (b) BB invocation and execution (interaction points); (c) BB access policies (security profile); (d) BB authoring, ownership, and licensing aspects; and e) BB service level agreements. The aim of this specification is to capture the BB characteristics that may be required when: (a) users (BB clients, citizens, developers) search for relevant components to build new applications upon them; and (b) during the application execution, when a BB has to be accessed and invoked providing the unambiguous definition of access policies and invocation protocols. Besides, the programmable resources defining the BB metadata should be exposed according to well-defined interfaces (URLs). For example: an `HTTP GET` issued to `{building_block}/spec/list` should return the list of specification formats it supports (it should include at least xwadl and usdl), or the following URLs gives access to the WADL [14] descriptions of the BB: `{building_block}/spec/xwadl`.

Besides, the Open Service Layer provides a set of key infrastructure components, referred to as Core Building Blocks. They expose operations to be used by both by the platform itself and by new building blocks. The most remarkable ones are:

- *Authentication and Authorization Control (AAC)* BB provides the functionality of user authentication and authorization across apps and tools in WeLive platform.
- *Logging BB* allows for tracing information regarding the platform-level and application-level events.

4 WeLive Co-creation Approach

The service co-creation and innovation approach in WeLive is based on the "Quadruple Helix" paradigm [15], where the fourth helix is the citizen, who closely collaborates with Industry, Government and Academia to co-create value added public services.

Through WeLive platform, stakeholders participate by contributing with new services, building blocks and dataset requests, by giving place to new data and apps and even by co-funding novel public app ideas. Stakeholders in a city consume the generated apps publicly available in the WeLive Marketplace and actively contribute and collaborate co-creating public services of high economic and social interest for a city.

During the first half of the project, first 18 months, the following co-creation process has been applied. Online questionnaires addressed to citizens, public servants and SMEs staff have been issued at each of the three cities and one region participating in the project to understand what new urban apps are most requested at each of them. In parallel, an analysis of each participating city strategy and the status of its IT and open data infrastructure was carried out. The analysis of the information gathered through these two channels was followed by the celebration of several focus group workshops where face to face contact with different types of stakeholders took place. In such workshops, the discussion was guided by selecting a couple of scenarios per city, based on the opinions of stakeholders and the city strategy analysis.

4.1 Bilbao's Co-creation Process Experience

With regards to Bilbao's case, in first place, questionnaires among different stakeholders (citizens, companies and public administrations) were distributed by e-mail. The following numbers of people were contacted: 271 citizens, 43 companies and 10 public administration representatives. Besides, the city strategy documents were explored. Looking at the questionnaire results and the city strategy, the topics of traffic, culture, health and tourism, were identified as most relevant for stakeholders.

As a second step, two motivating scenarios, based on the most relevant topics, were used as discussion points for the three focus groups sessions celebrated: (a) "*Collaboration in the Neighbourhood and Participation in municipal decision*" and (b) "*Collaborating on a more Efficient and Transparent City*". A workshop for each stakeholder group was celebrated where people participating in the initial survey and other representatives were invited. For each session, people were divided in groups of 4–5 people, each of them reflecting in one of the scenarios. At each session, the following steps were carried out: (a) *Inspiration phase* –project partners presented the project idea and the co-ideation approach of WeLive; (b) *Brainstorming* about ideas associated to the scenarios assigned to each group; (c) *Voting for ideas* by all groups; (d) Specific service or *use case definition*; (e) *Presentation of services conceived*; and (f) *Voting for services*.

From these focus group sessions, a selection of six potential new urban apps for the city of Bilbao were identified, three for each of the two scenarios.

4.2 Population of WeLive Environment for Bilbao

Based on the feasibility analysis of each of the candidate services, given that some relied on the assumption of existence of certain datasets in the public domain, three services have been implemented so far. In two of the identified services, i.e. Bilboenergy and Public Spent Dashboard, the datasets were not ready yet. The other apps required datasets existing or easily created, since they would be populated by the users themselves. Hence, WeLive instance for Bilbao was populated with the following artefacts:

1. *Datasets*. They were imported both from Bilbao Open Data[3] and Open Data Euskadi[4]. A total of 165 datasets are currently available in the ODS component as seen in https://dev.welive.eu/ods/organization/bilbao-city-council.
2. *Building blocks*. A range of BBs, both specific to the apps and generic across the whole project were created as referred later.
3. *Apps*. Three new apps were developed, published in WeLive marketplace and in Google Play, namely Bilbozkatu, BilON and Auzonet.
   - *Bilbozkatu* - a proposal box for citizens to make improvement suggestions for their neighbourhoods, which others can support or not. Its main features are: create proposal, vote in favour or against a proposal, comment and rate proposals and see proposals geo-located on a map. Internally, it makes use of the following BBs: Feedback BB, In-app questionnaire, AAC, Logging. A new dataset has been

[3] http://www.bilbao.net/opendata/es/inicio.
[4] http://opendata.euskadi.eus/w79-home/es.

created within ODS to support the voting campaigns. Information about neighbourhoods in Bilbao is retrieved from Bilbao Open Data.

- *BilbON* – app with points of interest (POI) in Bilbao classified in categories. Its main features are: a) display categories of POIs on a map, b) search for POIs by different criteria, c) see details of a POI or d) create new POIs. Internally it makes use of the following building blocks: In-App questionnaire, AAC, Logging. A new dataset was created within ODS to support the voting campaigns, whilst POIs datasets are obtained from Open Data Euskadi. Figure 4 shows snapshots of this app.
- *Auzonet* – app to share goods/items between neighbours. Its main features are: (a) offer a good or item, (b) demand a good or item, (c) rate other users and (d) chat with people who offers or demands an item. Internally, it makes use of the following BBs: Rating BB, In-App questionnaire, AAC, Logging. A new dataset has been created within ODS to support the exchange of articles among neighbours and rating of those exchanges.

Fig. 4. BilON co-created service launched through WeLive Player

5 WeLive Evaluation Methodology

WeLive project is being executed in two phases. In phase I, only the Open Innovation Area, Open Data Stack and WeLive Marketplace components have been made publicly available. This explains why the first developed apps have been the result of an open participation process, rather than relying exclusively on the platform. Figure 5 shows the timeline for the first phase of pilots, being executed. As can be seen, the execution, monitoring and evaluation of the pilots has been divided in two sub-phases: *pre-pilot sub-phase* – addressed to a controlled group of users that assess the platform and apps – and *pilot execution sub-phase* – addressed to the overall public.

5.1 Evaluation Tools and KPIs in WeLive

A set of tools have been created in order to evaluate WeLive tools and apps and measure their take-up along the pilots' execution. Firstly, data logs from apps are collected to give information about users' activity on the WeLive platform and their usage of different apps are automatically submitted to the Logging Core BB. For instance, an `ArtefactPublished` event notifies when an app, BB or dataset is published.

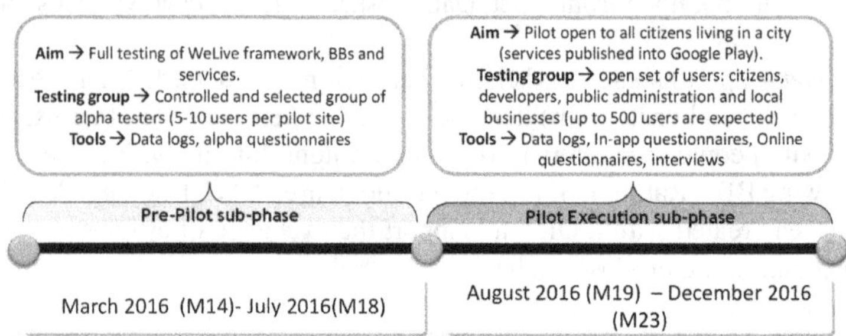

Fig. 5. 1st pilot phase evaluation sub-phases, aim, testing groups and tools used.

Secondly, a short intuitive one screen in-app questionnaire, including 5 questions and 1 comment box, which can be launched from each WeLive app has been created. The objective of the in-app questionnaire is to gather information about: (1) intuitiveness of an application; (2) usefulness of an application; and (3) acceptability of an application. An exemplary question is: Was this app useful for you?

Thirdly, a more extensive on-line questionnaire has been created to gather information about user experience and acceptability of WeLive concept and applications related to: (1) ethical, (2) legal, (3) economical, and (4) transparency aspects.

The generated data logs and the answers collected from in-app and online questionnaires serve to feed with values a range of Key Performance Indicators (KPIs) defined across the project. A set of generic KPIs associated to the different components and purposes of WeLive have been defined. For example: a) KPI1.2: Number of public services apps, building blocks and dataset ideas (per pilot): 64, or b) KPI3.1: Number of building blocks created with the help of the Open Service framework and Open Data Toolset (for all pilots): 9. Likewise, for each of the apps, a range of KPIs was defined to be able to assess the success of their deployment. For example, for BilbON app some of the KPIs are: (a) KPI.BIO.12: ' Number of times the app is started: > 150 or (b) KPI.BIO.14 ' Number of new POIs added: 80% of users create a POI. Observe that each defined KPI is associated to *a priori* defined target value (Fig. 6).

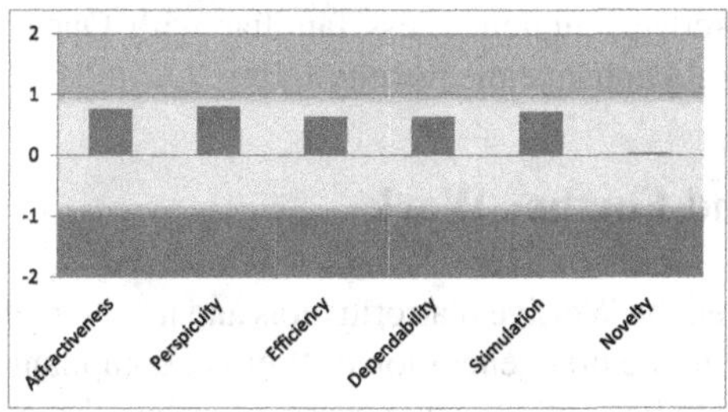

Fig. 6. Preliminary User Evaluation of WeLive solution.

5.2 Pre-pilot Sub-phase Execution and Evaluation

In this completed sub-phase, the technical reliability of the solution has been assessed and the population of WeLive at the four pilot sites has taken place. The aim is to ensure that WeLive platform tools and city or region apps are robust and functional enough to be made publicly available at each pilot site.

WeLive tools and apps were tested in the following aspects: usability and friendliness, proper behaviour (prosumer and social interaction) and in-app questionnaires launching and proper log generation. After alpha testers' identification, group creation and training, each country task force tested the city public services, WeLive player and framework components (Controller, OIA, ODS, CDV, MKT & ADS). The Apps/framework components testing included: usability and functionality issues identification, In-app questionnaires filling (only for the apps) and logs generation checking. Testers filled in an alpha script questionnaire[5]. Finally, a summary of the main issues identified and their recording in Redmine issue tracking system was performed.

Besides, the project experience of use (UX) has been assessed. UX according to the international standard ISO 9241-210 consists of the user's emotions, perceptions, preferences, physical and psychological responses, behaviour, and responses that result before, during or after use of a product. To get a first impression, the User Experience Questionnaire (UEQ) [16] was used, which aims to catch the immediate impression of a user towards a product. The UEQ contains 6 scales with 26 items, each item valued −3 to 3, e.g. *attractive −3…−2…1…0…1…2…3 unattractive*: (a) *Attractiveness*: Overall impression of product. Do users like or dislike the product?; (b) *Perspicuity*: Is it easy to get familiar or learn how to use the product?; (c) *Efficiency*: Can users solve their tasks without unnecessary effort?; d) *Dependability*: Does the user feel in control of the interaction?; and e) *Stimulation*: Is it exciting and motivating to use the product?

Opinions from 2 public servants and 7 SMEs were collected after celebrating workshops for each collective informing about WeLive tools and apps in Bilbao. The obtained results are close to 0.8 value in all aspects except novelty, which according to the UEQ authors is already considered as a positive evaluation. Continuous improvements of apps and platform during the pilot execution sub-phase should enhance the results by the end

[5] http://bit.ly/2b54FwX.

of the first pilot. Moreover, audience less familiar with Open Government will be approached which should enhance the novelty rating.

6 Conclusion and Further Work

This paper has presented the WeLive platform tools and its co-creation approach applied in order to given place to the first generation of WeLive compliant apps. The evaluation methodology designed to be applied in two phase pilots has also been outlined. The first preliminary evaluation results, obtained during the first iteration of trials, pre-pilot sub-phase, associated to the current version of the platform and the first available apps in the city of Bilbao have been presented.

Currently the project is embarked in actual pilot phase I execution sub-phase where actual measurements about the overall acceptability of the WeLive solution in terms of the project wide defined KPIs will be obtained. Future work will gain insights about the actual acceptance of the solution within 4 distinct European urban contexts.

Acknowledgements. This work has been carried out within WeLive project H2020-INSO-2014, 645845.

References

1. European Commission: 'Digital by Default or by Detour?' Assessing User Centric eGovernment performance in Europe. eGovernment Benchmark 2012 (2013). https://ec.europa.eu/digital-agenda/sites/digital-agenda/
2. Annual Growth Survey 2013: communication from the commission (2012). http://ec.europa.eu/europe2020/pdf/ags2013_en.pdf. Accessed 28 Nov
3. Annual Growth Survey 2014: communication from the commission (2014). http://ec.europa.eu/europe2020/pdf/2014/ags2014_en.pdf. Accessed 13 Nov
4. Cabinet Office, UK: Public Service Mutuals - The Next Steps (2012)
5. ITU, OECD: M-Government - mobile technologies for responsive governments and connected societies (2011). http://www.itu.int/pub/D-STR-GOV.M_GOV-2011
6. Baldwin, C., von Hippel, E.: Modeling a paradigm shift: from producer innovation to user and open collaborative innovation (2009)
7. Almirall, E., Wareham, J.: Living labs: arbiters of mid- and ground- level innovation. Technol. Anal. Strat. Manage. **23**(1), 87–102 (2011)
8. Open Data Institute: Open Data Barometer – 2013. Global Report (2013). http://www.opendataresearch.org/dl/odb2013/Open-Data-Barometer-2013-Global-Report.pdf
9. Capgemini Consulting: the open data economy unlocking economic value by opening government and public data (2013). https://www.capgemini-consulting.com/resource-file-access/resource/pdf/opendata_pov_6feb.pdf
10. Roden D.: Introducing Broad Data (2013). http://www.domo.com/blog/2013/03/introducing-broad-data/
11. Aguilera, U., López-de-Ipiña, D., Pérez-Velasco, J.: Collaboration-centred cities through urban apps based on open and user-generated data. Sensors **16**(7), 1022 (2016)
12. Dyche, J.: Data-as-a-service, explained and defined (2010). SearchDataManagement.com. Accessed 24 October

13. Linked USDL (2016). https://linked-usdl.org/
14. WADL Specification (2016). https://wadl.java.net/
15. European Commission, digital single market. open innovation 2.0. (2016). https://ec.europa.eu/digital-single-market/en/open-innovation-20
16. Rauschenberger, M., Schrepp, M., Cota, M.P., Olschner, S., Thomaschewski, J.: Efficient measurement of the user experience of interactive products - how to use the user experience questionnaire (UEQ). example: spanish language version. Int. J. Interact. Multimed. Artif. Intell. **2**(1), 39–45 (2013)

Violence Detection in Real Environments for Smart Cities

Joaquín García-Gómez, Marta Bautista-Durán, Roberto Gil-Pita(✉), Inma Mohino-Herranz, and Manuel Rosa-Zurera

Signal Theory and Communications Department, University of Alcalá, 28805 Alcalá de Henares (Madrid), Spain
{joaquin.garciagomez,marta.bautista}@edu.uah.es, roberto.gil@uah.es

Abstract. Violence continues being an important problem in the society. Thousands of people suffer its effects every day and statistics show this number has maintained or almost increased recently. In the modern environment of smart cities there is a necessity to develop a system capable of detecting if a violent situation is taking place or not. In this paper we present an automatic acoustic violence detection system for smart cities, integrating both signal processing and pattern recognition techniques. The proposed software has been implemented in three steps: feature extraction in time and frequency domain, genetic algorithm implementation in order to select the best features, and classification to take a binary decision. Results derived from the experiments show that MFCCs are the best features for violence detection, and others like pitch or short time energy have also a good performance. In other words, features that can distinguish between voiced and unvoiced frames seem to be a good election for violence detection in real environments.

Keywords: Violence detection · Audio processing · Audio features · Feature selection

1 Introduction

Defining the term 'violence' is not an easy task because it is differently understood depending on the person. The World Health Organization defines violence as "the intentional use of physical force or power, threatened or actual, against oneself, another person, or against a group or community, which either results in or has a high likelihood of resulting in injury, death, psychological harm, maldevelopment, or deprivation" [1]. Other related works define violence in very diverse ways, principally referring to physical violent situations. Some examples are: "physical violence or accident resulting in human injury or pain" [2], "a series of human actions accompanying with bleeding" [3] or "any situation or action that may cause physical or mental harm to one or more persons" [4]. However, anything produced in an injurious or damaging way might be described as violent.

C.R. García et al. (Eds.): UCAmI 2016, Part II, LNCS 10070, pp. 482–494, 2016.
DOI: 10.1007/978-3-319-48799-1_52

Violence is a broad concept that encompasses several categories. Depending on the nature of the violence, we can distinguish between physical, psychological or even sexual violence. Nowadays women and children are the largest and most vulnerable group of victims. Referring to the first one, recent researches show that 35 % of women around the world have suffered physical or sexual violence during their lives [5], and 43 % of women from the European Union declared suffering psychological violence at least once [6]. On the other hand, lots of children are abused every day in the schools. Last year, more than 9 % of students from Spain suffered bullying and approximately 21 % were usually insulted [7]. These statistics demonstrate how these situations continue being really relevant at present and this problem must be treated in order to prevent the tragical end sometimes it has.

The combination of audio and video have been successfully employed in automatic violence detection [2,3,8] in the development of modern smart cities. The use of video proves to be efficient, but unfortunately it brings problems such as computational cost, intrusiveness and poor coverage. It has been shown that audio can be also used to detect violence by itself [4], since violent situations might be preceded by other signs like arguments, shouts or an increase in the volume of the conversation. Related studies up to now have been done with pretended violence from films or games, but it can distort the generalization of the results in real violence, which is of great interest for the development of modern smart cities.

Bearing in mind with this fact, in this paper we present an automatic acoustic violence detection system able to detect violence in real environments in smart cities, integrating both signal processing and pattern recognition techniques. The proposed system is composed of some microphones recording the audio in those places where violent situations would taken place, like home for avoiding gender-based violence or school for bullying. The system monitors the real-time data and in case of detecting a set of consecutive violent frames, it sends a notice to the relevant person or authority. In our study the objective of violence detection is focused on real environments so the advantage of using only audio, apart from the simpler processing system and the low cost, is the small intrusiveness it has.

This paper is structured as follows. First, Sect. 2 introduces the implemented classification system, describing the structure of the detector (Subsect. 2.1), the feature extraction (Subsect. 2.2), the different used classifiers (Subsect. 2.3) and the selection of features by using genetic algorithms (Subsect. 2.4). Then, Sect. 3 describes the results, including the description of the database (Subsect. 3.1), the validation method employed (Subsect. 3.2) and the discussion of the results (Subsect. 3.3). To sum up, Sect. 4 presents the conclusions.

2 The Proposed System

The aim of this section is to explain the overall operation of the system, including how the detector is implemented and which features are taken into account. Furthermore, the used classifiers and the method of feature selection will be explained.

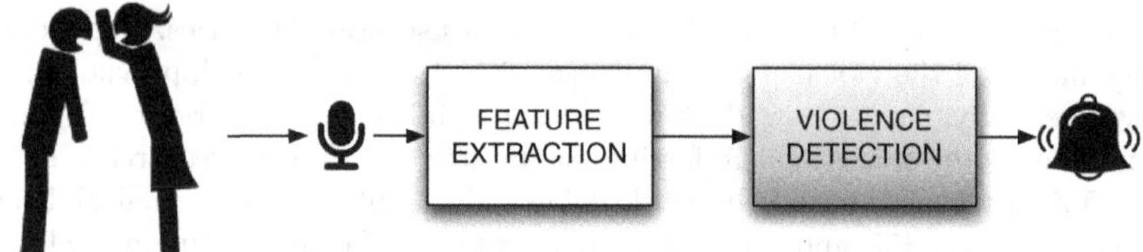

Fig. 1. Proposed system.

2.1 Structure of the Detector

The proposed system has the aim of resolving the violence detection problem in real environments of the smart city. As we stated above, the system will be only based on audio, which will be processed to extract useful information in real time and then the data will be classified to make a decision every T seconds. In Fig. 1 the scheme of the system is proposed. These steps will be explained in detail in the following sections.

2.2 Feature Extraction

The objective of the feature extraction task is to process the input audio signal to obtain useful information that helps the classifying algorithm to properly detect when a situation is violent or not. Features have been evaluated in frequency or time domain. In order to evaluate these features, the audio segments are divided into S frames of 400 ms length with an overlap of 95 %. The features considered in this paper are:

- **Mel-Frecuency Cepstral Coefficients (MFCCs).** The MFCCs are a set of perceptual parameters commonly used in speech recognition [9]. They are calculated from the Short Time Fourier Transform (STFT) and provide a compact representation of the spectral envelope, so most of the signal energy is concentrated in the first coefficients. Perceptual analysis emulates human ear non-linear frequency response by creating a set of filters on non-linearly spaced frequency bands [10]. Mel cepstral analysis uses the Mel scale and a cepstral smoothing in order to get the final smoothed spectrum. The number of cepstral coefficients calculated is 25, for a sampling frequency of 22,050 Hz. The statistics applied to these measurements are the mean and the standard deviation.
- **Delta Mel-Frequency Cepstral Coefficients.** This feature is calculated from MFCCs and is the difference between two of them [9]. Let us denote $MFCC_{n,i}$ as the n-th MFCC evaluated for the i-th time frame, then the Delta MFCC can be expressed using Eq. 1:

$$\Delta MFCC_{n,i} = MFCC_{n+1,i} - MFCC_{n-1,i}, \tag{1}$$

The statistics applied to this measure are mean and standard deviation.

- **Pitch.** Also named fundamental frequency, this feature determines the tone of the speech and can be used to distinguish a person from the other [10]. In this paper we estimate the pitch for every frame of 20 ms evaluating the main peaks of the autocorrelation of the error of a linear predictor with 10 coefficients [9]. The statistics applied to this feature are the mean and the standard deviation.
- **Harmonic Noise Rate (HNR).** HNR quantifies the purity of the speech in every frame of 400 ms length with an overlap of the 95 %. It measures the relationship between the harmonic energy produced by the vocal cords versus non-harmonic energy present in the signal [9]. The statistics applied to this feature are the mean and the standard deviation.
- **Short Therm Energy.** The short time energy is the energy of the short speech segment. Short time energy is a simple and effective classifying parameter for voiced and unvoiced frames [11]. It can be determined from the following expression:

$$N_j = \sum_{i=1}^{S} x_i^2, \tag{2}$$

  where S is the number of 400 ms frames with an overlap of 95 % in each segment. The statistics applied to this measure are the mean and the standard deviation.
- **Energy Entropy.** The energy entropy expresses abrupt changes in the energy level of the audio signal. This is useful for detecting violence due to rapid changes occurring in the tone of voice. To get this parameter the frames are subdivided into K small subframes. The equation of the energy entropy is defined as follows [4]:

$$EE_j = -\sum_{i=1}^{K} \sigma_i^2 log_2 \sigma_i^2, \tag{3}$$

  where σ_i^2 is the normalized energy calculated for each i-th subframe and EE_j is the energy entropy for every frame of 400 ms length with an overlap of 95 %. The statistics applied to the energy entropy are mean, standard deviation, the ratios of maximum to mean and maximum to median value.
- **Zero Crossing Rate.** Zero Crossing Rate (ZCR) is one of the most widely used time-domain audio features [4]. This feature is the relation between the number of zeros and the total length of the frame.

$$Z_j = \frac{1}{2S} \sum_{i=1 \ldots S} |sgn(x_i) - sgn(x_{i-1})| \tag{4}$$

  The statistics applied to this feature are the mean and the standard deviation. This measure is calculated in frames of 400 ms length with an overlap of 95 %.
- **Spectral Flux.** This feature is evaluated in the frequency domain. It represents the spectral change between successive frames [4].

$$F_j = \sum_{k=0 \ldots S-1} (N_{j,k} - N_{j-1,k})^2, \tag{5}$$

where $N_{j,k}$ is the spectral energy, obtained from the Fast Fourier Transform in the j-th frame and k-th samples. The statistics applied to this feature are mean and standard deviation.

- **Spectral Rolloff.** Spectral Rolloff is calculated in the frequency domain and is defined as the frequency $m_c^R(j)$ below which c% of the magnitude distribution of the Discrete Fourier Transform (DFT) X_k coefficients is concentrated for frame j. It represents the skewness of the spectral shape [4]. Different information can be extracted from music, speech or shots, so it might be interesting for violence detection. The equation is defined as follows:

$$\sum_{k=0}^{m_c^R(j)} |X_{jk}| = \frac{c}{100} \sum_{k=0}^{S-1} |X_{jk}| \quad (6)$$

- **Spectral Centroid.** Spectral Centroid is studied in the frequency domain and it is defined as the center of gravity of the magnitude spectrum of the STFT. This feature takes high values correspond with high frequencies [12]. The statistics applied to this feature are the mean and the standard deviation.
- **Ratio of Unvoiced Time Frames.** In the propose feature the number of unvoiced time frames is evaluated. This value is related to the presence or absence of clear or strong speech in the analyzed audio.

2.3 Classifiers

Three different classifiers are going to be considered in the study: The Least Squares Linear Detector (LSLD), the Least Squares Quadratic Detector (LSQD) and the Neural Networks based Detector.

LSLD uses linear decision boundaries, so it cannot differentiate among classes associated in very complex shapes. Let us consider a set of training patterns $\mathbf{x} = [x_1, x_2, ..., x_L]^T$, where each pattern is assigned to one of the classes (violence or non violence). In this type of classifier the decision rule is obtained through a set of K linear combinations of the training patters. In the particular case of only two classes (binary classifier), the number of required linear combinations is reduced to one (denoted y), and the decision is taken by thresholding the linear combination (Eq. 7).

$$y = w_0 + \sum_{n=1}^{L} w_n x_n, \quad (7)$$

where w_n are the weights and w_0 is a bias term. The mean squared error is minimized to determine the values of these weights by using the Wiener-Hopf equations [13].

On the other side, LSQD uses more complex boundaries, which allows to better discriminate among the specific classes. Nevertheless, they are implemented in a similar way. In fact, the essential difference is that the decision rule includes some quadratic combinations of the training patters, in other words, some products between the features. As a result, Eq. 8 is obtained equivalently to the Eq. 7 of linear classifier.

$$y = w_0 + \sum_{n=1}^{L} w_n x_n \sum_{n=1}^{L} \sum_{m=1}^{n} x_m x_n v_{mn}, \tag{8}$$

where v_{mn} are the quadratic weights. The minimization of the mean squared error allows determining the optimum weights, which are again obtained using the Wiener-Hopf equations [13].

Nevertheless, the number of features can become extremely big to be computed, resulting in too much time and computer resources. To avoid this problem a simplified version of the quadratic classifier has been implemented. It consists in taking just the square of the training patters. In this way the number of features is increased just at twice the original number. 9 is the final equation for the decision rule in the quadratic classifier.

$$y = w_0 + \sum_{n=1}^{L} w_n x_n \sum_{n=1}^{L} {x_n}^2 v_n \tag{9}$$

Related to the detector based on Neural Networks, it allows to implement more complex boundaries to separate the classes than the previous ones. A large number of neurons implies more complex boundaries to solve the problem, but it also implies lost of generalization due to overtraining. Thus, it is not useful to design an algorithm with a large number of them since the classifier could learn how to classify specifically the given database and might not be able to works correctly with other data. Because of that, a reduced number of neurons (5 hidden neurons) has been selected in the experiments of the paper.

It is important to highlight that in the problem at hand the errors associated to the different failures of the system does not have the same importance, and a Neyman Pearson architecture must be implemented. Thus, in order to implement a detector able to control the probability of false alarm of the detector, the value of the threshold applied at the output of the classifier must be selected so that a desired probability of false alarm is achieved. It should be noted that the considered concept of false alarm includes only false-positives, that is to say, the system detects violence and it does not exist.

2.4 Selecting Features

The Genetic Algorithm (GA) is inspired by the principles of genetic and natural selections with the aim of obtaining the best results for solving a problem [14]. The method is based on a random exchange of features of the individuals of a population that constitute the possible solutions for the problem. With that, the genetic algorithm is a search algorithm able to be applied on optimization problems in different areas [15].

This algorithm is splittted into four steps: at first, the population is created as a binary vector $\mathbf{f} = [f_1, ..., f_p]$ where each element indicates if this feature is selected or not. If the p-th element is 1 this feature is taken and not otherwise. With the population created, in the second step an adaptive function is defined to determine the adequacy of each individual to survive in the environment. This is called as 'selection step'. At third step the best individuals are selected by pairs (parents) in order to generate a new individual (son) composed by parts of them. This step is the 'crossover'. Then, the mutation takes place and some individuals of the population change their values in a little amount. At this point, the new population is created and the process will return to the 'selection step' to cyclically continue until it fulfills the algorithm criteria.

In our case the problem is to determinate which features will be the best to be applied to violence detection. There are a total of 51 features, but each individual only chooses a subset of them. The adaptive function has the aim of maximize the probability of detection associated to a probability of false alarm for a given detection system. In this point, only the LSLD and the LSQD have been considered in the feature selection process. MLPs have been discarded, since the training time of this kind of solutions make them not suitable for heuristic feature selection processes, such as the one described in this paper (please note in this point that the number of individuals evaluated is very large).

With this criterion the individuals will be ranked and only the best individuals survive and reproduce. The population is composed of 100 individuals, 10 of them will be chosen as parents, and they will generate the remaining 90 sons by crossover. After this, mutation changes a 4 percent of the genes. This process is repeated until a number of generations are reached (30 generations in our case). The whole process is repeated 10 times in order to avoid local minima, and the best individual of all is selected as final solution.

3 Results

In order to validate the proposed system, a set of experiments has been carried out using a database of audio files. These audio files have been divided in segments of 5 s length, with a sampling frequency of 22,050 Hz. Feature extraction has then been applied to obtain useful information from data. With the aim of selecting a reduced set of features, a genetic algorithm is used. Once the best features have been selected, a specifically trained classifier aims at giving the final decision. Figure 2 shows a block diagram describing the process carried out in the experiments. It is important to note that the computational cost is high just in the training step in contrast to the test one. As a result, in a practical implementation the time necessary to detect an alarm is approximately the set time (5 s in the proposed system).

3.1 Database Description

Real life violence presents specific characteristics, different from those found in non-real environments. This fact makes the use of state-of-the-art databases not suitable. Taking into account this issue, a new database has been developed for the experiments carried out in the study.

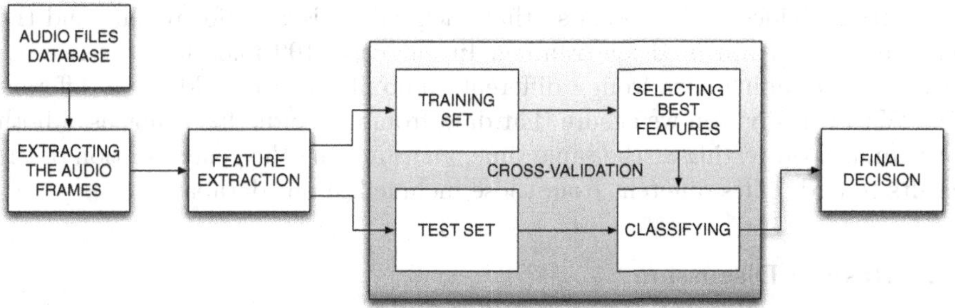

Fig. 2. Block diagram of the experiments.

To generate the mentioned database, some videos from *YouTube* platform have been downloaded and the audio content has been extracted. As a sampling frequency of 22,050 Hz is applied, the minimal frequency of the original audios has to be that one. In any other case, the audio has been discarded. Some segments of video corresponds to violent scenes, including shouting or fights between people. Most of them were recorded with mobile phone cameras and similar, so they don't have high quality. This is interesting since the study should be different in real world, where it usually appears background noise, compared to a fictional one, such as in films.

Once downloaded the file segments were labeled. It consisted in listening to the audios and noting where a scene was considered violent or not. This task was carried out by two people, comparing the results to make the labeled data more objective.

Table 1 summarizes the characteristics of the database.

Table 1. Summary of the database

Parameters	Value
Total duration	27,802 s
Violent duration	3,051 s
Percentage of violence	10.97 %
Number of audios	109
Minimum audio length	15 s
Maximum audio length	4,966 s

3.2 Validation Methods

To avoid loss of generalization of the results, a tailored version of k-fold cross-validation has been used in the experiments. In standard k-fold cross-validation the data is divided in k subsets so that each subset is used for testing and the remaining $k - 1$ are used for training. In our case, 109 folds have been used, each fold containing data from a different audio file, so each fold has a different size. With this division we ensure that data from any audio file is not used both for training and testing at the same time, guaranteeing the generalization of the results to audio files different from those included in our database.

3.3 Results Discussion

As it was stated above, two GA based feature selection strategies have been considered: the case of maximizing the probability of detection with an LSLD (labeled 'Linear FS') and the case with an LSQD (labeled 'Quadratic FS'). In each case, the three detectors described in this paper have been evaluated. The probability of false alarm considered in the optimization process has been 10 %, and 20 features have been selected in the feature selection process. Figure 3 shows the Probability of Detection versus Probability of False Alarm obtained for the different classifiers described in this paper. Results show the best performance of the LSQD with quadratic FS for high probability of false alarm, and the best performance of the MLP with linear FS for low probabilities of false alarm.

Concerning the selected features, it is interesting to evaluate the percentage of occurrence of each feature, in the case of both the linear FS process, and the

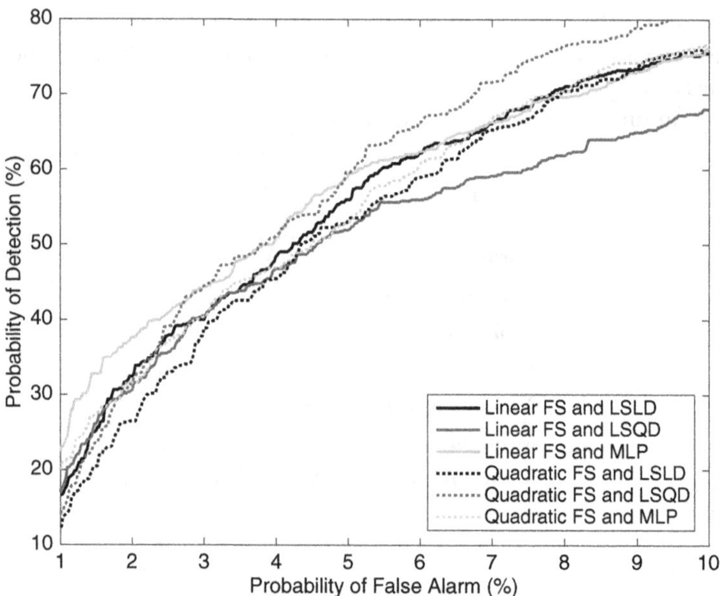

Fig. 3. Probability of Detection versus Probability of False Alarm obtained for the different experiments described in this paper.

Table 2. Summary of the selected features for the LSLD

Number	Measurement	Statistic	Percentage occurrence
1	MFCC 3	Standard deviation	100.00
2	Pitch	Mean	100.00
3	Energy Entropy	Standard deviation	100.00
4	Spectral Centroid	Mean	100.00
5	ΔMFCC 2	Standard deviation	99.07
6	Short Time Energy	Mean	99.07
7	Spectral Flux	Mean	99.07
8	MFCC 1	Standard deviation	98.13
9	MFCC 2	Standard deviation	96.26
10	Spectral Flux	Standard deviation	92.52
11	MFCC 1	Mean	78.50
12	ΔMFCC 5	Standard deviation	63.55
13	ΔMFCC 3	Mean	53.27
14	Energy Entropy	Standard deviation	50.46
15	Spectral Rolloff	Standard deviation	50.46
16	ΔMFCC 1	Standard deviation	48.59
17	MFCC 5	Standard deviation	42.99
18	Short Time Energy	Standard deviation	42.99
19	Spectral Rolloff	Median	41.12
20	ΔMFCC 4	Mean	36.44

quadratic FS process. Tables 2 and 3 show the most selected features, sorted by the percentage of occurrence for the linear FS and the quadratic FS.

From these tables we can appreciate that among the features analyzed in this paper, MFCCs are the most important features to obtain relevant information for violence detection. In fact, half of the selected features correspond to this kind of features in both LSLD and LSQD. In addition, as could be expected, the mean value of the pitch appears in high positions in both tables. Note in this point that pitch allows to determinate relevant characteristics such as tone of the speech, specially in situations like arguments where the fundamental frequency varies depending on the increasing volume of the conversation. On the other hand, the standard deviation of the pitch only appears in the case of the quadratic FS, which implies that this feature is only useful for quadratic detectors. With respect to ratio of unvoiced time frames (which has been originally proposed in this paper), it ranks 10th in the quadratic list, with an appearance rate of 94.39 %, which shows the importance of differentiating between voiced and unvoiced frames. For the same reason, statistics relative to the short time energy and energy entropy appear in both tables.

Table 3. Summary of the selected features for the LSQD

Number	Measurement	Statistic	Percentage of occurrence
1	MFCC 3	Standard deviation	100.00
2	ΔMFCC 2	Standard deviation	100.00
3	ΔMFCC 5	Standard deviation	100.00
4	Pitch	Mean	100.00
5	Short Time Energy	Mean	100.00
6	MFCC 1	Standard deviation	99.07
7	Short Time Energy	Standard deviation	97.20
8	MFCC 1	Mean	95.33
9	Pitch	Standard deviation	94.39
10	Ratio of unvoiced time frames	–	94.39
11	MFCC 3	Median	88.78
12	Energy Entropy	Standard deviation	79.44
13	Spectral Centroid	Mean	75.70
14	Energy Entropy	Max/Mean	70.09
15	ΔMFCC 3	Standard deviation	65.42
16	MFCC 2	Standard deviation	61.68
17	MFCC 5	Standard deviation	57.01
18	Spectral Centroid	Standard deviation	57.01
19	Zero Crossing Rate	Standard deviation	39.25
20	MFCC 4	Standard deviation	33.64

Another relevant measurement is the spectral centroid, whose mean appears in both tables, while the standard deviation is useful just in the LSQD. Related to spectral flux, it is an important feature for the linear detector because its mean ranks 7th and its standard deviation ranks 10th. However, none of them are selected in the quadratic detector, so we can conclude that spectral flux is only useful for linear detectors. The same applies to the spectral rolloff.

Comparing Tables 2 and 3 we can appreciate that 14 of the total features are the same in both tables, so in general most of the measurements can be used in both linear based and quadratic based detectors.

4 Conclusion

The purpose of this paper is to obtain a system aiming at violence detection through voice analysis in a real environment. To do this, different experiments have taken place with the aim of obtaining the best results in terms of probability of detection for a give probability of false alarm. The results derived from the experiments show that MFCCs are the best features for violence detection, and others like pitch or short time energy have also a good performance. In other words, features which can distinguish between voiced and unvoiced frames seem to be a good election for violence detection. Regarding to the classifiers, the results obtained does not seems to be clear in order to choose only one of them because its performance depends on the probability of false alarm in which the study is focused. It is important to note that the experiment has been carried out on a specifically created database, where the quality of the audio is not always suitable, and it has been labeled by two people, which could be not enough objective to determine if the content is violent or not.

The ongoing work will be focused on applying the proposed system to a broader database in order to validate its performance. That database should be checked by a higher number of people. Another improvement could be the extraction of more features, or even the use of other types of classifiers.

Acknowledgements. This work has been funded by the Spanish Ministry of Economy and Competitiveness (under project TEC2015-67387-C4-4-R, funds Spain/FEDER) and by the University of Alcala (under project CCG2015/EXP-056).

References

1. Krug, E.G., Mercy, J.A., Dahlberg, L.L., Zwi, A.B.: The world report on violence and health. Lancet **360**(9339), 1083–1088 (2002)
2. Demarty, C.H., Penet, C., Gravier, G., Soleymani, M.: The mediaeval 2012 affect task: violent scenes detection. In: Working Notes Proceedings of the MediaEval 2012 Workshop (2012)
3. Chen, L.H., Hsu, H.W., Wang, L.Y., Su, C.W.: Violence detection in movies. In: 2011 Eighth International Conference on Computer Graphics, Imaging and Visualization (CGIV), pp. 119–124. IEEE (2011)
4. Giannakopoulos, T., Kosmopoulos, D., Aristidou, A., Theodoridis, S.: Violence content classification using audio features. In: Antoniou, G., Potamias, G., Spyropoulos, C., Plexousakis, D. (eds.) SETN 2006. LNCS (LNAI), vol. 3955, pp. 502–507. Springer, Heidelberg (2006). doi:10.1007/11752912_55
5. World Health Organization, et al.: Department of reproductive health and research, london school of hygiene and tropical medicine, south african medical research council. Global and regional estimates of violence against women prevalence and health effects of intimate partner violence and non-partner sexual violence, Geneva, Switzerland. World Health Organization (2013)
6. Board, I.E., Implemention, I.: European union agency for fundamental rights (2006)
7. Sánchez, T., Idoia, P., et al.: Ciberadolescentes: reduciendo la morbimortalidad a través de la esalud (2016)
8. Schedi, M., Sjöberg, M., Mironică, I., Ionescu, B., Quang, V.L., Jiang, Y.G., Demarty, C.H.: Vsd2014: a dataset for violent scenes detection in hollywood movies and web videos. In: 2015 13th International Workshop on Content-Based Multimedia Indexing (CBMI), pp. 1–6. IEEE (2015)
9. Mohino, I., Gil-Pita, R., Álvarez, L.: Stress Detection Through Emotional Speech Analysis. Springer, New York (2011)

10. Gil-Pita, R., López-Garrido, B., Rosa-Zurera, M.: Tailored MFCCs for sound environment classification in hearing aids. In: Sulaiman, H.A., Othman, M.A., Othman, M.F.I., Rahim, Y.A., Pee, N.C. (eds.) Advanced Computer and Communication Engineering Technology. LNEE, vol. 315, pp. 1037–1048. Springer, Heidelberg (2015). doi:10.1007/978-3-319-07674-4_96
11. Jalil, M., Butt, F.A., Malik, A.: Short-time energy, magnitude, zero crossing rate and autocorrelation measurement for discriminating voiced and unvoiced segments of speech signals. In: 2013 International Conference on Technological Advances in Electrical, Electronics and Computer Engineering (TAEECE), pp. 208–212. IEEE (2013)
12. Tzanetakis, G., Cook, P.: Musical genre classification of audio signals. IEEE Trans. Speech Audio Process. **10**(5), 293–302 (2002)
13. Van Trees, H.L.: Detection, Estimation, and Modulation Theory. Wiley, Chichester (2004)
14. Haupt, R.L., Haupt, S.E.: Practical Genetic Algorithms. Wiley, Chichester (2004)
15. Holland, J., Goldberg, D.: Genetic Algorithms in Search, Optimization and Machine Learning. Addison-Wesley, Boston (1989)

MyMic – Mobile Application as a Replacement of Wireless Microphones Using UDP Over WiFi

Kholoud Elbatsh[1(✉)] and Tarek Eslim[2]

[1] Faculty of Computer Science and Information Technology, Gaza University, Gaza, Palestine
k.elbatsh@gu.edu.ps
[2] ALTARIQ Systems & Projects, Gaza, Palestine
tarek@altariq.ps

Abstract. Nowadays, most of event halls are prepared with normal wireless microphone system that depends mainly on FM radio frequencies. These systems have unexpected problems such as no enough microphones, interferences, weak signal, running out of battery life, unwanted noise, and feedback. Moreover, extra equipment is required if the speech needs recording.

The proposed solution is "MyMic". It is a mobile application developed by ALTARIQ Systems & Projects to solve the previous issues. The main idea of the application is using the smartphone connected to WiFi as a wireless mic. A control panel running on PC/Tablet (server) manages Mobiles (Clients); it receives the sound streams using UDP packets and sends processed sound stream to the sound system. The control panel allows multiple speakers simultaneously. System testing inside a hotel event hall was successful with clear sound of three simultaneous speaking users where noise values were 4.7 % in average.

Keywords: Mobile · Mobile application · WiFi · UDP · Wireless microphones · Sound stream · Sampling rate · Sample size · Noise

1 Introduction

MyMic is a mobile application developed to provide an innovative solution to replace wireless microphones on events, many places where people meet and want to talk in the mic; they wait to get the microphone. The microphone moves physically from persons to other. For example: Conferences, Meetings, Ceremonies & Outdoor events, and Lectures. It is an issue to have several mic units working over FM in the hall or meeting room, or Video Conference sound system. Then the proposed system solves the following issues:

- Microphones distribution and moving from person to other in order to talk.
- Microphone batteries that may out of charge and then be out of use.
- It is required to move the mic from person to another during the sessions.
- There is no easy way to record the speech live.

C.R. García et al. (Eds.): UCAmI 2016, Part II, LNCS 10070, pp. 495–503, 2016.
DOI: 10.1007/978-3-319-48799-1_53

To provide an effective solution, mobiles are the good choice because all people nowadays carry their mobiles most of the time especially outdoor. Each conference or event attendee will use his mobile as a mic.

Audio streaming using UDP packets over WiFi networks is the best technique, where mobiles always are connected and people is used to access these networks anywhere.

MyMic is considered as a Real Time Multimedia Applications (RTMA), they are applications that send and receive audio or video streams through communication networks. The received packets must be decoded before rendering the audio and the video at receiver terminal [1]. RTMAs are experiencing rapid development due to the growing popularity of audio and video applications, MyMic is a real time audio application over Wireless Local Area Network (WLAN), such as IEEE 802.11 (WiFi). RTMAs use the streaming technology to offer audio and video services via internet while MyMic offers the service without internet.

Audio Streaming is a technique to deliver audio that is distributed over telecommunications networks, and transmitted, through an Internet Protocol (IP) network, from the source to the destination. Some protocols provide basic network services support in the network layer, others work in the transport layer such as User Datagram Protocol (UDP) and Transmission Control Protocol (TCP) [1]. The Real-Time Streaming Protocol (RTSP) [2] and the Session Initiation Protocol (SIP) are examples of application layer protocols to control multimedia delivery. UDP protocol is used directly in the packet transmission of MyMic application.

Audio streaming is very sensitive to delay and jitter, and require high bandwidth. This means that audio streaming requires special network performance that is measured by many parameters such as packet loss, end to end delays, jitter, bandwidth, timeliness, reliability and cost. However, problems of wireless network such as shadowing, multipath fading and interferences still limiting the available bandwidth for the deployed applications. All the users of RTMAs seeks to receive high quality audio (clear audio), which is difficult since it is affected by many factors as the extended delay of voice, path, and echo [1].

It is important to talk about the main feature of the voice codec, which is bit rate (bps). It depends on the quality of the digitized voice and it is a critical parameter for voice transmission over WiFi. If the bit rate is not guaranteed, the signal may not play with the right quality. In these cases, cuts and delays that prevent the correct reception of the audio message may occur [3, 4].

So speech enhancement algorithms [5–9] are required to improve the Quality of Service (QoS) and Quality of Experience (QoE), some of them include noise removal [5, 10–12], echo canceller [13], and minimize delay and jitter.

This paper is structured as follows. First, Sect. 2 introduces the proposed system structure (Subsect. 2.1), the process of communication (Subsect. 2.2). Next, Sect. 3 talks about sound characteristics related to the system. Section 4 presents the implementation, explains testing environment and parameters, and some results. Later Sect. 5 is the conclusions.

2 The Proposed System

2.1 System Architecture

The proposed system architecture consists mainly of two components (Fig. 1):

1. **Mobile Application:** that turns the mobile as a mic, provide all user functions such as connection request and request for call.
2. **Tablet/Desktop application** (Control Panel): manages the mobile mics and speech requests, transfer the sound stream to the hall sound system, and records sound sessions.

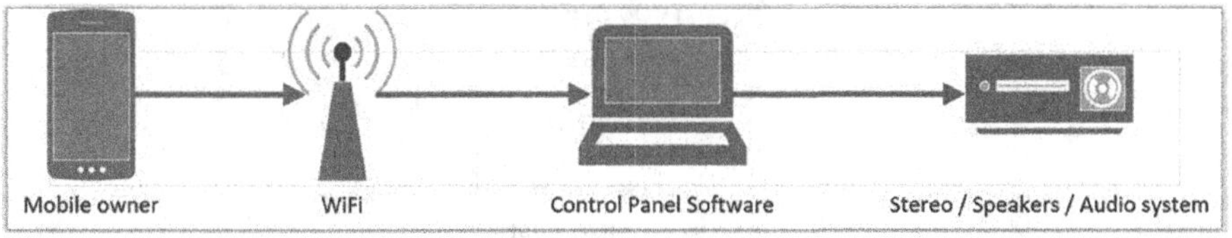

Fig. 1. System components

2.2 Process of Communication

The communication process starts when the admin executes the control panel software (Fig. 2) installed on a laptop or PC. Admin must "start server" and follow the next sequence steps:

Client Name	IP	Last Speech	Request to Talk	Talk/Mute	Allow/Suspend	Time Limit	Turns
User1	22.12.68.1	-	-			0	
User2	22.12.68.2	-	-			0	
User3	22.12.68.3	-	-			0	
User4	22.12.68.4	-	-			0	
User5	22.12.68.5	-	-			0	
User6	22.12.68.6	-	-			0	
User7	22.12.68.7	-	-			0	
User8	22.12.68.8	-	-			0	
User9	22.12.68.9	-	-			0	
User10	22.12.68.10	-	-			0	
User11	22.12.68.11	-	-			0	
User12	22.12.68.12	-	-			0	
User13	22.12.68.13	-	-			0	
User14	22.12.68.14	-	-			0	
User15	22.12.68.15	-	-			0	

Fig. 2. MyMic server

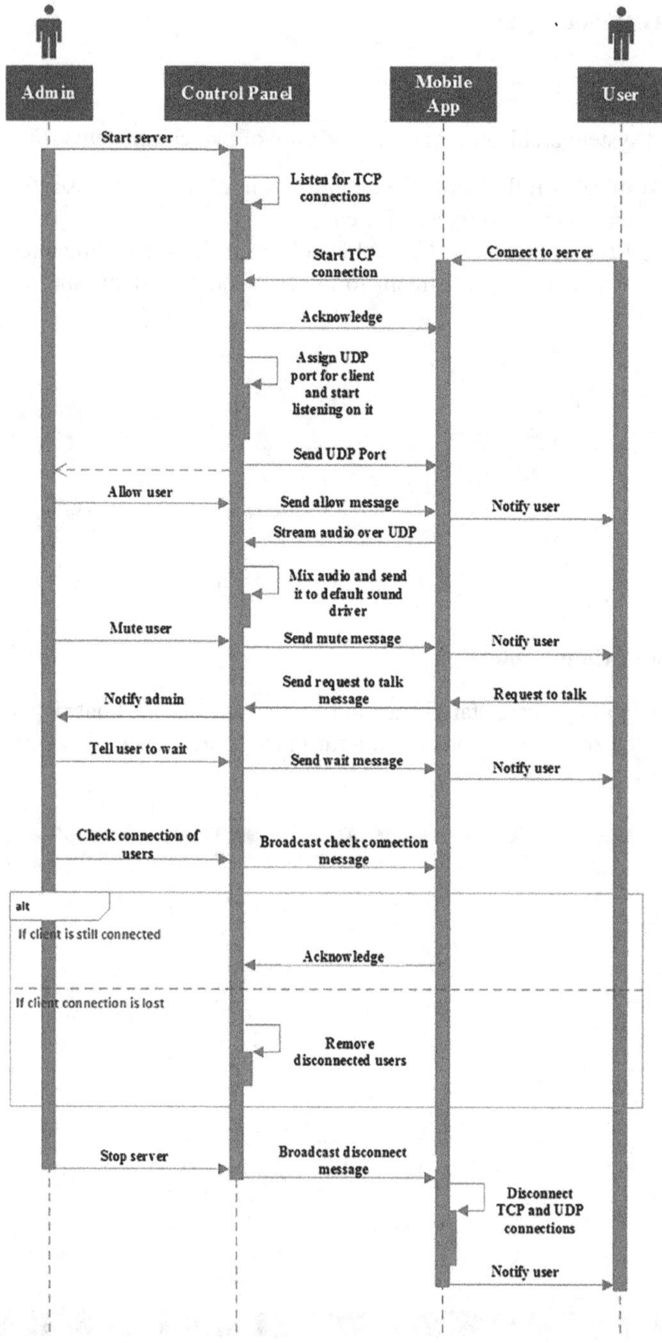

Fig. 3. Sequence diagram of communication process

- The server waits for any TCP connection request (Fig. 3) from any client (mobile app of attendee). On the setting, the admin determines the max number of users allowed to connect and talk, and the size of the audio UDP packet.
- The client or the mobile app initiates a TCP connection using the IP address it gets by scanning a QR code (Fig. 4) generated by the server instead of entering the IP address and port no (default TCP port no is 30006 in this case), the server acknowledged the connection and assign a UDP port no (start at 40000 by default and increase by one for each new user) for that client (Fig. 4). The server accepts unlimited number of client connections by the same process.

Fig. 4. QR code and server settings

- Each client connected to the server appears in the client list with the following properties and characteristics (Fig. 2):
  - **IP:** IP address of the client (mobile phone of attendance who is already connected).
  - **Last Speech:** Time of client last speech.
  - **Request to talk:** When client wants to talk, it turns to the green color and show the time of its request.
  - **Talk/Mute:** The admin can mute the sound of the client.
  - **Allow/Suspend:** The admin allows the client to talk by press this cell and suspend its speech when it is required.
  - **Time Limit:** The admin is allowed to determine the time limit of the client to talk, for example just 1 min enabling the good control of discussion time.
  - **Turns:** How many time the client has talked per session.
  - **Suspend all:** The admin to suspend all speakers at once.
  - **Record:** The admin uses this option to record the speech. The client will be notified on his mobile that the speech is being recorded.
- After that, in the control panel, the audio datagram packets are received in a buffer queue, processed and sent to the sound system instantly. When audio packet delay exceeds 300 ms, the packet is dropped.
- If the admin wants to stop the server, and disconnect all clients, he must press "stop server" button which was the "start server" button at the beginning.
- The admin always checks connections by "Refresh" button, it is a command that broadcast a check connection message for all connected clients (it wait for TCP

connection default time out), but in this case the admin press the "Refresh" button two times to filter all connected clients that did not reply.

In addition, a good advantage of the system is the ability to record all clients' speech which is very important for conferences, workshops, and any important event. All sound files are recorded in.wav format and stored in the application directory (Fig. 5).

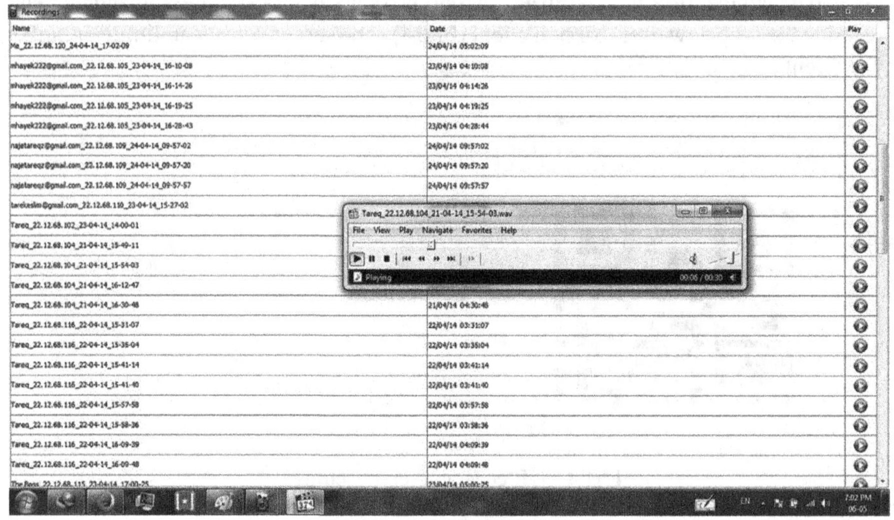

Fig. 5. Recorded audio

3 Sound Characteristics

Each mobile model has its hardware and software characteristics related to the microphones used, and the system built-in sound features. The system should be suitable to the minimum supported sound parameters such as sampling rate, and sample size.

To collect information about the most used mobile models in Gaza, a survey was conducted on 377 persons in the IT sector and the results show (Fig. 6) that 54 % of them use Samsung, 15 % iPhone, 10 % Sony, and 9 % Nokia.

For these models, sampling rate, sample size, and noise values are collected (Table 1), the minimum sampling rate is 44.1 kHz, and sample size is 16 bit, while the max is 192 kHz and 32 bit respectively. The audio quality of these models is evaluated by its noise and crosstalk noise that are −99.4 dB min and −88.2 dB max for noise, and −100 dB min and −53 dB max for crosstalk. Previous values are considered in the system to support all available models, it is set to 44.1 kHz for sampling rate, and 16 bit for sample size.

The audio is captured from the microphone as a Pulse-Code Modulation (PCM) raw format. Audio bytes are inserted into a buffer queue, where every buffer is 4 kilobytes in length. The Noise elimination feature is activated if it is a built-in feature of the mobile software.

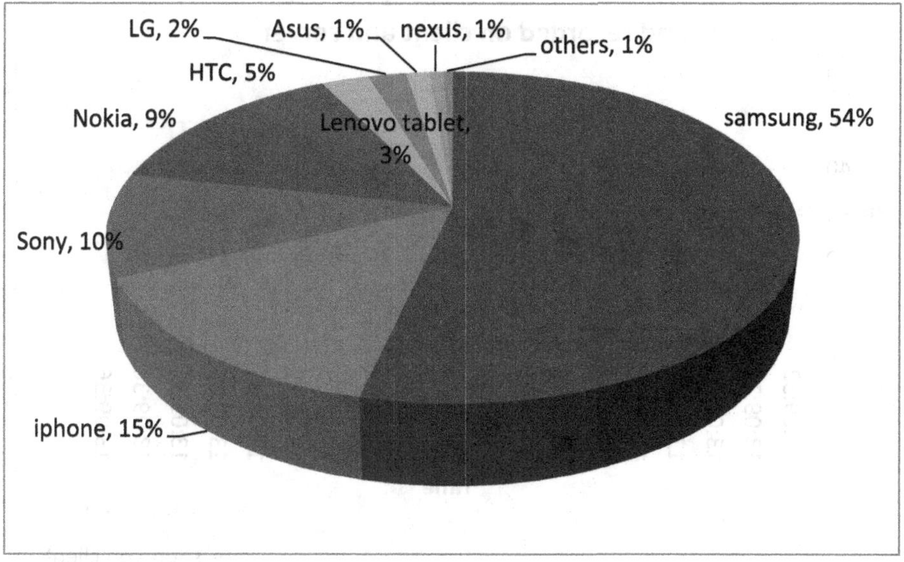

Fig. 6. The percentage of mobile models in use in Gaza

Table 1. Sound parameters on mobiles

	Sampling rate (kHz)	Sample size (bits)	Noise (dB)	Cross-talk noise (dB)
Min	44.1	16	−99.4	−100
Max	192	32	−88.2	−53

4 Implementation and Testing

The Android mobile application: Java is used for the TCP socket handling and processing using NDK [14] in Eclipse., C is used for UDP sockets, and C ++ and JNI [15] for the rest of audio processing code.

The control panel is programmed in Java except the audio processing code is in C# where special library for audio called (Naudio) [16] is used to convert the received PCM audio format to uncompressed wav format.

The application was tested in an events hall equipped with a WiFi router that supports speed of 300 Mbps, 15 mobile users were connected to the server, and made request to talk, three of them talked simultaneously, the sound was clear and no delay was noticed by human ears.

The three users said the same sentence and speeches were recorded on their mobile before transmitting and on the server (by the control panel) after receiving to compare between them and evaluate the noise. Figure 7 represents a comaprison for one of the mentioned users. The figure shows small noise values resulted from the transmition process over WiFi which in average equals 4.7 %

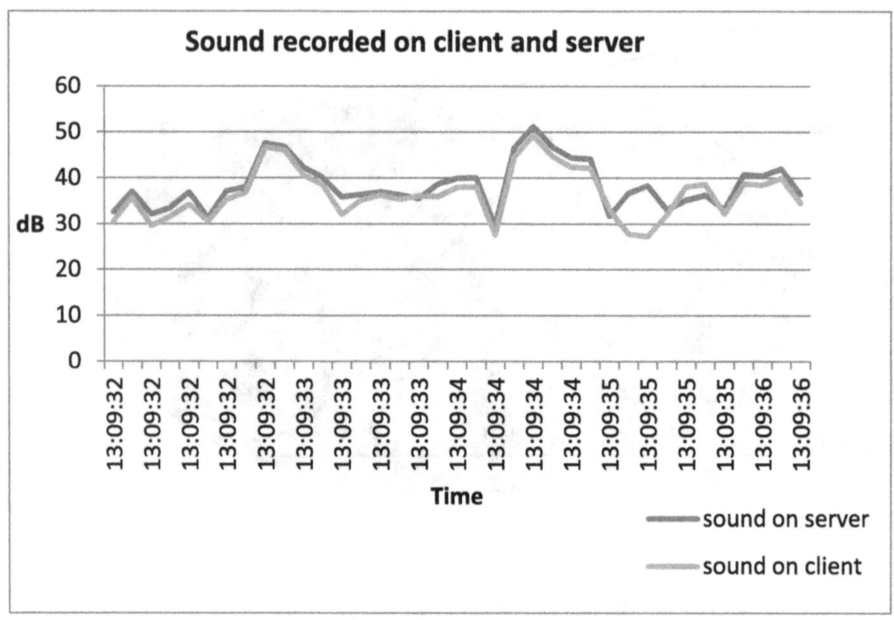

Fig. 7. Comparison between user speech recorded on mobile before transmitting and after receiving on server

Delay was tested inside the hall with a network tool on mobile device; it depends mainly on the network equipment and the design of the hall, some halls are prepared with a good network equipment and installations, others not.

Measured delay, noise, and echo, to evaluate the audio quality, using special software tools, are planned to be in the improvement and enhancement project.

5 Conclusion

MyMic is a mobile application designed and implemented to be a replacement of wireless microphones using UDP over WiFi. Clients connect to server by extract the server IP address and Port no from QR code generated from the control panel settings. It records voice in a PCM encoding, 16-bit sample size, and 44.1 kHz sampling rate, and transmits it to the control panel where the admin can control client sessions by permitting, suspend, and record their speeches.

Application parameters take in mind the minimum capabilities of the most used mobile models in Gaza market, and it is tested in an events hall with good results and clear sound where results show low noise values.

MyMic App was already developed and turned into commercial product, and ALTARIQ Systems & Projects has a project with Gaza University to improve and enhance the audio quality of MyMic.

Future work research for this issue will focus on many areas: the underlying transmission protocol, the WiFi network capabilities, mobile capabilities, and the audio quality improvement algorithms (noise and echo cancellation, and delay minimization).

Acknowledgments. The research work is under Bridges (Josoor) Project, it is supported by the Palestinian Information Technology Association of Companies (PITA) and The Palestinian Market Development Programme (PMDP).

References

1. Atalah, K.: Contributions to effective protocol design to mitigate continuous multimedia services short disruptions in WiFi networks. Ph.D. thesis, University of Las Palmas de Gran Canaria, Spain (2011)
2. Zingade, S., Joshi, R., Shendkar, R., Arora, P., Scholar, U.G.: DREAM–a data streaming application using RTP/RTSP in a local area network. Int. J. Eng. Sci. **6**, 2975 (2016)
3. Marrero, D.: Caracterización y modelado de prestaciones en redes inalámbricas para aplicaciones con calidad de servicio. Ph.D. thesis, University of Las Palmas de Gran Canaria, Spain (2015)
4. Shannon, J., O'Flaithearta, P., Cinar, Y., Melvin, H.: Enhancing multimedia QoE via more effective time synchronisation over 802.11 networks. In: Proceedings of the 7th International Conference on Multimedia Systems, p. 25. ACM (2016)
5. Premananda, B.S., Uma, B.V.: Speech enhancement algorithm to reduce the effect of background noise in mobile phones. Int. J. Wirel. Mob. Netw. **5**, 177 (2013)
6. Loizou, P.C.: Speech enhancement based on perceptually motivated Bayesian estimators of the magnitude spectrum. IEEE Trans. Speech Audio Process. **13**, 857–869 (2005)
7. Loizou, P.C.: Speech Enhancement: Theory and Practice. CRC Press, New York (2013)
8. Buera, L., Droppo, J., Acero, A.: Speech enhancement using a pitch predictive model. In: IEEE International Conference on Acoustics, Speech and Signal Processing, pp. 4885–4888. IEEE (2008)
9. Salih, E.A.: Speech Enhancement using Kalman filter in communication. Int. J. Math. Comput. Phys. Electr. Comput. Eng. **8**, 606–611 (2014). Speech Enhancement using Kalman filter in communication
10. Plapous, C., Claude, M., Pascal, S.: Improved signal-to-noise ratio estimation for speech enhancement. IEEE Trans. Audio Speech Lang. Process. **14**, 2098–2108 (2006)
11. Kashyap A., Prasad M.: Audio noise cancellation using Wiener Filter based LMS algorithm using Labview. Int. J. Emerg. Technol. Adv. Eng. **3** (2013)
12. van Meer, A.C.P., Garas, J., Sommen, P.C.W., van de Laar, J.L., Prodrive, B.V.: Implementation of a broadband multipoint acoustic noise canceller. In: Proceedings of ICSPAT-1998, Toronto (1998)
13. Hänsler, E., Gerhard, S.: An engineering guide to acoustic echo canceller. In: Hänsler, E., Gerhard, S. (eds.) Topics in Acoustic Echo and Noise Control: Selected Methods for the Cancellation Of Acoustical Echoes, The Reduction of Background Noise, and Speech Processing. Springer, Heidelberg (2006)
14. Android NDK. https://developer.android.com/ndk/index.html
15. Java Native Interface. http://docs.oracle.com/javase/7/docs/technotes/guides/jni/
16. C# audio library. https://naudio.codeplex.com/

Security

Design of a Semantic Framework to Modeling Human Behavior in Surveillance Context

Héctor F. Gómez A[1(✉)], Rafael Martínez-Tomás[2], Susana Arias Tapia[1], Víctor Hernández del Salto[1], Javier Sánchez Guerrero[1], J.A. Mocha-Bonilla[1], Patricio Ortiz Ortiz[1], David Castillo Salazar[1], Judith Nuñez Ramirez[1], and Cristina Páez Quinde[1]

[1] Facultad de Ciencias Humanas y de la Educación, Universidad Técnica de Ambato, Ambato, Ecuador
{hf.gomez,saarias,vhernandez,jsanchez,ja.mocha, patricioortizo,dr.castillo,judithdnunezr,mc.paez}@uta.edu.ec

[2] Dpto. Inteligencia Artificial, Universidad Nacional de Educación a Distancia, Juan del Rosal 16, 28040 Madrid, Spain
rmtomas@dia.uned.es

Abstract. Multi-sensory monitoring has developed significantly over the last decade. The main reason for this is because of two basic, social needs: security and health. Without doubt, there is a growing social need for security, for detecting dangerous situations, and criminal behavior detection (surveillance). We propose design a semantic framework to representing the human behavior in surveillance context. The principal goal, is have an easy semantic tool that allowing for knowledge engineers get semantic representations case study easy to analyze and reuse. We show examples of how easily and reuse is possible, however we are working on improving our framework, in order to make it much more manageable for the semantic use. Conclusions and future work of our research were generated to visualize what the new tools to be developed.

Keywords: Semantic framework · Ontology · Human behavior

1 Introduction

Horus, a multi-sensor framework for monitoring and detecting activities that integrates multisensory systems into one processing unit [1]. In summary, the hypothesis of this study is that ontological engineering and semantic technologies form a unique framework for the explicit representation of situations of high-level semantics, and facilitate a fast prototype of security and surveillance systems with a similar abstraction level to that of a human agent. This framework must meet the following requirements:

- Working with multisensory signals: [2], Buildingarchitecture [3], and TIME2 [4], and VERL semantic events [5].
- Represent knowledge. The ontology must be capable of conceptualizing the elements of the scenario and its relations.

C.R. García et al. (Eds.): UCAmI 2016, Part II, LNCS 10070, pp. 507–512, 2016.
DOI: 10.1007/978-3-319-48799-1_54

- Import ontologies. The structure is adapted to combine with other ontologies developed in different domains with the purpose of reusing knowledge representations in the various fields of science.
- The knowledge engineer establishes the relations among the activities and designs the semantic rules and axioms to infer a situation [7, 8].

This was achieved by identifying key technologies, approaches and issues. In Sect. 3, we describe the main characteristics of our proposal. In Sect. 4, we present our experimentation stage with examples to model the human behaviour. And in Sect. 5, we describe the conclusions and future works of this research.

2 Art State

The recognition of basic situations with low-level semantics such as trespassing perimeters, an object, or even a riot in video surveillance systems (SV) is not the only aim of this work. This study also ties to recognize more complex activities or situations of high-level semantics and higher abstraction. Going from sensor signals, and even images, to this type of interpretation involves a much higher level of semantics that can only be achieved by relating the information obtained to the information from the context. This interpretation always depends upon knowledge, capacity of expression, and the specific language of the expert. In this respect, there are solutions that have been proposed. Most of them are based on the use of structures that interrelate the various types of implied knowledge at different levels of description, starting with low-level semantics, and then, reaching a level that performs quality descriptions that help in the search and retrieval of activities and situations in security and surveillance systems [5, 9, 10]. This is not an exclusive problem of security and surveillance systems. Regarding interpretation of video sequences, other applications can be found; for example, applications related to information retrieval and automatic classification [2]. The SIMDA group has carried out projects that pro- pose the integration of different technologies and the semantic conceptualization of situations in different national projects: AVISA (2004), AVISADOS (2007) and INT3 (2010). The contribution of INT3 is essential for our study since one of their results is Horus. Horus is a modular architecture used for the management of multisensory input that incorporates a conceptualization model to share information of interest among multiple scenarios. The multisensory sources are mainly related to image sensors since these sensors are widely used for monitoring activities. However, other sensor technologies such as wireless sensor networks (WSN) are also integrated as generic objects in Horus. The Horus framework is distributed and hybrid. The remote nodes perform low-level processing as well as data retrieval; whereas a central node is in charge of gathering and fusing information. Horus includes detection of simple objects, and tracking and detection of activities. Its task is ambitious due to the great variety of scenarios and activities that can be used [1]. Ontologies seem appropriate for the aforementioned purpose due to their capacities of representation, of reuse, of consistency [5].

3 Methodology: CHAO Ontology

The ontology SSN2 is used to conceptualize SS. This ontology meets the standards necessary to conceptualize most of the physical sensors. The work of Horus is emulated in the experiments, starting from the sensor signal to infer activities of medium-level semantics. SSN2 has three modules that are in charge of: (a) relating an activity to a sensor event (this event is obtained from processing multisensory signals), (b) detailing techniques to process the signal, and (c) detailing the configurations necessary for the correct installation of the sensor. The scenario was conceptualized by using the Building architecture (BA) ontology, which not only conceptualizes the components of a scenario but also the spatial relations [3]. Term scenario will also be used as context. The scenarios consist of physical and architectural elements (e.g. floor, walls, and doors). By conceptualizing these elements, we can obtain more semantic details when the scenario participates in the inference of situations of high-level semantics. In order to conceptualize temporal relations among semantic activities, we worked with TIME2 [4]. TIME2 has been successfully used in some research works to model events [7]. Considering this, TIME2 ontology is also used in this study. With this ontology, we can answer questions related to the occurrence of an event or situation. This feature increases the detail of the modeling of high-level semantics. The class Event does not belong to this ontology, but this ontology is always referred because the spatial and temporal relations of an event that occurs at a certain place and time are applied in it. VERL, supported by CHAO, is used to model situations of high-level semantics, but his study works with se- mantic tools, making it necessary for the models to be exported to OWL. This tool is based on the structure for modeling situations proposed by VERL. The components of this structure can be seen on Fig. 1:

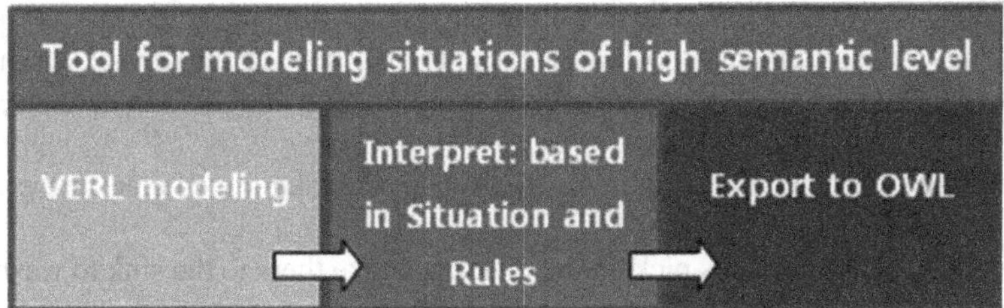

Fig. 1. Components of the situations frame-work

This tool is designed to take the conceptualizations of the SSN2, BA, and TIME2 ontologies. Additionally, events of different hierarchical level can be composed in this tool, as seen in Fig. 2. The tool create the event Changes_Zone ((Person, BuildingComponent) Meet (Person, BuildingComponent2)). This event is created with the temporal property of the situation (Person Inside BuildingComponent). Here, the person is taken as a mobile object since it is part of Mobile Objects in VERL. After that, the classes are created in OWL format according to the classes found. In addition, the existence of the spatial and temporal constraints is verified. Similarly, the parameters and axioms that the analyzed activity or situation needs are clearly established in OWL3. In the example,

Wandering in Protégé. The aim Meet min 1 is shown, which indicates that there must be two that are temporally coincident. The threshold of coincidence cannot be specified in an axiom, but it entered in the rules or algorithms in which it is necessary to use it infer or query some activity of interest.

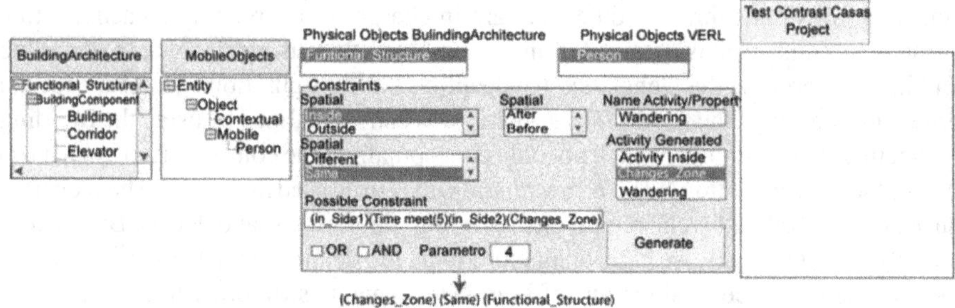

Fig. 2. Modeling of the activity wandering

4 Experimentation

In CASAS, the activities done between 12:00 and 12:45 are related to cooking lunch:

Making a telephone call and writing down a recipe: The participants walk by the dining room with a telephone in their hands. They look up a telephone number in the phone book, dial the number and listen to a voice message. The recorded messages are cuisine recipes that the participants write down on a notebook.

- Washing their hands: The participants walk by the kitchen and approach the sink to wash their hands. The use soap and dry their hands with a paper towel.
- Cooking: The participants cook oat- meal soup by following the recipe. For this, the participants pour a certain amount of water into a bowl and add the oatmeal, sugar and raisins.
- Eating: The participants eat the oat- meal soup and take a medicine in the dining room.
- Cleaning: The participants pick up the plates and take them to the sink to wash them with water and soap.

In the Figures below, the Protégé model is shown:

Figure 3 shows the result of the export of the VERL model. The tasks for preparing lunch are registered according to the activation of the sensors. The SWRL rule, which is executed to relate the sensors with the property Meet, is:

```
Sensor(?vSensor)∧activate_In(?vSensor,?vInstant)
∧ sqwrl:Difference(?vSensor,?vInstant,?Umbral) →
meet(?VSensor,?VInstant)
```

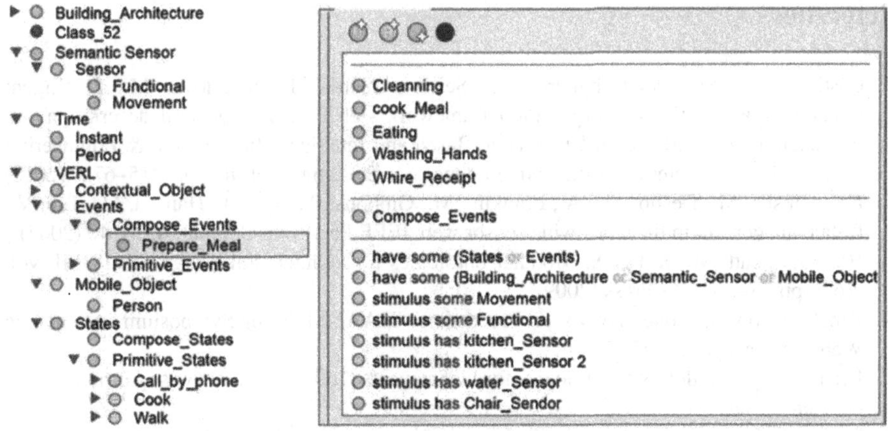

Fig. 3. Result of the composition of activities

The above rule uses the instances of the sensors and their activation time to verify if the difference between the activation instants is lower than the threshold. The cases of use analyze suspicious human behavior because the most important aspect of security and surveillance systems is the register of people's suspicious activities; however, objects or zones for another type of experiments can also be monitored.

5 Conclusions and Future Works

The work in this article started with the need to complete Horus by adding situation recognition. In fact, this study has made important contributions in this aspect. On the one hand, it was methodologically convenient to differentiate between events of medium and high- level semantics and those that had a low level. Therefore, on the basis of this theory, this study is not limited to a physical control system. On the other hand, from the theoretical point of view, the use of semantic technologies facilitates surveillance prototypes, modeling, and the implementation of a scenario and situations for the three hierarchical levels previously described. Both, the methods described and the semantic technologies used can be reused and they confirm the results of the experimentation phase. It was also possible to integrate the ontologies of specific scenarios, which are coherent with the methods, in CHAO. Because of the type of situations on which this study attempts to work, it is particularly important to find a weak suspicion [11, 12]. For example, in the process of monitoring people with Alzheimer's disease, it can be accepted that there are some false positives, but not false negatives since this would cause that a person would be wandering around without providing them with appropriate care. It was demonstrated that the proposal in this study can be useful to model various situations and reuse the components of the framework and the inference rules that work with a hierarchical, as it shows in our other research architecture of semantic levels. Moreover, it has been clearly demonstrated that the framework can be used to obtain sequences of high-level semantics with explicit knowledge.

References

1. Castillo, J., Fernández-Caballero, A., Serrano-Cuerda, J., Sokolova, M.: Intelligent monitoring and activity interpretation framework - INT3 Horus general description. In: Internacional Conference on Knowledge-Based and Intelligent Information & Engineering Systems. Lecture Notes in Artificial Intelligence, san Sebastian, vol. 40, pp. 6715–6727 (2012)
2. Balanzinska, M., Deshpande, A., Franklin, M., Gibbons, P., Gray, J., Hansen, M., Tao, V.: Data management in the worldwide sensor web. IEEE Pervasive Comput. **6**, 30–40 (2007)
3. Hois, J., Bhatt, M., Kutz, O.: Modular ontologies for architectural design. In: FOMI, vol. 6(66), pp. 66–77. IOS Press (2009)
4. Pan, E., Hobbs, J.: Time in owl-s. In: Proceedings of AAI-04 Spring Symposium on Semantic Web Services, pp. 25–42 (2004)
5. Bredmod, F., Maillot, N.: Ontologies for video events (2009). http://www-sop.inria.fr/orion/personnel/Van
6. Sunico, J.: Reconocimiento de imágenes: usuarios, segmentos de usuarios, gestos, emociones y empatía. http://jm.sunico.org/4007/06/48/reconocimiento-de-imagenes-usuarios-segmentos-de-usuarios-gestos-emociones-y-empatia/. Accessed 21 Sep 2008
7. Hu, W., Tan, T., Wang, L., Maybank, S.: A survey on visual surveillance of object moton and behaviors. IEEE Trans. Syst. Man Cybern. Part C **34**(3), 334–354 (2004)
8. Riboni, D., Pareschi, L., Radaelli, L., Bettini, C.: Is ontology-based activity recognition really effective? In: Pervasive Computing and Communicatiions Workshops, pp. 427–431 (2011)
9. Ayer, D., Chellapa, R.: Scenario recognition from video using a hierarchy of dynamic belief networks. IEEE (2000)
10. Botia, J., Villa, A., Plama, J.: Ambient assisted living system for in home monitoring of healthy. Expert Syst. Appl. **39**, 8136–9148 (2012)
11. Gómez A., H.F., Tomás, R.M., Tapia, S.A., Caballero, A.F., Ratté, S., Eras, A.G., González, P.L.: Identification of loitering human behaviour in video surveillance environments. In: Vicente, J.M.F., Álvarez-Sánchez, J.R., Paz López, F., Toledo-Moreo, F., Adeli, H. (eds.) Artificial Computation in Biology and Medicine. LNCS, vol. 9107, pp. 516–525. Springer, Heidelberg (2015)
12. Gómez, H., Martínez-Tomás, R., Tapia, S., Zamorano, M.: Using semantic technologies and the OSU ontology for modelling context and activities in multi-sensory surveillance systems. Int. J. Syst. Sci. **45**, 798–809 (2014)

Patients' Data Management System Through Identity Based Encryption

Alexandra Rivero-García(✉), Candelaria Hernández-Goya, Iván Santos-González, and Pino Caballero-Gil

Departamento de Ingeniería Informática y de Sistemas, Universidad de La Laguna, San Cristóbal de La Laguna, Tenerife, Spain
{ariverog,mchgoya,jsantosg,pcaballe}@ull.es

Abstract. In this paper a secure distributed system is proposed to manage patients' information in an emergency service in order to improve efficiency. Authentication, confidentiality and automatic and robust patient identification are provided. The system elements are NFC wristbands, assigned to patients, mobile devices assigned to medical staff and a server to manage the information and verify that its use is legitimate. Patient's identification is carried out through a keyed-Hash Message Authentication Code. In addition, a challenge-response protocol is proposed for mutual authentication of medical staff and the server using the FullIdent scheme Identity Based Encryption. The same scheme gives confidentiality to the system. The definition of this system provides a secure solution based on mHealth for managing patients in an emergency service.

Keywords: Identity Based Encryption (IBE) · mHealth · Keyed-Hash Message Authentication Code (HMAC) · Android · NFC

1 Introduction

Undoubtedly one of the most innovative paradigms of the last years in the health environment is the integration of mobile devices in healthcare (m-Health). Its significance stems from the flexibility provided by the system. However, the potential security problems that arise with mobile devices and their wireless interface must be specifically addressed due to the features of data handled. In [1] some of these problems and the corresponding recommendations to solve them are explained.

This paper presents a secure distributed patient management system in an emergency service with the primary goal of improving efficiency. Security services such as confidentiality and authentication are provided to protect communications and the access to patient records.

Patient misidentification is an issue to which health authorities have paid a lot of attention because of its consequences: medication errors, wrong surgical procedures, etc. [2]. In addition, statistics on this subject are worrying. For

C.R. García et al. (Eds.): UCAmI 2016, Part II, LNCS 10070, pp. 513–523, 2016.
DOI: 10.1007/978-3-319-48799-1_55

example, in the UK, the National Health Service received more than 24,000 statements on misidentifications of patients in 2006–2007 [3].

One of the bases of the proposal system is the use of NFC (Near Field Communication) [4], specifically NFC wristbands, for automatic patient identification. Unlike other technologies as RFID [5], Bluetooth or Wi-Fi [6], NFC is not oriented to the continuous data transmission. It is necessary a temporally contact between the devices that interact to allow the exchange of information in a quick and timely way. Although, at first, the distance factor for transmitting information may seem a limitation it is actually the key in this technology. The need for proximity between devices limits the types of attacks to develop. Besides, not requiring pairing between devices facilitate its use use by health staff.

NFC devices may operate in two different modes. On the one hand, in the active mode each device generates its own electromagnetic field (emulating the communication paradigm peer-to-peer). On the other hand, in the passive mode one device generates the electromagnetic field with its own power supply. In this way, it enables that other device starts the connection taking energy from the field generated to power its circuit. Then the passive device generates the response signal and transfers the data. This mode of operation matches with the RFID communication model and it is the one used in this proposal.

The other main components of the system are: a mobile device associated to a member of the medical staff, the server that hosts a web service and an NFC reader for allocating wristbands once patients have been identified.

2 Preliminaries

Recently, different tools to solve specific problems have been proposed in patient management. In [7] authors introduce a mutual authentication scheme to improve the security of medication automatic systems. RFID bracelets and cryptography based on elliptic curves are proposed there. The protocol used does not provide a mechanism for session key generation to protect confidentiality.

There are medical systems that base their operation on the use of NFC bracelets. In [8] an example is shown. In this case the bracelet is designed to be worn everyday by people. If there is an emergency that requires checking of medical data, it is directly read using a mobile application. A disadvantage of this application is that any user who has the application installed can perform an information query, because there is no any security mechanism implemented.

The authors of the publication [9] developed an attack on a mutual authentication system based on RFID tags in [10]. Specifically, they show that it is possible to trace the labels, for this reason patient privacy fails. At the same time a new protocol is defined, which solves the privacy problem and improves efficiency.

In [11] a system for the management of medical staff rounds is described. It uses NFC wristbands and mobile devices, but it does not specify whether security services are deployed or not.

Our system includes automatic patient identification, medical personnel authentication and confidentiality for communications between the mobile device and the server. Confidentiality between the mobile device and wristband is warranted by the need for proximity to establish the NFC connection.

3 Proposed System

Currently when a patient arrives to admissions in an emergency service, the staff identifies her/him. Generally, patient identification is performed by checking the social security card and/or the ID card and once this is done a plastic wristband is assigned to each patient.

Then the patient is evaluated by a health care staff member who analyses the information stored at the hospital entrance and adds the results of new assessments if any. Afterwards the patient may be treated by a specialist. During all these actions patient identification must be repeated.

This system has some drawbacks. Doctors should review patient's history before assisting her/him and they can make such consultation through printed documentation or using a computer. If paper documentation is used, it is usually generated as a batch for a set of patients. For example, ten medical records may be printed and a doctor can check and attend those ten patients. Once they are attended, the doctor should leave the records and repeat the process with a new group of patients. This arrangement has heterogeneous information because some data may be updated on computers and other data are kept in printed format.

Besides that updates made by doctors will not be updated instantaneously in the central system. In this approach health workers have to deal with many documentation which leads to consume time and resources. On the other hand, medical staff have to attend several patients and it may generate wrong patient identifications with serious consequences in some cases.

Some solutions to these conflicts are described in this work. Solutions are based on the implementation of a secure system based on NFC wristbands and mobile devices that allow us to eliminate misidentification and secondly, to rationalize time in patient care.

This proposal provides substantial changes to traditional system. When patient identification is performed for the first time, an NFC wristband is assigned to him/her, specifically a NTAG21x ICs [12] wristband which follows the pattern set by NFCForum (the association that regulates the NFC standards) [13]. This wristband has not patient sensitive data. The only data that the system saves on the wristband is an identifier assigned by the server. This identifier is generated through a process which will be discuss below. This generation takes into account the physical identifier of the card (similar to MAC number in computers) and the patient record identifier. It should be pointed out that this information will be written in the wristband in a completely secure way.

The code stored in the wristband allows any medical staff, with the right permissions, to access to the patient's record identifying the patient with the simple gesture of bringing a mobile device near to the wristband. Thanks to wristbands the system avoid confusion when identifying patients and increases efficiency in the development of medical tasks. Wristbands are fully recyclable, so when a patient leaves the hospital, it may be used with another patient.

The server manages access permissions to patient data on the basis of medical staff shifts.

Protection of patient data is a paramount objective in the healthcare environment. That is why security is one of the pillars of the described system. A HMAC tool is used for automatic patients' identification and identity-based cryptography to protect confidentiality of patient records.

3.1 Automatic Patient Identification

When a patient arrives to the emergency service he/she must be identified through his/her credentials. After that, an NFC wristband is assigned to him/her. Each patient will be identified through a HMAC generated by the server by using the physical wristband identifier and the patient history number. If a patient does not have a medical history in the system, it will be created automatically with some basic fields, such as name, age, country, and some initial information.

The NFC wristband is going to be read by a NFC reader. The procedure is illustrated in Fig. 1.

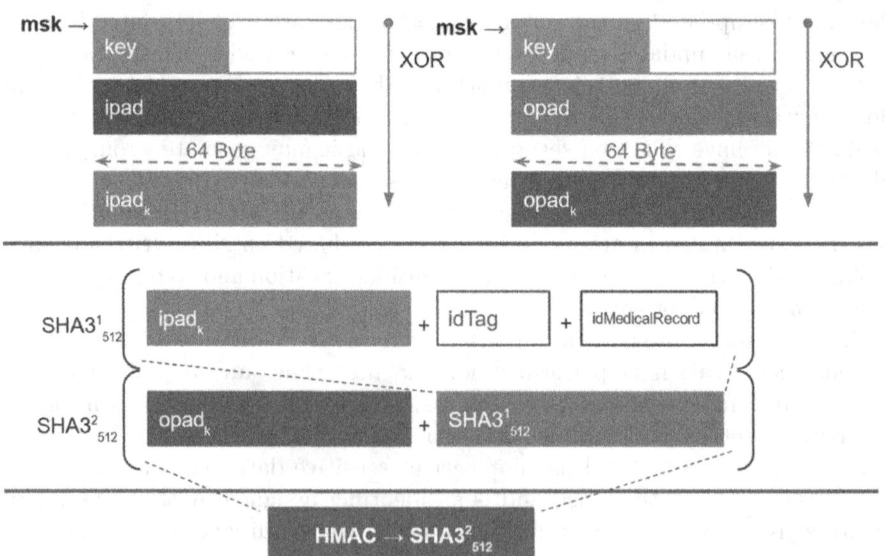

Fig. 1. HMAC generation

The system send the physical wristband identifier to the server and there two 64 bytes arrays are generated as in [14]. They are denoted as *ipad* and *opad* and some default values are assigned to them during the initialization of the HMAC generation. New arrays are generated through a XOR operation of previous ones and the master secret key (msk). The generation of the msk is explained below. The results are $ipad_k$ and $opad_k$. Then, with the physical wristband identifier (idTag) and the patient medical record the system is ready to generate the HMAC value. A hash function is applied to the concatenation of these fields and the $ipad_k$. The output of this hash concatenated with the $opad_k$ is the input to another hash function. The HMAC final result is:

$$HMAC(msk, K) = HASH((opad_k)||HASH(ipad_k)||M)$$

where, M is the concatenation of the physical wristband identifier and the patient medical record. Furthermore the hash function is a $SHA3_{512}$. The output of the function is the number stored in the NFC wristband, as patient identifier.

When access to patient data is required the NFC wristband should be read through a mobile application which sends the data of the physical wristband identifier and the HMAC to the server. The server verifies the authenticity of the bracelet and the access permissions. Then the authentication protocol described later in the paper is used each time a member of the medical staff needs to access to patients' data.

The protection of communications is achieved through an Identity Based Encryption (IBE). In this public key cryptography schemes any text can act as a valid public key and the system has a server devoted to generate private keys for health staff (PKG, Private Key Generator). This approach offers the advantage of simplifying management by not having to define a public key infrastructure. Furthermore, this type of scheme was chosen because of its low computational complexity and its efficiency in terms of memory and its usability. Figure 2 shows the communication flow.

3.2 Data Confidentiality

Authentication against the server is provided by using an Identity-Based Encryption scheme (IBE) as primitive. Concretely, the scheme proposed by Boneh-Franklin [15], the version named FullIdent scheme.

A crucial element in the proposal is a Private Key Generator (PKG), a server in charge of generating health staff private keys. The identifier for medical staff will be the number of registered medical practitioners (ID). Next, we describe the mathematical basic tools used as well as the notation included in the system description.

Definition 1 *(Bilinear map pairing).* Considering two cycling groups $(G, +)$ and $(G_T, \cdot)$ of the same prime order q, P a generator of G, there is a bilinear map paring $\hat{e} : G \times G \rightarrow G_T$ satisfying the following conditions:

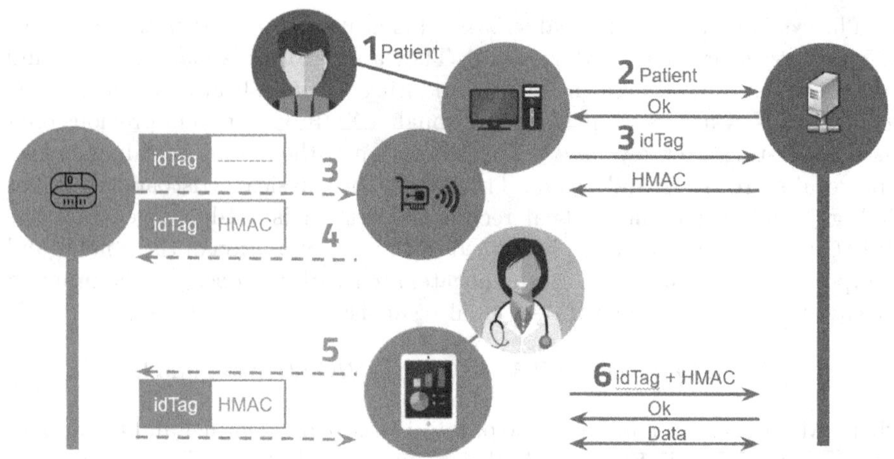

Fig. 2. Consulting medical history flow

- Bilinear: $\forall P, Q \in G$ and $\forall a, b \in \mathbb{Z}$, $\hat{e}(aP, bQ) = \hat{e}(P, Q)^{ab}$
- Non-degenerate: $\exists P_1, P_2 \in G$ that $\hat{e}(P_1, P_2) \neq 1$. This means if P is generator of G, then $\hat{e}(P, P)$ is a generator of Q.
- Computability: there exists an algorithm to compute $\hat{e}(P, Q), \forall P, Q \in G$

It should be pointed out that the key exchange between the server and the doctor, which will be explained below, is performed using the stream cipher SNOW_3G [16] under the session key obtained through an ECDH (Elliptic Curve Diffie-Hellman) [17]. This data exchange is critical to the security of subsequent connections as you can see in Fig. 3.

Some hash functions denoted as follows are also needed:

$$H_1 : \{0,1\}^* \rightarrow G^*, H_2 : G_T \rightarrow \{0,1\}^n$$
$$H_3 : \{0,1\}^n \times \{0,1\}^n \rightarrow \mathbb{Z}_q^*, H_4 : \{0,1\}^n \rightarrow \{0,1\}^n$$

where the size of the message is defined by n. Additional notation is also described: $x \xleftarrow{r} S$ stands for an element x randomly selected from a set S, $x \leftarrow y$ denotes the assignment of the value y to x and $||$ is used for concatenation.

The steps needed for the IBE scheme are the following:

SETUP: The initial parameters are established and the server generates the master public key (mpk, represented here as Q_{TA}) and the master secret key (msk, represented here as t). For that a prime q based on some private data $k \in \mathbb{Z}$, two groups G and G_T of order q and a bilinear pairing map $\hat{e} : G \times G \rightarrow G_T$ are selected. $P \in G$ is randomly selected and the hash functions H_1, H_2, H_3 and H_4 are also chosen.

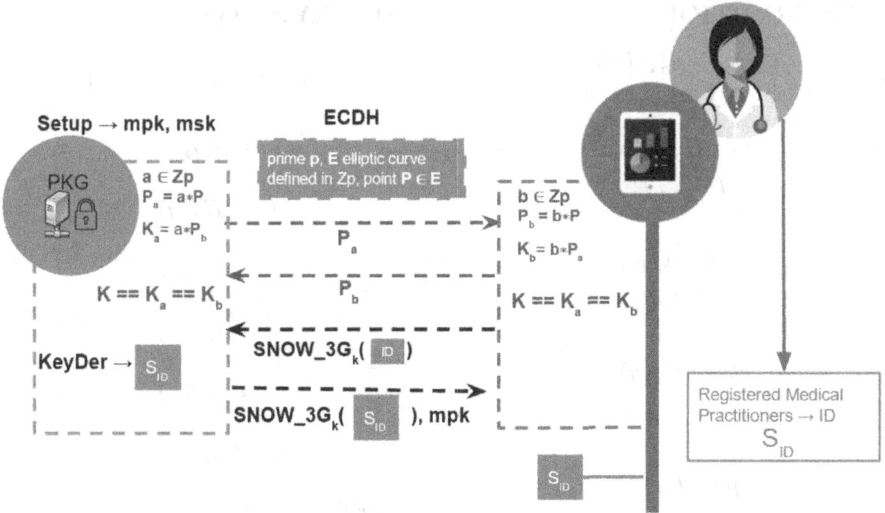

Fig. 3. Private key exchange

EXTRACT (ID): In this step the secret key for each member of the medical staff based on their ID is generated. The public key $Q_{ID} \in G$ and the secret key $S_{ID} \in G$ are calculated taking into account the master private key (t).

ENCRYPT (ID_b, m): All the messages $m \in \{0,1\}^n$ will be encrypted. The receiver's public key is generated taking into account ID_b (the identification ID of receiver b) because the message is encrypted with Q_{ID_b} giving as result σ (3-tuple : c, U, V).

DECRYPT (S_{ID_b}, σ): This step is similar to previous one, If everything is right, the message $m \in \{0,1\}^n$ will be returned. Otherwise, if there are some problems in the signature or in the encryption of m, $\perp$ is returned. The message is decrypted with the 3-tuple σ parsed and the receiver private key (S_{ID_b})

A formal description of all these steps as well as the elements exchanged follows.

SETUP

$$t \xleftarrow{r} \mathbb{Z}_q^*$$

$$Q_{TA} \leftarrow tP$$

EXTRACT

$$Q_{ID} \leftarrow H_1(ID)$$

$$S_{ID} \leftarrow tQ_{ID}$$

ENCRYPTION

$$Q_{ID_b} \leftarrow H_1(ID_b)$$
$$x \stackrel{r}{\leftarrow} \mathbb{Z}_q^*$$
$$r \leftarrow H_3(x||m)$$
$$U \leftarrow rP$$

$$S \leftarrow rQ_{TA}$$
$$y \leftarrow \hat{e}(S, Q_{ID_b})$$

$$k \leftarrow H_2(y)$$
$$V \leftarrow x \oplus k$$

$$p \leftarrow H_4(x)$$
$$c \leftarrow m \oplus p$$
$$\sigma \leftarrow (c, U, V)$$

DECRYPTION

$$split \quad \sigma \quad as \quad (c, U, V)$$

$$y \leftarrow \hat{e}(S_{ID_b}, U)$$

$$k \leftarrow H_2(y)$$

$$x \leftarrow V \oplus k$$

$$p \leftarrow H_4(x)$$

$$m \leftarrow c \oplus p$$

$$r \leftarrow H_3(x||m)$$

Verification: $U == rP$

Note: if the verification is successful m is returned, otherwise $\perp$ is returned.

Algorithm 1. IBE steps definition.

3.3 Authentication Scheme

A mutual authentication protocol is proposed through challenge-response [18] based on the previous IBE scheme. Authentication is performed whenever establishing communication is required. These utilities are described below.

1. The doctor sends an authentication request to the server:

$$ID \rightarrow PKG : Req_{ID}$$

2. The server randomly generates an integer $r \in \mathbb{Z}_q^*$ and this number is sent encrypted with the corresponding doctor public key:

$$PKG \rightarrow ID : a = E_{ID}(r)$$

3. The doctor decrypts the received message and sends the result to the server:

$$r' = S_{ID}(a)$$
$$ID \rightarrow PKG : r'$$

4. The server verify if $r == r'$. If everything is right, authentication is successful and the encrypted messages received including doctor's identifier will be accepted.

Server authentication against doctors will be symmetrical but using master keys. In Fig. 4 the authentication process is shown.

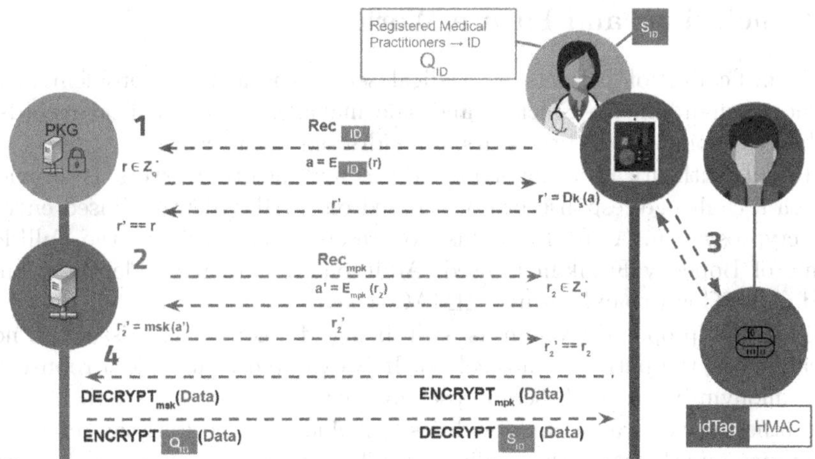

Fig. 4. Challenge-response protocol

4 Security Analysis

The proposed scheme provides protection against different attacks. Here we describe some of them.

A spoofing attack and/or cloning of the card will be hardly successful since it would involve the generation of the HMAC described involving the server master key, the ID card and the number of patient record. Even if an outsider obtains this information, the NFC wristband physical identifier and the number patient record are unique. Furthermore if the attacker corrupts the data, the system can detect it easily. It is because the server can know that the information does not catch with its own data. We have to take into account that the data saved on the NFC Tags is not sensible data, the information is the HMAC solution.

If someone wants to emulate the card from an Android device, it is required to change from being passive device to be an active one. Hence, the attack will be detected since the application has as restriction reading only passive NFC tags. The implementation using Android communications allows to distinguish the roles.

The Denial of Service (DoS) attacks by making requests to the server are restricted because only those requests associated to a legitimate staff number will take effect. Once the corresponding private key is assigned, additional requests from this number will not be attended.

Regarding a "Man in the Middle" attack, it would be easily detectable because the number of members who are allowed to make requests to the server is limited to those who are working at the time of the request.

5 Conclusions and Future Work

The identification of patients in medical services is a major problem in the healthcare environment. Efficient and safe management of medical records is another key point. These two issues are addressed in this work.

Mutual authentication involving server and health workers is provided through a challenge-response protocol based on a IBE (Identity-Based encryption) cryptosystem. Apart from this, to preserve confidentiality the FullIdent scheme of Boneh y Franklin is used. Additionally, patients's identification is based on NFC wristbands using a HMAC scheme.

Since the proposed system is still being developed, the issue of non-traceability of the patient is not solved. It is expected to include a robust and secure anonymity scheme based on pseudonyms.

Another new desirable functionalities to include may be statistics on medical information and the use of the application. The automatic assignment of patients to doctors seems to be a promising feature as well.

Acknowledgements. Research supported by TESIS2015010102, TESIS2015010106, RTC-2014-1648-8, TEC2014-54110-R, MTM-2015-69138-REDT and DIG02-INSITU.

References

1. TechTarget, mhealth security: best practices and industry trends, TechTarget, Technical report (2015)
2. Organization, W.H.: Patient safety solutions. http://goo.gl/EuAX51
3. Pablo-Comeche, D., Buitrago-Vera, C., Meneu, R.: Identificación inequívoca de pacientes. evaluación del lanzamiento y su implantación en los hospitales de la agencia valenciana de salud, Medicina Clínica, vol. 135, no. Julio 2010, pp. 1–6, 2010. http://dx.doi.org/10.1007/s10916-015-0362-8
4. Want, R.: Near field communication. IEEE Pervasive Comput. **3**, 4–7 (2011)
5. Finkenzeller, K., Handbook, R.: Radio-Frequency Identification Fundamentals and Applications. John Wiley & Son, Chippenham (1999)
6. Lee, J.-S., Su, Y.-W., Shen, C.-C.: A comparative study of wireless protocols: bluetooth,UWB, ZigBee, and Wi-Fi. In: 33rd Annual Conference of the IEEE on Industrial Electronics Society, IECON 2007. IEEE, pp. 46–51 (2007)
7. Jin, C., Xu, C., Zhang, X., Li, F.: A secure ECC-based RFID mutual authentication protocol to enhance patient medication safety. J. Med. Syst. **40**(1), 1–6 (2015). http://dx.doi.org/10.1007/s10916-015-0362-8
8. H. id: Health system platform (2012). https://www.healthid.com/
9. Lee, C.-I., Chien, H.-Y.: An elliptic curve cryptography-based rfid authentication securing e-health system. Int. J. Distrib. Sens. Netw. **11**, 1–7 (2015). http://dx.doi.org/10.1155/2015/642425
10. He, D., Kumar, N., Chilamkurti, N., Lee, J.-H.: Lightweight ECC based RFID authentication integrated with an ID verifier transfer protocol. J. Med. Syst. **38**(10), 1–6 (2014). http://dx.doi.org/10.1007/s10916-014-0116-z
11. Kstinger, H., Gobber, M., Grechenig, T., Tappeiner, B., Schramm, W.: Developing a NFC based patient identification and ward round system for mobile devices using the android platform. In: 2013 IEEE Point-of-Care Healthcare Technologies (PHT), pp. 176–179, January 2013

12. P. data sheet NTAG213, 215, 216, Nfc forum type 2 tag compliant ic with 144, 504, 888 bytes user memory (2015). http://www.who.int/patientsafety/solutions/patientsafety/PS-Solution2.pdf
13. NFCFORUM, Official web page (2016). http://nfc-forum.org/
14. Bellare, M., Canetti, R., Krawczyk, H.: Message authentication using hash functions: the HMAC construction. RSA Lab. Cryptobytes **2**(1), 12–15 (1996)
15. Boneh, D., Franklin, M.: Identity-based encryption from the weil pairing. In: Kilian, J. (ed.) CRYPTO 2001. LNCS, vol. 2139, pp. 213–229. Springer, Heidelberg (2001). doi:10.1007/3-540-44647-8_13
16. Santos-González, I., Rivero-García, A., Caballero-Gil, P., Hernández-Goya, C.: Alternative communication system for emergency situations. In: WEBIST, vol. 2, pp. 397–402 (2014)
17. Miller, V.S.: Use of elliptic curves in cryptography. In: Williams, H.C. (ed.) CRYPTO 1985. LNCS, vol. 218, pp. 417–426. Springer, Heidelberg (1986). doi:10.1007/3-540-39799-X_31
18. Menezes, A.J., Van Oorschot, P.C., Vanstone, S.A.: Handbook of Applied Cryptography. CRC Press, Boca Raton (1996)

Development of an Android Application to Combat Domestic Violence

José Ángel Concepción-Sánchez(✉), Pino Caballero-Gil, and Jezabel Molina-Gil

Department of Computer Engineering, University of La Laguna, 38200 La Laguna, Tenerife, Spain
{alu0100697414,pcaballe,jmmolina}@ull.edu.es

Abstract. Domestic violence is one of the most serious and widespread problems in our society. In the most dangerous cases, the use of special devices for GPS tracing is recommended. However, the truth is that they are used only in extreme cases. This work describes the idea and operation of a mobile application to combat domestic violence. Among the main technologies that are used in the implementation of the proposal are Android, BLE and LTE. If an offender gets close to a victim, even if the established threshold distance has not been broken, the victim is warned thanks to the application. Besides, if the threshold distance is broken, automatic streaming of a real-time video is sent to the police and a list of stored contacts are warned so that they can try to help to protect the victim till the police arrives.

Keywords: Security · Mobile application · Gender violence · Protection · Android · Bluetooth Low Energy · Long Term Evolution · Wi-Fi

1 Introduction

Currently, one of the most terrible problems in the world is domestic violence. For example, in Spain, in the last 10 years the annual average of fatalities has been 62. In addition, there are many other cases that do not end in death but victims are seriously injured. Thus, the number of victims of domestic violence in 2015 in Spain was 7.229, and the rate of victims of domestic violence was 1.3 per 1,000 women aged 14 and older, 2 per cent greater than the year before [1].

A few years ago, a system was developed based on GPS monitoring devices consisting of ankle bracelets to be attached to offenders [2,3], so that they allow notifying a control centre and the victim if a threshold distance between offender and victim is violated. Such a system is implemented only in cases of high or extreme risk, due to the lack of information or conviction among the judges, what causes that the vast majority of victims are not protected. Besides, this system is not effective in small cities because if the victim and the aggressor live in the same city, it can generate false alarms.

C.R. García et al. (Eds.): UCAmI 2016, Part II, LNCS 10070, pp. 524–529, 2016.
DOI: 10.1007/978-3-319-48799-1_56

The aforementioned facts mean that there is a serious problem in our society for which current solutions are not being effective.

This work aims not only at preventing unwanted situations between victims and aggressors, but also in conveying a sense of security to victims in their everyday life, so that they can go outside without being worried that their aggressors can appear suddenly. The proposed system is continuously checking the distance between them and if it gets too short, a warning is sent to the victim to the emergency services and to a list of contacts, so that this provides time to react. Unlike other proposals [4–6], the described proposal is based on an automatic smartphone application.

At the moment, this work is only a prototype and is not currently being used.

The next sections describe in more detail the operation procedure of the proposed system, the location and sharing system, and the technologies that are used, respectively. Finally, a brief conclusion and some open problems close this paper.

2 Proposal Operation

In this paper, a new Android application is described for protecting domestic violence victims from their aggressors. The two main features of the proposal are:

- The use of Bluetooth Low Energy (BLE) [7] to automatically detect the near presence of the aggressor. Compared to classic Bluetooth, BLE is intended to provide considerably reduced power consumption and cost while maintaining a similar communication range. About the security, this technology uses AES encryption and configurable security schemas.
- The use of Long Term Evolution (LTE) [8] to send streaming of a real-time video to the police. It is a standard for wireless communication of high-speed data for mobile phone and data terminals and it is based on the GSM/EDGE and UTMS/HSPA network technologies, increasing the capacity and speed using a different radio interface together with core network improvements.

The mobile application that is described in this work is an app location for the Android operating system (with possibility of portability to iOS and Windows Phone in the future) that uses BLE in the background to check whether the device attached to the aggressor (typically a BLE bracelet) is detected near the victim. Thus, if the application detects the aggressor, it can use two different levels of warning using Android notifications together with vibration and sound. These two levels are:

- Low level (caution): The aggressor has been detected in the vicinity, but does not exceed the signal strength required to alert the police. In this case, the victim may be aware in order to try to avoid unwanted situation of a meeting. See Fig. 1.
- High level (hazard): According to the signal strength of the devices, the aggressor is too close to the victim because he has exceeded the threshold distance. See Fig. 2.

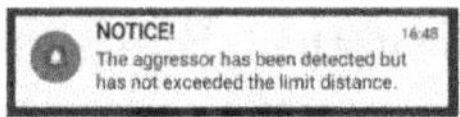

Fig. 1. Warning of attacker detection

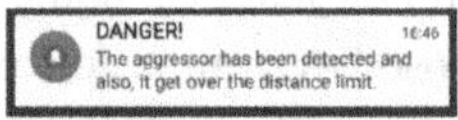

Fig. 2. Warning of attacker approach

In the high level of hazard warning, besides notifying the victim, the application starts a video recording that is sent in real time using 4G mobile technologies to the receiver station of the police. If the victim doesn't have their smartphone at hand, the audio of the video can still be used by the control centre to analize the situation and proceed accordingly.

In addition to the basic functionality of the application discussed above, the application has other elements of great interest:

- Panic Button: On the main page of the application there is a panic button, which is large enough so that the victim can instinctively press it and a call is automatically made to the emergency services. This is a detail of great interest because under high stress, it is difficult to dial a number or to select a contact.
- Contact List: The victim can configure a list of numbers to be notified by SMS if the attacker exceeds the second warning level, so that, for example, a neighbour can come to help while the police arrives.
- Recording and Streaming: The victim may choose to record and send a video to a control centre by pressing a programmed button.
- Privacy of the application: The application icon is hidden so the victim can have privacy. Neither the aggressor nor anyone can see it is installed. In addition, when the application is initialized, it is necessary to put a password to be able to access the app.
- Warning of Disabled Bluetooth: If the Bluetooth is turned off on the device, a warning will notify the user, as this will not allow the application to function. Meaning the victim will not know if the aggressor is getting near. This warning cannot be removed from the Android notification until Bluetooth is activated. See Fig. 3

Figure 4 shows two screenshots of the application in different situations.

Figure 5 shows a list of contacts to warn in dangerous situations.

In addition, we have also developed the part responsible for receiving streaming videos. To do this, we have made use of technologies such as NodeJS and

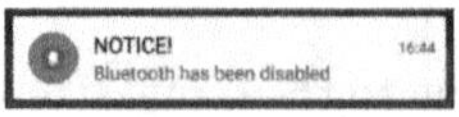

Fig. 3. Warning of disabled Bluetooth

Fig. 4. Screenshot in caution level and hazard level

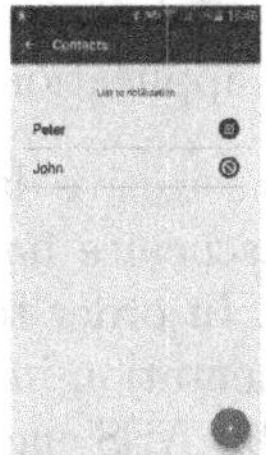

Fig. 5. List of contacts for warning

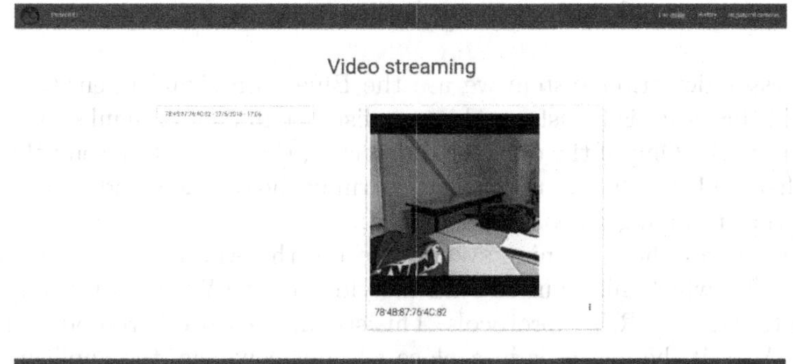

Fig. 6. Web application

Angular. Besides of receive videos that are sent via streaming from the mobile application, the web also saves a history of connections with contact information of the victim and all devices that have been used ever the system. See Fig. 6

3 Used Technologies

The main technologies used in this work are as follows:

- Android mobile operating system based on Linux, along with middleware applications focused to be used on mobile devices. It is the most operating system used in mobile phones, above of iOS and Windows phone.

- Bluetooth Low Energy: Also known as BLE or Bluetooth LE, it is a new digital technology developed for interoperable Bluetooth radio devices. The main difference from previous Bluetooth versions is that being LE allows working with very low power consumption, solving the problem of their predecessors. The maximum range for a BLE device class 1 is one hundred meters.
- LTE (Long Term Evolution): Also known as 4G, it is a wireless communication standard for transmitting high-speed data for mobile phones and data terminals. It offers much higher speeds than their predecessors and it is also safer than them.
- NodeJS, Angular, HTML5 and CSS3 for deploy the Web application.
- Wowza server: Responsible for receiving streaming video sent from the mobile applications, and where the web application connects for the videos.

Also, as the application handles sensitive data, especially when sending video recording, different cryptographic schemes have to be used to protect authenticity, confidentiality and integrity. In order to achieve it, the system has been enriched with an OpenSSL implementation including Elliptic Curve Diffie Hellman for secret key agreement, 256-bit AES encryption in CBC mode and Elliptic Curve Digital Signature Algorithm for signing/verifying.

4 Location and Streaming Systems

For aggressor detection system we use the Bluetooth signal intensity between them. This intensity is transformed into a distance in meters thanks to a mathematical formula. Only if the offender is detected, the application send the notification that we have already mentioned, warning the contacts and automatically starting the streaming video.

Moreover, for the streaming system, we use the Android library called libstreaming [9], which allows us to send the video to the Wowza streaming server through RTMP and RTSP protocols. This streaming video is reproduced in the website. Also, if the victim is in a place without coverage, the application will save automatically the video on her mobile device.

5 Conclusions

This work describes the implementation of a novel warning system to protect the people who are at a high risk of suffering domestic violence today but we don't discard that in a future, this plataform can be used for another society problems. The main goal of this proposal is to make the victim feel more safe because the developed application guarantees that if the offender gets close, even if the threshold distance has not been broken, the victim is warned so that protection measures can be taken, providing the user makes sure the application is working according to instructions. Besides, if the threshold distance is broken, an automatic streaming of a recording in real time is sent to the police while a list of stored contacts are warned so that they can try to help to protect the victim as the police arrives. Since this is part of a work in progress, further improvements for the application in the form of additional features are being developed. Also, another future work is to make the application available for iOS and Windows Phone operating systems.

Acknowledgments. Research supported by RTC-2014-1648-8 and TEC2004-54110-R projects.

References

1. Estadística de Violencia Doméstica y Violencia de Género Año (2015). http://www.ine.es/prensa/np972.pdf
2. Ellsberg, M., Arango, D.J., Morton, M., Gennari, F., Kiplesund, S., Contreras, M., Watts, C.: Prevention of violence against women and girls: what does the evidence say? Lancet **385**(9977), 1555–1566 (2015)
3. Whitfield, D.: The Magic Bracelet: Technology and Offender Supervision. Waterside Press, Hook (2001)
4. Chand, D., Nayak, S., Bhat, K.S., Parikh, S., Singh, Y., Kamath, A.A.: A mobile application for Women's Safety: WoSApp. In: IEEE Region 10 Conference, pp. 1–5 (2015)
5. Chang, J.C., Wang, P.S., Fan, K.H., Yang, S.R., Su, D.Y., Lin, M.S., Tseng, Y.C.: iMace: protecting females from sexual and violent offenders in a community via smartphones. In: Parallel Processing Workshops, pp. 71–74 (2011)
6. Monisha, D.G., Monisha, M., Pavithra, G., Subhashini, R.: Women safety device and application-FEMME. Indian J. Sci. Technol. **9**(10), 1–6 (2016)
7. Bluetooth Low Energy (BLE). http://hipertextual.com/2013/12/que-es-bluetooth-le
8. Low Term Evolution (LTE). http://www.3gpp.org/technologies/keywords-acronyms/98-lte
9. Libstreaming library. https://github.com/fyhertz/libstreaming

Video Game-Based Early and Quick Safety and Stability Assessment of Critical Physical Infrastructure Affected by Disasters

Roberto G. Aldunate[1(✉)], Oscar Hidalgo[2], Cesar Navarro[2], and Alfredo Valenzuela[2]

[1] College of Applied Health Sciences, University of Illinois at Urbana-Champaign, Urbana, IL, USA
aldunate@illinois.edu
[2] Fondef Project CA13i10331, Temuco, Chile
oscar.hidalgo218@gmail.com, cnavarronm@gmail.com, alfredo.valenzuela.r@gmail.com

Abstract. Earthquakes have a profound social and economic impact when they hit densely populated urban areas. Early and Quick Safety and Structural Stability Assessment of Critical Physical Infrastructure, affected by large-scale disasters such as earthquakes, is a key task that determines potential outcomes of further activities like urban search and rescue, and recovery of the urban area. This task needs to be conducted as efficient, effective, and consistent as possible. This article presents a preliminary and exploratory effort to understand the role that technology may play in improving assessment of critical physical infrastructure affected by disasters, through a video game-based simulator. Preliminary results include validation from subject matter experts from the Chilean Department of Transportation. The results of this work are encouraging for the development of a national standard capability on conducting assessment of critical physical infrastructure affected by disasters.

Keywords: Critical physical infrastructure · Video game · Structural stability

1 Introduction

Large-scale disasters, such as earthquakes, affecting urban areas may be devastating and have great economic impact [1–4]. In particular, the 2010 earthquake in Chile reduced the country economic growth between 0.1 and 0.5 % [5]. The first 72 h after an earthquake hits a densely populated urban area are critical for the response system, because after them the likelihood to find survivors becomes very scarce [6–8]. To quickly react to earthquake's consequences, rapid critical physical infrastructure (CPI) assessment methodologies have been created in the last four decades, and they are mostly based on recording visual inspection on paper, while training is conducted through traditional lectures [9, 10]. Currently, professionals ranging from experts to beginners may reach different outcomes when assessing CPI damage on large magnitude disasters [11]. Therefore, it is necessary to uniform knowledge transfer in order to develop a standard capability. On the other

C.R. García et al. (Eds.): UCAmI 2016, Part II, LNCS 10070, pp. 530–535, 2016.
DOI: 10.1007/978-3-319-48799-1_57

hand, as video game technology has been used for emergency management training and education on response to different types of disasters [12], the authors of this article anticipated this technology would provide promising benefits for the development of such a standardized capability. Thus, the preliminary and exploratory research and development effort presented in this article, framed within a Chilean Fondef Project (#CA13i10331), which successfully aimed at improving decision-making during response to disasters, focused on developing a video-game-based technology that facilitates the acquisition, analysis, and knowledge on CPI stability assessment.

2 Related Work

Methodologies for CPI assessment typically use inspection forms to classify and describe the post-earthquake condition as the ATC-20 of E.E.U.U., the Ministry of Construction of Japan, Italy and Mexico [13]. Chile has been collaborating with Japan, the US Federal Emergency Management Agency (FEMA), and California Emergency Management Agency [14], on CPI assessment training conducted by experts delivering the activity based on courses using limited material gathered from experiences from past disasters [15]. Literature review reveals that evolutionary computational techniques, such as artificial neural networks [11], and traditional computational tools are mostly used on data collection, building inventory data, analysis, GIS maps, expert system calibration [19, 20] with video game used mainly for problem-solving on emergency [21], but not for CPI stability assessment. Other tools, not using video game technology, related to CPI assessment are PEADAB Earthquake Damage Inspection Form (EDIF) [16], Post-Earthquake Information Management Systems from the National Earthquake Hazard Reduction Programs, USA [17, 18].

3 System Design and Prototype Implementation

The system to augment the capability on Early and Quick Safety and Structural Stability Assessment of Critical Physical Infrastructure (EQ-SSSA-CPI) relies on guidelines and procedures designed by the Chilean Department of Transportation (MOP), a web platform, and 3D video-game technology to build an immersive virtual environment.

3.1 Web-Based Simulator

The main components of the we-based CPI assessment tool are the Session Module, which allows the authentication of the user; the Assessment module, which allows the registration of the inspection conducted through the 3D CPI model; the Simulator module, which is the 3D immersive virtual environment; and the Assessment Management Building module, which provides a space for trainee's performance evaluation and expert's CPI profiles scheduling (Fig. 1).

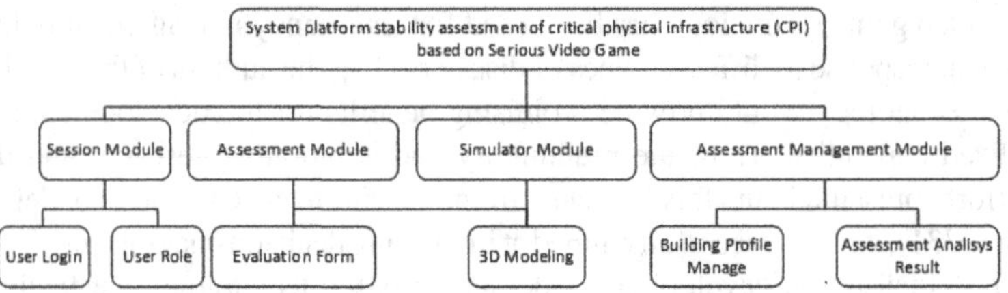

Fig. 1. System's modules and main components.

3.2 3D CPI Modeling Based on Traffic Light Model

The use of the traffic light model to assess CPI's structural stability is broadly used [22]. The semantics for this traffic light model is as follows: a green tag associated with a CPI instance means safe to proceed; a yellow tag means proceed with caution; and a red tag means do not proceed. A schematic representation on how this traffic light model is used to classify damage to a CPI component is depicted in Fig. 2.

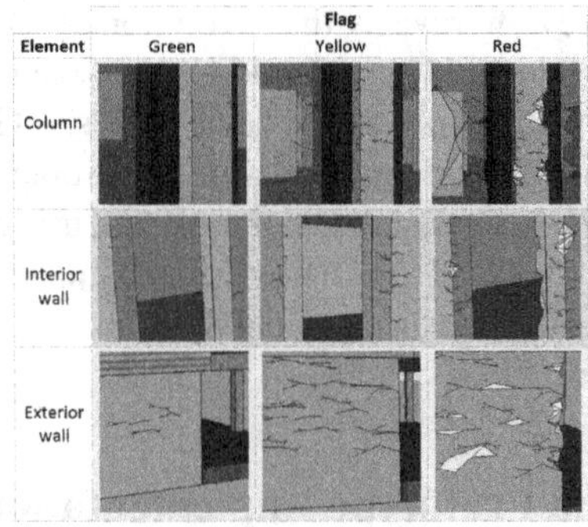

Fig. 2. Examples of traffic light model for CPI damage. (Color figure online)

3.3 System Architecture

A multi-layered architecture was designed for the development of the tool to conduct early stability assessment of the CPI. A data layer is used for access, administration and maintenance of the database. A persistence layer secures resources in the database. A business layer contains all operations and procedures related with logics, functionality and algorithms of the simulator. The control layer is a security element hosted between the presentation layer and business layer. Lastly, the presentation layer provides graphical user interface and user interaction.

3.4 Prototype Implementation

A prototype was built based on the design presented above. This prototype involves several technologies wrapped on a web platform, which allows the user to experience virtually the different effects that different types of earthquakes may have on the CPI.

The prototype has two types of sessions: (a) a session where the trainee will approach a set of CPI cases previously scheduled by the expert, and (b) the expert session, which allows the expert to review the assessment conducted by the trainee. For assessment, the system presents the user with the CPI profile within the Unity 3D plug-in, while the assessment forms are all available on HTML/JavaScript (Fig. 3).

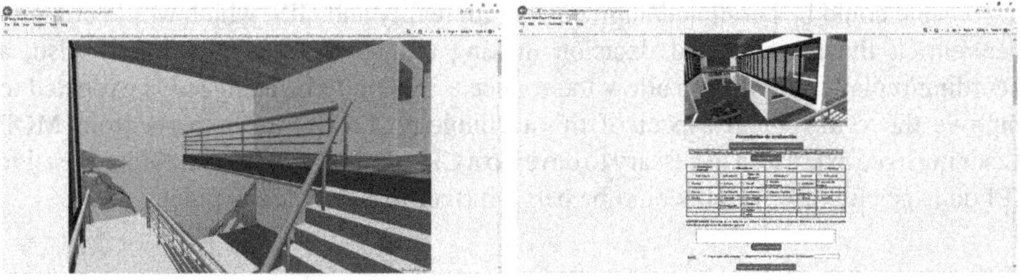

Fig. 3. Trainee session's screenshots.

4 Results

The video game-based prototype simulator was tested and evaluated by structural engineering experts, general engineers, and managers (N = 5), from the MOP Academy. The evaluation was conducted through a survey that containing questions grouped in 4 variables: functionality; usability; quality; and performance of this technology and every question was graded using a 1-5 scale, where every represented the following: 1- very bad, 2 - bad, 3 - neutral, 4 - good, and 5 - very good. The evaluation of these four variables by experts from MOP was, as shown in Fig. 4. Variables with very positive evaluation are the functionality and the online-performance of the prototype, while usability and general quality may be improved.

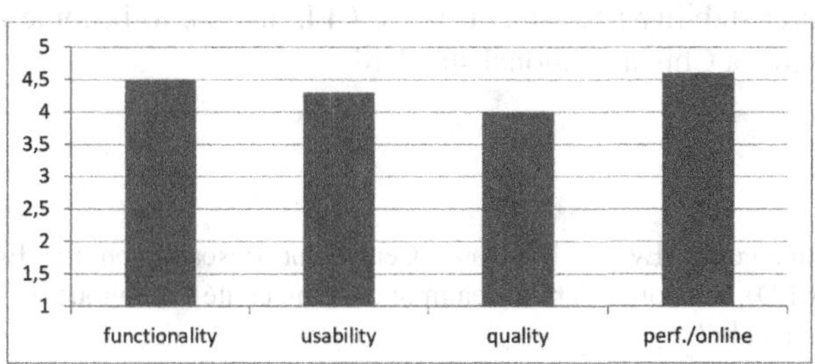

Fig. 4. Evaluation of serious video game bases simulator conducted by MOP Academy.

Experts and managers from MOP Academy have qualitatively expressed that they anticipate this type of technology represents a real opportunity to further develop a national standard capability. This opinion has been expressed in terms of perceiving that this technology provides easy access to practitioners, online web-based platform; easy to learn and use; young adults are familiar with videogame technology; and enables different teaching/training/learning methodologies.

5 Future Work

Further research includes the development of a mobile extension of the system, where video game could be paralleled/augmented with reality and GIS, which would complement/enrich the learning and decision making related to CPI assessment. Also, a recording/replay capability to allow the trainee's session to be analyzed is expected to improve the pedagogical aspect of this technology. Lastly, the experts from MOP Academy have expressed necessary to develop a CPI profile editor with a comprehensive CPI damages library, which would be part a further research/development.

6 Conclusion

This article presents a preliminary and exploratory effort to improve early and quick safety and structural stability assessment of critical physical infrastructure, based on integrating methodologies, guidelines and procedures utilized by the MOP Academy, and videogame and web technology. The simulator prototype allows to develop a competence among trainees that: (a) supports understanding on stability assessment of CPI affected by disasters like earthquakes; (b) the trainee can gather the CPI data while navigating through the virtual CPI; (c) facilitates training, debriefing, and correction of trainees learning by putting together trainee and expert; and (d) allows to classify a CPI based on the broadly utilized traffic model. Subject matter experts that participated in the calibration and evaluation phases have provided encouraging feedback on the functionality, usability, quality, and performance of a prototype for improving structural stability assessment of the CPI affected by disasters such as earthquakes. This article describes a proof of concept on the idea that video game technology has the potential to improve structural stability assessment of the CPI, and so, to become a foundational component towards a Chilean national standard.

References

1. EM-DAT: Emergency Events Database. Centre for Research on the Epidemiology of Disasters (CRED), School of Public Health of the Université Catholique de Louvain (2013). http://www.emdat.be/
2. Kim, V.: Japan damage could reach $235 billion, World Bank estimates. Los Angeles Times (2011). http://articles.latimes.com/2011/mar/21/world/la-fgw-japan-quake-world-bank-20110322

3. World Bank: The World Bank Supports Thailand's Post-Floods Recovery Effort (2011). http://www.worldbank.org/en/news/feature/2011/12/13/world-bank-supports-thailands-post-floods-recovery-effort
4. Robertson, C., Krauss, C.: Gulf Spill Is the Largest of Its Kind, Scientists Say. The New York Times Company (2010). http://www.nytimes.com/2010/08/03/us/03spill.html?_r=0
5. Barcena, A., Prado, A., Lopez, L., Samaniego, J.: The Chilean earthquake of 27 February 2010 - An Overview. United Nations Publication, Santiago, Chile (2010)
6. He, Z.J.: Golden ten minutes - a new concept of trauma emergency. Med. J. Chin. PLA **29**, 1009–1011 (2004)
7. He, Z.J., Ma, J.X.: Time efficiency of first-aid to war wound and trauma. Med. J. Chin. PLA **30**, 566–568 (2005)
8. Macintyre, A., Barbera, J.A., Smith, E.: Surviving collapsed structure entrapment after earthquakes: a "Time-to-Rescue" analysis. Prehosp. Disaster Med. **21**(1), 4–19 (2006)
9. Calvi, G.M., Pinho, R., Magenes, G., Bommer, J.J., Restrepo-Vélez, L.F., Crowley, H.: Development of seismic vulnerability assessment methodologies over the past 30 years. ISET J. Earthq. Technol. **43**(3), 75–104 (2006)
10. Carreño, M.L., Cardona, O.D., Barbat, A.H.: Computational tool for post-earthquake evaluation of damage in buildings. Earthq. Spectra **26**(1), 63–86 (2010)
11. Carreño, M.L., Cardona, O.D., Barbat, A.H.: New techniques applied to post-earthquake assessment of buildings. Intersections/Intersecţii Struct. Eng. Acad. Soc. **1**(4), 12–22 (2004)
12. Michael, D., Chen, S.: Serious Games that Educate, Train and Inform. Thompson Course Technology PTR, Boston (2005)
13. Taskin, B., Guler, K., Tugsal, U.M., Gencoglu, M., Celik, M., Hasgur, Z., Aydogan, M., Saygun, A.I.: A novel post-earthquake damage survey sheet - Part I-RC buildings. In: 15th World Conference on Earthquake Engineering, 15WCEE, Lisbon, Portugal (2012)
14. Chilean National Office for Emergency: Integral Management Balance. Oficina Nacional de Emergencia de Chile. Balance de Gestión Integral. Santiago, Chile (2010)
15. Tanaka, S., Shigekawa, K.: Development of training system for building damage assessment using actual buildings. J. Disaster Res. **9**(2), 188–197 (2014)
16. Agnastopoulos, S.A., Moretti, M.: Post-earthquake emergency assessment of building damage, safety and usability. Part 2: organisation. Soil Dyn. Earthq. Eng. **28**(3), 233–244 (2008)
17. National Earthquake Hazards Reduction Program (NEHRP): Strategic Plan for the National Earthquake Hazards Reduction Program. Fiscal Years 2009–2013. National Earthquake Hazards Reduction Program, U.S. (2008)
18. American Lifelines Alliance, ALA.: Post-Earthquake Information System (PIMS) Scoping Study. National Institute of Building Sciences, Washington, DC (2008)
19. Yasmin, T., Chourasia, A., Bhattacharyya, S.K., Parashar, J.: Fragility analysis for seismic vulnerability assessment of buildings: a review. Int. Res. J. Eng. Technol. **2**(6), 502–508 (2015)
20. Mohinuddin, M., Jahan, I., Alam, J.: Earth-quake vulnerability assessment of existing buildings in cox's-bazar using field survey & GIS. Int. J. Eng. Res. Technol. **3**(8), 1147–1156 (2014)
21. McCabe, I., Stephan, M., Cole, V., Kapralos, B., DeChamplain, A., Rosendale, E.: Blaze: a serious game for improving household fire safety awareness. In: 2012 IEEE International Games Innovation Conference, IGIC 2012, pp. 1–4. IEEE, Rochester, New York (2012)
22. Tang, A., Wen, A.: An intelligent simulation system for earthquake disaster assessment. Comput. Geosci. **35**(5), 871–879 (2009)

Algorithms for Lightweight Key Exchange

Rafael Álvarez([✉]), Juan Santonja, and Antonio Zamora

Department of Computer Science and Artificial Intelligence (DCCIA), University of Alicante (Campus de San Vicente), Ap. 99, 03080 Alicante, Spain
{ralvarez,zamora}@dccia.ua.es, jsl2@alu.ua.es

Abstract. Public-key cryptography is too slow for general purpose encryption, with most applications limiting its use as much as possible. Some secure protocols, especially those that enable forward secrecy, make a much heavier use of public-key cryptography, increasing the demand for lightweight cryptosystems that can be implemented in low powered or mobile devices. This performance requirements are even more significant in critical infrastructure and emergency scenarios where peer-to-peer networks are deployed for increased availability and resiliency. We benchmark several public-key key-exchange algorithms, determining those that are better for the requirements of critical infrastructure and emergency applications.

Keywords: Public-key · Key exchange · Lightweight cryptography · Elliptic curve

1 Introduction

Public-key cryptography is very demanding in terms of computing power but unavoidable in most modern secure applications, even those intended for low power or mobile devices. For this reason, public-key cryptography has been considered too slow for general purpose encryption, with applications employing public-key cryptography exclusively to securely share keys for the much faster standard symmetric-key cryptography (see [8,13]); limiting, in this way, the use of public-key cryptography as much as possible.

With the recent aim of perfect forward secrecy in many protocols, however, this model is no longer possible since these algorithms generate new key pairs and exchange secret keys per session and sometimes even per message (see [11,12,17]); therefore increasing the demand for lighter weight public-key cryptography especially for peer-to-peer applications involving mobile wireless devices.

Moreover, secure communication protocols based on peer-to-peer and other types of *ad-hoc* networking combined with forward secrecy are especially useful in critical infrastructure and emergency situations since they can enable improved coverage, resiliency, connectivity, security, anonymity and data privacy in these challenging applications.

In this paper we analyze the performance of several commonly used and state-of-the-art public-key key-exchange protocols in order to find those most suitable for critical infrastructure and emergency applications.

C.R. García et al. (Eds.): UCAmI 2016, Part II, LNCS 10070, pp. 536–543, 2016.
DOI: 10.1007/978-3-319-48799-1_58

2 Description

Since public-key cryptography is usually very slow for general purpose encryption, most secure data-communication protocols resort to public-key cryptography exclusively to securely share secret values that can be, in turn, used as keys for much faster symmetric-key cryptography (see [8,13]). We describe in the following some public-key protocols that are commonly used for symmetric key agreement, with a special focus on performance.

2.1 RSA

Extremely popular, RSA is one of the first practical public-key cryptosystems (first published in 1977 by Ron Rivest, Adi Shamir and Leonard Adleman) and bases it security on the difficulty of factoring the product of two large prime numbers. Whether breaking RSA is as hard as the factoring problem is still an open question; although, if the public key is large enough, only someone with the knowledge of these two prime numbers can decode the message in a feasible way.

Unlike the other algorithms considered in this paper, RSA is a full public-key cryptosystem capable of directly supporting data encryption/decryption, key exchange and digital signature. As other public-key cryptosystems, RSA is too slow for general purpose data encryption, so it is mainly used to securely exchange symmetric keys and other small values. For more information see [3,13].

2.2 Diffie-Hellman

The Diffie-Hellman (DH) key exchange protocol was originally conceptualized by Ralph Merkle and designed by Whitfield Diffie and Martin Hellman in 1975. Its security is based on the discrete logarithm problem, which is considered unfeasible for groups with large enough order; unlike RSA, the DH key exchange protocol is not a full public-key cryptosystem and only enables for the exchange of a secret value that can be used for symmetric keys or other purposes, but does not support data encryption/decryption or digital signature directly.

The shared value is dependent on the asymmetric key pairs of both ends of the conversation, so new keys must be generated if a new secret is required. Protocols that achieve forward secrecy (see [11,12]) generate new key pairs for each session, discarding the old ones for each new session; the DH key exchange protocol is a common choice for these protocols since key pair generation is very fast. See [7,13] for additional information.

2.3 Elliptic Curve Diffie-Hellman

As in Sect. 2.2, the elliptic curve Diffie-Hellman (ECDH) key exchange protocol allows both ends of a conversation to establish a shared secret. It is an adaptation of the DH key exchange protocol but employing elliptic curve cryptography, which has some advantages related to key length and overall performance.

The ECDH protocol requires that both parties agree, prior to secure communication, on domain parameters and each party must generate a suitable key pair consisting of a private key d (a randomly selected integer in a certain interval) and a public key Q (a point in the curve). These public keys can either be static (and trusted via certificate) or ephemeral (usually referred to as ECDHE) that are temporary and not authenticated.

The National Institute for Standards and Technology (NIST) standardized some elliptic curves suitable for cryptography (see [15]) in different security levels. Elliptic curve cryptography is a vast and complex field, for more information see [4,9,14].

2.4 Curve25519

Also referred to as X25519, Curve25519 is a ECDH key exchange protocol targeting the 128 bit security level and offering vastly improved performance compared to the traditional NIST elliptic curves. It was released by Daniel J. Bernstein in 2005 and constructed in such a way that it avoids many common problems in its implementation; eliminating, by default, many side channel attacks and issues with poor-quality random-number generators.

Besides pure performance, some suspicious aspects of the NIST's P curve constants (there have been some concerns regarding their origin) have increased the popularity of Curve25519, making it the default for modern protocols like WhatsApp [17] and Signal [12] protocols, among others. For more detailed information regarding Curve25519, see [1,2,5].

2.5 FourQ

FourQ is a high-performance elliptic curve that also targets the 128-bit security level. It is a fairly recent state-of-the-art design, being released by Microsoft Research in 2015 (see [6,10]); therefore, it is not used yet in standard or well-known protocols.

Its high performance stems from a four-dimensional decomposition minimizing the total number of elliptic curve group operations, extended twisted Edwards coordinates enabling the fastest known elliptic curve addition formulas, and extremely fast arithmetic modulo the Mersenne prime $p = 2^{127} - 1$. With this optimizations, FourQ is claimed to be between 4 to 5 times faster than NIST P-256 curve and 2 to 3 times faster than Curve25519.

3 Results

In this section, we analyze the performance of several public-key algorithms in terms of key pair generation and secret exchange (key agreement). These two operations form the basis of most secure protocols that involve communication over insecure channels and are a suitable performance benchmark for such cases.

All benchmarks have been performed employing optimized implementations on an Intel Core i7-5930k CPU with 32 GB of RAM running Windows 10 Enterprise 64-bit, with all measurements computed as the average over 100 cycles of each specific operation and take into account a single side of the conversation (a single key pair generation and the calculation of a single party of the secret exchange).

In the case of RSA, the exchanged secret was 32 byte (256 bit) long, and the exchange was performed by simple encryption with the recipient's public key; in the rest of the algorithms, the exchanged secret was the expected length per the algorithm's design and parametrization.

We have targeted the 128 bit symmetric-equivalent security level as shown in Table 1, which details the key length required for different public-key cryptography algorithms in order to be as secure as a certain symmetric key length (see [16]). For this reason, we have taken the following key lengths for each algorithm:

- RSA (3072 bit),
- Diffie-Hellman (3072 bit),
- Elliptic curve Diffie-Hellman (NIST P-256, which has a 256 bit key length),
- Curve25519 (key length is fixed at 256 bit),
- FourQ (key length is fixed at 256 bit).

Table 1. Required key length in bits for equivalent security

Symmetric	RSA/DH	ECDH
80	1024	160
112	2048	224
128	3072	256
192	7680	384
256	15360	512

3.1 Key Pair Generation

We can see in Fig. 1 that RSA is severely impacted by the long bit length required to maintain the security level target. Standard Diffie-Hellman is a bit slower than the elliptic curve variants, which all seem to be equivalent at this scale, but it is much quicker than RSA.

If we only take into account the elliptic curve Diffie-Hellman based algorithms, shown in Fig. 2, we can see that the standard NIST P-256 curve is several times slower than Curve25519, and that FourQ is almost 2 times faster than Curve25519.

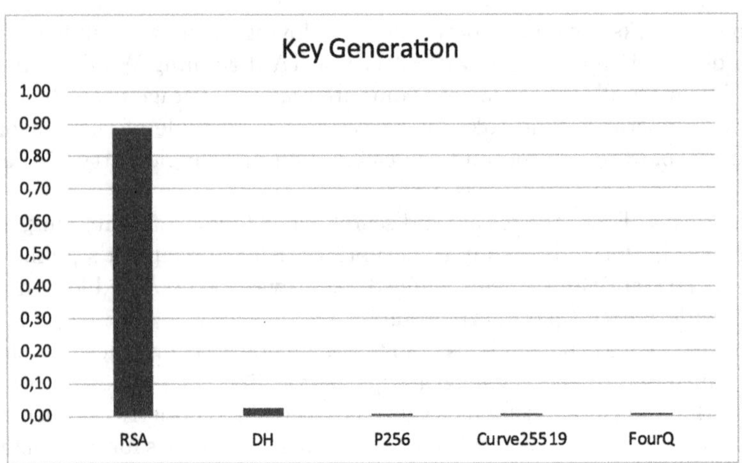

Fig. 1. Time required *(in seconds)* for the generation of a single key pair.

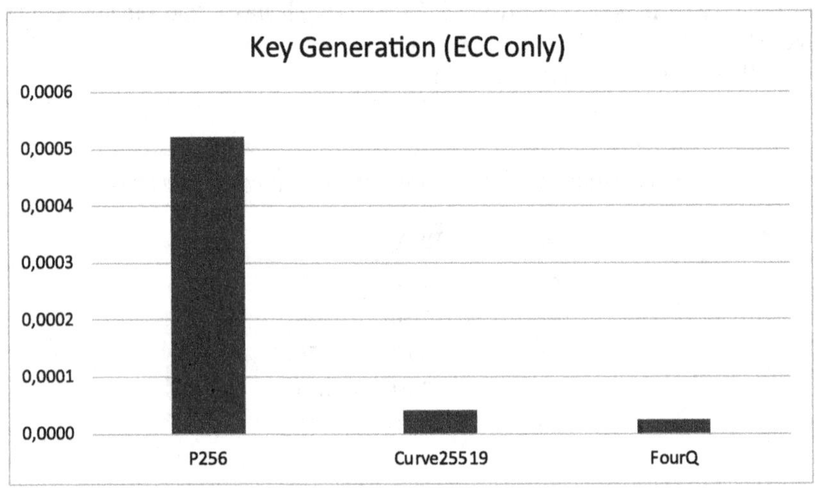

Fig. 2. Time required *(in seconds)* for the generation of a single key pair *(elliptic curve algorithms only)*.

3.2 Secret Key Exchange

In the case of the secret value exchange operation, the situation is reversed from the previous section with standard Diffie-Hellman being much slower than the rest of the algorithms and RSA being a bit slower than the elliptic curve variants (see Fig. 3). It should be remarked that the overall times required for secret exchange are much less than the times required for key pair generation.

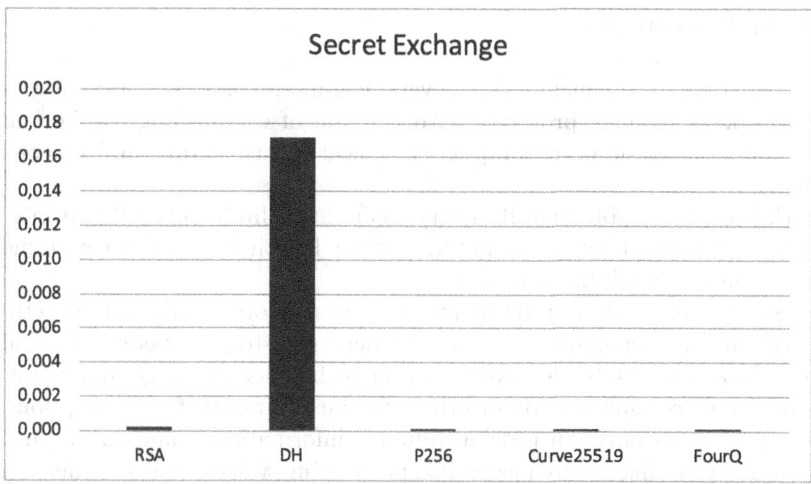

Fig. 3. Time required *(in seconds)* for the exchange of a secret key on a single side of the communication.

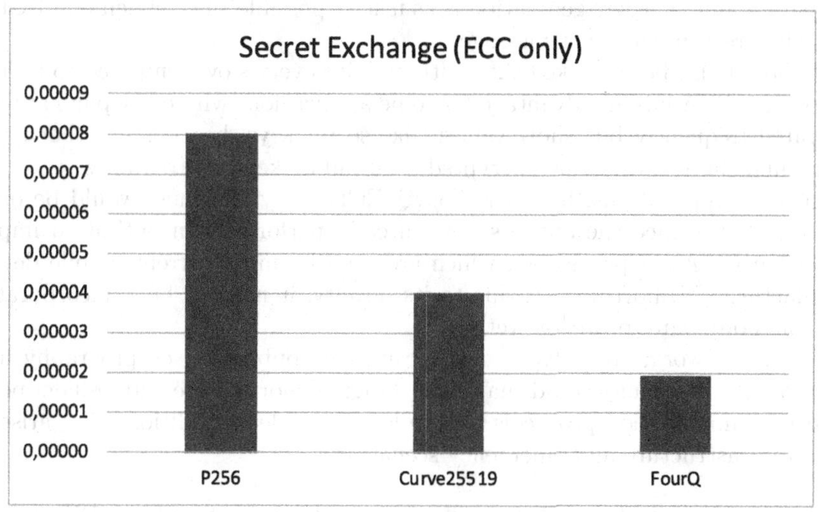

Fig. 4. Time required *(in seconds)* for the exchange of a secret key on a single side of the communication *(elliptic curve algorithms only)*.

Moreover, focusing exclusively on the elliptic curve Diffie-Hellman variants (Fig. 4), we find again that there are very tangible performance benefits with the Curve25519 and, especially, Four$\mathbb{Q}$ ECDH schemes.

4 Conclusions

In this paper we have benchmarked several commonly used and state-of-the-art public-key key-exchange protocols with the aim of establishing the best algorithms for lightweight cryptography in critical infrastructure and emergency scenarios.

With the results obtained, it is very clear that elliptic curve algorithms not only present a certain advantage in terms of key length but, also, a very tangible improvement in overall performance.

These performance improvements are even more significant in critical infrastructure and emergency scenarios where peer-to-peer networks of small wireless devices might be deployed in order to increase coverage and resiliency to power, cable communication or other standard infrastructure disruptions. In this way, these systems can provide valuable information, communication, and coordination tools like secure messaging, positioning, voice or video conferencing, etc. Therefore, lighter weight cryptography means more efficient use of computing power and also battery capacity which might be a deciding factor.

In those cases, where communication protocols implement forward secrecy, it is paramount that key generation is as fast as possible since ephemeral ECDH key pairs are generated per message.

It should also be remarked that, although it is very slow compared to ECDH algorithms, RSA has an advantage for some applications where key pairs are not generated frequently but short values (like secret keys, beacons or other types of granular data) have to be encrypted with public-key cryptography.

In most applications, however, Four$\mathbb{Q}$ ECDH key exchange would be optimal, especially since the authors have already performed an optimized implementation for ARM processors, which are used by most current mobile device manufacturers. Unfortunately, due to its novelty, it has not been incorporated into common secure protocols yet.

As future work, the advent of very efficient public-key cryptography and forward secrecy schemes could enable the design of more secure and resilient peer-to-peer communication protocols for the less-than-ideal conditions that arise in critical infrastructure and emergency scenarios.

Acknowledgement. Research partially supported by the Spanish MINECO and FEDER under Project Grant TEC2014-54110-R.

References

1. Bernstein, D.J.: Curve25519: new Diffie-Hellman speed records. In: Yung, M., Dodis, Y., Kiayias, A., Malkin, T. (eds.) PKC 2006. LNCS, vol. 3958, pp. 207–228. Springer, Heidelberg (2006). doi:10.1007/11745853_14
2. Bernstein, D.J., Birkner, P., Joye, M., Lange, T., Peters, C.: Twisted edwards curves. In: Vaudenay, S. (ed.) AFRICACRYPT 2008. LNCS, vol. 5023, pp. 389–405. Springer, Heidelberg (2008)

3. Boneh, D.: Twenty years of attacks on the RSA cryptosystem. Not. Am. Math. Soc. **46**(2), 203–213 (1999)
4. Brown, M., Hankerson, D., López, J., Menezes, A.: Software implementation of the NIST elliptic curves over prime fields. In: Naccache, D. (ed.) CT-RSA 2001. LNCS, vol. 2020, pp. 250–265. Springer, Heidelberg (2001)
5. Chou, T.: Fastest Curve25519 implementation ever. In: Workshop on Elliptic Curve Cryptography Standards (2015). http://www.nist.gov/itl/csd/ct/ecc-workshop.cfm
6. Costello, C., Longa, P.: FourQ: four-dimensional decompositions on a Q-curve over the Mersenne prime. In: Advances in Cryptology — ASIACRYPT (2015, to appear). http://eprint.iacr.org/2015/565
7. Diffie, W., Hellman, M.E.: New directions in cryptography. IEEE Trans. Inf. Theor. **22**(6), 644–654 (1976)
8. Galbraith, S.D.: Mathematics of Public Key Cryptography. Cambridge University Press, Cambridge (2012)
9. Koblitz, A.H., Koblitz, N., Menezes, A.: Elliptic curve cryptography: the serpentine course of a paradigm shift. J. Number Theor. **131**(5), 781–781 (2011). Elsevier
10. Longa, P.: FourQNEON: faster elliptic curve scalar multiplications on ARM processors. TechReport MSR-TR-2016-25 (2016). http://research.microsoft.com/apps/pubs/?id=266450
11. Marlinspike, M.: Advanced cryptographic ratcheting. Open Whisper Systems (2013). https://whispersystems.org/blog/advanced-ratcheting/
12. Marlinspike, M.: Signal on the outside, signal on the inside. Open Whisper Systems (2016). https://whispersystems.org/blog/signal-inside-and-out/
13. Menezes, A.J., Oorschot, P.C., Vanstone, S.A.: Handbook of Applied Cryptography. CRC Press, Boca Raton (1996)
14. Menezes, A., Vanstone, S.A., Okamoto, T.: Reducing elliptic curve logarithms to logarithms in a finite field. In: Proceedings of the 23rd Annual ACM Symposium on Theory of Computing, pp. 80–89. ACM (1991)
15. Various: Federal Information Processing Standards Publication 186-4. Announcingthe Digital Signature Standard (DSS). FIPS 186-4, Nationa Institute of Standards and Technology (2013). http://nvlpubs.nist.gov/nistpubs/FIPS/NIST.FIPS.186-4.pdf
16. Various: Elliptic Curve Cryptography. OpenSSL Wiki (2016). https://wiki.openssl.org/index.php/Elliptic_Curve_Cryptography
17. Various: WhatsApp. Encryption Overview. Technical white paper, WhatsApp (2016). https://www.whatsapp.com/security/WhatsApp-Security-Whitepaper.pdf

Resilient Grouping Proofs with Missing Tag Identification

Mike Burmester[1(✉)] and Jorge Munilla[2]

[1] Department of Computer Science, Florida State University, Tallahassee, FL 32306, USA
burmester@cs.fsu.edu

[2] Departamento de Ingeniería de Comunicaciones, Universidad de Málaga, Andalucía Tech, Spain
munilla@ic.uma.es

Abstract. The adoption of RFID (Radio Frequency Identification) technology has greatly improved the efficiency of inventory control, supply-chain management and logistics. With RFID group scanning, an RFID reader scans a group of RFID tagged objects to generate a grouping proof of "simultaneous" presence. Shipments may have to be tracked remotely by readers that are not necessarily trusted. In this paper we extend earlier work on grouping proofs and group codes to capture resilient group scanning with untrusted readers. We present a two-pass anonymous grouping proof (of integrity) for the scanned objects of a (not necessarily complete) collection of RFID tagged objects that identifies missing objects. The proof is generated by an untrusted reader and can be checked by a verifier, a trusted entity. We only assume that RFID tags are able to generate pseudorandom numbers and compute one-way hash functions.

Keywords: RFID grouping proofs · Group codes · Inventory control · Anonymity · Missing tag identification · Forward error correction · Erasure codes

1 Introduction

RFID (Radio-Frequency Identification) is a wireless technology that has stimulated numerous applications in fields such as inventory control, supply-chain management and logistics, and identified new challenges and opportunities. A typical RFID deployment has three main components: tags or transponders, which are electronic data storage devices attached to objects to be identified; readers or interrogators, that manage tag population, read data from and write data to tags; and a verifier that is a trusted entity that exchanges tag information with the readers and processes data according to specific task applications. Most tags are passive with no power of their own but get the energy needed to operate from a reader.

C.R. García et al. (Eds.): UCAmI 2016, Part II, LNCS 10070, pp. 544–555, 2016.
DOI: 10.1007/978-3-319-48799-1_59

Although initial designs of RFID systems focused on performance reliability, the technology has found use in applications that require the implementation of security mechanisms that: (*i*) take into account features such as the vulnerability of the radio channel, the constrained power of devices, the low-cost and limited functionality of tags and the request-response operation mode; and (*ii*) make tags resistant to privacy/confidentiality threats, malicious traceability and loss of data integrity.

When RFID technology is used for supply-chain management, concerns regarding the monitoring of tags and the transfer of ownership of tags need to be addressed. If the transfer is permanent, or even temporal, ownership transfer protocols may be used [2,3]. However there are cases when the owner does not want to cede control. For example, a manufacturer may use the services provided by a carrier who, in turn, uses other carriers to ship products. In such cases it is important that the owner can periodically check the integrity of a shipment via the carrier. This requirement is referred to as *group scanning*, and involves multiple tags generating a *grouping proof* of "simultaneous" presence in the range of an RFID reader [4,5]. There are practical scenarios where grouping proofs can substantially expand the capabilities of RFID based systems. For example, products may need to be shipped together in pallets and one may want to track their integrity through the supply-chain.

Our contribution: We present an anonymous RFID grouping proof of integrity of a group of tagged objects G with missing tag identification that supports tag privacy (in particular, untraceability) such that (Fig. 1):

a. The verifier can authorize an untrusted reader to inspect G and identify any missing objects.
b. The authorization is for one only inspection, and the tags of G are untraceable while the group is not inspected.
c. If a subgroup G' of G is scanned by the reader, then the reader can generate a grouping proof of integrity for G' and identify the missing tags of $G \backslash G'$ (there are restrictions on the size $|G'/G|$—Sect. 4).
d. Only the verifier (a trusted entity) can check the proof.
e. The reader cannot generate a (valid) grouping proof of G with missing tag identification for an unauthorized inspection.

This extends earlier work [19] in which a grouping proof is only generated when the scanned group is complete. With such proofs it is not possible for the verifier to check the integrity of incomplete scanned groups, or identify missing tags.

The rest of this paper is organized as follows. In Sect. 2 we review the literature for RFID grouping proofs and group codes. In Sect. 3 we discuss grouping proof deployments and capabilities, erasure codes, the threat model and our design criteria. In Sect. 4 we present a two-round anonymous grouping proof of integrity with missing tag identification. In Sect. 5 we discuss security aspects and in Sect. 6 we summarize our main results.

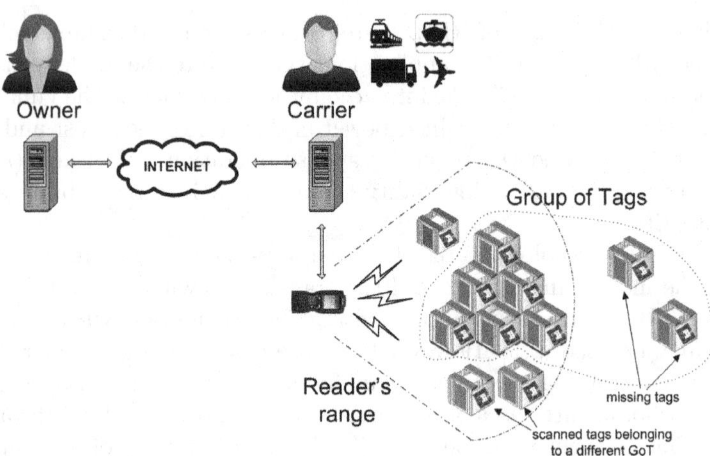

Fig. 1. An untrusted carrier can compile a grouping proof of integrity for the objects of a pallet that the Owner can verify, and identify any missing objects (tags of the pallet that are missing—beyond the reader's range).

2 Background

In 2004 Ari Juels defined a new RFID application called a yoking-proof that generates evidence of simultaneous presence of two tags in the range of an RFID reader. These were extended to grouping proofs for multiple tags—see *e.g.* [8]. In 2008 Huang and Ku [9] presented a grouping proof that uses a random number generator and a cyclic redundancy code. This had several weaknesses, some of which were addressed by Chien et al. [10] who, in turn, proposed a new grouping proof. Peris-Lopez *et al.* [6] proposed guidelines for securing grouping proofs as well as a yoking-proof protocol (for two tags). Liu *et al.* [4] proposed a grouping proof for distributed RFID applications with trusted readers. This is vulnerable to de-synchronization and privacy leaks [11].

While grouping proofs provide integrity evidence for complete groups of tags they do not address incomplete groups. In particular, they do not provide any information about missing tags. Sato *et al.* [12] proposed a group code that makes it possible to find the identifiers of missing tags, without requiring a packaging list or an external database. This code uses Gallager low-density parity check (LDPC) codes for forward error correction [13]. However the randomised nature of LDPC codes makes it difficult to get specific decoding guarantees. To address this, Su *et al.* [14] used strongly selective families (SSF). Su and Tonguz [15] proposed a variant that uses the Chinese remainder theorem to construct non-regular generating matrices. Another modification proposed by Su [16] uses resolvable transversal designs to generate parity-check matrices and group splitting to improve performance. Mabrouk and Couderc [17] propose a group code that is based on Reed-Solomon (RS) codes. However the size of the blocks and the partitioning of the redundancy is not optimal. Burmester and Munilla [18] analyzed the memory-erasure tradeoff of group codes and considered optimized approximations for practical settings. Finally Burmester and Munilla [19] proposed a grouping proof that uses optimized RS codes to identify missing tags when the scanned group of tags is not complete. The present paper extends the results in [18,19] by integrating grouping proofs with optimized group codes so that a grouping proof of a (possibly incomplete) scanned group of tagged objects is always generated, as well as a list of the identifiers of any missing tagged objects.

3 Grouping Proofs and Design Criteria

3.1 Group Scanning and Grouping Proofs with Missing Tag Identification

A typical deployment of an RFID grouping proof involves: a *group of tags* G (GoT); a *verifier*, the owner of G that knows the private information stored by the tags; and a *reader*, that is controlled by the carrier whose services are contracted by the owner and has physical possession of G, but does not control G.

A grouping proof for G with missing tag identification provides evidence of temporal events that corroborate the "simultaneous" presence (in practice, within the same interval window) of the tags of a scanned subgroup G' of G, and identifies the missing tags of $G \backslash G'$. This extends the traditional notion of grouping proofs for which $G' = G$ (with no missing tags) to capture resilient applications that address the risks involved in loss, theft or damage in supply chain management.

In Sect. 3.5 we shall discuss our threat model and in Sect. 4.1 our requirements for grouping proofs with missing tag identification. In particular, DoS attacks and attacks in which an adversarial reader tries to forge a grouping proof with missing tag identification by dropping some of the scanned tags and obtaining identifiers for the missing tags.

3.2 Capabilities of Group Scanning Parties

Passive UHF tags are the most common for supply-chain applications. They have no power of their own, operate in the far field, and backscatter communication [20]. We shall assume that tags are able to perform basic symmetric-key cryptographic operations such as selecting pseudo-random numbers and evaluating a pseudo-random function. On-board clocks are beyond the capabilities of most tags, but the activity time span of a tag during a single session can be limited using techniques such as measuring the discharge rate of capacitors [7]. By contrast readers and verifiers/servers are able to perform complex cryptographic operations.

3.3 Erasure Codes

Let $\mathbb{F}_q$ be a finite field of order q, $q = p^m$, p a prime, m a positive integer. A q-ary erasure channel (q-EC) is a memoryless channel that on input $a \in \mathbb{F}_q$, outputs symbol a or no symbol at all. They are used to model data loss in digital networks, and when retransmission are not either possible or simply convenient, forward error correction may be used to recover the missing information.

A q-ary (n, k, s) erasure code is a linear forward error correction code that encodes source (input) data $x = (x_1, \ldots, x_k) \in \mathbb{F}_q^k$ to encoded data $y = (y_1, \ldots, y_n) \in \mathbb{F}_q^n$, in such a way that the source data can be recovered if no more than s blocks $y_i \in \mathbb{F}_q$ are missing. In a *systematic* code the source data is embedded in the encoded data. Typically, $y_i = x_i$, for $i = 1, \ldots, k$. We must have $s \leq n–k$ (Singelton bound); the optimal case $s = (n-k)$ is reached with Maximum Distance Separable (MDS) codes. The most common MDS codes are the Reed-Solomon (RS) codes that are cyclic over $\mathbb{F}_q$, $q = p^m > n$, with minimum distance $d = n-k + 1$ $(s = d-1)$.

3.4 Optimized Group Codes

In our protocol in Sect. 4 the concept of forward error correction as applied to erasure codes is adapted to address the transportation of RFID tagged objects that are exposed to risks during transmission that may involve loss, theft or damage. We shall use an $RS(n, k)$ code over $\mathbb{F}_{2^m}$, $2 \leq m \leq 16$ (according to RFC 6865 [21]), to encode the identifiers $(id_1, \ldots, id_{n_g})$ of n_g RFID tags so that we can recover up to $s_t = (n-k)/(n/n_g)$ identifiers of missing tags. For this application the source data $x = id_1 \| \cdots \| id_{n_g}$ is an $n_g \ell$ bit string, where ℓ is the binary length of the identifiers id_i. We rearrange x into k blocks $x_i \in \mathbb{F}_{2^m}$ (depending on the implementation, some blocks x_i can be padded with zeros if necessary). Then x is encoded to get an RS codeword $y = (y_1, \ldots, y_n)$, with n/n_g blocks stored (written) in the memory of each tag_i, so that we can recover s_t missing tag identifiers. These n/n_g blocks stored in tag_i are denoted by ID_i and provide the identifying information provided by id_i as well as redundancy information w_i that allows to recover the missing tags—see Fig. 2.

To identify the missing tags, the data collected (read) from the tags is used to generate a codeword y' with erasures. Thus, RS decoding can only be performed if the scanned identifiers y_i are ordered correctly, such that y and y' agree on all non-erased positions. For this purpose control information is needed: the identifier ID_i of each tag_i is extended to include some extra bits that define its order i when it was encoded. As an example suppose that $RS(150, 120)$ over $GF(2^8)$ is used with a group of $n_g = 10$ tags. Then $k/n_g = 12$ bytes are allocated for the tag identifiers ID_i (*i.e.* 96 bits as specified in the EPC Gen2v2 standard [1]), that are then extended to $n/n_g = 15$ bytes to recover up to $s_t = (150 - 120)/15 = 2$ missing tags. In this case 4 bits are sufficient for control information (order of the tag), so that 124 bits are needed for the extended tag identifiers. For larger groups, with say $n_t = 100$ tags and up to $s_t = 60$ missing tags, we can use the $RS(2000, 800)$ code over $GF(2^{12})$: in this case the

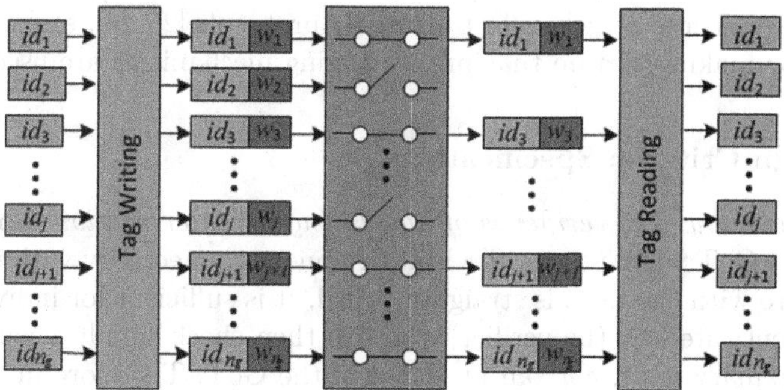

Fig. 2. The write-transmit-read process with forward error correction in a RFID tag-erasure model.

$k/n_g = 8$ symbols $= 12$ bytes of the identifiers ID_i are extended to $n/n_g =$ 20 symbols = 30 bytes. For a detailed analysis and discussion of optimal group codes see [18].

Note that for optimal codes the complexity of encoding and decoding is quadratic in n, so that high values for the number of tags and/or missing tags increases the computational burden of the readers. This increase however does not affect RFID tags (except that it could require more memory).

3.5 Threat Model for RFID Systems

RFID wireless channels are particularly vulnerable because tags are restricted to lightweight cryptographic protection. We assume the Byzantine threat model in which the adversary controls the communication channels, and may eavesdrop, block, modify and or inject messages in any communication between tags and readers. By contrast, the communication channel between high level entities (*i.e.* readers and verifiers) is secure since fully-fledged cryptographic techniques can be used. However, these channels may or may not enjoy continuous connectivity. Thus, during an interrogation the verifier may be online or offline, and different solutions for the grouping proof problem are required in each case.

Several types of attacks against RFID systems have been described in the literature. Some are well known on other platforms. In particular, the adversary may attempt to perform impersonation, DoS, interleaving and reflection attacks and other passive or active attacks. The unique aspects of RFID applications highlight other vulnerabilities such as unauthorized tracking, a privacy concern in which the adversary tries to trace and/or recognize the tags of a collection. There are also attacks on RFID systems that are usually excluded from the security model, such as *online man-in-the-middle relay attacks* [22] and *side channel* or *power analysis* [23] attacks. In particular, if no distance-bounding mechanism [24] is used, our protocol in Sect. 4 will be subject to active attacks that involve relaying flows between tags faster than the time interval defined by the tag timers. These attacks affect all RFID protocols [25,26], and can only be addressed by making certain that precise timing mechanisms are used.

3.6 Design Criteria: Specifications

Batch connectivity: The verifier is offline during the interrogation. Checking the integrity of a GoT when the verifier has permanent connectivity with the reader, and therefore with the tags, is straightforward. It is sufficient for individual tags to get authenticated by the verifier, who can then check simultaneous presence by using auxiliary data, *e.g.*, an identifier of the GoT. Therefore in this paper, we focus on offline solutions. In this case, the interactions of the verifier are restricted to: (*i*) broadcasting a challenge that is valid for a (short) time span and, (*ii*) checking responses from the tags that are compiled and sent from time to time by the readers.

Balanced loading: A grouping proof should be computed in a balanced, distributed way. No tag will assume the role of a "centralized" verifier. The tags of a GoT have similar hardware capabilities and the computation load per tag should be balanced.

Messages must include destination information (possibly private) to allow unicast/multicast communication. This is particularly important for anonymity: each message must contain information that allows tags to decide if they are the intended recipient.

3.7 Design Criteria: Assumptions

The tags of a GoT are not compromised. Consequently they can share private information. This does not mean that tags cannot be compromised; but if this happens then it is not possible to generate evidence that will corroborate simultaneous presence in any meaningful way.

Simultaneity is defined by valid interrogation intervals specified by the verifier. Grouping proofs use session numbers, counters or timestamps provided by the verifier. RFID communication is a sequential process and interrogation simultaneity can only be captured by an "exposure-time" window: events are considered as happening simultaneously if they take place within this window.

4 An Anonymous Grouping Proof Protocol with Missing Tag Identification

Our grouping proof is based on the design criteria in the previous sections and provides anonymity.

4.1 Requirements

a. *The verifier can check the integrity of a group of scanned tags*: that the tags were scanned simultaneously (during the same session defined by the activation time of the tags) within a time window defined by a counter T_s.
b. *The reader can also check the integrity of the group and obtain the identifiers of any missing tags*, but does not share any private keys with the tags and should not be able to access or even trace the tags beyond the lifetime of T_s.
c. *The reader is reliable but not trusted.* The reader will scan and process all tags in its range but may also try to forge a grouping proof. In practice, this assumption is justified because the carrier is liable for any additional missing items and therefore has no motivation to increase the set of missing tags.
d. Tags can only generate (pseudo) random numbers and evaluate a one-way hash function: h.

The security objectives are twofold: (i) the verifier (owner) must be able to check the integrity of a group of shipped items, while (ii) the reader (carrier) must be able to recover the identifiers of missing tags if the shipment is compromised.

Protocol Description

The verifier V stores for each group $G = \{tag_1, \ldots, tag_{n_g}\}$ of tags that it owns the tuple: $(T_s, k_g, \{(k_i, ID_i)\}_{i=1}^{n_g})$, where T_s is a counter value, k_g a group key, and (k_i, ID_i) the private key and identifier of tag_i (Sect. 3.4). Each tag_i of G stores in non-volatile memory: (k_g, k_i, ID_i), and a counter T_i that is initialized to the same value T_s for all tags of G. The reader R initially does not share any information with the tags of G.

The protocol is initiated by the verifier V who sends to the reader R a scanning request (T_s, T_s', k_s), where T_s is a fresh value of a counter, $T_s' = h(k_s, T_s)$ is an authenticator and $k_s = h(k_g, T)$ is the session key. The protocol has two rounds—see Fig. 3.

Round 1. The reader R broadcasts to all tags in its range (T_s, T_s') and sets a timer. Each tag_i in the range of R, computes $k_s = h(k_g, T_s)$, and checks the integrity of T_s by verifying that $T_s' = h(k_s, T_s)$ and that $T_s > T_i$. If any of these fail, tag_i returns random values ("$*$" in Fig. 3). Otherwise, it updates its counter to T_s, draws a random number r_i and computes the authenticator $r_i' = h(k_s, r_i)$. Then it sends (r_i, r_i') to R and sets a timer. The active period of each tag_i is defined by its timer: volatile values are discarded on timeout.

The received values r_i are used by the reader R to identify (singulate) tags in this session(session pseudonym). For every r_i, R checks its integrity by verifying that $r_i' = h(k_s, r_i)$, and if this holds stores them in a list L_1. On timeout R computes a session challenge $R_s = h(T, r_{j_1}, \ldots, r_{j_u})$, where $(j_1, \ldots, j_u) \subseteq (1, \ldots, n_g)$ are the indeces of the group of scanned tags, and the authenticator $R_s' = h(k_s, R_s)$. This round incorporates the randomness provided by the verifier's challenge T_s and the randomness provided by the tags r_i,

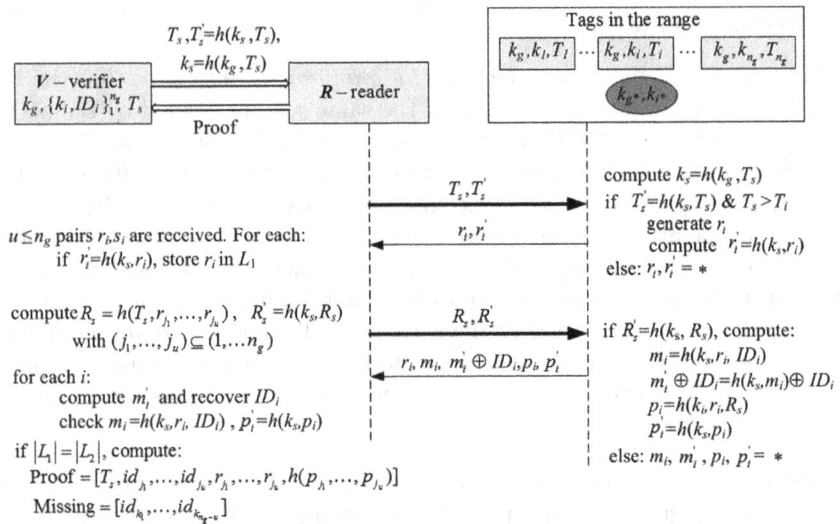

Fig. 3. Flows of the anonymous grouping proof of integrity for the subgroup of scanned tags $tag_{j_1},\ldots,tag_{j_u}$ that identifies the missing tag_j, $j \in \{1,\ldots,n_g\}\backslash\{j_1,\ldots,j_u\}$.

which prevent replay attacks. The challenge T_s defines the scanning period for the verifier, and simultaneity by defining the validity period of the nonces r_i.

Round 2. The reader R broadcasts R_s, R_s' to all tags in its range. Each tag_i in the range of R that has not timed out, checks that $R_s' = h(k_s, R_s)$ and if so, computes:

$$m_i = h(k_s, r_i, ID_i),\ h(k_s, m_i) \oplus ID_i = m_i' \oplus ID_i,$$
$$p_i = h(k_i, r_i, R_s),\ p_i' = h(k_s, p_i),$$

and sends $(m_i, m_i' \oplus ID_i, p_i, p_i')$ to R and timeouts.

R computes $m_i' = h(k_s, m_i)$ and retrieves ID_i. Then it checks that $m_i = h(k_s, r_i, ID_i)$ and $p_i' = h(k_s, p_i)$. If these are correct, R stores the corresponding identifiers ID_i in a list L_2. On timeout R checks that $|L_1| = |L_2|$, and if so compiles the grouping proof: $(T, id_{j_1},\ldots,id_{j_u}, r_{j_1},\ldots,r_{j_u}, h(p_{j_1},\ldots,p_{j_u})$ and obtains the missing tag identifiers id_j, by RS decoding the $u(n/n_g)$ blocks of the scanned identifiers $ID_{j_1},\ldots,ID_{j_u}$ in L_2 as described in Sect. 3.4. Then R sends privately to the verifier V the grouping proof for the group of scanned tags and the list of the $(n_g - u)$ missing tags, provided that it is within the correction capabilities of the implemented forward error correction mechanism; i.e. $(n_g - u) < (n-k)/(n/n_g)$ for $RS(n,k)$.

To validate the grouping proof, the verifier V first uses the value T_s to retrieve the tuple $(k_g, \{k_i, ID_i\}_{i=1}^{n_g})$ (one lookup). Then V computes $R_s = h(T_s, r_{j_1},\ldots,r_{j_u})$ using the values r_{j_i} given in the proof and the corresponding $p_{j_i} = h(k_{j_i}, r_{j_i}, R_s)$. Finally V checks that the value of $h(p_{j_1},\ldots,p_{j_u})$ in the proof is correct, and that the values of the missing tags are correct.

We shall assume that the keys k_g, k_i, k_s, the challenges T, R_s and the random numbers r_i, all have the same bit length κ, which is the *security parameter* of the protocol. This protocol has just two rounds and only requires the tags to be able to generate random numbers and compute a hash function.

5 Security Analysis

5.1 Privacy

An adversary that physically tracks a group G of tagged objects can determine which executions are linked to G; this cannot be prevented. Similarly an adversarial reader that is authorized to inspect G can link the inspected tags. Unlinkability concerns the periods during which physical tracking or authorized inspection is interrupted.

Formally, unlinkability is defined in terms of an indistinguishability experiment $\texttt{PrivK}^{link}_{\mathcal{A},\Pi}(\kappa)$ that involves a probabilistic polynomial time (PPT) adversary $\mathcal{A}$ and a grouping proof Π. During the experiment $\mathcal{A}$ has access to simulated executions of Π, initialised with security parameter κ and random secret keys, and can interact with executions as specified in the threat model. Eventually $\mathcal{A}$ identifies two tags: tag^0 and tag^1 and is challenged with a grouping proof interrogation $\texttt{int}_b$ involving tag^b, b is a random bit. $\mathcal{A}$ outputs a bit b'. If $b'=b$ then the output of the experiment is 1 ($\mathcal{A}$ wins), otherwise it is 0.

Definition. A grouping proof provides *unlinkability* if: $\forall$ PPT $\mathcal{A}$: Prob$[\texttt{PrivK}^{link}_{\mathcal{A},\Pi}(\kappa) = 1] = \frac{1}{2} + \mathsf{neglible}$, where the probabilities are taken over the coin tosses of $\mathcal{A}$, the random bits and the coins tosses used in the simulation of Π.

Proof of unlinkability (sketch). Every tag_i will update its counter T_i and draw a fresh (pseudo) random number r_i after responding to the reader's challenge. Consequently the responses of tag^0, tag^1 in the interrogations $\texttt{int}_0, \texttt{int}_1$ are (pseudo) random and cannot be distinguished with probability better than $1/2+$ $\mathsf{negligible}$.

5.2 Informal Discussion of Common Attacks

Replay attacks. The use of the counter value T_s prevents replay attacks: if an adversarial reader re-uses T_s, the tags that received this earlier will have updated their counter and will not respond. If a expired, but never sent to the tags, T_s is sent then the tags will respond (only this time) and a proof will be generated but this will not be accepted by the verifier (T_s is not valid). Similarly a replayed response r_i, r'_i for a previous counter value T_s will not be valid.

Forging grouping proofs. An adversarial reader may use a counter value T_s for a subgroup G'' of the scanned tags of G and succeed in generating identifiers for the "missing" tags $G \backslash G''$. Assumption 4.1 (reliable but not necessarily trusted) prevents such attacks.

Impersonation attacks on tags are prevented by using private keys k_i. Impersonation attacks on a reader will not yield a valid proof: only readers that have access to the one-time challenge (T_s, k_s) of the verifier can interrogate the group of tags. The values p_i $(= h(k_i, r_i, R_s))$ from different sessions cannot be used to compose a proof since they involve the session nonces r_i of interrogated tags and the challenge of the reader R_s $(= h(T_s, r_{j_1}, \ldots, r_{j_u}))$ that depends on the counter T_s which specifies the validity time window. Note that all tags set timers in Round 1 of the protocol, and after timeout will not respond.

De-synchronization attacks. If a protocol execution completes successfully then all tags will share the same counter value. No tag will accept a previously used T_s. Even if tags do not share the same counter value (*e.g.*, because of an interrupted interrogation), there are no synchronization concerns.

6 Conclusion

Several RFID grouping proofs have been proposed in the literature. Many assume communication models, capabilities and design principles that either are not properly defined or are not practical. In this paper we address the group scanning problem in a strong adversarial setting. We define basic design criteria for anonymous group scanning and present a two pass anonymous grouping proof of integrity for scanned (not necessarily complete) collections of tagged objects with missing tag identification generated by an untrusted reader that the verifier (a trusted entity) can verify. The proof resists replay, impersonation and de-synchronization attacks.

Acknowledgments. This material is based in part upon work supported by: (a) the National Science Foundation under Grant Numbers CNS 1347113, DUE 1241525, 1027217 and DGE 1538850, (b) the NSA/DHS under grant BAA-003-15, (c) Universidad de Málaga and (d) Spanish MINECO and FEDER under project TEC2014-54110-R.

References

1. EPC-Global: Radio-Frequency Identity Protocols, Generation-2.V2. UHF RFID. Technical report, April 2015
2. Kapoor, G., Piramuthu, S.: Single RFID tag ownership transfer protocols. IEEE Trans. Syst. Man Cybern. Part C **42**(2), 164–173 (2012)
3. Jorge Munilla, F.G., Susilo, W.: Cryptanalysis of an EPCC1G2 standard compliant ownership transfer protocol. Wirel. Pers. Commun. **72**, 245–258 (2013)
4. Liu, H., Ning, H., Zhang, Y., He, D., Xiong, Q., Yang, L.T.: Grouping-proofs-based authentication protocol for distributed RFID systems. IEEE Trans. Parallel Distrib. Syst. **24**(7), 1321–1330 (2013)
5. Burmester, M., Munilla, J.: RFID grouping-proofs. In: Security and Trends in Wireless Identification and Sensing Platform Tags: Advancements in RFID. IGI Global (2013)

6. Peris-Lopez, P., Orfila, A., Hernandez-Castro, J.C., van der Lubbe, J.C.A.: Flaws on RFID grouping-proofs. guidelines for future sound protocols. J. Netw.Comput. Appl. **34**(3), 833–845 (2011). http://dx.doi.org/10.1016/j.jnca.2010.04.008
7. Juels, A.: Yoking-proofs for RFID tags. In: PERCOMW 2004: Proceedings of the Second IEEE Annual Conference on Pervasive Computing and Communications Workshops, Washington, DC, pp. 138–142. IEEE Computer Society, USA (2004)
8. Piramuthu, S.: On existence proofs for multiple RFID tags. In: IEEE International Conference on Pervasive Services, Workshop on Security, Privacy and Trust in Pervasive and Ubiquitous Computing - SecPerU 2006, June 2006. IEEE Computer Society Press, IEEE, Lyon, France (2006)
9. Huang, H.-H., Ku, C.-Y.: A RFID grouping proof protocol for medication safety of inpatient. J. Med. Syst. **33**, 467 (2008)
10. Chien, H.-Y., Yang, C.-C., Wu, T.-C., Lee, C.-F.: Two RFID-based solutions to enhance inpatient medication safety. J. Med. Syst. **35**(3), 369–375 (2011)
11. Burmester, M., Munilla, J.: Distributed group authentication for RFID supply management. IACR Cryptol. ePrint Arch. **2013**, 779 (2013)
12. Sato, Y., Igarashi, Y., Mitsugi, J., Nakamura, O., Murai, J.: Identification of missing objects with group coding of RF tags. In: 2012 IEEE International Conference on RFID, pp. 95–101, April 2012
13. Gallager, R.G.: Low-density parity-check codes. IRE Trans. Inf. Theory **8**(1), 21–28 (1962)
14. Su, Y.-S., Lin, J.-R., Tonguz, O.K.: Grouping of RFID tags via strongly selective families. IEEE Commun. Lett. **17**(6), 1120–1123 (2013)
15. Su, Y.-S., Tonguz, O.K.: Using the Chinese remainder theorem for the grouping of RFID tags. IEEE Trans. Commun. **61**(11), 4741–4753 (2013)
16. Su, Y.-S.: Extended grouping of RFID tags based on resolvable transversal designs. IEEE Signal Process. Lett. **21**(4), 488–492 (2014)
17. Ben Mabrouk, N., Couderc, P.: EraRFID: reliable RFID systems using erasure coding. In: 2015 IEEE International Conference on RFID, pp. 121–128, April 2015
18. Burmester, M., Munilla, J.: Tag memory-erasure tradeoff of RFID grouping codes. IEEE Commun. Lett. **99**, 1–4 (2016)
19. Burmester, M., Munilla, J.: An anonymous RFID grouping-proof with missing tag identification. In: 10th Annual IEEE International Conference on RFID (IEEE RFID 2016), Orlando, Florida, 3–5 May 2016, pp. 1–8. IEEE (2016)
20. Paret, D.: RFID and Contactless Smart Card Applications. Wiley, UK (2005)
21. Roca, V., Cunche, M., Lacan, J., Bouabdallah, A., Matsuzono, K.: Simple reed-solomon forward error correction (FEC) scheme for FECFRAME. Technical report (2013)
22. Bengio, S., Brassard, G., Desmedt, Y., Goutier, C., Quisquater, J.-J.: Secure implementations of identification systems. J. Cryptol. **4**(3), 175–183 (1991)
23. Mangard, S., Popp, T., Oswald, M.E.: Power Analysis Attacks - Revealing the Secrets of Smart Cards. Springer, USA (2007). ISBN: 0-387-30857-1
24. Kim, C.H., Avoine, G., Koeune, F., Standaert, F.-X., Pereira, O.: The swiss-knife RFID distance bounding protocol. In: Lee, P.J., Cheon, J.H. (eds.) ICISC 2008. LNCS, vol. 5461, pp. 98–115. Springer, Heidelberg (2009)
25. Munilla, J., Ortiz, A., Peinado, A.: Distance bounding protocols with void-challenges for RFID. In: Workshop on RFID Security - RFIDSec 2006, Graz, Austria, July 2006
26. Duc, D.N., Kim, K.: On the security of RFID group scanning protocols. IEICE Trans. **93–D**(3), 528–530 (2010)

Author Index

Printed in the United States
By Bookmasters